A Developer's Guide to the Semantic Web

Liyang Yu

A Developer's Guide to the Semantic Web

Second Edition

 Springer

Liyang Yu
Delta Air Lines
Atlanta
USA

ISBN 978-3-662-43795-7   ISBN 978-3-662-43796-4 (eBook)
DOI 10.1007/978-3-662-43796-4
Springer Heidelberg New York Dordrecht London

Library of Congress Control Number: 2014950052

Printed on acid-free paper

Springer is part of Springer Science+Business Media (www.springer.com)

To my parents, Zaiyun Du my mother and Hanting Yu my father.

The truth is, they cannot read this dedication without someone translating it. However, this is never a problem for them, since there is something in this world that goes beyond the boundary of all languages and all cultures, and still remains the same to all human hearts. It lets my parents understand every word I have said here without the need of any translation at all.

It is the love they have been giving me. I will never be able to pay them back enough, and I can only wish that I will be their son in my next life, so I can continue to love them, and be loved.

Preface to the First Edition

Objectives of the Book

This book is all about the Semantic Web.

From its basics, the Semantic Web can be viewed as a collection of standards and technologies that allow machines to understand the meaning (semantics) of information on the Web. It represents a new vision about how the Web should be constructed so its information can be processed automatically by machines on a large scale.

This exciting vision opens the possibility of numerous new applications on the Web. Since 2001, there have been many encouraging results in both academic world and real application world. A whole suite of standards, technologies, and related tools have been specified and developed around the concept of the Semantic Web.

However, such an extensive and rapid progress of the Semantic Web has presented a steep learning curve for those who are new to the Semantic Web. Understanding its related concepts, learning the core standards and key technical components, and finally reaching the point where one can put all these into real development work requires a considerable amount of effort.

To facilitate this learning process, a comprehensive and easy-to-follow text is a must. This book, *A Developer's Guide to the Semantic Web*, serves this exact purpose. It provides an in-depth coverage on both the *What-Is* and *How-To* aspects of the Semantic Web. From this book, you will not only obtain a solid understanding about the Semantic Web but also learn how to combine all the pieces together to build new applications on the Semantic Web. More specifically,

- It offers a complete coverage of all the core standards and technical components of the Semantic Web. This coverage includes RDF, RDFS, OWL (both OWL 1 and OWL 2), and SPARQL (including features offered by SPARQL 1.1). Other related technologies are also covered, such as Turtle, Microformats, RDFa, GRDDL, and SKOS.

- It provides an in-depth description of multiple well-known applications and projects in the area of the Semantic Web, such as FOAF, semantic Wiki, SearchMonkey by Yahoo!, Rich Snippets by Google, Open Linked Data Project, and DBpedia Project.
- It explains the key concepts, core standards, and technical components in the context of examples. In addition, the readers will be taken in a step-by-step fashion through the development of each example. Hopefully for the first time ever, such teaching method will ease the learning curve for those who have found the Semantic Web a daunting topic.
- It includes several complete programming projects, which bridge the gap between *What-Is* and *How-To*. These example applications are real coding projects and are developed from the scratch. In addition, the code generated by these projects can be easily reused in the readers' future development work.

Intended Readers

The book is written with the following readers in mind:

- Software engineers and developers who are interested in learning the Semantic Web technology in general.
- Web application developers who have the desire and/or needs to study the Semantic Web and build semantic Web applications.
- Researchers working in research institutes who are interested in the Semantic Web research and development.
- Undergraduate and graduate students from computer science departments, whose focus of work is in the area of the Semantic Web.
- Practitioners in related engineering fields. For example, Data Mining engineers whose work involves organizing and processing a large amount of data by machines.

The prerequisites needed to understand this book includes the following:

- Working knowledge of Java programming language.
- Basic understanding of the Web, including its main technical components such as URL, HTML, and XML.

Structure of the Book

This book is organized as follows:

- Chapters 1–6 covers the basic concept, the core standards, and technical components of the Semantic Web. The goal of these chapters is to show you the *What-Is* aspect about the Semantic Web.

Chapter 1 introduces the concept of the Semantic Web by using a simple example. With this example, the difference between the traditional Web and the Semantic Web is clearly revealed. Further discussion in this chapter helps you to establish a solid understanding about the concept of the Semantic Web.

Chapter 2 covers RDF in great detail to give you a sound technical foundation to further understand the Semantic Web. If you are not familiar with RDF, you should not skip this chapter, since everything else is built upon RDF. In addition, Turtle format is presented in this chapter, which will be used to understand the material presented in Chap. 6.

Chapter 3 goes on with other RDF-related technologies, including Microformats, RDFa and GRDDL. If you prefer to get a full picture about the Semantic Web as quickly as possible, you can skip this chapter. However, the material presented in this chapter will be necessary in order to understand Chap. 8.

Chapter 4 presents RDF Schema and also introduces the concept of ontology. You should not skip this chapter since Chap. 5 is built upon this chapter. SKOS is also presented in this chapter; you can skip it if you are not working with any existing vocabularies in knowledge management field.

Chapter 5 discusses OWL in great detail and covers both OWL 1 and OWL 2. This is one of the key chapters in this book and should not be skipped. Unless RDF Schema can satisfy the needs of your application, you should spend enough time to understand OWL, which will give you the most updated information about latest ontology development language.

Chapter 6 covers SPARQL. This is another chapter that you should carefully read. Working on the Semantic Web without using SPARQL is like working with database systems without knowing SQL. Notice SPARQL 1.1 is covered in this chapter as well. At the time of this writing, SPARQL 1.1 has not become a standard yet, so when you are reading this book, notice the possible updates.

- Chapters 7–11 provides an in-depth discussion of some well-known semantic Web applications/projects in the real application world. These chapters serve as a transition from knowing What-Is to understanding *How-To* in the world of the Semantic Web.

Chapter 7 presents FOAF (Friend Of A Friend) project. The FOAF ontology is arguably the most widely used ontology at this point. The goal of this chapter is to introduce you to a real world example in the social networking area. Since the modeling of this domain does not require any specific domain knowledge, it is easy to follow and you can therefore focus on appreciating the power of the Semantic Web. This chapter should not be skipped, not only because of the popularity of the FOAF ontology but also because this ontology has been used frequently in the later chapters as well.

Chapter 8 presents Google's Rich Snippets and Yahoo!'s searchMonkey; both are using RDFa and Microformats as the main tools when adding semantic markups. These are important examples, not only because they are currently the

major semantic Web applications developed by leading players in the field, but
also they show us the benefits of having the added semantics on the Web.

Chapter 9 discusses the topic of Semantic Wiki, together with a real world
example. This chapter represents the type of the Semantic Web applications built
by using manual semantic markup. After reading this chapter, you should not
only see the power of the added semantics but also start to understand those
situations where manual semantic markup can be a successful solution.

Chapter 10 presents DBpedia in great detail. DBpedia is a well-known project
in the Semantic Web community, and a large number of real world semantic
Web applications take advantage of the DBpedia datasets directly or indirectly.
Also, DBpedia gives an example of automatic semantic markup. Together with
Chap. 9, where manual semantic markup is used, you have a chance to see both
methods at work.

Chapter 11 discusses the Linked Open Data project (LOD) as an real world
implementation example of the Web of Data concept. For the past several years,
LOD has attracted tremendous attention from both the academic world and real
application world. In fact, DBpedia, as a huge dataset, stays in the center of LOD
cloud. Therefore, LOD together with DBpedia, becomes a must for anyone who
wants to do development work on the Semantic Web. More specifically, this
chapter covers both the production and the consumption aspects of Linked Data;
it also provides application examples that are built upon LOD cloud. In addition,
this chapter explains how to access LOD programmatically, which should be
very useful to your daily development work.

• Chapters 12–15 is the section of *How-To*. After building a solid foundation for
development work on the Semantic Web, this section presents three different
running applications that are created from scratch. The methods, algorithms, and
concrete classes presented in these chapters will be of immediate use to your
future development work.

Chapter 12 helps to build a foundation for your future development work on
the Semantic Web. More specifically, it covers four major tool categories you
should know, namely, development frameworks, reasoners, ontology engineering tools, and other tools such as search engines for the Semantic Web. This
chapter also discusses some related development methodology for the Semantic
Web, such as the Ontology-driven Software Development Methodology. Furthermore, since ontology development is the key of this methodology, this
chapter also presents an ontology development guide that you can use.

Chapter 13 covers a popular development framework named Jena, to prepare
you for your future development work on the Semantic Web. More specifically,
this chapter starts from how to setup Jena development environment and then
presents a `Hello World` example to get you started. In what follows, this
chapter covers the basic operation every semantic Web application needs, such
as creating RDF models, handling persistence, querying RDF dataset, and

inferencing with ontology models. After reading this chapter, you will be well prepared for real development work.

Developing applications for the Semantic Web requires a set of complex skills, and this skill set lands itself on some basic techniques. In Chap. 13, you have learned some basics. Chapter 14 continues along the same path by building an agent that implements the Follow-Your-Nose algorithm on the Semantic Web. After all, most semantic Web applications will have to be based on the Web, so moving or crawling from one dataset to another on the Web with some specific goals in mind is a routine task. Follow-Your-Nose method is one such basic technique. Besides implementing this algorithm, Chap. 14 also introduces some useful operations, such as how to remotely access SPARQL endpoints.

Chapter 15 presents two additional semantic Web applications from scratch. The first application helps you to create an e-mail list that you can use to enhance the security of your e-mail system. The second one is a ShopBot that runs on the Semantic Web, and you can use it to find products that satisfy your own specific needs. These two projects are both discussed in great detail, showing how applications on the Semantic Web are built. This includes RDF documents handling, ontology handling, inferencing based on ontologies, and SPARQL query handling, just to name a few.

Where to Get the Code

The source code for all the examples and application projects in this book can be downloaded from the author's personal Web site, www.liyangyu.com.

Acknowledgment

My deepest gratitude goes to a remarkable person in my life, Dr. Weirong Ding, for supporting me in all the ways that one can ever wish to be supported. It is not nearly as possible to list all the supports she gave me, but her unreserved confidence in my knowledge and talents has always been a great encouragement for me to finish this book. Being the first reader of this book, she has always been extremely patient with many of my ideas and thoughts, and interestingly enough, her patience has made her a medical doctor who is also an expert of the Semantic Web. And to make the readers of this book become experts of the Semantic Web, I would like to share something she always says to me: "never give yourself excuses and always give 200% of yourself to reach what you love."

I would like to thank Dr. Jian Jiang, a good friend of mine, for introducing me to the field of the Semantic Web, for many interesting and insightful discussions along the road of this book.

My gratitude is also due to Mr. Ralf Gerstner, Senior Editor at Springer. As a successful IT veteran himself, he has given me many valuable suggestions about the content and final organization of this book. The communication with him is always quite enjoyable: it is not only prompt and efficient but also very insightful and helpful. It is simply my very good luck to have a chance to work with an editor like Ralf.

Finally, I would like to express my love and gratitude to my beloved parents, for their understanding and endless love. They always give me the freedom I need, and they accept my decisions even when they cannot fully understand them. In addition, I wanted to thank them for being able to successfully teach me how to think and speak clearly and logically when I was at a very young age, so I can have one more dream fulfilled today.

Delta Air Lines, Atlanta, USA   Liyang Yu

Preface to the Second Edition

In the three years since the first edition of this book was published, I have received numerous email messages from readers all over the world commenting on the book and suggesting how it could be improved. Meanwhile, the Semantic Web world has been developing and experiencing exciting changes and improvements, noticeably some new standards such as SPARQL 1.1 and RDB2RDF, and also new developments such as schema.org and important real-world applications that built upon schema.org. In addition, I have also built up a large file of ideas based on my own research in the area and my own experience gained when building semantic Web applications for a variety of organizations. It is indeed a good time to update the book and make all these new material available to our readers.

The most obvious changes in this second edition are the new chapters described as follows.

- *schema.org and Semantic Markup (Chap. 10).* schema.org has been extremely important and popular since the day it was launched (June of 2011). Developed by Google, Yahoo, and Bing, it is considered as the first mainstream support of the vision of the Semantic Web. This new chapter covers everything about schema.org, including its background and rationale, its vocabulary, and the markup languages recommended. It also includes two examples to showcase some real-world applications built upon schema.org (Google-rich snippets and LRMI Project).
- *Social Network and the Semantic Web (Chap. 11).* It is not surprising that most of us are more or less related to the Web by participating in some kind of social network sites. It might however be surprising to realize that the Semantic Web technology has actually been playing a key role in these social network sites. This chapter focuses on this topic and helps to understand how the Semantic Web technology has been changing the way social networking sites work. More specifically, this chapter uses three most popular social networking sites, namely, Facebook, Twitter, and Pinterest as examples, and examines their *semantic components* in great detail. For Facebook, we take a look at the *Open Graph protocol*; for Twitter, we study *Twitter cards*; and for Pinterest, we focus

on *rich pins*. This not only shows how the idea of the Semantic Web can help social networking sites, but also serves as examples to the developers, so they can draw inspiration and come up with their own applications.

- *Other Recent Applications: data.gov and Wikidata (Chap. 12)*. This chapter uses two more recent developments to further illustrate how the idea of the Semantic Web can be applied to the Web and data that surround us. The first example is data.gov. We discuss the background of data.gov, how it is related to the Semantic Web, and examples are included to show the benefits of using the Semantic Web technologies on government open data. The second example is wikidata, a popular project that has been constantly under the spotlight recently. The relationship between Wikipedia, DBpedia, and wikidata is first discussed, followed by a close look at the semantic components inside wikidata. This will be another eye-opening project to the readers, because the Semantic Web components used in wikidata have indeed changed how Wikipedia is constructed and maintained.
- *Getting Started: Change Your Data Into Structured Data (Chap. 13)*. This chapter is motivated by questions from our readers. For example, if one is not consuming public RDF data, how should one create his/her own RDF content? If all existing structured data are stored in database tables, how should this structured information be converted into RDF content? Which ontology should be used? Is there a way to understand a complex ontology that is created by someone else? This chapter attempts to answer all these questions, in preparation for the readers to start their own development work. A main focus of this chapter is the RDB2RDF W3C standard, which is discussed in great detail and example implementation is also represented in a way that the readers can directly follow it in their own development work.
- *A Search Engine that Supports Rich Snippets (Chap. 17)*. This chapter is added as another example of developing semantic Web applications. It is important because (1) it directly shows how the Semantic Web idea can be used to enhance the performance of a search engine and (2) the implementation in this chapter can be directly adapted to build customized search engines that support rich snippets for different organizations.

Among the new material in existing chapters, Chap. 6, *SPARQL: Querying the Semantic Web*, has been greatly enhanced by covering the language features of the new standard, SPARQL 1.1, more thoroughly and completely. Compared to the first edition of this book, the coverage of SPARQL 1.1 in this second edition has changed from 14 to more than 40 pages.

Besides the above enhancement, most existing chapters are updated with new links, new figures if necessary, and new version numbers if applicable.

Finally, this second edition is organized into three parts. Part I, *Core of the Semantic Web*, containing Chaps. 1–6, covers the foundation of the Semantic Web, Part II, *Applied Semantic Web*, containing Chaps. 7–12, describes some application examples and latest development in the area of the Semantic Web, and Part III, *Building Your Own Applications on the Semantic Web*, containing Chaps. 13–18, offers concrete development guidelines and detailed descriptions of the necessary technical foundations, together with real projects and coding examples. This new layout clearly shows how the whole book is organized, with the goal of helping the readers to more easily conquer the learning curve needed to master the world of the Semantic Web.

Delta Air Lines, Atlanta, USA   Liyang Yu

Contents

Part I
Core of the Semantic Web

Chapter 1
A Web of Data: Toward the Idea
of the Semantic Web

If you are reading this book, chances are that you are a software engineer who makes a living by developing applications on the Web—or, more precisely, on the Web that we currently have.

And yes, there is another kind of Web. It is built on top of the current Web, and is called *the Semantic Web*. As a Web application developer, your career on the Semantic Web will be more exciting and fulfilling.

This book will prepare you well for your development work on the Semantic Web. This chapter tells you exactly what the Semantic Web is, and why it is important for you to learn everything about it.

We get started by presenting a simple example to illustrate the differences between the current Web and the Semantic Web. You can consider this example as a development assignment. Once you start to ponder the issues such as what exactly do we need to change on the current Web to finish this assignment, you are well on your way to seeing the basic picture of the Semantic Web.

With this basic understanding about the Semantic Web, we continue by discussing how much more it can revolutionize the way we use the Web, and further change the patterns as we conduct our development work on the Web. We then formally introduce the concept of the Semantic Web, and hopefully this concept will seem to be much more intuitive to you.

This chapter will build a solid foundation for you to understand the rest of this book. When you have finished the whole book, come back read this chapter again. You should be able to acquire a deeper appreciation of the idea of the Semantic Web. By then, I hope you will have also formed your own opinion about the vision of the Semantic Web, and with what you will have learned from this book, you will be ready to start your own exciting journey of exploring more and creating more on the Semantic Web.

© Springer-Verlag Berlin Heidelberg 2014

L. Yu, *A Developer's Guide to the Semantic Web*,
DOI 10.1007/978-3-662-43796-4_1

1.1   A Motivating Example: Data Integration on the Web

Data integration on the Web refers to the process of combining and aggregating information resources on the Web so they could be collectively useful to us. In this section, we use a concrete example to see how data integration can be implemented on the Web, and why it is so interesting to us.

1.1.1   A Smart Data Integration Agent

Here is our goal: for a given resource (which could be a person, an idea, an event or a product, such as a digital camera), we would like to know everything that has been said about it. More specifically, we would like to accomplish this goal by collecting as much information as possible about this resource, and we will then understand it by making queries against the collected information.

To make this more tangible, let me use myself as the resource. In addition, assume we have already built a "smart" agent, which will walk around the Web and try to find everything about me on our behalf.

To get our smart agent started, we feed it with the URL of my personal homepage as the starting point of its journey on the Web:

```
http://www.liyangyu.com
```

Now, our agent downloads this page, and tries to collect information from this page. This is also the point where everything gets more interesting:

- If my Web page were a traditional Web document, our agent would not be able to collect anything that is much use at all.

More specifically, the only thing our agent is able to understand on this page are those HTML language constructs, such as `<p>`, `<br>`, `<href>`, `<table>`, `<li>`, etc. Besides telling a Web browser about how to present my Web page, these HTML constructs do not convey any useful information about the underlying resource. Therefore, other than these HTML tokens, to our agent, my whole Web page simply represents a string of characters that look no different from any other Web document.

- However, let us assume my Web page is not a traditional Web document: besides the HTML constructs, it actually contains some "statements" that can be collected by our agent.

More specifically, all these statements follow the same simple structure, and each represents one aspect of the given resource. For example, List 1.1 shows some example statements that have been collected:

List 1.1 Some of the statements collected by our smart agent from my personal
Web page

```
ns0:LiyangYu ns0:name "Liyang Yu".
ns0:LiyangYu ns0:nickname "LaoYu".
ns0:LiyangYu ns0:author <ns0:_x>.
ns0:_x ns0:ISBN "978-1584889335".
ns0:_x ns0:publisher <http://www.crcpress.com>.
```

At this point, let's not worry about the issues such as how these statements are
added to my Web page, and how our agent collects them. Let us simply assume
when our agent visits my Web page, it can easily discover these statements.

Notice ns0 represent a namespace, so we know that everything with ns0 as its
prefix is collected from the same Web page. ns0:LiyangYu represents a resource
that is described by my Web page, in the case, this resource is me.

With this said, the first statement in List 1.1 can be read like this:

resource ns0:LiyangYu has a ns0:name whose value is Liyang Yu.

or, like this:

resource ns0:LiyangYu has a ns0:name property, whose value is Liyang Yu.

The second way to read a given statement is perhaps more intuitive. With this in
mind, each statement actually adds one *property–value* pair to the resource that is
being described. For example, the second statement claims the ns0:nickname
property of resource ns0:LiyangYu has a value given by LaoYu.

The third statement in List 1.1 is a little bit unusual. When specifying the value
of ns0:author property for resource ns0:LiyangYu, instead of using a simple
character string as its value (as in the first two statements in List 1.1), it uses another
resource, and this resource is identified by ns0:_x. To make this fact more obvious,
ns0:_x is included by <>.

Statement 4 in List 1.1 specifies the value of ns0:ISBN property of resource
ns0:_x, and the last statement in List 1.1 specifies the value of ns0:publisher
property of the same resource. Notice again, the value of this property is not a
character sting, but another resource identified by http://www.crcpress.com.

The statements in List 1.1 probably still make sense to our human eyes no matter
how ugly they look. The really interesting question is, how much does our agent
understand of these statements?

Not much at all. However, without too much understanding about these statements, our agent can indeed organize them into a graph format, as shown in Fig. 1.1
(notice more statements have been added to the graph).

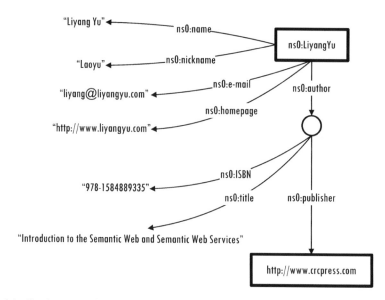

Fig. 1.1 Graph generated by our agent after visiting my personal Web page

After the graph shown in Fig. 1.1 is created, our agent declares its success on my personal Web site and moves on to the next one. It will repeat the same process again when it hits the next Web document.

Let us say that the next Web site our agent hits is www.amazon.com. Similarly, if Amazon were still the Amazon of today, our agent could not do much either. In fact, it can retrieve information about this ISBN number, 978-1584889335, by using Amazon Web Services.[1] For now, let us say our agent does not know how to do that.

However, again assume Amazon is already a new Amazon. Our agent can therefore collect lots of statements, which follow the same format as shown in List 1.1. Furthermore, some of the statements that have been collected are shown in List 1.2.

List 1.2 Statements collected by our agent from amazon.com

```
ns1:book-1584889330 ns1:ISBN "978-1584889335".
ns1:book-1584889330 ns1:price USD62.36.
ns1:book-1584889330 ns1:customerReview "4.5 star".
```

---

[1] http://aws.amazon.com/

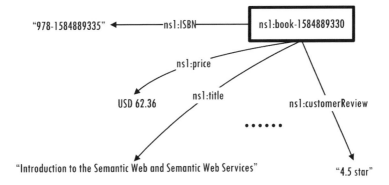

Fig. 1.2 Graph generated by our agent after visiting amazon.com

Notice similarly to the namespace prefix `ns0`, `ns1` represents another namespace prefix. And now, our agent can again organize these statements into a graph form (Fig. 1.2; notice more statements have been added to the graph).

To human eyes, one important fact is already quite obvious: `ns0:_x`, as a resource in Fig. 1.1, represents exactly the same item denoted by the resource named `ns1:book-1584889330` in Fig. 1.2. And once we have made this connection, we can start to see other facts easily. For example, a person who has a homepage with URL `http://www.liyangyu.com` has a book published, and the current price of that book is US$62.36 on Amazon. Obviously, this fact is not explicitly stated on either one of the Web sites; our human minds have integrated the information from both `www.liyangyu.com` and `www.amazon.com` to reach this conclusion.

For our agent, similar data integration is not difficult either. In fact, our agent sees the ISBN number, `978-1584889335`, showing up in both Figs. 1.1 and 1.2, and it therefore makes a connection between these two appearances (Fig. 1.3). It then automatically adds the following new statement to its original statement collection:

`ns0:_x sameAs ns1:book-1584889330.`

And once this is done, for our agent, Figs. 1.1 and 1.2 are already "glued" together by overlapping the `ns0:_x` node with the `ns1:book-1584889330` node. This gluing process is exactly the data integration process on the Web.

Now, without going into the details, it is not difficult to convince ourselves that our agent can answer lots of questions that we might have. For example, what is the price of the book written by a person whose homepage is given by this URL, `http://www.liyangyu.com`?

This is indeed very encouraging. And this is not all.

Let us say now that our agent hits `www.LinkedIn.com`. Similarly, if LinkedIn were still the LinkedIn of today, our agent could not do much. However, again

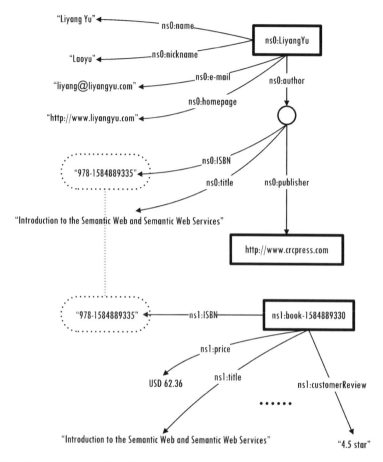

Fig. 1.3 Our agent can combine Figs. 1.1 and 1.2 automatically

assume LinkedIn is a new LinkedIn, and our agent is able to collect quite a few statements from this Web site. Some of them are shown in List 1.3.

List 1.3 Statements collected by our agent from LinkedIn

```
ns2:LiyangYu ns2:email "liyang@liyangyu.com".
ns2:LiyangYu ns2:workPlaceHomepage "http://www.delta.com".
ns2:LiyangYu ns2:connectedTo <ns2:Connie>.
```

The graph created by the agent is shown in Fig. 1.4 (notice more statements have been added to the graph).

For human readers, we know ns0:LiyangYu and ns2:LiyangYu represent exactly the same resource, because both these two resources have the same

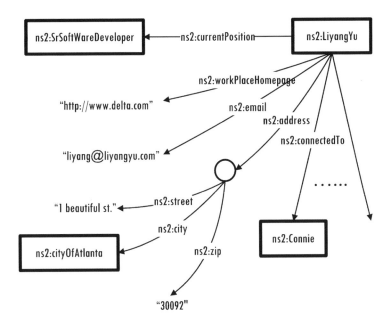

Fig. 1.4 Graph generated by our agent after visiting LinkedIn.com

e-mail address. For our agent, just by comparing the two identifies (ns0:LiyangYu vs. ns2:LiyangYu) does not ensure the fact that these two resources are the same.

However, if we can "teach" our agent the following fact:

if the e-mail property of resource A has the same value as the e-mail property of resource B, then resource A and B are the same resource.

our agent will be able to automatically add the following new statement to its current statement collection:

ns0:LiyangYu sameAs ns2:LiyangYu.

With the creation of this new statement, our agent has in fact integrated Figs. 1.1 and 1.4 by overlapping node ns0:LiyangYu with node ns2:LiyangYu. Clearly, this integration process is exactly the same as the one where Figs. 1.1 and 1.2 are connected together by overlapping node ns0:_x with node ns1:book-1584889330. And now, Figs. 1.1, 1.2 and 1.4 are all connected.

At this point, our agent is able to answer even more questions. The following are just some of them:

- What is Laoyu's workplace homepage?
- How much does it cost to buy Laoyu's book?
- In what city does Liyang live?

And clearly, to answer these questions, the agent must depend on the integrated graph, rather than on any single one. For example, to answer the first question, the agent has to go through the following link that runs across different graphs:

```
ns0:LiyangYu ns0:nickname "LaoYu".
ns0:LiyangYu sameAs ns2:LiyangYu.
ns2:LiyangYu ns2:workPlaceHomepage "http://www.delta.com".
```

Once the agent reaches the last statement, it can present an answer to us. You should be able to understand how the other questions are answered by mapping out the similar path as shown above.

Obviously, the set of questions that our agent is able to answer grows when it hits more Web documents. We can continue to move on to another Web site in order to add more statements to our agent's collection. However, the idea is clear: automatic data integration on the Web can be quite powerful, and can help us a lot when it comes to information discovery and retrieval.

1.1.2 Is Smart Data Integration Agent Possible?

The question is also clear: is it even possible to build a smart data integration agent such as the one we just discussed? Human do this kind of information integration on the Web on a daily basis, and now, we are in fact hoping to program a machine to this for us.

To answer this question, we have to understand what exactly has to be there to make our agent possible.

Let us go back to the basics. Our agent, after all, is a piece of software that works on Web. So to make it possible, we have to work on two parties: the Web and the agent.

Let us start with the Web. Recall that we have assumed that our agent is able to collect some statements from various Web sites (see Lists 1.1, 1.2 and 1.3). Therefore, each Web site has to be different from its traditional form, and changes have to be made. Without going into the details, here are some changes we need to have on each Web site:

- Each statement collected by our agent represents a piece of knowledge. There-fore, there has to be a way (a model) to represent knowledge on the Web. Furthermore, this model of representing knowledge has to be easily and readily processed (understood) by machines.
- This model has to be accepted as a standard by all the Web sites. Otherwise, statements contained in different Web sites would not share a common pattern.
- There has to be a way to create these statements on each Web site. For example, they could be either manually added or automatically generated.

- The statements contained in different Web sites cannot be completely arbitrary. For example, they should be created by using some common terms and relationships, at least for a given domain. For instance, to describe a person, we have some common terms such as name, birthday and homepage, etc.
- There has to be a way to define these common terms and relationships that specifies some kind of agreement on these common terms and relationships. Different Web sites, when creating their statements, will use these terms and relationships.
- And perhaps more to be included.

With these changes on the Web, a new breed of Web will be available for our agent. And in order to take advantage of this new Web, our agent has to be changed as well. For example,

- Our agent has to be able to understand each statement that it collects. One way to accomplish this is by understanding the common terms and relationships that are used to create these statements.
- Our agent has to be able to conduct reasoning based on its understanding of the common terms and relationships. For example, knowing the fact that resources A and B have the same e-mail address and considering the knowledge expressed by the common terms and relationships, it should be able to conclude that A and B are in fact the same resource.
- Our agent should be able to process some common queries that are submitted against the statements it has collected. After all, without providing a query interface, the collected statements will not be of too much use to us.
- And perhaps more to be included as well.

Therefore, here is our conclusion: yes, our agent is possible, provided that we can implement all the above (and possibly more).

1.1.3 The Idea of the Semantic Web

At this point, the Semantic Web can be understood as follows: the Semantic Web provides the technologies and standards that we need to make our agent possible, including all the things we have listed in the previous section. It can be understood as a brand new layer built on top of the current Web, and it adds machine-understandable meanings (or "semantics") to the current Web. Thus the name the *Semantic* Web.

The Semantic Web is certainly more than automatic data integration on a large scale. In the next section, we position it in a more general setting, and we then summarize the concept of the Semantic Web, which we hope will look more natural to you.

1.2   A More General Goal: A Web Understandable to Machines

1.2.1   How Do We Use the Web?

In the early days of the Web, it could be viewed as a set of Web sites that offer a collection of Web documents, and the goal was to get the content pushed out to its audiences. It acted like a one-way street: people read whatever was out there, with the goal of getting information they could use in a variety of ways.

Today, the Web has become much more interactive. First, more and more of what is now known as user-generated content has emerged on the Web, and a host of new Internet companies were created around this trend as well. More specifically, instead of only reading the content, people are now using the Web to create content and also to interact with each other by using social networking sites over Web platforms. And certainly, even if we don't create any new content or participate in any social networking sites, we can still enjoy the Web a lot: we can chat with our friends, we can shop online, we can pay our bills online and we can also watch a tennis game online, just to name a few.

Second, the life of a Web developer has also changed a lot. Instead of offering merely static Web contents, today's Web developer is capably of building Web sites that can execute complex business transactions, from paying bills online to booking a hotel room and airline tickets.

Third, more and more Web sites have started to publish structured content so that different business entities can share their content to attract and accomplish more transactions online. For example, Amazon and eBay both are publishing structured data via Web Service standards from their databases, so other applications can be built on top of these contents.

With all this being said, let us summarize what we do on today's Web at a higher level, and this will eventually reveal some critical issues we are having on the Web. Notice that our summary is mainly related to how we consume the available information on the Web, and we are not going to include activities such as chatting with friends or watching a tennis game online—these are nice things you can do on the Web, but are not much related to our purpose here.

Now, to put it simply, searching, information integration and Web data mining are the three main activities we conduct using the Web.

1.2.1.1   Searching

This is probably the most common usage of the Web. The goal is to locate some specific information or resources on the Web. For instance, finding different recipes for making margaritas, locating a local agent who might be able to help us buy a house, etc., are all good examples of searching.

Quite often though, searching on the Web can be very frustrating. At the time of this writing, for instance, using a common search engine (Google, for example), let us search the word SOAP with the idea that, in our mind, SOAP is a W3C standard for Web services. Unfortunately, we get about 63,200,000 listings back and soon find this result hardly helpful: there are listings for dish detergents, facial soaps and even soap operas! Only after sifting through multiple listings and reading through the linked pages are we able to find information about the W3C's SOAP specifications.

The reason for this situation is that search engines implement their search based on the core concept of "which documents contain the given keyword", and as long as a given document contains the keyword, it is included in the candidate set and is later presented back to the user as the search result. It is then up to the user to read and interpret the results to extrapolate any useful information.

1.2.1.2 Information Integration

We have seen an example of information integration in Sect. 1.1.1, and we have also created an imaginary agent to help us accomplish our goal. In this section, we take a closer look at this common task on the Web.

Let us say that you decide to try some Indian food for your weekend dining out. You first search the Web to find a list of restaurants specializing in Indian cuisine, you then pick one restaurant and you write down the address. Now if you don't see a map associated with the selected restaurant, you need to go to your favorite map utility to get the driving directions from your house to the restaurant. This process is a simple integration process: you first get some information (the address of the restaurant), and you use it to get more information (the directions), and they collectively help you to enjoy a nice evening dining out.

Another similar but more complex example is to create a holiday plan, which pretty much every one of us has done. Today, it is safe to say that we all have to do this manually: search for a place that fits not only our interests, but also our budget, and then find the hotel, flights and finally cars. The information from these different steps is then combined together to create a perfect plan for our vacation, hopefully.

Clearly, to conduct this kind of information integration manually is a somewhat tedious process. It would be more convenient if we could finish the process with more help from the machine. For example, we can specify what we need to some application, which then helps us out by conducting the necessary steps for us. For the vacation example, the application can help us even more: after creating our itinerary (including the flights, hotels and cars), it searches the Web to add related information such as daily weather, local maps, driving directions, city guides, so on and so forth.

Another good example of information integration is the application that makes use of Web services. As a developer who mainly works on Web applications, Web service should not be a new concept. For example, company A can provide a set of Web services via its Web site, and company B can write Java code (or whatever language of their choice) to consume these services so to search company A's product database on the fly. For instance, when provided with several keywords that should appear in a book title, the service returns a list of books whose titles contain the given keywords.

Clearly, company A is providing structured data for another application to consume. It does not matter which language company A has used to build its Web services and what platform these services are running on; nor does it matter which language company B is using and what platform company B is on. As long as company B follows the related standards, this integration can happen smoothly and nicely.

In fact, our perfect vacation example can also be accomplished by using a set of Web services. More specifically, finding a vacation location, booking a hotel room, buying air tickets and finally making a reservation at a car rental company can all be accomplished by consuming the right Web services.

On today's Web, this type of integration often involves different Web services. Often the related services have to be manually located and integrated (normally, this integration is implemented at the development phase). It would be much quicker, cleaner, more powerful and more maintainable if we could have some application that could help us to find the appropriate services on the fly and also invoke these services dynamically to accomplish our goal.

1.2.1.3   Web Data Mining

Intuitively speaking, data mining is the nontrivial extraction of useful information from a large (and normally distributed) dataset or database. Given that the Web can be viewed as a huge distributed database, the concept of Web data mining refers to the activity of getting useful information from Web.

Web data mining might not be as interesting as searching sounds to a casual user, but it could be very important and even be the daily work of those who work as analysts or developers for different companies and research institutes.

One example of Web data mining is as follows. Let us say that we are currently working as consultants for the air traffic control group at Hartsfield–Jackson Atlanta International Airport, reportedly the busiest airport in the United States. The management group in the control tower wants to understand how weather conditions may affect the takeoff rate on the runways, with the takeoff rate defined as the number of aircraft that have taken off in a given hour. Intuitively, severe weather conditions will force the control tower to shut down the airport, so the takeoff rate will go down to zero, and moderate weather conditions will just make the takeoff rate low.

For a task like this, we suggest that we gather as much historical data as possible and analyze them to find the pattern of the weather effects. We are told that historical data (the takeoff rates at different major airports for the past, say, 5 years) does exist, but they are published in different Web sites. In addition, the data we need on these Web sites are normally mingled together with other data that we do not need.

To handle this situation, we will develop a specific application that acts like a crawler: it will visit these Web sites one by one, and once it reaches a Web site, it will identify the data we need and only collect the needed information (historical takeoff rates) for us. After it collects these rates, it will store them into the data format that we want. Once it finishes with one Web site, it will move on to the next one until it has visited all the Web sites that we are interested in.

Clearly, this application is a highly specialized piece of software that is normally developed on a case-by-case basis. Inspired by this example, you might want to code up your own agent, which will visit all the related Web sites to collect some specific stock information, and report back to you, say, every 10 min. By doing so, you don't have to open up a browser every 10 min to check the stock prices, risking the possibility that your boss will catch you visiting these Web sites, yet you can still follow the latest changes in the stock market.

This stock-watcher application you have developed is yet another example of Web data mining. Again, it is a very specialized piece of software, and you might have to recode it if something important has changed on the Web sites that it routinely visits. And yes, it would much nicer if the application could understand the meaning of the Web pages on the fly so you do not have to change your code so often.

By now, we have talked about the three major activities that you can do and normally might do with the Web. You might be a casual visitor to the Web, or you might be a highly trained professional developer, but whatever you do with the Web more or less falls into one of these three categories.

The next question then is, what are the common difficulties that we have experienced in these activities? Does any solution exist to these difficulties? What would we do if we had the magic power to change the way the Web is constructed so that we did not have to experience these difficulties at all?

Let us talk about this in the next section.

1.2.2   What Stops Us From Doing More?

Let us go back to the first main Web activity: search. Among the three major activities, search is probably the most popular one. It is interesting that this activity in fact shows the difficulty of the current Web in a most obvious way: whenever we do a search, we want to get only relevant results; that is, we want to minimize the human work that is required when trying to find the appropriate documents.

However, the conflict also starts from here: the current Web is entirely aimed at human readers, and it is purely display-oriented. In other words, the Web has been constructed in such a way that it is oblivious to the actual information content on any given Web site. Web browsers, Web servers and even search engines do not actually distinguish weather forecasts from scientific papers, and cannot even tell a personal home page from a major corporate Web site. Search engines are therefore forced to do keyword-matching only: as long as a given document contains the keyword(s), it will be included in the candidate set that is later presented to the user as the search result.

If we had the magic power, we would reconstruct the whole Web such that computers could not only present the information that is contained the Web documents, but could also understand the very information they are presenting so they could make intelligent decisions on our behalf. For example, search engines would filter the pages before they present them back to us, if they were not able to directly give us the answer back.

For the second activity, integration, the main difficulty is that there is too much manual work involved in the integration process. If the Web were constructed in such a way that the meaning of each Web document could be retrieved from a collection of statements, our agent would be able to understand each page. As a result, information integration would become amazingly fun and easy, as we showed in Sect. 1.1.1.

Information integration implemented by using Web services may seem quite different at the first glance. However, to automatically composite and invoke the necessary Web services, the first step is to *discover* them in a more efficient and automated manner. Currently, this type of integration is difficult to implement mainly because the discovery process of its components is far from efficient.

The reason, again, as you can guess, is that although all the services needed to be integrated do exist on the Web, the Web is not programmed to understand and remember the meanings of any of these services. As far as the Web is concerned, all these components are created equal, and there is no way for us to teach our computers to understand the meaning of each component, at least on the current Web.

What about the last activity, namely, Web data mining? The truth is, Web data mining applications are not scalable, and they have to be implemented at a very high price, if they can be implemented at all.

More specifically, each Web data mining application is highly specialized and has to be specially developed for that application context. For a given project in a specific domain, only the development team knows the meaning of each data element in the data source and how these data elements should interact together to present some useful information. The developers have to program these meanings into the data mining software before setting it off to work; there is no way to let the mining application learn and understand these meanings on the fly. In addition, the underlying decision tree has to be preprogrammed into the application as well.

Also, even for a given specific task, if the meaning of the data element changes (this can easily happen given the dynamic nature of Web documents), the mining application has to be changed accordingly since it cannot learn the meaning of the data element dynamically. All of these practical concerns have made Web data mining a very expensive task to perform.

Now, if the Web were built to remember all the meanings of data elements, and in addition, if all these meanings could be understood by a computer, we would then program the mining software by following a completely different pattern. We can even build a generic framework for some specific domain so that once we have a mining task in that domain, we can reuse it all the time—Web data mining would not be as expensive as today.

Now, we have finally reached an interesting point. Summarizing the above discussion, we have come to an understanding of an important fact: our Web is constructed in such a way that its documents only contain enough information for a machine to present them, not to understand them.

Now the question is the following: is it still possible to reconstruct the Web by adding some information into the documents stored on the Web, so that machines can use this extra information to understand what a given document is really about?

The answer is yes, and by doing so, we in fact change the current (traditional) Web into something we call the *Semantic Web*—the main topic of this chapter and this whole book.

1.2.3   Again, the Idea of the Semantic Web

At this point, the Semantic Web can be understood as follows: the Semantic Web provides the technologies and standards that we need to make the following possible:

- it adds machine-understandable meanings to the current Web, so that
- computers can understand the Web documents and therefore can automatically accomplish tasks that have been otherwise conducted manually, on a large scale.

With all the intuitive understanding of the Semantic Web, we are now ready for a formal definition of the Semantic Web, which is the main topic of the next section.

1.3   The Semantic Web: A First Look

1.3.1   The Concept of the Semantic Web

First, the word "semantics" is related to the word *syntax*. In most languages, syntax is how you say something, where *semantics* is the meaning behind what you have said. Therefore, the Semantic Web can be understood as the "the Web of meanings", which echoes what we have learned so far.

At the time of this writing, there is no formal definition of the Semantic Web yet. And it often means different things to different groups of individuals. Nevertheless, the term "Semantic Web" was originally coined by World Wide Web Consortium[2]

---

[2] http://www.w3.org/

(W3C) director Sir Tim Berners-Lee, and was formally introduced to the world by the May 2001 *Scientific American* article "The Semantic Web" (Berners-Lee et al. 2001):

> The Semantic Web is an extension of the current Web in which information is given well-defined meaning, better enabling computers and people to work in cooperation.

There has been a dedicated team of people at W3C working to improve, extend and standardize the idea of the Semantic Web. This is now called *W3C Semantic Web Activity*.[3] According to this group, the Semantic Web can be understood as follows:

> The Semantic Web provides a common framework that allows data to be shared and reused across application, enterprise, and community boundaries.

For us, and for the purpose of this book, we can understand the Semantic Web as the following:

> The Semantic Web is a collection of technologies and standards that allow machines to understand the meaning (semantics) of information on the Web.

To see this, recall Sect. 1.1.2 has described some requirements for both the current Web and agents, in order to bring the concept of the Semantic Web into reality. If we understand the Semantic Web as a collection of technologies and standards, Table 1.1 summarizes how those requirements summarized in Sect. 1.1.2 can be mapped to the Semantic Web's major technologies and standards.

Table 1.1 may not make sense at this point, but all the related technologies and standards are covered in detail in the upcoming chapters of this book. When you finish this book and come back to review Table 1.1, you should be able to understand it much more easily.

1.3.2   The Semantic Web, Linked Data and the Web of Data

Linked Data and the *Web of Data* are concepts that are closely related to the concept of the Semantic Web. We take a brief look at these terms in this section. You will see more details about Linked Data and Web of Data in later chapters.

The idea of Linked Data was originally proposed by Tim Berners-Lee, and his 2006 Linked Data Principles[4] is considered to be the official and formal introduction of the concept itself. At its current stage, Linked Data is a W3C-backed movement that focus on connecting data sets across the Web, and it can be viewed as a subset of the Semantic Web concept, which is all about adding meanings to the Web.

---

[3] http://www.w3.org/2001/sw/

[4] http://www.w3.org/DesignIssues/LinkedData.html

Table 1.1 Requirements in Sect. 1.1.2 mapped to Semantic Web technologies and standards

Requirements	Semantic Web technologies and standards
Each statement collected by our agent represents a piece of knowledge. Therefore, there has to be a way (a model) to represent knowledge on the Web site. And furthermore, this model of representing knowledge has to be easily and readily processed (understood) by machines	Resource Description Framework (RDF)
This model has to be accepted as a standard by all the Web sites; therefore, statements contained in different Web sites all looked "similar" to each other	Resource Description Framework (RDF)
There has to be a way to create these statements on each Web site, for example, they can be either manually added or automatically generated	Semantic markup, RDFa, Microformats
The statements contained in different Web sites cannot be too arbitrary. For example, they should be created by using some common terms and relationships, perhaps on the basis of a given domain. For instance, to describe a person, we have some common terms such as name, birthday and homepage, etc.	Domain-specific ontologies/ vocabularies
There has to be a way to define these common terms and relationships, and there has to be some kind of agreement on these common terms and relationships. Different Web sites, when creating their statements, will use these terms and relationships	RDF Schema (RDFS), Web Ontology Language (OWL)
Our agent has to be able to understand each statement that it collects. One way to accomplish this is by understanding the common terms and relationships that are used to create these statements	Supporting tools for ontology processing
Our agent has to be able to conduct reasoning based on its understanding of the common terms and relationships. For example, knowing the fact that resources A and B have the same e-mail address and considering the knowledge expressed by the common terms and relationships, it should be able to decide that A and B are in fact the same resource	Reasoning based on ontologies
Our agent should be able to process some common queries that are submitted against the statements it has collected. After all, without providing a query interface, the collected statements will not be of much use to us	SPARQL query language

To understand the concept of Linked Data, think about the motivating example presented in Sect. 1.1.1. More specifically, our agent has visited several pages and has collected a list of statements from each Web site. These statements, as we know now, represented the added meaning to that particular Web site. This has given us the impression that the added structure information for machines has to be associated with some hosting Web site, and has to be either manually created or automatically generated.

In fact, there is no absolute need that machines and human beings have to share the same Web site. Therefore, it is also possible to *directly* publish some structured information online (a collection of machine-understandable statements, for example) without having them related to any Web site at all. Once this is done, these statements as a dataset are ready to be harvested and processed by applications.

Of course, such a dataset is not of much use if it does not link to other datasets. Therefore, one important design principle is to make sure each such dataset has outgoing links to other datasets.

As a result, publishing structured data online and adding links among these datasets are the key aspects of the Linked Data concept. The Linked Data principles have specified the steps of accomplishing these key aspects. Without going into the details of Linked Data principles, understand that the term Linked Data refers to a set of best practices for publishing and connecting structured data on the Web.

What is the relationship between Linked Data and the Semantic Web? Once you finish this book (Linked Data is covered in Chap. 9), you should have a much better understanding. For now, let us simply summarize their relationship without much discussion:

- Linked Data is published by using Semantic Web technologies and standards.
- Similarly, Linked Data is linked together by using Semantic Web technologies and standards.
- The Semantic Web is the goal, and Linked Data provides the means to reach the goal.

Another important concept is the Web of Data. At this point, we can understand Web of Data as an interchangeable term for the Semantic Web. In fact, the Semantic Web can be defined as a collection of standard technologies to realize a Web of Data. In other words, if Linked Data is realized by using the Semantic Web standards and technologies, the result would be a Web of Data.

1.3.3   Some Basic Things About the Semantic Web

Before we set off into the world of the Semantic Web, there are some useful information resources you should know about. We list them in this section.

- http://www.w3.org/2001/sw/

This is the W3C Semantic Web Activity's official Web site. It has quite a lot of information, including a short introduction, the latest publications (articles and interviews), presentations, links to specifications and links to different working groups.

- http://www.w3.org/2001/sw/SW-FAQ

This is the W3C Semantic Web Frequently Asked Questions page. This is certainly very helpful to you if you have just started to learn the Semantic Web.

Again, when you finish this whole book, come back to this FAQ, take yet another look, and you will find that you have a much better understanding at that point.

- http://www.w3.org/2001/sw/interest/

This is the W3C Semantic Web Interest Group, which provides a public forum to discuss the use and development of the Semantic Web, with the goal of supporting developers. Therefore, this could a useful resource for you when you start your own development work.

- http://www.w3.org/2013/data/

This is the W3C Semantic Web Activity News Web site. From here, you can follow the news related to Semantic Web activity, especially news and progress about specifications and specification proposals.

- http://www.w3.org/2001/sw/wiki/Main_Page

This is the W3C Semantic Web Community Wiki page. It has quite a lot of information for anyone who is interested in the Semantic Web. It has links to a set of useful sites, such as events in the Semantic Web community, semantic Web tools, people in the Semantic Web community and popular ontologies, just to name a few. Make sure to check out this page if you are looking for related resources during the course of your study of this book.

- http://iswc2013.semanticweb.org/

There are a number of different conferences in the world of the Semantic Web. Among these conferences, the International Semantic Web Conference (ISWC) is a major international forum at which research on all aspects of the Semantic Web is presented, and the above is their official Web site. The ISWC conference started in 2001, and it has been the major conference ever since. Check out this conference to follow the latest research activities.

With all this being said, we are now ready to start the book. Again, you can find a roadmap of the whole book in the Preface, and you can download all the code examples for this book from www.liyangyu.com.

Reference

Berners-Lee T, Hendler J, Lassila O (2001) The semantic Web. Sci Am 284(5):34–43

Chapter 2
The Building Block for the Semantic Web: RDF

This chapter is probably the most important chapter in this whole book: it covers the Resource Description Framework (RDF) in detail; RDF is the building block for the Semantic Web. A solid understanding of RDF provides the key to the whole technical world that defines the foundation of the Semantic Web: once you have gained the understanding of RDF, all the rest of the technical components will become much easier to comprehend, and in fact, much more intuitive as well.

This chapter covers all the main aspects of RDF, including its concept, its abstract model, its semantics, its language constructs and features, together with ample real-world examples. This chapter also introduces available tools you can use when creating or understanding RDF models. Make sure you understand this chapter well before you move on. In addition, have some patience when reading this chapter: some concepts and ideas may look unnecessarily complex at the first glance, but eventually you will start to see the reasons behind them.

Let's get started.

2.1 RDF Overview

2.1.1 RDF In Official Language

The Resource Description Framework (RDF) was originally created in early 1999 by W3C as a standard for encoding metadata. The name, Resource Description Framework, was formally introduced in the corresponding W3C specification document that outlines the standard.[1]

---

[1] Resource Description Framework (RDF) Model and Syntax Specification, a W3C Recommendation, 22 February 1999. http://www.w3.org/TR/1999/REC-rdf-syntax-19990222/

© Springer-Verlag Berlin Heidelberg 2014
L. Yu, *A Developer's Guide to the Semantic Web*,
DOI 10.1007/978-3-662-43796-4_2

As we discussed earlier, the current Web is built for human consumption, and it is not machine-understandable at all. It is therefore very difficult to automate anything on the Web, at least on a large scale. Furthermore, given the huge amount of information the Web contains, it is also impossible to manage it manually. A solution proposed by W3C is to use metadata to describe the data contained on the Web, and the fact that this metadata itself is machine-understandable enables automated processing of the related Web resources.

With the above consideration in mind, RDF was proposed in 1999 as a basic model and foundation for creating and processing metadata. Its goal is to define a mechanism for describing resources that makes no assumptions about a particular application domain (domain independent), and therefore can be used to describe information about any domain. The final result is that the RDF concept and model can directly help to promote interoperability between applications that exchange machine-understandable information on the Web.

As we discussed in Chap. 1, the concept of the Semantic Web was formally introduced to the world in 2001, and the goal of the Semantic Web is to make the Web machine-understandable. The obvious logical connection between the Semantic Web and RDF has greatly changed RDF: the scope of RDF has since then involved into something that is much greater. As can be seen throughout this book, RDF is not only used for encoding metadata about Web resources, but it is also used for describing *any* resources and their relations existing in the real world.

This much larger scope of RDF has been summarized in the updated RDF specifications published in 2004 by the RDF Core Working Group[2] as part of the W3C Semantic Web Activity.[3] This updated RDF specification comprises six documents (Table 2.1). These six documents have since then jointly replaced the original Resource Description Framework specification (1999 Recommendation), and they together became the new RDF W3C Recommendation on February 10, 2004.

Based on these official documents, RDF can be defined as follows:

• RDF is a language for representing information about resources in the World Wide Web (*RDF Primer*);

Table 2.1 RDF W3C Recommendation, February 10, 2004

Specification	Recommendation
RDF primer	10 February 2004
RDF test cases	10 February 2004
RDF concept	10 February 2004
RDF semantics	10 February 2004
RDF schema	10 February 2004
RDF syntax	10 February 2004

---

[2] RDFCore Working Group, W3C Recommendations, http://www.w3.org/2001/sw/RDFCore/
[3] W3C Semantic Web Activity, http://www.w3.org/2001/sw/

- RDF is a framework for representing information on the Web (*RDF Concept*);
- RDF is a general-purpose language for representing information in the Web (*RDF Syntax, RDF Schema*);
- RDF is an assertional language intended to be used to express propositions using precise formal vocabularies, particularly those specified using RDFS, for access and use over the World Wide Web, and is intended to provide a basic foundation for more advanced assertional languages with a similar purpose (*RDF Semantics*).

At this point, it is probably not easy to truly understand what RDF is based on these official definitions. Let us keep these definitions in mind, and once you have finished this chapter, review these definitions; you should find yourself having a better understanding of them.

For now, let us move on to some more explanation in plain English about what exactly RDF is and why we need it. This explanation will be much easier to understand and will give you enough background and motivation to continue reading the rest of this chapter.

2.1.2 RDF in Plain English

Let us forget about RDF for a moment, and consider those Web sites where we can find reviews of different products (such as Amazon.com, for example). Similarly, there are also Web sites that sponsor discussion forums where a group of people get together to discuss the pros and cons of a given product. The reviews published at these sites can be quite useful when you are trying to decide whether you should buy a specific product or not.

For example, I am a big fan of photography, and I have recently decided to upgrade my equipment—to buy a Nikon single lens reflex (SLR) or digital SLR (DSLR) camera so I will have more control over how a picture is taken, and therefore have more opportunity to show my creative side. However, most if not all Nikon SLR models are quite expensive, so to spend money wisely, I have read quite a lot of reviews, with the goal of choosing the one particular model that fits my needs the best.

You have probably had the same experience with some other product. Also, you would likely agree with me that reading these reviews takes a lot of time. In addition, even after reading quite a few reviews, you still may not be sure: could I have missed some reviews that would be very useful?

Now, imagine you are a quality engineer who works for Nikon. Your assignment is to read all these reviews and summarize what people have said about Nikon SLR cameras, and report back to Nikon headquarter so the design department can make better designs based on these reviews. Obviously, you can do your job by reading as many reviews as you can, and manually create a summary report and submit it to your boss. However, this is not only tedious, but also quite demanding: you could spend the whole morning reading, and only have covered a couple dozen reviews, with hundreds more to go!

One way to solve this problem is to write an application that reads all these reviews for you and generates a report automatically, all in a matter of a couple of minutes. Better yet, you could run this application as often as you want, just to gather the latest reviews. This is a great idea with only one flaw: such an application is not easy to develop, since the reviews published online are intended for human eyes to consume, not for machines to read.

Now, in order to solve this problem once and for all so as to make sure you have a smooth and successful career path, you start to consider the following key issue:

Assuming all the review publishers are willing to accept and follow some standard when they publish their reviews, what standard would make it easier to develop such an application?

Notice the words we used were *standard* and *easier*. Indeed, although writing such an application is difficult, there is in fact nothing stopping us from actually doing it, even on the current Web and without any standard. For example, screen-scraping can be used to read reviews from Amazon.com's review page (Fig. 2.1).

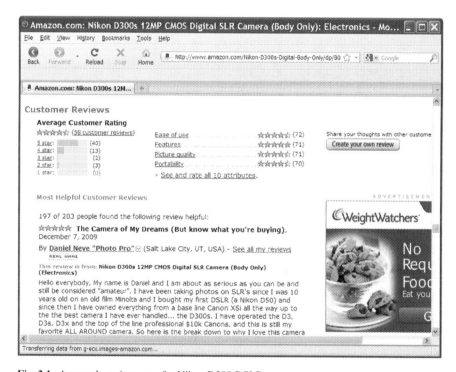

Fig. 2.1 Amazon's review page for Nikon D300 DSLR camera

On this page, a screen-scraping agent can pick up the fact that 40 customers have assigned 5 stars to Nikon D300 (a DSLR camera by Nikon), and 4 attributes are currently used for reviewing this camera: *Ease of use*, *Features*, *Picture quality* and *Portability*.

Once we have finished coding the agent that understands the reviews from Amazon.com, we can move on to the next review site. It is likely that we will have to add another new set of rules to our agent so it can understand the published reviews on that specific site. The same is true for the next site, and so on and so forth.

There is indeed quite a lot of work, and obviously, it is also not a scalable way to develop an application. In addition, when it comes to the maintenance of this application, it could be more difficult than the initial development work. For instance, a small change on any given review site can easily break the logic that is used to understand that site, and you will find yourself constantly being busy changing and fixing the code.

And this is exactly why a standard is important: once we have a standard that all the review sites follow, it is much easier to write an application to collect the distributed reviews and come up with a summary report.

Now, what exactly is this standard? Perhaps it is quite challenging to come up with a complete standard right away, but it might not be too difficult to specify some of the things we would want such a standard to have:

• It should be flexible enough to express any information anyone can think of.

Obviously, each reviewer has different things to say about a given Nikon camera, and whatever she/he wants to say, the standard has to provide a way to allow it. Perhaps the graph shown in Fig. 2.2 is a possible choice—any new information can be added to this graph freely: just add to it as you wish.

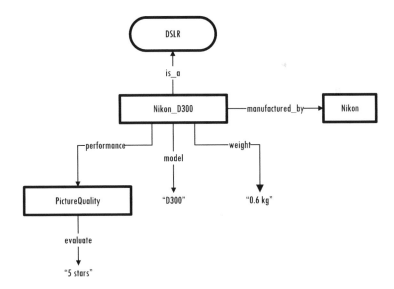

Fig. 2.2 A graph is flexible and can grow easily

Table 2.2 Tabular notation
of the graph in Fig. 2.2

Start node	Edge label	End node
Nikon_D300	is_a	DSLR
Nikon_D300	manufactured_by	Nikon
Nikon_D300	performance	PictureQuality
Nikon_D300	model	"D300"
Nikon_D300	weight	"0.6 kg"
PictureQuality	evaluate	"5 stars"

To represent this graph as structured information is not as difficult as you think:
the tabular notation shown in Table 2.2 is exactly equivalent to the graph shown in
Fig. 2.2.

More specifically, each row in the table represents one arrow in the graph,
including the start node, the edge with the arrow and the end node. The first column,
therefore, has the name of the start node, the second column has the label of the
edge, and the third column has the name of the end node. Clearly, no matter how the
graph grows and no matter how complex it becomes, Table 2.2 will always be able
to represent it correctly.

- It should provide a mechanism to connect the distributed information (knowledge) over the Web.

Now that every reviewer can publish his/her review freely and a given review
can be represented by a graph as we discussed above, the standard has to provide a
way so that our application, when visiting each review graph, is able to decide
precisely which product this review is talking about. After all, reviews created by
reviewers are distributed all over the Web, and different reviewers can use different
names for exactly the same product. For example, one reviewer can call it "Nikon
D300", another reviewer can use "Nikon D-300" and the next one simply names it
"D300". Our standard has to provide a way to eliminate this ambiguity so our
application can process the reviews with certainty.

- More requirements you can think of?

Yes, there are probably more requirements you would like to add to this
standard, but you have gotten the point. And, as you have guessed, W3C has long
realized the need for such a standard, and the standard has been published and
called RDF.

So, in plain English, we can define RDF as follows:

RDF is a standard published by W3C that can be used to represent distributed
information/knowledge in a way that computer applications can use and
process it in a scalable manner.

At this point, the above definition of RDF is good enough for us to continue. With more and more understanding about RDF, the following will become more and more obvious to you:

- RDF is the basic building block for supporting the vision of the Semantic Web;
- RDF is for the Semantic Web what HTML has been for the Web.

And the reason for RDF being the building block for the Semantic Web lies in the fact that knowledge represented using the RDF standard is structured, i.e., it is machine-understandable. This further means that RDF allows interoperability among applications exchanging machine-understandable information on the Web, and this, as you can tell, it is the fundamental idea of the Semantic Web.

2.2   The Abstract Model of RDF

In previous section, we mentioned the six documents comprising the RDF specification (Table 2.1). These documents taken together describe different aspects of RDF. One fundamental concept of RDF is its abstract model that is used to represent knowledge about the world. In this section, we learn this abstract model in detail.

2.2.1   The Big Picture

Before we get into the details, let us first take a look at the big picture of this abstract model, so it will be easier for you to understand the rest of its content.

The basic idea is straightforward: RDF uses this abstract model to decompose information/knowledge into small pieces, with some simple rules about the semantics (meaning) of each one of these pieces. The goal is to provide a general method that is simple and flexible enough to express any fact, yet structured enough that computer applications can operate with the expressed knowledge.

This abstract model has the following key components:

- statement
- subject and object resources
- predicate

And we will now discuss each one of these components, and then put them together to gain understanding of the abstract model as a whole.

Fig. 2.3 Graph structure of
RDF statement

2.2.2 Statement

As we have discussed, the key idea of RDF's abstract model is to break information
into small pieces, and each small piece has clearly defined semantics so that a
machine can understand it and do useful things with it. Now, using RDF's terminology, a given small piece of knowledge is called a *statement*, and the implementation of the above key idea can be expressed as the following rule:

*Rule #1: Knowledge (or information) is expressed as a list of statements; each
statement takes the form of Subject-Predicate-Object, and this order should never
be changed.*

Therefore, a RDF statement must have the following format:

```
subject predicate object
```

where the `subject` and `object` are names for two things in the world, with the
`predicate` being the name of a relation that connects these two things. Figure 2.3
shows the graph structure of a statement.

Notice that Fig. 2.3 shows a directed graph: the subject is contained in the oval
on the left, the object is the oval on the right, and the predicate is the label on the
arrow, which points from the subject to the object.

With this said, the information contained in Table 2.2 can be expressed as the
following statements shown in List 2.1.

List 2.1 Expressing Table 2.2 as a collection of RDF statements

subject	predicate	object
Nikon_D300	is_a	DSLR
Nikon_D300	manufactured_by	Nikon
Nikon_D300	performance	PictureQuality
Nikon_D300	model	"D300"
Nikon_D300	weight	"0.6 kg"
PictureQuality	evaluate	"5 stars"

Notice that since a statement always consists of three fixed components, it is also
called a *triple*. Therefore, in the world of RDF, each statement or triple represents a
single fact, a collection of statements or triples represents some given piece of
information or knowledge, and a collection of statements is called a *RDF graph*.

Now, is this abstract model flexible enough to represent any knowledge? The answer is yes, as long as that given knowledge can be expressed as a labeled and directed graph as shown in Fig. 2.2. And clearly, any new fact can be easily added to an existing graph to make it more expressive. Furthermore, without any loss to its original meaning, any such graph can be represented by a tabular format as shown in Table 2.2, which can then be expressed as a collection of RDF statements as shown in List 2.1, representing a concrete implementation of the RDF abstract model.

For any given RDF statement, both its `subject` and `object` are simple names for things in the world, and they are said to *refer to* or *denote* these things. Notice that these things can be anything, concrete or abstract. For example, the first statement in List 2.1 has both its `subject` and `object` refer to concrete things, while the third statement in List 2.1 has its `object` refer to `PictureQuality`, an abstract thing (concept).

In the world of RDF, the thing that a given `subject` or `object` denotes, be it concrete or abstract, is called a *resource*. Therefore, a resource is anything that is being described by RDF statements.

With this said, both `subject` and `object` in a statement are all names for resources. The question now is how do we come up with these names? This turns out to be a very important aspect of the RDF abstract model. Let us discuss this in detail in the next section.

2.2.3   Resource and Its URI Name

Let us go back to List 2.1, which contains a list of statements about the Nikon D300 camera as a resource in the real world. Imagine it is a review file created by one of the reviewers, and that this review is intended to be published on the Web.

Now, once this review is put on the Web, the resource names in this review, such as `Nikon_D300`, will present a problem. More specifically, it is quite possible that different reviewers may use different names to represent the same resource, namely, a Nikon D300 camera in this case. For example, one might use `Nikon-D300` instead of `Nikon_D300`. Even such a small difference will become a big problem for an application that tries to aggregate the reviews from different reviewers: it does not know these two reviews are in fact evaluating the same resource.

On the flip side of the coin, it is also possible that two different documents may have used the same name to represent different resources. In other words, a single name has different meanings. Without even seeing any examples, we all understand this semantic ambiguity is exactly what we want to avoid in order for any application to work correctly on the Web.

The solution proposed by RDF's abstract model is summarized in Rule #2 as follows:

Rule #2: The name of a resource must be global and should be identified by Uniform Resource Identifier (URI).

We are all familiar with URL (*Uniform Resource Locator*), and we use it all the time to locate a Web page we want to access. The reason why we can use URL to locate a Web resource is because it represents the network location of this given Web resource.

However, there is a subtle fact about URLs that most of us are not familiar with: a URL is often used to identify a Web resource that can be *directly* retrieved on the Web. For example, my personal home page has a URL as given by the following:

```
http://www.liyangyu.com
```

This URL is not only used to identify my home page, but also is used to retrieve it from the Web.

On the other hand, there are also lots of resources in the world that can be identified on the Web, but cannot be directly retrieved from the Web. For example, I myself as a person can be identified on the Web, but cannot be directly retrieved from the Web. Similarly, a Nikon D300 camera can be identified on the Web, yet we cannot retrieve it from the Web either. Therefore, for these resources, we cannot simply use URLs to represent them.

Fortunately, the Web provides a more general form of identifier for this purpose called the Uniform Resource Identifier (URI). In general, URLs can be understood as a particular kind of URI. Therefore, a URI can be created to identify anything that can be retrieved directly from the Web, and can also be created to represent anything that is not network-accessible, such as a human being, a building or even an abstract concept that does not physically exist, such as the picture quality of a given camera.

The reason why RDF's abstract model decides to use URIs to identify resources in the world should become obvious to you at this point. The RDF model has to be extremely flexible since anyone can talk about anything at any time; it does not matter whether you can retrieve that resource on the Web or not. Furthermore, since any collection of RDF statements is intended to be published on the Web, using URIs to identify the subjects and objects in these statements is simply a natural fit.

Another benefit of using URIs to represent subject and object resources is related to their global uniqueness. Imagine we can collect all the URIs in the whole world, and let us call this collection the space of all names. Clearly, we can partition this whole name space into different sections simply by looking at their owners. For example, the organization W3C is the owner for all URIs that start with http:// www.w3c.org/. And by convention, only W3C will create any new URI that start with http://www.w3c.org/. This guarantees the global uniqueness of URIs and certainly prevents name clashes. If you create a URI using this convention, you can rest assured no one will use the same URI to denote something else.

Given all this, what does a URI look like? In the world of RDF, by convention, there are two different types of URIs we can use to identify a given resource, namely a *hash URI* and a *slash URI*. A slash URI is simply a normal URI that we are all familiar with; and a hash URI consists of the following components:

```
normal URI + # + fragment identifier
```

For example, to identify Nikon D300 as a resource on the Web, List 2.2 uses both the hash URI and the slash URI:

List 2.2 Use URI to identify Nikon D300 on the Web as a resource

```
http://www.liyangyu.com/camera/Nikon_D300
http://www.liyangyu.com/camera#Nikon_D300
```

The first URI in List 2.2 is a slash URI, and the second one is a hash URI. For this hash URI, its normal URI is given by `http://www.liyangyu.com/camera`, and its fragment identify is given by `Nikon_D300`.

Notice some times a hash URI is also called a *URI reference*, or *URIref*. At the time of this writing, hash URI seems to be the name that is more and more widely used.

Now, an obvious question: what is the different between a hash URI and a slash URI? Or, when naming a given resource, should we use a hash URI or should we use a slash URI?

In order to answer this question, we in fact have to answer another question first: if we type the URIs contained in List 2.2 (both the hash one and the slash one) into a Web browser, do we actually get anything back? Or, should we be expecting to get anything back at all?

Before 2007, there was no expectation that actual content should be served at that location, since URIs do not require the entities being identified to be actually retrievable from the Web. Therefore, the fact that URIs look like web addresses is totally incidental; they are merely verbose names for resources.

However, since early 2007, especially with the development of the Linked Data project, dereferencing URIs in RDF models should return some content back, so that both human readers and applications can make use of the returned information.

You can see more about the Linked Data project and understand more about URIs in Chap. 9. For now, it is important to remember that URIs in RDF models should be dereferenceable URIs. Therefore, if you mint a URI, you are actually required to put something at that address so that RDF clients can access that page and get some information back.

With this new requirement, the difference between a hash URI and a slash URI starts to become more significant. Since you are going to see all the details in Chap. 9, let us simply state the conclusion here without too much explanation: it is easier to make sure a hash URI is also a dereferencable URI, since you can easily accomplish this without any content negotiation mechanism. However, to make a slash URI dereferenceable, content negotiation is normally needed.

With all this being said, for the rest of this chapter we are going to use hash URI. Furthermore, if we do create a new URI, we will not worry about serving content at that location—you will learn how to do that in Chap. 9.

Now, with the understanding that all the resources should be named by using URIs, we can revisit List 2.1 and rename all the resources there. List 2.3 shows the resources and their URI names.

List 2.3 Using URIs to name resources

```
original name       URI name
Nikon_D300          http://www.liyangyu.com/camera#Nikon_D300
DSLR                http://www.liyangyu.com/camera#DSLR
Nikon               http://www.dbpedia.org/resource/Nikon
PictureQuality      http://www.liyangyu.com/camera#PictureQuality
```

Notice that all the new URIs we have created contain the following domain,

```
http://www.liyangyu.com/
```

except for the URI for Nikon, the manufacturer of the camera. And this URI looks like this:

```
http://www.dbpedia.org/resource/Nikon
```

In fact, we did not coin this URI; it is an existing one. So why should we use an existing URI to represent Nikon? The reason is very simple: if a given resource has a URI that identifies it already, we should reuse this existing URI whenever we can. In our case, we happen to know that the above URI created by DBpedia project[4] (DBpedia is a well-known application in the world of the Semantic Web; you can see more details about it in Chap. 8) does represent Nikon, and it is indeed the same Nikon we are talking about. Therefore, we have decided to use it instead of inventing our own.

This does open up another whole set of questions. For example, is it good to always reuse URIs, or should we sometimes invent our own? If reuse is desirable,

---

[4] http://dbpedia.org/About

then for a given resource, how do we know if there already exists a URI? How do we find it? What if there are multiple URIs existing for this single resource?

At this point, we are not going into the details of the answers to these questions, since they are all covered in later chapters. For now, one thing important to remember is to always reuse URIs, and only invent your own if you absolutely have to.

And as you can tell, for the rest of the resources in List 2.3, we have simply chosen to invent our own URIs, because the main goal here is to show you the concept of the RDF abstract model. If we were to build a real project about reviewing cameras, we would have searched for existing URIs first (details presented in Chap. 9). For your information, the following is an existing URI that represents Nikon D300 camera. Again, this URI was minted by the DBpedia project:

```
http://dbpedia.org/resource/Nikon_D300
```

Also notice that both URIs created by DBpedia, i.e., the one representing Nikon and the above one identifying Nikon D300 camera, are all slash URIs. The URIs that we created in List 2.3 are all hash URIs.

Now, before we can rewrite the statements listed in List 2.1, we do have one more issue to cover: if we use URIs to represent resources as required by RDF abstract model, all the resources will inevitably have fairly long names. This is not quite convenient and not quite readable either.

The solution to this issue is quite straightforward: a full URI is usually abbreviated by replacing it with its XML *qualified name* (*QName*). Recall in the XML world, a QName contains a *prefix* that maps to a namespace URI, followed by a colon and then a *local name*. Using our case as an example, we can declare the following two namespace prefixes as shown in List 2.4:

List 2.4 Namespace prefixes for our example review

```
prefix          namespace
myCamera        http://www.liyangyu.com/camera#
dbpedia         http://www.dbpedia.org/resource/
```

And now, the following full URI,

```
http://www.liyangyu.com/camera#Nikon_D300
```

can be written as

```
myCamera:Nikon_D300
```

and similarly, this full URI

```
http://www.dbpedia.org/resource/Nikon
```

can be written as

```
dbpedia:Nikon
```

As you will see later in this chapter, there are different serialization formats for RDF models, and the precise rules for abbreviation depend on the RDF serialization syntax being used. For now, this QName notation is fine. And remember, namespaces possess no significant meanings in RDF; they are merely a tool to abbreviate long URI names.

Now we can rewrite the statements listed in List 2.1. After replacing the simple names we have used in List 2.1, the new statements are summarized in List 2.5.

List 2.5 RDF statements using URIs as resource names

subject	predicate	object
myCamera:Nikon_D300	is_a	myCamera:DSLR
myCamera:Nikon_D300	manufactured_by	dbpedia:Nikon
myCamera:Nikon_D300	performance	myCamera:PictureQuality
myCamera:Nikon_D300	model	"D300"
myCamera:Nikon_D300	weight	"0.6 kg"
myCamera:PictureQuality	evaluate	"5 stars"

Looking at List 2.5, you might start to think about the predicate column: do we have to use URI to name predicate as well? The answer is yes, and it is indeed very important to do so. Let us discuss this more in the next section.

2.2.4 Predicate and Its URI Name

In a given RDF statement, predicate denotes the relation between the subject and object. The RDF abstract model requires the usage of URIs to identify predicates, rather than using strings (or words) such as "has" or "is_a" to identify predicates.

With this said, we can change rule #2 to make it more complete:

Rule #2: The name of a resource must be global and should be identified by Uniform Resource Identifier (URI). The name of predicate must also be global and should be identified by URI as well.

Using URIs to identify predicates is important for a number of reasons. The first reason is similar to the reason why we should use URIs to name subjects and objects. For example, one group of reviewers who reviews cameras may use string `model` to indicate the fact that Nikon D300 has D300 as its model number, and another group of reviewers who mainly reviews television sets could also have used `model` to mean the specific model number of a given TV set. A given application seeing these `model` strings will have difficulty distinguishing their meanings. On the other hand, if the predicates for the camera reviewers and TV reviewers are named respectively as follows:

```
http://www.liyangyu.com/camera#model
http://www.liyangyu.com/TV#model
```

it will then be clear to the application that these are distinct predicates.

Another benefit of using URIs to name predicates comes from the fact that this enables the predicates to be treated as resources as well. This, in fact, has a far-reaching effect down the road. More specifically, if a given predicate is seen as a resource, we can then add RDF statements with this predicate's URI as subject, just as we do for any other resource. This means that additional information about the given predicate can be added. As we will see in later chapters, by adding this additional information, we can specify some useful facts about this predicate. For example, we can add the fact that this given predicate is the same as another predicate, or that it is a subpredicate of another predicate, or it is an inverse predicate of another predicate, so on and so forth. This additional information turns out to be one of the main factors that are responsible for the reasoning power provided by RDF models, as you will see in later chapters.

The third benefit, which will also become more obvious later, is that using URIs to name subjects, predicates, and objects in RDF statements promotes the development and use of shared vocabularies on the Web. Recall that we have been using the following URI to denote Nikon as a company that has manufactured the Nikon D300:

```
http://www.dbpedia.org/resource/Nikon
```

Similarly, if we could find an existing URI that denotes `model` as a predicate, we could have used it instead of inventing our own. In other words, by discovering and using vocabularies already used by others to describe resources implies a shared understanding of those concepts, and that will eventually make the Web much more machine friendly. Again, we will discuss this more in the chapters yet to come.

Now, with all this said, let us name our predicates (List 2.6):

List 2.6 Using URIs to name predicates

original name	URI name
is_a	http://www.liyangyu.com/camera#is_a
manufactured_by	http://www.liyangyu.com/camera#manufactured_by
performance	http://www.liyangyu.com/camera#performance
model	http://www.liyangyu.com/camera#model
weight	http://www.liyangyu.com/camera#weight
evaluate	http://www.liyangyu.com/camera#evaluate

With these new predicate names, List 2.5 can be rewritten. For example, the first statement can be written as the following:

subject: myCamera:Nikon_D300
predicate: myCamera:is_a
object: myCamera:DSLR

You can finish the rest statements in List 2.5 accordingly.

So far at this point, we have covered two basic rules about the abstract RDF model. Before we move on to other aspects of the abstract model, we would like to present a small example to show you that these two rules have already taken you farther than you might have realized.

2.2.5 RDF Triples: Knowledge That Machines Can Use

Let us take a detour here, just to see how RDF statements (triples) can be used by machines. With the statements in List 2.5, let us ask the machine the following questions:

- What predicates did the reviewer use to describe Nikon D300?
- What performance measurements have been used for Nikon D300?

The first question can be expressed in the following RDF format:

```
question = new RDFStatement();
question.subject = myCamera:Nikon_D300;
question.predicate = myCamera:*;
```

Notice myCamera:* is used as a wild card. The pseudo-code in List 2.7 can help the computer to answer the question:

List 2.7 Pseudo-code to answer questions

```
// format my question
question = new RDFStatement();
question.subject   = myCamera:Nikon_D300;
question.predicate = myCamera:*;

// read all the review statements and store them in statement ar-
ray
RDFStatement[] reviewStatements = new RDFStatement[6];
reviewStatements[0].subject   = myCamera:Nikon_D300;
reviewStatements[0].predicate = myCamera:is_a;
reviewStatements[0].object = myCamera:DSLR;
reviewStatements[1].subject   = myCamera:Nikon_D300;
reviewStatements[1].predicate = myCamera:manufactured_by;
reviewStatements[1].object = dbpedia:Nikon;
reviewStatements[2].subject   = myCamera:Nikon_D300;
reviewStatements[2].predicate = myCamera:performance;
reviewStatements[2].object = myCamera:PictureQuality;
reviewStatements[3].subject   = myCamera:Nikon_D300;
reviewStatements[3].predicate = myCamera:model;
reviewStatements[3].object = "D300";
reviewStatements[4].subject   = myCamera:Nikon_D300;
reviewStatements[4].predicate = myCamera:weight;
reviewStatements[4].object = "0.6 kg";
reviewStatements[5].subject   = myCamera:PictureQuality;
reviewStatements[5].predicate = myCamera:evaluate;
reviewStatements[5].object = "5 stars";

// answer the question!
foreach s in reviewStatements[] {
   if ( (s.subject==question.subject || question.subject=='*') &&
         (s.predicate==question.predicate || question.predicate ==
         '*') ) {
      System.out.println(s.predicate.toString());
   }
};
```

Runing this code gives us the following answer:

```
myCamera:is_a
myCamera:manufactured_by
myCamera:performance
```

```
myCamera:model
myCamera:weight
```

meaning that the reviewer has defined all the above predicates for Nikon D300. Now, to answer the second question, all you have to change is the question itself:

```
question = new RDFStatement();
question.subject = myCamera:Nikon_D300;
question.predicate = myCamera:performance;
```

and also change the output line in List 2.7 to the following:

```
System.out.println(s.subject.toString());
```

and the answer will be returned to you:

```
myCamera:PictureQuality
```

meaning that the reviewer has used `myCamera:PictureQuality` as the performance measurement to evaluate Nikon D300.

In fact, try out some other questions, such as who is the manufacturer of Nikon D300, what model number does it have, etc. You will see the code does not have to change much at all. And clearly, based on the knowledge presented in the RDF statements (Table 2.2), machines can indeed conduct some useful work for us. It is also not hard for us to imagine some more interesting examples if we can add more RDF statements with more complex predicates and objects.

2.2.6   RDF Literals and Blank Node

We are not totally done with the abstract RDF model yet. In this section, we describe two important components of abstract model: RDF literals and blank node. First, let us summarize all the terminologies we have learned so far.

2.2.6.1   Basic Terminologies So Far

One difficulty about learning RDF comes from the fact that it has lots of terminologies and synonyms. To make our learning easier, let us summarize these terminologies and their synonyms in this section.

So far, we have learned the following:

Subject:	used to denote *resource* in the world, must be identified by URI, and also called *node*, or *start node* in an RDF graph;
Object:	used to denote *resource* in the world, must be identified by URI, and also called *node*, or *end node* in an RDF graph;
Predicate:	used to denote the relation between subject and object, must be identified by URI, also called *edge* in an RDF graph.

This summary certainly needs to grow. For example, you might have already noticed that the following statement does not completely follow the above summary:

Subject	Predicate	Object
myCamera:Nikon_D300	myCamera:model	"D300"

Since its object obviously takes a string as its value, instead of another resource. Also, the string value has nothing to do with URIs. In addition, there are two more similar statements in our list:

Subject	Predicate	Object
myCamera:Nikon_D300	myCamera:weight	"0.6 kg"
myCamera:PictureQuality	myCamera:evaluate	"5 stars"

Before we explain all these issues, let us first see something new:

- *predicate*: also called *property*, i.e., predicate and property are synonyms.

This is a quite intuitive change. To see this, consider the following statement,

Subject	Predicate	Object
myCamera:Nikon_D300	myCamera:is_a	myCamera:DSLR

which can be read as follows:

resource myCamera:Nikon_D300 and resource myCamera:DSLR are related by a predicate called myCamera:is_a.

Now, besides understanding predicate as a relation between the subject and object resource, we can also perceive it as putting some constraint on one of the attributes (properties) of the subject resource. In our case, the myCamera:is_a attribute (property) of the subject takes resource myCamera:DSLR as its value. With this said, the above statement can be read in a different way:

myCamera:is_a is a *property* of resource myCamera:Nikon_D300 and resource myCamera:DSLR is the *value* of this property.

Fig. 2.4 Graph structure of RDF statement (equivalent to Fig. 2.3)

Now we can change the names of the components in a RDF statement to make it more consistent with the above reading:

Resource	Property	Value
myCamera:Nikon_D300	myCamera:is_a	myCamera:DSLR

and with this said, Fig. 2.3 is completely equivalent to Fig. 2.4.
And now,

- *object*: also called property *value*, and both literal strings and resources can be used as property value. If a resource is used as its value, this resource may or may not be identified by a URI. If it is not represented by a URI, it is called a *blank node*.

Notice that the object in one statement can become the subject in another statement (such as myCamera:PictureQuality, for example). Therefore, a blank node object in one statement can become a blank node subject in another statement.
To summarize what we have learned:

Subject:	can be URI named resource, or a blank node;
Object:	also called property value, can be URI named resource, literal or blank node;
Predicate:	also called property, must be URI named resource.

And now we understand why we can have statements that use string values as their objects. Let us move on to learn more about literals and blank nodes, two important concepts in the abstract RDF model.

2.2.6.2 Literal Values

RDF literals are simple raw text data, and they can be used as property values. As we have seen in List 2.7, "D300", "0.6 kg" and "5 stars" are all examples of literal values. Other common examples include people's names and book ISBN numbers.

A literal value can be optionally localized by attaching a language tag, indicating in which language the raw text is written. For example, "Dr."@en, the literal value Dr. with an English language tag, or "Dott."@it, the same with an Italian language tag.

A literal value can also be optionally typed by using a URI that indicates a datatype, and this datatype information can be used by the RDF document parser to understand how to interpret the raw text. The datatype URI can be any URI, but quite often you will see that datatypes defined in XML Schema are being used.

To add a datatype to a literal value, put the literal value in quotes, and then use two carets, followed by the datatype URI. List 2.8 shows some examples of using both the language tag and datatype URIs:

List 2.8 Examples of using language tags and datatypes on RDF literal values

```
"D300"

"D300"@en

"D300"@it

"D300"^^<http://www.w3.org/2001/XMLSchema#string>
```

In List 2.8, the first line uses simple raw text without any language tag and any datatype; it is therefore an untyped literal value without any language tag. Line 2 and 3 are also untyped literal values, but they do have language tags. Line 4 is a typed literal value, and its full datatype URI is also written out.

Notice that an untyped literal, regardless of whether it has a language tag or not, is completely different from a typed literal. Therefore, the literal value on line 1 and the literal value on line 4 are considered two different things and are not related to each other at all. In fact, all the four literal values in List 2.8 are not related, therefore the four statements in List 2.9 are completely different, and no one can be inferred from the others.

List 2.9 Completely different statements (all the property values are different)

```
resource: myCamera:Nikon_D300
property: myCamera:model
value: "D300"

resource: myCamera:Nikon_D300
property: myCamera:model
value: "D300"@en

resource: myCamera:Nikon_D300
property: myCamera:model
value: "D300"@it

resource: myCamera:Nikon_D300
property: myCamera:model
value: "D300"^^<http://www.w3.org/2001/XMLSchema#string>
```

For a typed literal, the purpose of its datatype URI is to tell the parser or an application how to map the raw text string to values. It is therefore possible that two typed literals that appear different can be mapped to the same value. For example, the two statements in List 2.10 are equivalent:

List 2.10   Two identical statements

```
resource: myCamera:Nikon_D300
property: myCamera:weight
value: "0.6"^^<http://www.w3.org/2001/XMLSchema#float>

resource: myCamera:Nikon_D300
property: myCamera:weight
value: "0.60"^^<http://www.w3.org/2001/XMLSchema#float>
```

We discuss more about datatypes and typed literals in later sections. But before we move on, here is one more thing to remember: literals are only used as object values; they can never be used as subjects.

2.2.6.3   Blank Nodes

A *blank node* is a node (denotes either a subject or an object) that does not have a URI as its identifier, i.e., a nameless node. It in fact happens quite often in RDF models, and it is also called an *anonymous node* or a *bnode*. List 2.11 shows one example of a blank node:

List 2.11   Blank node example

resource	property	value
myCamera:Nikon_D300	myCamera:reviewed_by	_:anon0
_:anon0	foaf:givenname	"liyang"
_:anon0	foaf:family_name	"yu"

First off, foaf:givenname and foaf:family_name are just QNames, and they have used a new namespace, namely, foaf, that you have not seen yet. At this point, understand that both foaf:givenname and foaf:family_name are simply abbreviated URIs that represent properties. And obviously, these two properties are used to denote a person's first and last name.

Now, these three statements in List 2.11 have expressed the following fact:

this Nikon D300 camera (myCamera:Nikon_D300) is reviewed by (myCamera:reviewed_by) some specific resource in the world. This resource has a property called foaf:givenname whose value is liyang, it also has a property called foaf:family_name whose value is yu.

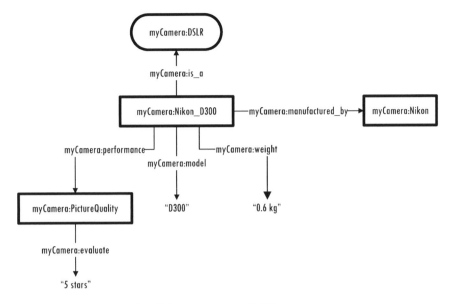

Fig. 2.5 Graph representation of the statements in List 2.5

And obviously, the blank node here represents this specific resource. Notice that when we say a node is a blank node, we refer to the fact that it does not have a URI as its name. However, in real RDF documents, it will most likely be assigned a local identifier so that it could be referred within the same document scope. In our example, this local identifier is given by _:anon0.

By now, we all know that a list of RDF statements can be represented by a RDF graph (and vice versa). For example, Fig. 2.5 shows the graph generated by representing the statement in List 2.5.

Now, if we add the statements in List 2.11 to the graph shown in Fig. 2.5, we get Fig. 2.6:

As you can tell, the local name of the blank node is not included in the graph, and it is now a real blank node—probably that is why the name was created at the first place.

The main benefit of using blank nodes is the fact that blank nodes provide a way to model the so-called *n-ary (n-way) relationship* in RDF models.

To see this, first understand that RDF only models *binary* relationships. For example, the following statement,

Resource	Property	Value
myCamera:Nikon_D300	myCamera:reviwed_by	"liyang yu"

represents a binary relationship, i.e., the relationship between a camera and the literal string that represents its reviewer. Now, there could be another reviewer who

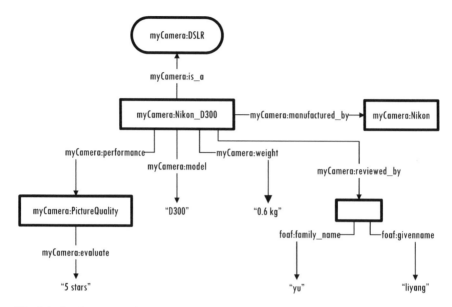

Fig. 2.6 Graph representation of the statements in Lists 2.5 and 2.11

has the same name. In order to eliminate this ambiguity, we decide that we will add more details to the reviewer. This time, not only will we spell out the first name and last name (as in List 2.11), we will also add an e-mail address of the reviewer, so we can be quite certain to whom we are referring.

However, by doing so, the camera is no longer related to a single literal string, instead, it is related to a collection of components (a last name, a first name and an e-mail address). In other words, the original binary relationship has now become an *n*-ary relationship ($n = 3$, to be more precise). So how does RDF model this *n*-way relationship?

The solution is to create another resource to represent this collection of components, and the original subject keeps its binary relationship to this newly created resource. Meanwhile, each one of the ·components in this collection can become a separate property of the new resource (List 2.12):

List 2.12 Modeling a three-way relationship between camera and reviewer

```
resource                property                value
myCamera:Nikon_D300 myCamera:reviewed_by new_resource_URI
new_resource_URI        foaf:givenname          "liyang"
new_resource_URI        foaf:family_name        "yu"
new_resource_URI        foaf:mbox               <mailto:liyang@liyangyu.com>
```

Again, `foaf:mbox` is just another QName that represents e-mail address property (more about `foaf` namespace in later chapters). Also, `new_resource_URI` is the new URI we have created, and it represents the collection of the three components. The important fact is that we have now successfully modeled a three-way relationship between a given camera and its reviewer.

As you can easily imagine, there are lots of similar scenarios like this in the real world, where we have to model *n*-ary relationships. Clearly, for each such *n*-ary relationship, there will be a new URI invented, which means we have to invent numerous URIs such as `new_resource_URI`. However, since most of these new URIs will never be referred from outside the graph, it is not necessary for them to have URIs at all. This is exactly the concept of blank node, and this is how blank nodes can help us to model a given *n*-ary relationship.

Again, as we have mentioned, most RDF processors automatically assign a local node identifier to a blank node, which is needed when the RDF statements are written out. In addition, other statements within the same document can make reference to this blank node if necessary. Of course, a blank node is not accessible from outside the graph, and it is not considered when data aggregation is performed.

Before we move on, here is one more thing to remember: blank nodes can only be used as subjects or objects; they cannot be used as properties.

2.2.7   A Summary So Far

Up to this point, we have covered the basic components of abstract RDF model. Before we move on, the following is a summary of what we have learned so far.

- RDF offers an abstract model and framework that tells us how to decompose information/knowledge into small pieces.
- One such small piece of information/knowledge is represented as a statement which has the form (subject, predicate, object). A statement is also called a triple.
- A given RDF model can be expressed either as a graph, or as a collection of statements or triples.
- Each statement maps to one edge in the graph. Therefore, the subject and object of a given statement are also called nodes, and its predicate is also called an edge.
- Subjects and objects denote resources in the real world. Predicates denote the relationship between subjects and objects.
- Predicates are also called properties, and objects are also called property values. Therefore, a statement also has the form (resource, property, propertyValue).

- URIs are used to name resources and properties. For a given resource or property, if there is an existing URI to name it, you should reuse it instead of inventing your own.
- An RDF statement can only model a binary relationship. To model an *n*-ary relationship, intermediate resources are introduced and blank nodes are quite often used.
- An object can take either a simple literal or another resource as its value. If a literal is used as its value, the literal can be typed or untyped, and can also have an optional language tag.

If you are comfortable with the above, move on. Otherwise, review the material in this section, and make sure you understand it completely.

2.3 RDF Serialization: RDF/XML Syntax

The RDF data model we have covered so far provides an abstract and conceptual framework for describing resources in a way that machines can process. The next step is to define some serialization syntax for creating and reading concrete RDF models, so applications can start to write and share RDF documents.

The W3C specifications define an XML syntax for this purpose. It is called RDF/XML, and is used to represent an RDF graph as an XML document. Notice that this is not the only serialization syntax that is being used. For example, Notation 3 (or N3) as a non-XML serialization format, is also introduced by W3C, and is widely used among the Semantic Web developers. This section concentrates on RDF/XML syntax only, and other formats will be discussed in later sections.

2.3.1 The Big Picture: RDF Vocabulary

As we have discussed, RDF uses URIs instead of words to name resources and properties. In addition, RDF refers to a set of URIs (often created for a specific purpose) as a *vocabulary*. Furthermore, all the URIs in such a vocabulary normally share a common leading string, which is used as the common prefix in these URIs' QNames. This prefix often becomes the namespace prefix for this vocabulary, and the URIs in this vocabulary are formed by appending individual local names to the end of this common leading string.

In order to define RDF/XML serialization syntax, a set of URIs are created and are given specific meanings by RDF. This group of URIs becomes RDF's own

vocabulary of terms, and it is called the *RDF vocabulary*. More specifically, the
URIs in this RDF vocabulary all share the following lead strings:

```
http://www.w3.org/1999/02/22-rdf-syntax-ns#
```

By convention, this URI prefix string is associated with namespace prefix `rdf:`,
and is typically used in XML with the prefix `rdf`. For this reason, this vocabulary is
also referred to as the `rdf:` vocabulary.

The terms in `rdf:` vocabulary are listed in List 2.13. Understanding the syntax of
RDF/XML means to understand the meaning of these terms and how to use them
when creating a concrete RDF model in XML format.

List 2.13 Terms in the RDF vocabulary

> Syntax names:
> `rdf:RDF, rdf:Description, rdf:ID, rdf:about, rdf:parseType,`
> `rdf:resource, rdf:li, rdf:nodeID, rdf:datatype`
>
> Class names:
> `rdf:Seq,  rdf:Bag,  rdf:Alt,  rdf:Statement,  rdf:Property,`
> `rdf:XMLLiteral, rdf:List`
>
> Property names:
> `rdf:subject,    rdf:predicate,    rdf:object,    rdf:type,`
> `rdf:value, rdf:first, rdf:rest_n` (where *n* is a decimal integer
> greater than zero with no leading zeros).
>
> Resource names:
> `rdf:nil`

From now on, `rdf:`*name* will be used to indicate a term from the RDF vocabulary, and its URI can be formed by concatenating the RDF namespace URI and
name itself. For example, the URI of `rdf:type` is given as below:

```
http://www.w3.org/1999/02/22-rdf-syntax-ns#type
```

2.3.2 Basic Syntax and Examples

As we have discussed, RDF/XML is the normative syntax for writing RDF models.
In this section, we describe the RDF/XML syntax, and most of the example
statements we are going to use come from List 2.5.

2.3.2.1 `rdf:RDF`, `rdf:Description`, `rdf:about` and `rdf:` resource

Now, let us start with the first statement in List 2.5:

Subject	Predicate	Object
myCamera:Nikon_D300	myCamera:is_a	myCamera:DSLR

List 2.14 shows the RDF/XML presentation of a RDF model that contains only this single statement:

List 2.14 RDF/XML presentation of the first statement in List 2.5

```
1: <?xml version="1.0"?>
2: <rdf:RDF
2a:     xmlns:rdf="http://www.w3.org/1999/02/22-rdf-syntax-ns#"
3:      xmlns:myCamera="http://www.liyangyu.com/camera#">
4: <rdf:Description
4a:     rdf:about="http://www.liyangyu.com/camera#Nikon_D300">
5:    <myCamera:is_a
5a:     rdf:resource="http://www.liyangyu.com/camera#DSLR"/>
6: </rdf:Description>
7: </rdf:RDF>
```

Since this is our very first RDF model expressed in XML format, let us explain it carefully.

Line 1 should look familiar. It says that this document is in the XML format; it also indicates which version of XML this document is in. Line 2 creates a `rdf:RDF` element, indicating this XML document is intended to represent a RDF model, which ends at the end tag, `</rdf:RDF>`. In general, whenever you want to create a XML document representing an RDF model, `rdf:RDF` should always be the root element of your XML document.

Line 2 also includes a XML namespace declaration by using an `xmlns` attribute, which specifies that prefix `rdf:` is used to represent the RDF namespace URI reference, i.e., `http://www.w3.org/1999/02/22-rdf-syntax-ns#`. Based on the discussion in Sect. 2.3.1, we know that any tag with the form of `rdf:name` is a term from the RDF vocabulary given in List 2.13. For instance, term `rdf:Description` (on line 4) is taken from the RDF vocabulary, and its URI name should be constructed by concatenating RDF namespace URI reference and local name. Therefore, its URI name is given by the following:

`http://www.w3.org/1999/02/22-rdf-syntax-ns#Description`

Line 3 adds a new `xmlns` attribute that declares another XML namespace. It specifies that prefix `myCamera:` should be used to represent the namespace URI given by `http://www.liyangyu.com/camera#`. Any term that has the name `myCamera:name` is therefore a term taken from this namespace.

At this point, the opening `<rdf:RDF>` tag is closed, indicated by the ">" sign at the end of line 3. In general, this is a typical routine for all RDF/XML documents, with the only difference being more or less namespace declarations in different RDF documents.

Now, any statement in a given RDF model is a description of a resource in the real world, with the resource being the subject of the statement. The term `rdf:Description` translates this fact into RDF/XML syntax. It indicates the start of a description of a resource, and it uses the `rdf:about` attribute to specify the resource that is being described, as shown on line 4.

In general, this kind of XML node in a given RDF/XML document is called a *resource XML node*. In this example, it represents a subject of a statement. You can understand line 4 as the following:

`<rdf:Description rdf:about` = "URI of the statement's subject">

Now, given the fact that tag `rdf:Description` indicates the start of a statement, `</rdf:Description>` must signify the end of a statement. Indeed, line 6 shows the end of our statement.

With this being said, line 5 has to specify the property and property value of the statement. It does so by using a `myCamera:is_a` tag to represent the property. Since the property value in this case is another resource, `rdf:resource` is used to identify it by referring to its URI.

Notice that line 5 is nested within the `rdf:Description` element, therefore, the property and property value specified by line 5 apply to the resource specified by the `rdf:about` attribute of the `rdf:Description` element.

In general, the node created by line 5 is called a *property XML node*. Clearly, each property XML node represents a single statement. Notice a given property node is always contained within a resource XML node, which represents the subject of the statement.

Now, after all the above discussion, lines 4–6 can be viewed as the following:

```
4: <rdf:Description rdf:about="URI of the statement's subject">
5:    <predicateURI rdf:resource="URI of the statement's object"/>
6: </rdf:Description>
```

and can be read like this:

This is a description about a resource named `myCamera:Nikon_D300`, which is an instance of another resource, namely, `myCamera:DSLR`.

At this point, we have finished our first RDF/XML document, which has only one statement. We will keep adding statements into this document until we have covered all the RDF vocabulary features.

2.3.2.2   `rdf:type` and Typed Nodes

Now, take a look at the statement in List 2.14. In order to express the knowledge that the Nikon D300 is a digital SLR, we had to invent a property called `myCamera:is_a`. It is not hard to imagine that this kind of requirement is quite common in other applications as well. For example, we will want to express the fact that a certain resource is a person, another resource is a book, so on and so forth. It then seems reasonable for the RDF vocabulary to provide some term just for this purpose, so a given application does not have to invent its own.

In RDF vocabulary, `rdf:type` exists to identify the type of a given resource. List 2.15 shows the term `rdf:type` in use.

List 2.15   Using `rdf:type` to specify the type of a given resource

```
1: <?xml version="1.0"?>
2: <rdf:RDF
2a:     xmlns:rdf="http://www.w3.org/1999/02/22-rdf-syntax-ns#"
3:     xmlns:myCamera="http://www.liyangyu.com/camera#">
4:    <rdf:Description
4a:        rdf:about="http://www.liyangyu.com/camera#Nikon_D300">
5:      <rdf:type
5a:          rdf:resource="http://www.liyangyu.com/camera#DSLR"/>
6:    </rdf:Description>
7: </rdf:RDF>
```

This is obviously a better choice: instead of inventing our own home-made property (`myCamera:is_a`), we are now using a common term from the RDF vocabulary. Figure 2.7 shows the graph representation of the statement in List 2.15.

The subject node in Fig. 2.7 is often called a *typed node* in a graph, or *typed node element* in RDF documents. Assigning a type to a resource has far-reaching implication than you might have realized now. As we will see in later sections

Fig. 2.7   Graph representation of the statement in List 2.15

and chapters, it is one of the reasons why we claim the RDF model represents structured information that machines can understand.

In fact, once we have the term `rdf:type` at our disposal, we can often write the statement in List 2.15 in a simpler format without using `rdf:Description`. List 2.16 shows the detail.

List 2.16 A simpler form of List 2.15

```
1: <?xml version="1.0"?>
2: <rdf:RDF
2a:      xmlns:rdf="http://www.w3.org/1999/02/22-rdf-syntax-ns#"
3:       xmlns:myCamera="http://www.liyangyu.com/camera#">
4:   <myCamera:DSLR
4a:       rdf:about="http://www.liyangyu.com/camera#Nikon_D300">
5:   </myCamera:DSLR>
6: </rdf:RDF>
```

List 2.16 is equivalent to List 2.15. In fact, most RDF parsers will change List 2.16 back to List 2.15 when they operate on the document. In addition, some developers believe the format in List 2.15 is clearer.

Now, let us take the rest of the statements from List 2.5 and add them to our RDF/XML document. List 2.17 shows the document after we have added the next statement.

List 2.17 Adding one more statement from List 2.5 to List 2.15

```
1: <?xml version="1.0"?>
2: <rdf:RDF
2a:      xmlns:rdf="http://www.w3.org/1999/02/22-rdf-syntax-ns#"
3:       xmlns:myCamera="http://www.liyangyu.com/camera#">
4:
5:   <rdf:Description
5a:       rdf:about="http://www.liyangyu.com/camera#Nikon_D300">
6:     <rdf:type
6a:         rdf:resource="http://www.liyangyu.com/camera#DSLR"/>
7:   </rdf:Description>
8:
9:   <rdf:Description
9a:       rdf:about="http://www.liyangyu.com/camera#Nikon_D300">
10:    <myCamera:manufactured_by
10a:       rdf:resource="http://www.dbpedia.org/resource/Nikon"/>
11:   </rdf:Description>
12:
13: </rdf:RDF>
```

The new statement added is expressed on lines 9–11. With the understanding of the first statement (lines 5–7), this new statement does not require too much explanation. However, we can make this a little bit more concise: since the two statements have the same subject, they can be combined together, as shown in List 2.18.

List 2.18 A simpler form of List 2.17

```
1:  <?xml version="1.0"?>
2:  <rdf:RDF
2a:     xmlns:rdf="http://www.w3.org/1999/02/22-rdf-syntax-ns#"
3:      xmlns:myCamera="http://www.liyangyu.com/camera#">
4:
5:   <rdf:Description
5a:      rdf:about="http://www.liyangyu.com/camera#Nikon_D300">
6:     <rdf:type
6a:        rdf:resource="http://www.liyangyu.com/camera#DSLR"/>
7:     <myCamera:manufactured_by
7a:        rdf:resource="http://www.dbpedia.org/resource/Nikon"/>
8:   </rdf:Description>
9:
10: </rdf:RDF>
```

Now, moving on to the rest of the statements from List 2.5 does require some new knowledge, which is explained in the next section.

2.3.2.3   Using Resource as Property Value

The next statement uses a resource called myCamera:PictureQuality as the value of its myCamera:performance property, which is not something totally new at this point. The two statements in the current RDF document (lines 6 and 7, List 2.18) are all using resources as their objects. However, there is a little bit more about this myCamera:PictureQuality resource: it has a property that needs to be described, as shown by the last statement in List 2.5.

List 2.19 shows one way to implement this:

List 2.19 Example of using resource as property value

```
1: <?xml version="1.0"?>
2: <rdf:RDF
2a:    xmlns:rdf="http://www.w3.org/1999/02/22-rdf-syntax-ns#"
3:       xmlns:myCamera="http://www.liyangyu.com/camera#">
4:
5:   <rdf:Description
5a:       rdf:about="http://www.liyangyu.com/camera#Nikon_D300">
6:      <rdf:type
6a:          rdf:resource="http://www.liyangyu.com/camera#DSLR"/>
7:      <myCamera:manufactured_by
7a:         rdf:resource="http://www.dbpedia.org/resource/Nikon"/>
8:      <myCamera:performance rdf:resource=
8a:             "http://www.liyangyu.com/camera#PictureQuality"/>
9:   </rdf:Description>
10:
11: <rdf:Description
11a:   rdf:about="http://www.liyangyu.com/camera#PictureQuality">
12:   <myCamera:evaluate>5 stars</myCamera:evaluate>
13: </rdf:Description>
14:
15: </rdf:RDF>
```

This approach first uses a rdf:resource attribute on myCamera:performance property, and this attribute points to the URI of the resource that is used at the object of this property (line 8). This object resource is further described separately by using a new rdf:Description node at the top-level of the document (lines 11–13).

Another way to represent resource as property value is to simply put the description of the object resource into the property XML node that uses this resource as the object value, as shown in List 2.20.

List 2.20 Another format when using resource as property value

```
1: <?xml version="1.0"?>
2: <rdf:RDF
2a:    xmlns:rdf="http://www.w3.org/1999/02/22-rdf-syntax-ns#"
3:       xmlns:myCamera="http://www.liyangyu.com/camera#">
4:
5:   <rdf:Description
5a:       rdf:about="http://www.liyangyu.com/camera#Nikon_D300">
6:      <rdf:type
6a:           rdf:resource="http://www.liyangyu.com/camera#DSLR"/>
7:      <myCamera:manufactured_by
7a:         rdf:resource="http://www.dbpedia.org/resource/Nikon"/>
```

```
8:       <myCamera:performance>
9:         <rdf:Description rdf:about=
9a:              "http://www.liyangyu.com/camera#PictureQuality">
10:           <myCamera:evaluate>5 stars</myCamera:evaluate>
11:         </rdf:Description>
12:       </myCamera:performance>
13:   </rdf:Description>
14:
15: </rdf:RDF>
```

Clearly, lines 9–11 map to lines 11–13 in List 2.19. In fact, this pattern can be used recursively until all the resources have been described. More specifically, if myCamera:PictureQuality as a resource uses another resource as its property value (instead of literal value "5 stars" as shown on line 10), that resource can again be described inside the corresponding property XML node, and so on.

2.3.2.4   Using Untyped Literals as Property Values, rdf:value and rdf:parseType

We now move on to the next statement in List 2.5, where a literal string is used as the value of myCamera:model property. Again, this is not new. We have learned how to use a literal value as the object of a property XML node (line 10, List 2.20). Specially, the value is simply put inside the XML element.

At this point, List 2.21 shows the document that includes all the statements from List 2.5 so far.

List 2.21 RDF/XML document that includes all the statements from List 2.5

```
1: <?xml version="1.0"?>
2: <rdf:RDF
2a:     xmlns:rdf="http://www.w3.org/1999/02/22-rdf-syntax-ns#"
3:      xmlns:myCamera="http://www.liyangyu.com/camera#">
4:
5:   <rdf:Description
5a:        rdf:about="http://www.liyangyu.com/camera#Nikon_D300">
6:     <rdf:type
6a:          rdf:resource="http://www.liyangyu.com/camera#DSLR"/>
7:     <myCamera:manufactured_by
7a:          rdf:resource="http://www.dbpedia.org/resource/Nikon"/>
8:     <myCamera:performance>
9:         <rdf:Description rdf:about=
9a:              "http://www.liyangyu.com/camera#PictureQuality">
```

```
10:            <myCamera:evaluate>5 stars</myCamera:evaluate>
11:        </rdf:Description>
12:      </myCamera:performance>
13:      <myCamera:model>D300</myCamera:model>
14:      <myCamera:weight>0.6 kg</myCamera:weight>
15:   </rdf:Description>
16:
17: </rdf:RDF>
```

Lines 13 and 14 show how literal values are used. For example, line 14 tells us property `myCamera:weight` has a literal value of `0.6 kg`.

However, given the fact that the Web is such a global resource itself, it might not be a good idea to use a literal value such as `0.6 kg`. When we do this, we in fact assume that anyone who accesses this property will be able to understand the unit that is being used, which may not be a safe assumption to make. A better or safer solution is to explicitly express the value and the unit in separate property values. In other words, the value of `myCamera:weight` property would need to have two components: the literal for the decimal value and an indication of the unit of measurement (kg). Notice in this situation, the decimal value itself can be viewed as the main value of `myCamera:weight` property, whilst the unit component exists just to provide additional contextual information that qualifies the main value.

To implement this solution, we need to model such a qualified property as a new structured value. More specifically, a totally separate resource should be used to represent this structured value as a whole. This new resource should have properties representing the individual components of the structured value. In our example, it should have two properties: one for the decimal value, the other for the unit. This new resource is then used as the object value of the original statement.

RDF vocabulary provides a predefined `rdf:value` property just for this use case. List 2.22 shows to use it:

List 2.22 Using `rdf:value` to represent literal value

```
1: <?xml version="1.0"?>
2: <rdf:RDF
2a:     xmlns:rdf="http://www.w3.org/1999/02/22-rdf-syntax-ns#"
3:      xmlns:uom="http://www.example.org/units#"
4:      xmlns:myCamera="http://www.liyangyu.com/camera#">
5:
6:    <rdf:Description
6a:        rdf:about="http://www.liyangyu.com/camera#Nikon_D300">
7:      <rdf:type
7a:          rdf:resource="http://www.liyangyu.com/camera#DSLR"/>
8:      <myCamera:manufactured_by
8a:          rdf:resource="http://www.dbpedia.org/resource/Nikon"/>
9:      <myCamera:performance>
```

```
10:        <rdf:Description rdf:about=
10a:            "http://www.liyangyu.com/camera#PictureQuality">
11:          <myCamera:evaluate>5 stars</myCamera:evaluate>
12:        </rdf:Description>
13:      </myCamera:performance>
14:      <myCamera:model>D300</myCamera:model>
15:      <myCamera:weight>
16:        <rdf:Description>
17:          <rdf:value>0.6</rdf:value>
18:          <uom:units
18a:             rdf:resource="http://www.example.org/units#kg"/>
19:        </rdf:Description>
20:      </myCamera:weight>
21:    </rdf:Description>
22:
23:  </rdf:RDF>
```

Now, property `myCamera:weight` is using a resource (lines 16–19) as its value. This resource, as we discussed earlier, has two properties. The first property is the predefined `rdf:value` property, its value is 0.6 (line 17). The other one is the `uom:units` property defined in the `uom` namespace (line 3). The value of this property is another resource, and `http://www.example.org/units#kg` is the URI of this resource.

Another interesting part of List 2.22 is the name of the resource given by lines 16–19. Notice that on line 16, `<rdf:Description>` tag does not have anything like `rdf:about` attribute. Therefore, this resource is an *anonymous* resource (we discussed the concept of anonymous resources in Sect. 2.2.6.3).

Why is the resource used by `myCamera:weight` property made to be anonymous? This is because its purpose is to provide a context for the other two properties to exist, and other RDF documents have no need to use or add any new details to this resource. Therefore, there is simply no need to give this resource an identifier.

In RDF models, there is an easier way to implicitly create a blank node. It is considered to be a shorthand method provided by RDF. This involves the use of `rdf:parseType` keyword from the RDF vocabulary, as shown in List 2.23:

List 2.23 Using `rdf:parseType` to represent literal value

```
1:  <?xml version="1.0"?>
2:  <rdf:RDF
2a:      xmlns:rdf="http://www.w3.org/1999/02/22-rdf-syntax-ns#"
3:      xmlns:uom="http://www.example.org/units#"
4:      xmlns:myCamera="http://www.liyangyu.com/camera#">
5:
6:    <rdf:Description
6a:        rdf:about="http://www.liyangyu.com/camera#Nikon_D300">
7:      <rdf:type
7a:          rdf:resource="http://www.liyangyu.com/camera#DSLR"/>
```

```
8:      <myCamera:manufactured_by
8a:        rdf:resource="http://www.dbpedia.org/resource/Nikon"/>
9:      <myCamera:performance>
10:       <rdf:Description rdf:about=
10a:          "http://www.liyangyu.com/camera#PictureQuality">
11:        <myCamera:evaluate>5 stars</myCamera:evaluate>
12:       </rdf:Description>
13:      </myCamera:performance>
14:      <myCamera:model>D300</myCamera:model>
15:      <myCamera:weight rdf:parseType="Resource">
16:        <rdf:value>0.6</rdf:value>
17:        <uom:units
17a:           rdf:resource="http://www.example.org/units#kg"/>
18:      </myCamera:weight>
19:    </rdf:Description>
20:
21: </rdf:RDF>
```

List 2.23 is identical to List 2.22. `rdf:parseType="Resource"` on line 15 is used as the attribute of the `myCamera:weight` element. It indicates to the RDF parser that the contents of the `myCamera:weight` element (lines 16 and 17) should be interpreted as the description of a new resource (a blank node), and should be treated as the value of property `myCamera:weight`. Without seeing a nested `rdf:Description` tag, the RDF parser creates a blank node as the value of the `myCamera:weight` property, and then uses the enclosed two elements as the properties of that blank node. Obviously, this is exactly what we wish the parser to accomplish.

2.3.2.5 Using Typed Literal Values and `rdf:datatype`

We have mentioned typed literal values, but have not had a chance to use them yet in our RDF document. Let us take a look at typed literals in this section.

Line 16 of List 2.23 uses `0.6` as the value of the `rdf:value` property. Here `0.6` is a plain untyped literal, and only we know that the intention is to treat it as a decimal number; there is no information in List 2.23 that explicitly indicates that. However, sometimes, it is important for the RDF parser or the application to know how to explain the plain value.

The solution is to use the `rdf:datatype` keyword from the RDF vocabulary. Notice that RDF/XML syntax does not provide any data type system of its own, such as data types for integers, real numbers, strings, dates, etc. It instead borrows an external data type system, and currently, it is the XML schema datatypes. The reason is also very simple: since XML enjoys such a great success, its schema datatypes would most likely to be interoperable among different software agents.

Now let us use `rdf:datatype` to clearly indicate that the value `0.6` should be treated as a decimal value, as shown in List 2.24:

List 2.24 Example of using `rdf:datatype`

```
1: <?xml version="1.0"?>
2: <rdf:RDF
2a:     xmlns:rdf="http://www.w3.org/1999/02/22-rdf-syntax-ns#"
3:      xmlns:uom="http://www.example.org/units#"
4:      xmlns:myCamera="http://www.liyangyu.com/camera#">
5:
6:   <rdf:Description
6a:        rdf:about="http://www.liyangyu.com/camera#Nikon_D300">
7:     <rdf:type
7a:          rdf:resource="http://www.liyangyu.com/camera#DSLR"/>
8:     <myCamera:manufactured_by
8a:          rdf:resource="http://www.dbpedia.org/resource/Nikon"/>
9:     <myCamera:performance>
10:      <rdf:Description rdf:about=
10a:          "http://www.liyangyu.com/camera#PictureQuality">
11:        <myCamera:evaluate>5 stars</myCamera:evaluate>
12:      </rdf:Description>
13:     </myCamera:performance>
14:     <myCamera:model
14a:       rdf:datatype="http://www.w3.org/2001/XMLSchema#string">
15:        D300</myCamera:model>
16:     <myCamera:weight rdf:parseType="Resource">
17:       <rdf:value rdf:datatype=
17a:          "http://www.w3.org/2001/XMLSchema#decimal">
18:          0.6</rdf:value>
19:       <uom:units
19a:           rdf:resource="http://www.example.org/units#kg"/>
20:     </myCamera:weight>
21:   </rdf:Description>
22:
23: </rdf:RDF>
```

As shown at line 17 in List 2.24, property `rdf:value` now has an attribute named `rdf:datatype` whose value is the URI of the datatype. In our example, this URI is `http://www.w3.org/2001/XMLSchema#decimal`. The result is that the value of the `rdf:value` property, namely, `0.6`, will be treated as a decimal value as defined in the XML schema data types.

Notice there is no absolute need to use `rdf:value` in the above example. A user-defined property name can be used instead of `rdf:value`, and the `rdf:datatype` attribute can still be used together with that user-defined property. Line 14 shows one example: it specifies literal D300 should be interpreted as a string. In fact, RDF does not associate any special meaning with rdf:value; it is simply provided as a convenience for use in the cases as described by our example.

Also notice that since http://www.w3.org/2001/XMLSchema#decimal is used as an attribute value, it has to be written out, rather than using any shorthand abbreviation. However, this makes the line quite long and might hurt readability in some cases. To improve the readability, some RDF documents would use XML entities.

More specifically, an XML entity can associate a name with a string of characters, and this name can be referenced anywhere in the XML document. When XML processors reach such a name, they replace the name with the character string, which normally represents the real content. Since we can make the name really short, this provides us with the ability to abbreviate the long URI.

To declare the entity, we can do the following:

```
<!DOCTYPE
     rdf:RDF [<!ENTITY xsd "http://www.w3.org/2001/XMLSchema#">]>
```

A reference name xsd is defined here to be associated with the namespace URI that contains the XML schema data types. We can use &xsd; (notice the ";", it is necessary) anywhere in the RDF document to represent the above URI. Using this abbreviation, we have the following more readable version, as shown in List 2.25:

List 2.25 A more readable version of List 2.24

```
1: <?xml version="1.0"?>
2: <!DOCTYPE
2a: rdf:RDF [<!ENTITY xsd "http://www.w3.org/2001/XMLSchema#">]>
3:
4: <rdf:RDF
4a:      xmlns:rdf="http://www.w3.org/1999/02/22-rdf-syntax-ns#"
5:       xmlns:uom="http://www.example.org/units#"
6:       xmlns:myCamera="http://www.liyangyu.com/camera#">
7:
8:   <rdf:Description
8a:        rdf:about="http://www.liyangyu.com/camera#Nikon_D300">
9:     <rdf:type
9a:          rdf:resource="http://www.liyangyu.com/camera#DSLR"/>
10:    <myCamera:manufactured_by
10a:         rdf:resource="http://www.dbpedia.org/resource/Nikon"/>
11:    <myCamera:performance>
12:      <rdf:Description rdf:about=
12a:             "http://www.liyangyu.com/camera#PictureQuality">
```

```
13:          <myCamera:evaluate>5 stars</myCamera:evaluate>
14:        </rdf:Description>
15:      </myCamera:performance>
16:      <myCamera:model
16a:            rdf:datatype="&xsd;string">D300</myCamera:model>
17:      <myCamera:weight rdf:parseType="Resource">
18:        <rdf:value rdf:datatype="&xsd;decimal">0.6</rdf:value>
19:        <uom:units
19a:            rdf:resource="http://www.example.org/units#kg"/>
20:      </myCamera:weight>
21:    </rdf:Description>
22:
23:  </rdf:RDF>
```

2.3.2.6   `rdf:nodeID` and More About Anonymous Resources

In Sect. 2.3.2.3 we talked about blank nodes. For example, List 2.22, lines 16–19 represents a blank node. As you can see, that blank node is embedded inside the XML property node, `myCamera:weight`, and is used as the property value of this node.

This kind of embedded blank node works well most of the time, but it does have one disadvantage: it cannot be referenced from any other part of the same document. In some cases, we do have the need to make reference to a blank node within the same document.

To solve this problem, RDF/XML syntax provides another way to represent a blank node: use the so-called blank node identifier. The idea is to assign a *blank node identifier* to a given blank node, so it can be referenced within this particular RDF document, and still remains unknown outside the scope the document.

This blank node identifier method uses the RDF keyword `rdf:nodeID`. More specifically, a statement using a blank node as its subject value should use an `rdf:Description` element together with an `rdf:nodeID` attribute instead of an `rdf:about` or `rdf:ID` (discussed in later section) attribute. By the same token, a statement using a blank node as its object should also use a property element with an `rdf:nodeID` attribute instead of an `rdf:Resource` attribute. List 2.26 shows the detail:

List 2.26 Use `rdf:nodeID` to name a blank node

```
 1: <?xml version="1.0"?>
 2: <rdf:RDF
2a:     xmlns:rdf="http://www.w3.org/1999/02/22-rdf-syntax-ns#"
 3:     xmlns:uom="http://www.example.org/units#"
 4:     xmlns:myCamera="http://www.liyangyu.com/camera#">
 5:
 6:   <rdf:Description
6a:       rdf:about="http://www.liyangyu.com/camera#Nikon_D300">
 7:     <rdf:type
7a:         rdf:resource="http://www.liyangyu.com/camera#DSLR"/>
 8:     <myCamera:manufactured_by
8a:        rdf:resource="http://www.dbpedia.org/resource/Nikon"/>
 9:     <myCamera:performance>
10:       <rdf:Description rdf:about=
10a:           "http://www.liyangyu.com/camera#PictureQuality">
11:         <myCamera:evaluate>5 stars</myCamera:evaluate>
12:       </rdf:Description>
13:     </myCamera:performance>
14:     <myCamera:model>D300</myCamera:model>
15:     <myCamera:weight rdf:nodeID = "youNameThisNode"/>
16:   </rdf:Description>
17:
18:   <rdf:Description rdf:nodeID = "youNameThisNode">
19:     <rdf:value>0.6</rdf:value>
20:     <uom:units
20a:         rdf:resource="http://www.example.org/units#kg"/>
21:   </rdf:Description>
22:
23: </rdf:RDF>
```

Notice that the blank node in List 2.22 (lines 16–19) has been given a local identifier called `youNameThisNode`, and the resource named `youNameThisNode` is then described on lines 18–21. We purposely name this identifier to be `youNameThisNode`, just to show you that you can name this node whatever you want to. The real benefit is that this resource now has a local identifier, so it can be referenced from other places within the same document. Although in this particular case, it's not referenced by any other resource except for being the object of property `myCamera:weight`, you should be able to imagine the cases where a blank node could be referenced multiple times.

Blank nodes are very useful in RDF, and we will see more examples of using blank node in later sections. In addition, notice that `rdf:nodeID` is case-sensitive. For example, an RDF parser will flag an error if you have mistakenly written it as `rdf:nodeId`. In fact, every single term in the RDF vocabulary is case-sensitive, so make sure they are right.

2.3.2.7 `rdf:ID`, `xml:base` and RDF/XML Abbreviation

By now, you probably have already realized one thing about RDF/XML syntax: it is quite verbose and quite long. In this section, we discuss the things you can do to make it shorter.

We have already seen RDF/XML abbreviations in the previous section. For example, compare List 2.17 with List 2.18. In List 2.18, multiple properties are nested within the `rdf:Description` element that identifies the subject, and in List 2.17, each property requires a separate statement, and these statements all share the same subject.

Another abbreviation we have seen is to use ENTITY declaration (together with DOCTYPE declaration at the beginning of a given RDF/XML document). List 2.25 presented one such example.

The last abbreviation we have seen involves the so-called *long form* of RDF/XML syntax. More specifically, List 2.15 uses the `rdf:Description` together with `rdf:about` combination to describe a resource, and this form is called the long form. On the other hand, List 2.16 is an abbreviation of this long form, and they are equivalent to each other. Most RDF parsers will translate the abbreviated from into the long form first before any processing is done.

A new abbreviation of the long form that we have not seen yet is to use the `rdf:ID` term from the RDF vocabulary, as shown in List 2.27 (notice that since we only want to show the use of `rdf:ID`, we did not include other properties as described in List 2.26):

List 2.27 Example of using `rdf:ID`

```
1: <?xml version="1.0"?>
2: <rdf:RDF
2a:     xmlns:rdf="http://www.w3.org/1999/02/22-rdf-syntax-ns#"
3:      xmlns:myCamera="http://www.liyangyu.com/camera#">
4:
5:   <rdf:Description rdf:ID="Nikon_D300">
6:     <rdf:type
6a:         rdf:resource="http://www.liyangyu.com/camera#DSLR"/>
7:     <myCamera:manufactured_by
7a:         rdf:resource="http://www.dbpedia.org/resource/Nikon"/>
8:   </rdf:Description>
9:
10: </rdf:RDF>
```

Comparing List 2.27 to List 2.18, you can see the difference. Instead of using `rdf:about`, RDF keyword `rdf:ID` is used to identify the resource that is being described by this RDF document (line 5).

This does make the statement shorter, at least there is no long URI needed for the resource. However, to use `rdf:ID`, we have to be very careful. More specifically, `rdf:ID` only specifies a fragment identifier; the complete URI of the subject is obtained by concatenating the following 3 pieces together:

in-scope base URI + "#" + `rdf:ID` value

Since the in-scope base URI is not explicitly stated in the RDF document (more on this later), it is then provided by the RDF parser based on the location of the file. In this example, since `http://www.liyangyu.com/rdf/review.rdf` is the location, and `http://www.liyangyu.com/rdf/review.rdf#Nikon-D300` is then used as the URI of the subject.

Clearly, using `rdf:ID` results in a relative URI for the subject, and the URI changes if the location of the RDF document changes. This seems to be contradicting to the very meaning of URI: it is the unique and global identifier of a resource, and how can it change based on the location of some file then?

The solution is to explicitly state the in-scope base URI. Specifically, we can add the `xml:base` attribute in the RDF document to control which base is used to resolve the `rdf:ID` value. Once an RDF parser sees the `xml:base` attribute, it generates the URI by using the following mechanism:

`xml:base` + "#" + `rdf:ID` value

List 2.28 shows the details (line 4):

List 2.28 Example of using `xml:base`

```
 1: <?xml version="1.0"?>
 2: <rdf:RDF
2a:     xmlns:rdf="http://www.w3.org/1999/02/22-rdf-syntax-ns#"
 3:     xmlns:myCamera="http://www.liyangyu.com/camera#"
 4:     xml:base="http://www.liyangyu.com/camera#">
 5:
 6:   <rdf:Description rdf:ID="Nikon_D300">
 7:     <rdf:type
7a:         rdf:resource="http://www.liyangyu.com/camera#DSLR"/>
 8:     <myCamera:manufactured_by
8a:         rdf:resource="http://www.dbpedia.org/resource/Nikon"/>
 9:   </rdf:Description>
10:
11: </rdf:RDF>
```

`rdf:ID` (together with `xml:base`) can also be used in the short form (see List 2.16), as shown in List 2.29:

List 2.29 Example of using `xml:base` with the short form

```
1: <?xml version="1.0"?>
2: <rdf:RDF
2a:     xmlns:rdf="http://www.w3.org/1999/02/22-rdf-syntax-ns#"
3:         xmlns:myCamera="http://www.liyangyu.com/camera#"
4:         xml:base="http://www.liyangyu.com/camera#">
5:
6:     <myCamera:DSLR rdf:ID="Nikon_D300">
7:         <myCamera:manufactured_by
7a:             rdf:resource="http://www.dbpedia.org/resource/Nikon"/>
8:     </myCamera:DSLR>
9:
10: </rdf:RDF>
```

In both List 2.28 and List 2.29, the subject will have the following URI,

```
http://www.liyangyu.com/camera#Nikon_D300
```

which is what we wanted, and it will not change when the location of the RDF document changes.

As a summary, Lists 2.15, 2.16, 2.28 and 2.29 are all equivalent forms. However, it might be a good idea to use `rdf:about` instead of `rdf:ID`, since it provides an absolute URI for the resource. Also, that URI is taken verbatim as the subject, which certainly avoids all potential confusion.

At this point, we have covered the most frequently used RDF/XML syntax, which you certainly need in order to understand the rest of the book. We discuss some other capabilities provided by RDF/XML syntax in the next few sections to complete the description of the whole RDF picture.

2.3.3 Other RDF Capabilities and Examples

RDF/XML syntax also provides some additional capabilities, such as representing a group of resources, and making statements about statements. In this section, we take a brief look at these capabilities.

2.3.3.1 RDF Containers: `rdf:Bag, rdf:Seq, rdf:Alt` and `rdf:li`

Let us say that a Nikon D300 camera can be reviewed based on the following criteria (it is certainly oversimplified to apply only three measurements when it comes to reviewing a camera, but it is good enough to make our point clear):

- effective pixels,
- image sensor format and
- picture quality.

How do we express this fact in RDF?

RDF/XML syntax models this situation by the concept of *container*. A container is a resource that contains things, and each one of these things is called a *member* in the container. A member can be represented by either a resource or a literal.

The following three types of containers are provided by RDF/XML syntax using a predefined container vocabulary:

- `rdf:Bag`
- `rdf:Seq`
- `rdf:Alt`

A resource can have type `rdf:Bag`. In this case, the resource represents a group of resources or literals, the order of these members is not significant, and there could be duplicated members as well. For example, the review criteria presented above can be model by using `rdf:Bag`.

A `rdf:Seq` type resource is the same as a `rdf:Bag` resource, except the order of its members is significant. For instance, if we want to show which criterion is more important than the others, we will have to represent them using `rdf:Seq`.

`rdf:Alt` is also a container. However, items in this container are alternatives. For example, it can be used to describe a list of alternative stores where you can find a Nikon D300 camera.

Let us take a look at the example shown in List 2.30:

List 2.30 Example of using `rdf:Bag`

```
1: <?xml version="1.0"?>
2: <!DOCTYPE rdf:RDF
2a:     [<!ENTITY myCamera "http://www.liyangyu.com/camera#">]>
3:
4: <rdf:RDF
4a:    xmlns:rdf="http://www.w3.org/1999/02/22-rdf-syntax-ns#"
5:        xmlns:myCamera="http://www.liyangyu.com/camera#">
6:
7:   <rdf:Description
7a:        rdf:about="http://www.liyangyu.com/camera#Nikon_D300">
8:      <myCamera:hasReviewCriteria>
9:       <rdf:Description>
10:        <rdf:type rdf:resource=
10a:          "http://www.w3.org/1999/02/22-rdf-syntax-ns#Bag"/>
11:          <rdf:li rdf:resource="&myCamera;EffectivePixel"/>
12:          <rdf:li rdf:resource="&myCamera;ImageSensorFormat"/>
13:          <rdf:li rdf:resource="&myCamera;PictureQuality"/>
```

```
14:          </rdf:Description>
15:        </myCamera:hasReviewCriteria>
16:   </rdf:Description>
17:
18: </rdf:RDF>
```

To express the fact that a Nikon D300 camera can be reviewed based a given set of criteria, a property called myCamera:hasReviewCriteria has been assigned to Nikon D300 (line 8), and this property's value is a resource whose type is rdf:Bag (line 10). Furthermore, rdf:li is used to identify the members of this container resource, as shown on lines 11–13. Notice that lines 7–16 are one single statement, with the container resource represented by a blank node.

Figure 2.8 shows the corresponding graph representation of List 2.30.

Notice that rdf:li is a property provided by RDF/XML syntax for us to use, so we do not have to explicitly number each membership property. Under the hood, a given RDF parser will normally generate properties such as rdf:_1, rdf:_2 and rdf:_3 (as shown in Fig. 2.8) to replace rdf:li. In this case, since the members are contained in a rdf:Bag, these numbers should be ignored by the applications creating or processing this graph. Notice that RDF models do not regulate the processing of List 2.30; it is up to the applications to handle it in the way that it is intended to.

The example of rdf:Seq, including the RDF/XML syntax and the graph representation, is exactly the same as List 2.30, except that the container type is changed to rdf:Seq. Again, notice that properties such as rdf:_1, rdf:_2 and rdf:_3, so

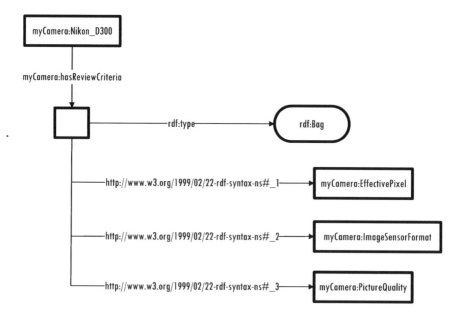

Fig. 2.8 Graph representation of the statements in List 2.30

on and so forth, are generated by the RDF parser to replace rdf:li, and it is up to the applications to correctly interpret the sequence.

The syntax and graph representation of rdf:Alt are also exactly the same except that you need to use rdf:Alt as the type of the container resource. And again, it is up to the application to understand that only one member should be taken, and it should be identified by rdf:_1.

In summary, these three types of containers are predefined by RDF/XML syntax for you to use. You should, however, use them according to their "intended usage"; RDF/XML itself does not provide any check at all. In fact, this container vocabulary is created with the goal to help make data representation and processing more interoperable, but applications are not required to use them. They can choose their own way to describe groups of resources if they prefer.

2.3.3.2   RDF Collections: rdf:first, rdf:rest, rdf:nil and rdf:List

In the last section, we discussed the container class. The problem with a RDF container is that it is not closed: a container includes the identified resources as its members, it never excludes other resources to be members. Therefore, it could be true that some other RDF documents may add additional members to the same container.

To solve this problem, RDF uses a pre-defined *collection vocabulary* to describe a group that contains only the specified resources as members. Its vocabulary includes the following keywords:

- rdf:first
- rdf:rest
- rdf:List
- rdf:nil

To express the fact that "*only* effective pixels, image sensor format and picture quality can be used as criteria to review a given Nikon D300 camera", the above keywords can be used as shown in Fig. 2.9.

Clearly, the members of a given container are all linked together by repeatedly using rdf:first, rdf:rest, until the end (indicated by rdf:nil, a resource that is of type rdf:List). Notice how the blank nodes are used in this structure (Fig. 2.9). Obviously, there is no way to add any new members into this container, since other RDF documents will not be able to access the blank nodes here. This is how RDF/XML syntax can guarantee the underlying container is closed.

Since ideally every closed container should follow the same pattern as shown in Fig. 2.9, RDF/XML provides a special notation to make it easier to describe a closed container. More specifically, there is no need to explicitly use rdf:first, rdf:rest and rdf:nil keywords; all we need to do is to use the attribute rdf:parseType with its value set to be Collection, as shown in List 2.31:

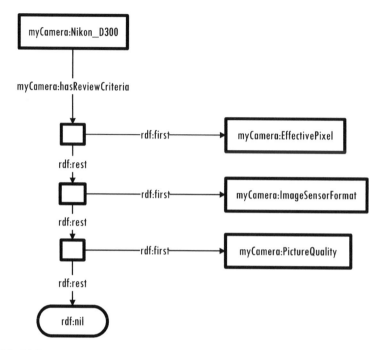

Fig. 2.9 RDF collection vocabulary

List 2.31 Example of using RDF collection

```
1: <?xml version="1.0"?>
2: <!DOCTYPE rdf:RDF
2a:       [<!ENTITY myCamera "http://www.liyangyu.com/camera#">]>
3:
4: <rdf:RDF
4a:     xmlns:rdf="http://www.w3.org/1999/02/22-rdf-syntax-ns#"
5:     xmlns:myCamera="http://www.liyangyu.com/camera#">
6:
7:   <rdf:Description
7a:       rdf:about="http://www.liyangyu.com/camera#Nikon_D300">
8:     <myCamera:hasReviewCriteria rdf:parseType="Collection">
9:     <rdf:Description rdf:about="&myCamera;EffectivePixel"/>
10:    <rdf:Description
10a:        rdf:about="&myCamera;ImageSensorFormat"/>
11:    <rdf:Description rdf:about="&myCamera;PictureQuality"/>
12:    </myCamera:hasReviewCriteria>
13:   </rdf:Description>
14:
15: </rdf:RDF>
```

A RDF parser that sees List 2.31 will then automatically generate the structure shown in Fig. 2.9.

Notice that it is possible, however, to manually use `rdf:first`, `rdf:rest` and `rdf:nil` keywords to construct a closed container, without using the notation shown in List 2.31. If you decide to do so, it is your responsibility to make sure you have created the pattern as shown in Fig. 2.9, and you have used blank nodes so no other RDF document can access the list and modify it. Therefore, the best solution is indeed to use this special notation offered by RDF/XML syntax.

2.3.3.3 RDF Reification: `rdf:statement`, `rdf:subject`, `rdf:predicate` and `rdf:object`

At this point, we have covered most of the terms in RDF vocabulary. In this section, we discuss the remaining terms, more specifically, `rdf:statement`, `rdf:subject`, `rdf:predicate` and `rdf:object`.

In fact, these four terms make up the built-in vocabulary used for describing RDF statements. Therefore, if we need to describe RDF statements using RDF, this vocabulary provides the terms we would like to use.

For example, for a given RDF statement, we might want to record information such as when this statement is created and who has created it, and so on. A description of a statement using this vocabulary is often called a *reification* of the statement, and accordingly, this vocabulary is also called RDF *reification vocabulary*.

Let us take a look at one example. The following statement from List 2.5,

```
myCamera:Nikon_D300 myCamera:manufactured_by dbpedia:Nikon
```

states the fact that the Nikon D300 camera is manufactured by Nikon Corporation. A reification of this statement is shown in List 2.32.

List 2.32 Reification example

```
myCamera:statement_01    rdf:type        rdf:Statement
myCamera:statement_01    rdf:subject     myCamera:Nikon_D300
myCamera:statement_01    rdf:predicate   myCamera:manufactured_by
myCamera:statement_01    rdf:object      dbpedia:Nikon
```

In List 2.32, `myCamera:statement_01` is a URI that is assigned to the statement that is being described, i.e.,

```
myCamera:Nikon_D300 myCamera:manufactured_by dbpedia:Nikon
```

And the first statement in List 2.32 says the resource identified by `myCamera:statement_01` is an RDF statement. The second statement says that the subject of this RDF statement is identified by resource `myCamera:Nikon_D300`. The third statement says the predicate of this RDF statement is given by `myCamera:manufactured_by`, and the last statement says the object of the statement refers to the resource identified by `dbpedia:Nikon`.

Obviously, this reification example has used four statements to describe the original statement. This usage pattern is often referred to as the conventional use of the RDF reification vocabulary. Since it always involves four statements, it is also called a *reification quad*.

Now, to record provenance information about the original statement, we can simply add additional statements to this quad, as shown in List 2.33:

List 2.33 Adding provenance information using reification

```
myCamera:statement_01 rdf:type        rdf:Statement
myCamera:statement_01 rdf:subject     myCamera:Nikon_D300
myCamera:statement_01 rdf:predicate   myCamera:manufactured_by
myCamera:statement_01 rdf:object      dbpedia:Nikon
myCamera:statement_01 dc:creator      http://www.liyangyu.com#liyang
```

As you can see, the last statement in List 2.33 is added to show the creator of the original statement, and `http://www.liyangyu.com#liyang` is the URI identifying this creator.

Notice `dc:creator` is another existing URI (just like `dbpedia:Nikon` is an existing URI representing Nikon Corporation) taken from a vocabulary called Dublin Core. We will discuss Dublin Core in more detail in the next section. For now, understanding that `dc:creator` represents the creator of a given document is good enough.

You can certainly add more statements into List 2.33 to record more provenance information about the original statement, such as the date when the original statement was created, etc.

The usage of reification vocabulary is fairly straightforward. However, using it does require some caution. Recall that we have assigned a URI to the original statement (`myCamera:statement_01`), so it can be represented as a resource, and new RDF statements can be created to describe it. However, this kind of logic connection only exists in our mind. The URI is completely arbitrary, and there is no built-in mechanism in RDF to understand that this URI is created to represent a particular statement in a given RDF graph.

As a result, it is up to the RDF application to handle this, and it has to be done with care. For example, given the statements in List 2.34, an RDF application may try to match `rdf:subject`, `rdf:predicate` and `rdf:object` taken from List 2.33 to a statement so as to decide whether the reification in List 2.33 is used on this particular statement. However, there could be multiple statements in different RDF models, and all these statements will be matched successfully; it is therefore hard to decide exactly which one is the candidate. For example, different camera reviewers can make the same statement in their reviews (in RDF format), and our RDF application built on all these reviews will find multiple matches. Therefore, for a given statement, we cannot simply depend on matching its `rdf:subject`, `rdf:predicate` and `rdf:object` components. Most likely, more application-specific assumptions may have to be made to make this work.

In addition, notice that other applications receiving these RDF documents may not share the same application-specific understanding, and therefore may not be able to interpret these statements correctly.

With all this being said, RDF reification is still useful and remains an important topic, mainly because it provides one way to add provenance information, which is important to handle the issue of trust on the Web. For now, understand it and in your own development work, use it with care.

2.4 Other RDF Sterilization Formats

2.4.1 Notation-3, Turtle and N-Triples

By now, there is probably one important aspect of RDF that we have not emphasized enough: RDF is an abstract data model, and RDF standard itself does not specify its representation. The recommended and perhaps the most popular representation of a RDF model is the XML serialization format (noted as RDF/XML), as we have seen so far.

However, RDF/XML is not designed for human eyes. For instance, it is hard to read, and can be quite long as well. There are indeed other RDF serialization formats, such as *Notation-3* (or *N3*), *Turtle* and *N-Triples*.

Notation-3 is a non-XML serialization of the RDF model and is designed with human-readability in mind. It is therefore much more compact and readable than the XML/RDF format.

Since Notation-3 has several features that are not necessary for serialization of RDF models (such as its support for RDF-based rules), Turtle was created as a simplified and RDF-only subset of Notation-3. In addition, N-Triples is another simpler format than either Notation-3 or Turtle, and therefore it offers another alternative to developers.

In this section, we focus mainly on the Turtle format because of its popularity among developers. In addition, as you will see in Chap. 6, SPARQL has borrowed almost everything from Turtle to form its own query language. Therefore, understanding Turtle will make us comfortable with the syntax used in SPARQL query language as well.

2.4.2 Turtle Language

Formally speaking, Turtle represents *Terse RDF Triple Language*. It is a text-based syntax for serialization of the RDF model. You can find a complete discussion about Turtle here:

```
http://www.w3.org/TeamSubmission/turtle/
```

And you should know the following about Turtle in general:

- The URI that identifies the Turtle language is given by:

```
http://www.w3.org/2008/turtle#turtle
```

- The XML (Namespace name, local name) pair that identifies Turtle language is as follows:

```
http://www.w3.org/2008/turtle#, turtle
```

- The suggested namespace prefix is ttl, and a Turtle document should use ttl as the file extension.

2.4.2.1   Basic Language Features

Now, let us take a brief look at the Turtle language. First, a Turtle document is a collection of RDF statements, and each statement has a format that is called a triple:

```
<subject> <predicate> <object> .
```

Notice,

- each statement has to end with a period;
- the subject must be represented by a URI;
- the predicate must be represented by a URI;
- the object can be either a URI or a literal;
- a URI must be surrounded in <> brackets, which are used to delineate a given URI.

A given literal may have a language or a datatype URI as its suffix, but it is not allowed to have both. If it is given a language suffix, the suffix is created by an @ together with the language tag. For example:

```
"this is in English"@en
```

If it is given a datatype suffix, ^^ is used:

```
"10"^^<http://www.w3.org/2001/XMLSchema#decimal>
"foo"^^<http://example.org/mydatatype/sometype>
```

Notice that a literal does not have to be appended by a datatype URI or language tag. For example, these two literals are perfectly legal:

```
"10"
"foo"
```

With all this said, List 2.34 shows some triple examples in the Turtle format (notice the period at the end of each statement):

List 2.34 Triple examples in Turtle format

```
<http://www.liyangyu.com/foaf.rdf#liyang>
<http://xmlns.com/foaf/0.1/name> "liyang yu" .

<http://www.liyangyu.com/foaf.rdf#liyang>
<http://xmlns.com/foaf/0.1/interest>
<http://dbpedia.org/resource/Semantic_Web> .
```

And this is the main idea for Turtle. However, there are lots of abbreviations and shortcuts that can make the RDF Turtle documents much more compact and still readable. Let us discuss these features next.

2.4.2.2 Abbreviations and Shortcuts: Namespace Prefix, Default Prefix and @base

Obviously, full URIs are long and somewhat unreadable. To make them shorter and also more readable, we can define a namespace prefix so we don't have to write the long common part of the URI over and over. The general format for defining namespace prefix is given as below:

@prefix *pref*: <*uri*> .

where `pref` is the shortcut for `uri`. For example,

@prefix **foaf:** <http://xmlns.com/foaf/0.1/> .
@prefix **liyang:** <http://www.liyangyu.com/foaf.rdf#> .

and now the two statements in List 2.34 can be rewritten as in List 2.35:

List 2.35 Statements in List 2.34 rewritten using namespace prefix

```
@prefix foaf: <http://xmlns.com/foaf/0.1/> .
@prefix liyang: <http://www.liyangyu.com/foaf.rdf#> .

liyang:liyang foaf:name "liyang yu" .
liyang:liyang foaf:interest
              <http://dbpedia.org/resource/Semantic_Web> .
```

which are obviously much more readable and compact as well.

Another way to abbreviate namespace is to create a default namespace prefix, acting as the "main" namespace for a Turtle document. For example, if we are creating or working on a FOAF document (more about FOAF in Chap. 7), making a FOAF namespace as the default (main) namespace is a good choice. To create a default namespace, we can use the same general form, but without a `pref` string:

```
@prefix : <uri> .
```

for instance,

```
@prefix : <http://xmlns.com/foaf/0.1/> .
```

will set `<http://xmlns.com/foaf/0.1/>`as the default namespace, and List 2.35 will be changed to List 2.36:

List 2.36 Statements in List 2.35 rewritten using default namespace prefix

```
@prefix : <http://xmlns.com/foaf/0.1/> .
@prefix liyang: <http://www.liyangyu.com/foaf.rdf#> .

liyang:liyang :name "liyang yu" .
liyang:liyang :interest
                <http://dbpedia.org/resource/Semantic_Web> .
```

In other words, any URI identifier starting with `:` will be in the default namespace. Notice in some documents, `@base` directive is also used to allow abbreviation of URIs. It could be confusing if you are not familiar with this since it somewhat feels like a default namespace prefix, but in fact it is not. Let us talk about this a little bit more.

The key point to remember about `@base` is this: whenever it appears in a document, it defines the base URI against which all relative URIs are going to be resolved. Let us take a look at List 2.37:

List 2.37 Example of using `@base`

```
1:   <subj0> <pred0> <obj0> .
2:   @base <http://liyangyu.com/ns0/> .
3:   <subj1> <http://liyangyu.com/ns0/pred1> <obj1> .
4:   @base <foo/> .
5:   <subj2> <pred2> <obj2> .
6:   @predix : <bar#> .
7:   :subj3 :pred3 :obj3 .
8:   @predix : <http://liyangyu.com/ns1/> .
9:   :subj4 :pred4 :obj4 .
```

How should this be resolved? Clearly, line 1 is a triple that all of its components are using relative URIs, therefore all these URIs should be resolved against the current @base value. Since there is no explicit definition of @base yet, the location of this document will be treated as the current base. Assuming this document locates at http://liyangyu.com/data/, line 1 will be resolve to the following:

```
<http://liyangyu.com/data/subj0>
<http://liyangyu.com/data/pred0>
<http://liyangyu.com/data/obj0> .
```

Since line 2 has specified a new base value, line 3 will be resolved to the following:

```
<http://liyangyu.com/ns0/subj1>
<http://liyangyu.com/ns0/pred1>
<http://liyangyu.com/ns0/obj1> .
```

Notice pred1 does not need to resolve, since it has an absolute URI.

Now, line 4 again uses @base to define a relative URI, which will be resolved against the current base; in other words, line 4 is equivalent to the following:

```
@base <http://liyangyu.com/ns0/foo/> .
```

therefore, line 5 will then be resolved using this new base URI:

```
<http://liyangyu.com/ns0/foo/subj2>
<http://liyangyu.com/ns0/foo/pred2>
<http://liyangyu.com/ns0/foo/obj2> .
```

Line 6 defines a default namespace prefix:

```
@predix : <bar#> .
```

and since it is again a relative URI, it has to be resolved against the current base first. Therefore, this default namespace will have the following resolved URI:

```
@predix : <http://liyangyu.com/ns0/foo/bar#> .
```

Therefore, the triple on line 7 will be resolved to this:

```
<http://liyangyu.com/ns0/foo/bar#subj3>
<http://liyangyu.com/ns0/foo/bar#pred3>
<http://liyangyu.com/ns0/foo/bar#obj3> .
```

Finally, line 8 defines another default namespace, and since it is an absolute URI already, it does not have to be resolved against the current base. Line 9 is resolved to this:

```
<http://liyangyu.com/ns1/subj4>
<http://liyangyu.com/ns1/pred4>
<http://liyangyu.com/ns1/obj4> .
```

This should have cleared up the confusion around @base directive and default namespace prefix, and this has also completed the discussion about URI abbreviation. Let us talk about some other frequently used abbreviations.

2.4.2.3 Abbreviations and Shortcuts: Token a, Comma and Semicolons

Token a in Turtle is always equivalent to the following URI:

```
<http://www.w3.org/1999/02/22-rdf-syntax-ns#type>
```

therefore,

```
liyang:liyang rdf:type foaf:Person .
```

can be written as follows:

```
liyang:liyang a foaf:Person .
```

Both commas and semicolons can be used to make a given document shorter. More specifically, if two or more statements with the same subject and predicate are made, we can combine the statements and separate different objects by one or more commas. For example, consider List 2.38:

List 2.38 A Turtle document that has two statements with the same subject and predicate

```
@prefix foaf: <http://xmlns.com/foaf/0.1/> .
@prefix liyang: <http://www.liyangyu.com/foaf.rdf#> .

liyang:liyang foaf:name "liyang yu" .
liyang:liyang foaf:interest
              <http://dbpedia.org/resource/Semantic_Web> .
liyang:liyang foaf:interest <http://semantic-mediawiki.org/> .
```

can be changed to List 2.39, which is equivalent yet has a shorter form:

List 2.39 Combine the two statements in List 2.38

```
@prefix foaf: <http://xmlns.com/foaf/0.1/> .
@prefix liyang: <http://www.liyangyu.com/foaf.rdf#> .

liyang:liyang foaf:name "liyang yu" .
liyang:liyang foaf:interest
              <http://dbpedia.org/resource/Semantic_Web>,
              <http://semantic-mediawiki.org> .
```

If we have the same subject but different predicates in more than one statement, we can use semicolons to make them shorter. For example, List 2.39 can be further rewritten as shown in List 2.40:

List 2.40 Using; to rewrite List 2.39

```
@prefix foaf: <http://xmlns.com/foaf/0.1/> .
@prefix liyang: <http://www.liyangyu.com/foaf.rdf#> .

liyang:liyang foaf:name "liyang yu" ;
              foaf:interest <http://www.foaf-project.org/>,
                            <http://semantic-mediawiki.org> .
```

2.4.2.4 Turtle Blank Nodes

Last but not least, let us discuss blank nodes. Some literature does not recommend using blank nodes, but in some cases, they can be very handy. In Turtle, a blank node is denoted by [], and you can use it as either the subject or the object. For example, List 2.41 says "there exists a person named liyang yu":

List 2.41 Using a blank node as the subject

```
@prefix foaf: <http://xmlns.com/foaf/0.1/> .

[] a foaf:Person;
   foaf:name "liyang yu" .
```

In List 2.41, a blank node is used as the subject. If you decide to serialize this model using the RDF/XML format, you will get document shown in List 2.42:

List 2.42 Express the statement in List 2.41 using the RDF/XML format

```
<?xml version="1.0"?>
<rdf:RDF xmlns:foaf="http://xmlns.com/foaf/0.1/"
         xmlns:rdf="http://www.w3.org/1999/02/22-rdf-syntax-ns#">
   <foaf:Person>
      <foaf:name>liyang yu</foaf:name>
   </foaf:Person>
</rdf:RDF>
```

and it will have the following underlying triples:

```
_:bnode0 <http://www.w3.org/1999/02/22-rdf-syntax-ns#type>
         <http://xmlns.com/foaf/0.1/Person> .
_:bnode0 <http://xmlns.com/foaf/0.1/name> "liyang yu" .
```

We can also use blank nodes to represent objects. For example, the Turtle statement in List 2.43 says "Liyang is a person and he knows another person named Connie":

List 2.43 Use blank node as the object

```
@prefix foaf: <http://xmlns.com/foaf/0.1/> .
@prefix liyang: <http://www.liyangyu.com/foaf.rdf#> .

liyang:liyang a foaf:Person;
                  foaf:knows [
                        a foaf:Person;
                        foaf:name "connie".
                        ].
```

Again, in RDF/XML format, the statements in List 2.43 will look like the ones shown in List 2.44:

List 2.44 Express the statement in List 2.43 using RDF/XML format

```
<?xml version="1.0"?>
<rdf:RDF xmlns:foaf="http://xmlns.com/foaf/0.1/"
         xmlns:liyang="http://www.liyangyu.com/foaf.rdf#"
         xmlns:rdf="http://www.w3.org/1999/02/22-rdf-syntax-ns#">
<foaf:Person rdf:about="http://www.liyangyu.com/foaf.rdf#liyang">
   <foaf:knows>
     <foaf:Person>
        <foaf:name>connie</foaf:name>
     </foaf:Person>
   </foaf:knows>
</foaf:Person>

</rdf:RDF>
```

and underlying triples are also listed here:

```
<http://www.liyangyu.com/foaf.rdf#liyang>
<http://www.w3.org/1999/02/22-rdf-syntax-ns#type>
<http://xmlns.com/foaf/0.1/Person> .

_:bnode0 <http://www.w3.org/1999/02/22-rdf-syntax-ns#type>
         <http://xmlns.com/foaf/0.1/Person> .
_:bnode0 <http://xmlns.com/foaf/0.1/name> "connie" .

         <http://www.liyangyu.com/foaf.rdf#liyang>
         <http://xmlns.com/foaf/0.1/knows> _:bnode0 .
```

You can tell how compact the Turtle format is!

2.5   Fundamental Rules of RDF

Since we have covered most of the content about RDF, it is time for us to summarize the basic rules of RDF. There are three basic rules, and they are critically related to some of the most important aspects of the Semantic Web. At this point, these closely related aspects are:

1. RDF represents and models information and knowledge in a way that machines can understand.
2. Distributed RDF graphs can be aggregated to facilitate new information discovery.

In this section, we examine the three basic RDF rules. The goal is to establish a sound understanding of why these basic RDF rules provide the foundation to the above aspects of the Semantic Web.

2.5.1   Information that Is Understandable by Machines

Let us start from Rule 1. We have seen this rule already, where it was presented to describe the abstract RDF model. Here we will look at it again from a different perspective: it plays an important role when making machines understand the knowledge expressed in RDF statements. Here is this rule again:

Rule #1: Knowledge (or information) is expressed as a list of statements, and each statement takes the form of Subject-Predicate-Object, *and this order should never be changed.*

Before we get into details on this part, let us take a look at this triple pattern once more time.

Since the value of a property can be a literal or a resource, a given RDF statement can take the form of alternating sequence of resource–property, as shown in List 2.45:

List 2.45 The pattern of RDF statement

```
1: <rdf:Description rdf:resources="#resource-0">
2:    <someNameSpace:property-0>
3:       <rdf:Descrption rdf:resource="#resource-1">
4:          <someNameSpace:property-1>
5:             <rdf:Description rdf:resource="#resource-2">
6:                <someNameSpace:property-2>
7:                   ...
8:                </someNameSpace:property-2>
9:             </rdf:Description>
10:          </someNameSpace:property-1>
11:       </rdf:Description>
12:    </someNameSpace:property-0>
13: </rdf:Description>
```

In List 2.45, `#resource-0` has a property named `property-0`, and its value is another resource described using lines 3–11 (`#resource-1`). Furthermore, `#resource-1` has a property named `property-1` whose value is yet another resource described using lines 5–9. This pattern can go on and on, however, the `Resource-Property-Value` structure is never changed.

Why this order is so important? Because if we follow this order when we creating RDF statements, an RDF-related application will be able to understand the meaning of these statements. To see this, let us study the example shown in List 2.46:

List 2.46 One simple statement about Nikon D300

```
1: <?xml version="1.0"?>
2:
3: <rdf:RDF
3a:     xmlns:rdf="http://www.w3.org/1999/02/22-rdf-syntax-ns#"
4:      xmlns:myCamera="http://www.liyangyu.com/camera#">
5:
6:    <rdf:Description
6a:        rdf:about="http://www.liyangyu.com/camera#Nikon_D300">
7:       <myCamera:effectivePixel>12.1M</myCamera:effectivePixel>
8:    </rdf:Description>
9:
10: </rdf:RDF>
```

List 2.46 is equivalent to the following RDF statement:

```
myCamera:Nikon-D300 myCamera:effectivePixel 12.1M
```

We, as human readers, understand its meaning. For a given application, the above triple looks more like this:

```
$#!6^:af#@dy $#!6^:3pyu9a 12.1M
```

However, the application does understand the structure of a RDF statement, so the following is true as far as the application is concerned:

$#!6^:af#@dy is the subject
$#!6^:3pyu9a is the property
12.1M is the value

And now, here is the interesting part: the application also has a vocabulary it can access, and the following fact is stated in this vocabulary:

property `$#!6^:3pyu9a` is used exclusively on resource whose type is `$#!6^:Af5%`

We will see what exactly this vocabulary is (in fact, it is called an RDF schema), and we will also find out how to express the above fact by using this vocabulary in Chap. 4. For now, let us just assume the above fact is well-expressed in the vocabulary.

Now given all this, the application, without really associating any special meaning to the above statement, can draw the following conclusion:

resource `$#!6^:af#@dy` is an instance of resource `$#!6^:Af5%`

When the application shows the above conclusion to the screen, to human eyes, that conclusion looks like the following:

`Nikon-D300` is an instance of `DSLR`

which makes perfect sense!

The key point here is that a given application cannot actually associate any special meanings to the RDF statements. However, with the fixed structure of statements and some extra work (the vocabulary, for instance), the logical pieces of meaning can be mechanically maneuvered by the given application. It therefore can act as if it *does* understand these statements. In fact, in Chaps. 4 and 5, once we understand more about RDF schema and OWL, we will see more examples of this exciting inference power.

2.5.2   Distributed Information Aggregation

The second and third rules are important for distributed information aggregation. Here is again Rule #2:

Rule #2: The name of a resource must be global and should be identified by a Uniform Resource Identifier (URI). The name of the predicate must also be global and should be identified by URI as well.

And Rule #3 is given below:

Rule #3: I can talk about any resource at my will, and if I chose to use an existing URI to identify the resource I am talking about, then the following is true:

- *the resource I am talking about and the resource already identified by this existing URI are exactly the same thing or concept;*
- *everything I have said about this resource is considered to be additional knowledge about that resource.*

These two rules together provide the foundation for distributed information aggregation. At this point, they seem to be trivial and almost like a given. However, they are the key idea behind the Linked Open Data project (Chap. 9), and they are the starting point for new knowledge discovery. We will see lots of these exciting facts in the later chapters. For now, a simple comparison of the traditional Web and the "Web of RDF documents" may give you a better understanding of their importance.

Recall the situation in the current Web. One of the things about the Internet that is quite attractive to all of us is that you can talk about anything you want, and you can publish anything you want. When you do this, you can also link your document to any other pages you would like to.

For example, assume on my own Web site (www.liyangyu.com), I have offered a review about Nikon D300, and I also linked my page to a digital camera review site. Someone else perhaps did the same and has a link to the same digital camera review site as well. What will this do to this review site? Not much at all, except that some search engines will realize the fact that quite a few pages have linked to it, and the rank of this site should be adjusted to be a little bit more important. But this is pretty much all of it, and the final result is still the same: the Web is a huge distributed information storage place, from which getting information is normally pretty hard.

On the other hand, on the "Web of RDF documents", things can be quite different. For example, based on the above rule, all the RDF documents containing a resource identified by the same known URI can be connected together. This connection is implemented based on this URI, which has a well-defined meaning. Even though these RDF documents are most likely distributed everywhere on the Web, however, each one of them presents some knowledge about that resource, and adding them together can produce some very powerful results.

More specifically, when I publish my review of D300, all I need to do is to use a URI to represent this resource. Anyone else who wants to review the same camera has to use the same URI. These reviews can then be automatically aggregated to produce the summary one might want to have. An example along this path is discussed in the next section.

One last point before we move on. It is clear to us now only named resources can be aggregated. Therefore, anonymous resources cannot be aggregated. The reason is simple: if a resource in a document is anonymous, an aggregation tool will not be able to tell if this resource is talking about some resource that has already been defined and described. This is probably one disadvantage of using anonymous resources.

2.5.3 A Hypothetical Real World Example

It is now a good time to go back to our original question: as a quality engineer who is working for Nikon, my assignment is to read all these reviews and summarize what people have said about Nikon SLR cameras. I will have to report back to Nikon's design department, so they can make better designs based on these reviews.

And as we have discussed, we need a standard so that we can develop an application that will read all these reviews and generate a report automatically.

Now, with the RDF standard being in place, how should I proceed with this task? The following steps present one possible solution I can use:

Step 1. Create a group of URIs to represent Nikon's digital camera products.

At this point, you should understand why this step is necessary. The following are some possible choices for these URIs:

```
http://www.liyangyu.com/camera#Nikon_D300
http://www.liyangyu.com/camera#Nikon_D90
http://www.liyangyu.com/camera#Nikon_D60
```

Obviously, we should be reusing URIs as much as we can. For example, the following URIs taken from DBpedia are good choices:

```
http://dbpedia.org/resource/Nikon_D300
http://dbpedia.org/resource/Nikon_D90
http://dbpedia.org/resource/Nikon_D60
```

However, for this hypothetical example, we are fine with making up new URIs.

Step 2. Provide a basic collection of terms that one can use to review a camera.

This step is also a critical step, and we will see a lot more about this step in later chapters. For now, we can understand this step like this: with only the URIs to represent different cameras, reviewers themselves are not able to share much of their knowledge and common language about cameras.

To make a common language among the reviewers, we can provide some basic terms for them to use when reviewing cameras. The following are just two example terms at this point:

```
http://www.liyangyu.com/camera#model
http://www.liyangyu.com/camera#weight
```

and we can add more terms and collect these terms together to create a vocabulary for the reviewers to use.

Do you recall that the RDF model should be flexible enough that anyone can say anything about a resource? What if some reviewer wants to say something about a camera, and the term she/he wants to use is not included in our vocabulary? The solution is simple: she/he can simply download the vocabulary, add that term and then upload the vocabulary for all the reviewers to use, as simple as this.

Now, a key question arises. Assume I have already developed an automatic tool that can help me read all these reviews and generate a summary report. If the vocabulary is undergoing constant update, do I have to change my application constantly as well?

The answer is no. Probably it is not easy to see the reason at this point, but this is exactly where the flexibility is. More specifically, with a set of common URIs and a shared vocabulary, distributed RDF graphs can be created by different sources on the Web, and applications operating on these RDF models are extremely robust to the change of the shared vocabulary.

You will see this more clearly in later chapters. For now, understand this is a concrete implementation of one of the design goals of RDF standard: it has to be flexible enough that anyone can say anything about a given resource.

Step 3. Make sure the reviewers will use the given set of URIs and the common vocabulary when they publish their reviews on the Web.

This is probably the most difficult step: each reviewer has to learn RDF, and has to use the given URIs to represent cameras. In addition, they have to use the given vocabulary as well, although they do have the flexibility of growing the vocabulary as discussed above.

The issue of how to make sure they will accept this solution is beyond the scope of this book—it is a not related to the technology itself. Rather, it is about the acceptance of the technology.

With this said, we will simply assume the reviewers will happily accept our solution. To convince yourself about this assumption, think about the very reason of being a reviewer. For any reviewer, the goal is to make sure her/his voice is heard by both the consumers and the producers of a given product. And if this reviewer is not publishing her/his review in an RDF document by using the given URIs and vocabulary, her/his review will never be collected; therefore she/he will not have a chance to make a difference about that product at all.

Step 4. Build the application itself and use it to collect reviews and generate reports.

This is, in fact, the easy part. This application first acts like a crawler that visits some popular review sites to collect all the RDF documents. Once the documents are collected, all the statements in these RDF documents are grouped based on their subjects. i.e., those statements that have the same subject are grouped together regardless of which RDF document they are originally from, and this is exactly what data aggregation is.

Clearly, one such group represents all the reviews for a given camera, if the URI that represents that camera is used as the subject. Once this is done, a report about this camera can be generated by querying the statements in this group.

Let us take a look at a small example. Imagine the application has collected the statements shown in List 2.5 already. In addition, it has also collected the statements shown in List 2.47 from another reviewer:

List 2.47 Statements about Nikon D300 from another reviewer

subject	predicate	object
myCamera:Nikon_D300	myCamera:effectivePixel	"12.1M"
myCamera:Nikon_D300	myCamera:shutterrange	"30s - 1/8000s"
myCamera:Nikon_D300	myCamera:wb	"auto"

Clearly, the statements from List 2.5 and the statements from List 2.47 are all about the same Nikon D300 camera, so these statements can be aggregated together into a single group.

Now repeat the same procedure as described above. Obviously, more and more statements about the Nikon D300 will be collected from different reviewers and will be added to the same statement group. It is not hard to imagine this group will contain quite a large number of statements once our application has visited enough review sites.

Once the application stops its crawling on the Web, we can implement different queries against the collected statements in this group. To see how this can be done, take a look at the example code (List 2.7) presented in Sect. 2.2.5. The only difference now is that we have many more statements than the simple test case discussed in Sect. 2.2.5. Therefore, more interesting results can be expected. Clearly, you can implement different queries, but the basic idea remains the same.

As a side note, recall we claimed that any new terms added by reviewers would not disturb the application itself. To see this, consider the query *what properties did the reviewers use to describe Nikon D300?* This query is important to Nikon's design department, since it shows the things that consumers would care about for a given camera. As you can tell, to implement this query, a simple pattern-match is done as shown in List 2.7, and only the subject has to be matched; the property part is what we want to collect for this query. Obviously, the reviewers can add new terms (properties), and these added new terms will not require any change to the code.

Finally, it is interesting to think about this question: exactly what do all the reviewers have to agree upon to make this possible?

Surprisingly, the only two things all the reviewers have to agree upon are the following:

- Reviewers have to agree to use RDF.
- Reviewers have to agree to use the given URIs instead of inventing their own.

What about the basic vocabulary that reviewers use to review cameras? We don't have to reach an agreement on that at all—one can add new properties without disturbing the application, as we have just discussed. Furthermore, adding a new term does not require any agreement from other reviewers either. We do provide an initial version of the vocabulary, however, it is merely a starting point for reviewers to use, not something that everyone has to agree upon.

In addition, the pseudo-code in List 2.7 does not need to know anything about the nature of the data in the statements in order to make use of it. Imagine even we change to another application domain, the pseudo-code in List 2.7 will not change much at all.

To summarize our point: with the help from RDF standard, we can indeed create an application that can help us to finish our job with much more ease.

2.6   More About RDF

As this point, you have gained a fairly solid understanding of RDF. Before we move on to the next chapter, we have several more issues to cover here, and some of them have probably already been on your mind for quite a while.

2.6.1   Dublin Core: Example of Predefined RDF Vocabulary

In this chapter, we have used terms from the Dublin Core (DC) vocabulary without formally introducing it. Chances are you will see terms from the Dublin Core vocabulary in different RDF documents quite often. So in this section, let us focus on the Dublin Core vocabulary.

To put it simply, Dublin Core is a set of predefined URIs representing different properties of a given document. Since they are widely used in RDF documents, they can also be understood as another set of predefined RDF vocabulary.

Dublin Core was developed in the *March 1995 Metadata Workshop* sponsored by the Online Computer Library Center (OCLC) and the National Center for Supercomputing Applications (NCSA). The workshop itself was held in Dublin,

Table 2.3 Element examples in the Dublin Core Metadata Scheme

Element name	Element description
Creator	This element represents the person or organization responsible for creating the content of the resource, e.g., authors in the case of written documents
Publisher	This element represents the entity responsible for making the resource available in its present form; it can be a publishing house, a university department, etc.
Contributor	This element represents the person or organization not specified in a Creator element who has made significant intellectual contributions to the resource but whose contribution is secondary to any person or organization specified in a Creator element, e.g., editor, transcriber, illustrator
Title	This element represents the name given to the resource, usually by the Creator
Subject	This element represents the topic of the resource. Normally this will be expressed as keywords or phrases that describe the subject or content of the resource
Date	This element represents the date associated with the creation or availability of the resource
Identifier	This element is a string or number that uniquely identifies the resource. Examples include URLs, Purls and ISBN, or other formal names
Description	This element is a free text description of the content of the resource, and has flexible format, including abstracts or other content descriptions
Language	This element represents the language used by the document
Format	This element identifies the data format of the document. This information can be used to identify the software that might be needed to display or operate the resource, e.g., postscript, HTML, text, jpeg, XML

Ohio; hence the name Dublin Core. Currently, it is maintained by the Dublin Core Metadata Initiative[5] project.

Dublin Core has 15 elements, which are called the Dublin Core Metadata Element Set (DCMES). It is proposed as the minimum number of metadata elements required to facilitate the discovery of document-like objects in a networked environment such as the Internet. Table 2.3 shows some of these terms.

Generally speaking, if we are using RDF to describe a document, or maybe part of our RDF document is to describe a document, we should use Dublin Core predicates as much as we can. For example, Title predicate, Creator predicate, are all good choices.

Notice that the URIs in Dublin Core vocabulary all have the following lead strings:

```
http://www.purl.org/metadata/dublin-core#
```

---

[5] http://dublincore.org/

By convention, this URI prefix string is associated with namespace prefix `dc:`, and is typically used in XML with the prefix `dc`.

For example, List 2.48 is a simple RDF description about my personal Web page. The two statements use Dublin Core terms to indicate the creator of this Web site and the date this site was created (lines 8 and 9):

List 2.48 Example of using Dublin Core terms

```
1:  <?xml version="1.0"?>
2:  <!DOCTYPE rdf:RDF
2a:          [<!ENTITY xsd "http://www.w3.org/2001/XMLSchema#">]>
3:
4:  <rdf:RDF
4a:     xmlns:rdf="http://www.w3.org/1999/02/22-rdf-syntax-ns#"
5:      xmlns:dc="http://www.purl.org/metadata/dublin-core#">
6:
7:    <rdf:Description rdf:about="http://www.liyangyu.com">
8:      <dc:creator>Liyang Yu</dc:creator>
9:      <dc:date rdf:datatype="&xsd;date">2006-09-10</dc:date>
10:   </rdf:Description>
11:
12: </rdf:RDF>
```

We can certainly add more if we want to describe more information. But you see how easy it is to use: you just need to specify the Dublin Core namespace and use it anywhere you want in your document.

2.6.2   XML vs. RDF?

The relationship between XML and RDF can be described quite simply: RDF and XML are not much related at all.

RDF, as you have seen, is a standard for describing things in the real world. More importantly, these descriptions can be processed by machines on a large scale. To serialize an RDF abstract model, different serialization formats are available. Among these formats, RDF/XML is recommended by W3C and is used in most documents. Therefore, the only connection between RDF and XML is the fact that RDF uses the XML syntax and its namespace concept.

Given this relationship between XML and RDF, perhaps a better question to ask is why can XML not accomplish what RDF has accomplished?

There are several reasons behind this. First of all, XML provides very limited semantics, and even for this limited semantics, it is quite ambiguous. This fact is nicely summarized as follows:

YU, LIYANG.

DEVELOPER'S GUIDE TO THE SEMANTIC WEB.

2ND ED.   Cloth   829 P.
HEIDELBERG: SPRINGER, 2014

GUIDEBOOK. INCL. COMPANION WEB SITE.

LCCN 2014950052
 ISBN 3662437953   **Library PO#** SLIP ORDERS

		List	89.99 USD
6207 UNIV OF TEXAS/SAN ANTONIO		**Disc**	17.0%
App. Date 8/19/15 CSC.APR	6108-09	**Net**	74.69 USD

SUBJ: 1. SEMANTIC WEB. 2. SEMANTIC WEB--RESEARCH.

CLASS TK5105.888   DEWEY# 025.04   LEVEL ADV-AC

YBP Library Services

YU, LIYANG.

DEVELOPER'S GUIDE TO THE SEMANTIC WEB.

2ND ED.   Cloth   829 P.
HEIDELBERG: SPRINGER, 2014

GUIDEBOOK. INCL. COMPANION WEB SITE.

LCCN 2014950052
 ISBN 3662437953   **Library PO#** SLIP ORDERS

		List	89.99 USD
6207 UNIV OF TEXAS/SAN ANTONIO		**Disc**	17.0%
App. Date 8/19/15 CSC.APR	6108-09	**Net**	74.69 USD

SUBJ: 1. SEMANTIC WEB. 2. SEMANTIC WEB--RESEARCH.

CLASS TK5105.888   DEWEY# 025.04   LEVEL ADV-AC

XML is only the first step to ensuring that computers can communicate freely. XML is an alphabet for computers and as everyone traveling in Europe knows, knowing the alphabet doesn't mean you can speak Italian or French.—*Business Week*, March 18, 2002

The key point here is XML is by far the best format to share data on the Web and exchange information between different platforms and applications. However, it does not have enough restrictions to successfully express semantics.

Let us look at one example. How do we use XML to express the following knowledge, "the author of *A Developer's Guide to the Semantic Web* is Liyang Yu"? Using XML, you have several ways to do this (List 2.49).

List 2.49 Ambiguity of XML document

```
<!-- form 1 -->
<author>
  <fistName>Liyang</fistName>
  <lastName>Yu</lastName>
  <book>
    <title>A Developer's Guide to the Semantic Web</title>
  </book>
</author>

<!-- form 2 -->
<author>
  <name>Liyang Yu</name>
  <book>
    <title>A Developer's Guide to the Semantic Web</title>
  </book>
</author>

<!-- form 3 -->
<author>
  <name>Liyang Yu</name>
  <book>A Developer's Guide to the Semantic Web</book>
</author>
```

Clearly, there is no agreement on the structure one can use. This makes an automatic agent that is intended to work on a large scale virtually impossible, if not prohibitively expensive.

On the other hand, using RDF to express the same idea is very straightforward, and it leaves no space for any ambiguity, as shown in List 2.50.

List 2.50 Using RDF to express the fact described in List 2.49

```
1: <rdf:RDF
1a:     xmlns:rdf="http://www.w3.org/1999/02/22-rdf-syntax-ns#"
2:      xmlns:dc="http://www.purl.org/metadata/dublin-core#">
3:
4: <rdf:Description
4a:      rdf:about="http://www.liyangyu.com/book#SemanticWeb">
5:   <dc:title>A Developer's Guide to the Semantic Web</dc:title>
6:   <dc:creator>Liyang Yu</dc:creator>
7: </rdf:Description>
8:
9: </rdf:RDF>
```

The only thing you can change in List 2.50 is the URI that represents the book (line 4). For example, you have to mint one if it does not already exist. Any RDF application can easily characterize this structure and understand which part of the structure is the subject, the property and the value of that property.

Second, parsing XML statements heavily depends on the tree structure, which is not quite scalable on a global basis. To be more specific, you can easily make up some XML document so the representation of this document in a machine's memory depends on the data structures such as tree and character strings. In general, these data structures can be quite hard to handle, especially when the amount is large.

An RDF statement presents a very simple data structure—a directly labeled graph which has long been a very well understood data structure in the field of computer science. It is also quite scalable for a large data set. The nodes of the graph are the resources or literals, the edges are the properties, and the labels are URIs of nodes and edges. You can certainly change the graph into a collection of triples (subject–predicate–object), which fits into the framework of relational database very well. All these are quite attractive compared to XML documents.

The third reason, which is even more important, is that using the RDF format promotes the development and usage of standardized vocabularies (or, ontologies, as you will see in the later chapters). The more you understand about the Semantic Web, the more you will appreciate the importance of these vocabularies. The following are some of the benefits of using standard vocabularies:

- Without a shared vocabulary, it is always possible that same word can mean different concepts and different words can refer to the same concept.
- Without a shared vocabulary, distributed information will likely remain isolated. An application that is capable of processing this distributed information on a global scale will be very hard to build.
- Without a shared vocabulary, machine inferencing will be difficult to implement. Therefore new knowledge discovery will be difficult to do.
- And much more, as we will see in the later chapters.

At this point, the above might not seem quite clear and convincing. However, as your understanding of the Semantic Web grows, these points will become more obvious to you.

As a conclusion, XML is unequaled as an information exchange format over the Internet. But by itself, it simply does not provide what we need for the construction of the Semantic Web.

If you are still not convinced, do this small experiment. Take the hypothetical example we discussed earlier, and pretend there is no RDF standard at all. In other words, replace all the RDF documents with XML documents, see how many more constraints you need to artificially impose to make it work, and how many more case-specific code you need to write. You will see the benefit of the RDF abstract model quite easily.

2.6.3 Use a RDF Validator

One last thing before we move on to the next chapter: use a RDF validator.

As you have seen by now, RDF/XML syntax can be quite convoluted and error-prone, especially when you are creating RDF documents by hand. One good idea is to use a validator whenever you can.

There are a number of available validators; you can choose any one you like. For example, I have been using the RDF validator provided by W3C for quite a while. This validator can be accessed at `http://www.w3.org/RDF/Validator/`.

Figure 2.10 shows its current look and feel.

To use this validator, simply paste the RDF document into the document window, and click the `Parse RDF` button. You can also ask for an RDF graph by making the corresponding selection using the `Triples and/or Graph` dropdown list. You can further specify the graph format in the `Graph format` dropdown list, as shown in Fig. 2.10.

If there are indeed any errors in your document, the validator flags them by telling you the lines and columns where the errors occur. You can always make changes to your RDF document and submit it again, until you have a valid RDF document.

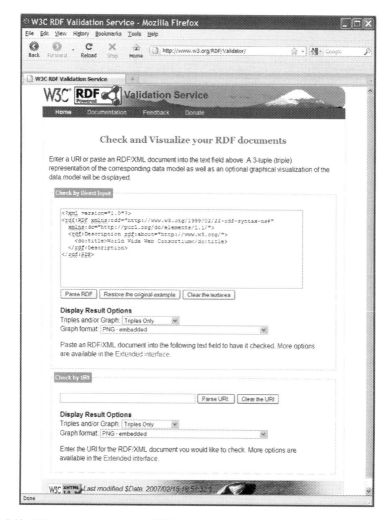

Fig. 2.10   RDF validator provided by W3C

2.7   Summary

In this chapter, we have learned RDF, the building block for the Semantic Web.

The first thing we should understand from this chapter is the RDF abstract model. More specifically, this abstract model includes the following main points:

- it provides a framework for us to represent knowledge in a way that can be processed by machines;
- it involves important concepts such as resource, statement (triple), subject, object, predicate and RDF graph;

- it has fundamental rules that one should follow when using RDF model to represent structured information on the Web. These rules include that the structure of a statement has to be in the form of subject-predicate-object, and URIs should be used to identify subject, predicate and object.

In order for us to create and operate with concrete RDF documents, this chapter also covers the two major RDF serialization formats, including RDF/XML syntax and Turtle language. We should have learned the following:

- the concept of RDF vocabulary, and why this vocabulary is important when it comes to RDF serialization;
- understanding of the main features of RDF/XML syntax, including all the language constructs (terms from the RDF vocabulary) that can be used to represent a RDF model;
- understanding of the main features of Turtle language, and how to use it to represent a RDF model.

This chapter also discusses why RDF is the choice for expressing knowledge that machines can understand. Examples are used to show the power of RDF, and a detailed discussion about distributed information aggregation using RDF is also included. We should have learned the following main points:

- what exactly it means when we claim RDF graphs can be understood by machines;
- why the fundamental rules about RDF are important in order for machines to understand and operate with RDF graphs;
- why URI reuse is important for distributed information aggregation.

Finally, this chapter discusses some related issues about RDF. This includes the following:

- Dublin Core, as an example of another predefined RDF vocabulary;
- the relationship between XML and RDF, and
- tools and support you can use when working with concrete RDF models.

At this point, make sure you have established a clear understanding about all these main points included in this summary. If not, review the material in this chapter before you move on.

Chapter 3
Other RDF-Related Technologies: Microformats, RDFa and GRDDL

3.1 Introduction: Why Do We Need These?

So far at this point, we have learned the concept of the Semantic Web, and we have learned RDF. Let us think about these two for a moment.

Recall the vision of the Semantic Web is to add meaning into the current Web so machines can understand its contents. Based on what we have learned about RDF, we understand that RDF can be used to express the meaning of a Web document in a machine-processable way. More specifically, for a given Web document, we can create a set of RDF triples to describe its meaning, and somehow indicate to the machine that these RDF statements are created for the machine to understand this document.

Although we are not quite there yet, it is not hard for us to understand the feasibility of this idea. In fact, it is called *semantic markup*, as we will see in later chapters.

However, there is one obvious flaw with this approach: it is simply too complex for most of us. More specifically, to finish this markup process, we have to first create a collection of RDF statements to describe the meaning of a Web document, then put them into a separate file, and finally, we have to somehow link the original Web document to this RDF file. Is there a simpler way of doing all these?

The answer is yes, and that is to use microformats or RDFa. They are simpler since microformats or RDFa constructs can be *directly* embedded into XHTML to convey the meaning of the document itself, instead of collecting them into separate documents.

This in fact plays an important role in the grand plan for the Semantic Web, since a single given Web page is now readable not only by human eyes, but also by machines. A given application that understands microformats or RDFa can perform tasks that are much more complex than those performed by the applications that are built solely based on screen scraping. In fact, in Chap. 10, we will see Google's Rich Snippets, a direct result of microformats or RDFa.

© Springer-Verlag Berlin Heidelberg 2014
L. Yu, *A Developer's Guide to the Semantic Web*,
DOI 10.1007/978-3-662-43796-4_3

To understand how GRDDL (pronounced "*griddle*") fits into the picture, think about the semantic information an XHTML page contains when it is embedded with microformats or RDFa constructs. It will be quite useful if we can obtain RDF statements from this XHTML page automatically. GRDDL is a tool that can help us to accomplish this. Once we can do this, the RDF statements harvested from these XHTML pages can be aggregated together to create even more powerful applications.

And these are the reasons why we need microformats, RDFa and GRDDL. If you skip this chapter for now, you can still continue learning the core technology components of the Semantic Web. However, you need to understand this chapter in order to fully understand Chap. 10.

3.2 Microformats

3.2.1 Microformats: The Big Picture

To put it simply, microformats are a way to embed specific semantic data into the HTML content that we have today, so when a given application accesses this content, it will be able to tell what this content is about.

We are all familiar with HTML pages that represent people, so let us start from here. Let us say we would like to use microformats to add some semantic data about people. To do so, we need the so-called hCard microformat, which offers a group of constructs you can use to markup the content:

- a root class called vcard;
- a collection of properties, such as fn (formatted name) and n (name), and quite a few others.

We will see more details about hCard microformat in the next section. For now, understand that hCard microformat can be used to markup the page content where a person is described. In fact, hCard microformat is not only used for people, it can also be used to markup content about companies, organizations and places, as we will see in the next section.

Now, what if we would like to markup some other content? For example, some event described in a Web document? In this case, we will need to use the hCalendar microformat, which also provides a group of constructs we can use to markup the related content:

- a root class called vcalendar;
- a collection of properties, such as dtstart, summary, location, and quite a few others.

By the same token, if we would like to markup a page content that contains a person's resume, we then need to use the hResume microformat. What about hRecipe microformat? Obviously, it is use for adding markups to a page content where a cooking recipe is described.

By now, the big picture about microformats is clear, and we can define microformats as follows:

> Microformats are a collection of individual microformats, with each one of them representing a specific domain (such as person, event, location, etc.) that can be described by a Web content page. Each one of these microformats provides a way of adding semantic markup to these Web pages, so that the added information can be extracted and processed by software applications.

With this definition in mind, it is understandable that the microformats collection is always growing: there are existing microformats that cover a number of domains, and for the domains that have not been covered yet, new microformats are created to cover them.

For example, hCard microformat and hCalendar microformat are stable microformats, while hResume microformat and hRecipe microformat are still in draft state. In fact, there is a microformats community that is actively working on new microformats. You can always find the latest news from their official Web site,[1] including a list of stable microformats and a list of draft ones that are under discussion.

Finally, notice that microformats are not a W3C standard or recommendation. They are offered by an open community, and are open standards originally licensed under Creative Commons Attribution. They have been placed into the public domain since December 29, 2007.

3.2.2   Microformats: Syntax and Examples

In this section, we take a closer look at how to use microformats to markup a given Web document. As we discussed earlier, microformats are a collection of individual microformats, and to present each one of them in this chapter is not only impossible but also unnecessary. In fact, understanding one such microformat will be enough; the rest of them are quite similar when it comes to actually using them to markup a page.

With this said, we focus on the hCard microformat in this section since at the time of this writing, the hCard microformat is one of the most popular and well-established microformats. We will begin with an overview of hCard microformat, followed by some necessary HTML knowledge, and as usual, we will learn hCard by examples.

---

[1] http://microformats.org

3.2.2.1   From `vCard` to `hCard` Microformat

`hCard` microformat has its root in `vCard`, and can be viewed as a `vCard` representation in HTML, hence the letter *h* in `hCard` (HTML `vCard`). It is therefore helpful to have a basic understanding about `vCard`.

`vCard` is a file format standard that specifies how basic information about a person or an organization should be presented, including name, address, phone numbers, e-mail addresses, URLs, etc. This standard was originally proposed in 1995 by the Versit Consortium, which included Apple, AT&T Technologies, IBM and Siemens as its members. In late 1996, this standard was passed on to the Internet Mail Consortium, and since then it has been used widely in address book applications to facilitate the exchange and backup of contact information.

To date, this standard has been given quite a few extensions, but its basic idea remains the same: `vCard` has defined a collection of properties to represent a person or an organization. Table 3.1 shows some of these properties.

Since this standard was formed before the advent of XML, the syntax is just simple text that contains property–value pairs. For example, my own `vCard` object can be expressed as shown in List 3.1.

List 3.1 My `vCard` object

```
BEGIN:VCARD
FN:Liyang Yu
N:Yu;Liyang;;;
URL:http://www.liyangyu.com
END:VCARD
```

First, notice this `vCard` object has a `BEGIN:VCARD` element and an `END:VCARD` element, which mark the scope of the object. Inside the object, the `FN` property has a value of `Liyang Yu`, which is used as the display name. The `N` property represents the structured name, in the order of first, last, middle names, prefixes and suffixes, separated by semicolons. This can be parsed by a given

Table 3.1 Example properties contained in `vCard` standard

Property name	Property description	Semantic
N	Name	The name of the person, place or thing associated with the `vCard` object.
FN	Formatted name	The formatted name string associated with the `vCard` object.
TEL	Telephone	Phone number string for the associated `vCard` object.
EMAIL	E-mail	E-mail address associated with the `vCard` object.
URL	URL	A URL that can be used to get online information about the `vCard` object.

Table 3.2 Examples of vCard properties mapped to hCard properties

vCard property	hCard properties and subproperties
FN	fn
N	n with subproperties: family-name, given-name, additional-name, honorific-prefix, honorific-suffix
EMAIL	email with subproperties: type, value
URL	url

application in order to understand each component in the person's name. Finally, URL is the URL of the Web site that provides more information about the vCard object.

With understanding of the vCard standard, it is much easier to understand the hCard microformat, since it is built directly on the vCard standard. More specifically, the properties supported by the vCard standard are mapped directly to the properties and subproperties contained in the hCard microformat, as shown in Table 3.2.

Notice Table 3.2 does not include all the property mappings, which you can find on the microformats' official Web site (see Sect. 3.2.1). As a high-level summary, hCard properties can be grouped into six categories:

- personal information properties: this includes properties such as fn, n, nickname, etc.;
- address properties: this includes properties such as adr, with subproperties such as street-address, region and postal-code, etc.;
- telecommunication properties: this includes properties such as email, tel and url, etc.;
- geographical properties: this includes properties such as geo, with subproperties such as latitude and longitude;
- organization properties: this includes properties such as logo, org, with subproperties such as organization-name and organization-unit;
- annotation properties: this include properties such as title, note and role, etc.

With the above mapping in place, the next issue is to represent a vCard object (contained within BEGIN:VCARD and END:VCARD) in hCard microformat. To do so, hCard microformat uses a root class called vcard, and in HTML content, an element with a class name of vcard is itself called an hCard.

Now, we are ready to take a look at some examples to understand how exactly we can use the hCard microformat to markup some page content.

3.2.2.2   Using **hCard** Microformat to Markup Page Content

Let us start with a very simple example. Suppose that in one Web page, we have some HTML code as shown in List 3.2:

List 3.2 Example HTML code without `hCard` microformat markup

```
... <!-- other HTML code -->
<div>
    <a href="http://www.liyangyu.com/">Liyang Yu</a>
</div>
... <!-- other HTML code -->
```

Obviously, for our human eyes, we understand that the above link is pointing to a Web site that describes a person named Liyang Yu. However, any application that sees this code does not really understand that, except for showing a link on the screen as follows:

Liyang Yu

Now let us use the `hCard` microformat to add some semantic information to this link. The basic rules when doing markup can be summarized as follows:

- Use `vcard` as the class name for the element that needs to be marked up, and this element now becomes an `hCard` object.
- The properties of an `hCard` object are represented by elements inside the `hCard` object. An element with class name taken from a property name represents the value of that property. If a given property has subproperties, the values of these subproperties are represented by elements inside the element for that given property.

Based on these rules, List 3.3 shows one possible markup implemented by using `hCard` microformat.

List 3.3 `hCard` microformat markup added to List 3.2

```
... <!-- other HTML code -->
<div class="vcard">
   <div class="fn">Liyang Yu</div>
   <div class="n">
      <div class="given-name">Liyang</div>
      <div class="family-name">Yu</div>
   </div>
   <div class="url">http://www.liyangyu.com</div>
</div>
... <!-- other HTML code -->
```

This markup is not hard to follow. For example, the root class has a name given by `vcard`, and the property names are used as class names inside it. And certainly, this simple markup is able to make a lot of difference to an application: any application that understands the hCard microformat will be able to understand the fact that this is a description of a person, with the last name, first name and URL given.

If you open up List 3.3 using a browser, you will see it is a little bit different from the original look and feel. Instead of a clickable name, it actually shows the full name, first name, last name and the URL separately. So let us make some changes to our initial markup, without losing the semantics, of course.

First, a frequently used trick when implementing markup for HTML code comes from the fact that class (also including rel and rev attributes) attribute in HTML can actually take a space-separated list of values. Therefore, we can combine fn and n to reach something as shown in List 3.4:

List 3.4 An improved version of List 3.3

```
... <!-- other HTML code -->
<div class="vcard">
   <div class="n fn">
      <div class="given-name">Liyang</div>
      <div class="family-name">Yu</div>
   </div>
   <div class="url">http://www.liyangyu.com</div>
</div>
... <!-- other HTML code -->
```

This is certainly some improvement; at least we don't have to encode the name twice. However, if you open up List 3.4 in a browser, it still does not show the original look. To go back to its original look, we at least need to make use of element <a> together with its href attribute.

In fact, microformats do not force the content publishers to use specific elements; we can choose any element and use it together with the class attribute. Therefore, List 3.5 is our best choice:

List 3.5 Final hCard microformat markup for List 3.2

```
... <!-- other HTML code -->
<div class="vcard">
   <a class="n fn url" href="http://www.liyangyu.com">
      <span class="given-name">Liyang</span>
      <span class="family-name">Yu</span>
   </a>
</div>
... <!-- other HTML code -->
```

And this is it: if you open up List 3.5 from a Web browser, you get exactly the original look and feel. And certainly, any application that understands hCard microformat will be able to understand what a human eye can see: this is a link to a Web page that describes a person, whose last name is Yu, and first name is Liyang.

List 3.6 is another example of using hCard microformat. It is more complex and certainly more interesting. We present it here so you can get more understanding about using the hCard microformat to markup content files.

List 3.6   A more complex hCard microformat markup example

```
<div id="hcard-liyang-yu" class="vcard">
   <a class="n fn url" href="http://www.liyangyu.com">
      <span class="given-name">Liyang</span>
      <span class="family-name">Yu</span>
   </a>
   <div class="org">Delta Air Lines</div>
   <div class="tel">
      <span class="type">work</span>
      <span class="value">404.773.8994</span>
   </div>
   <div class="adr">
     <div class="street-address">1030 Delta Blvd.</div>
     <span class="locality">Atlanta</span>,
     <span class="region">GA</span>
     <span class="postal-code">30354</span>
     <div class="country-name">USA</div>
   </div>
   <a class="email" href="mailto:liyang.yu@delta.com">
      liyang.yu@delta.com
   </a>

</div>
```

And List 3.7 shows the result rendered by a Web browser.

List 3.7   Rendering result of List 3.6

Liyang Yu
Delta Air Lines
work 404.773.8994
1030 Delta Blvd.
Atlanta, GA 30354
USA
liyang.yu@delta.com

3.2.3   Microformats and RDF

At this point, we have learned the hCard microformat. With what you have learned here, it is not hard for you to explore other microformats on your own.

In this section, we will first summarize the benefits offered by microformats, and more importantly, we will also take a look of the relationship between microformats and RDF.

3.2.3.1   What's So Good About Microformats?

First off, microformats do not require any new standards; instead, they leverage existing standards. For example, microformats reuse HTML tags as much as possible, since almost all the HTML tags allow class attributes to be used.

Second, the learning curve is minimal for content publishers, who continue to mark up their Web documents as they normally would. The only difference is that they are now invited to make their documents more semantically rich by using class attributes with standardized properties values, such as those from the hCard microformat as we have discussed.

Third, the added semantic markup has no impact on the document's presentation, if it is done right.

Last, and perhaps most important, is the fact that this small change in the markup process brings a significant change to the whole Web world. The added semantic richness can be utilized by different applications, since applications can start to understand at least part of the document on the Web now. We will see some exciting applications in Chaps. 10 and 11, and it is also possible that at the time you are reading this book, more applications built upon microformats have become available to us.

With this said, how are microformats related to RDF? Do we still need RDF at all? Let us answer these questions in the next section.

3.2.3.2   Microformats and RDF

Obviously, the primary advantage microformats offer over RDF is that we can embed metadata directly in the XHTML documents. This not only reduces the amount of markup we need to write, but also provides one single content page for both human readers and machines. The other advantage of microformats is that microformats have a simple and intuitive syntax, therefore they do not need much of a learning curve compared to RDF.

However, microformats were not designed to cover the same scope as RDF was, and they simply do not work on the same exact level. To be more specific, the following are something offered by RDF, but not by microformats (notice at this point, you may not be able to fully appreciate all the items in the list, but after you read more of this book, you will be able to):

- RDF does not depend on predefined "formats", and it has the ability to utilize, share and even create any number of vocabularies.
- With the help from these vocabularies, RDF statements can participate in reasoning processes and new facts can be discovered by machines.
- Resources in RDF statements are represented as URIs, allowing a linked data Web to be created.
- RDF itself is infinitely extensible and open-ended.

You can continue to grow this list once you learn more about microformats and RDF from this book and your real development work. However, understanding microformats is also a must, and this will at least enable you to pick up the right tool for the right situation.

3.3 RDFa

3.3.1 RDFa: The Big Picture

With what we have learned so far, the big picture of RDFa is quite simple to understand: it is just another way to directly add semantic data into XHTML pages. Unlike microformats, which reuse the existing `class` attribute on most HTML tags, RDFa provides a set of new attributes that can be used to carry the added markup data. Therefore, in order to use RDFa to embed the markup data within the Web documents, some attribute-level extensions to XHTML have to be made. In fact, this is also the reason for the name: RDF*a* means RDF in HTML *a*ttributes.

Notice that unlike microformats, RDFa is a W3C standard. More specifically, it became a W3C standard on October 14, 2008, and you can find the main standard document on W3C official Web site.[2] Based on this document, RDFa is officially defined as follows:

> RDFa is a specification for attributes to express structured data in any markup language.

Another W3C RDFa document, *RDFa for HTML Authors*,[3] has provided the following definition of RDFa:

> RDFa is a thin layer of markup you can add to your web pages that make them understandable for machines as well as people. By adding it, browsers, search engines, and other software can understand more about the pages, and in so doing offer more services or better results for the user.

---

[2] http://www.w3.org/TR/2008/REC-rdfa-syntax-20081014/

[3] http://www.w3.org/MarkUp/2009/rdfa-for-html-authors

Once you have finished Sect. 3.3, you should be able to understand both these definitions better.

3.3.2 RDFa Attributes and RDFa Elements

First off, attributes introduced by RDFa have names. For example, `property` is one such attribute. Obviously, when we make reference to this attribute, we say attribute `property`. In order to avoid repeating the word attribute too often, attribute `property` is often written as `@property`. You will see this a lot if you read about RDFa. And in what follows, we will write `@attributeName` to represent one attribute whose name is given by `attributeName`.

The following attributes are used by RDFa at the time of this writing:

```
about
content
datatype
href
property
rel
resource
rev
role
src
typeof
```

Some of them are used more often than others, as we will discuss in later sections. Before we get into the detail, let us first understand with what XHTML elements these attributes can be used.

The rule is very simple: you can use these attributes with just about any element. For example, you can use them on `div` element, on the `p` element, or even on the `h2` (or `h3`, etc.) element. In real practice, there are some elements that are more frequently used with these attributes.

The first such element is the `span` element. It is a popular choice for RDFa simply because you can insert it anywhere in the body of an XHTML document. `link` and `meta` elements are also popular choices, since you can use them to add RDFa markups to the `head` element of an HTML document. This is in fact one of the reasons why RDFa is gaining popularity: these elements have been used to add metadata to the `head` element for years; therefore, any RDFa-aware software can extract useful metadata from them with only minor modifications needed.

The last frequently used element when it comes to adding RDFa markup into the content is the `a` linking element. With what you have learned about RDF from Chap. 2, it is not hard for you to see the reason here: a linking element actually expresses a relationship between one resource (the one where it is stored) and another (the resource it links to). In fact, as you will see in the examples, we can always use @rel on a link element to add more information about the relationship, and this information serves as the predicate of a triple stored in that a element.

3.3.3   RDFa: Rules and Examples

In this section we explain how to use RDFa to markup a given content page, and we also summarize the related rules when using the RDFa attributes. We will not cover all the RDFa attributes as listed in Sect. 3.3.2, but what you will learn here should be able to get you far in the world of RDFa if you so desire.

3.3.3.1   RDFa Rules

Before we set off to study the usage of each RDFa attribute, let us understand its basic rules first. Notice that at this point, these rules may seem unclear to you, but you will start to understand them better when we start to see more examples.

As we learned in Chap. 2, any given RDF statement has three components: subject, predicate and object. It turns out that RDFa attributes are closely related to these components:

- attributes rel, rev and property are used to represent predicates;
- for attribute rel, its subject is the value of about attribute, and its object is the value of href attribute;
- for attribute rev, its subject and object are reversed compared to rel: its subject is the value of href attribute, and its object is the value of about attribute;
- for attribute property, its subject is the value of about attribute, and its object is the value of content attribute.

Now recall the fact that we always have to be careful about the object of a given RDF statement: its object can either take a literal string as its value, or it can use another resource (identified by a URI) as it value. How is this taking effect when it comes to RDFa? Table 3.3 summarizes the rules:

Based on Table 3.3, if the object of an RDF statement takes a literal string as its value, this literal string will be the value of content attribute. Furthermore, the subject of that statement is identified by the value of about attribute, and the predicate of that statement is given by the value of property attribute. If the object of a RDF statement takes a resource (identified by a URI) as its value, the URI will be the value of href attribute. Furthermore, the subject of that statement is identified by the value of about attribute, and the predicate of that statement is given by the value of rel attribute.

Let us see some examples along this line. Assume I have posted an article about the Semantic Web on my Web site. In that post, I have some simple HTML code as shown in List 3.8.

Table 3.3 RDFa attributes as different components of a RDF statement

Object values	Subject attribute	Predicate attribute	Object
Literal strings	`about`	`property`	Value of `content` attribute
Resource (identified by URI)	`about`	`rel`	Value of `href` attribute

List 3.8 Some simple HTML code in my article about the Semantic Web

```
<div>
    <h2>This article is about the Semantic Web and written by
Liyang.</h2>
</div>
```

This can be easily understood by a human reader of the article. First, it says this article is about the Semantic Web; second, it says the author of this article is Liyang. Now I would like to use RDFa to add some semantic markup so machines can see these two facts. One way to do this is shown in List 3.9.

List 3.9 Use RDFa to markup the content HTML code in List 3.8

```
<div xmlns:dc="http://purl.org/dc/elements/1.1/">
    <p>This article is about <span about="http://www.liyangyu.com
/article/theSemanticWeb.html" rel="dc:subject" href="http://dbpe-
dia.org/resource/Semantic_Web"/>the Semantic Web and written by
<span about="http://www.liyangyu.com/article/theSemanticWeb.html"
property="dc:creator" content="Liyang"/>Liyang.</p>
</div>
```

Recall dc represents the Dublin Core vocabulary namespace (review Chap. 2 for more understanding about Dublin Core). We can pick up the RDFa markup segments from List 3.9, and show them in List 3.10:

List 3.10 RDFa markup text taken from List 3.9

```
<span about="http://www.liyangyu.com/article/theSemanticWeb.html"
rel="dc:subject"
href="http://dbpedia.org/resource/Semantic_Web"/>

<span about="http://www.liyangyu.com/article/theSemanticWeb.html"
property="dc:creator" content="Liyang"/>
```

Clearly, in the first `span` segment, the object is a resource identified by a URI. Therefore, `@rel` and `@href` have to be used as shown in List 3.10. Notice `http://dbpedia.org/resource/Semantic_Web` is used as the URI identifying the object resource. This is an URI created by DBpedia project (discussed in Chap. 8) to represent the concept of the Semantic Web. Here we are reusing this URI instead of inventing our own. To see more details about reusing URIs, review Chap. 2.

On the other hand, in the second `span` segment, the object is represented by a literal string. Therefore, `@property` and `@content` have to be used.

The last rule we need to discuss here is about attribute `about`. At this point, we understand attribute `about` is used to represent the subject of the RDF statement. But for a given XHTML content marked up by RDFa, how does an RDFa-aware application exactly identify the subject of the markup? This can be summarized as follows:

- If attribute `about` is used explicitly, then the value represented by `about` is the subject.
- If a RDFa-aware application does not find `about` attribute, it will assume the `about` attribute on the nearest ancestor element represents the subject.
- If an RDFa-aware application searches through all the ancestors of the element with RDFa markup information, and does not find an `about` attribute, then the subject is an empty string, and effectively indicates the current document.

These rules about subject are in fact quite intuitive, especially the last one, given that lots of a document's markup information will be typically about the document itself.

With all this understanding about RDFa rules, we can now move on to the example of RDFa markup.

3.3.3.2 RDFa Examples

In this section, we use examples to show how semantic markup information can be added by using RDFa attributes. Notice we will be able to cover only a subset of ways to add RDFa metadata in an XHTML document, it is however enough to get your far if you decide to explore more on yourself.

A common usage of RDFa attributes is to add *inline* semantic information. This is in fact the original motivation that led to the creation of RDFa: how to take human-readable Web page content and make it machine-readable. List 3.9 is a good example of this inline markup. You can compare List 3.8 with List 3.9; List 3.8 is the original page content that is written for human-eyes, and List 3.9 is what we have after inline RDFa markup. Notice the presentation rendered by any Web browser is not altered at all.

Another example is to markup the HTML code shown in List 3.2. It is a good exercise for us since we have already marked up List 3.2 using `hCard` microformats, and using RDFa to markup the same HTML content shows the difference between the two.

List 3.11 shows the RDFa markup of List 3.2. It accomplishes the same goal as shown in List 3.5. It tells an RDFa-aware application the following: this is a link to the homepage of a person whose first name is Liyang, and whose last name is Yu.

List 3.11 RDFa markup for the HTML code shown in List 3.2

```
... <!-- other HTML code -->
<div xmlns:foaf="http://xmlns.com/foaf/0.1/">
   <a about="http://www.liyangyu.com#liyang"
      rel="foaf:homepage"
      href="http://www.liyangyu.com/">Liyang Yu</a>
   <span property="foaf:firstName" content="Liyang"/>
   <span property="foaf:lastName" content="Yu"/>
</div>
... <!-- other HTML code -->
```

Again, if you open up the above with a Web browser, you see the same output as given by List 3.2. With what we have learned so far, understanding List 3.11 should not be difficult at all.

Notice that FOAF vocabulary is used for RDFa to markup the content; we covered FOAF briefly in Chap. 2, and you will see a detailed discussion of FOAF in Chap. 7. For now, just remember that FOAF is a vocabulary, with a collection of words that one can use to describe people and their basic information.

This is in fact an important difference between microformats and RDFa. More specifically, when using microformats to markup a given document, the possible values for the properties are predefined. For example, if hCard microformat is used, only hCard properties and subproperties can be used in the markup (see List 3.5 for example). However, this is not true for RDFa markup: you can in fact use anything as the values for the attributes. For example, List 3.11 could have been written as shown in List 3.12.

List 3.12 Another version of List 3.11

```
... <!-- other HTML code -->
<div xmlns:yu="http://www.liyangyu.com/yu">
   <a about="http://www.liyangyu.com#liyang"
      rel="yu:myHomepage"
      href="http://www.liyangyu.com/">Liyang Yu</a>
   <span property="yu:myFirstName" content="Liyang"/>
   <span property="yu:myLastName" content="Yu"/>
</div>
... <!-- other HTML code -->
```

However, this is not a desirable solution at all. In order for any RDFa-aware application to understand the markup in List 3.12, that application has to understand your vocabulary first. And clearly, if all the Web publishers went ahead and invented their own keywords, the world of available keywords would have become quite messy. Therefore, it is always the best choice to use words from a well-recognized vocabulary when it comes to markup your page. Again, FOAF vocabulary is one such well-accepted vocabulary, and if you use it in your markup (as shown in List 3.11), chances are any application that understands RDFa will be able to understand FOAF as well.

In fact, this flexibility of the possible values of RDFa attributes is quite useful for many markup requirements. For example, assume in my Web site, I have the following HTML snippet as shown in List 3.13.

List 3.13 HTML code about my friend, Dr. Ding

```
... <!-- other HTML code -->
<div>
<p>My friend, Dr. Ding, also likes to play tennis.</p>
</div>
... <!-- other HTML code -->
```

And I would like to markup the code in List 3.13 so that machines will understand these facts: first, I have a friend whose name is Dr. Ding, second, Dr. Ding likes to play tennis.

You can certainly try to use microformats to reach the goal; however, RDFa seems to be quite easy to use, as shown in List 3.14.

List 3.14 RDFa markup of List 3.13

```
... <!-- other HTML code -->
<div xmlns:foaf="http://xmlns.com/foaf/0.1/">
<p>My friend, <span about="http://www.liyangyu.com#liyang" rel=
"foaf:knows" href="http://www.example.org#ding">Dr.Ding</span>,
also likes to play <span about="http://www.example.org#ding" rel=
"foaf:interest" href="http://dbpedia.org/resource/Tennis">tennis.
</span></p>
<span about="http://www.example.org#ding" property="foaf:title"
content="Dr."/>    <span    about="http://www.ex-ample.org#ding"
proerty="foaf:lastName" content="Ding"/>
</div>
... <!-- other HTML code -->
```

Again, notice `http://dbpedia.org/resource/Tennis` is used as the URI identifying tennis as a sport. This is also a URI created by the DBpedia project, as you will see in later chapters. We are reusing this URI since it is always good to reuse existing ones. On the other hand, `http://www.example.org#ding` is a URI that we invented to represent Dr. Ding, since there is no URI for this person yet.

An application which understands RDFa will generate the RDF statements as shown in List 3.15 from List 3.14 (expressed in Turtle format).

List 3.15 RDF statements generated from the RDFa markup in 114

```
@prefix foaf: <http://xmlns.com/foaf/0.1/>.

<http://www.liyangyu.com#liyang>
foaf:knows <http://www.example.org#ding>.
<http://www.example.org#ding>
foaf:interest <http://dbpedia.org/resource/Tennis>.
<http://www.example.org#ding> foaf:title "Dr.".
<http://www.example.org#ding> foaf:lastName "Ding".
```

So far, all the examples we have seen are about inline markup. Sometimes, RDFa semantic markup can also be added about the containing document without explicitly using attribute `about`. Since this is a quite common use case of RDFa, let us take a look at one such example.

List 3.16 shows the markup that can be added to the document header:

List 3.16 RDFa markup about the containing document

```
<html xmlns:dc="http://purl.org/dc/elements/1.1/">
   <head>
      <meta property="dc:title" content="Liyang Yu's Homepage"/>
      <meta property="dc:creator" content="Liyang Yu"/>
   </head>
   <body>
<!-- body of the page -->
```

Clearly, there is no `about` attribute used. Based on the RDFa rules we discussed earlier, when no subject is specified, an RDFa-aware application assumes an empty string as the subject, which represents the document itself.

As this point, we have covered the following RDFa attributes: `about`, `content`, `href`, `property` and `rel`. These are all frequently used attributes, and understanding these can get you quite far.

The last attribute we would like to discuss here is attribute `typeof`. It is quite important and useful since it presents a case where a blank node is created. Let us take a look at one example.

Assume on my homepage, I have the following HTML code to identify myself as shown in List 3.17.

List 3.17 HTML code that identifies me

```
<div>
   <p>Liyang Yu</p>
   <p>E-mail: <a
      href="mailto:liyang@liyangyu.com">liyang@liyangyu.com</a>
</div>
```

We would now like to use RDFa to markup this part so the machine will understand that this whole `div` element is about a person whose name is `Liyang Yu` and whose e-mail address is `liyang@liyangyu.com`.

List 3.18 shows this markup:

List 3.18 RDFa markup of the HTML code shown in List 3.17

```
<div typeof="foaf:Person"
     xmlns:foaf="http://xmlns.com/foaf/0.1/">
   <p property="foaf:name">Liyang Yu</p>
   <p>E-mail: <a rel="foaf:mbox"
       href="mailto:liyang@liyangyu.com">liyang@liyangyu.com</a>
</div>
```

Notice the usage of attribute `typeof`. More specifically, this RDFa attribute is designed to be used when we need to declare a new data item with a certain type. In this example, this type is the `foaf:Person` type. For now, just understand `foaf:Person` is another keyword from the FOAF vocabulary, and it represents human being as a class called `Person`. Again, you will see more about FOAF vocabulary in a later chapter.

Now, when `typeof` is used as one attribute on the `div` element, the whole `div` element represents a data item whose type is `foaf:Person`. Therefore, once reading this line, any RDFa-aware application will be able to understand this `div` element is about a person. In addition, `foaf:name` and `foaf:mbox` are used with @property and @rel respectively to accomplish our goal to make machines understand this information, as you should be familiar with by now.

Notice we did not specify attribute `about` like we have done in the earlier examples. So what would be the subject for these properties then? In fact, attribute `typeof` on the enclosing `div` does the trick: it implicitly sets the subject of the properties marked up within that `div`. In other words, the name and e-mail address are associated with a new node of type `foaf:Person`. Obviously, this new node does not have a given URI to represent itself; it is therefore a blank node. Again, this is a trick you will see quite often if you are working with RDFa markup, so make sure you are comfortable with it.

The last question before we move on: if this new node is a blank node, how do we use it when it comes to data aggregation? For example, the markup information here could be quite important: it could be some supplemental information about a resource we are interested in. However, without a URI identifying it, how do we relate this information to the correct resource at all?

In this case, the answer is yes, we can indeed relate this markup information to another resource that exists outside the scope of this document. The secret lies in the `foaf:mbox` property. As you will see in Chap. 5, this property is an inverse functional property, and that is how we know which resource should be the subject of this markup information, even the subject itself is represented by a blank node.

3.3.4 RDFa and RDF

3.3.4.1 What's So Good About RDFa?

In Sect. 3.2.3.1, we discussed the benefits offered by microformats. In fact all these are still true for RDFa, and we can add one more here: RDFa is useful because microformats only exist as a collection of centralized vocabularies. More specifically, what if we want to markup a web page about a resource, for which there is no microformat available to use? In that case, RDFa is always a better choice, since you can in fact use any vocabulary for your RDFa markup.

In this chapter, we only see the Dublin Core vocabulary and the FOAF vocabulary. However, as you will see after you finish more chapters, there are quite a lot of vocabularies out there, covering different domains, and all are available to you when it comes to using RDFa to markup a given page. In fact, you can even invent your own if it is necessary (again, more on this later).

3.3.4.2 RDFa and RDF

At this point in the book, RDFa and RDF can be understood as the same thing. To put it simply, RDFa is just a way of expressing RDF triples inside given XHTML pages.

However, RDFa does make it much easier for people to express semantic information in conjunction with normal web pages. For instance, while there are many ways to express RDF (such as in serialized XML files that live next to standard web pages), RDFa helps machines and humans read exactly the same content. This is one of the major motivations for the creation of RDFa.

It might be a good idea to come back to this topic after you have finish the whole book. By then, you will have a better understanding of the whole picture. For example, having an HTML representation and a separate RDF/XML representation (or N3 and Turtle, etc.) is still a good solution for many cases, where HTTP content negotiation is often used to decide which format should be returned to the client (details in Chap. 9).

3.4 GRDDL

3.4.1 GRDDL: The Big Picture

As we discussed in Sect. 3.1, Gleaning Resource Descriptions from Dialects of Languages (GRDDL) is a way (a markup format, to be more precise) that enables users to obtain RDF triples out of XML documents (called *XML dialects*), in particular XHTML documents. The following GRDDL terminology is important for us to understand GRDDL:

- *GRDDL-aware agent*: a software agent that is able to recognize the GRDDL transformations and run these transformations to extract RDF.
- *GRDDL Transformation*: an algorithm for getting RDF from a source document.

GRDDL became a W3C recommendation on September 11, 2007.[4] In this standard document, GRDDL is defined as the following:

GRDDL is a mechanism for Gleaning Resource Descriptions from Dialects of Languages. The GRDDL specification introduces markup based on existing standards for declaring that an XML document includes data compatible with RDF and for linking to algorithms (typically represented in XSLT), for extracting this data from the document.

You can also find more information about GRDDL from the official Web site of the W3C GRDDL Working Group.[5]

In this section, we take a quick look at GRDDL, and introduce the markup formats needed for extracting markup information created by using microformats and RDFa. What you learn from here will give you enough if you decide to go further into GRDDL.

The last words before we move on: do not bury your semantic markup data in (X)HTML pages. Instead, when you publish a document that contains markup data,

---

[4] http://www.w3.org/TR/2007/REC-grddl-20070911/

[5] http://www.w3.org/2001/sw/grddl-wg/

do reference GRDDL profiles and/or transformations for their extraction. You will see how to do this in the next two sections.

3.4.2   Using GRDDL with Microformats

There are a number of ways to reference GRDDL in a document where microformats markup data is added. Referencing GRDDL transformations directly in the head of the HTML document is probably the easiest implementation: only two markup lines are needed.

More specifically, the first thing is to add a `profile` attribute to the `head` element to indicate the fact that this document contains GRDDL metadata. List 3.19 shows how to do this.

List 3.19 Adding a `profile` attribute for GRDDL transformation

```
<html xmlns="http://www.w3.org/1999/xhtml" xml:lang="en">
<head profile="http://www.w3.org/2003/g/data-view">
  <title>Liyang Yu's Homepage</title>
</head>
<body>
<!-- body of the page -->
```

In HTML, `profile` attribute in `head` element is used to link a given document to a description of the metadata schema that document uses. The URI for GRDDL is given by the following,

```
http://www.w3.org/2003/g/data-view
```

And by including this URI as shown in List 3.19, we declare that the metadata in the markup can be interpreted using GRDDL.

The second step is to add a `link` element containing the reference to the appropriate transformation. More specifically, recall that microformats are a collection of individual microformats such as the `hCard` microformat and the `hCalendar` microformat. Therefore, when working with markup data added by using microformats, it is always necessary to name the specific GRDDL transformation.

Let us assume the document in List 3.19 contains `hCard` microformat markups. Therefore, the `link` element has to contain the reference to the specific transformation for converting HTML containing `hCard` patterns into RDF. This is shown in List 3.20.

List 3.20 Adding `link` element for GRDDL transformation (`hCard` microformat)

```
<html xmlns="http://www.w3.org/1999/xhtml" xml:lang="en">
<head profile="http://www.w3.org/2003/g/data-view">
   <title>Liyang Yu's Homepage</title>
   <link rel="transformation"
        href="http://www.w3.org/2006/vcard/hcard2rdf.xsl"/>
</head>
<body>
<!-- body of the page -->
```

These two steps are all there is to it: the `profile` URI tells a GRDDL-aware application to look for a `link` element whose `rel` attribute contains the token `transformation`. Once the agent finds this element, the agent should use the value of `href` attribute on that element to decide how to extract the `hCard` microformat markup data as RDF triples from the enclosing document.

What if `hCalendar` microformat markup has been used in the document? If that is the case, we should use the following transformation as the value of `href` attribute:

```
http://www.w3.org/2002/12/cal/glean-hcal.xsl
```

3.4.3   Using GRDDL with RDFa

With what we learned from Sect. 3.4.2, it is now quite easy to use GRDDL with RDFa. The first step is still the same, i.e., we need to add a `profile` attribute to the `head` element, as shown in List 3.19. For the second step, as you have guessed, we will have to switch the transformation itself (List 3.21).

List 3.21 Adding `link` element for GRDDL transformation (RDFa)

```
<html xmlns="http://www.w3.org/1999/xhtml" xml:lang="en">
<head profile="http://www.w3.org/2003/g/data-view">
   <title>Liyang Yu's Homepage</title>
   <link rel="transformation"
   href="http://www.w3.org/2001/sw/grddl-wg/td/RDFa2RDFXML.xsl"/>
</head>
<body>
<!-- body of the page -->
```

3.5 Summary

This chapter covers the technical details of both microformats and RDFa. GRDDL, a popular markup format which automatically converts microformats and RDFa markup information into RDF triples, is also included.

From this chapter, you should have learned the following main points:

- the concepts of microformats and RDFa, and how they fit into the whole idea of the Semantic Web;
- the language constructs of both microformats and RDFa, and how to markup a given (X)HTML page by using these constructs;
- the advantages and limitations of both microformats and RDFa, and their relationships to RDF;
- the concept of GRDDL, how it fits into the idea of the Semantic Web, and how to use GRDDL to automatically extract markup data from (X)HTML pages.

With all this said, the final goal is for you to understand these technical components, and also to be able to pick the right one for a given development assignment.

Chapter 4
RDFS and Ontology

Even after you have read the previous two chapters carefully, you probably still have lots of unanswered questions. This chapter is a natural continuation of Chaps. 2 and 3, especially Chap. 2. After reading this chapter, you should have answers to most of your questions.

This chapter covers all the main aspects of the Resource Description Framework Schema (RDFS), including its concepts, its semantics, its language constructs and features, and certainly, real-world examples. Here we also formally introduce the concept of ontology, together with a description of the Simple Knowledge Organization System (SKOS). Again, make sure you understand the content in this chapter, since what you learn here is important for you to continue on with Chap. 5.

4.1 RDFS Overview

4.1.1 RDFS in Plain English

Unlike the previous chapter, we will start this chapter by discussing RDFS in plain English. In this section, our goal is to answer the following two questions:

- Why do we need RDFS, and
- What is RDFS?

Let us go back to Chap. 2 and take another look at List 2.25, the RDF/XML representation of List 2.5. The following questions may come to your mind:

- Line 9 of List 2.25 says `myCamera:Nikon_D300` is an instance (by using predicate `rdf:type`) of the resource identified by URI `myCamera:DSLR`, but where is this `myCamera:DSLR` resource defined? What does it look like?

© Springer-Verlag Berlin Heidelberg 2014
L. Yu, *A Developer's Guide to the Semantic Web*,
DOI 10.1007/978-3-662-43796-4_4

- If we use object-oriented concepts, `myCamera:DSLR` can be understood as a class. Now, if `myCamera:DSLR` represents a class, are there any other classes that are defined as its super classes or subclasses?
- The rest of List 2.25 uses several properties (such as `myCamera:model` and `myCamera:weight`) to describe `myCamera:Nikon_D300`. Are there any other properties that we can use to describe `myCamera:Nikon_D300`? How do we know these properties exist for us to use in the first place?

You can ask more questions like these. The last question, in particular, raises an important issue: when we describe a real-world resource such as `myCamera:Nikon_D300`, what are the things (predicates) we can use to describe it? If we all say something about it, and furthermore, if we all go on to invent our own things to say about it, there will be no common language shared among us. And in that case, any given application cannot go too much further beyond simply aggregating the distributed RDF models.

A common language or shared vocabulary seems to be the key there. More specifically, if properties such as `myCamera:model` and `myCamera:weight` are used to describe a camera, that is because somewhere, in some document, someone has defined that these are indeed the predicates we can use to describe it. There are possibly more terms defined for us to use, and it is our choice which predicates to use when publishing our own descriptions. Therefore, this common language can make sure of one important thing for us: everything we say about a given resource, we have a reason to say it.

Clearly at this stage, what seems to be missing for our RDF documents is such a common language, or a vocabulary, where classes, subclasses, properties and relations between these classes and properties are defined. As you might have guessed, RDFS is such a language that we can use to define a vocabulary, which can then be used to structure the RDF documents we create.

Vocabulary is not something totally new to us at this point; we have used the word vocabulary in previous chapters for a number of times. For example, all the RDF terms we covered in Chap. 2 are elements from RDF vocabulary, and Dublin Core is another vocabulary. We have used both to create RDF documents in the previous two chapters. Now, for a given specific application domain (such as photography), we may need some application-specific vocabularies, and this is where we use the RDFS.

Therefore, in plain English, we can define RDFS as follows:

RDFS is a language one can use to create a vocabulary (often the created vocabulary is domain-specific), so when distributed RDF documents are created in this domain, terms from this vocabulary can be used. Therefore, everything we say, we have a reason to say it.

At this point, we understand how RDFS fits into the world of RDF. We will also see how it works together with RDF to create more structured and machine-understandable documents on the Web in the coming sections of this chapter. For now, let us move on to see the official definition of RDFS.

4.1.2   RDFS in Official Language

RDFS or RDF Schema is a W3C standard; its initial version[1] was originally published by W3C in April 1998. With the change of RDF standards (see Chap. 2), W3C released the final RDFS recommendation[2] in February 2004, and it is included in the six documents published as the updated RDF specifications as shown in Table 2.1. Various abbreviations such as RDF(S), RDF-S or RDF/S can be used to refer to the same RDF Schema.

Based on this official document, RDFS can be defined as follows:

RDFS is recommendation from W3C and it is an extensible knowledge representation language that one can use to create a vocabulary for describing classes, subclasses and properties of RDF resources.

With this definition, RDFS can be understood as RDF's vocabulary description language. As a standard, RDFS provides language constructs that can be used to describe classes and properties within a specific application domain, for example, what is a DSLR class, and what is property model, and how could it be used to describe a resource. Notice that the language constructs in RDFS are themselves classes and properties; in other words, RDFS provides standard classes and properties that can be used to describe classes and properties in a specific domain.

To further help you understand what RDFS is, let us move on to some more explanations and examples in the next section. Before we can discuss its language features and constructs, a solid understanding about it is needed.

4.2   RDFS + RDF: One More Step Toward Machine-Readable

In this section, we discuss more about the reason why RDFS is needed. This will not only enhance your understanding about RDFS, it will also help you to put the pieces together to understand the world of the Semantic Web.

4.2.1   A Common Language to Share

The first important fact about RDFS is that RDFS can be used to define a vocabulary, a common language everyone can use. The goal? Everything we say, we have a reason to say it.

---

[1] http://www.w3.org/TR/1998/WD-rdf-schema-19980409/

[2] http://www.w3.org/TR/rdf-schema/

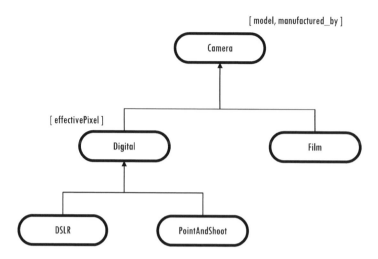

Fig. 4.1 A small vocabulary for the domain of photography

Let us take a look at one example. Figure 4.1 shows a small vocabulary in the world of photography:

Notice in this tiny vocabulary, an oval box is used to represent a specific resource type, and the arrow from one oval box to another oval box means that the first oval box is a subtype of the second oval box. The properties that one can use to describe a given resource type are included in [], and are placed beside that specific oval box.

With all this said, this simple vocabulary tells us the following fact:

We have a resource call **Camera**, and **Digital** and **Film** are its two subresources. Also, resource **Digital** has two subresources, **DSLR** and **PointAndShoot**. Resource **Camera** can be described by properties called **model** and **manufactured_by**, and resource **Digital** can be described by a property called **effectivePixel**.

Again, DSLR is short for Digital Single Lens Reflex, which is a type of camera that is more often used by professional photographers, and tends to be expensive as well. On the other hand, a *Point And Shoot* camera, also called a compact camera, is often used by non-professionals, and it normally offers functionalities such as autofocus and autoexposure setting.

Now, if we want to describe Nikon D300 as a DSLR, we know what we can say about it. List 4.1 shows one such example.

List 4.1 A simple description of Nikon D300

```
1:  <?xml version="1.0"?>
2:  <rdf:RDF
2a:      xmlns:rdf="http://www.w3.org/1999/02/22-rdf-syntax-ns#"
3:       xmlns:myCamera="http://www.liyangyu.com/camera#">
4:
5:  <rdf:Description
5a:      rdf:about="http://www.liyangyu.com/camera#Nikon_D300">
6:    <rdf:type
6a:        rdf:resource="http://www.liyangyu.com/camera#DSLR"/>
7:    <myCamera:model>Nikon D300</myCamera:model>
8:    <myCamera:manufactured_by
         rdf:resource="http://www.dbpedia.org/resource/Nikon"/>
9:    <myCamera:effectivePixel>12.3</myCamera:effectivePixel>
10: </rdf:Description>
11:
12: </rdf:RDF>
```

As we see from Fig. 4.1, resource `Camera` can be described by properties named `manufactured_by` and `model`. Why can we use them to describe Nikon D300, an instance of `DSLR`, not `Camera` (lines 7 and 8)? The reason is really simple: any property that can be used to describe the base type can also be used to describe any subtype of this base type. Again, anything we say here, we have a reason to say.

On the other hand, we will not be able to use a term if that term is not defined in the vocabulary. If we have to do so, we will then need to grow the vocabulary accordingly.

Now, imagine someone else from the same application domain has come up with another RDF document describing the same camera (or another camera). Whatever the resource being described might be, all these documents now share the same terms. Notice that when we say the same terms are shared, it is not that all the documents will use exactly the same terms to describe resource—one document might use different properties compared to the other document, but all the properties available to use are included in the given vocabulary. The result is that any application that "knows" this vocabulary will be able to process these documents with ease. This is an obvious benefit of having a common vocabulary.

Another important benefit of having a vocabulary defined is to facilitate machine understanding, as discussed in the next section.

4.2.2   Machine Inferencing Based on RDFS

A vocabulary created by using RDFS can facilitate inferencing on the RDF documents that make use of this vocabulary. To see this, let us go back to List 4.1 to understand what inferences machines can make.

The inferencing for this case is based on line 6, which says the resource identified by `http://www.liyangyu.com/camera#Nikon_D300` is a `DSLR`. Given the vocabulary in Fig. 4.1, the following inferences can be made:

- Resource `http://www.liyangyu.com/camera#Nikon_D300` is a `Digital` camera, and
- Resource `http://www.liyangyu.com/camera#Nikon_D300` is a `Camera`,

which is all done by the machine, and these inferred conclusions can be critical information for many applications. In fact, a lot more inferencing can be done when a vocabulary is defined, and we will see more examples during the course of this chapter.

At this point, you have seen all the important aspects of RDFS, especially why we need it. The rest is to understand its syntax, which we cover in coming sections. And the good news is, RDFS itself can be written in the RDF/XML format, and any vocabulary created using RDFS can also be written in the RDF/XML format, so it is not totally new.

4.3   RDFS Core Elements

In this section, we cover the syntax of RDFS, together with examples. Our goal is to build a camera vocabulary by using RDFS terms, with the one shown in Fig. 4.1 as our starting point.

4.3.1   The Big Picture: RDFS Vocabulary

First, as we have discussed, RDFS is a collection of terms we can use to define classes and properties for a specific application domain. Just like RDF terms and Dublin Core terms, all these RDFS terms are identified by predefined URIs, and all these URIs share the following leading string:

`http://www.w3.org/2000/01/rdf-schema#`

and by convention, this URI prefix string is associated with namespace prefix `rdfs:`, which is typically used in RDF/XML format with the prefix `rdfs`.

Second, all these RDFS terms can be divided into the following groups based on their purposes:

- Classes

This group includes RDFS terms that can be used to define classes. More specifically, the following terms are included here: `rdfs:Resource`, `rdfs:Class`, `rdfs:Literal`, `rdfs:Datatype`.

- Properties

This group includes RDFS terms that can be used to define properties, and the following terms are included: `rdfs:range`, `rdfs:domain`, `rdfs:subClassOf`, `rdfs:subPropertyOf`, `rdfs:label` and `rdfs:comment`.

- Utilities

As its name suggests, this group of RDFS terms are used for miscellaneous purposes, as we will see later in this chapter. For now, understand that this group contains the following terms: `rdfs:seeAlso` and `rdfs:isDefinedBy`.

4.3.2 Basic Syntax and Examples

4.3.2.1 Defining Classes

First off, `rdfs:Resource` represents the root class, and every other class defined using RDFS terms is a subclass of this class. In practice, this term is rarely used; it mainly acts as a logic root to hold everything together: all things described by RDF are instances of class `rdfs:Resource`.

To define a class in a vocabulary, `rdfs:Class` is used. For our camera vocabulary, List 4.2 shows the definition of the `Camera` class.

List 4.2 Definition of the `Camera` class

```
1: <?xml version="1.0"?>
2: <rdf:RDF
2a:     xmlns:rdf="http://www.w3.org/1999/02/22-rdf-syntax-ns#"
3:      xmlns:rdfs="http://www.w3.org/2000/01/rdf-schema#"
4:      xmlns:myCamera="http://www.liyangyu.com/camera#">
5:
6: <rdf:Description
6a:     rdf:about="http://www.liyangyu.com/camera#Camera">
7:    <rdf:type
7a:   rdf:resource="http://www.w3.org/2000/01/rdf-schema#Class"/>
8: </rdf:Description>
9:
10: </rdf:RDF>
```

Let us understand List 4.2 line by line. First of all, everything is defined between `<rdf:RDF>` and `</rdf:RDF>`, indicating this document is either a RDF document (as we have seen in Chap. 2) or a RDF schema document (as seen here). Lines 2–4 have defined several namespaces, and the new one here is the `rdfs` namespace (line

3), which includes all the predefined terms in RDF Schema. Line 4 defines the namespace for our camera vocabulary.

Now, the key lines are lines 6–8. Line 6 defines a new resource by using the term `rdf:Description` from RDF vocabulary, and this new resource has the following URI:

`http://www.liyangyu.com/camera#Camera`

Line 7 specifies the type property of this resource by using RDF term `rdf:type`, and its value is another resource (indicated by using RDF term `rdf:resource`), which has the following URI:

`http://www.w3.org/2000/01/rdf-schema#Class`

Obviously, this URI is a predefined term in RDFS vocabulary and its QName is given by `rdfs:Class`. Now, we have defined a new class, and we can read it as follows:

Here we declare: this resource, `http://www.liyangyu.com/camera#Camera`, is a class.

Notice `Camera` class is by default a subclass of `rdfs:Resource`, the root class of all classes. In addition, pay attention not to mix together these two terms: `rdfs:Resource` and `rdf:resource`. `rdfs:Resource` is a class defined in RDFS as we have discussed above, and `rdf:resource` is simply an XML attribute that goes together with a specific property element (in List 4.2, it is used together with `rdf:type` property element) to indicate the fact that the property's value is another resource. Also, `rdf:resource` is case-sensitive, i.e., cannot be written as `rdf:Resource`. If you do so, your validator will raise a red flag at it for sure.

Sometimes, you will see `rdf:ID` is used instead of `rdf:about`. For example, List 4.3 is equivalent to List 4.2, and List 4.3 uses `rdf:ID`:

List 4.3 Use `rdf:ID` to define `Camera` class

```
1: <?xml version="1.0"?>
2: <rdf:RDF
2a:     xmlns:rdf="http://www.w3.org/1999/02/22-rdf-syntax-ns#"
3:      xmlns:rdfs="http://www.w3.org/2000/01/rdf-schema#"
4:      xmlns:myCamera="http://www.liyangyu.com/camera#"
5:      xml:base="http://www.liyangyu.com/camera#">
6:
7: <rdf:Description rdf:ID="Camera">
8:     <rdf:type
8a:    rdf:resource="http://www.w3.org/2000/01/rdf-schema#Class"/>
9: </rdf:Description>
10:
11: </rdf:RDF>
```

Notice the use of line 5. It is always a good practice (almost necessary) to use `xml:base` together with `rdf:ID`, as we discussed in Chap. 2. Since using `rdf:ID` makes the line shorter, from now on, we will be using `rdf:ID` more.

In fact, there is a short form you can use, which is equivalent to both Lists 4.2 and 4.3. This short form is shown in List 4.4.

List 4.4 Short form that is equivalent to Lists 4.2 and 4.3

```
1: <?xml version="1.0"?>
2: <rdf:RDF
2a:     xmlns:rdf="http://www.w3.org/1999/02/22-rdf-syntax-ns#"
3:      xmlns:rdfs="http://www.w3.org/2000/01/rdf-schema#"
4:      xmlns:myCamera="http://www.liyangyu.com/camera#"
5:      xml:base="http://www.liyangyu.com/camera#">
6:
7:   <rdfs:Class rdf:ID="Camera">
8:   </rdfs:Class>
9:
10: </rdf:RDF>
```

This short form not only looks cleaner, but also looks more intuitive: `rdfs:Class` is used to define a class and `rdf:ID` is used to provide a name for the class being defined (lines 7 and 8). And of course, if you prefer to use `rdf:about` instead of `rdf:ID`, List 4.4 will become List 4.5, which again is equivalent to Lists 4.2 and 4.3.

List 4.5 A short form using `rdf:about`

```
1: <?xml version="1.0"?>
2: <rdf:RDF
2a:     xmlns:rdf="http://www.w3.org/1999/02/22-rdf-syntax-ns#"
3:      xmlns:rdfs="http://www.w3.org/2000/01/rdf-schema#"
4:      xmlns:myCamera="http://www.liyangyu.com/camera#">
5:
6: <rdfs:Class rdf:about="http://www.liyangyu.com/camera#Camera">
7: </rdfs:Class>
8:
9: </rdf:RDF>
```

Notice in List 4.5, `xml:base` is not needed anymore.

To define more classes, we can simply add more class definitions by using `rdfs:Class` as shown in List 4.6:

List 4.6 Adding class `Lens` into the vocabulary

```
1: <?xml version="1.0"?>
2: <rdf:RDF
2a:     xmlns:rdf="http://www.w3.org/1999/02/22-rdf-syntax-ns#"
3:      xmlns:rdfs="http://www.w3.org/2000/01/rdf-schema#"
4:      xmlns:myCamera="http://www.liyangyu.com/camera#"
5:      xml:base="http://www.liyangyu.com/camera#">
6:
7: <rdfs:Class rdf:about="http://www.liyangyu.com/camera#Camera">
8: </rdfs:Class>
9:
10: <rdfs:Class rdf:about="http://www.liyangyu.com/camera#Lens">
11: </rdfs:Class>
12:
13: <rdfs:Class rdf:about="http://www.liyangyu.com/camera#Body">
14: </rdfs:Class>
15:
16: <rdfs:Class
16a:        rdf:about="http://www.liyangyu.com/camera#ValueRange">
17: </rdfs:Class>
18:
19: </rdf:RDF>
```

Notice that in List 4.6, we have defined class `Lens`, `Body` and `ValueRange`; the reason for having these classes will become clear in later sections of this chapter.

So much for the top-level classes at this point. Let us move on to subclasses. To define subclasses, we need to use `rdfs:subClassOf` property defined in RDF Schema. List 4.7 shows the details.

List 4.7 Subclass definitions are added

```
1: <?xml version="1.0"?>
2: <rdf:RDF
2a:     xmlns:rdf="http://www.w3.org/1999/02/22-rdf-syntax-ns#"
3:      xmlns:rdfs="http://www.w3.org/2000/01/rdf-schema#"
4:      xmlns:myCamera="http://www.liyangyu.com/camera#"
5:      xml:base="http://www.liyangyu.com/camera#">
6:
7: <rdfs:Class rdf:about="http://www.liyangyu.com/camera#Camera">
8: </rdfs:Class>
9:
10: <rdfs:Class rdf:about="http://www.liyangyu.com/camera#Lens">
11: </rdfs:Class>
12:
13: <rdfs:Class rdf:about="http://www.liyangyu.com/camera#Body">
14: </rdfs:Class>
15:
16: <rdfs:Class
16a:      rdf:about="http://www.liyangyu.com/camera#ValueRange">
17: </rdfs:Class>
18:
19: <rdfs:Class
19a:      rdf:about="http://www.liyangyu.com/camera#Digital">
20:     <rdfs:subClassOf rdf:resource="#Camera"/>
21: </rdfs:Class>
22:
23: <rdfs:Class rdf:about="http://www.liyangyu.com/camera#Film">
24:     <rdfs:subClassOf rdf:resource="#Camera"/>
25: </rdfs:Class>
26:
27: <rdfs:Class rdf:about="http://www.liyangyu.com/camera#DSLR">
28:     <rdfs:subClassOf rdf:resource="#Digital"/>
29: </rdfs:Class>
30:
31: <rdfs:Class
31a:     rdf:about="http://www.liyangyu.com/camera#PointAndShoot">
32:     <rdfs:subClassOf rdf:resource="#Digital"/>
33: </rdfs:Class>
34:
35: <rdfs:Class
35a:      rdf:about="http://www.liyangyu.com/camera#Photographer">
36:     <rdfs:subClassOf
36a:          rdf:resource="http://xmlns.com/foaf/0.1/Person"/>
37: </rdfs:Class>
38:
39: </rdf:RDF>
```

Lines 19–37 define some subclasses that are used in our vocabulary. First off, notice how the base class is identified in the `rdfs:subClassOf` property. For instance, line 19 defines a class, `Digital`, and line 20 uses the `rdfs:subClassOf` property to specify the base class of `Digital` is `Camera`. The way `Camera` is identified is as follows:

```
<rdfs:subClassOf rdf:resource="#Camera"/>
```

This is perfectly fine in this case since when a RDF parser sees `#Camera`, it assumes that class `Camera` must have been defined in the same document (which is true here). To get the URI of class `Camera`, it concatenates `xml:base` and this name together to get the following:

```
http://www.liyangyu.com/camera#Camera
```

This is clearly the right URI for this class, and this is also the reason why we need to add line 5 to specify the base URI to use when concatenation is done. Of course, you can always do the following to specify the full URI of the base class:

```
<rdfs:Class rdf:about="http://www.liyangyu.com/camera#Digital">
    <rdfs:subClassOf
        rdf:resource="http://www.liyangyu.com/camera#Camera"/>
</rdfs:Class>
```

And this is often used when the base class is defined in some other document. In fact, lines 35–37 provide a perfect example, where class `Photographer` is being defined as a subclass of `Person`. Since base class `Person` is not defined in this vocabulary, we use its full URI to identify this class, as shown by line 36. We will see class `Person` later in this book; it is a key class created by the popular FOAF project, which is presented in Chap. 7.

The rest of the subclass definitions can be understood similarly. For now, we have defined the following subclasses: `Digital`, `Film`, `DSLR`, `PointAndShoot` and `Photographer`.

Another important fact about `rdfs:subClassOf` property is that you can use it multiple times when defining a class. If you do so, all the base classes introduced by `rdfs:subClassOf` will be ANDed together to create the new class. For instance, let us say you have already defined a class called `Journalist`; you can now define a new class called `Photojournalist` as follows:

```
<rdfs:Class
        rdf:about="http://www.liyangyu.com/camera#Photojournalist">
    <rdfs:subClassOf rdf:resource="#Photographer"/>
    <rdfs:subClassOf rdf:resource="#Journalist"/>
</rdfs:Class>
```

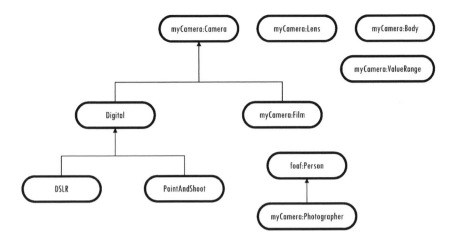

Fig. 4.2 Classes defined for our camera ontology

This means class Photojournalist is a subclass of *both* Photographer class and Journalist class. Therefore, any instance of Photojournalist is an instance of Photographer and Journalist at the same time.

4.3.2.2 Defining Properties

At this point, we have defined all the classes we need for our camera vocabulary. Figure 4.2 summarizes all these classes and their relationships:

Notice all the classes in Fig. 4.2 are "floating" around: except for the base-class and subclass relationship, there seem to be no other bounds among them. In fact, the bounds, or the relationships among these classes, will be expressed by properties. Let us now move on to define these properties.

To define a property, rdf:Property type is used, and rdf:about in this case specifies the URI of the property. Furthermore, rdfs:domain and rdfs:range together indicate how the property should be used. Let us take a look at List 4.8.

List 4.8 Define property `owned_by`

```
1: <?xml version="1.0"?>
2: <rdf:RDF
2a:      xmlns:rdf="http://www.w3.org/1999/02/22-rdf-syntax-ns#"
3:       xmlns:rdfs="http://www.w3.org/2000/01/rdf-schema#"
4:       xmlns:myCamera="http://www.liyangyu.com/camera#"
5:       xml:base="http://www.liyangyu.com/camera#">
6:
7:
... // classes, sub-classes definitions as shown in List 4.7
38:
39:  <rdf:Property
41a:      rdf:about="http://www.liyangyu.com/camera#owned_by">
40:      <rdfs:domain rdf:resource="#DSLR"/>
41:      <rdfs:range rdf:resource="#Photographer"/>
42:  </rdf:Property>
43:
44: </rdf:RDF>
```

As shown in List 4.8, lines 39–42 define the property called `owned_by`. We can read this as follows:

> We define a property called `owned_by`. It can only be used to describe the characteristics of class `DSLR`, and its possible values can only be instances of class `Photographer`.

or equivalently,

subject: `DSLR`
predicate: `owned_by`
object: `Photographer`

The new RDFS terms here are `rdfs:domain` and `rdfs:range`. More specifically, property `rdfs:domain` is used to specify which class the property being defined can be used with. It is optional, so you can declare property `owned_by` like this:

```
<rdf:Property
    rdf:about="http://www.liyangyu.com/camera#owned_by">
  <rdfs:range rdf:resource="#Photographer"/>
</rdf:Property>
```

This means property `owned_by` can be used to describe any class. For instance, you can say something like "a `Person` is `owned_by` a `Photographer`". In most cases, this is not what we want, and the definition with `rdfs:domain` as shown in

List 4.8 is much better. It says that `owned_by` can only be used on the instances of class `DSLR`.

Notice when defining a property, multiple `rdfs:domain` properties can be specified. In that case, we are indicating that the property can be used with a resource that is an instance of *every* class defined by `rdfs:domain` property. For example,

```
<rdf:Property
     rdf:about="http://www.liyangyu.com/camera#owned_by">
  <rdfs:domain rdf:resource="#DSLR"/>
  <rdfs:domain rdf:resource="#PointAndShoot"/>
  <rdfs:range rdf:resource="#Photographer"/>
</rdf:Property>
```

This says property `owned_by` can only be used with something that is a `DSLR` camera *and* a `PointAndShoot` camera at the same time. In fact, a DSLR camera can be used as a point-and-shoot camera, so the above definition does hold.

As for `rdfs:range`, all the above discussion is true. First of all, it is optional, like the following:

```
<rdf:Property
     rdf:about="http://www.liyangyu.com/camera#owned_by">
  <rdfs:domain rdf:resource="#DSLR"/>
</rdf:Property>
```

This says property `owned_by` can be use with `DSLR` class, but its value can be anything. Therefore, in our RDF document, we can add a statement that says a DSLR camera is owned by another DSLR camera, which certainly does not make much sense. Therefore, most likely, we will need to use at least one `rdfs:range` property when defining a property.

We can also use multiple `rdfs:range` properties such as the following (assume we have already defined a class call `Journalist`):

```
<rdf:Property
     rdf:about="http://www.liyangyu.com/camera#owned_by">
  <rdfs:domain rdf:resource="#DSLR"/>
  <rdfs:range rdf:resource="#Photographer"/>
  <rdfs:range rdf:resource="#Journalist"/>
</rdf:Property>
```

This says property `owned_by` can be used to depict `DSLR`s, and its value has to be someone who is a `Photographer` and `Journalist` at the same time. In other words, this someone has to be a photojournalist.

With all this said, we can continue to define other properties used in our camera vocabulary, as shown in List 4.9.

List 4.9 Camera vocabulary with properties defined

```
1: <?xml version="1.0"?>
2: <rdf:RDF
2a:     xmlns:rdf="http://www.w3.org/1999/02/22-rdf-syntax-ns#"
3:      xmlns:rdfs="http://www.w3.org/2000/01/rdf-schema#"
4:      xmlns:myCamera="http://www.liyangyu.com/camera#"
5:      xml:base="http://www.liyangyu.com/camera#">
6:
7:
    ... // classes/sub-classes definitions as shown in List 4.7
38:
39: <rdf:Property
39a:    rdf:about="http://www.liyangyu.com/camera#owned_by">
40:   <rdfs:domain rdf:resource="#DSLR"/>
41:   <rdfs:range rdf:resource="#Photographer"/>
42: </rdf:Property>
43:
44: <rdf:Property
44a:  rdf:about="http://www.liyangyu.com/camera#manufactured_by">
45:   <rdfs:domain rdf:resource="#Camera"/>
46: </rdf:Property>
47:
48: <rdf:Property
48a:    rdf:about="http://www.liyangyu.com/camera#body">
49:   <rdfs:domain rdf:resource="#Camera"/>
50:   <rdfs:range rdf:resource="#Body"/>
51: </rdf:Property>
52:
53: <rdf:Property
53a:    rdf:about="http://www.liyangyu.com/camera#lens">
54:   <rdfs:domain rdf:resource="#Camera"/>
55:   <rdfs:range rdf:resource="#Lens"/>
56: </rdf:Property>
57:
58: <rdf:Property
58a:    rdf:about="http://www.liyangyu.com/camera#model">
59:   <rdfs:domain rdf:resource="#Camera"/>
60:   <rdfs:range
60a:    rdf:resource="http://www.w3.org/2001/XMLSchema#string"/>
61: </rdf:Property>
62:
63: <rdf:Property
63a:   rdf:about="http://www.liyangyu.com/camera#effectivePixel">
```

```
64:     <rdfs:domain rdf:resource="#Digital"/>
65:    <rdfs:range
65a:     rdf:resource="http://www.w3.org/2001/XMLSchema#decimal"/>
66: </rdf:Property>
67:
68: <rdf:Property
68a:     rdf:about="http://www.liyangyu.com/camera#shutterSpeed">
69:     <rdfs:domain rdf:resource="#Body"/>
70:     <rdfs:range rdf:resource="#ValueRange"/>
71: </rdf:Property>
72:
73: <rdf:Property
73a:     rdf:about="http://www.liyangyu.com/camera#focalLength">
74:     <rdfs:domain rdf:resource="#Lens"/>
75:     <rdfs:range
75a:     rdf:resource="http://www.w3.org/2001/XMLSchema#string"/>
76: </rdf:Property>
77:
78: <rdf:Property
78a:     rdf:about="http://www.liyangyu.com/camera#aperture">
79:     <rdfs:domain rdf:resource="#Lens"/>
80:     <rdfs:range rdf:resource="#ValueRange"/>
81: </rdf:Property>
82:
83: <rdf:Property
83a:     rdf:about="http://www.liyangyu.com/camera#minValue">
84:     <rdfs:domain rdf:resource="#ValueRange"/>
85:     <rdfs:range
85a:     rdf:resource="http://www.w3.org/2001/XMLSchema#float"/>
86: </rdf:Property>
87:
88: <rdf:Property
88a:     rdf:about="http://www.liyangyu.com/camera#maxValue">
89:     <rdfs:domain rdf:resource="#ValueRange"/>
90:     <rdfs:range
90a:     rdf:resource="http://www.w3.org/2001/XMLSchema#float"/>
91: </rdf:Property>
92:
93: </rdf:RDF>
```

As shown in List 4.9, we have defined four properties related to Camera class. Property body can be used on a Camera instance, and it takes a Body instance as its value (lines 48–51). lens property is defined similarly (lines 53–56): it can be used on a Camera instance, and it takes a Lens instance as its value. Together these two properties specify the fact that any given camera will always have a body and lens, which is quite intuitive indeed.

Another property that is shared by all cameras is the `model` property, as shown on lines 58–61. Finally, notice the definition of property `manufactured_by`, which does not have property `rdfs:range` defined (lines 44–46). As we have discussed, it is almost always better to have `rdfs:range`, but for simplicity, we are not going to have it here.

Property `effectivePixel` is only applicable to digital cameras; therefore its `rdfs:domain` property points to `Digital` class as seen on lines 63–66.

We know that for any given camera body and its lens, there are three parameters that are often used to specify its performance: shutter speed (a parameter that can be adjusted on the camera's body), focal length of the lens and aperture of the lens. Therefore, we need to define all these properties for our camera vocabulary to be useful.

Property `focalLength` is defined on lines 73–76. It is used on instances of `Lens` class, and it takes a string as its value, such as 50 mm. Notice that for a zoom lens, i.e., a lens with changeable focal length, this definition will not be enough, since there has to be a way to specify the range of the changeable focal lengths. For now, let us assume we only consider non-zoom lens, and our definition will be fine.

Another parameter for lens is aperture, which indeed has a range. For instance, 2.8–22 can be the typical range of aperture values for a given lens. Taking this into account, we have defined property `aperture` as shown on lines 78–81. It is used on instances of `Lens` class, and its value should take an instance of `ValueRange` class. Notice the same method is used for shutter speed parameter: property `shutterSpeed` is used on `Body` class, and its value also takes an instance of `ValueRange` class (lines 68–71).

Finally, we need to include range information in `ValueRange` class. To implement this, lines 83–91 define two more properties: `minValue` and `maxValue`. These two properties will be used on instances of `ValueRange` class, and by using these two properties, we will be able model the fact that some parameters take a range of values instead of a single value.

Up to this point, we have added the related properties into our camera vocabulary. Together with the class definitions shown in Fig. 4.2, this now becomes a complete vocabulary, and we can also update Fig. 4.2 and change it to Fig. 4.3.

Again, in Fig. 4.3, the properties that can be used to describe a given resource type are included in [], and are placed beside that specific oval box. The value range of that property is also included. For example, property `myCamera:body` can be used on `myCamera:Camera` class, and its value can be an instance of type `myCamera:Body`. Notice if there are no constraints on the values a given property can assume, there will be no value specified for that property. Notice that property `myCamera:manufactured_by` is one such example.

In fact, properties not only describe the relationship among classes, they are also the more interesting part in a vocabulary: they are the key factors when it comes to reasoning based on vocabularies. Let us discuss this more in the next few sections.

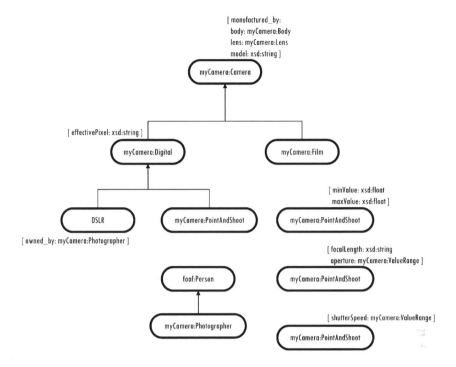

Fig. 4.3 Our camera ontology so far

4.3.2.3 More About Properties

First off, properties are inheritable from base classes to subclasses. More specifically, remember class `Digital` has a property called `effectivePixel`, and it also has two subclasses, namely, `DSLR` and `PointAndShoot`. Then do these sub-classes also have the property `effectivePixel`? In other words, can we use `effectivePixel` to describe a `DSLR` instance? The answer is yes, since a subclass always inherits properties from its base class.

Therefore, class `DSLR` and `PointAndShoot` both have a property called `effectivePixel`.

In fact, taken one step further, a class always inherits properties from *all* its base classes. For instance, we can use `model` property on class `Camera`, and since `Camera` is also a base class of `DSLR` (although not a direct base class), we can then `model` property on class `DSLR` as well.

The second important issue about property is the subproperty. We can define a property to be a subproperty of another property, and this is done by using `rdfs:subPropertyOf`. For example, the `model` property describes the "name" of a camera. However, the manufacturer could sell the same model using different model names. For instance, the same camera sold in North America could have a different model name than the one sold in Asia. Therefore, we can define another property, say, officialModel, to be a subproperty of model:

```
<rdf:Property
    rdf:about="http://www.liyangyu.com/camera#officialModel">
    <rdfs:subPropertyOf rdf:resource="#model"/>
</rdf:Property>
```

This declares the property officialModel as a specialization of property model. Property officialModel inherits rdfs:domain and rdfs:range values from its base property model. However, you can narrow the domain and/or the range as you wish.

We can also use multiple rdfs:subPropertyOf when defining a property. If we do so, we are declaring the property being defined has to be a subproperty of *each* of the base properties.

The third issue about property is that we have been using the abbreviated form to define properties. It is important to know this since you might see the long form in other documents. List 4.10 shows the long form one can use to define a property.

List 4.10 Long form used to define property owned_by

```
<rdf:Description
    rdf:about="http://www.liyangyu.com/camera#owned_by">
  <rdf:type rdf:resource=
      "http://www.w3.or/1999/02/22-rdf-syntx-ns#Property"/>
  <rdfs:domain rdf:resource="#DSLR"/>
  <rdfs:range rdf:resource="#Photographer"/>
</rdf:Description>
```

The fourth issue we would like to mention might also be something you have realized already: the separation of class definitions and property definitions in our vocabulary. Those who are used to the object-oriented world might find this fact uncomfortably strange.

For instance, if we are using any object-oriented language (such as Java or C++), we may define a class called DigitalCamera, and we will then encapsulate several properties to describe a digital camera. These properties will be defined at the same time we define the class, and they are defined in the class scope as its member variables. Normally, these properties are not directly visible to the outside world.

For RDF schema, it is quite a different story. We define a class, and very often we also indicate its relationships to other classes. However, this is it: we never declare its member variables, i.e., the properties it may have. A class is just an entity who may have relationships to other entities. What is inside this entity, i.e., its member variables/properties, is simply unknown.

The truth is, we declare properties separately and associate the properties with classes if we wish to do so. Properties are never owned by any class; they are never local to any class either. If we do not associate a given property to any class, this property is simply independent and can be used to describe any class.

What is the reason behind this? What is the advantage of separating the class definition and property definition? Before you read on, think about it, you should be able to figure out the answer by now.

The answer is Rule #3 that we discussed in Chap. 2. Let me put it here again:

Rule #3:

I can talk about any resource at will, and if I choose to use an existing URI to identify the resource I am talking about, then the following is true:

- The resource I am talking about and the resource already identified by this existing URI are exactly the same thing or concept.

- Everything I have said about this resource is considered to be additional knowledge about that resource.

And more specifically, the separation of the class definition and property definition is just an implementation of this rule. The final result is that the application we build will have more power to automatically process the distributed information, together with a stronger inferencing engine.

To see this, think about the case where someone else would like to add some new properties into our camera vocabulary, and then publish RDF documents that use these newly added properties. The camera reviewers example in Chap. 2 fits into this example perfectly. For example, those reviewers will have an initial vocabulary they can use to publish their reviews, and they also enjoy the freedom to come up with new terms to describe a given camera.

Adding new properties to an existing vocabulary can be understood as an implementation of Rule #3 as well: anyone, anywhere and anytime can talk about a resource by adding more properties to it.

And here is an important fact: adding new properties does not disturb any existing application, and no change is needed to any existing application each time a new property is added. The reason behind this fact is the separation of class definitions and property definitions. If the definition of class were not separate from the definition of property, this would not have been accomplished.

The final point about property is related to an important programming trick that you should know. Let us modify owned_by property as follows:

```
<rdf:Property rdf:ID="owned_by">
    <rdfs:domain rdf:resource="#Digital"/>
    <rdfs:domain rdf:resource="#Film"/>
    <rdfs:range rdf:resource="#Photographer"/>
</rdf:Property>
```

If we define the `owned_by` property like this, we are saying `owned_by` is to be used with instances that are *both* digital cameras and film cameras at the same time. Clearly, such a camera has not been invented yet. Actually, what we wanted to express here is the fact that a photographer can own a digital camera or a film camera or both. How do we accomplish this?

Given that a subclass inherits all the properties associated with its base class, we can associate `owned_by` property with the base class:

```
<rdf:Property rdf:ID="owned_by">
   <rdfs:domain rdf:resource="#Camera"/>
   <rdfs:range rdf:resource="#Photographer"/>
</rdf:Property>
```

Since both `Digital` and `Film` are subclasses of `Camera`, they all inherit property `owned_by`. Now we can use the `owned_by` property with `Digital` class *or* `Film` class, and this has solved our problem.

Before we move on to the next section, here is one last thing we need to be cautious about: `Class` is in the `rdfs` namespace and `Property` is in the `rdf` namespace, and this is not a typo in the above lists.

4.3.2.4   RDFS Data Types

As we discussed earlier, property `rdfs:range` is used to specify the possible values of a property being declared. In some cases, the property being defined can simply have *plain* or *untyped* string as its value, represented by `rdfs:Literal` class contained in RDFS vocabulary. For example, property `model` could have been defined as follows, and it could then use any string as its value:

```
<rdf:Property
       rdf:about="http://www.liyangyu.com/camera#model">
   <rdfs:domain rdf:resource="#Camera"/>
   <rdfs:range
    rdf:resource="http://www.w3.org/2001/01/rdf-schema#Literal"/>
</rdf:Property>
```

However, using `rdfs:Literal` is not a recommended solution for most cases. A better idea is to always provide *typed* values if you can. For example, we have specified the valid value for the `model` property has to be strings specified by the XML schema, as shown in List 4.9, lines 58–61. More specifically, the full URI of this data type is given by the following:

```
http://www.w3.org/2001/XMLSchema#string
```

and we can use this URI directly in our schema without explicitly indicating that it represents a datatype (as we have done in List 4.9). However, it is always useful to clearly declare that a given URI represents a datatype, as shown here:

```
<rdf:Property
     rdf:about="http://www.liyangyu.com/camera#model">
  <rdfs:domain rdf:resource="#Camera"/>
  <rdfs:range
     rdf:resource="http://www.w3.org/2001/XMLSchema#string"/>
</rdf:Property>
<rdfs:Datatype
     rdf:about="http://www.w3.org/2001/XMLSchema#string"/>
```

The next example shows that using `rdfs:Datatype` is not only a good practice, but it is also necessary in some cases. For instance, the following could be another definition of `effectivePixel` property:

```
<rdf:Property
    rdf:about="http://www.liyangyu.com/camera#effectivePixel">
  <rdfs:domain rdf:resource="#Digital"/>
  <rdfs:range
     rdf:resource="http://www.liyangyu.com/camera#MegaPixel"/>
</rdf:Property>
<rdfs:Datatype
       rdf:about="http://www.liyangyu.com/camera#MegaPixel">
  <rdfs:subClassOf
     rdf:resource="http://www.w3.org/2001/XMLSchema#decimal"/>
</rdfs:Datatype>
```

When a RDF schema parser reaches the above code, it first concludes the property `effectivePixel`'s value should come from a resource with the following URI:

```
http://www.liyangyu.com/camera#MegaPixel
```

And once it reaches the next couple of lines, it realizes this URI is in fact identifying an `rdfs:Datatype` instance, which has a base class given by this URI, `http://www.w3.org/2001/XMLSchema#decimal`. The parser then concludes that `effectivePixel` should always use a typed literal as its value.

Notice when `rdfs:Datatype` is used in our RDF schema document to indicate a data type, the corresponding RDF instance statements should then use `rdf:datatype` property as follows:

```
<model rdf:datatype="http://www.w3.org/2001/XMLSchema#string">
   Nikon_D300
</model>
<effectivePixel
      rdf:datatype="http://www.liyangyu.com/camera#MegaPixel">
   12.3
</effectivePixel>
```

A related topic here is the usage of `rdfs:XMLLiteral`. Remember, in most cases, its use should be avoided. To make our discussion complete, let us briefly talk about the reason here.

First understand that `rdfs:XMLLiteral` denotes a well-formed XML string, and it is always used together with `rdf:parseType="Literal"`. For instance, if you used `rdfs:XMLLiteral` in an RDF schema document to define some property, the RDF statements which describe an instance of this property must use `rdf:parseType="Literal"`. Let us see an example.

Suppose we have defined a new property called `features` as follows:

```
<rdf:Property rdf:ID="features">
   <rdfs:domain rdf:resource="#Digital"/>
   <rdfs:range rdf:resource=
       "http://www.w3.org/1999/02/22-rdf-syntax-ns#XMLLiteral"/>
</rdf:Property>
```

An example RDF statement could be as this:

```
<features rdf:parseType="Literal">
   Nikon D300 is <bold>good!</bold>, also, ...
</features>
```

Notice the usage of `rdf:parseType="Literal"`, which indicates the value here is a well-formed XML content.

Now, notice that although the content is a well-formed XML content, it does not have the `resource/property/value` structure in general. And as you have already learned, this structure is one of the main reasons why a given application can understand the content. Therefore, if we use XML paragraph as the value of some property, we have to accept the fact that no tools will be able to understand its meaning well. So, avoid using `XMLLiteral` if you can.

4.3.2.5 RDFS Utility Vocabulary

Up to this point, we have covered the most important classes and properties in RDF schema. In this section, we take a look at some utility classes and properties defined in RDFS vocabulary, and as you will see in the later chapters, some of these terms are quite useful. As a summary, the following terms are covered in this section:

```
rdfs:seeAlso
rdfs:isDefinedBy
rdfs:label
rdfs:comment
```

rdfs:seeAlso is a property that can be used on any resource, and it indicates another resource may provide additional information about the given resource. For example, List 4.11 shows one RDF document that uses this property:

List 4.11 Example of using rdfs:seeAlso

```
1:  <?xml version="1.0"?>
2:  <rdf:RDF
2a:     xmlns:rdf="http://www.w3.org/1999/02/22-rdf-syntax-ns#"
3:      xmlns:rdfs="http://www.w3.org/2000/01/rdf-schema#"
4:      xmlns:myCamera="http://www.liyangyu.com/camera#">
5:
6:  <rdf:Description
6a:      rdf:about="http://www.liyangyu.com/camera#Nikon_D300">
7:     <rdf:type
7a:         rdf:resource="http://www.liyangyu.com/camera#DSLR"/>
8:     <rdfs:seeAlso
8a:         rdf:resource="http://dbpedia.org/resource/Nikon_D300"/>
9:  </rdf:Description>
10:
11: </rdf:RDF>
```

Line 8 says this: to understand more about the resource identified by this URI,

```
http://www.liyangyu.com/camera#Nikon_D300
```

you can take a look at the resource identified at this URI:

```
http://dbpedia.org/resource/Nikon_D300
```

Notice that rdfs:seeAlso has no formal semantics defined. In real application, it only implies the fact that these two URIs are somehow related to each other; it is then up to the application to decide how to handle this situation.

For our case, recall the above URI is created by DBpedia to represent exactly the same resource, namely, Nikon D300 camera. Therefore, these two URIs are considered to be URI aliases, and an application can act accordingly. For example, the application can retrieve an RDF document from the second URI and collect more information from this new document — this is a typical example of information aggregation based on URI aliases. As you will see in later chapters, this is also one of the key concepts in the world of linked data.

`rdfs:isDefinedBy` is quite similar to `rdfs:seeAlso`, and it is actually a `rdfs:subPropertyOf` of `rdfs:seeAlso`. It is intended to specify the primary source of information about a given resource. For example, the following statement,

```
subject rdfs:isDefinedBy object
```

says that the `subject` resource is defined by the `object` resource, and more specifically, this `object` resource is supposed to be an original or authoritative description of the resource.

The last two properties you may encounter in documents are `rdfs:label` and `rdfs:comment`. `rdfs:label` is used to provide a class/property name for human eyes, and similarly, `rdfs:comment` provides a human-readable description of the property/class being defined. One example is shown in List 4.12.

List 4.12 Example of using `rdfs:label` and `rdfs:comment`

```
1: <rdf:Property rdf:ID="officialModel">
2:    <rdfs:subPropertyOf rdf:resource="#model"/>
3:    <rdfs:label xml:lang="EN">officialModelName</rdfs:label>
4:    <rdfs:comment xml:lang="EN">
4a:        this is the official name of the camera.
4b:        the manufacturer may use different names when
4c:        the camera is sold in different regions/countries.
5:    </rdfs:comment>
6: </rdf:Property>
```

Their usage is quite straightforward and does not require much of an explanation.

4.3.3 Summary So Far

4.3.3.1 Our Camera Vocabulary

At this point, we have finished our discussion about RDFS core terms, and our final product is a simple camera vocabulary defined by using RDFS terms. List 4.13 shows the complete vocabulary. Compared to List 4.9, List 4.13 includes all the data type information. Notice Fig. 4.3 does not change; it is still the graphical representation of our camera ontology.

List 4.13 Our camera vocabulary

```
1: <?xml version="1.0"?>
2: <rdf:RDF
2a:     xmlns:rdf="http://www.w3.org/1999/02/22-rdf-syntax-ns#"
3:      xmlns:rdfs="http://www.w3.org/2000/01/rdf-schema#"
4:      xmlns:myCamera="http://www.liyangyu.com/camera#"
5:      xml:base="http://www.liyangyu.com/camera#">
6:
7: <rdfs:Class rdf:about="http://www.liyangyu.com/camera#Camera">
8: </rdfs:Class>
9:
10: <rdfs:Class rdf:about="http://www.liyangyu.com/camera#Lens">
11: </rdfs:Class>
12:
13: <rdfs:Class rdf:about="http://www.liyangyu.com/camera#Body">
14: </rdfs:Class>
15:
16: <rdfs:Class
16a:       rdf:about="http://www.liyangyu.com/camera#ValueRange">
17: </rdfs:Class>
18:
19: <rdfs:Class
19a:       rdf:about="http://www.liyangyu.com/camera#Digital">
20:    <rdfs:subClassOf rdf:resource="#Camera"/>
21: </rdfs:Class>
22:
23: <rdfs:Class rdf:about="http://www.liyangyu.com/camera#Film">
24:    <rdfs:subClassOf rdf:resource="#Camera"/>
25: </rdfs:Class>
26:
27: <rdfs:Class rdf:about="http://www.liyangyu.com/camera#DSLR">
28:    <rdfs:subClassOf rdf:resource="#Digital"/>
29: </rdfs:Class>
30:
31: <rdfs:Class
31a:     rdf:about="http://www.liyangyu.com/camera#PointAndShoot">
32:    <rdfs:subClassOf rdf:resource="#Digital"/>
33: </rdfs:Class>
34:
35: <rdfs:Class
35a:       rdf:about="http://www.liyangyu.com/camera#Photographer">
36:    <rdfs:subClassOf
36a:           rdf:resource="http://xmlns.com/foaf/0.1/Person"/>
37: </rdfs:Class>
```

```
38:
39: <rdf:Property
39a:      rdf:about="http://www.liyangyu.com/camera#owned_by">
40:    <rdfs:domain rdf:resource="#DSLR"/>
41:    <rdfs:range rdf:resource="#Photographer"/>
42: </rdf:Property>
43:
44: <rdf:Property
44a:  rdf:about="http://www.liyangyu.com/camera#manufactured_by">
45:    <rdfs:domain rdf:resource="#Camera"/>
46: </rdf:Property>
47:
48: <rdf:Property
48a:      rdf:about="http://www.liyangyu.com/camera#body">
49:    <rdfs:domain rdf:resource="#Camera"/>
50:    <rdfs:range rdf:resource="#Body"/>
51: </rdf:Property>
52:
53: <rdf:Property
53a:      rdf:about="http://www.liyangyu.com/camera#lens">
54:    <rdfs:domain rdf:resource="#Camera"/>
55:    <rdfs:range rdf:resource="#Lens"/>
56: </rdf:Property>
57:
58: <rdf:Property
58a:      rdf:about="http://www.liyangyu.com/camera#model">
59:    <rdfs:domain rdf:resource="#Camera"/>
60:    <rdfs:range
60a:      rdf:resource="http://www.w3.org/2001/XMLSchema#string"/>
61: </rdf:Property>
62: <rdfs:Datatype
62a:       rdf:about="http://www.w3.org/2001/XMLSchema#string"/>
63:
64: <rdf:Property
64a:    rdf:about="http://www.liyangyu.com/camera#effectivePixel">
65:    <rdfs:domain rdf:resource="#Digital"/>
66:    <rdfs:range
66a:      rdf:resource="http://www.liyangyu.com/camera#MegaPixel"/>
67: </rdf:Property>
68: <rdfs:Datatype
68a:       rdf:about="http://www.liyangyu.com/camera#MegaPixel">
```

```
69:    <rdfs:subClassOf
69a:     rdf:resource="http://www.w3.org/2001/XMLSchema#decimal"/>
70: </rdfs:Datatype>
71:
72: <rdf:Property
72a:      rdf:about="http://www.liyangyu.com/camera#shutterSpeed">
73:    <rdfs:domain rdf:resource="#Body"/>
74:    <rdfs:range rdf:resource="#ValueRange"/>
75: </rdf:Property>
76:
77: <rdf:Property
77a:      rdf:about="http://www.liyangyu.com/camera#focalLength">
78:    <rdfs:domain rdf:resource="#Lens"/>
79:    <rdfs:range
79a:     rdf:resource="http://www.w3.org/2001/XMLSchema#string"/>
80: </rdf:Property>
81: <rdfs:Datatype
81a:      rdf:about="http://www.w3.org/2001/XMLSchema#string"/>
82:
83: <rdf:Property
83a:      rdf:about="http://www.liyangyu.com/camera#aperture">
84:    <rdfs:domain rdf:resource="#Lens"/>
85:    <rdfs:range rdf:resource="#ValueRange"/>
86: </rdf:Property>
87:
88: <rdf:Property
88a:      rdf:about="http://www.liyangyu.com/camera#minValue">
89:    <rdfs:domain rdf:resource="#ValueRange"/>
90:    <rdfs:range
90a:     rdf:resource="http://www.w3.org/2001/XMLSchema#float"/>
91: </rdf:Property>
92: <rdfs:Datatype
92a:      rdf:about="http://www.w3.org/2001/XMLSchema#float"/>
93:
94: <rdf:Property
94a:      rdf:about="http://www.liyangyu.com/camera#maxValue">
95:    <rdfs:domain rdf:resource="#ValueRange"/>
96:    <rdfs:range
96a:     rdf:resource="http://www.w3.org/2001/XMLSchema#float"/>
97: </rdf:Property>
98: <rdfs:Datatype
98a:      rdf:about="http://www.w3.org/2001/XMLSchema#float"/>
99:
100: </rdf:RDF>
```

At the beginning of this chapter, we said that vocabulary like this can help machines to make inferences, based on the knowledge expressed in the vocabulary. We will discuss this inferencing power in a later section. For now, let us understand this first: how is the knowledge expressed in the vocabulary?

4.3.3.2   Where Is the Knowledge?

So far in this chapter, we have created a simply camera vocabulary by using some predefined classes and properties from RDF Schema. So how is the knowledge encoded in this vocabulary?

And here is the answer: in a given vocabulary, the meaning of a term is expressed and understood by defining the following:

- all the properties that can be used on it, and
- the types of those objects that can be used as the values of these properties.

For example, let us take a look at term `Camera`. As far as any application is concerned, a `Camera` is something like this:

- It is a class.
- We can use property `manufactured_by` on it, and any resource can be the value of this property.
- We can use property `body` on it, with a `Body` instance as this property's value.
- We can use property `lens` on it, with a `Lens` instance as this property's value.
- We can use property `model` on it, with an XML string as this property's value.

And similarly, for any application, a `Digital` camera is something like this:

- It is a class.
- We can use property `manufactured_by` on it, and any resource can be the value of this property.
- We can use property `body` on it, with a `Body` instance as this property's value.
- We can use property `lens` on it, with a `Lens` instance as this property's value.
- We can use property `model` on it, with an XML string as this property's value.
- We can use property `effectivePixel` on it, with an XML decimal as this property's value.

You can come up with the meaning of the word `DSLR` just as above.

How can the knowledge be used and understood by applications? Before we move on to this topic, let us take a look at a new concept: ontology.

4.4   The Concept of Ontology

Ontology plays a critical role for the Semantic Web, and it is necessary to understand ontology in order to fully appreciate the idea of the Semantic Web. Its concept, however, seems quite abstract and hard to grasp from the beginning. It does take a while to get used to, but the more you know it, the more you see the value of it.

4.4.1 What Is Ontology

First off, understand we have already built an ontology: List 4.13 is in fact a tiny ontology in the domain of photography.

There are many definitions of ontology, perhaps each single one of these definitions starts from a different angle of view. And some of these definitions can be confusing as well. For example, the most popular definition of ontology is "ontology is a formalization of a conceptualization"!

For us, in the world of the Semantic Web, the definition presented in the W3C's OWL Use Cases and Requirements Documents[3] is good enough (you will learn all about Web Ontology Language OWL in the next chapter):

> An ontology formally defines a common set of terms that are used to describe and represent a domain . . . An ontology defines the terms used to describe and represent an area of knowledge.

Several things need to be made clear from this definition. First of all, ontology is domain-specific, and it is used to describe and represent *an area of* knowledge. A domain is simply a specific subject area or area of knowledge, such as the area of photography, medicine, real estate, education, etc.

Second, ontology contains terms and the relationships among these terms. Terms are often called classes, or concepts, and these words are interchangeable. The relationships between these classes can be expressed by using a hierarchical structure: super-classes represent higher-level concepts, and subclasses represent finer concepts. The finer concepts have all the attributes and features that the higher concepts have.

Third, besides the above relationships among the classes, there is another level of relationship expressed by using a special group of terms: properties. These property terms describe various features and attributes of the concepts, and they can also be used to associate different classes together. Therefore, the relationships among classes are not only super-class or subclass relationships, but also relationships expressed in the term of properties.

By having the terms and the relationships among these terms clearly defined, ontology encodes the knowledge of the domain in such a way that the knowledge can be understood by a computer. This is the basic idea of ontology.

4.4.2 The Benefits of Ontology

We can summarize the benefits of ontology as follows (and you should be able to come up with most of the items in this list):

---

[3] "OWL Web Ontology Language Use Cases and Requirements", http://www.w3.org/TR/webont-req/

- It provides a common and shared understanding/definition about certain key concepts in the domain.
- It offers the terms one can use when creating RDF documents in the domain.
- It provides a way to reuse domain knowledge.
- It makes the domain assumptions explicit.
- Together with ontology description languages (such as RDFS and OWL, which we will learn in the next chapter), it provides a way to encode knowledge and semantics such that machines can understand.
- It makes automatic large-scale machine processing possible.

When you have made more progress in this book, you will have more understanding about these benefits, and you will be able to add more as well.

It is now a good time to discuss some related concepts and introduce an important vocabulary, SKOS, which can be very useful when it comes to development work on the Semantic Web.

4.5   Building the Bridge to Ontology: SKOS

We have discussed the concept of ontology in the previous section. In this section, we will take a small detour to understand the Simple Knowledge Organization System (SKOS), a model and vocabulary that is used to bridge the world of Knowledge Organization Systems (KOS) and the Semantic Web.

If you are doing development work on the Semantic Web, it is likely that you will have a chance to see or use SKOS. In addition, understanding SKOS will enhance your understanding about ontology, and it will also give you a chance to better appreciate the benefit of having ontologies on the Semantic Web.

4.5.1   Knowledge Organization Systems (KOS)

If you have experience working with those so-called KOSs, you may be familiar with some well-understood knowledge organizing schemes such as taxonomies, thesauri, subject headers and other types of controlled vocabulary. These schemes are not all the same, but they all allow the organization of concepts into concept schemes where it is also possible to indicate relationships between the terms contained in the scheme.

You have probably already started to consider the relationships between these schemes and ontologies. What is the difference between these schemes and ontologies? Is there a way to build a bridge between these two so we can express KOSs in a machine-understandable way, within the framework of the Semantic Web?

To understand these interesting questions, let us first get more understanding about some basic schemes that are widely used in a variety of knowledge organization systems. We will concentrate on two of these schemes, namely taxonomy and thesaurus. When we have a good understanding of these schemes, we can move on to study the relationships between these schemes and ontologies.

First, understand that KOS is a general term that refers to, among other things, a set of elements, often structured and controlled, that can be used for describing objects, indexing objects, browsing collections, etc. KOSs are commonly found in cultural heritage institutions such as libraries and museums. They can also be used in other scientific areas; examples include biology and chemistry, where naming and classifying are important.

More specifically, taxonomies and thesauri are typical examples of KOSs.

- Taxonomy

Based on its Greek roots, taxonomy is the science of classification. Originally, it referred only to the classification of organisms. Now, it is often used in a more general way, referring to the classification of things or concepts, as well the schemes underlying such a classification. In addition, taxonomy normally has some hierarchical relationships embedded in its classifications.

Table 4.1 shows a small example of a taxonomy of American cities, categorized according to a hierarchy of regions and states in the United States. Notice just a few cities are included to show the example.

- Thesaurus

Thesaurus can be understood as a extension to taxonomy: it takes taxonomy as described above, allowing subjects to be arranged in a hierarchy and in addition, it adds the ability to allow other statements be made about the subjects. Table 4.2 shows some examples.

The following is a small example, which can helps us to put the above together:

```
Tennis
    RT Courts
    BT Sports
Sports
    BT Activity
    NT Tennis
    NT Football
    NT Basketball
```

Region	State	City
Southwest	California	San Francisco
		Los Angeles
	Arizona	Tucson
		Phoenix
Midwest	Indiana	Ft. Wayne
		West Lafayette
	Illinois	Chicago
		Milwaukee

Table 4.1 A small example of taxonomy of American cities

Table 4.2 A thesaurus allows statements to be made about the subjects

Thesaurus term	Meaning
BT	Short for "broader term", refers to the term above the current one in the hierarchy and must have a wider or less specific meaning.
NT	Short for "narrower term", an inverse property of BT. In fact, a taxonomy is a thesaurus that only uses the BT/NT properties to build a hierarchy. Therefore, every thesaurus contains a taxonomy.
SN	Short for "scope note", a string attached to the term explaining its meaning within the thesaurus.
USE	Refers to another term that is to be preferred instead of this term, implying that the terms are synonymous. For example, if we have a term named "Resource Description Framework", we can put a USE property referring to another term named "RDF". This means that we have the term Resource Description Framework, but RDF means the same thing, and we encourage the use of term RDF instead of this one.
UF	An inverse property of USE.
TT	Short for "top term", referring to the topmost ancestor of this current term.
RT	Short for "related term", referring to a term that is related to this term, without being a synonym of it or a broader/narrower term.

Now that we understand both taxonomy and thesaurus as examples of KOSs, the question is, why do we need these schemes? How do they help us in real life?

KOSs can be useful in many ways. The following is just to name a few:

- They can make search more robust (instead of simple keywords matching, related words, for example, can also be considered).
- They can help to build more intelligent browsing interfaces (following the hierarchical structure, and explore broader/narrower terms, etc.).
- They can help us to formally organize our knowledge for a given domain, therefore promote reuse of the knowledge and also facilitate data interoperability.

With all these said, let us continue on to understand how KOSs are related to ontologies, and why we are interested in KOSs in the world of the Semantic Web.

4.5.2   Thesauri vs. Ontologies

To understand how KOSs are related to ontologies, we use the example of thesauri vs. ontologies. There are quite a few KOSs in the application world, and concentrating on one of them makes our discussion a lot easier. In addition, taxonomies are just special thesauri; therefore, comparing thesauri with ontologies includes taxonomies as well.

- KOSs are used for knowledge organization, while ontologies are used for knowledge representation.

Compared to ontologies, KOSs' descriptive capability is simply far too weak, which is also the reason why KOSs cannot be used to represent knowledge. More specifically, the broader/narrower relationship used to build the hierarchy is essentially the only relationship offered by a taxonomy. A thesaurus extends this with the BT/RT and UF/USE relationships, and the SN property, which allows them to better describe the terms. However, the descriptive power offered by these language constructs is still very limited.

- KOSs are semantically much less rigorous than ontologies, and no formal reasoning can be conducted by just having KOSs.

As we will learn later, ontologies are based upon description logic; therefore logical inferencing can be conducted. However, in KOSs, relationships between concepts are semantically weak. For example, ontologies can specify an *is-a* relationship, while in thesauri, the hierarchical relation can represent anything from is-a to *part-of*, depending on the interpretations rooted from the domain and application.

With all this said, KOSs cannot match up with ontologies when it comes to fully representing the knowledge in the ways that the Semantic Web requires. However, there is indeed a need to port KOSs to the Semantic Web. Some of the reasons can be summarized as follows:

- Porting KOSs into the Semantic Web means these schemes are machine-readable and can be exploited in a much more effective and intelligent way.
- Porting KOSs into the shared space offered by the Semantic Web promotes reuse of these schemes, and further promotes interoperability.
- Porting KOSs into the Semantic Web allows KOSs to leverage all the new ideas and technologies originating from the Semantic Web. For example, part of the implementation of porting KOSs to the Semantic Web means to have each single concept represented by a URI, and therefore uniquely identified on the Web. Furthermore, "similar" concepts contained in different KOS schemes can be linked together, which will then form a distributed, heterogeneous global concept scheme. Obviously, this global scheme can be used as the foundation for new applications that allow meaningful navigation between KOSs.

You will come up with other benefits when you have more experience with the Semantic Web and KOSs. For now, the key question is how to port these existing KOSs to the Semantic Web so that machines can understand them? This gives raise to SKOS, a vocabulary built specifically for this purpose, as we discuss in the next few sections.

4.5.3   Filling the Gap: SKOS

4.5.3.1   What Is SKOS?

Simple Knowledge Organization Systems, or SKOS, is an RDF vocabulary for representing KOSs, such as taxonomies, thesauri, classification schemes and subject heading lists. It is used to port existing KOSs into the shared space of the Semantic Web; therefore they can be published on the Web, they can be machine-readable and can be exchanged between software applications.

SKOS has been developed by W3C Semantic Web Development Working Group (SWDWG), and has an official Web site[4] that contains all the information related to SKOS. It became a W3C standard on August 18, 2009. This standard includes the following specifications:

- SKOS Reference W3C Recommendation;
- SKOS Primer W3C Working Group Note;
- SKOS Use Cases and Requirements W3C Working Group Note, and
- SKOS RDF files.[5]

Recall the Dublin Core vocabulary we discussed in Chap. 2: whenever we would like to use RDF statements to describe a document, we should use the terms from Dublin Core vocabulary. SKOS is the vocabulary we should use when we try to publish a given KOS into the shared space of the Semantic Web.

Notice the URIs in SKOS vocabulary all have the following lead strings:

```
http://www.w3.org/2004/02/skos/core#
```

By convention, this URI prefix string is associated with namespace prefix `skos:`, and it is typically used in different sterilization formats with the prefix `skos`.

4.5.3.2   SKOS Core Constructs

In this section, we discuss the core constructs of SKOS, which includes the following:

- Conceptual resources should be identified by URIs, and can be explicated noted as concepts.
- Concepts can be labeled with lexical strings in one or more natural languages.
- Concepts can be documented with different types of notes.
- Concepts can be semantically related to each other in informal hierarchies.
- Concepts can be aggregated into concept schemes.

---

[4] http://www.w3.org/2004/02/skos/

[5] http://www.w3.org/2004/02/skos/vocabs

These are not all the SKOS features offered by the SKOS model, but they are enough to represent most KOSs on the Semantic Web. For the rest of this section, we use Turtle for our examples, and the following namespaces are needed. We now list these namespaces here so they need not be included in every single example.

```
@prefix skos: <http://www.w3.org/2004/02/skos/core#> .
@prefix rdf: <http://www.w3.org/1999/02/22-rdf-syntax-ns#> .
@prefix rdfs: <http://www.w3.org/2000/01/rdf-schema#> .
@prefix foaf: <http://xmlns.com/foaf/0.1/> .
@prefix dc: <http://purl.org/dc/elements/1.1/>.
@prefix ex: <http://www.example.com/> .
@prefix ex1: <http://www.example.com/1/> .
@prefix ex2: <http://www.example.com/2/> .
```

Concept is a fundamental element in any given KOS. SKOS introduces the class `skos:Concept`, so that we can use it to state that a given resource is a concept. To do so, we first create (or reuse) a URI to uniquely identify the concept, and we then use one RDF statement to assert that the resource, identified by this URI, is of type `skos:Concept`.

For example, the following RDF statement says tennis is a `skos:Concept`:

```
<http://dbpedia.org/resource/Tennis> rdf:type skos:Concept .
```

Instead of creating a URI to represent tennis as a concept, we reuse the URI for tennis created by DBpedia (we will see more about the DBpedia project in Chap. 8). Clearly, using SKOS to publish concept schemes makes it easy to reference the concepts in resource descriptions on the Semantic Web. In this particular example, for the resource `http://dbpedia.org/resource/Tennis`, besides everything that has been said about it, we know it is also a `skos:Concept`.

The first thing to know about `skos:Concept` is that SKOS allows us to use labels on a given concept. Three label properties are provided: `skos:prefLabel`, `skos:altLabel` and `skos:hiddenLabel`. They are all subproperties of the `rdfs:label` property, and they are all used to link a `skos:Concept` to an RDF plain literal, which is formally defined as a character string combined with an optional language tag. More specifically,

- `skos:prefLabel` property is used to assign a preferred lexical label to a concept.

This preferred lexical label should contain terms used as descriptors in indexing systems, and is normally used in a KOS to unambiguously represent the underlying concept. Therefore, it is recommend that no two concepts in the same KOS be given the same preferred lexical label for any given language tag.

- skos:altLabel property is used when synonyms, near-synonyms or abbreviations need to be represented.
- skos:hiddenLabel property is used mainly for indexing and/or searching capabilities.

For example, the character string as the value of this property is accessible to applications performing text-based indexing and searching operations, but is not visible otherwise. A good example is to include misspelled variants of the preferred label. List 4.14 shows how these properties are used for the concept tennis:

List 4.14 Different label properties used for tennis concept

```
<http://dbpedia.org/resource/Tennis> rdf:type skos:Concept;
      skos:prefLabel "tennis"@en;
      skos:altLabel "Lawn_Tennis"@en;
      skos:hiddenLabel "Tenis"@en.
```

The second characterizations of concepts are the human-readable documentation properties defined for a given concept; skos:scopeNote, skos:definition, skos:example and skos:historyNote are examples of these properties. And all these properties are subproperties of skos:note property. These properties are all quite straightforward and do not require much explanation.

For example, the skos:definition property is used to provide a complete explanation of the intended meaning of a concept. Notice that the organization of these properties, with skos:note as their root, offers a straightforward way to retrieve all the documentation associated with one single concept. For instance, to find all the documentation for a concept, all we need to find is all the subproperty values of the skos:note property.

At this point, List 4.15 is the latest definition of our tennis concept:

List 4.15 Use skos:definition in our tennis concept

```
<http://dbpedia.org/resource/Tennis> rdf:type skos:Concept;
      skos:prefLabel "tennis"@en;
      skos:altLabel "Lawn_Tennis"@en;
      skos:hiddenLabel "Tenis"@en;
      skos:definition "Tennis is a sport usually played between
two players or between two teams of two players each.Each player
uses a racket that is strung to strike a hollow rubber ball
covered with felt past a net into the opponent's court."@en.
```

Now, let us take a look at some semantic relationships that can be specified when defining a concept using SKOS. For a given KOS, the meaning of a concept is defined not just by the natural-language words in its labels, but also by its relationships to other concepts in the same KOS. To map these relationships to a machine-readable level, three standard properties: `skos:broader`, `skos:narrower` and `skos:related` are offered by SKOS vocabulary. More specifically,

- `skos:broader` and `skos:narrower` together are used for representing the hierarchical structure of the KOS, which can either be an is-a relationship (similar to a class and subclass relationship), or a part-of relationship (one concept represents a resource that is a part of the resource represented by another concept).

For example, List 4.16 shows the usage of `skos:broader`:

List 4.16 Use `skos:broader` in our tennis concept

```
<http://dbpedia.org/resource/Tennis> rdf:type skos:Concept;
      skos:prefLabel "tennis"@en;
      skos:altLabel "Lawn_Tennis"@en;
      skos:hiddenLabel "Tenis"@en;
      skos:broader <http://dbpedia.org/resource/Racquet_sport>.
```

Based on List 4.16, `http://dbpedia.org/resource/Racquet_sport`, is another concept that is broader in meaning. Again, the URI of this new concept is taken from DBpedia, another example of URI reuse.

Notice that the `skos:broader` property does not explicitly indicate its direction, and it should be read as "has broader concept". In other words, the subject of a `skos:broader` statement is the more specific concept, and the object is the more general one.

Also notice that `skos:broader` and `skos:narrower` are each other's inverse property. You will see more about inverse property in later chapters, but for now, understand that if an inferencing engine reads List 4.16, it will be able to add the following inferred statement automatically:

```
<http://dbpedia.org/resource/Racquet_sport> skos:narrower
<http://dbpedia.org/resource/Tennis>.
```

meaning that the subject has a narrower concept identified by the object.

Notice that the SKOS vocabulary does not specify `skos:broader` and `skos:narrower` as transitive properties.

For example, `http://dbpedia.org/resource/Tennis`, as a concept, has `http://dbpedia.org/resource/Racquet_sport` as its broader concept. And this later concept itself has `http://dbpedia.org/resource/Sport` as a broader concept.

Therefore, `http://dbpedia.org/resource/Tennis` should have another boarder concept called `http://dbpedia.org/resource/Sport`. This chain of transitivity does make sense, but we can also find examples where such transitivity does not make sense. Therefore, `skos:broader` and `skos:narrower` are not formally considered as transitive properties.

- `skos:related` is used for nonhierarchical links, but for associative relationship between two concepts.

List 4.17 shows one example of using `skos:related`.

List 4.17 Use `skos:related` in our tennis concept

```
<http://dbpedia.org/resource/Tennis> rdf:type skos:Concept;
      skos:prefLabel "tennis"@en;
      skos:altLabel "Lawn_Tennis"@en;
      skos:hiddenLabel "Tenis"@en;
      skos:broader <http://dbpedia.org/resource/Racquet_sport>;
      skos:related
   <http://dbpedia.org/reource/International_Tennis_Federation>.
```

List 4.17 claims that `http://dbpedia.org/resource/Tennis` is related to another concept given by the following URI:

```
http://dbpedia.org/resource/International_Tennis_Federation
```

Understand that `skos:related` is a symmetric property (you will see symmetric property in later chapters). Therefore, an inferencing engine is able to add the following statement based on List 4.17:

```
<http://dbpedia.org/reource/International_Tennis_Federation>
   skos:related
<http://dbpedia.org/resource/Tennis>.
```

Again, notice that the SKOS vocabulary does not specify `skos:related` to be a transitive property, as in the case for `skos:broader` and `skos:narrower`.

At this point, we have covered those related terms in SKOS vocabulary so we understand how to define a concept, label a concept, add documentation notes about a concept, and also how to specify semantic relationships about a concept. Obviously, for a given KOS, there will be multiple concepts and these concepts are logically contained together by the same KOS to form a vocabulary. SKOS offers `skos:ConceptScheme` class and other related terms to model this aspect of a vocabulary. Let us take a look at these constructs.

First, the following shows how to define a concept scheme that represent a vocabulary:

```
ex:myTennisVocabulary rdf:type skos:ConceptScheme;
   dc:creater ex:liyangYu.
```

This declares a vocabulary (concept scheme) named `myTennisVocabulary`. And by using `skos:inScheme` property, we can add our tennis concept into this vocabulary, as shown in List 4.18:

List 4.18 Use `skos:ConceptScheme` and `skos:inScheme` to build vocabulary

```
ex:myTennisVocabulary rdf:type skos:ConceptScheme;
   dc:creater ex:liyangYu.

<http://dbpedia.org/resource/Tennis> rdf:type skos:Concept;
      skos:inScheme ex:myTennisVocabulary;
      skos:prefLabel "tennis"@en;
      skos:altLabel "Lawn_Tennis"@en;
      skos:hiddenLabel "Tenis"@en;
      skos:broader <http://dbpedia.org/resource/Racquet_sport>;
      skos:related
    <http://dbpedia.org/reource/International_Tennis_Federation>.
```

We can now add more concepts (and labels for concepts, relationships between concepts, etc.) as we wish, just like what we have done in List 4.18, until we have covered all the concepts and relationships in a given KOS. This way, we can create a vocabulary that represents a given KOS. The final result is that the given KOS has now been converted to a machine-readable RDF document, and can be shared and reused on the Semantic Web. This process is called *mapping* a KOS onto the Semantic Web.

`skos:hasTopConcept` is another very useful property provided by the SKOS vocabulary. This can be used to provide an "entry point" that we can use to access the machine-readable KOS. List 4.19 shows how:

List 4.19 Use `skos:hasToConcept` to provide an entry point of the vocabulary

```
ex:myTennisVocabulary rdf:type skos:ConceptScheme;
   skos:hasTopConcept <http://dbpedia.org/resource/Tennis>;
   dc:creater ex:liyangYu.

<http://dbpedia.org/resource/Tennis> rdf:type skos:Concept;
      skos:inScheme ex:myTennisVocabulary;
      skos:prefLabel "tennis"@en;
      skos:altLabel "Lawn_Tennis"@en;
      skos:hiddenLabel "Tenis"@en;
      skos:broader <http://dbpedia.org/resource/Racquet_sport>;
      skos:related
    <http://dbpedia.org/reource/International_Tennis_Federation>.
```

Now, an application can query the value of `skos:hasTopConcept` property, and use the returned concept and its `skos:broader` and `skos:narrower` properties to explore the whole vocabulary. Notice multiple `skos:hasTopConcept` properties can be defined for a given concept scheme.

4.5.3.3   Interlinking Concepts by Using SKOS

At this point, we understand that we can use SKOS to map a traditional KOS onto
the Semantic Web. The key difference between a traditional KOS and its
corresponding Semantic Web version is that the latter is machine-readable. When
we claim a given KOS is machine-readable, we mean the following facts:

- every SKOS concept is identified by a URI, and
- everything is expressed using RDF statements, which can be processed by
  machines.

The fact that every concept is uniquely identified by a URI makes it possible to
state that two concepts from different schemes have some semantic relations. With
the help of these interlinking concepts, applications such as information retrieval
packages can start to make use of several KOSs at the same time. In fact, linking
concepts contained in different KOSs is considered to be a key benefit of publishing
KOSs on the Semantic Web.

SKOS vocabulary provides the following terms one can use to build the inter-
links between concepts:

- `skos:exactMatch` and `skos:closeMatch`
- `skos:broadMatch`, `skos:narrowMatch` and `skos:relatedMatch`

Using property `skos:closeMatch` means that the two concepts are close enough
in meaning and they can be used interchangeably in applications that are built upon
the two schemes containing these two concepts. For example, List 4.20 shows how
this property is used:

List 4.20 Use `skos:closeMatch` to link a concept in another vocabulary

```
ex:myTennisVocabulary rdf:type skos:ConceptScheme;
   skos:hasTopConcept <http://dbpedia.org/resource/Tennis>;
   dc:creater ex:liyangYu.

<http://dbpedia.org/resource/Tennis> rdf:type skos:Concept;
     skos:inScheme ex:myTennisVocabulary;
     skos:prefLabel "tennis"@en;
     skos:altLabel "Lawn_Tennis"@en;
     skos:hiddenLabel "Tenis"@en;
     skos:closeMatch ex2:Tennis;
     skos:broader <http://dbpedia.org/resource/Racquet_sport>;
     skos:related
    <http://dbpedia.org/reource/International_Tennis_Federation>.
```

This says, among other things, that `http://dbpedia.org/resource/Tennis`
concept is a close match to another concept named `ex2:Tennis`.

Notice that `skos:closeMatch` is not transitive, which is also the main difference between `skos:closeMatch` and property `skos:exactMatch`. More specifically, `skos:exactMatch` is a subproperty of `skos:closeMatch`, and it indicates the two concepts have equivalent meanings. Therefore, any application that makes use of this property can expect an even stronger link between schemes. In addition, `skos:exactMatch` is indeed declared as a transitive property, as you might have guessed.

For `skos:broadMatch`, `skos:narrowMatch` and `skos:relatedMatch`, their usage is quite straightforward and does not need much explanation. Also,

- `skos:broachMatch` is a subproperty of `skos:broader`;
- `skos:narrowMatch` is a subproperty of `skos:narrower`; and
- `skos:relatedMatch` is a subproperty of `skos:related`.

With this said, for example, a statement which asserts a `skos:broadMatch` between two concepts is treated as a statement that declares a `skos:broader` between these two concepts.

At this point, we have finished the discussion of the SKOS vocabulary. We have not covered everything about it, but what we have learned here will be enough to get you started. In summary, you can use the SKOS vocabulary to map a given KOS to the Semantic Web and change it to be machine-readable, and therefore bridge the world of taxonomies and thesauri and other controlled vocabularies to the world of the Semantic Web.

4.6 Another Look at Inferencing Based on RDF Schema

We have discussed the benefits offered by ontologies on the Semantic Web. In order to convince ourselves, let us take another look at our camera ontology to see how it can make machines more intelligent. In addition, not only will we see more reasoning power provided by our camera ontology, but we will also find things that can be improved—this points to another new building block called OWL, which is presented in the next chapter in detail.

4.6.1 RDFS Ontology Based Reasoning: Simple, Yet Powerful

Early this chapter (Sect. 4.2.2), we used an example to show you how reasoning is done by using the camera ontology (we called it camera vocabulary back then). In this section, we present this reasoning ability in a more formal way, together with the extra reasoning examples that we did not cover in the previous sections.

More specifically, with the help of the camera ontology, a given application can accomplish reasoning in the following ways:

• Understand a resource's class type by reading the property's `rdfs:domain` tag.

When we define a property **P**, we normally use `rdfs:domain` to specify exactly which class this property **P** can be used to describe; let us use **C** to denote this class. Now for a given resource identified by a specific URI, if our application detects property **P** is indeed used to describe this resource, our application can then conclude the resource represented by this particular URI must be an instance of class **C**. We have an example for this type of reasoning presented in Sect. 4.2.2, as you have seen.

• Understand a resource's class type by reading the property's `rdfs:range` tag.

When we define a property **P**, we normally use `rdfs:range` to specify exactly what possible values this property can assume. More specifically, this value can be a typed or untyped literal, and can also be an instance of a given class **C**. Now when parsing a resource, if our application detects property **P** is used to describe this resource, and the value of **P** of this resource is represented by a specific URI pointing to another resource, our application can then conclude the resource represented by this particular URI must be an instance of class **C**.

To see how this works, take a look at the simple RDF document presented in List 4.21.

List 4.21 A simple RDF document using camera ontology

```
1: <?xml version="1.0"?>
2: <rdf:RDF
2a:     xmlns:rdf="http://www.w3.org/1999/02/22-rdf-syntax-ns#"
3:      xmlns:myCamera="http://www.liyangyu.com/camera#">
4:
5: <rdf:Description
5a:     rdf:about="http://www.liyangyu.com/camera#Nikon_D300">
6:    <myCamera:lens rdf:resource=
6a:      "http://dbpedia.org/resource/Nikon_17-35mm_f/2.8D_ED-
6b:      IF_AF-S_Zoom-Nikkor"/>
7: </rdf:Description>
8:
9: </rdf:RDF>
```

This is a very simple RDF document: it only uses one property, namely, `myCamera:lens` to describe the given resource (line 6). However, based on the definition of this property (lines 53–56, List 4.13), an application is able to make the following reasoning:

`http://dbpedia.org/resource/Nikon_17-35mm_f/2.8D_ED-IF_AF-S_Zoom-Nikkor` is an instance of class `myCamera:Lens`.

Again, notice that we have used an existing URI from DBpedia to represent a Nikon zoom lens, the reason being the same: we should reuse URI as much as we can.

In fact, our application, based on the definition of property `myCamera:lens`, can also make the following reasoning:

`http://www.liyangyu.com/camera#Nikon_D300` is an instance of class `myCamera:Camera`.

- Understand a resource's super-class type by following the class hierarchy described in the ontology.

This can be viewed as extension to the above two reasoning scenarios. In both of the above cases, the final result is that the class type of some resource has been successfully identified. Now our application can scan the class hierarchy defined in the ontology; if the identified class has one or more super-classes defined in the ontology, our application can then conclude that this particular resource is not only an instance of the identified class, but also an instance of all the super-classes.

- Understand more about the resource by using the `rdfs:subPropertyOf` tag.

Let us use an example to illustrate this reasoning. Suppose we have defined the following property:

```
<rdf:Property rdf:ID="parent">
    <rdfs:domain rdf:resource="#Person"/>
    <rdfs:range rdf:resource="#Person"/>
</rdf:Property>
<rdf:Property rdf:ID="mother">
    <rdfs:subClassOf rdf:resouce="#parent"/>
</rdf:Property>
```

This defines two properties, namely, `parent` and `mother`, with `mother` being a subproperty of `parent`. Assume we have a resource in the RDF statement document:

```
<Person rdf:ID="Liyang">
    <mother>
        <Person rdf:resource="#Zaiyun"/>
    </mother>
</Person>
```

When parsing this statement, an application realizes the fact that `Liyang`'s `mother` is `Zaiyun`. One step further, since `mother` is a subproperty of `parent`, it then concludes that `Liyang`'s parent is also `Zaiyun`. This can be very useful in some cases.

The above are the four main ways a given application can make inferences based on the given ontology, together with the instance document. These are indeed simple yet very powerful already.

4.6.2 Good, Better and Best: More Is Needed

RDF schema is quite impressive indeed: you can use its terms to define ontologies, and having these ontologies defined, our application can conduct reasoning on the run. However, there is still something missing when you use RDFS vocabulary to define ontologies.

For example, what if we have two classes representing the same concept? For example, we have a DSLR class in our camera ontology, and we know DSLR represents Digital Single Lens Reflex; it will be quite useful if we could define another class named DigitalSingleLensReflex, and also indicate in our ontology that these two classes represent exactly the same concept in life. However, using RDF schema, it is not possible to accomplish this.

Another example is that there are no cardinality constraints available using RDF schema. For example, effectivePixel is a property that is used to describe the image size of a digital camera. For one particular camera, there should be only one effectivePixel value. However, in our RDF document, we can use multiple effectivePixel properties on a single digital camera instance!

Therefore, there is indeed a need to extend RDF schema to allow for the expression of more complex relationships among classes and of more precise constraints on specific classes and properties. In other words, we need a more advanced language that is able to do the following:

- express relationships among classes defined in different documents across the Web;
- construct new classes by unions, intersections and complements of other existing classes;
- add constraints on the number and type for properties of classes;
- determine if all members of a class will have a particular property, or if only some of them might;
- and more.

This new language is called OWL, and it is the main topic of the next chapter, so read on.

4.7 Summary

In this chapter, we have learned about RDFS, another important building block for the Semantic Web. The first thing we should understand from this chapter is how RDFS fits into the whole concept of the Semantic Web. More specifically, this includes the following main points:

- It provides a collection of terms (RDFS vocabulary) that one can use to build ontologies.
- With these ontologies, RDF documents can be created by using shared knowledge and common terms, i.e., whatever we say, we have a reason to say it.

In order for us to create ontologies by using RDFS, this chapter also covers the main language features of RDFS. We should have learned the following:

- the concept of RDFS vocabulary, and how it is related to other vocabularies, such as RDF vocabulary, and Dublin Core vocabulary;
- understanding of the key terms contained in RDFS vocabulary, and how to use them to develop domain-specific ontologies.

This chapter also discusses the concept of ontologies, and further introduces another vocabulary called SKOS. We should have learned the following main points:

- the concept of ontology, and the reason for having ontologies for the Semantic Web;
- the concept of SKOS, and how to use SKOS vocabulary to map an existing KOS onto the Semantic Web, and certainly, the benefit of doing so.

Finally, this chapter shows the reasoning power provided by ontologies. This includes the following:

- the meaning of a given term is expressed by the properties that can be used on this term, and the values these properties can assume;
- machines can understand such meanings, and four different ways of reasoning can be implemented by machines based on this understanding;
- RDF Schema can be improved in a number of different ways.

In the next chapter, we present OWL, essentially a much more advanced version of RDFS, and you will have more chances to see how machines can understand meanings by conducting useful reasoning on the fly.

Chapter 5
OWL: Web Ontology Language

This chapter is a natural extension of Chap. 4. As a key technical component in the world of the Semantic Web, the Web Ontology Language OWL is the most popular language to use when creating ontologies. In this chapter, we cover OWL in great detail, and after finishing this chapter, you will be quite comfortable when it comes to defining ontologies using OWL.

5.1 OWL Overview

5.1.1 OWL in Plain English

OWL is currently the most popular language to use when creating ontologies. Since we have already established a solid understanding about RDF Schema, understanding OWL becomes much easier.

The purpose of OWL is exactly the same as RDF Schema: to define ontologies that include classes, properties and their relationships for a specific application domain. When anyone wants to describe any resource, these terms can be used in the published RDF documents; therefore, everything we say, we have a reason to say it. And furthermore, a given application can implement reasoning processes to discover implicit or unknown facts with the help of the ontologies.

However, compared to RDF schema, OWL provides us with the capability to express much more complex and richer relationships. Therefore, we can construct applications with a much stronger reasoning ability. For this reason, we often want to use OWL for the purpose of ontology development. RDF Schema is still a valid choice, but it's obvious limitation compared to OWL will always make it a second choice.

In plain English, we can define OWL as follows:

© Springer-Verlag Berlin Heidelberg 2014
L. Yu, *A Developer's Guide to the Semantic Web*,
DOI 10.1007/978-3-662-43796-4_5

OWL = RDF Schema + new constructs for better expressiveness

And remember, since OWL is built upon RDF Schema, all the terms contained in RDFS vocabulary can still be used when creating OWL documents.

Before we move on to the official definition of OWL, let us spend a few lines on its interesting acronym. Clearly, the natural acronym for Web Ontology Language would be WOL instead of OWL. The story dates back to December 2001, the days when the OWL group was working on OWL. Prof. Tim Finin, in an e-mail dated December 27, 2001,[1] suggested the name OWL based on these considerations: OWL has just one obvious pronunciation that is also easy on the ear, it yields good logos, it suggests wisdom and it can be used to honor the *One World Language* project, an Artificial Intelligence project at MIT in the mid 1970s. The name OWL since then has been accepted as it formal name.

5.1.2   OWL in Official Language: OWL 1 and OWL 2

Behind the development of OWL, there is actually quite a long history that dates back to the 1990s. Back then, a number of research efforts were set up to explore how the idea of *knowledge representationSee* KR (KR) from the area of Artificial Intelligence*See* AI (AI) could be used on the Web to make machines understand its content. These efforts resulted in a variety of languages. Among them, noticeably two languages called Simple HTML Ontology Extensions (SHOE*See* SHOE) and Ontology Inference Layer (OIL*See* OIL) later on become part of the foundation of OWL.

Meanwhile, another project named the DARPA Agent Markup Language*See* DAML, (DAML, where *DARPA* represents US Defense Advanced Research Projects Agency) was started in late 1990 with the goal of creating a machine-readable representation for the Web. The main outcome of the DAML project was the DAML language, an agent markup language based on RDF.

Based on DAML, SHOE and OIL, a new Web ontology language named DAML +OIL was developed by a group called "US/UK ad hoc Joint Working Group on Agent Markup Languages". This group was jointly funded by DARPA under the DAML program and the European Union's Information Society Technologies (IST) funding project. DAML+OIL since then has become the whole foundation of OWL language.

The OWL language started as a research-based revision of the DAML+OIL web ontology language. W3C created the Web Ontology Working Group[2] in November 2001, and the first working drafts of the abstract syntax, reference and synopsis were published in July 2002. The OWL documents became a formal W3C

---

[1] http://lists.w3.org/Archives/Public/www-webont-wg/2001Dec/0169.html

[2] http://www.w3.org/2007/OWL/wiki/OWL_Working_Group

recommendation on February 10, 2004. The recommendation includes the following documents[3]:

- OWL Web Ontology Language Overview
- OWL Web Ontology Language Guide
- OWL Web Ontology Language Reference
- OWL Web Ontology Language Semantics and Abstract Syntax
- OWL Web Ontology Language Test Cases
- OWL Web Ontology Language Use Cases and Requirements

The standardization of OWL has since then sparked the development of OWL ontologies in a number of fields including medicine, biology, geography, astronomy, defense and the aerospace industry. For example, in the life sciences community, OWL is extensively used and has become a de facto standard for ontology development and data exchange.

On the other hand, the numerous contexts in which OWL language has been applied have also revealed its deficiencies from a user's point of view. For instance, ontology engineers have identified some major limitations of its expressiveness, which is obviously needed for real development work. Also, OWL tool designers have come up with their list of some practical limitations of the OWL language as well.

In response to these comments and requests from the real users, it was decided that an incremental revision of OWL was needed, and was provisionally called OWL 1.1. Accordingly, the initial version of OWL language is referred to as OWL 1.

The 2005 OWL Experiences and Directions Workshop[4] created a list of new features to be provided by OWL 1.1. The actual development of these new features was then undertaken by an informal group of language users and developers. The deliverables of their work were submitted to W3C as a member submission, and as the same time, a new W3C OWL Working Group[5] was officially formed in September 2007.

Under the auspices of the Working Group, the original member submission has evolved significantly. In April 2008, the Working Group decided to call the new language OWL 2, and the initial 2004 OWL standard continues to be called OWL 1.

On October 27, 2009, OWL 2 became a W3C standard,[6] with the following core specifications:

- OWL 2 Web Ontology Language Structural Specification and Functional-Style Syntax
- OWL 2 Web Ontology Language Mapping to RDF Graphs
- OWL 2 Web Ontology Language Direct Semantics

---

[3] http://www.w3.org/2004/OWL/#specs

[4] http://www.mindswap.org/2005/OWLWorkshop/

[5] http://www.w3.org/2007/OWL/wiki/OWL_Working_Group

[6] http://www.w3.org/TR/2009/REC-owl2-overview-20091027/

- OWL 2 Web Ontology Language RDF-Based Semantics
- OWL 2 Web Ontology Language Conformance
- OWL 2 Web Ontology Language Profiles

These core specifications are part of the W3C OWL 2 Recommendations, and they are mainly useful for ontology tool designers. For example, in order to implement an OWL 2 validator or a reasoner that understands OWL 2, one has to be familiar with these specifications. For developers like us, this chapter will help you to learn how to use OWL 2 to develop your own ontology documents.

With the understanding of the history behind OWL, let us take a look at its official definition. W3C's OWL 2 Primer[7] has given a good definition of OWL:

> The W3C OWL 2 Web Ontology LanguageSee OWL (OWL) is a Semantic Web language designed to represent rich and complex knowledge about things, groups of things, and relations between things. OWL is a computational logic-based language such that knowledge expressed in OWL can be reasoned with by computer programs either to verify the consistency of that knowledge or to make implicit knowledge explicit.

If you don't fully understand this definition at this point, rest assured that it will gradually shape up during the course of this chapter. In this chapter, we will cover the details of OWL language, and you will be able to define ontologies on your own, and understand existing ontologies that are written by using OWL.

5.1.3   From OWL 1 to OWL 2

With the discussion of OWL history in place, we understand OWL 2 is the latest standard from W3C. In fact, OWL 1 can be considered as a subset of OWL 2, and all the ontologies that are created by using OWL 1 will be recognized and understood by any application that can understand OWL 2.

However, OWL 1 still plays a special role, largely for some historical reasons. More specifically, up to this point, most practical-scale and well-known ontologies are written in OWL 1, and most ontology engineering tools, including development environments for the Semantic Web, are equipped with the ability to understand OWL 1 ontologies only. Therefore, in this chapter, we will make a clear distinction between OWL 1 and OWL 2: the language constructs of OWL 1 will be covered first, followed by the language constructs of OWL 2. Once you have finished the part about OWL 1, you should be able to understand most of the ontologies in the real Semantic Web world. With a separate section covering OWL 2, you can get a clear picture about what has been improved since OWL 1.

Also notice that for the rest of this chapter, we will use the names OWL and OWL 2 interchangeably. We will always explicitly state OWL 1 if necessary.

---

[7] http://www.w3.org/TR/2009/REC-owl2-primer-20091027/

5.2   OWL 1 and OWL 2: The Big Picture

Form this point through the rest of this chapter, we will cover the syntax of OWL, together with examples. Our goal is to rewrite our camera vocabulary developed in Chap. 4, and by doing so, we will cover most of the OWL language features.

Similar to RDFS, OWL can be viewed as a collection of terms we can use to define classes and properties for a specific application domain. These predefined OWL terms all have the following URI as their leading string (applicable to both OWL 1 and OWL 2),

```
http://www.w3.org/2002/07/owl#
```

and by convention, this URI prefix string is associated with namespace prefix `owl:`, and is typically used in RDF/XML documents with the prefix `owl`.

For the rest of this section, we will discuss several important concepts related to OWL, so we will be ready for the rest of this chapter.

5.2.1   Basic Notions: Axiom, Entity, Expression and IRI Names

An *axiom* is a basic statement that an OWL ontology has. It represents a basic piece of knowledge. For example, a statement like "the `Digital` camera class is a subclass of the `Camera` class" is an axiom. Clearly, any given OWL ontology can be viewed as a collection of axioms. Furthermore, this ontology asserts that all its axioms are true.

Clearly, each axiom, as a statement, will have to involve some class, some property and sometimes, some individual. For example, one axiom can claim that a Nikon D300 camera is an individual of class `Digital` camera, and another axiom can state that a `Photographer` individual can `own` a given camera. These classes, properties and individuals can be viewed as the atomic constituents of axioms, and these atomic constituents are also called *entities*. Sometimes, in OWL, individual entity is also called object, and class entity is called category and property entity is called relation.

As we will see in this chapter, a key feature of OWL is to combine different class entities and/or property entities to create new class entities and property entities. The combinations of entities to form complex descriptions about new entities are called *expressions*. In fact, expressions are a main reason why we claim OWL language has a much more enhanced expressiveness compared to ontology language such as RDFS.

The last concept we would like to mention here is the *IRI* names, which you will encounter when reading OWL 2-related literature.

As we know at this point, URIs are the standard mechanism for identifying resources on the Web. For the vision of the Semantic Web, we have been using

URIs to represent classes, properties and individuals, as shown in Chaps. 2 and 4. This URI system fits well into the Semantic Web for the following two main reasons:

1. It provides a mechanism to uniquely identify a given resource.
2. It specifies a uniform way to retrieve machine-readable descriptions about the resource being identified by the URI.

The first point here should be fairly clear (refer to Chap. 2 for details), and the second point will be covered in detail in Chap. 9.

Internationalized Resource Identifiers (IRIs)*See* IRI are just like URIs except that they can make use of the whole range of Unicode characters. As a comparison, URIs are limited to the ASCII subset of the characters, which only has 127 characters. In addition, the ASCII subset itself is based on the needs of English-speaking users, which presents some difficulty for non-English users. And these considerations have been the motivation of IRIs.

There are standard ways to convert IRIs to URIs, and vice versa. Therefore, an IRI can be coded into a URI, which is quite helpful when we need to use the IRI in a protocol that accepts only URIs (such as the HTTP protocol).

For our immediate purpose in this chapter, IRIs are interchangeable with URIs, and there is not much need to make a distinction between these two. However, understanding IRIs is helpful, especially if you are doing development using a language other than English.

5.2.2 Basic Syntax Forms: Functional-Style, RDF/XML Syntax, Manchester Syntax and XML Syntax

OWL specifications provide various syntaxes for persisting, sharing and editing ontologies. These syntaxes could be confusing for someone new to the language. In this section, we give a brief description of each syntax form so you understand which one will work the best for your needs.

- Functional-Style syntax

It is important to realize the fact that the OWL language is not defined by using a particular concrete syntax, but rather it is defined in a high-level structural specification that is then mapped into different concrete syntaxes. By doing so, it is possible to clearly describe the essential language features without getting into the technical details of exchange formats.

Once the structural specification is complete, it is necessary to move toward some concrete syntaxes. The first step of doing so is the Functional-Style syntax. This syntax is designed for translating the structural specification to various other syntaxes, and it is often used by OWL tool designers. In general, it is not intended to be used as an exchange syntax, and as OWL language users, we will not be seeing or using this syntax often.

• RDF/XML syntax

This is the syntax we are familiar with, and it is also the sterilization format we have been using throughout the book. Most well-known ontologies written in OWL 1 use this syntax as well. In addition, this is the only syntax that is mandatory to be supported by all OWL tools. Therefore, as a developer, you should be familiar with this syntax. We will be using this syntax for the rest of this chapter as well.

• Manchester syntax

The Manchester syntax provides a textual-based representation of OWL ontologies that is easy to read and write. The motivation behind Manchester syntax was to design a syntax that could be used for editing class expressions in tools such as Protégé and the like. Since it is quite successful in these tools, it has been extended to represent a complete ontology.

Manchester syntax is fairly easy to learn, and it has a compact format that is easy to read and write as well. We will not be using this format in this book. With what you will learn from using the RDF/XML format, understanding Manchester syntax will not present too much of a challenge at all.

• OWL/XML

Although RDF/XML syntax is the normative format specified by the W3C OWL standard, it is not easy to work with. More specifically, it is difficult to use existing XML tools for tasks other than parsing and rendering it. Even standard XML tools such as Xpath and XSLT will not work well with RDF/XML representations of ontologies. In order to take advantage of existing XML tools, a more regular and simple XML format is needed. OWL/XML is such a format for representing OWL ontologies. Its main advantage is that it conforms to an XML schema, and therefore it is possible to use existing XML tools such as Xpath and XSLT for processing and querying tasks. In addition, parsing can be done more easily than in RDF/XML syntax.

In this book, we will not use this format. Again, once you are familiar with the RDF/XML format, understanding OWL/XML syntax will not be too hard.

5.3 OWL 1 Web Ontology Language

In this section, we concentrate on the language constructs offered by OWL 1. Again, all these constructs are now part of OWL 2, and any ontology created by using OWL 1 will continue to be recognized and understood by any application that understands OWL 2.

Fig. 5.1 Relationship
between top classes

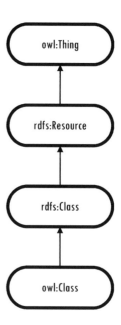

5.3.1 Defining Classes: The Basics

Recall in RDF Schema, the root class of everything is `rdfs:Resource`. In the world
of OWL 1, `owl:Thing` is the root of all classes, it is also the base class of `rdfs:`
`Resource`. Furthermore, `owl:Class` is defined by OWL 1 so that we can use it to
define classes in OWL 1 ontologies, and `owl:Class` is a subclass of `rdfs:Class`.
The relationship between all these top classes can therefore be summarized in
Fig. 5.1:

Now, to declare one of our camera ontology's top classes using OWL 1, such as
`Camera`, we can do the following:

```
<rdf:Description
    rdf:about="http://www.liyangyu.com/camera#Camera">
  <rdf:type rdf:resource="http://www.w3.org/2002/07/owl#Class"/>
</rdf:Description>
```

And the following is an equivalent format:

```
<owl:Class rdf:about="http://www.liyangyu.com/camera#Camera">
</owl:Class>
```

To define all the classes in our camera ontology, List 5.1 will be good enough:

List 5.1 Class definitions for our camera ontology using OWL 1

```
1: <?xml version="1.0"?>
2: <rdf:RDF
2a:    xmlns:rdf="http://www.w3.org/1999/02/22-rdf-syntax-ns#"
3:     xmlns:rdfs="http://www.w3.org/2000/01/rdf-schema#"
4:     xmlns:owl="http://www.w3.org/2002/07/owl#"
5:     xmlns:myCamera="http://www.liyangyu.com/camera#"
6:     xml:base="http://www.liyangyu.com/camera#">
7:
8:  <owl:Class rdf:about="http://www.liyangyu.com/camera#Camera">
9:  </owl:Class>
10:
11: <owl:Class rdf:about="http://www.liyangyu.com/camera#Lens">
12: </owl:Class>
13:
14: <owl:Class rdf:about="http://www.liyangyu.com/camera#Body">
15: </owl:Class>
16:
17: <owl:Class
17a:     rdf:about="http://www.liyangyu.com/camera#ValueRange">
18: </owl:Class>
19:
20: <owl:Class
20a:     rdf:about="http://www.liyangyu.com/camera#Digital">
21:   <rdfs:subClassOf rdf:resource="#Camera"/>
22: </owl:Class>
23:
24: <owl:Class rdf:about="http://www.liyangyu.com/camera#Film">
25:   <rdfs:subClassOf rdf:resource="#Camera"/>
26: </owl:Class>
27:
28: <owl:Class rdf:about="http://www.liyangyu.com/camera#DSLR">
29:   <rdfs:subClassOf rdf:resource="#Digital"/>
30: </owl:Class>
31:
32: <owl:Class
32a:     rdf:about="http://www.liyangyu.com/camera#PointAndShoot">
33:   <rdfs:subClassOf rdf:resource="#Digital"/>
34: </owl:Class>
35:
36: <owl:Class
36a:     rdf:about="http://www.liyangyu.com/camera#Photographer">
37:   <rdfs:subClassOf
37a:         rdf:resource="http://xmlns.com/foaf/0.1/Person"/>
38: </owl:Class>
39:
40: </rdf:RDF>
```

Looks like we are done: we have just finished using OWL 1 terms to define all the classes used in our camera ontology.

Notice that List 5.1 only contains a very simple class hierarchy. OWL 1 offers much greater expressiveness than we have just utilized. Let us explore these features one by one, and in order to show how these new features are used, we will also change our camera ontology from time to time.

5.3.2   Defining Classes: Localizing Global Properties

In Chap. 4, we defined properties by using RDFS terms. For example, recall the definition of owned_by property,

```
<rdf:Property
     rdf:about="http://www.liyangyu.com/camera#owned_by">
  <rdfs:domain rdf:resource="#DSLR"/>
  <rdfs:range rdf:resource="#Photographer"/>
</rdf:Property>
```

Notice that rdfs:range imposes a global restriction on owned_by property, i.e., the rdfs:range value applies to Photographer class and all subclasses of Photographer class.

However, there will be cases where we actually would like to localize this global restriction on a given property. Clearly, RDFS terms will not be able to help us to implement this. OWL 1, on the other hand, provides ways to localize a global property by defining new classes, as we show in this section.

5.3.2.1   Value Constraints: owl:allValuesFrom

Let us go back to our definition of owned_by property. More specifically, we have associated this property with two classes, DSLR and Photographer, in order to express the knowledge "DSLR is owned_by Photographer".

Let us say we now want to express the following fact: DSLR, especially an expensive one, are normally used by professional photographers. For example, the body alone of some high-end digital SLRs can cost as much as $5,000.00.

To accomplish this, we decide to define a new class called ExpensiveDSLR, as a subclass of DSLR. We would also like to define two more classes, Professional and Amateur, as subclasses of Photographer. These two classes represent professional and amateur photographers, respectively. List 5.2 shows the definitions of these two new classes.

List 5.2 New class definitions are added: `Professional` and `Amateur`

```
1: <?xml version="1.0"?>
2: <rdf:RDF
2a:     xmlns:rdf="http://www.w3.org/1999/02/22-rdf-syntax-ns#"
3:      xmlns:rdfs="http://www.w3.org/2000/01/rdf-schema#"
4:      xmlns:owl="http://www.w3.org/2002/07/owl#"
5:      xmlns:myCamera="http://www.liyangyu.com/camera#"
6:      xml:base="http://www.liyangyu.com/camera#">
7:
8:
   ... same as List 5.1

38:
39:
40: <owl:Class
40a:     rdf:about="http://www.liyangyu.com/camera#Professional">
41:     <rdfs:subClassOf rdf:resource="#Photographer"/>
42: </owl:Class>
43:
44: <owl:Class
44a:     rdf:about="http://www.liyangyu.com/camera#Amateur">
45:     <rdfs:subClassOf rdf:resource="#Photographer"/>
46: </owl:Class>
47:
48: </rdf:RDF>
```

Does this ontology successfully express our idea? Not really. Since `owned_by` has `DSLR` as its `rdfs:domain` and `Photographer` as its `rdfs:value`, and given the fact that `ExpensiveDSLR` is a subclass of `DSLR`, and `Professional` and `Amateur` are both subclasses of `Photographer`, these new subclasses all inherit the `owned_by` property. Therefore, we can indeed say something like this:

`ExpensiveDSLR owned_by Professional`

which is what we wanted. However, we cannot exclude the following statement either:

`ExpensiveDSLR owned_by Amateur`

How do we modify the definition of `ExpensiveDSLR` to make sure it can be owned *only* by `Professional`? OWL 1 uses `owl:allValuesFrom` to solve this problem, as shown in List 5.3.

List 5.3 Use `owl:allValuesFrom` to define `ExpensiveDSLR` class

```
1: <owl:Class
1a:    rdf:about="http://www.liyangyu.com/camera#ExpensiveDSLR">
2:   <rdfs:subClassOf rdf:resource="#DSLR"/>
3:   <rdfs:subClassOf>
4:     <owl:Restriction>
5:       <owl:onProperty rdf:resource="#owned_by"/>
6:       <owl:allValuesFrom rdf:resource="#Professional"/>
7:     </owl:Restriction>
8:   </rdfs:subClassOf>
9: </owl:Class>
```

To understand how List 5.3 defines `ExpensiveDSLR` class, we need to understand `owl:Restriction` first.

`owl:Restriction` is an OWL 1 term used to describe an anonymous class, which is defined by adding some restriction on some property. Furthermore, all the instances of this anonymous class have to satisfy this restriction; hence the term `owl:Restriction`.

The restriction itself has two parts. The first part is about to which property this restriction is applied to, and this is specified by using `owl:onProperty` property. The second part is about the property constraint itself, or, exactly what is the constraint. Two kinds of property restrictions are allowed in OWL: *value constraints* and *cardinality constraints*. A value constraint puts constraints on the range of the property, while a cardinality constraint puts constraints on the number of values a property can take. We will see value constraints in this section and cardinality constraints in the coming sections.

One way to specify a value constraint is to use the built-in OWL 1 property called `owl:allValuesFrom`. When this property is used, the value of the restricted property has to all come from the specified class or data range.

With all this said, List 5.3 should be easier to understand. Lines 4–7 use `owl:Restriction` to define an anonymous class; the constraint is applied on `owned_by` property (this is specified by using `owl:onProperty` property on line 5), and the values for `owned_by` property must all come from instances of class `Professional` (this is specified by using `owl:allValuesFrom` property on line 6). Therefore, lines 4–7 can be read as follows:

lines 4–7 have defined an anonymous class which has a property `owned_by`, and all values for `owned_by` property must be instances of `Professional`.

With this, List 5.3 can be read as follows:

Here is a definition of class `ExpensiveDSLR`: it is a subclass of `DSLR`, and a subclass of an anonymous class which has a property `owned_by` and all values for this property must be instances of `Professional`.

It does take a while to get used to this way of defining new classes. Once you are used to it, you can simply read List 5.3 like this:

Here is a definition of class `ExpensiveDSLR`: it is a subclass of `DSLR` and it has a property named `owned_by`, and only instances of class `Professional` can be the value for this property.

Therefore, by adding constraints on a given property, we have defined a new class that satisfies our needs. In fact, this new way of defining classes is frequently used in OWL ontologies, so make sure you understand it and feel comfortable with it as well.

5.3.2.2 Enhanced Reasoning Power 1

In this chapter, we are going to talk about OWL's reasoning power in more detail, so you will see more sections like this one coming up frequently. The following should be clear before we move on.

First off, when we say an application can understand a given ontology, we mean that the application can parse the ontology and create a list of axioms based on the ontology, and all the facts are expressed as RDF statements. You will see how this is accomplished in later chapters, but for now, just assume this can be easily done.

Second, when we say an application can make inferences, we refer to the fact that the application can add new RDF statements into the existing collection of statements. The newly added statements are not mentioned anywhere in the original ontology or original instance document.

Finally, when we say instance document, we refer to an RDF document that is created by using the terms presented in the given ontology. Also, when we present this instance document, we will only show the part that is relevant to that specific reasoning capability being discussed. The rest of the instance file that is not related to this specific reasoning capability will not be included.

With all this being said, we can now move on to take a look at the reasoning power provided by `owl:allValuesFrom` construct. Let us say our application sees the following instance document:

```
<myCamera:ExpensiveDSLR
         rdf:about="http://dbpedia.org/resource/Canon_EOS-1D">
    <myCamera:owned_by
         rdf:resource="http://www.liyangyu.com/people#Liyang"/>
    <myCamera:owned_by
         rdf:resource="http://www.liyangyu.com/people#Connie"/>
</myCamera:ExpensiveDSLR>
```

The application will be able to add the following facts (in Turtle format):

```
<http://www.liyangyu.com/people#Liyang> rdf:type
myCamera:Professional.
<http://www.liyangyu.com/people#Connie> rdf:type
myCamera:Professional.
```

Notice that it is certainly true that our application will also be able to add quite a few other facts, such as `http://www.liyangyu.com/people#Liyang` must also be `myCamera:Photographer`, and also `http://dbpedia.org/resource/Canon_EOS-1D` must be a `myCamera:DSLR`, just to name a few. Here, we are not going to list all these added facts; instead, we will only concentrate on the new facts that are related to the OWL 1 language feature that is being discussed.

5.3.2.3   Value Constraints: `owl:someValuesFrom`

In last section, we used `owl:allValuesFrom` to make sure that `ExpensiveDSLRs` are those cameras that can only be owned by `Professionals`. Now, let us loosen up this restriction by allowing some `Amateurs` to buy and own `ExpensiveDSLRs` as well. However, we still require that at least one of the owners has to be a `Professional`. OWL 1 uses `owl:someValuesFrom` to express this idea, as shown in List 5.4.

List 5.4 Use `owl:someValuesFrom` to define `ExpensiveDSLR` class

```
1: <owl:Class
1a:      rdf:about="http://www.liyangyu.com/camera#ExpensiveDSLR">
2:    <rdfs:subClassOf rdf:resource="#DSLR"/>
3:    <rdfs:subClassOf>
4:       <owl:Restriction>
5:          <owl:onProperty rdf:resource="#owned_by"/>
6:          <owl:someValuesFrom rdf:resource="#Professional"/>
7:       </owl:Restriction>
8:    </rdfs:subClassOf>
9: </owl:Class>
```

This can be read like this:

A class called `ExpensiveDSLR` is defined. It is a subclass of `DSLR`, and it has a property called `owned_by`. Furthermore, at least one value of the `owned_by` property is an instance of `Professional`.

With what we have learned from the previous section, this does not require much explanation.

5.3.2.4 Enhanced Reasoning Power 2

Our application sees the following instance document:

```
<myCamera:ExpensiveDSLR
          rdf:about="http://dbpedia.org/resource/Canon_EOS-1D">
  <myCamera:owned_by
          rdf:resource="http://www.liyangyu.com/people#Liyang"/>
</myCamera:ExpensiveDSLR>
```

The application will be able to add the following facts:

```
<http://www.liyangyu.com/people#Liyang> rdf:type
myCamera:Professional.
```

If our application sees the following instance document:

```
<myCamera:ExpensiveDSLR
          rdf:about="http://dbpedia.org/resource/Canon_EOS-1D">
  <myCamera:owned_by
          rdf:resource="http://www.liyangyu.com/people#Liyang"/>
  <myCamera:owned_by
          rdf:resource="http://www.liyangyu.com/people#Connie"/>
</myCamera:ExpensiveDSLR>
```

then *at least* one of the following two statements is true (it could be that both are true):

```
<http://www.liyangyu.com/people#Liyang> rdf:type
myCamera:Professional.
<http://www.liyangyu.com/people#Connie> rdf:type
myCamera:Professional.
```

It is important to understand the difference between `owl:allValuesFrom` and `owl:someValuesFrom`. Think about it on your own, and we will summarize the difference in a later section.

5.3.2.5 Value Constraints: `owl:hasValue`

Another way OWL 1 uses to localize a global property in the context of a given class is to use `owl:hasValue`. So far, we have defined `ExpensiveDSLR` as being a `DSLR` that is owned by a professional photographer (List 5.3), or owned by at least one professional photographer (List 5.4). These definitions are fine, but they are not straightforward. In fact, we can use a more direct approach to define what it means to be an expensive DSLR.

Let us first define a property called `cost` like this:

```
<owl:DatatypeProperty
      rdf:about="http://www.liyangyu.com/camera#cost">
  <rdfs:domain rdf:resource="#Digital"/>
  <rdfs:range
          rdf:resource="http://www.w3.org/2001/XMLSchema#string"/>
</owl:DatatypeProperty>
```

Since we have not yet reached the section about defining properties, let us not worry about the syntax here. For now, understand this defines a property called `cost`, which is used to describe `Digital` and its value will be a string of your choice. For instance, you can take `expensive` or `inexpensive` as its value.

Clearly, `DSLR` and `PointAndShoot` are all subclasses of `Digital`; therefore they can all use property `cost` in the way they want. In other words, `cost` as a property is global. Now in order to directly express the knowledge that "an `ExpensiveDSLR` is expensive", we can specify the fact that the value of `cost`, when used with `ExpensiveDSLRs`, should always be `expensive`. We can use `owl:hasValue` to implement this idea, as shown in List 5.5.

List 5.5 Use `owl:hasValue` to define `ExpensiveDSLR` class

```
 1: <owl:Class
1a:      rdf:about="http://www.liyangyu.com/camera#ExpensiveDSLR">
 2:    <rdfs:subClassOf rdf:resource="#DSLR"/>
 3:    <rdfs:subClassOf>
 4:      <owl:Restriction>
 5:        <owl:onProperty rdf:resource="#cost"/>
 6:        <owl:hasValue
6a:        rdf:datatype="http://www.w3.org/2001/XMLSchema#string">
 7:            expensive
 8:        </owl:hasValue>
 9:      </owl:Restriction>
10:    </rdfs:subClassOf>
11: </owl:Class>
```

This defines class `ExpensiveDSLR` as follows:

A class called `ExpensiveDSLR` is defined. It is a subclass of `DSLR`, and every instance of `ExpensiveDSLR` has a `cost` property whose value is `expensive`.

Meanwhile, instances of DSLR or PointAndShoot can take whatever cost value they want (i.e., expensive or inexpensive), indicating that they can be expensive or inexpensive. This is exactly what we want.

It is now a good time to take a look at the differences between these three properties. More specifically, whenever we decide to use owl:allValuesFrom, it is equivalent to declare that "all the values of this property must be of this type, but it is all right if there are no values at all". Therefore, the property instance does not even have to appear. On the other hand, using owl:someValuesFrom is equivalent to saying "there must be some values for this property, and at least one of these values has to be of this type. It is okay if there are other values of other types". Clearly, using an owl:someValuesFrom restriction on a property implies this property has to appear at least once, whereas an owl:allValuesFrom restriction does not require the property to show up at all.

Finally, owl:hasValue says "regardless of how many values a class has for a particular property, at least one of them must be equal to the value that you specify". It is therefore very much the same as owl:someValuesFrom except it is more specific because it requires a particular instance instead of a class.

5.3.2.6   Enhanced Reasoning Power 3

Our application sees the following instance document (notice the definition of ExpensiveDSLR is given in List 5.5):

```
<myCamera:DSLR
          rdf:about="http://dbpedia.org/resource/Canon_EOS-1D">
   <myCamera:cost
      rdf:datatype="http://www.w3.org/2001/XMLSchema#string">
      expensive</myCamera:cost>
</myCamera:DSLR>
```

The application will be able to add the following facts:

```
< http://dbpedia.org/resource/Canon_EOS-1D > rdf:type
myCamera:ExpensiveDSLR .
```

Notice the original instance document only shows the class type as DSLR, and the application can assert the more accurate type would be ExpensiveDSLR.

5.3.2.7   Cardinality Constraints: owl:cardinality, owl:min (max)Cardinality

Another way to define class by adding restrictions on properties is to constrain the cardinality of a property based on the class on which it is intended to be used.

In this section, we will add cardinality constraints to some of our existing class definitions in our camera ontology. By doing so, not only will we learn how to use the cardinality constraints, our camera ontology will also become more accurate.

In our camera ontology, class `Digital` represents a digital camera, and property `effectivePixel` represents the picture resolution of a given digital camera, and this property can be used on instances of `Digital` class. Obviously, when defining `Digital` class, it would be useful to indicate that there can be only one `effectivePixel` value for any given digital camera. We cannot accomplish this by using RDFS vocabulary; however, OWL 1 does allow us to do so, as shown in List 5.6.

List 5.6 Definition of class `Digital` using `owl:cardinality` constraint

```
1: <owl:Class rdf:about="http://www.liyangyu.com/camera#Digital">
2:    <rdfs:subClassOf rdf:resource="#Camera"/>
3:    <rdfs:subClassOf>
4:      <owl:Restriction>
5:        <owl:onProperty rdf:resource="#effectivePixel"/>
6:        <owl:cardinality rdf:datatype=
6a:          "http://www.w3.org/2001/XMLSchema#nonNegativeInteger">
7:          1
8:        </owl:cardinality>
9:      </owl:Restriction>
10:   </rdfs:subClassOf>
11: </owl:Class>
```

This defines class `Digital` as follows:

A class called `Digital` is defined. It is a subclass of `Camera`; it has a property called `effectivePixel`; there can be only one `effectivePixel` value for an instance of `Digital` class.

and notice that we need to specify that the literal "1" is to be interpreted as a non-negative integer using `rdf:datatype` property. Also, be aware that this does not place any restrictions on the number of occurrences of `effectivePixel` property in any instance document. In other words, a given instance of `Digital` class (or its subclass) can indeed have multiple `effectivePixel` values, however, when it does, these values must all be equal.

What about `model` property? Clearly, each camera should have at least one `model` value, but it can have multiple `model` values: as we have discussed, the exact same camera, when sold in Asia or North America, can indeed have different model values. To take this constraint into account, we can modify the definition of Camera class as shown in List 5.7.

List 5.7 Definition of class Camera using owl:minCardinality constraint

```
1: <owl:Class rdf:about="http://www.liyangyu.com/camera#Camera">
2:   <rdfs:subClassOf>
3:     <owl:Restriction>
4:       <owl:onProperty rdf:resource="#model"/>
5:       <owl:minCardinality rdf:datatype=
5a:        "http://www.w3.org/2001/XMLSchema#nonNegativeInteger">
6:       1
7:       </owl:minCardinality>
8:     </owl:Restriction>
9:   </rdfs:subClassOf>
10: </owl:Class>
```

And you can use owl:minCardinality together with owl:maxCardinality to specify a range, as shown in List 5.8, which says that a camera should have a least one model value, but cannot have more than three.

List 5.8 Definition of class Camera using owl:minCardinality and owl: maxCardinality constraints

```
1: <owl:Class rdf:about="http://www.liyangyu.com/camera#Camera">
2:   <rdfs:subClassOf>
3:     <owl:Restriction>
4:       <owl:onProperty rdf:resource="#model"/>
5:       <owl:minCardinality rdf:datatype=
5a:        "http://www.w3.org/2001/XMLSchema#nonNegativeInteger">
6:       1
7:       </owl:minCardinality>
8:       <owl:maxCardinality rdf:datatype=
8a:        "http://www.w3.org/2001/XMLSchema#nonNegativeInteger">
9:       3
10:      </owl:maxCardinality>
11:     </owl:Restriction>
12:   </rdfs:subClassOf>
13: </owl:Class>
```

5.3.2.8   Enhanced Reasoning Power 4

Our application sees the following statement from one instance document (notice the definition of `Digital` is given in List 5.6):

```
<myCamera:Digital
        rdf:about="http://www.liyangyu.com/camera#Nikon_D300">
   <myCamera:effectivePixel rdf:resource=
        "http://www.example.org/digitalCamera#pixelValue12.3"/>
</myCamera:Digital>
```

And it has also collected this statement from another instance document:

```
<myCamera:Digital
        http://www.liyangyu.com/camera#Nikon_D300">
   <myCamera:effectivePixel rdf:resource=
        "http://dbpedia.org/resource/Nikon_D300_Resolution"/>
</myCamera:Digital>
```

The application will be able to add the following fact:

```
<http://www.example.org/digitalCamera#pixelValue12.3>
owl:sameAs <http://dbpedia.org/resource/Nikon_D300_Resolution>.
```

Notice `owl:sameAs` means the two given resources are exactly the same. In other words, the following two URIs are URI aliases to each other:

```
http://www.example.org/digitalCamera#pixelValue12.3
http://dbpedia.org/resource/Nikon_D300_Resolution
```

Lists 5.7 and 5.8 yield similar reasoning power. As you can easily see them by yourself, we are not going to discuss them in much detail here.

5.3.3   Defining Classes: Using Set Operators

In the previous sections, we have defined classes by placing constraints on properties, including property value constraints and cardinality constraints. OWL 1 also gives us the ability to construct classes by using set operators. In this section, we briefly introduce these operators so you have more choices when it comes to defining classes.

5.3.3.1 Set Operators

The first operator is `owl:intersectionOf`. Recall the definition of Expensive
DSLR presented in List 5.5; we can rewrite this definition as shown in List 5.9.

List 5.9 Definition of class `ExpensiveDSLR` using `owl:intersectionOf`

```
1:  <owl:Class
1a:      rdf:about="http://www.liyangyu.com/camera#ExpensiveDSLR">
2:      <owl:intersectionOf rdf:parseType="Collection">
3:         <owl:Class rdf:about="#DSLR"/>
4:         <owl:Restriction>
5:           <owl:onProperty rdf:resource="#cost"/>
6:           <owl:hasValue rdf:datatype=
6a:               "http://www.w3.org/2001/XMLSchema#string">
7:             expensive
8:           </owl:hasValue>
9:         </owl:Restriction>
10:     </owl:intersectionOf>
11: </owl:Class>
```

Based on what we have learned so far, List 5.9 is quite straightforward: lines 4–9
define an anonymous class using `owl:Restriction` pattern. This class represents
all the individuals that have cost property, and the value for this property is
expensive. Line 3 includes class DSLR into the picture, which represents all the
DSLR cameras. Line 2 then claims the new class, ExpensiveDSLR, represents all the
individuals that are in the intersection of these two sets of individuals. Therefore,
we can read List 5.9 as follows:

> A class called ExpensiveDSLR is defined. It is the intersection of DSLR class
> and an anonymous class that has a property called cost, and this property has
> the value expensive.

Or, we can simply read List 5.9 as this:

> A class called ExpensiveDSLR is defined. It is a DSLR for which cost is
> expensive.

So what is the difference between List 5.5 and List 5.9? Notice List 5.5 uses
multiple `owl:subClassOf` terms, and in OWL 1, this means qualified individuals
should all come from a *subset* of the final intersection of all the classes specified by
the multiple `owl:subClassOf` terms. On the other hand, List 5.9 means that
qualified individuals should all come from the final intersection of the classes

included in the class collection (line 2 of List 5.9). So there is indeed some subtle difference between these two definitions. However, as far as reasoning is concerned, these two definitions will produce the same inferred facts.

The second operator is the `owl:unionOf` operator. For example, although most photographers today mainly use digital cameras, still they may keep their film cameras around in case they do need them. Therefore if we define a class called `CameraCollection` to represent a photographer's camera collection, it could be defined as shown in List 5.10.

List 5.10 Definition of class `CameraCollection` using `owl:unionOf`

```
1: <owl:Class
1a:   rdf:about="http://www.liyangyu.com/camera#CameraCollection">
2:    <owl:unionOf rdf:parseType="Collection">
3:       <owl:Class rdf:about="#Digital"/>
4:       <owl:Class rdf:about="#Film"/>
5:    </owl:unionOf>
6: </owl:Class>
```

List 5.10 says `CameraCollection` should include both the extension of `Digital` and the extension of `Film`, and clearly, this is exactly what we want.

The last set operator is the `owl:complementOf` operator. A good example is the set of professional photographers and the set of amateur photographers; they are exactly the complement of each other. Therefore, we can rewrite the definition of `Amateur` photographer as shown in List 5.11.

List 5.11 Definition of class `Amateur` using `owl:complementOf`

```
1: <owl:Class rdf:about="http://www.liyangyu.com/camera#Amateur">
2:   <owl:intersectionOf rdf:parseType="Collection">
3:      <owl:Class rdf:about="http://xmlns.com/foaf/0.1/Person"/>
4:      <owl:Class>
5:        <owl:complementOf rdf:resource="#Professional"/>
6:      </owl:Class>
7:   </owl:intersectionOf>
8: </owl:Class>
```

This says that an `Amateur` is a `Person` who is not a `Professional`, and notice we have used `owl:intersectionOf` as well to make the definition correct.

5.3.3.2 Enhanced Reasoning Power 5

Like other OWL 1 language features, using set operators to define class also provides enhanced reasoning power. Since there are indeed quite a few related to using set operators, we will discuss the related ones without using concrete examples.

More specifically, the following are some of these enhanced reasoning conditions:

- If a class C_0 is the owl:intersectionOf a list of class C_1, C_2 and C_3, then C_0 is subclass of each one of C_1, C_2 and C_3.
- If a class A is the owl:intersectionOf a list of classes and class B is the owl:intersectionOf another list of classes, class A is a subclass of class B if every constituent class of A is a subclass of some constituent class of B.
- If a class C_0 is the owl:unionOf a list of class C_1, C_2 and C_3, then each one of C_1, C_2 and C_3, is a subclass of C_0.
- If a class A is the owl:unionOf a list of classes and class B is the owl:unionOf another list of classes, class A is a subclass of class B if every constituent class of B is a super-class of some constituent class of A.
- If a class A is owl:complementOf a class B, then all the subclasses of A will be owl:disjointWith class B.

Notice this is not a complete list, but the above will give you some idea about reasoning based on set operators.

5.3.4 Defining Classes: Using Enumeration, Equivalent and Disjoint

Besides all the methods we have learned so far about defining classes, OWL 1 still has more ways that we can use:

- construct a class by enumerating its instances;
- specify a class is equivalent to another class, and
- specify a class is disjoint from another class.

We discuss the details in this section.

5.3.4.1 Enumeration, Equivalent and Disjoint

Defining classes by enumeration could be quite useful for many cases. To see why, let us recall the methods we have used when defining the ExpensiveDSLR class. So far we have defined the class ExpensiveDSLR by saying that it has to be owned by a professional photographer, or, its cost property has to take the value expensive, etc. All these methods are a *descriptive* way to define a class: as long as an instance satisfies all the conditions, it is a member of the defined class.

The drawback of this descriptive method is the fact that there could be a large number of instances qualified, and sometimes, it takes computing time to make the decision of qualification. In some cases, it will be more efficient and useful if we can explicitly enumerate which are the qualified members; which will simply present a more accurate semantics for many applications. The `owl:oneOf` property provided by OWL 1 can be used to accomplish this. List 5.12 shows how.

List 5.12 Definition of class `ExpensiveDSLR` using `owl:oneOf`

```
1: <owl:Class
1a:      rdf:about="http://www.liyangyu.com/camera#ExpensiveDSLR">
2:    <rdfs:subClassOf rdf:resource="#DSLR"/>
3:    <owl:oneOf rdf:parseType="Collection">
4:      <myCamera:DSLR
4a:              rdf:about="http://dbpedia.org/resource/Nikon_D3"/>
5:      <myCamera:DSLR
5a:         rdf:about="http://dbpedia.org/resource/Canon_EOS-1D"/>
6:    </owl:oneOf>
7: </owl:Class>
```

It is important to understand that no other individuals can be included in the extension of class `ExpensiveDSLR`, except for the instances listed on lines 4 and 5. Therefore, if you do decide to use enumeration to define this class, you might want to add more instances there. Also, notice that `Nikon_D3` (line 4) is not a typo, it is indeed a quite expensive DSLR, and this URI is taken from DBpedia project, similar to the URI on line 5.

Since each individual is referenced by its URI, it is fine not to use a specific type for it, and just use `owl:Thing` instead. Therefore, List 5.13 is equivalent to List 5.12.

List 5.13 Definition of class `ExpensiveDSLR` using `owl:oneOf`

```
1: <owl:Class
1a:      rdf:about="http://www.liyangyu.com/camera#ExpensiveDSLR">
2:    <rdfs:subClassOf rdf:resource="#DSLR"/>
3:    <owl:oneOf rdf:parseType="Collection">
4:      <owl:Thing
4a:         rdf:about="http://dbpedia.org/resource/Nikon_D3"/>
5:      <owl:Thing
5a:         rdf:about="http://dbpedia.org/resource/Canon_EOS-1D"/>
6:    </owl:oneOf>
7: </owl:Class>
```

The last thing to remember is the syntax: we need to use `owl:oneOf` together with `rdf:parseType` to tell the parser that we are in fact enumerating all the members of the class being defined.

We can also define a class by using `owl:equivalentClass` property, which indicates that two classes have precisely the same instances. For example, List 5.14 declares another class called `DigitalSLR`, and it is exactly the same as `DSLR` class:

List 5.14 Use `owl:equivalentClass` to define class `DigitalSLR`

```
1: <owl:Class
1a:     rdf:about="http://www.liyangyu.com/camera#DigitalSLR">
2:     <owl:equivalentClass rdf:resource="#DSLR"/>
3: </owl:Class>
```

More often, property `owl:equivalentClass` is used to explicitly declare that two classes in two different ontology documents are in fact equivalent classes. For example, if another ontology document defines a class called `DigitalSingle-LensReflex`, and we would like to claim our class, `DSLR`, is equivalent to this class, we can accomplish this as shown in List 5.15.

List 5.15 Use `owl:equivalentClass` to specify two classes are equivalent

```
1: <owl:Class rdf:about="http://www.liyangyu.com/camera#DSLR">
2:     <rdfs:subClassOf rdf:resource="#Digital"/>
3:     <owl:equivalentClass rdf:resource=
3a:         "http://www.example.org#DigitalSingleLensReflex"/>
4: </owl:Class>
```

Now, in any RDF document, if we have described an instance that is of type `DSLR`, it is also an instance of type `DigitalSingleLensReflex`.

Finally, OWL 1 also provides a way to define the fact that two classes are not related in any way. For instance, in our camera ontology, we have defined `DSLR` and `PointAndShoot` as subclasses of `Digital`. To make things simpler and without worrying about the fact that a `DSLR` camera in many cases can be simply used as a `PointAndShoot` camera, we can define `DSLR` to be disjoint from the `PointAndShoot` class, as shown in List 5.16:

List 5.16 Use `owl:disjointWith` to specify two classes are disjoint

```
1: <owl:Class rdf:about="http://www.liyangyu.com/camera#DSLR">
2:    <rdfs:subClassOf rdf:resource="#Digital"/>
3:    <owl:equivalentClass rdf:resource=
3a:        "http://www.example.org#DigitalSingleLensReflex"/>
4:    <owl:disjointWith rdf:resource="#PointAndShoot"/>
5: </owl:Class>
```

Once a given application sees this definition, it will understand that any instance of `DSLR` can never be an instance of the `PointAndShoot` camera. Also notice that `owl:disjointWith` by default is a symmetric property (more on this later): if `DSLR` is disjoint with `PointAndShoot`, then `PointAndShoot` is disjoint with `DSLR`.

5.3.4.2 Enhanced Reasoning Power 6

Similar to set operators, we will list some related reasoning powers here without using concrete examples:

- If a class c_0 is `owl:oneOf` a list of class c_1, c_2 and c_3, then each of c_1, c_2 and c_3 has `rdf:type` given by c_0.
- If a class A is `owl:equivalentClass` to class B, then a `owl:sameAs` relationship will be asserted between these two classes.
- If a class A is `owl:disjointWith` class B, then any subclass of A will be `owl:disjointWith` with class B.

Again, this is certainly not a complete list, and you will see others in your future work for sure.

5.3.5 Our Camera Ontology So Far

Let us summarize our latest camera ontology (with only the class definitions) as shown in List 5.17. Notice that in previous sections, in order to show the related language features of OWL 1, we have discussed different ways to define classes. To avoid unnecessary complexities, we have not included all of them into our current camera ontology.

List 5.17 Our current camera ontology, with class definitions only

```
1: <?xml version="1.0"?>
2: <!DOCTYPE rdf:RDF [
3:     <!ENTITY owl "http://www.w3.org/2002/07/owl#" >
4:     <!ENTITY xsd "http://www.w3.org/2001/XMLSchema#" >
5:     <!ENTITY rdfs "http://www.w3.org/2000/01/rdf-schema#" >
6:     <!ENTITY myCamera "http://www.liyangyu.com/camera#" >
7: ]>
8:
9: <rdf:RDF
9a:    xmlns:rdf="http://www.w3.org/1999/02/22-rdf-syntax-ns#"
10:    xmlns:rdfs="http://www.w3.org/2000/01/rdf-schema#"
11:    xmlns:owl="http://www.w3.org/2002/07/owl#"
12:    xmlns:myCamera="http://www.liyangyu.com/camera#"
13:    xml:base="http://www.liyangyu.com/camera#">
14:
15: <owl:Class rdf:about="&myCamera;Camera">
16:   <rdfs:subClassOf>
17:     <owl:Restriction>
18:       <owl:onProperty rdf:resource="&myCamera;model"/>
19:       <owl:minCardinality
19a:           rdf:datatype="&xsd;nonNegativeInteger">
20:           1
21:       </owl:minCardinality>
22:     </owl:Restriction>
23:   </rdfs:subClassOf>
24: </owl:Class>
25:
26: <owl:Class rdf:about="&myCamera;Lens">
27: </owl:Class>
28:
29: <owl:Class rdf:about="&myCamera;Body">
30: </owl:Class>
31:
32: <owl:Class rdf:about="&myCamera;ValueRange">
33: </owl:Class>
34:
35: <owl:Class rdf:about="&myCamera;Digital">
36:   <rdfs:subClassOf rdf:resource="&myCamera;Camera"/>
37:   <rdfs:subClassOf>
38:     <owl:Restriction>
39:       <owl:onProperty
39a:           rdf:resource="&myCamera;effectivePixel"/>
40:       <owl:cardinality
40a:           rdf:datatype="&xsd;nonNegativeInteger">
41:           1
```

```
42:         </owl:cardinality>
43:       </owl:Restriction>
44:     </rdfs:subClassOf>
45: </owl:Class>
46:
47: <owl:Class rdf:about="&myCamera;Film">
48:    <rdfs:subClassOf rdf:resource="&myCamera;Camera"/>
49: </owl:Class>
50:
51: <owl:Class rdf:about="&myCamera;DSLR">
52:    <rdfs:subClassOf rdf:resource="&myCamera;Digital"/>
53: </owl:Class>
54:
55: <owl:Class rdf:about="&myCamera;PointAndShoot">
56:    <rdfs:subClassOf rdf:resource="&myCamera;Digital"/>
57: </owl:Class>
58:
59: <owl:Class rdf:about="&myCamera;Photographer">
60:    <rdfs:subClassOf
60a:        rdf:resource="http://xmlns.com/foaf/0.1/Person"/>
61: </owl:Class>
62:
63: <owl:Class rdf:about="&myCamera;Professional">
64:    <rdfs:subClassOf rdf:resource="&myCamera;Photographer"/>
65: </owl:Class>
66:
67: <owl:Class rdf:about="&myCamera;Amateur">
68:    <owl:intersectionOf rdf:parseType="Collection">
69:       <owl:Class rdf:about="http://xmlns.com/foaf/0.1/Person"/>
70:       <owl:Class>
71:         <owl:complementOf
71a:            rdf:resource="&myCamera;Professional"/>
72:       </owl:Class>
73:    </owl:intersectionOf>
74: </owl:Class>
75:
76: <owl:Class rdf:about="&myCamera;ExpensiveDSLR">
77:    <rdfs:subClassOf rdf:resource="&myCamera;DSLR"/>
78:    <rdfs:subClassOf>
79:       <owl:Restriction>
80:         <owl:onProperty rdf:resource="&myCamera;owned_by"/>
81a:             rdf:resource="&myCamera;Professional"/>
82:       </owl:Restriction>
83:    </rdfs:subClassOf>
84: </owl:Class>
85:
86: </rdf:RDF>
```

5.3.6 Define Properties: The Basics

Up to this point, for our project of rewriting the camera ontology using OWL 1, we have finished defining the necessary classes. It is now the time to define all the necessary properties.

Recall when creating ontologies using RDF schema, we have the following terms to use when it comes to describing a property:

```
rdfs:domain
rdfs:range
rdfs:subPropertyOf
```

With only three terms, a given application already shows impressive reasoning power. And more importantly, as we saw in Chap. 4, most of the reasoning power comes from the understanding of the properties by the application.

This shows an important fact: richer semantics embedded into the properties will directly result in greater reasoning capabilities. This is the reason why OWL 1, besides continuing to use these three methods, has greatly enhanced the ways to characterize a property, as we will see in this section.

The first thing to notice is the fact that defining properties using OWL 1 is quite different from defining properties using RDF schema. More specifically, when using RDFS terms, the general procedure is to define the property first and then use it to connect two things together: a given property can either connect one resource to another resource, or connect one resource to a typed or untyped value. Both connections are done by using the term `rdf:Property`.

In the world of OWL 1, two different classes are used to implement these two different connections:

- `owl:ObjectProperty` is used to connect a resource to another resource;
- `owl:DatatypePropery` is used to connect a resource to an `rdfs:Literal` (untyped) or an XML schema built-in datatype (typed) value.

In addition, `owl:ObjectProperty` and `owl:DatatypeProperty` are both subclasses of `rdf:Property`. For example, List 5.18 shows the definitions of `owned_by` property and `model` property (taken from List 4.13):

List 5.18 Definitions of `owned_by` and `model` property, as shown in List 4.13

```
<rdf:Property
    rdf:about="http://www.liyangyu.com/camera#owned_by">
  <rdfs:domain rdf:resource="#DSLR"/>
  <rdfs:range rdf:resource="#Photographer"/>
</rdf:Property>

<rdf:Property rdf:about="http://www.liyangyu.com/camera#model">
  <rdfs:domain rdf:resource="#Camera"/>
  <rdfs:range
      rdf:resource="http://www.w3.org/2001/XMLSchema#string"/>
</rdf:Property>
<rdfs:Datatype
    rdf:about="http://www.w3.org/2001/XMLSchema#string"/>
```

In OWL 1, these definitions will look like the ones shown in List 5.19:

List 5.19 Use OWL 1 terms to define `owned_by` and `model` property

```
<owl:ObjectProperty
    rdf:about="http://www.liyangyu.com/camera#owned_by">
  <rdfs:domain rdf:resource="#DSLR"/>
  <rdfs:range rdf:resource="#Photographer"/>
</owl:ObjectProperty>

<owl:DatatypeProperty
    rdf:about="http://www.liyangyu.com/camera#model">
  <rdfs:domain rdf:resource="#Camera"/>
  <rdfs:range
      rdf:resource="http://www.w3.org/2001/XMLSchema#string"/>
</owl:DatatypeProperty>
<rdfs:Datatype
    rdf:about="http://www.w3.org/2001/XMLSchema#string"/>
```

Notice that except using `owl:ObjectProperty` and `owl:DatatypeProperty`, the basic syntax of defining properties in both RDF schema and OWL 1 is quite similar. In fact, at this moment, we can go ahead define all the properties that appear in List 4.13. After defining these properties, we have a whole camera ontology written in OWL 1 on our hands. Our finished camera ontology is given in List 5.20.

List 5.20 Our camera ontology defined in OWL 1

```
1: <?xml version="1.0"?>
2: <!DOCTYPE rdf:RDF [
3:     <!ENTITY owl "http://www.w3.org/2002/07/owl#" >
4:     <!ENTITY xsd "http://www.w3.org/2001/XMLSchema#" >
5:     <!ENTITY rdfs "http://www.w3.org/2000/01/rdf-schema#" >
6:     <!ENTITY myCamera "http://www.liyangyu.com/camera#" >
7: ]>
8:
9: <rdf:RDF
9a:     xmlns:rdf="http://www.w3.org/1999/02/22-rdf-syntax-ns#"
10:     xmlns:rdfs="http://www.w3.org/2000/01/rdf-schema#"
11:     xmlns:owl="http://www.w3.org/2002/07/owl#"
12:     xmlns:myCamera="http://www.liyangyu.com/camera#"
13:     xml:base="http://www.liyangyu.com/camera#">
14:
15:   <owl:Class rdf:about="&myCamera;Camera">
16:    <rdfs:subClassOf>
17:     <owl:Restriction>
18:      <owl:onProperty rdf:resource="&myCamera;model"/>
19:      <owl:minCardinality
19a:          rdf:datatype="&xsd;nonNegativeInteger">
20:         1
21:      </owl:minCardinality>
22:     </owl:Restriction>
23:    </rdfs:subClassOf>
24:   </owl:Class>
25:
26:   <owl:Class rdf:about="&myCamera;Lens">
27:   </owl:Class>
28:
29:   <owl:Class rdf:about="&myCamera;Body">
30:   </owl:Class>
31:
32:   <owl:Class rdf:about="&myCamera;ValueRange">
33:   </owl:Class>
34:
35:   <owl:Class rdf:about="&myCamera;Digital">
36:    <rdfs:subClassOf rdf:resource="&myCamera;Camera"/>
37:    <rdfs:subClassOf>
38:      <owl:Restriction>
```

```
39:         <owl:onProperty
39a:            rdf:resource="&myCamera;effectivePixel"/>
40:         <owl:cardinality
40a:            rdf:datatype="&xsd;nonNegativeInteger">
41:          1
42:         </owl:cardinality>
43:       </owl:Restriction>
44:     </rdfs:subClassOf>
45: </owl:Class>
46:
47: <owl:Class rdf:about="&myCamera;Film">
48:     <rdfs:subClassOf rdf:resource="&myCamera;Camera"/>
49: </owl:Class>
50:
51: <owl:Class rdf:about="&myCamera;DSLR">
52:     <rdfs:subClassOf rdf:resource="&myCamera;Digital"/>
53: </owl:Class>
54:
55: <owl:Class rdf:about="&myCamera;PointAndShoot">
56:     <rdfs:subClassOf rdf:resource="&myCamera;Digital"/>
57: </owl:Class>
58:
59: <owl:Class rdf:about="&myCamera;Photographer">
60:     <rdfs:subClassOf
60a:            rdf:resource="http://xmlns.com/foaf/0.1/Person"/>
61: </owl:Class>
62:
63: <owl:Class rdf:about="&myCamera;Professional">
64:     <rdfs:subClassOf rdf:resource="&myCamera;Photographer"/>
65: </owl:Class>
66:
67: <owl:Class rdf:about="&myCamera;Amateur">
68:     <owl:intersectionOf rdf:parseType="Collection">
69:       <owl:Class
69a:            rdf:about="http://xmlns.com/foaf/0.1/Person"/>
70:       <owl:Class>
71:         <owl:complementOf
71a:            rdf:resource="&myCamera;Professional"/>
72:       </owl:Class>
73:     </owl:intersectionOf>
74: </owl:Class>
75:
76: <owl:Class rdf:about="&myCamera;ExpensiveDSLR">
77:     <rdfs:subClassOf rdf:resource="&myCamera;DSLR"/>
```

```
78:    <rdfs:subClassOf>
79:      <owl:Restriction>
80:        <owl:onProperty rdf:resource="&myCamera;owned_by"/>
81:        <owl:someValuesFrom
81a:             rdf:resource="&myCamera;Professional"/>
82:      </owl:Restriction>
83:    </rdfs:subClassOf>
84:  </owl:Class>
85:
86:  <owl:ObjectProperty rdf:about="&myCamera;owned_by">
87:    <rdfs:domain rdf:resource="&myCamera;DSLR"/>
88:    <rdfs:range rdf:resource="&myCamera;Photographer"/>
89:  </owl:ObjectProperty>
90:
91:  <owl:ObjectProperty rdf:about="&myCamera;manufactured_by">
92:    <rdfs:domain rdf:resource="&myCamera;Camera"/>
93:  </owl:ObjectProperty>
94:
95:  <owl:ObjectProperty rdf:about="&myCamera;body">
96:    <rdfs:domain rdf:resource="&myCamera;Camera"/>
97:    <rdfs:range rdf:resource="&myCamera;Body"/>
98:  </owl:ObjectProperty>
99:
100: <owl:ObjectProperty rdf:about="&myCamera;lens">
101:    <rdfs:domain rdf:resource="&myCamera;Camera"/>
102:    <rdfs:range rdf:resource="&myCamera;Lens"/>
103: </owl:ObjectProperty>
104:
105: <owl:DatatypeProperty rdf:about="&myCamera;model">
106:    <rdfs:domain rdf:resource="&myCamera;Camera"/>
107:    <rdfs:range rdf:resource="&xsd;string"/>
108: </owl:DatatypeProperty>
109: <rdfs:Datatype rdf:about="&xsd;string"/>
110:
111: <owl:ObjectProperty rdf:about="&myCamera;effectivePixel">
112:    <rdfs:domain rdf:resource="&myCamera;Digital"/>
113:    <rdfs:range rdf:resource="&myCamera;MegaPixel"/>
114: </owl:ObjectProperty>
115: <rdfs:Datatype rdf:about="&myCamera;MegaPixel">
116:    <rdfs:subClassOf rdf:resource="&xsd;decimal"/>
117: </rdfs:Datatype>
118:
119: <owl:ObjectProperty rdf:about="&myCamera;shutterSpeed">
120:    <rdfs:domain rdf:resource="&myCamera;Body"/>
```

```
121:    <rdfs:range rdf:resource="&myCamera;ValueRange"/>
122: </owl:ObjectProperty>
123:
124: <owl:DatatypeProperty rdf:about="&myCamera;focalLength">
125:    <rdfs:domain rdf:resource="&myCamera;Lens"/>
126:    <rdfs:range rdf:resource="&xsd;string"/>
127: </owl:DatatypeProperty>
128: <rdfs:Datatype rdf:about="&xsd;string"/>
129:
130: <owl:ObjectProperty rdf:about="&myCamera;aperture">
131:    <rdfs:domain rdf:resource="&myCamera;Lens"/>
132:    <rdfs:range rdf:resource="&myCamera;ValueRange"/>
133: </owl:ObjectProperty>
134:
135: <owl:DatatypeProperty rdf:about="&myCamera;minValue">
136:    <rdfs:domain rdf:resource="&myCamera;ValueRange"/>
137:    <rdfs:range rdf:resource="&xsd;float"/>
138: </owl:DatatypeProperty>
139: <rdfs:Datatype rdf:about="&xsd;float"/>
140:
141: <owl:DatatypeProperty rdf:about="&myCamera;maxValue">
142:    <rdfs:domain rdf:resource="&myCamera;ValueRange"/>
143:    <rdfs:range rdf:resource="&xsd;float"/>
144: </owl:DatatypeProperty>
145: <rdfs:Datatype rdf:about="&xsd;float"/>
146:
147: </rdf:RDF>
```

At this point, we have just finished rewriting our camera ontology using OWL 1 by adding the property definitions. Compared to the ontology defined using RDFS (List 4.13), List 5.20 includes a couple of new classes. I will leave it to you to update Fig. 4.3 to show these changes.

Now, this is only part of the whole picture. OWL 1 provides much richer features when it comes to property definitions. We will discuss these features in detail in the next several sections, but here is a quick look at these features:

- a property can be symmetric;
- a property can be transitive;
- a property can be functional;
- a property can be inverse functional;
- a property can be the inverse of another property.

5.3.7 Defining Properties: Property Characteristics

5.3.7.1 Symmetric Properties

A symmetric property describes the situation where if a resource R1 is connected to resource R2 by property P, then resource R2 is also connected to resource R1 by the same property. For instance, we can define a property friend_with for Photographer class, and if photographer A is friend_with photographer B, photographer B is certainly friend_with photographer A. This is shown in List 5.21:

List 5.21 Example of symmetric property

```
1: <owl:ObjectProperty
1a:     rdf:about="http://www.liyangyu.com/camera#friend_with">
2:   <rdf:type rdf:resource=
2a:       "http://www.w3.org/2002/07/owl#SymmetricProperty"/>
3:   <rdfs:domain rdf:resource="#Photographer"/>
4:   <rdfs:range rdf:resource="#Photographer"/>
5: </owl:ObjectProperty>
```

The key to indicate this property is a symmetric property lies in line 2. The definition in List 5.21 says the follows: friend_with is an object property which should be used to describe instances of class Photographer, its values are also instances of class Photographer, and it is a symmetric property.

Notice List 5.21 does have a simpler form, as shown in List 5.22:

List 5.22 Example of symmetric property using a simpler form

```
1: <owl:SymmetricProperty
1a:     rdf:about="http://www.liyangyu.com/camera#friend_with">
2:   <rdfs:domain rdf:resource="#Photographer"/>
3:   <rdfs:range rdf:resource="#Photographer"/>
4: </owl:SymmetricProperty>
```

It is important to know and understand the long form shown in List 5.21. One case where this long form is useful is the case when you need to define a property to be of several types, for example, a property that is symmetric and also functional (the functional property will be explained soon). In that case, the long form is the choice, and we just have to use multiple rdf:type elements.

Notice `owl:SymmetricProperty` is a subclass of `owl:ObjectProperty`. Therefore, `rdfs:range` of a symmetric property can only be a resource, and cannot be a literal or data type.

5.3.7.2 Enhanced Reasoning Power 7

Our application sees the following instance document:

```
<myCamera:Photographer
          rdf:about="http://www.liyangyu.com/people#Liyang">
   <myCamera:friend_with
          rdf:resource="http://www.liyangyu.com/people#Connie"/>
</myCamera:Photographer>
```

The application will be able to add the following two statements:

```
<http://www.liyangyu.com/people#Connie> rdf:type
myCamera:Photographer.
```

```
<http://www.liyangyu.com/people#Connie> myCamera:friend_with
<http://www.liyangyu.com/people#Liyang>.
```

5.3.7.3 Transitive Properties

A transitive property describes the situation where, if a resource `R1` is connected to resource `R2` by property `P`, and resource `R2` is connected to resource `R3` by the same property, then resource `R1` is also connected to resource `R3` by property `P`.

This can be a very useful feature in some cases. For example, photography is a fairly expensive hobby for most of us, and which camera to buy depends on which one offers a better ratio of quality to price. Therefore, even though a given camera is very expensive, if it provides excellent quality and performance, the ratio could be high. On the other hand, a `PointAndShoot` camera has a very appealing price but it may not offer you that much room to discover your creative side; therefore may not have a high ratio at all.

Let us define a new property called `betterQPRatio` to capture this part of the knowledge in our camera ontology. Obviously, this property should be able to provide us a way to compare two different cameras. Furthermore, we will also declare it to be a transitive property; therefore if camera `A` is `betterQPRatio` than camera `B`, and camera `B` is `betterQPRatio` than camera `C`, it should be true that Camera `A` is `betterQPRatio` than camera `C`.

List 5.23 shows the syntax we use in OWL 1 to define such a property:

List 5.23 Example of transitive property

```
1: <owl:ObjectProperty
1a:     rdf:about="http://www.liyangyu.com/camera#betterQPRatio">
2:   <rdf:type rdf:resource=
2a:      "http://www.w3.org/2002/07/owl#TransitiveProperty"/>
3:   <rdfs:domain rdf:resource="#Camera"/>
4:   <rdfs:range rdf:resource="#Camera"/>
5: </owl:ObjectProperty>
```

Not much explanation is needed. Again, `owl:TransitiveProperty` is a sub-class of `owl:ObjectProperty`. Therefore, `rdfs:range` of a transitive property can only be a resource, and cannot be a literal or a data type.

5.3.7.4 Enhanced Reasoning Power 8

Our application collects the following statement from one instance document:

```
<myCamera:DSLR
          rdf:about="http://www.liyangyu.com/camera#Nikon_D300">
  <myCamera:betterQPRatio
          rdf:resource="http://www.liyangyu.com/camera#Nikon_D70"/>
</myCamera:DSLR>
```

and in another RDF document, our application finds this statement:

```
<DSLR rdf:about="http://www.liyangyu.com/camera#Nikon_D70"
      xmlns="http://www.liyangyu.com/camera#">
  <betterQPRatio>
    <DSLR rdf:about=
             "http://www.liyangyu.com/camera#Nikon_D40"/>
  </betterQPRatio>
</DSLR>
```

our application will add the following statement:

```
<http://www.liyangyu.com/camera#Nikon_D300>
myCamera:betterQPRatio
<http://www.liyangyu.com/camera#Nikon_D40>.
```

Notice the usage of the namespace in the second instance file. Since the namespace attribute (`xmlns`) is added, there is no need to use QNames, which is used in the first instance file.

Furthermore, although these two statements are from two different instance files, our application is still able to draw the conclusion based on our camera ontology. Clearly, distributed information over the Web is integrated and processed by the machine because of two facts: first, we have expressed the related knowledge in our ontology, and second, even though the information is distributed all over the Web, the idea of using URIs to identify resources is the clue that connects them all.

5.3.7.5 Functional Properties

A functional property describes the situation where, for any given instance, there is at most one value for a property. In other words, it defines a many-to-one relation: there is at most one unique `rdfs:range` value for each `rdfs:domain` instance.

A good example would be our `manufactured_by` property. A camera includes a lens and a camera body, both of which include a number of different parts, and these parts can indeed be made in different countries around the world. If we ignore this complexity at this point, we can simply say that one given camera can only have one manufacturer, such as Nikon D300 is manufactured by Nikon Corporation. Clearly, different cameras can be manufactured by the same manufacturer.

List 5.24 shows a revised definition of `manufactured_by` property:

List 5.24 Example of functional property

```
1: <owl:ObjectProperty
1a:     rdf:about="http://www.liyangyu.com/camera#manufactured_by">
2:    <rdf:type rdf:resource=
2a:        "http://www.w3.org/2002/07/owl#FunctionalProperty"/>
3:    <rdfs:domain rdf:resource="#Camera"/>
4: </owl:ObjectProperty>
```

To see another example of a functional property, let us revisit the definition of property `effectivePixel`. Clearly, for a given digital camera, it has only one `effectivePixel` value, and we have indicated this fact by defining `Digital` and `effectivePixel` as shown in List 5.25:

List 5.25 Definitions of `Digital` class and `effectivePixel` property

```
<owl:Class rdf:about="http://www.liyangyu.com/camera#Digital">
  <rdfs:subClassOf rdf:resource="#Camera"/>
  <rdfs:subClassOf>
    <owl:Restriction>
      <owl:onProperty rdf:resource="#effectivePixel"/>
      <owl:cardinality rdf:datatype=
          "http://www.w3.org/2001/XMLSchema#nonNegativeInteger">
          1
      </owl:cardinality>
    </owl:Restriction>
  </rdfs:subClassOf>
</owl:Class>

<owl:ObjectProperty
    rdf:about="http://www.liyangyu.com/camera#effectivePixel">
  <rdfs:domain rdf:resource="#Digital"/>
  <rdfs:range
      rdf:resource="http://www.liyangyu.com/camera#MegaPixel"/>
</owl:ObjectProperty>
<rdfs:Datatype
    rdf:about="http://www.liyangyu.com/camera#MegaPixel">
  <rdfs:subClassOf
      rdf:resource="http://www.w3.org/2001/XMLSchema#decimal"/>
</rdfs:Datatype>
```

As you can see, `owl:cardinality` is used to accomplish the goal. In fact, this is equivalent to the following definitions shown in List 5.26:

List 5.26 Definition of `Digital` class and `effectivePixel` property (equivalent to List 5.25)

```
<owl:Class rdf:about="http://www.liyangyu.com/camera#Digital">
  <rdfs:subClassOf rdf:resource="#Camera"/>
</owl:Class>

<owl:FunctionalProperty
    rdf:about="http://www.liyangyu.com/camera#effectivePixel">
  <rdfs:domain rdf:resource="#Digital"/>
  <rdfs:range
      rdf:resource="http://www.liyangyu.com/camera#MegaPixel"/>
</owl:FunctionalProperty>
<rdfs:Datatype
    rdf:about="http://www.liyangyu.com/camera#MegaPixel">
  <rdfs:subClassOf
      rdf:resource="http://www.w3.org/2001/XMLSchema#decimal"/>
</rdfs:Datatype>
```

Therefore, a class with a property that has an `owl:cardinality` equal to 1 is the same as the class which has the same property defined as a functional property. OWL not only provides us with a much richer vocabulary to express more complex knowledge, but also gives us different routes to accomplish the same goal.

Notice `owl:FunctionalProperty` is a subclass of `rdf:Property`. Therefore, `rdfs:range` of a functional property can be a resource, a literal or a data type.

5.3.7.6   Enhanced Reasoning Power 9

Our application collects the following statement from one instance document:

```
<myCamera:DSLR
          rdf:about="http://www.liyangyu.com/camera#Nikon_D300">
  <myCamera:manufactured_by
            rdf:resource="http://dbpedia.org/resource/Nikon"/>
</myCamera:DSLR>
```

and in another RDF document, our application finds this statement:

```
<DSLR rdf:about="http://www.liyangyu.com/camera#Nikon_D300"
      xmlns="http://www.liyangyu.com/camera#">
<manufactured_by rdf:resource=
                  "http://www.freebase.com/view/en/nikon"/>
</DSLR>
```

our application will add the following statement:

```
<http://dbpedia.org/resource/Nikon> owl:sameAs
<http://www.freebase.com/view/en/nikon>.
```

Since property `manufactured_by` is defined as a functional property, and since the two instance files are both describing the same resource identified by `myCamera:Nikon_D300`, it is therefore straightforward to see the reason why the above statement can be inferred.

Notice that the URI `http://dbpedia.org/resource/Nikon`, coined by DBpedia, represents Nikon Corporation. Similarly, the following URI was created by freebase[8] to represent the same company,

```
http://www.freebase.com/view/en/nikon
```

---

[8] http://www.freebase.com/

and freebase is another experimental Web site in the area of the Semantic Web. Understanding the fact these two URIs represent the same company in real life is not a big deal for human minds and eyes. However, for machines to understand this fact is great progress, and we can easily imagine how much this will help us in a variety of applications.

5.3.7.7   Inverse Property

An inverse property describes the situation where if a resource R1 is connected to resource R2 by property P, then the inverse property of P will connect resource R2 to resource R1.

A good example in our camera ontology is the property owned_by. Clearly, if a camera is owned_by a Photographer, than we can define an inverse property of owned_by, say, own, to indicate that the Photographer own the camera. This example is given in List 5.27.

List 5.27   Example of inverse property

```
1: <owl:ObjectProperty
1a:     rdf:about="http://www.liyangyu.com/camera#owned_by">
2:   <rdfs:domain rdf:resource="#DSLR"/>
3:   <rdfs:range rdf:resource="#Photographer"/>
4: </owl:ObjectProperty>
5: <owl:ObjectProperty
5a:     rdf:about="http://www.liyangyu.com/camera#own">
6:   <owl:inverseOf rdf:resource="#owned_by"/>
7:   <rdfs:domain rdf:resource="#Photographer"/>
8:   <rdfs:range rdf:resource="#DSLR"/>
9: </owl:ObjectProperty>
```

Notice that compared to the definition of property owned_by, property own's values for rdfs:domain and rdfs:range are flipped from that in owned_by. Also note that owl:inverseOf is a property, not a class (recall that owl:FunctionalProperty is a subclass of rdf:Property). Therefore, it cannot be used to connect any rdfs:domain to any rdfs:range; it is only used as a constraint when some other property is being defined, as shown in List 5.27.

5.3.7.8   Enhanced Reasoning Power 10

Our application collects the following statement from a given instance document:

```
<myCamera:Photographer
          rdf:about="http://www.liyangyu.com/people#Liyang">
  <myCamera:own
      rdf:resource="http://www.liyangyu.com/camera#Nikon_D300"/>
</myCamera:Photographer>
```

and once it realizes the fact that own is an inverse property of owned_by, it will add the following statement, without us doing anything:

```
<http://www.liyangyu.com/camera#Nikon_D300> myCamera:owned_by
<http://www.liyangyu.com/people#Liyang>.
```

5.3.7.9   Inverse Functional Property

Recall the functional property discussed earlier: for a given rdfs:domain value, there is a unique rdfs:range value. An inverse functional property, as its name suggests, is just the opposite of functional property: for a given rdfs:range value, the value of the rdfs:domain property must be unique.

Let us go back to the camera review example, and also assume the reviewers themselves are often photographers. We would like to assign a unique reviewer ID to each photographer, so when they submit a review for a given camera, they can add their reviewer IDs into the submitted RDF documents.

The reviewerID property, in this case, should be modeled as an inverse functional property. Therefore, if two photographers have the same reviewerID, these two photographers should be the same person. List 5.28 shows the definition of reviewerID property.

List 5.28 Example of inverse functional property

```
1: <owl:DatatypeProperty
1a:     rdf:about="http://www.liyangyu.com/camera#reviewerID">
2:   <rdf:type rdf:resource=
2a:   http://www.w3.org/2002/07/owl#InverseFunctionalProperty"/>
3:   <rdfs:domain rdf:resource="#Photographer"/>
4:   <rdfs:range
4a:     rdf:resource="http://www.w3.org/2001/XMLSchema#string"/>
5: </owl:DatatypeProperty>
6: <rdfs:Datatype
6a:     rdf:about="http://www.w3.org/2001/XMLSchema#string"/>
```

In fact, we can make an even stronger statement about photographers and their reviewer IDs: not only is one reviewer ID is used to identify just one photographer, each photographer has only one reviewer ID. Therefore, we can define the `reviewerID` property as both a functional and an inverse functional property as shown in List 5.29.

List 5.29 A property can be both a functional and an inverse functional property

```
1: <owl:DatatypeProperty
1a:     rdf:about="http://www.liyangyu.com/camera#reviewerID">
2:   <rdf:type rdf:resource=
2a:     "http://www.w3.org/2002/07/owl#FunctionalProperty"/>
3:   <rdf:type rdf:resource=
3a:   "http://www.w3.org/2002/07/owl#InverseFunctionalProperty"/>
4:   <rdfs:domain rdf:resource="#Photographer"/>
5:   <rdfs:range
5a:     rdf:resource="http://www.w3.org/2001/XMLSchema#string"/>
6: </owl:DatatypeProperty>
7: <rdfs:Datatype
7a:     rdf:about="http://www.w3.org/2001/XMLSchema#string"/>
```

It is important to understand the difference between functional and inverse functional properties. A good example you can use to make the difference clear is the birthdate property: any given person can have only one birthdate; therefore, birthdate is a functional property. Is the birthdate property also an inverse functional property? Certainly not, because many people can have the same birthdate; if it were indeed an inverse functional property, then for a given date, only one person could be born on that date.

Similarly, e-mail as a property, should be an inverse functional property, because an e-mail address belongs to only one person. However, e-mail cannot be a functional property since one person can have several e-mail accounts, like most of us do.

Most ID-like properties are functional properties and inverse functional properties at the same time. For example, think of social security number, student ID, driver's license and passport number, just to name a few.

Finally, notice that `owl:InverseFunctionalProperty` is a subclass of `rdf:Property`. Therefore, `rdfs:range` of an inverse functional property can be a resource, a literal or a data type.

5.3.7.10 Enhanced Reasoning Power 11

Our application collects the following statement from one instance document:

```
<myCamera:Photographer
         rdf:about="http://www.liyangyu.com/camera#Liyang">
  <myCamera:reviewerID>reviewer-0910</myCamera:reviewerID>
</myCamera:Photographer>
```

and in another RDF document, our application finds this statement:

```
<myCamera:Photographer
         rdf:about="http://liyangyu.com/foaf.rdf#Liyang">
  <myCamera:reviewerID>reviewer-0910</myCamera:reviewerID>
</myCamera:Photographer>
```

our application will add the following statement:

```
<http://www.liyangyu.com/camera#Liyang> owl:sameAs
<http://liyangyu.com/foaf.rdf#Liyang>.
```

Since property `reviewerID` is defined as an inverse functional property, the reason behind the above statement is obvious.

5.3.8 Camera Ontology Written Using OWL 1

At this point, we have covered most of the OWL 1 language features, and our current version of the camera ontology is given in List 5.30. Notice that the class definitions are not changed (compared to List 5.17), but we have added some new properties and also modified some existing properties.

List 5.30 Camera ontology written in OWL 1

```
1: <?xml version="1.0"?>
2: <!DOCTYPE rdf:RDF [
3:     <!ENTITY owl "http://www.w3.org/2002/07/owl#" >
4:     <!ENTITY xsd "http://www.w3.org/2001/XMLSchema#" >
5:     <!ENTITY rdfs "http://www.w3.org/2000/01/rdf-schema#" >
6:     <!ENTITY myCamera "http://www.liyangyu.com/camera#" >
7: ]>
8:
9: <rdf:RDF
9a:     xmlns:rdf="http://www.w3.org/1999/02/22-rdf-syntax-ns#"
10:     xmlns:rdfs="http://www.w3.org/2000/01/rdf-schema#"
11:     xmlns:owl="http://www.w3.org/2002/07/owl#"
12:     xmlns:myCamera="http://www.liyangyu.com/camera#"
13:     xml:base="http://www.liyangyu.com/camera#">
14:
15:   <owl:Class rdf:about="&myCamera;Camera">
16:     <rdfs:subClassOf>
17:       <owl:Restriction>
18:         <owl:onProperty rdf:resource="&myCamera;model"/>
19:         <owl:minCardinality
20:             rdf:datatype="&xsd;nonNegativeInteger">
21:           1
22:         </owl:minCardinality>
23:       </owl:Restriction>
24:     </rdfs:subClassOf>
25:   </owl:Class>
26:
27:   <owl:Class rdf:about="&myCamera;Lens">
28:   </owl:Class>
29:
30:   <owl:Class rdf:about="&myCamera;Body">
31:   </owl:Class>
32:
33:   <owl:Class rdf:about="&myCamera;ValueRange">
34:   </owl:Class>
35:
36:   <owl:Class rdf:about="&myCamera;Digital">
37:     <rdfs:subClassOf rdf:resource="&myCamera;Camera"/>
38:     <rdfs:subClassOf>
39:       <owl:Restriction>
40:         <owl:onProperty
41:         <owl:cardinality
42:             rdf:datatype="&xsd;nonNegativeInteger">
43:           1
44:         </owl:cardinality>
```

```
45:      </owl:Restriction>
46:     </rdfs:subClassOf>
47:  </owl:Class>
48:
49:  <owl:Class rdf:about="&myCamera;Film">
50:     <rdfs:subClassOf rdf:resource="&myCamera;Camera"/>
51:  </owl:Class>
52:
53:  <owl:Class rdf:about="&myCamera;DSLR">
54:     <rdfs:subClassOf rdf:resource="&myCamera;Digital"/>
55:  </owl:Class>
56:
57:  <owl:Class rdf:about="&myCamera;PointAndShoot">
58:     <rdfs:subClassOf rdf:resource="&myCamera;Digital"/>
59:  </owl:Class>
60:
61:  <owl:Class rdf:about="&myCamera;Photographer">
62:     <rdfs:subClassOf
62a:          rdf:resource="http://xmlns.com/foaf/0.1/Person"/>
63:  </owl:Class>
64:
65:  <owl:Class rdf:about="&myCamera;Professional">
66:     <rdfs:subClassOf rdf:resource="&myCamera;Photographer"/>
67:  </owl:Class>
68:
69:  <owl:Class rdf:about="&myCamera;Amateur">
70:     <owl:intersectionOf rdf:parseType="Collection">
71:       <owl:Class
71a:           rdf:about="http://xmlns.com/foaf/0.1/Person"/>
72:       <owl:Class>
73:         <owl:complementOf
73a:             rdf:resource="&myCamera;Professional"/>
74:       </owl:Class>
75:     </owl:intersectionOf>
76:  </owl:Class>
77:
78:  <owl:Class rdf:about="&myCamera;ExpensiveDSLR">
79:     <rdfs:subClassOf rdf:resource="&myCamera;DSLR"/>
80:     <rdfs:subClassOf>
81:       <owl:Restriction>
82:         <owl:onProperty rdf:resource="&myCamera;owned_by"/>
83:         <owl:someValuesFrom
83a:             rdf:resource="&myCamera;Professional"/>
84:       </owl:Restriction>
```

```
85:      </rdfs:subClassOf>
86:   </owl:Class>
87:
88:   <owl:ObjectProperty rdf:about="&myCamera;owned_by">
89:     <rdfs:domain rdf:resource="&myCamera;DSLR"/>
90:     <rdfs:range rdf:resource="&myCamera;Photographer"/>
91:   </owl:ObjectProperty>
92:
93:   <owl:ObjectProperty rdf:about="&myCamera;manufactured_by">
94:     <rdf:type rdf:resource="&owl;FunctionalProperty"/>
95:     <rdfs:domain rdf:resource="&myCamera;Camera"/>
96:   </owl:ObjectProperty>
97:
98:   <owl:ObjectProperty rdf:about="&myCamera;body">
99:     <rdfs:domain rdf:resource="&myCamera;Camera"/>
100:    <rdfs:range rdf:resource="&myCamera;Body"/>
101: </owl:ObjectProperty>
102:
103: <owl:ObjectProperty rdf:about="&myCamera;lens">
104:    <rdfs:domain rdf:resource="&myCamera;Camera"/>
105:    <rdfs:range rdf:resource="&myCamera;Lens"/>
106: </owl:ObjectProperty>
107:
108: <owl:DatatypeProperty rdf:about="&myCamera;model">
109:    <rdfs:domain rdf:resource="&myCamera;Camera"/>
110:    <rdfs:range rdf:resource="&xsd;string"/>
111: </owl:DatatypeProperty>
112: <rdfs:Datatype rdf:about="&xsd;string"/>
113:
114: <owl:ObjectProperty rdf:about="&myCamera;effectivePixel">
115:    <rdfs:domain rdf:resource="&myCamera;Digital"/>
116:    <rdfs:range rdf:resource="&myCamera;MegaPixel"/>
117: </owl:ObjectProperty>
118: <rdfs:Datatype rdf:about="&myCamera;MegaPixel">
119:    <rdfs:subClassOf rdf:resource="&xsd;decimal"/>
120: </rdfs:Datatype>
121:
122: <owl:ObjectProperty rdf:about="&myCamera;shutterSpeed">
123:    <rdfs:domain rdf:resource="&myCamera;Body"/>
124:    <rdfs:range rdf:resource="&myCamera;ValueRange"/>
125: </owl:ObjectProperty>
126:
127: <owl:DatatypeProperty rdf:about="&myCamera;focalLength">
128:    <rdfs:domain rdf:resource="&myCamera;Lens"/>
```

```
129:    <rdfs:range rdf:resource="&xsd;string"/>
130: </owl:DatatypeProperty>
131: <rdfs:Datatype rdf:about="&xsd;string"/>
132:
133: <owl:ObjectProperty rdf:about="&myCamera;aperture">
134:   <rdfs:domain rdf:resource="&myCamera;Lens"/>
135:   <rdfs:range rdf:resource="&myCamera;ValueRange"/>
136: </owl:ObjectProperty>
137:
138: <owl:DatatypeProperty rdf:about="&myCamera;minValue">
139:   <rdfs:domain rdf:resource="&myCamera;ValueRange"/>
140:   <rdfs:range rdf:resource="&xsd;float"/>
141: </owl:DatatypeProperty>
142: <rdfs:Datatype rdf:about="&xsd;float"/>
143:
144: <owl:DatatypeProperty rdf:about="&myCamera;maxValue">
145:   <rdfs:domain rdf:resource="&myCamera;ValueRange"/>
146:   <rdfs:range rdf:resource="&xsd;float"/>
147: </owl:DatatypeProperty>
148: <rdfs:Datatype rdf:about="&xsd;float"/>
149:
150: <owl:ObjectProperty rdf:about="&myCamera;own">
151:   <owl:inverseOf rdf:resource="&myCamera;owned_by"/>
152:   <rdfs:domain rdf:resource="&myCamera;Photographer"/>
153:   <rdfs:range rdf:resource="&myCamera;DSLR"/>
154: </owl:ObjectProperty>
155:
156: <owl:DatatypeProperty rdf:about="&myCamera;reviewerID">
157:   <rdf:type rdf:resource="&owl;FunctionalProperty"/>
158:   <rdf:type rdf:resource="&owl;InverseFunctionalProperty"/>
159:   <rdfs:domain rdf:resource="&myCamera;Photographer"/>
160:   <rdfs:range rdf:resource="&xsd;string"/>
161: </owl:DatatypeProperty>
162: <rdfs:Datatype rdf:about="&xsd;string"/>
163:
164: </rdf:RDF>
```

5.4 OWL 2 Web Ontology Language

In this section, we discuss the latest W3C standard, the OWL 2 language. We first discuss the new features in general, and then move on to each individual language feature. Similarly, we use examples to illustrate the usage of these new features.

5.4.1   What Is New in OWL 2

OWL 2 offers quite an impressive list of new features, which can be roughly categorized into the following five major categories:

1. Syntactic sugar to make some common statements easier to construct.

   These features are called syntactic sugar because these new constructs do not alter the reasoning process built upon the ontology that uses these constructs; they are there to make the language easier to use. You will see more details in the next few sections.

2. New constructs that improve expressiveness.

   These features indeed increase the expressiveness. Examples include a collection of new properties, such as reflexive property, irreflexive property and asymmetric property, just to name a few. Also, the new qualified cardinality constraints greatly enhance the expressiveness of the language, as do the new features such as property chains and keys.

3. Extended support for datatypes.

   This includes more built-in datatypes being offered by OWL 2. In addition, OWL 2 allows users to define their own datatypes when creating ontologies. As you will see in later sections, these features can be very powerful to use.

4. Simple metamodeling capabilities and extended annotation capabilities.

   The metamodeling capability includes a new feature called punning. Annotation is also quite powerful in OWL 2. More specifically, you can add annotation to axioms, add domain and range information to annotation properties, and you can also add annotation information to annotations themselves.

5. New sublanguages: the profiles.

   Another feature offered by OWL 2 is its sublanguages, namely, OWL 2 EL, OWL 2 QL and OWL 2 PL. These language profiles offer different levels of tradeoff between expressiveness and efficiency, and therefore offer more choices to the users.

5.4.2   New Constructs for Common Patterns

This part of the new features is commonly referred to as the *syntactic sugar*, meaning that these features are simply shorthand; they do not change the expressiveness or the semantics. You can accomplish the same goals using OWL 1, but these constructs can make your ontology document more concise, as you will see in this section.

5.4.2.1 Common Pattern: Disjointness

In OWL 1, we can use `owl:disjointWith` to specify the fact that two classes are disjoint (see List 5.16). However, this can be used only on two classes. Therefore, to specify that several classes are mutually disjoint, `owl:disjointWith` has to be used on all the possible class pairs. For instance, if we have four classes, we need to use `owl:disjointWith` altogether six times.

OWL 2 provides a new construct called `owl:AllDisjointClasses` so we can do this with more ease. For example, List 5.16 specifies the fact that `DSLR` and `PointAndShoot` are disjoint to each other. For illustration purpose, let us say now we want to specify the fact that `Film` camera, `DSLR` camera and `PointAndShoot` camera are all disjoint (here we make the things a lot simpler by ignoring the fact that a `DSLR` camera can be used as a `PointAndShoot` camera, and also that a `Film` camera can be a `PointAndShoot` camera). List 5.31 shows how this has to be done using OWL 1's `owl:disjointWith` construct:

List 5.31 Using OWL 1's `owl:disjontWith` to specify three classes are pairwise disjoint

```
<owl:Class rdf:about="&myCamera;DSLR">
  <owl:disjointWith rdf:resource="&myCamera;PointAndShoot"/>
</owl:Class>

<owl:Class rdf:about="&myCamera;DSLR">
  <owl:disjointWith rdf:resource="&myCamera;Film"/>
</owl:Class>

<owl:Class rdf:about="&myCamera;PointAndShoot">
  <owl:disjointWith rdf:resource="&myCamera;Film"/>
</owl:Class>
```

Using OWL 2's construct, this can be as simple as shown in List 5.32.

List 5.32 Example of using `owl:AllDisjointClasses`

```
<owl:AllDisjointClasses>
  <owl:members rdf:parseType="Collection">
    <owl:Class rdf:about="&myCamera;DSLR"/>
    <owl:Class rdf:about="&myCamera;PointAndShoot"/>
    <owl:Class rdf:about="&myCamera;Film"/>
  </owl:members>
</owl:AllDisjointClasses>
```

If we have four classes which are pairwise disjoint, instead of following the pattern shown in List 5.31 and using six separate statements, we can simply add one more line in List 5.32.

Another similar feature is OWL 2's `owl:disjointUnionOf` construct. Recall List 5.10, where we defined one class called `CameraCollection`. This class obviously includes both the extension of `Digital` and the extension of `Film`. However, List 5.10 does not specify the fact that any given camera cannot be a digital camera and at the same time a film camera as well.

Now, again for simplicity, let us assume that `Film` camera, `DSLR` camera and `PointAndShoot` camera are all disjoint; what should we do if we want to define our `CameraCollection` class as a union of class `Film`, class `DSLR` and class `PointAndShoot`, and also indicate the fact that all these classes are pairwise disjoint?

If we do this by using only OWL 1 terms, we can first use `owl:unionOf` to include all the three classes, and then we can use three pairwise disjoint statements to make the distinction clear. However, this solution is as concise as the one shown in List 5.33, which uses OWL 2's `owl:disjointUnionOf` operator.

List 5.33 Example of using `owl:disjointUnionOf` operator

```
<owl:Class rdf:about="&myCamera;CameraCollection">
  <owl:disjointUnionOf>
    <owl:members rdf:parseType="Collection">
      <owl:Class rdf:about="&myCamera;DSLR"/>
      <owl:Class rdf:about="&myCamera;PointAndShoot"/>
      <owl:Class rdf:about="&myCamera;Film"/>
    </owl:members>
  </owl:disjointUnionOf>
  </owl:Class>
```

As we discussed at the beginning of this section, these constructs are simply shortcuts which do not change semantics or expressiveness. Therefore, there is no change in the reasoning power. Any reasoning capability we mentioned when discussing OWL 1 is still applicable here.

5.4.2.2   Common Pattern: Negative Assertions

Another important syntax enhancement from OWL 2 is the so-called *negative fact assertions*. To understand this, recall that OWL 1 provides the means to specify the value of a given property for a given individual; however, it does not offer a construct to *directly* state that an individual does not hold certain values for certain properties. It is true that you can still use only OWL 1's constructs to do this; however, that is normally not the most convenient and straightforward way.

To appreciate the importance of negative fact assertions, consider this statement: Liyang as a photographer does *not* own a Canon EOS-7D camera. This kind of native property assertions are very useful since they can explicitly claim that some fact is not true. In a world with open-end assumptions where anything is possible, this is certainly important.

Since `owl:ObjectProperty` and `owl:DatatypeProperty` are the two possible types of a given property, OWL 2 therefore provides two constructs as follows:

```
owl:NegativeObjectPropertyAssertion
owl:NegativeDataPropertyAssertion
```

List 5.34 shows how to use `owl:NegativePropertyAssertion` to specify the fact that Liyang as a photographer does *not* own a Canon EOS-7D camera (notice that namespace definitions are omitted, which can be found in List 5.30).

List 5.34 Example of using `owl:NegativePropertyAssertion`

```
1: <myCamera:Photographer rdf:about="http://liyangyu.com#liyang">
2: </myCamera:Photographer>
3:
4: <myCamera:DSLR
4a:          rdf:about="http://dbpedia.org/resource/Canon_EOS_7D">
5: </myCamera:DSLR>
6:
7:  <owl:NegativeObjectPropertyAssertion>
8:    <owl:sourceIndividual rdf:resource=
8a:                          "http://liyangyu.com#liyang"/>
9:    <owl:assertionProperty rdf:resource="&myCamera;own"/>
10:    <owl:targetIndividual rdf:resource=
10a:                         "http://dbpedia.org/resource/Canon_EOS_7D"/>
11: </owl:NegativeObjectPropertyAssertion>
```

Notice that lines 1–2 define the `Photographer` resource, and lines 4–5 define the `DSLR` resource. Again, `http://dbpedia.org/resource/Canon_EOS_7D` was coined by DBpedia project, and we are reusing it here to represent the Canon EOS-7D camera. Lines 7–11 state that the `Photographer` resource does not own the `DSLR` resource.

Obviously, the following OWL 2 constructs have to be used together to specify that two individuals are not connected by a property:

```
owl:NegativeObjectPropertyAssertion
owl:sourceIndividual
owl:assertionProperty
owl:targetIndividual
```

Similarly, `owl:NegativeDataPropertyAssertion` is used to say one resource does not have a specific value for a given property. For example, we can say Nikon D300 does not have an `effectivePixel` of 10, as shown in List 5.35.

List 5.35 Example of using owl:NegativeDataPropertyAssertion

```
1:   <owl:NegativeDataPropertyAssertion>
2:     <owl:sourceIndividual
2a:        rdf:resource="http://dbpedia.org/resource/Nikon_D300"/>
3:     <owl:assertionProperty rdf:resource="effectivePixel"/>
4:     <owl:targetValue
4a:        rdf:datatype="http://www.liyangyu.com/camera#MegaPixel">
5:        10
6:     </owl:targetValue>
7:   </owl:NegativeDataPropertyAssertion>
```

Again, as a summary, the following OWL 2 constructs have to be used together to finish the task:

```
owl:NegativeDataPropertyAssertion
owl:sourceIndividual
owl:assertionProperty
owl:targetValue
```

5.4.3 Improved Expressiveness for Properties

Recall that compared to RDF Schema, one of the main features offered by OWL 1 is the enhanced expressiveness around property definition and restrictions. These features have greatly improved the reasoning power as well.

Similarly, OWL 2 offers even more constructs for expressing additional restrictions on properties and new characteristics of properties. These features have become the centerpiece of the OWL 2 language, and we cover them in great detail in this section.

5.4.3.1 Property Self Restriction

OWL 1 does not allow the fact that a class is related to itself by some property. However, this feature can be useful in many applications. A new property called `owl:hasSelf` is offered by OWL 2 for this reason.

More specifically, `owl:hasSelf` has the type of `rdf:Property`, and its `rdfs:range` can be any resource. Furthermore, a class expression defined by using `owl:hasSelf` restriction specifies the class of all objects that are related to themselves via the given property.

Our camera ontology does not have the need to use `owl:hasSelf` property, but let us take a look at one example where this property can be useful.

For instance, in computer science, a thread is defined as a running task within a given program. Since a thread can create another thread, multiple tasks can be running at the same time. If we were to define an ontology for computer programming, we could use List 5.36 to define a class called `Thread`:

List 5.36 Example of `owl:hasSelf`

```
<owl:Class rdf:about="&myExample;Thread">
  <owl:equivalentClass>
    <owl:Restriction>
      <owl:onProperty rdf:resource="&myExample;create"/>
      <owl:hasSelf rdf:datatype="&xsd;boolean">true</owl:hasSelf>
    </owl:Restriction>
  </owl:equivalentClass>
</owl:Class>
```

which expresses the idea that all threads can create threads.

5.4.3.2   Property Self Restriction: Enhanced Reasoning Power 12

Our application sees the following statement from an instance document (notice the definition of `Thread` is given in List 5.36):

```
<myExample:Thread
    rdf:about="http://www.liyangyu.com/myExample#webCrawler">
</myExample:Thread>
```

The application will be able to add the following fact automatically:

```
<http://www.liyangyu.com/myExample#webCrawler>
myExample:create <http://www.liyangyu.com/myExample#webCrawler>.
```

5.4.3.3   Property Cardinality Restrictions

Let us go back to List 5.30 and take a look at the definition of `Professional` class. Now, instead of simply saying it is a sub-class of `Photographer`, we would like to say that any object of `Professional` photographer should own at least one `DSLR` camera. This can be done by using terms from the OWL 1 vocabulary, as shown in List 5.37.

List 5.37 A new definition of `Professional` class in our camera ontology

```
<owl:Class rdf:about="&myCamera;Professional">
  <rdfs:subClassOf rdf:resource="&myCamera;Photographer"/>
  <rdfs:subClassOf>
    <owl:Restriction>
      <owl:onProperty rdf:resource="&myCamera;own"/>
      <owl:minCardinality rdf:datatype="&xsd;nonNegativeInteger">
        1
      </owl:minCardinality>
    </owl:Restriction>
  </rdfs:subClassOf>
</owl:Class>
```

This is obviously a more expressive definition. Also, given the `rdfs:range` value of property `own` is specified as `DSLR` (see List 5.30), we know that any camera owned by a `Professional` photographer has to be a `DSLR` camera.

Now, what if we want to express the idea that a `Professional` photographer is someone who owns at least one `ExpensiveDSLR` camera? It turns out this is not doable by solely using the terms from the OWL 1 vocabulary, since it does not provide a way to further specify the class type of the instances to be counted, which is required for this case.

Similar requirements are quite common for other applications. For example, we may have the need to specify the fact that a marriage has exactly two persons, one is a female and one is a male. These category of cardinality restrictions are called *qualified cardinality restrictions*, where not only the count of some property is specified, but also the class type (or data range) of the instances to be counted has to be restrained.

OWL 2 provides the following constructs to implement qualified cardinality restrictions:

```
owl:minQualifiedCardinality
owl:maxQualifiedCardinality
owl:qualifiedCardinality
```

List 5.38 shows how `owl:minQualifiedCardinality` is used to define the class `Professional` photographer.

List 5.38 Example of using `owl:minQualifiedCardinality` constraint

```
<owl:Class rdf:about="&myCamera;Professional">
  <rdfs:subClassOf rdf:resource="&myCamera;Photographer"/>
  <rdfs:subClassOf>
    <owl:Restriction>
      <owl:minQualifiedCardinality
          rdf:datatype="&xsd;nonNegativeInteger">
        1
      </owl:minQualifiedCardinality>
      <owl:onProperty rdf:resource="&myCamera;own"/>
      <owl:onClass rdf:resource="&myCamera;ExpensiveDSLR"/>
    </owl:Restriction>
  </rdfs:subClassOf>
</owl:Class>
```

Comparing List 5.38 with List 5.37, you can see that `owl:onClass` is the key construct, which is used to specify the type of the instance to be counted.

Notice that `owl:minQualifiedCardinality` is also called the *at-least* restriction, for obvious reasons. Similarly, `owl:maxQualifiedCardinality` is the *at-most* restriction and `owl:qualifiedCardinality` is the *exact* cardinality restriction. We can replace the at-least restriction in List 5.38 with the other two restrictions respectively to create different definitions of `Professional` class. For example, when `owl:maxQualifiedCardinality` is used, a `Professional` can own at most one `ExpensiveDSLR`, and when `owl:qualifiedCardinality` is used, exactly one `ExpensiveDSLR` should be owned.

5.4.3.4   Property Cardinality Restrictions: Enhanced Reasoning Power 13

Qualified cardinality restrictions can greatly improve the expressiveness of a given ontology, and therefore, the reasoning power based on the ontology is also enhanced.

In the medical field, for example, using qualified cardinality restrictions, we can specify in an ontology the fact that a human being has precisely two limbs which are of type `Leg` and two limbs which are of type `Arm`. It is not hard to imagine this kind of precise information can be very useful for any application that is built to understand this ontology.

Let us understand more about this reasoning power by again using our camera ontology example. Our application sees the following statement from an instance document (notice the definition of `Professional` is given in List 5.38):

```
<myCamera:Professional
          rdf:about="http://www.liyangyu.com/people#Liyang">
</myCamera:Professional>
```

The application will be able to add the following two statements:

```
<http://www.liyangyu.com/people#Liyang> myCamera:own _x.
_x rdf:type myCamera:ExpensiveDSLR.
```

If we submit a query to ask who owns an expensive DSLR camera, this resource, http://www.liyangyu.com/people#Liyang, will be returned as one solution, even though the instance document does not explicitly claim this fact.

5.4.3.5 More About Property Characteristics: Reflexive, Irreflexive and Asymmetric Properties

Being reflexive in real life is quite common. For example, any set is a subset of its self. Also, in a given ontology, every class is its own subclass. If you use a reasoner on our camera ontology given in List 5.30 (we will see how to do this in later chapters), you can see statement like the following,

```
<http://www.liyangyu.com/camera#Camera> rdfs:subClassOf
<http://www.liyangyu.com/camera#Camera> .
```

These are all example of reflexive relations. Furthermore, properties can be reflexive, which means a reflexive property relates everything to itself. For this purpose, OWL 2 provides the owl:ReflexiveProperty construct so that we can use it to define reflexive properties.

For the purpose of our camera ontology, none of the properties we have so far is a reflexive property. Nevertheless, the following shows one example of how to define http://example.org/example1#hasRelative as a reflexive property:

```
<owl:ReflexiveProperty
     rdf:about="http://example.org/example1#hasRelative"/>
```

Clearly, every person has himself or herself as a relative, including any individual from the animal world. Also, understand that owl:ReflexiveProperty is a subclass of owl:ObjectProperty. Therefore, rdfs:range of a reflexive property can only be a resource, and cannot be a literal or a data type.

With the understanding or reflexive property, it is easier to understand an irreflexive property. More precisely, no resource can be related to itself by an irreflexive property. For example, nobody can be his own parent:

```
<owl:IrreflexiveProperty
     rdf:about="http://example.org/example1#hasParent"/>
```

Again, `owl:IrreflexiveProperty` is a subclass of `owl:ObjectProperty`. Therefore, `rdfs:range` of an irreflexive property can only be a resource, and cannot be a literal or a data type.

Finally, let us discuss asymmetric properties. Recall by using OWL 1 terms, we can define symmetric properties. For example, if resource `A` is related to resource `B` by this property, resource `B` will be related to `A` by the same property as well.

Besides symmetric relationships, there are asymmetric ones in the real world. A property is an asymmetric property if it connects `A` with `B`, but never connects `B` with `A`.

A good example is the `owned_by` property. Based on the definition in List 5.30, a `DSLR` camera is owned by a `Photographer`. Furthermore, we understand that the `owned_by` relationship should not go the other way around, i.e., a `Photographer` instance is `owned_by` a `DSLR` camera. To ensure this, `owned_by` can also be defined as a asymmetric property, as shown in List 5.39.

List 5.39 Example of using `owl:AsymmetricProperty`

```
<owl:AsymmetricProperty rdf:about="&myCamera;owned_by">
  <rdfs:domain rdf:resource="&myCamera;DSLR"/>
  <rdfs:range rdf:resource="&myCamera;Photographer"/>
</owl:AsymmetricProperty>
```

Again, `owl:AsymmetricProperty` is a subclass of `owl:ObjectProperty`. Therefore, `rdfs:range` of a asymmetric property can only be a resource, rather than a literal or a data type.

5.4.3.6 More About Property Characteristics: Enhanced Reasoning Power 14

The benefits of these property characteristics are quite obvious. For example, a major benefit is related to the open-world assumption that OWL makes. In essence, the open-world assumption means that from the absence of a statement alone, a deductive reasoner cannot infer that the statement is false.

This assumption implies a significant amount of computing work for any given reasoner, simply because there are so many unknowns. Therefore, if we can eliminate some unknowns, we will achieve better computing efficiency.

`owl:IrreflexiveProperty` and `owl:AsymmetricProperty` can help us in this regard. There will be more statements tagged with a clear `true`/`false` flag, and more queries can be answered with certainty. Notice, for example, asymmetric is stronger than simply not symmetric.

`owl:ReflexiveProperty` can also help us when it comes to reasoning. First notice that it is not necessarily true that every two individuals who are related by a reflexive property are identical. For example, the following statement

```
<http://www.liyangyu.com/people#Liyang> example1:hasRelative
<http://www.liyangyu.com/people#Connie>.
```

is perfectly fine, and the subject and object of this statement each represent a different resource in the real world.

Furthermore, at least the following statements can be added by a given application that understands a reflexive property:

```
<http://www.liyangyu.com/people#Liyang> example1:hasRelative
<http://www.liyangyu.com/people#Liyang>.
<http://www.liyangyu.com/people#Connie> example1:hasRelative
<http://www.liyangyu.com/people#Connie>.
```

Therefore, for a given query about `example1:hasRelative`, you will see more statements (facts) returned as solutions.

5.4.3.7   Disjoint Properties

In Sect. 5.4.2.1, we presented some OWL 2 language constructs that one can use to specify that a set of classes are mutually disjoint. Experiences from real applications suggest that it is also quite useful to have the ability to express the same disjointness of properties. For example, two properties are disjoint if there are no two individual resources that can be connected by both properties.

More specifically, OWL 2 offers the following constructs for this purpose:

```
owl:propertyDisjointWith
owl:AllDisjointProperties
```

`owl:propertyDisjointWith` is used to specify that two properties are mutually disjoint, and it is defined as a property itself. Also, `rdf:Property` is specified as the type for both its `rdfs:domain` and `rdfs:range` value. Given the fact that both `owl:ObjectProperty` and `owl:DatatypeProperty` are subclasses of `rdf:Property`, `owl:propertyDisjointWith` can therefore be used to specify the disjointness of both data type properties and object properties.

A good example from our camera ontology is the `owned_by` and `own` property. Given this statement,

```
<http://dbpedia.org/resource/Nikon_D300> myCamera:owned_by
<http://www.liyangyu.com/people#Liyang>.
```

we know the following statement should not exist:

```
<http://dbpedia.org/resource/Nikon_D300> myCamera:own
<http://www.liyangyu.com/people#Liyang>.
```

Therefore, property `owned_by` and property `own` should be defined as disjoint properties. List 5.40 shows the improved definition of property `owned_by`.

List 5.40   Example of using `owl:propertyDisjointWith`

```
<owl:AsymmetricProperty rdf:about="&myCamera;owned_by">
  <owl:propertyDisjointWith rdf:resource="&myCamera;own"/>
  <rdfs:domain rdf:resource="&myCamera;DSLR"/>
  <rdfs:range rdf:resource="&myCamera;Photographer"/>
</owl:AsymmetricProperty>
```

The syntax of using `owl:propertyDisjointWith` on data type properties is quite similar to the one shown in List 5.40, and we will not present any example here.

`owl:AllDisjointProperties` has a similar syntax as its counterpart, i.e., `owl:AllDisjointClasses`. For example, the following shows how to specify that a given group of object properties are pairwise disjoint:

```
<owl:AllDisjointProperties>
  <owl:members rdf:parseType="Collection">
    <owl:ObjectProperty rdf:about="&example;property1"/>
    <owl:ObjectProperty rdf:about="&example;property2"/>
    <owl:ObjectProperty rdf:about="&example;property3"/>
  </owl:members>
</owl:AllDisjointProperties>
```

Finally, notice that `owl:AllDisjointProperties` can be used on data type properties with the same syntax as shown above.

5.4.3.8   Disjoint Properties: Enhanced Reasoning Power 15

The benefits of disjoint properties are again related to the open-world assumption, and these properties can help us to eliminate unknowns. For example, given the definition of `owned_by` property as shown in List 5.40 and the following statement,

```
<http://dbpedia.org/resource/Nikon_D300> myCamera:owned_by
<http://www.liyangyu.com/people#Liyang>.
```

an application will be able to flag the following statement to be false:

```
<http://dbpedia.org/resource/Nikon_D300> myCamera:own
<http://www.liyangyu.com/people#Liyang>.
```

5.4.3.9 Property Chains

Property chain is a very useful feature introduced by OWL 2. It provides a way for us to define a property in terms of a chain of object properties that connect resources.

One common example used to show the power of property chain is the `hasUncle` relationship. More specifically, assume we have defined the following object properties:

```
example:hasParent rdf:type owl:ObjectProperty.
example:hasBrother rdf:type owl:ObjectProperty.
```

where `example` is a namespace prefix. Now, given the following statements,

```
example:Joe rdf:type foaf:Person;
                      example:hasParent example:John.
example:John rdf:type foaf:Person;
                      example:hasBrother example:Tim.
```

and as human readers, we should be able to understand the fact that Joe has an uncle named Tim.

How can we make our application understand this fact? We could have defined a new property, `example:hasUncle`, as follows:

```
example:hasUncle rdf:type owl:ObjectProperty.
```

And then we could have added one statement to explicitly specify the following fact:

```
example:Joe example:hasUncle example:Tim.
```

This is, however, not the preferred solution. First, an application should be smart enough to infer this fact, and manually adding it seems to be redundant. Second, we can add the facts that are obvious to us, but what about the facts that are not quite obvious? One of the main benefits of having ontology is to help us to find all the implicit facts, especially those that are not too apparent to us.

OWL 2 offers us the property chain feature for this kind of situation. Instead of defining `example:hasUncle` property as above, we can define it by using a property chain as shown in List 5.41 (notice that List 5.41 also includes the definitions of `example:hasParent` and `example:hasBrother` properties).

List 5.41 Example of using `owl:propertyChainAxiom`

```
<owl:ObjectProperty rdf:about="&example;hasParent">
</owl:ObjectProperty>

<owl:ObjectProperty rdf:about="&example;hasBrother">
</owl:ObjectProperty>

<rdf:Description rdf:about="&example;hasUncle">
  <owl:propertyChainAxiom rdf:parseType="Collection">
    <owl:ObjectProperty rdf:about="&example;hasParent"/>
    <owl:ObjectProperty rdf:about="&example;hasBrother"/>
  </owl:propertyChainAxiom>
</rdf:Description>
```

List 5.41 defines `example:hasUncle` as a property chain consisting of `example:hasParent` and `example:hasBrother`; any time `example:hasParent` and `example:hasBrother` exist, `example:hasUncle` exists. Therefore, if resource A `example:hasParent` resource B and resource B `example:hasBrother` resource C, then A `example:hasUncle` resource C, a fact that we no longer need to add manually.

With this basic understanding about property chain, let us explore how we can use it in our camera ontology.

If you are into the art of photography, you probably use SLR cameras. An SLR camera, as we know, has a camera body and a removable lens. Therefore, a photographer normally owns a couple of camera bodies, and a collection of camera lenses. One of these lenses will be mounted to one particular camera body to make up a complete camera.

Using our current camera ontology, we can have the following statements:

```
<http://www.liyangyu.com/people#Liyang> myCamera:own
<http://www.liyangyu.com/camera#Nikon_D300>.


<http://www.liyangyu.com/camera#Nikon_D300> myCamera:lens
<http://www.liyangyu.com/camera#Nikon_Lens_10-24mm>.
```

which specify the fact that `http://www.liyangyu.com/people#Liyang` owns a Nikon D300 camera, which uses a Nikon 10–24 mm zoom lens.

As human readers, by reading these two statements, we also understand that `http://www.liyangyu.com/people#Liyang` not only owns the Nikon D300 camera, but also owns the Nikon 10–24 mm zoom lens.

To let our application understand this fact, instead of adding a simple `myCamera:hasLens` property and then manually adding a statement to explicitly specify the lens and photographer ownership, the best solution is to use the property chain to define `myCamera:hasLens` property as shown in List 5.42.

List 5.42 Use property chain to define `myCamera:hasLens` property

```
<rdf:Description rdf:about="&myCamera;hasLens">
  <owl:propertyChainAxiom rdf:parseType="Collection">
    <owl:ObjectProperty rdf:about="&myCamera;own"/>
    <owl:ObjectProperty rdf:about="&myCamera;lens"/>
  </owl:propertyChainAxiom>
</rdf:Description>
```

With this definition in place, machine can reach the same understanding as we have, without the need to manually add the statement.

With the knowledge about property chains, we need to think carefully when defining properties. It is always good to consider the choices between whether to define it as a simple property, or to use property chain for the property. Using property chain will make our ontology more expressive and powerful when inferences are made. Finally, notice that property chain is only used on object properties, not on data type properties.

5.4.3.10   Property Chains: Enhanced Reasoning Power 16

The reasoning power provided by property chain is quite obvious. Given the definition of `myCamera:hasLens` (see List 5.42), if our application sees the following statements:

```
<http://www.liyangyu.com/people#Liyang> myCamera:own
<http://www.liyangyu.com/camera#Nikon_D300>.
```

```
<http://www.liyangyu.com/camera#Nikon_D300> myCamera:lens
<http://www.liyangyu.com/camera#Nikon_Lens_10-24mm>.
```

it will add the following statement automatically:

```
<http://www.liyangyu.com/people#Liyang> myCamera:hasLens
<http://www.liyangyu.com/camera#Nikon_Lens_10-24mm>.
```

5.4.3.11   Keys

OWL 2 allows keysSee owl003AhasKey to be defined for a given class. The `owl:hasKey` construct, more specifically, can be used to state that each named instance of a given class is uniquely identified by a property or a set of properties, which can be both data properties or object properties, depending on the specific application.

For example, in our camera ontology, we can use the `myCamera:reviewerID` property as the key for `Photographer` class, as shown in List 5.43.

List 5.43 Example of using `owl:hasKey`

```
<owl:Class rdf:about="&myCamera;Photographer">
  <owl:intersectionOf rdf:parseType="Collection">
    <owl:Class rdf:about="http://xmlns.com/foaf/0.1/Person"/>
    <owl:Class>
      <owl:hasKey rdf:parseType="Collection">
        <owl:DatatypeProperty rdf:about="&myCamera;reviewerID"/>
      </owl:hasKey>
    </owl:Class>
  </owl:intersectionOf>
</owl:Class>
```

With this definition in place, we can use `myCamera:reviewerID` property to uniquely identify any named `myCamera:Photographer` instance. Notice that in this example, we don't have the need to use multiple properties as a key, but you can if your application requires it (notice the `rdf:parseType` attribute for `owl:hasKey` construct).

It is also important to understand the difference between `owl:hasKey` and the `owl:InverseFunctionalProperty` axiom. The main difference is that the property or properties used as the key can only be used with those named individuals of the class on which `owl:hasKey` is defined. On the other hand, it is often true that an `owl:InverseFunctionalProperty` is used on a blank node, as we will see in Chap. 7.

5.4.3.12 Keys: Enhanced Reasoning Power 17

The benefit of having `owl:hasKey` is quite obvious: if two named instances of the class have the same values for each key property (or a single key property), these two individuals are the same. This can be easily understood without any example.

Notice that this is quite useful if two instances of the class are actually harvested from different instance documents over the Web. The identical key values of these two individuals tell us that these two instances, although each has a different URI, actually represent the same resource in the real world. This is one of the reasons why a Linked Data Web is possible, as we will see in later chapters.

5.4.4 Extended Support for Datatypes

As we know, OWL 1 depends on XML Schema (represented by `xsd:` prefix) for its built-in datatypes, and it has generally been working well. However, with more experience gained from ontology development in practice, some further

Table 5.1 Datatypes supported by OWL 2

Category	Supported datatypes
Decimal numbers and integers	`xsd:decimal, xsd:integer, xsd:nonNegativeInteger, xsd:nonPositiveInteger, xsd:positiveInteger, xsd:negativeInteger, xsd:long, xsd:int, xsd:short, xsd:byte, xsd:unsignedLong, xsd:unsignedInt, xsd:unsignedShort, xsd:unsignedByte`
Float-point numbers	`xsd:double, xsd:float`
Strings	`xsd:string, xsd:normalizedString, xsd:token, xsd:language, xsd:Name, xsd:NCName, xsd:NMTOKEN`
Boolean values	`xsd:boolean`
Binary data	`xsd:hexBinary, xsd:base64Binary`
IRIs	`xsd:anyURI`
Time instants	`xsd:dateTime, xsd:dateTimeStamp`
XML literals	`rdf:XMLLiteral`

requirements about datatypes have been identified. These new requirements can be summarized as follows:

- A wider range of supported datatypes is needed.
- The capability of adding constraints on datatypes should be supported.
- The capability of creating new user-defined datatypes is also required.

OWL 2 has provided answers to these requirements. The related new features are covered in this section in detail.

5.4.4.1 Wider Range of Supported Datatypes and Extra Built-in Datatypes

OWL 2 provides a wider range of supported datatypes, which are again borrowed from XML Schema Datatypes. Table 5.1 summarizes all the datatypes currently supported by OWL 2, and for details, you can refer to the related OWL 2 specification.[9]

Two new built-in types, namely, `owl:real` and `owl:rational`, are added by OWL 2. The definitions of these two types are shown in Table 5.2.

5.4.4.2 Restrictions on Datatypes and User-Defined Datatypes

OWL 2 allows users to define new datatypes by adding constraints on existing ones. The constraints are added via the so-called *facets*, another concept borrowed from XML schema.

---

[9] http://www.w3.org/TR/2009/REC-owl2-syntax-20091027/

Table 5.2 Two new built-in datatypes of OWL 2

Datatype	Definition
owl:real	The set of all real numbers
owl: rational	The set of all rational numbers, it is a subset of owl:real, and it contains the value of xsd:decimal

Restrictions on XML elements are called facets. The four bounds facets, for example, restrict a value to a specified range:

```
xsd:minInclusive, xsd:minExclusive
xsd:maxInclusive, xsd:maxExclusive
```

Notice that xsd:minInclusive and xsd:maxInclusive specify boundary values that are included in the valid range, and values that are outside the valid range are specified by xsd:minExclusive and xsd:maxExclusive facets.

Obviously, the above four bounds facets can be applied only to numeric types; other datatypes may have their own specific facets. For instance, xsd:length, xsd:minLength and xsd:maxLength are the three length facets that can be applied to any of the string-based types.

We will not get into much more detail about facets, but you can always learn more about them from the related XML Schema specifications. For our purpose, we are more interested in the fact that OWL 2 allows us to specify restrictions on datatypes by means of constraining facets.

More specifically, owl:onDatatype and owl:withRestrictions are the two main OWL 2 language constructs for this purpose. By using these constructs, we can, in fact, define new datatypes.

Let us take a look at one such example. We will define a new datatype called AdultAge, where the age has a lower bound of 18 years old. List 5.44 shows how this is done.

List 5.44 Example of using owl:onDatatype and owl:with Restrictions to define new datatype

```xml
<rdfs:Datatype rdf:about="&example;AdultAge">
  <owl:onDatatype rdf:resource="&xsd;integer"/>
  <owl:withRestrictions rdf:parseType="Collection">
    <rdf:Description>
      <xsd:minInclusive
          rdf:datatype="&xsd;integer">18</xsd:minInclusive>
    </rdf:Description>
  </owl:withRestrictions>
</rdfs:Datatype>
```

With this definition, AdultAge, as a user-defined datatype, can be used as the rdfs:range value for some property, like any other built-in datatype. To make this more interesting, we can use another facet to add an upper bound, thereby creating another new datatype called PersonAge, as shown in List 5.45.

List 5.45 Another example of using owl:onDatatype and owl: withRestrictions to define new datatype

```
<rdfs:Datatype rdf:about="&example;PersonAge">
  <owl:onDatatype rdf:resource="&xsd;integer"/>
  <owl:withRestrictions rdf:parseType="Collection">
    <rdf:Description>
      <xsd:minInclusive
          rdf:datatype="&xsd;integer">0</xsd:minInclusive>
    </rdf:Description>
    <rdf:Description>
      <xsd:maxInclusive
          rdf:datatype="&xsd;integer">150</xsd:maxInclusive>
    </rdf:Description>
  </owl:withRestrictions>
  </rdfs:Datatype>
```

In our camera ontology, we can change the definition of myCamera:MegaPixel datatype to make it much more expressive. For example, we can say that any digital camera's effective pixel value should be somewhere between 1.0 megapixel and 24.0 megapixel, as shown in List 5.46:

List 5.46 Define myCamera:MegaPixel as a new datatype

```
<rdfs:Datatype rdf:about="&myCamera;MegaPixel">
  <owl:onDatatype rdf:resource="&xsd;integer"/>
  <owl:withRestrictions rdf:parseType="Collection">
    <rdf:Description>
      <xsd:minInclusive
          rdf:datatype="&xsd;decimal">1.0</xsd:minInclusive>
    </rdf:Description>
    <rdf:Description>
      <xsd:maxInclusive
          rdf:datatype="&xsd;decimal">24.0</xsd:maxInclusive>
    </rdf:Description>
  </owl:withRestrictions>
</rdfs:Datatype>
```

Similarly, we can define another new datatype called `myCamera:CameraModel`, which, for example, should be an `xsd:string` with `xsd:maxLength` no longer than 32 characters. We will leave this as an exercise for you — at this point, it should be not difficult at all.

5.4.4.3   Data Range Combinations

Just as new classes can be constructed by combining existing ones, new datatypes can be created by combining existing datatypes. OWL 2 provides the following constructs for this purpose:

```
owl:datatypeComplementOf
owl:intersectionOf
owl:unionOf
```

These are quite straightforward to understand. `owl:unionOf`, for example, creates a new datatype by using a union on existing data ranges.

List 5.47 shows the definition of a new datatype called `MinorAge`, which is created by combining two existing datatypes:

List 5.47 Example of using `owl:intersectionOf` and `owl:datatypeComplementOf` to define new datatype

```
<rdfs:Datatype rdf:about="&example;MinorAge">
  <owl:equivalentClass>
    <owl:intersectionOf rdf:parseType="Collection">
      <rdfs:Datatype rdf:about="&example;PersonAge"/>
      <rdfs:Datatype>
        <owl:datatypeComplementOf
             rdf:resource="&example;AdultAge"/>
      </rdfs:Datatype>
    </owl:intersectionOf>
  </owl:equivalentClass>
</rdfs:Datatype>
```

Therefore, a person who has a `MinorAge` is younger than 18 years old.

5.4.5 Punning and Annotations

5.4.5.1 Understanding Punning

OWL 1 (more specifically, OWL 1 DL) has strict rules about separation of namespaces. For example, a URI cannot be typed as both a class and an individual in the same ontology.

OWL 2 relaxes this requirement: you can the same IRI for entities of different kinds, thus treating, for example, a resource as both a class and an individual of a class. This feature is referred to as *punning*.

Let us take a look at one example. Recall we have borrowed this URI from DBpedia project, `http://dbpedia.org/resource/Nikon_D300`, to represent a Nikon D300 camera. And obviously, it is an instance of class `myCamera:DSLR`:

```
<myCamera:DSLR
        rdf:about="http://dbpedia.org/resource/Nikon_D300"/>
```

However, there is not just one Nikon D300 camera in the world, Nikon must have produced thousands of them. For example, I have one Nikon D300 myself. I can use the following URI to represent this particular Nikon D300:

```
http://liyangyu.com/resource/Nikon_D300
```

Therefore, it is natural for me to make the following statement:

```
<rdf:Description
    rdf:about="http://www.liyangyu.com/camera#Nikon_D300">
  <rdf:type
    rdf:resource="http://dbpedia.org/resource/Nikon_D300"/>
</rdf:Description>
```

Clearly, `http://dbpedia.org/resource/Nikon_D300` represents a class in this statement. Therefore, this same URI can represent both a class and an individual resource.

Notice, however, the reasoning engine will interpret them as two different and independent entities, that is, entities that are not logically connected but just happen to have the same-looking name. Statements we make about the individual nature of Nikon D300 do not affect the class nature of Nikon D300, and vice versa.

There are also some restrictions in OWL 2 about punning:

- One IRI cannot denote both a datatype property and an object project.
- One IRI cannot be used for both a class and a datatype.

So why is punning useful to us? To put it simply, punning can be used for stating facts about classes and properties themselves.

For example, when we treat `http://dbpedia.org/resource/Nikon_D300` as an instance of class `myCamera:DSLR`, we are using `myCamera:DSLR` as a metaclass. In fact, punning is also referred to as *metamodelingSee* punning.

Metamodeling is related to annotations (more about annotation in the next section). They both provide ways to associate additional information with classes and properties, and the following rules-of-the-thumb are often applied to determine when to use which construct:

- Metamodeling should be used when the information attached to entities should be considered as part of the domain.
- Annotations should be used when the information attached to entities should not be considered as part of the domain and should not contribute to the logical consequences of the underlying ontology.

As a quick example, the facts that my Nikon D300 is a specific instance of the class of Nikon D300 and Nikon D300 in general is a digital SLR camera are statements about the domain. These facts are therefore better represented in our camera ontology by using metamodeling. In contrast, a statement about who created the IRI that represents a Nikon D300 camera does not describe the actual domain itself, and it should be represented via annotation.

5.4.5.2   OWL Annotations, Axioms About Annotation Properties

Annotation is not something new, but it is enhanced by OWL 2. In this section, we first discuss annotations by OWL 1 (you can still find them in ontologies created by using OWL 1), and we then cover annotation constructs provided by OWL 2.

OWL 1 allows classes, properties, individuals and ontology headers to be annotated with useful information such as labels, comments, authors, creation date, etc. This information could be important if the ontology is to be reused by someone else.

Notice that OWL 1 annotation simply associates property–value pairs to ontology entities, or to the entire ontology itself. This information is merely for human eyes and is not part of the semantics of the ontology, and will therefore be ignored by most reasoning engines. The commonly used annotation constructs offered by OWL 1 are summarized in Table 5.3.

These constructs are quite straightforward and easy to use. For example, the following shows annotation property `rdfs:comment` is used to add information to `myCamera:Lens` class, providing a natural language description of its meaning:

```
<owl:Class rdf:about="&myCamera;Lens">
   <rdfs:comment>represents the set of all camera lenses.
   </rdfs:comment>
</owl:Class>
```

Table 5.3 OWL 1's annotation properties

Annotation property	Usage
owl: versionInfo	Provides basic information for version control purpose
rdfs:label	Supports a natural language label for the resource/property
rdfs:comment	Supports a natural language comment about a resource/property
rdfs:seeAlso	Provides a way to identify more information about the resource
rdfs: isDefinedBy	Provides a link pointing to the source of information about the resource

You will see more examples of using these properties in later chapters.

OWL 1 also offers the ability to create user-defined annotation properties. More specifically, a user-defined annotation property should be defined by using the owl: AnnotationProperty construct, before we can use this property. List 5.48 shows an example of using a user-defined annotation property:

List 5.48 Example of using owl:AnnotationProperty to declare a user-defined annotation property

```
1: <?xml version="1.0"?>
2: <rdf:RDF
2a:     xmlns:rdf="http://www.w3.org/1999/02/22-rdf-syntax-ns#"
3:     xmlns:rdfs="http://www.w3.org/2000/01/rdf-schema#"
4:     xmlns:owl="http://www.w3.org/2002/07/owl#"
5:     xmlns:dc="http://www.purl.org/metadata/dublin-core#"
6:     xmlns:myCamera="http://www.liyangyu.com/camera#"
7:     xml:base="http://www.liyangyu.com/camera#">
8:
9:  <owl:AnnotationProperty rdf:about=
9a:           "http://www.purl.org/metadata/dublin-core#date">
10: </owl:AnnotationProperty>
11:
12: <owl:Class rdf:about="http://www.liyangyu.com/camera#Lens">
13:    <dc:date rdf:datatype=
13a:                "http://www.w3.org/2001/XMLSchema#date">
13b:    2009-09-10</dc:date>
14: </owl:Class>
```

The goal is to annotate the date on which class Lens was created. To do so, we reuse the terms in Dublin Core and explicitly declare dc:date as a user-defined annotation property (lines 9–10) and then use it on class Lens (line 13) to signal the date when this class is defined.

With the understanding about annotations in OWL 1, let us take a look at what is offered by OWL 2. An obvious improvement is that OWL 1 did not allow annotations of axioms, but OWL 2 does. As a summary, OWL 2 allows for annotations on ontologies, entities (classes, properties and individuals), anonymous individuals, axioms and also on annotations themselves.

Without covering all these new features in detail, we will concentrate on how to add annotation information on axioms and how to make statements about annotations themselves.

To add annotation information about a given axiom, we need the following OWL 2 language constructs:

```
owl:Axiom
owl:annotatedSource
owl:annotatedProperty
owl:annotatedTarget
```

List 5.49 shows some possible annotation on the following axiom:

```
<owl:Class rdf:about="&myCamera;DSLR">
  <rdfs:subClassOf rdf:resource="&myCamera;Digital"/>
</owl:Class>
```

List 5.49 Annotations on a given axiom

```
<owl:Axiom>
  <owl:annotatedSource rdf:resource="&myCamera;DSLR"/>
  <owl:annotatedProperty rdf:resource="&rdfs;subClassOf"/>
  <owl:annotatedTarget rdf:resource="&myCamera;Digital"/>
  <rdfs:comment>
    States that every DSLR is a Digital camera.
  </rdfs:comment>
</owl:Axiom>
```

This probably reminds you of the RDF reification vocabulary that we discussed in Chap. 2. They indeed share some similarities. For example, such annotations are often used in tools to provide natural language text to be displayed in `help` windows.

OWL 2 also allows us to add axioms about annotation properties. For example, we can specify the domain and range of a given annotation property. In addition, annotation properties can participate in an annotation property hierarchy. All these can all be accomplished by using the constructs that you are already familiar with: `rdfs:subPropertyOf`, `rdfs:domain` and `rdfs:range`.

If an annotation property's `rdfs:domain` value has been specified, that annotation property can only be used to add annotations to the entities whose type is the specified type. Similarly, if the `rdfs:range` property of an annotation property has been specified, the added annotation information can only assume values that have the type specified by its `rdfs:range` property. Since these are all quite straightforward, we will skip the examples.

Finally, understand that the annotations we have discussed here carry no semantics in the OWL 2 Direct Semantics (more on this in later sections), with the exception of axioms about annotation properties. These special axioms have no semantic meanings in the OWL 2 Direct Semantics, but they do have the standard RDF semantics in the RDF-based Semantics, via the mapping RDF vocabulary.

5.4.6   Other OWL 2 Features

5.4.6.1   Entity Declarations

As developers, we know most programming languages require us to declare a variable first before we can actually use it. However, this is not the case when developing ontologies using OWL 1: we can use any entity, such as a class, an object property or an individual anywhere in the ontology without any prior announcement.

This can be understood as a convenience for the developers. However, the lack of error checking could also be a problem. In practice, for example, if any entity were mistyped in a statement, there would be no way of catching that error at all.

For this reason, OWL 2 has introduced the notion of *entity declaration*. The idea is that every entity contained in an ontology should be declared first before it can be used in that ontology. Also, a specific type (class, datatype property, object property, datatype, annotation property or individual) should be associated with the declared entity. With this information, OWL 2 supporting tools can check for errors and consistency before the ontology is actually being used.

For example, in our camera ontology, the class `myCamera:Camera` should be declared as follows before its complete class definition:

```
<owl:Class rdf:about="&myCamera;Camera"/>
```

Similarly, the following statements declare a new datatype, an object property and a user-defined annotation property:

```
<rdfs:Datatype rdf:about="&myCamera;MegaPixel"/>
<owl:ObjectProperty rdf:about="&myCamera;own"/>
<owl:AnnotationProperty
    rdf:about="http://www.purl.org/metadata/dublin-core#date"/>
```

To declare an individual, a new OWL construct, `owl:NamedIndividual` can be used. The following statement declares a Nikon D300 camera will be specified in the ontology as an individual:

```
<owl:NamedIndividual
    rdf:about="http://dbpedia.org/resource/Nikon_D300"/>
```

Table 5.4 Top and bottom object/data properties

Type	Usage
`owl:topObjectProperty` (universal object property)	All pairs of individuals are connected by `owl:topObjectProperty`
`owl:bottomObjectProperty` (empty object property)	No individuals are connected by `owl:bottomObjectProperty`
`owl:topDataProperty` (universal data property)	All individuals are connected with all literals by `owl:topDataProperty`
`owl:bottomDataProperty` (empty data property)	No individual is connected with a literal by `owl:bottomDataProperty`

Finally, understand that these declarations are optional, and they do not affect the meanings of OWL 2 ontologies and therefore have no effect on reasoning either. However, using declaration is always recommended to ensure the quality of the ontology.

5.4.6.2   Top and Bottom Properties

OWL 1 has built-in top and bottom entities for classes, namely, `owl:Thing` and `owl:Nothing`. `owl:Thing` represents an universal class, and `owl:Nothing` represents an empty class.

In addition to the above class entities, OWL 2 provides top and bottom object and data properties. These constructs and their usage are summarized in Table 5.4.

5.4.6.3   Imports and Versioning

Imports and versioning are important aspects of the ontology management task. In this section, we first discuss how imports and versioning are handled in OWL 1, since quite a lot of ontologies are created when only OWL 1 is available. We then examine the new features of imports and versioning provided by OWL 2.

To understand handling imports and versioning in OWL 1, we first must understand several related concepts. One of these concepts is the ontology name, which is typically contained in a section called *ontology header*.

The ontology header of a given ontology is part of the ontology document, and it describes the ontology itself. For example, List 5.50 can be the ontology header of our camera ontology:

List 5.50 Ontology header of our camera ontology

```
1: <owl:Ontology rdf:about="">
2:    <owl:versionInfo>v.10</owl:versionInfo>
3:    <rdfs:comment>our camera ontology</rdfs:comment>
4: </owl:Ontology>
```

Line 1 of List 5.50 declares an RDF resource of type `owl:Ontology`, and the name of this resource is given by its `rdf:about` attribute. Indeed, as with anything else in the world, an ontology can be simply treated as a resource. Therefore, we can assign a URI to it and describe it by using the terms from the OWL vocabulary.

Notice in List 5.50, the URI specified by `rdf:about` attribute points to an empty string. In this case, the base URI specified by `xml:base` attribute (line 13, List 5.30) will be taken as the name of this ontology. This is also part of the reason why we have line 13 in List 5.30.

With this said, the following statement will be created by any parser that understands OWL ontology:

`<http://www.liyangyu.com/camera> rdf:type owl:Ontology.`

and a given class in this ontology, such as `Camera` class, will have the following URI:

`http://www.liyangyu.com/camera``#Camera`

Similarly, a given property in this ontology, such as `model` property, will have the following URI:

`http://www.liyangyu.com/camera``#model`

and this is exactly what we want to achieve.

Now, with this understanding about the name of a given ontology, let us study how `owl:imports` works in OWL 1. List 5.51 shows a new ontology header which uses `owl:imports` construct:

List 5.51 Our camera ontology header which uses `owl:imports`

```
1: <owl:Ontology rdf:about="">
2:    <owl:versionInfo>v.10</owl:versionInfo>
3:    <rdfs:comment>our camera ontology</rdfs:comment>
4:    <owl:imports
4a:       rdf:resource="http://www.example.org/exampleOntology"/>
5: </owl:Ontology>
```

Clearly, line 4 of List 5.51 tries to import another ontology into our camera ontology. Notice this is used only as an example to show the usage of `owl:imports` construct; there is currently no real need for our camera ontology to import another ontology yet.

First off, understand `owl:imports` is a property with class `owl:Ontology` as both its `rdfs:domain` and `rdfs:range` value. It is used to make reference to another

OWL ontology that contains definitions, and those definitions are considered part of the definitions of the importing ontology. The `rdf:resource` attribute of `owl:imports` specifies the URI (name) of the ontology being imported.

In OWL 1, importing another ontology is done by "name and location". In other words, the importing ontology is required to contain a URI that points to the location of the imported ontology, and this location should match with the name of the imported ontology as well.

One way to understand this "name and location" rule is to think about the possible cases where our camera ontology (List 5.30) is imported by other ontologies. For example, every such importing ontology has to have a statement like this:

```
<owl:imports rdf:resource="http://www.liyangyu.com/camera"/>
```

The importing ontology then expects our camera ontology to have a name specified by `http://www.liyangyu.com/camera`, and our camera ontology has to be located at `http://www.liyangyu.com/camera` as well. This is why we use an empty `rdf:about` attribute (see List 5.50) and at the same time, we specify the `xml:base` attribute on line 13 of List 5.30. By doing so, we can guarantee the location and the name of our camera ontology match each other (since the value of `xml:base` is taken as the name of the ontology), and every importing ontology can find our camera ontology successfully.

This coupling of names and locations in OWL 1 works well when ontologies are published at a fixed location on the Web. However, applications quite often use ontologies off-line (the ontology has been downloaded to some local ontology repositories before hand). Also, ontologies can be moved to other locations. Therefore, in real application world, ontology names and their locations may not match at all.

This has forced the users to manually adjust the names of ontologies and the `owl:imports` statements in the importing ontologies. This is obviously a cumbersome solution to the situation. In addition, these problems get more acute when considering the multiple versions of a given ontology. The specification of OWL 1 provides no guidelines on how to handle such cases at all.

OWL 2's solution is quite simple: it specifies that importing another ontology should be implemented by the location, rather than the name, of the imported ontology.

To understand this, we need to start from ontology version management in OWL. More specifically, in OWL 1, a simple construct called `owl:versionInfo` is used for version management, as shown on line 2 of List 5.51. In OWL 2, on the other hand, a new language construct, `owl:versionIRI`, is introduced to replace `owl:versionInfo`. For example, our camera ontology can have a ontology header as shown in List 5.52.

List 5.52 Ontology header of our camera ontology using

```
<owl:Ontology rdf:about="">
  <owl:versionIRI>
    http://www.liyangyu.com/camera/v1
  </owl:versionIRI>
  <rdfs:comment>our camera ontology</rdfs:comment>
</owl:Ontology>
```

With the usage of `owl:versionIRI`, each OWL 2 ontology has two identifiers: the usual ontology IRI that identifies the name of the ontology, and the value of `owl:versionIRI`, which identifies a particular version of the ontology.

In our case (List 5.52), since the `rdf:about` attribute points to an empty string, the IRI specified by `xml:base` attribute (line 13, List 5.30) is taken as the name of this ontology, which will remain stable. The second identifier for this ontology, i.e., `http://www.liyangyu.com/camera/v1`, is used to represent the current version.

OWL 2 has specified the following rules when publishing an ontology:

- An ontology should be stored at the location specified by its `owl:versionIRI` value.
- The latest version of the ontology should be located at the location specified by the ontology IRI.
- If no version IRI is ever used, the ontology should be located at the location specified by the ontology IRI.

With this said, the importing schema is quite simple:

- If it does not matter which version is desired, the ontology IRI should be the used as the `owl:imports` value.
- If a particular version is needed, the particular version IRI should be used as the `owl:imports` value.

In OWL 2, this is called the "importing by location" rule. With this schema, publishing a new current version of an ontology involves placing the new ontology at the appropriate location as identified by the version IRI, and replacing the ontology located at the ontology URI with this new ontology.

Before we move on to the next topic, there are two more things we need to know about `owl:imports`. First off, notice `owl:imports` property is transitive, that is, if ontology A imports ontology B, and B imports C, then ontology A imports both B and C.

Second, it is true that `owl:imports` property includes other ontologies whose content is assumed to be part of the current ontology, and the imported ontologies provide definitions that can be used directly. However, `owl:imports` does not provide any shorthand notation when it comes to actually using the terms from the imported ontology. Therefore, it is common to have a corresponding namespace declaration for any ontology that is imported.

5.4.7   OWL Constructs in Instance Documents

There are several terms from the OWL vocabulary that can be used in instance documents. These terms can be quite useful, and we cover them here in this section.

The first term is `owl:sameAs`, which is often used to link one individual to another, indicating the two URI references actually refer to the same resource in the world. Obviously, it is unrealistic to assume everyone will use the same URI to represent the same resource; thus URI aliases cannot be avoided in practice, and `owl:sameAs` is a good way to connect these aliases together.

List 5.53 describes Nikon D300 camera as a resource, and it also indicates that the URI coined by DBpedia in fact represents exactly the same resource:

List 5.53 Example of using `owl:sameAs`

```
1:  <?xml version="1.0"?>
2:  <rdf:RDF
2a:      xmlns:rdf="http://www.w3.org/1999/02/22-rdf-syntax-ns#"
3:       xmlns:rdfs="http://www.w3.org/2000/01/rdf-schema#"
4:       xmlns:owl="http://www.w3.org/2002/07/owl#"
5:       xmlns:myCamera="http://www.liyangyu.com/camera#">
6:
7:  <rdf:Description
7a:       rdf:about="http://www.liyangyu.com/camera#Nikon_D300">
8:       <rdf:type
8a:          rdf:resource="http://www.liyangyu.com/camera#DSLR"/>
9:       <owl:sameAs
9a:          rdf:resource="http://dbpedia.org/resource/Nikon_D300"/>
10: </rdf:Description>
11:
12: </rdf:RDF>
```

Based on List 5.53, the following two URIs actually represent the same camera, namely, the Nikon D300:

```
http://www.liyangyu.com/camera#Nikon_D300
http://dbpedia.org/resource/Nikon_D300
```

If you happen to have read some earlier documents about OWL, you might have come across another OWL term called `owl:sameIndividualAs`. In fact, `owl:sameAs` and `owl:sameIndividualAs` have the same semantics, and in the published W3C standards, `owl:sameAs` has replaced `owl:sameIndividualAs`. Therefore, avoid using `owl:sameIndividualAs`, and use `owl:sameAs` instead.

owl:sameAs can also be used to indicate that two classes denote the same concept in the real world. For example, List 5.54 defines a new class called DigitalSingleLensReflex, and it has the same intentional meaning as the class DSLR:

List 5.54 Use owl:sameAs to define a new class DigitalSingleLens Reflex

```
1: <?xml version="1.0"?>
2: <rdf:RDF
2a:    xmlns:rdf="http://www.w3.org/1999/02/22-rdf-syntax-ns#"
3:     xmlns:rdfs="http://www.w3.org/2000/01/rdf-schema#"
4:     xmlns:owl="http://www.w3.org/2002/07/owl#"
5:     xmlns:myCamera="http://www.liyangyu.com/camera#">
6:
7: <owl:Class rdf:about=
7a:    "http://www.liyangyu.com/camera#DigitalSingleLensReflex">
8:   <owl:sameAs
8a:       rdf:resource="http://www.liyangyu.com/camera#DSLR"/>
9: </owl:Class>
10:
11: </rdf:RDF>
```

Notice the definition in List 5.55 is quite different from the one in List 5.54:

List 5.55 Use owl:equivalentClass to define class DigitalSingleLensReflex

```
1: <?xml version="1.0"?>
2: <rdf:RDF
2a:    xmlns:rdf="http://www.w3.org/1999/02/22-rdf-syntax-ns#"
3:     xmlns:rdfs="http://www.w3.org/2000/01/rdf-schema#"
4:     xmlns:owl="http://www.w3.org/2002/07/owl#"
5:     xmlns:myCamera="http://www.liyangyu.com/camera#">
6:
7: <owl:Class rdf:about=
7a:    "http://www.liyangyu.com/camera#DigitalSingleLensReflex">
8:   <owl:equivalentClass
8a:       rdf:resource="http://www.liyangyu.com/camera#DSLR"/>
9: </owl:Class>
10:
11: </rdf:RDF>
```

List 5.55 defines a new class by using `owl:equivalentClass`. With the term `owl:equivalentClass`, the two classes, namely, `DigitalSingleLensReflex` and `DSLR`, will now have the same class extension (the set of all the instances of a given class is called its extension); however, they do not necessarily denote the same concept at all.

Also notice that `owl:sameAs` is not only used in instance documents, it can be used in ontology documents as well, as shown in List 5.54.

`owl:differentFrom` property is another OWL term that is often used in instance documents. It is the opposite of `owl:sameAs`, and it is used to indicate that two URIs refer to different individuals. List 5.56 shows one example:

List 5.56 Example of using `owl:differentFrom`

```
1:  <?xml version="1.0"?>
2:  <rdf:RDF
2a:     xmlns:rdf="http://www.w3.org/1999/02/22-rdf-syntax-ns#"
3:      xmlns:rdfs="http://www.w3.org/2000/01/rdf-schema#"
4:      xmlns:owl="http://www.w3.org/2002/07/owl#"
5:      xmlns:myCamera="http://www.liyangyu.com/camera#">
6:
7:  <rdf:Description
7a:      rdf:about="http://www.liyangyu.com/camera#Nikon_D3X">
8:    <rdf:type
8a:        rdf:resource="http://www.liyangyu.com/camera#DSLR"/>
9:    <owl:differentFrom
9a:      rdf:resource="http://www.liyangyu.com/camera#Nikon_D3S"/>
10: </rdf:Description>
11:
12: </rdf:RDF>
```

The code snippet in List 5.56 clearly states the following two URIs represent different resources in the real world, so there is no confusion even though these two URIs do look like each other a lot (notice that D3X and D3S are both real DSLRs by Nikon):

```
http://www.liyangyu.com/camera#Nikon_D3X
http://www.liyangyu.com/camera#Nikon_D3S
```

The last OWL term to discuss here is `owl:AllDifferent`, a special built-in OWL class. To understand it, we need to again mention the so-called *Unique-Names* assumption, which typically holds in the world of database applications, for example. More specifically, this assumption says that individuals with different names are indeed different individuals.

However, this is not the assumption made by OWL, which actually follows the non-unique-names assumption: even if two individuals (or classes or properties) have different names, they can still be the same individual. This can be derived by inference, or explicitly asserted by using `owl:sameAs`, as shown in List 5.53. The reason why we adopt the non-unique-names assumption in the world of the Semantic Web is simply because it is the most plausible one to make in the given environment.

However, there are some cases where the unique-names assumption does hold. To model this situation, one solution is to repeatedly use `owl:differentFrom` on all the individuals. However, this solution will likely create a large number of statements, since all individuals have to be declared pairwise disjoint.

A special class called `owl:AllDifferent` is provided for this kind of situation. This class has one built-in property called `owl:distinctMembers`, and an instance of `owl:AllDifferent` is linked to a list of individuals by property `owl:distinctMembers`. The intended meaning of such a statement is that all individuals included in the list are all different from each other. An example is given in List 5.57.

List 5.57 Example of using `owl:AllDifferent` and `owl:distinct Members`

```
1: <?xml version="1.0"?>
2: <rdf:RDF
2a:    xmlns:rdf="http://www.w3.org/1999/02/22-rdf-syntax-ns#"
3:     xmlns:rdfs="http://www.w3.org/2000/01/rdf-schema#"
4:     xmlns:owl="http://www.w3.org/2002/07/owl#"
5:     xmlns:myCamera="http://www.liyangyu.com/camera#">
6:
7:  <owl:AllDifferent>
8:   <owl:distinctMembers rdf:parseType="Collection">
9:    <myCamera:DSLR
9a:      rdf:about="http://www.liyangyu.com/camera#Nikon_D3"/>
10:    <myCamera:DSLR
10a:     rdf:about="http://www.liyangyu.com/camera#Nikon_D3X"/>
11:    <myCamera:DSLR
11a:     rdf:about="http://www.liyangyu.com/camera#Nikon_D3S"/>
12:    <myCamera:DSLR
12a:    rdf:about="http://www.liyangyu.com/camera#Nikon_D300S"/>
13:    <myCamera:DSLR
13a:     rdf:about="http://www.liyangyu.com/camera#Nikon_D300"/>
14:    <myCamera:DSLR
14a:     rdf:about="http://www.liyangyu.com/camera#Nikon_D700"/>
15:   </owl:distinctMembers>
16: </owl:AllDifferent>
```

Clearly, List 5.57 has accomplished the goal with much more ease. Remember, `owl:distinctMembers` is a special syntactical construct added for convenience and should always be used together with an `owl:AllDifferent` instance as its subject.

5.4.8 OWL 2 Profiles

5.4.8.1 Why Do We Need All These?

An important issue when designing an ontology language is the tradeoff between its expressiveness and the efficiency of the reasoning process. It is generally true that the richer the language is, the more complex and time-consuming the reasoning becomes. Sometimes, the reasoning can become complex enough that it is computationally impossible to finish the reasoning process. The goal therefore is to design a language that has sufficient expressiveness and that is also simple enough to be supported by reasonably efficient reasoning engines.

This is also inevitably the case with OWL: some of its constructs are very expressive; however, they can lead to uncontrollable computational complexities. The tradeoff between the reasoning efficiency and the expressiveness has led to the definitions of different subsets of OWL, and each one of these subsets is aimed at the different levels of this tradeoff.

This has also been the case for OWL 1. Again, since quite a lot ontologies were created when only OWL 1 was available, we first briefly discuss the OWL 1 language subsets, and we then move on to the profiles provided by OWL 2.

5.4.8.2 Assigning Semantics to OWL Ontology: Description Logic vs. RDF-Based Semantics

Once we have an ontology written in OWL (be it OWL 1 or OWL 2), we have two alternative ways to assign meanings to this ontology. The first one is called the *Direct Model–Theoretic Semantics*; the other one is called *RDF-based semantics*.

The reason behind this dual-assignment was largely due to the fact that OWL was originally designed to use a notational variant of Description Logic*See* DL (DL), which has been extensively investigated in the literature, and its expressiveness and computational properties are well-understood. Meanwhile, it was also very important for OWL to be semantically compatible with existing Semantic Web languages such as RDF and RDFS. The semantic differences between DL and RDF made it difficult to satisfy both requirements, and the solution chosen by W3C was to provide two coexisting semantics for OWL, therefore two ways of assigning semantics to a given OWL ontology.

For OWL 1, this dual-assignment directly results in two different dialects of OWL 1, namely *OWL 1 DL* and *OWL 1 Full*. More specifically, OWL 1 DL refers to the OWL 1 ontologies interpreted by using Direct Semantics, and OWL 1 Full refers to those interpreted by using RDF-based semantics.

This dual-assignment continues to be true in OWL 2. Similarly, *OWL 2 DL* refers to the OWL 2 ontologies that have their semantics assigned by using Direct Semantics, and *OWL 2 Full* refers to those ontologies that have their semantics assigned by using RDF-based semantics.

5.4.8.3   Three Faces of OWL 1

At this point, we understand OWL 1 has two different language variants: OWL 1 DL and OWL 1 Full.

OWL 1 DL is designed for users who need maximum expressiveness together with guaranteed computational completeness and *decidability*, meaning that all conclusions are guaranteed to be computable and all computations will be finished in finite time. To make sure this happens, OWL 1 DL supports all OWL 1 language constructs, but they can be used under certain constraints. For example, one such constraint specifies that a class may be a subclass of many classes, but it cannot be an instance of any class (more details coming up).

On the other hand, OWL 1 Full provides maximum expressiveness; there are no syntactic restrictions on the usage of the built-in OWL 1 vocabulary and the vocabulary elements defined in the ontology. However, since it uses the RDF-compatible semantics, its reasoning can be undecidable. In addition, it does not have the constraints that OWL 1 DL has, thereby adding an extra source of undecidability. At the time of this writing, no complete implementation of OWL 1 Full exists, and it is not clear whether OWL 1 Full can be implemented at all in practice.

With the above being said, OWL 1 DL seems to be a good choice if a decidable reasoning process is desired. However, reasoning in OWL 1 DL has a high worst-case computational complexity. To ease this concern, a fragment of OWL 1 DL was proposed by the OWL Working Group, and this subset of OWL 1 DL is called *OWL 1 Lite*.

Therefore, the *three faces of OWL 1* are given by OWL 1 Lite, OWL 1 DL and OWL 1 Full. The following summarizes the relations between these three faces:

- Every legal OWL 1 Lite feature is a legal OWL 1 DL feature; therefore, every legal OWL 1 Lite ontology is a legal OWL 1 DL ontology.
- OWL 1 DL and OWL 1 Full have the same language features; therefore every legal OWL 1 DL ontology is a legal OWL 1 Full ontology.
- Every valid OWL 1 Lite conclusion is a valid OWL 1 DL conclusion.
- Every valid OWL 1 DL conclusion is a valid OWL 1 Full conclusion.

Let us now discuss OWL 1's three faces in more detail. This will not only help you to understand ontologies that are developed by using only OWL 1 constructs, it will also help you to better understand OWL 2 language profiles as well.

- OWL 1 Full

The entire OWL 1 language we have discussed in this chapter is called OWL 1 Full, with every construct we have covered in this chapter being available to the ontology developer. It also allows us to combine these constructs in arbitrary ways with RDF and RDF schema, including mixing the RDF schema definitions with OWL definitions. Any legal RDF document is therefore a legal OWL 1 Full document.

- OWL 1 DL

As we mentioned, OWL 1 DL has the same language feature as OWL 1 Full does, but it has restrictions about the ways in which the constructs from OWL 1 and

RDF can be used. More specifically, the following rules must be observed when building ontologies:

– No arbitrary combination is allowed: a resource can be only a class, a datatype, a datatype property, an object property, an instance or a data value, and not more than one of these. In other words, a class cannot be at the same time a member of another class (no punning is allowed).
– Restrictions on functional property and inverse functional property: recall these two properties are subclasses of `rdf:Property`, therefore they can connect resource to resource or resource to value. However, in OWL 1 DL, they can only be used with object properties, not datatype properties.
– Restriction on transitive property: `owl:cardinality` cannot be used with transitive properties or their subproperties because these subproperties are transitive properties by implication.
– Restriction on `owl:imports`: if `owl:imports` is used by an OWL 1 DL ontology to import an OWL 1 Full ontology, the importing ontology will not be qualified as an OWL 1 DL.

In addition, OWL 1 Full does not put any constraints on annotation properties; however, OWL 1 DL does:

– Object properties, datatype properties, annotation properties and ontology properties must be mutually disjoint. For example, a property cannot be at the same time a datatype property and an annotation property.
– Annotation properties must not be used in property axioms. In other words, no subproperties or domain/range constraints for annotation properties can be defined.
– Annotation properties must be explicitly declared, as shown in List 5.48.
– The object of an annotation property must be either a data literal, a URI reference or an individual; nothing else is permitted.

• OWL 1 Full

OWL 1 Lite is a further restricted subset of OWL 1 DL, and the following are some of the main restrictions:

– The following constructs are not allowed in OWL Lite: `owl:hasValue`, `owl:disjointWith`, `owl:unionOf`, `owl:complementOf`, `owl:oneOf`.
– Cardinality constraints are more restricted: `owl:minCardinality` and `owl:maxCardinality` cannot be used; `owl:cardinality` can be used, but with value to be either 0 or 1.
– `owl:equivalentClass` statement can no longer be used to relate anonymous classes, but only to connect class identifiers.

Remember, you can always find a full list of the features supported by the three faces of OWL 1 from OWL 1's official specifications. It is up to you to understand each version in detail and thus make the right decision in your design and development work.

Recall that List 5.30 is an ontology written only by using OWL 1 features. Let us decide what face this ontology has. Clearly, it is not OWL 1 Lite since we used `owl:hasValue`, and it is also not OWL 1 DL since we also used functional property on `owl:DatatypeProperty`. Therefore, our camera ontology shown in List 5.30 is an OWL 1 Full version ontology.

There are indeed tools that can help you to decide the particular species of a given OWL 1 ontology. For example, you can find one such tool as this location:

`http://www.mygrid.org.uk/OWL/Validator`

You can try to validate our camera ontology and see its species decided by this tool. This will certainly enhance your understanding about OWL 1 species.

5.4.8.4   Understanding OWL 2 Profiles

Recall we mentioned that for any ontology created by using OWL 1, we had two alternative ways to assign semantics to this ontology. The same situation still holds for OWL 2. In addition, the first method is still called the Direct Model-Theoretic Semantics, and it is specified by the W3C recommendation OWL 2 Web Ontology Language Direct Semantics.[10] The second one is again called RDF-based Semantics, and it is specified by the W3C recommendation OWL 2 Web Ontology Language RDF-Based Semantics.[11] Also, *OWL 2 DL* refers to those OWL 2 ontologies interpreted by using Direct Semantics, and *OWL 2 Full* refers to those ontologies interpreted by using RDF-based semantics. Another way to understand this is to consider the fact that the direct model-theoretic semantics assigns meaning to OWL 2 ontologies by using Description Logic, therefore the name OWL 2 DL.

The differences between these two semantics are generally quite slight. For example, given an OWL 2 DL ontology, inferences drawn using Direct Semantics remain valid inferences under RDF-based semantics. As developers, we need to understand the following about OWL 2 DL vs. OWL 2 Full:

- OWL 2 DL can be viewed as a syntactically restricted version of OWL 2 Full. The restrictions are added and designed to make the implementation of OWL 2 reasoners easier.

More specifically, the reasoners built upon OWL 2 DL can return all "yes or no" answers to any inference request, while OWL 2 Full can be undecidable. At the time of this writing, there are production quality reasoners that cover the entire OWL 2 DL language, but there are no such reasoners for OWL 2 Full yet.

- Under OWL 2 DL, annotations have no formal meaning. However, under OWL Full, there are some extra inferences that can be drawn.

In addition to OWL 2 DL, OWL 2 further specifies language profiles. An OWL 2 *profile* is a trimmed down version of the OWL 2 language that trades some

---

[10] http://www.w3.org/TR/2009/REC-owl2-direct-semantics-20091027/

[11] http://www.w3.org/TR/2009/REC-owl2-rdf-based-semantics-20091027/

expressive power for efficiency of reasoning. In computational logic, profiles are usually called *fragment*s or *sublanguage*s.

The OWL 2 specification offers three different profiles, and they are called *OWL 2 EL*, *OWL 2 QL* and *OWL 2 RL*. To guarantee a scalable reasoning capability, each one of these profiles has its own limitations regarding its expressiveness. In the next section, we take a closer look at all these three profiles, and we also briefly summarize the best scenarios for using each specific profile. For the details of each profile, you can always consult OWL 2's official specification, i.e., OWL 2 Web Ontology Language Profiles.[12]

5.4.8.5   OWL 2 EL, QL and RL

- OWL 2 EL

OWL 2 EL is designed with very large ontologies in mind. For example, life sciences commonly require applications that depend on large ontologies. These ontologies normally have a huge number of classes and complex structural descriptions. Classification is the main goal of the related applications. With the restrictions added by OWL 2 EL, the complexity of reasoning algorithms (including query answering algorithms) is known to be worst-case polynomial; therefore these algorithms are often called *PTime-complete* algorithms.

More specifically, the following key points summarize the main features of OWL 2 EL:

- allow `owl:someValuesFrom` to be used with class expression or data range;
- allow `owl:hasValue` to be used with individual or literal;
- allow the use of self-restriction `owl:hasSelf`;
- property domains, class/property hierarchies, class intersections, disjoint classes, property chains and keys are fully supported.

And these features are not supported by OWL 2 EL:

- `owl:allValuesFrom` is not supported on both class expression and data range;
- none of the cardinality restrictions is supported;
- `owl:unionOf` and `owl:complementOf` are not supported;
- disjoint properties are not supported;
- irreflexive object properties, inverse object properties, functional and inverse functional object properties, symmetric object properties and asymmetric object properties are not supported;
- the following datatypes are not supported: `xsd:double`, `xsd:float`, `xsd:nonPositiveInteger`, `xsd:positiveInteger`, `xsd:short`, `xsd:long`, `xsd:int`, `xsd:byte`, `xsd:unsignedLong`, `xsd:boolean`, `xsd:unsignedInt`, `xsd:`

---

[12] http://www.w3.org/TR/2009/REC-owl2-profiles-20091027/

negativeInteger, `xsd:unsignedShort`, `xsd:unsignedByte` and `xsd:language`.

- OWL 2 QL

OWL 2 QL is designed for those applications that involve classical databases and that also need to work with OWL ontologies. For these applications, the interoperability of OWL with database technologies becomes their main concern because the ontologies used in these applications are often used to query large sets of individuals. Therefore, querying answering against large volumes of instance data is the most important reasoning task for these applications.

OWL 2 QL can guarantee polynomial-time performance as well, and this performance is again based on the limited expressive power. Nevertheless, the language constructs supported by OWL 2 QL can represent key features of Entity-relationship and UML diagrams; therefore, it can be used directly as a high level database schema language as well.

More specifically, the following key points summarize the main features of OWL 2 QL:

- allow `owl:someValuesFrom` to be used, but with restrictions (see below);
- property domains and ranges, property hierarchies, disjoint classes or equivalence of classes (only for subclass-type expressions), symmetric properties, reflexive properties, irreflexive properties, asymmetric properties and inverse properties are supported.

And these features are not supported by OWL 2 QL:

- `owl:someValuesFrom` is not supported when used on a class expression or a data range in the subclass position;
- `owl:allValuesFrom` is not supported on both class expression and data range;
- `owl:hasValue` is not supported when used on an individual or a literal;
- `owl:hasKey` is not supported;
- `owl:hasSelf` is not supported;
- `owl:unionOf` and `owl:oneOf` are not supported;
- none of the cardinality restrictions is supported;
- property inclusions involving property chains;
- transitive property, functional and inverse functional properties are not supported;
- the following datatypes are not supported: `xsd:double`, `xsd:float`, `xsd:nonPositiveInteger`, `xsd:positiveInteger`, `xsd:short`, `xsd:long`, `xsd:int`, `xsd:byte`, `xsd:unsignedLong`, `xsd:boolean`, `xsd:unsignedInt`, `xsd:negativeInteger`, `xsd:unsignedShort`, `xsd:unsignedByte` and `xsd:language`.

- OWL 2 RL

OWL 2 RL is designed for those applications that require scalable reasoning without sacrificing too much expressive power. Therefore, OWL 2 applications that

Table 5.5 Syntactic restrictions on class expressions in OWL 2 RL

Subclass expressions	Super-class expressions
A class other than `owl:Thing`	A class other than `owl:Thing`
An enumeration of individuals (`owl:oneOf`)	Intersection of classes (`owl:intersectionOf`)
Intersection of class expressions (`owl:intersectionOf`)	Negation (`owl:complementOf`)
Union of class expressions (`owl:unionOf`)	Universal quantification to a class expression (`owl:allValuesFrom`)
Existential quantification to a class expression (`owl:someValuesFrom`)	Existential quantification to an individual (`owl:hasValue`)
Existential quantification to a data range (`owl:someValuesFrom`)	At-most 0/1 cardinality restriction to a class expression
Existential quantification to an individual (`owl:hasValue`)	Universal quantification to a data range (`owl:allValuesFrom`)
Existential quantification to a literal (`owl:hasValue`)	Existential quantification to a literal (`owl:hasValue`)
	At-most 0/1 cardinality restriction to a data range

are willing to trade the full expressiveness of the language for efficiency, and RDF (S) applications that need some added expressiveness from OWL 2 are all good candidates for this profile. OWL 2 RL can also guarantee polynomial-time performance.

The design goal of OWL 2 RL is achieved by restricting the use of constructs to certain syntactic positions. Table 5.5, taken directly from OWL 2's official profile specification document, uses `owl:subClassOf` as an example to show the usage patterns that must be followed by the subclass and super-class expressions used with `owl:subClassOf` axiom.

All axioms in OWL 2 RL are constrained in the similar pattern. And furthermore:

- property domains and ranges only for subclass-type expressions; property hierarchies, disjointness, inverse properties, symmetry and asymmetric properties, transitivity properties, property chains, functional and inverse functional properties, irreflexive properties fully supported;
- disjoint unions of classes and reflexive object properties are not supported;
- finally, `owl:real` and `owl:rational` as datatypes are not supported.

5.4.9 Our Camera Ontology in OWL 2

As this point, we have covered the major features offered by OWL 2. Our camera ontology (List 5.30) has also been rewritten using OWL 2 features, as shown in List 5.58. At this point, there are not many tools that support OWL 2 ontologies yet, so we simply list the new camera ontology here and leave it to you to validate it and decide its species, once the related tools are available.

List 5.58 Our camera ontology written using OWL 2 features

```
1: <?xml version="1.0"?>
2: <!DOCTYPE rdf:RDF [
3:     <!ENTITY owl "http://www.w3.org/2002/07/owl#">
4:     <!ENTITY xsd "http://www.w3.org/2001/XMLSchema#">
5:     <!ENTITY rdfs "http://www.w3.org/2000/01/rdf-schema#">
6:     <!ENTITY myCamera "http://www.liyangyu.com/camera#">
7: ]>
8:
9: <rdf:RDF
9a:     xmlns:rdf="http://www.w3.org/1999/02/22-rdf-syntax-ns#"
10:     xmlns:rdfs="http://www.w3.org/2000/01/rdf-schema#"
11:     xmlns:owl="http://www.w3.org/2002/07/owl#"
12:     xmlns:xsd="http://www.w3.org/2001/XMLSchema#"
13:     xmlns:myCamera="http://www.liyangyu.com/camera#"
14:     xml:base="http://www.liyangyu.com/camera#">
15:
16:     <owl:Ontology rdf:about="">
17:         <owl:versionIRI>
18:             http://www.liyangyu.com/camera/v1
19:         </owl:versionIRI>
20:         <rdfs:comment>our camera ontology</rdfs:comment>
21:     </owl:Ontology>
22:
23:     <owl:Class rdf:about="&myCamera;Camera"/>
24:     <owl:Class rdf:about="&myCamera;Lens"/>
25:     <owl:Class rdf:about="&myCamera;Body"/>
26:     <owl:Class rdf:about="&myCamera;ValueRange"/>
27:     <owl:Class rdf:about="&myCamera;Digital"/>
28:     <owl:Class rdf:about="&myCamera;Film"/>
29:     <owl:Class rdf:about="&myCamera;DSLR"/>
30:     <owl:Class rdf:about="&myCamera;PointAndShoot"/>
31:     <owl:Class rdf:about="&myCamera;Photographer"/>
32:     <owl:Class rdf:about="&myCamera;Professional"/>
33:     <owl:Class rdf:about="&myCamera;Amateur"/>
34:     <owl:Class rdf:about="&myCamera;ExpensiveDSLR"/>
35:
36:     <owl:AsymmetricProperty rdf:about="&myCamera;owned_by"/>
37:     <owl:ObjectProperty rdf:about="&myCamera;manufactured_by"/>
38:     <owl:ObjectProperty rdf:about="&myCamera;body"/>
39:     <owl:ObjectProperty rdf:about="&myCamera;lens"/>
40:     <owl:DatatypeProperty rdf:about="&myCamera;model"/>
41:     <owl:ObjectProperty rdf:about="&myCamera;effectivePixel"/>
42:     <owl:ObjectProperty rdf:about="&myCamera;shutterSpeed"/>
43:     <owl:DatatypeProperty rdf:about="&myCamera;focalLength"/>
```

```
44:    <owl:ObjectProperty rdf:about="&myCamera;aperture"/>
45:    <owl:DatatypeProperty rdf:about="&myCamera;minValue"/>
46:    <owl:DatatypeProperty rdf:about="&myCamera;maxValue"/>
47:    <owl:ObjectProperty rdf:about="&myCamera;own"/>
48:    <owl:DatatypeProperty rdf:about="&myCamera;reviewerID"/>
49:
50:    <rdfs:Datatype rdf:about="&xsd;string"/>
51:    <rdfs:Datatype rdf:about="&myCamera;MegaPixel"/>
52:    <rdfs:Datatype rdf:about="&xsd;float"/>
53:
54:    <owl:Class rdf:about="&myCamera;Camera">
55:      <rdfs:subClassOf>
56:        <owl:Restriction>
57:          <owl:onProperty rdf:resource="&myCamera;model"/>
58:          <owl:minCardinality
59:                   rdf:datatype="&xsd;nonNegativeInteger">
60:           1
61:          </owl:minCardinality>
62:        </owl:Restriction>
63:      </rdfs:subClassOf>
64:    </owl:Class>
65:
66:    <owl:Class rdf:about="&myCamera;Lens">
67:    </owl:Class>
68:
69:    <owl:Class rdf:about="&myCamera;Body">
70:    </owl:Class>
71:
72:    <owl:Class rdf:about="&myCamera;ValueRange">
73:    </owl:Class>
74:
75:    <owl:Class rdf:about="&myCamera;Digital">
76:      <rdfs:subClassOf rdf:resource="&myCamera;Camera"/>
77:      <rdfs:subClassOf>
78:        <owl:Restriction>
79:          <owl:onProperty
79a:              rdf:resource="&myCamera;effectivePixel"/>
80:          <owl:cardinality
81:              rdf:datatype="&xsd;nonNegativeInteger">
82:            1
83:          </owl:cardinality>
84:        </owl:Restriction>
85:      </rdfs:subClassOf>
```

```
 86:    </owl:Class>
 87:
 88:    <owl:Class rdf:about="&myCamera;Film">
 89:      <rdfs:subClassOf rdf:resource="&myCamera;Camera"/>
 90:    </owl:Class>
 91:
 92:    <owl:Class rdf:about="&myCamera;DSLR">
 93:      <rdfs:subClassOf rdf:resource="&myCamera;Digital"/>
 94:    </owl:Class>
 95:
 96:    <owl:Class rdf:about="&myCamera;PointAndShoot">
 97:      <rdfs:subClassOf rdf:resource="&myCamera;Digital"/>
 98:    </owl:Class>
 99:
100:    <owl:Class rdf:about="&myCamera;Photographer">
101:      <owl:intersectionOf rdf:parseType="Collection">
102:        <owl:Class
102a:            rdf:about="http://xmlns.com/foaf/0.1/Person"/>
103:        <owl:Class>
104:          <owl:hasKey rdf:parseType="Collection">
105:            <owl:DatatypeProperty
105a:                rdf:about="&myCamera;reviewerID"/>
106:          </owl:hasKey>
107:        </owl:Class>
108:      </owl:intersectionOf>
109:    </owl:Class>
110:
111:
112:    <owl:Class rdf:about="&myCamera;Professional">
113:      <rdfs:subClassOf rdf:resource="&myCamera;Photographer"/>
114:      <rdfs:subClassOf>
115:        <owl:Restriction>
116:          <owl:minQualifiedCardinality
116a:              rdf:datatype="&xsd;nonNegativeInteger">
117:            1
118:          </owl:minQualifiedCardinality>
119:          <owl:onProperty rdf:resource="&myCamera;own"/>
120:          <owl:onClass rdf:resource="&myCamera;ExpensiveDSLR"/>
121:        </owl:Restriction>
122:      </rdfs:subClassOf>
123:    </owl:Class>
124:
125:
126:    <owl:Class rdf:about="&myCamera;Amateur">
```

```
127:      <owl:intersectionOf rdf:parseType="Collection">
128:        <owl:Class
128a:            rdf:about="http://xmlns.com/foaf/0.1/Person"/>
129:        <owl:Class>
130:          <owl:complementOf
130a:              rdf:resource="&myCamera;Professional"/>
131:        </owl:Class>
132:      </owl:intersectionOf>
133:    </owl:Class>
134:
135:    <owl:Class rdf:about="&myCamera;ExpensiveDSLR">
136:      <rdfs:subClassOf rdf:resource="&myCamera;DSLR"/>
137:      <rdfs:subClassOf>
138:        <owl:Restriction>
139:          <owl:onProperty rdf:resource="&myCamera;owned_by"/>
140:          <owl:someValuesFrom
140a:              rdf:resource="&myCamera;Professional"/>
141:        </owl:Restriction>
142:      </rdfs:subClassOf>
143:    </owl:Class>
144:
145:    <owl:AsymmetricProperty rdf:about="&myCamera;owned_by">
146:      <owl:propertyDisjointWith rdf:resource="&myCamera;own"/>
147:        <rdfs:domain rdf:resource="&myCamera;DSLR"/>
148:        <rdfs:range rdf:resource="&myCamera;Photographer"/>
149:    </owl:AsymmetricProperty>
150:
151:    <owl:ObjectProperty rdf:about="&myCamera;manufactured_by">
152:      <rdf:type rdf:resource="&owl;FunctionalProperty"/>
153:        <rdfs:domain rdf:resource="&myCamera;Camera"/>
154:    </owl:ObjectProperty>
155:
156:    <owl:ObjectProperty rdf:about="&myCamera;body">
157:      <rdfs:domain rdf:resource="&myCamera;Camera"/>
158:      <rdfs:range rdf:resource="&myCamera;Body"/>
159:    </owl:ObjectProperty>
160:
161:    <owl:ObjectProperty rdf:about="&myCamera;lens">
162:      <rdfs:domain rdf:resource="&myCamera;Camera"/>
163:      <rdfs:range rdf:resource="&myCamera;Lens"/>
164:    </owl:ObjectProperty>
165:
166:    <owl:DatatypeProperty rdf:about="&myCamera;model">
167:      <rdfs:domain rdf:resource="&myCamera;Camera"/>
```

```
168:      <rdfs:range rdf:resource="&xsd;string"/>
169:    </owl:DatatypeProperty>
170:    <rdfs:Datatype rdf:about="&xsd;string"/>
171:
172:    <owl:ObjectProperty rdf:about="&myCamera;effectivePixel">
173:      <rdfs:domain rdf:resource="&myCamera;Digital"/>
174:      <rdfs:range rdf:resource="&myCamera;MegaPixel"/>
175:    </owl:ObjectProperty>
176:
177:    <rdfs:Datatype rdf:about="&myCamera;MegaPixel">
178:      <owl:onDatatype rdf:resource="&xsd;integer"/>
179:      <owl:withRestrictions rdf:parseType="Collection">
180:        <rdf:Description>
181:          <xsd:minInclusive rdf:datatype="&xsd;decimal">
182:            1.0
183:          </xsd:minInclusive>
184:        </rdf:Description>
185:        <rdf:Description>
186:          <xsd:maxInclusive rdf:datatype="&xsd;decimal">
187:            24.0
188:          </xsd:maxInclusive>
189:        </rdf:Description>
190:      </owl:withRestrictions>
191:    </rdfs:Datatype>
192:
193:    <owl:ObjectProperty rdf:about="&myCamera;shutterSpeed">
194:      <rdfs:domain rdf:resource="&myCamera;Body"/>
195:      <rdfs:range rdf:resource="&myCamera;ValueRange"/>
196:    </owl:ObjectProperty>
197:
198:    <owl:DatatypeProperty rdf:about="&myCamera;focalLength">
199:      <rdfs:domain rdf:resource="&myCamera;Lens"/>
200:      <rdfs:range rdf:resource="&xsd;string"/>
201:    </owl:DatatypeProperty>
202:    <rdfs:Datatype rdf:about="&xsd;string"/>
203:
204:    <owl:ObjectProperty rdf:about="&myCamera;aperture">
205:      <rdfs:domain rdf:resource="&myCamera;Lens"/>
206:      <rdfs:range rdf:resource="&myCamera;ValueRange"/>
207:    </owl:ObjectProperty>
208:
209:    <owl:DatatypeProperty rdf:about="&myCamera;minValue">
210:      <rdfs:domain rdf:resource="&myCamera;ValueRange"/>
211:      <rdfs:range rdf:resource="&xsd;float"/>
```

```
212:  </owl:DatatypeProperty>
213:  <rdfs:Datatype rdf:about="&xsd;float"/>
214:
215:  <owl:DatatypeProperty rdf:about="&myCamera;maxValue">
216:    <rdfs:domain rdf:resource="&myCamera;ValueRange"/>
217:    <rdfs:range rdf:resource="&xsd;float"/>
218:  </owl:DatatypeProperty>
219:  <rdfs:Datatype rdf:about="&xsd;float"/>
220:
221:  <owl:ObjectProperty rdf:about="&myCamera;own">
222:    <owl:inverseOf rdf:resource="&myCamera;owned_by"/>
223:    <rdfs:domain rdf:resource="&myCamera;Photographer"/>
224:    <rdfs:range rdf:resource="&myCamera;DSLR"/>
225:  </owl:ObjectProperty>
226:
227:  <owl:DatatypeProperty rdf:about="&myCamera;reviewerID">
228:    <rdf:type rdf:resource="&owl;FunctionalProperty"/>
229:    <rdf:type rdf:resource="&owl;InverseFunctionalProperty"/>
230:    <rdfs:domain rdf:resource="&myCamera;Photographer"/>
231:    <rdfs:range rdf:resource="&xsd;string"/>
232:  </owl:DatatypeProperty>
233:  <rdfs:Datatype rdf:about="&xsd;string"/>
234:
235:  <rdf:Description rdf:about="&myCamera;hasLens">
236:    <owl:propertyChainAxiom rdf:parseType="Collection">
237:      <owl:ObjectProperty rdf:about="&myCamera;own"/>
238:      <owl:ObjectProperty rdf:about="&myCamera;lens"/>
239:    </owl:propertyChainAxiom>
240:  </rdf:Description>
241:
242:  </rdf:RDF>
```

Compare this ontology with the one shown in List 5.30; the differences you see are part of the new features offered by OWL 2.

5.5 Summary

We have covered OWL in this chapter, including both OWL 1 and OWL 2. As an ontology development language, OWL fits into the world of the Semantic Web just as RDFS does. However, compared to RDFS, OWL provides a much greater expressiveness, together with much more powerful reasoning capabilities.

The first part of this chapter presents OWL 1, since most of the available ontologies are written by using OWL 1, and quite a few development tools at this point still only support OWL 1. More specifically, you should understand the following main points about OWL 1:

- understand the key terms and related language constructs provided by OWL 1, and understand how to use these terms and language constructs to define classes and properties;
- understand the enhanced expressiveness and reasoning power offered by OWL 1 ontologies, compared to the ontologies defined by using RDFS.

The second part of this chapter focuses on OWL 2. Make sure you understand the following about OWL 2:

- new features provided by OWL 2, such as a collection of new properties, extended support for datatypes and simple metamodeling capabilities, etc.;
- understand how to use the added new features to define ontologies with more expressiveness and enhanced reasoning power.

This chapter also discusses the topic of OWL language profiles. Make sure you understand the following main points about OWL profiles:

- the concept of OWL language profiles, and why these profiles are needed;
- language features and limitations of each profile, and which specific profile should be selected for a given task.

With the material presented in this chapter and Chap. 4, you should be technically sound when it comes to ontology development. In Chap. 14, we present a methodology that will help you further with ontology design and development. Together, this will prepare you well for your work on the Semantic Web.

Chapter 6
SPARQL: Querying the Semantic Web

This chapter covers SPARQL, the last core component of the Semantic Web. With SPARQL, you will be able to locate specific information on the machine-readable Web, and the Web can therefore be viewed as a gigantic database, as many of us have been dreaming about.

This chapter will cover all the main aspects of SPARQL, including its concepts, its main language constructs and features, and certainly, real world examples and related tools you can use when querying the semantic Web. Once you are done with this chapter, you will have a complete tool collection that you can use to continue exploring the world of the Semantic Web.

6.1 SPARQL Overview

6.1.1 SPARQL in Official Language

SPARQL (pronounced "sparkle") is an RDF query language and data access protocol for the Semantic Web. Its name is an acronym that stands for *SPARQL Protocol and RDF Query Language*.*See* SPARQL SPARQL 1.0[1] was standardized by W3C's SPARQL Working Group (formerly known as the RDF Data Access Working Group) on January 15, 2008. You can follow the group's activities from the official Web site:

```
http://www.w3.org/2009/sparql/wiki/Main_Page
```

which also lists the specifications contained in the official W3C Recommendation.

---

[1] http://www.w3.org/TR/rdf-sparql-query/

© Springer-Verlag Berlin Heidelberg 2014
L. Yu, *A Developer's Guide to the Semantic Web*,
DOI 10.1007/978-3-662-43796-4_6

The W3C SPARQL 1.0 consists of three separate specifications. The first one, *SPARQL Query Language specification*,[2] makes up the core. Together with this language specification is the *SPARQL Query XML Results Format specification*,[3] which describes an XML format for serializing the results of a SPARQL query (including both SELECT and ASK queries). The third specification is the *SPARQL Protocol for RDF specification*[4] that uses WSDL 2.0 to define simple HTTP and SOAP protocols for remotely querying RDF databases.

SPARQL 1.1 became a W3C standard on March 21, 2013.[5] It has altogether 11 documents:

1. SPARQL 1.1 Overview
2. SPARQL 1.1 Query Language
3. SPARQL 1.1 Update
4. SPARQL 1.1 Service Description
5. SPARQL 1.1 Federated Query
6. SPARQL 1.1 Query Results JSON Format
7. SPARQL 1.1 Query Results CSV and TSV Formats
8. SPARQL Query Results XML Format (Second Edition)
9. SPARQL 1.1 Entailment Regimes
10. SPARQL 1.1 Protocol
11. SPARQL 1.1 Graph Store HTTP Protocol

The main focus of this chapter is on SPARQL query language itself, including both SPARQL 1.0 and SPARQL 1.1. The first half of the chapter will focus on SPARQL 1.0. This is necessary since SPARQL 1.1, as far as query language specification goes, has focused on adding more features to SPARQL 1.0, instead of replacing it. It is therefore still necessary to fully understand SPARQL 1.0 first.

The second half of the chapter includes the main language features offered by SPARQL 1.1. These new features are very useful, and understanding them will make sure you become even more productive with SPARQL.

6.1.2   SPARQL in Plain Language

At this point, we have learned RDF, a model and data format that we can use to create structured content for machine to read. We have also learned RDF schema and the OWL language, and we can use these languages to create ontologies.

With ontologies, anything we say in our RDF documents, we have a reason to say. And more importantly, since the RDF documents we create all share these common ontologies, it becomes much easier for machines to make inferences based

---

[2] http://www.w3.org/TR/rdf-sparql-query/

[3] http://www.w3.org/TR/rdf-sparql-XMLres/

[4] http://www.w3.org/TR/rdf-sparql-protocol/

[5] http://www.w3.org/TR/sparql11-query/

on these RDF contents, therefore generating even more RDF statements, as we saw in the last chapter.

As a result, there will be more and more content being expressed in RDF format. And indeed, for the last several years, a large amount of RDF documents have been published on the Internet, and a machine-readable Web has started to take shape. Following all this is the need to locate specific information on this data Web.

A possible solution is to build a new kind of search engine that works on this emerging Semantic Web. Since the underlying Web is machine-readable, this new search engine will have much better performance than that delivered by the search engines working in the traditional Web environment.

However, this solution will not be able to take full advantage of the Semantic Web. More specifically, a search engine does not directly give us answers; instead, it returns to us a collection of pages that might contain the answer. Since we are working on a machine-readable Web, why not directly ask for the answer?

Therefore, to push the solution one step further, we need a query language that we can use on this data Web. By simply submitting a query, we should be able to directly get the answer.

SPARQL query language is what we are looking for. In plain English,

SPARQL is a query language that we can use to query the RDF data content, and SPARQL also provides a protocol that we need to follow if we want to query a remote RDF data set.

The benefits of having a query language such as SPARQL are also obvious. To name a few,

- to query RDF graphs to get specific information;
- similarly, to query a remote RDF server and to get streaming results back;
- to run automated regular queries again RDF datasets to generate reports;
- to enable application development at a higher level, i.e., applications can work with SPARQL query results, not directly with RDF statements.

6.1.3 RDF Datasets and SPARQL Endpoints

First, understand that a SPARQL query is executed against an *RDF dataset* that represents a collection of graphs. An RDF dataset contains one default graph, which does not have a name, and zero or more named graphs, where each named graph is identified by an IRI. An RDF dataset may contain zero named graphs, but it always contains one default graph. A query can work with the default graph; it can also just work with the named graphs, as we will see in later this chapter. The graph that is being used for matching a graph pattern is the *active graph*, which often can simply be the default graph in the RDF Dataset.

A *SPARQL endpoint* can be understood as an interface that users (human or applications) can access to query a RDF dataset by using SPARQL query language. For human users, this endpoint could be a standalone or Web-based application.

For applications, this endpoint takes the form of a set of APIs that can be used by the calling agent.

A SPARQL endpoint can be configured to return results in a number of different formats. For instance, when used by human users in an interactive way, it presents the results in the form of an HTML table, which is often constructed by applying XSL transforms to the XML result returned by the endpoint. When accessed by applications, the results are serialized into machine-processable formats, such as RDF/XML or Turtle, just to name a few.

SPARQL endpoints can be categorized as *generic* endpoints versus *specific* endpoints. A generic endpoint works against any RDF dataset, which could be stored locally or be accessible from the Web. A specific endpoint is tied to one particular dataset, and this dataset cannot be switched to another endpoint.

In this chapter, our main goal is to learn SPARQL's language features; we will need a SPARQL endpoint that works in a command-line fashion so we can test our queries right away. Later in this book, we will see how to query RDF statements by using programmable SPARQL endpoints in a soft agent.

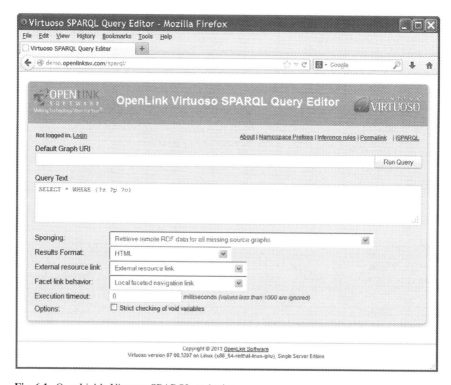

Fig. 6.1 OpenLink's Virtuoso SPARQL endpoint

There are quite a few SPARQL endpoints available on the Web.[6] We will use OpenLink's Virtuoso Live Demo Server[7] as our endpoint. Figure 6.1 shows the look-and-feel of this endpoint at the time of this writing.

To use this endpoint, make sure to choose "Retrieve remote RDF data for all missing source graphs", as shown in Fig. 6.1.

6.2 SPARQL 1.0 Query Language

Now, we are ready to study the query language itself. We need to select an RDF data file first, and use it as our example throughout this section. This example data file has to be clear enough for us to understand; yet it cannot be too trivial to reflect the power of the SPARQL 1.0 query language.

Let us take Dan Brickley's FOAF document[8] as our example. FOAF represents a project called *Friend Of A Friend*, and Dan Brickley is one of the two founders of this project. We have a whole chapter coming up to discuss FOAF in detail; for now, understanding the following about FOAF is good enough for you to continue:

- The goal of the FOAF project is to build a social network using the Semantic Web technology, so we can do experiments with it and build applications that are not easily built under traditional the Web.
- The core element of the FOAF project is the FOAF ontology, a collection of terms that can be used to describe a person: name, homepage, e-mail address, interests and people he/she knows, etc.
- Anyone can create an RDF document to describe himself/herself by using this FOAF ontology, and he/she can join the friends network as well.

Dan Brickley's FOAF document is therefore a collection of RDF statements that he created to describe himself, and the terms he used to do so are from FOAF ontology. You can find his file at this URL:

```
http://danbri.org/foaf.rdf
```

And since the file is quite long, List 6.1 only shows part of it, so you can get a feeling about what a FOAF document looks like. Note that Dan Brickley can change his FOAF document at any time; therefore at the time you are reading this book, the exact content of this RDF document could be different. However, the main idea is the same, and all the queries against this file will still be valid.

---

[6] http://www.w3.org/wiki/SparqlEndpoints

[7] http://demo.openlinksw.com/sparql/

[8] http://danbri.org/foaf.rdf

List 6.1 Part of Dan Brickley's FOAF document

```
 1:  <?xml version="1.0"?>
 2:
 3:  <rdf:RDF
 4:      xml:lang="en"
 5:      xmlns:wot="http://xmlns.com/wot/0.1/"
 6:      xmlns:owl="http://www.w3.org/2002/07/owl#"
 7:      xmlns:rdf="http://www.w3.org/1999/02/22-rdf-syntax-ns#"
 8:      xmlns:dct="http://purl.org/dc/terms/"
......

10:      xmlns="http://xmlns.com/foaf/0.1/"
......

18:    <Person rdf:ID="danbri">
19:      <foaf:name>Dan Brickley</foaf:name>
20:      <foaf:nick>danbri</foaf:nick>
21:      <owl:sameAs rdf:resource="http://foaf.me/danbri#me"/>
22:
......

30:      <mbox rdf:resource="mailto:danbri@danbri.org"/>
31:      <mbox rdf:resource="mailto:danbri@porklips.org"/>
32:
......

160: <!-- connections to other peoples -->
......

166:      <knows>
167:        <Person>
168:          <mbox rdf:resource=
168a:            "mailto:libby.miller@bristol.ac.uk"/>
169:          <mbox rdf:resource="mailto:libby@asemantics.com"/>
170:        </Person>
171:      </knows>
172:
......

175:      <knows>
176:        <Person rdf:about=
176a:              "http://www.w3.org/People/Berners-Lee/card#i">
177:          <name>Tim Berners-Lee</name>
```

```
178:          <isPrimaryTopicOf rdf:resource=
178a:              "http://en.wikipedia.org/wiki/Tim_Berners-Lee"/>
179:          <homepage rdf:resource=
179a:              "http://www.w3.org/People/Berners-Lee/"/>
180:          <mbox rdf:resource="mailto:timbl@w3.org"/>
181:         <rdfs:seeAlso rdf:resource=
181a:              "http://www.w3.org/People/Berners-Lee/card"/>
182:       </Person>
183:     </knows>
184:
......

457:    </Person>
458:  </rdf:RDF>
459:
```

As you can see, he has included his name and nickname (lines 19, 20), and his e-mail addresses (lines 30, 31). He has also used `foaf:knows` to include some of this friends, as shown on lines 166–171, and lines 175–183. Note a default namespace is declared in line 10, and that default namespace is the FOAF ontology namespace (see Chap. 7 for details). As a result, he can use terms from the FOAF ontology without adding any prefix, such as `Person`, `knows`, `mbox`, `plan`, etc.

6.2.1   The Big Picture

SPARQL 1.0 provides four different forms of query:

- `SELECT` query
- `ASK` query
- `DESCRIBE` query
- `CONSTRUCT` query

Among these forms, the `SELECT` query is the most frequently used query form. In addition, all these query forms are based on two basic SPARQL concepts: the triple pattern and the graph pattern. Let us understand these two concepts first before we start to look at SPARQL queries.

6.2.1.1   Triple Pattern

As we have learned, the RDF model is built on the concept of triple, a 3-tuple structure consisting of subject, predicate and object. Likewise, SPARQL is built upon the concept of *triple pattern*, which is also written as subject, predicate and object, and has to be terminated with a full stop. The difference between RDF triples and SPARQL triple patterns is that a SPARQL triple pattern can include variables: any or all of the subject, predicate and object values in a triple pattern can be a variable. Clearly, an RDF triple is also a SPARQL triple pattern.

The second line in the following example is a SPARQL triple pattern (note that Turtle syntax is used here):

```
@prefix foaf: <http://xmlns.com/foaf/0.1/> .
<http://danbri.org/foaf.rdf#danbri> foaf:name ?name .
```

As you can tell, the subject of this triple pattern is Dan Brickely's URI, the predicate is `foaf:name` and the object component of this triple pattern is a variable, identified by the ? character in front of a string `name`.

Note that a SPARQL variable can be prefixed with either a ? character or a $ character, and these two are interchangeable. In this book, we will use the ? character. In other words, a SPARQL variable is represented by the following format:

```
?variableName
```

where the ? character is necessary, and `variableName` is given by the user.

The best way to understand a variable in a triple pattern is to view it as a placeholder that can match any value. More specifically, here is what happens when the above triple pattern is used against an RDF graph:

0. Create an empty RDF document, call it `resultSet`.
1. Get the next triple from the given RDF graph; if there are no more triples, return the `resultSet`.
2. Match the current triple with the triple pattern: if both the subject and the predicate of the current triple match the given subject and predicate in the triple pattern, the actual value of the object from the current triple will *bind* to the variable called `name`, and therefore create a new concrete triple that will be collected into the `resultSet`.
3. Go back to step 1.

Obviously, the above triple pattern can be read as followings:

find the value of `foaf:name` property defined for RDF resource identified by `http://danbri.org/foaf.rdf#danbri`.

And based on the above steps, it is clear that all possible bindings are included. Therefore, if we have multiple instances of `foaf:name` property defined for `http://danbri.org/foaf.rdf#danbri`, all these multiple bindings will be returned.

It is certainly fine to have more than one variable in a triple pattern. For example, the following triple pattern has two variables:

`<http://danbri.org/foaf.rdf#danbri> `**`?property ?name .`**

And it means to find all the properties and their values that have been defined to the resource identified by `http://danbri.org/foaf.rdf#danbri`.

It is also fine to have all components as variables:

`?subject ?property ?name .`

This triple pattern will then match all triples in a given RDF graph.

6.2.1.2 Graph Pattern

Another important concept in SPARQL is called the *graph pattern*. Similar to a triple pattern, a graph pattern is also used to select triples from a given RDF graph, but it can specify a much more complex "selection rule" compared to a simple triple pattern.

First, a collection of triple patterns is called a graph pattern. In SPARQL, { and } are used to specify a collection of triple patterns. For example, the following three triple patterns present one graph pattern:

```
{
    ?who foaf:name ?name .
    ?who foaf:interest ?interest .
    ?who foaf:knows ?others .
}
```

To understand how a graph pattern is used to select resources from a given RDF graph, we need to remember one key point about the graph pattern: if a given variable shows up in multiple triple patterns within the graph pattern, its value in all these patterns has to be the same. In other words, each resource returned must be able to substitute into all occurrences of the variable. More specifically:

0. Create an empty set called `resultSet`.
1. Get the next resource from the given RDF graph. If there are no more resources left, return `resultSet` and stop.

2. Process the first triple pattern:

   - If the current resource does not have a property instance called `foaf:name`, goto 6.
   - Otherwise, bind the current resource to variable `?who`, and bind the value of property `foaf:name` to variable `?name`.

3. Process the second triple pattern:

   - If the current resource (represented by variable `?who`) does not have a property instance called `foaf:interest`, go to 6.
   - Otherwise, bind the value of property `foaf:interest` to variable `?interest`.

4. Process the third triple pattern:

   - If the current resource (represented by variable `?who`) does not have a property instance called `foaf:knows`, go to 6.
   - Otherwise, bind the value of property `foaf:knows` to variable `?others`.

5. Collect the current resource into `resultSet`.
6. Go to 1.

Based on these steps, it is clear that this graph pattern in fact tries to find any resource that has all three of the desired properties defined. The above process will stop its inspection at any point and move on to a new resource if the current resource does not have any of the required properties defined.

You should be able to understand other graph patterns in a similar way just by remembering this basic rule: within a graph pattern, a variable must always be bound to the same value no matter where it shows up.

And now, we are ready to dive into the world of SPARQL query language.

6.2.2 SELECT Query

The SELECT query form is used to construct standard queries, and it is probably the most popular form among the four. In addition, most of its features are shared by other query forms.

6.2.2.1 Structure of a SELECT Query

List 6.2 shows the structure of a SPARQL SELECT query:

List 6.2 The structure of a SPARQL SELECT query

```
# base directive
BASE <URI>

# list of prefixes
PREFIX pref: <URI>
...


# result description
SELECT ...

# graph to search
FROM ...

# query pattern
WHERE {

    ...
}

# query modifiers
ORDER BY ...
```

As shown in List 6.2, a SELECT query starts with a BASE directive and a list of PREFIX definitions that may contain an arbitrary number of PREFIX statements. These two parts are optional, and they are used for URI abbreviations. For example, if you assign a label pref to a given URI, then the label can be used anywhere in a query in place of the URI itself. Also notice that pref is simply a label; we can name it whatever we want. This is all quite similar to the Turtle language abbreviations we discussed in Chap. 2, and we will see more details about these two parts in the upcoming query examples.

The SELECT clause comes next. It specifies which variable bindings, or data items, should be returned from the query. As a result, it "picks up" what information to return from the query result.

The FROM clause tells the SPARQL endpoint against which graph the search should be conducted. As you will see later, this is also an optional item—in some cases, there is no need to specify the dataset that is being queried against.

The WHERE clause contains the graph patterns that specify the desired results; it tells the SPARQL endpoint what to query for in the underlying data graph. Notice the WHERE clause is not optional, although the WHERE keyword itself is

optional. However, for clarity and readability, it is a good idea not to omit
WHERE.

The last part is generally called query modifiers. The main purpose is to tell the
SPARQL endpoint how to organize the query results. For instance, the ORDER BY
clause and LIMIT clause are examples of query modifiers. Obviously, query modifiers are also optional.

6.2.2.2 Writing Basic **SELECT** Query

As we have discussed, our queries will be issued against Dan Brickley's FOAF
document. And our first query will accomplish the following: since FOAF ontology
has defined a group of properties that one can use to describe a person, it would be
interesting to see which of these properties are actually used by Brickley. List 6.3
shows the query.

List 6.3 What FOAF properties did Dan Brickley use to describe himself?

```
1: base <http://danbri.org/foaf.rdf>
2: prefix foaf: <http://xmlns.com/foaf/0.1/>

3: select *
4: from <http://danbri.org/foaf.rdf>
5: where
6: {
7:   <#danbri> ?property ?value.
8: }
```

Since this is our first query, let us study it in greater detail. First, notice that
SPARQL is not case-sensitive, so all the keywords can be either in small letters or
capital letters.

Now, lines 1 and 2 are there for abbreviation purposes. Line 1 uses the
BASE keyword to define a base URI against which all relative URIs in the
query will be resolved, including the URIs defined with the PREFIX keyword.
In this query, PREFIX keyword specifies that foaf will be the shortcut for an
absolute URI (line 2), so the URI foaf stands for does not have to be resolved
against the BASE URI.

Line 3 specifies which data items should be returned by the query. Notice that
only variables in the graph pattern (lines 6–8) can be chosen as returned data items.

In this example, we would like to return both the property names and their values, so we should have written the SELECT clause like this:

```
select ?property ?value
```

Since ?property and ?value are the only two variables in the graph pattern, we don't have to specify them one by one as shown above; we can simply use a * as a wildcard for all the variables, as shown on line 3.

Line 4 specifies the data graph against which we are doing our search. Notice Virtuoso SPARQL endpoint can be used as either a generic or a specific SPARQL endpoint, and in this chapter, we will always explicitly specify the location of Brickley's FOAF document.

Line 5 is the where keyword, indicating that the search criteria are next, and lines 6–8 gives the criteria represented by a graph pattern. Since we have discussed the concepts of triple pattern and graph pattern already, we understand how they are used to select the qualified triples. For this particular query, the graph pattern should be quite easy to follow. More specifically, this graph pattern has only one triple pattern, and it tries to match all the property instances and their values that are ever defined for the resource representing Brickley in real life.

Note that the resource representing Brickley has a relative URI as shown on line 7, and it is resolved by concatenating the BASE URI with this relative URI. The resolved URI is given by,

```
http://danbri.org/foaf.rdf#danbri
```

which is the one that Brickley has used in his FOAF file.

Now you can put List 6.3 into the query box as shown in Fig. 6.1 and click the Run Query button; you should be able to get the results back. Figure 6.2 shows part of the result.

From the result, we can see which properties have been used. For instance, foaf:knows and foaf:mbox are the most commonly used ones. Other properties such as foaf:name, foaf:nick, foaf:homepage, foaf:holdsAccount are also used.

Note that Brickley's FOAF file could be under constant updates, so at the time you are trying this query, you might not see the same result as shown in Fig. 6.2. Also, we will not continue to show the query results from now on unless it is necessary to do so, so this chapter won't be too long.

Let us try another simple query: find all the people known by Brickley. List 6.4 shows the query.

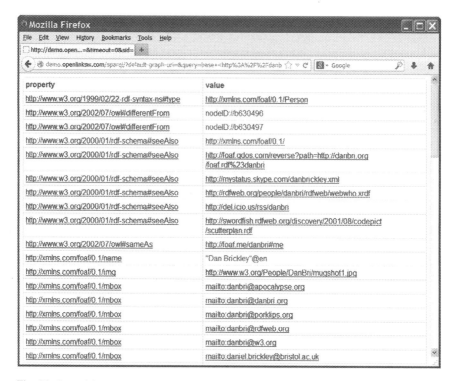

Fig. 6.2 Part of the query result when running the query in List 6.3

List 6.4 Find all the people known by Dan Brickley

```
base <http://danbri.org/foaf.rdf>
prefix foaf: <http://xmlns.com/foaf/0.1/>

select *
from <http://danbri.org/foaf.rdf>
where
{
   <#danbri> foaf:knows ?friend .
}
```

Try to run the query, and right away you will see the problem: the query itself is right, but the result does not really tell us anything: there are way too many blank nodes.

In fact, it is quite often that when we include a friend we know in our FOAF documents, instead of using his/her URI, we simply use a blank node to represent this friend. For example, in List 6.1, one friend, Libby Miller, is represented by a blank node. As we will see in Chap. 7, even a blank node is used to represent a friend, as long as `foaf:mbox` property value is also included for this resource, any application will be able to recognize the resource.

Let us change List 6.4 to accomplish the following: find all the people known by Brickley, and show their names, e-mail addresses and homepage information. List 6.5 is the query that can replace the one in List 6.4:

List 6.5 Find all the people known by Brickley, show their names, e-mail addresses and homepage information

```
base <http://danbri.org/foaf.rdf>
prefix foaf: <http://xmlns.com/foaf/0.1/>

select *
from <http://danbri.org/foaf.rdf>
where
{
    <#danbri> foaf:knows ?friend .
    ?friend foaf:name ?name .
    ?friend foaf:mbox ?email .
    ?friend foaf:homepage ?homepage .
}
```

The graph pattern in List 6.5 contains four triple patterns. Also, variable `?friend` is used as the object in the first triple pattern, but it is used as subject of the other three triple patterns. This is the so-called object-to-subject transfer in SPARQL queries. By doing this transfer, we can traverse multiple links in the RDF graph.

If we run this query against Brickley's FOAF graph, we see the names, e-mails and homepages of Brickley's friends, which makes the result much more readable, as shown in Fig. 6.3.

However, the number of friends showing up in this result is much less than the number indicated by the result from running the query in List 6.4 — looks like some friends are missing. What is wrong? We will leave the answer to the next section, but before that, let us try some more SPARQL queries.

Some of Brickley's friends have their pictures posted on the Web, and let us say for some reason we are interested in the formats of these pictures. The query shown in List 6.6 tries to find all of the picture formats that have been used by Brickley's friends:

friend	name	email	homepage
http://www.w3.org/People/Berners-Lee/card#i	"Tim Berners-Lee"@en	mailto:timbl@w3.org	http://www.w3.org/People/Berners-Lee/
nodeID://b630499	"Dean Jackson"@en	mailto:dean@w3.org	http://www.grorg.org/dean/
nodeID://b630499	"Dean Jackson"@en	mailto:dino@grorg.org	http://www.grorg.org/dean/
nodeID://b630506	"Edd Dumbill"@en	mailto:edd@usefulinc.com	http://heddley.com/edd/
nodeID://b630506	"Edd Dumbill"@en	mailto:edd@xml.com	http://heddley.com/edd/
nodeID://b630506	"Edd Dumbill"@en	mailto:edd@xmlhack.com	http://heddley.com/edd/
nodeID://b630507	"Martin Poulter"@en	mailto:m.l.poulter@bristol.ac.uk	http://www.weird.co.uk/martin/
nodeID://b630511	"Eric Miller"@en	mailto:em@w3.org	http://purl.org/net/eric/

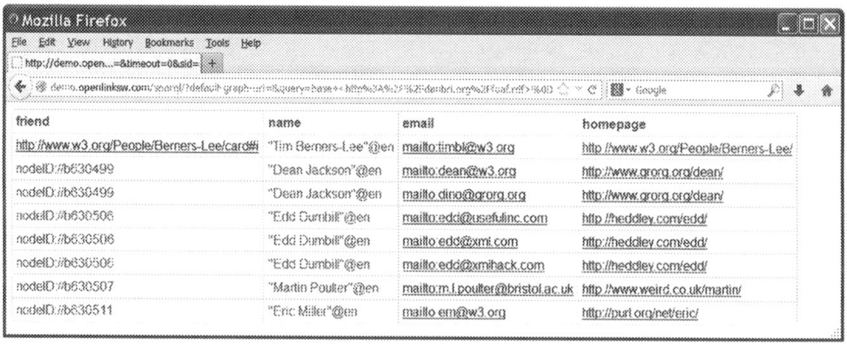

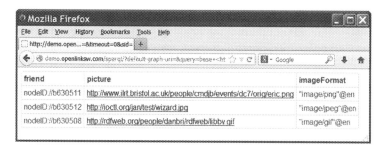

Fig. 6.3 Result from running the query shown in List 6.5

List 6.6 Find all the picture formats used by Brickley's friends

```
base <http://danbri.org/foaf.rdf>
prefix foaf: <http://xmlns.com/foaf/0.1/>
prefix dc: <http://purl.org/dc/elements/1.1/>

select *
from <http://danbri.org/foaf.rdf>
where
{
   <#danbri> foaf:knows ?friend .
   ?friend foaf:depiction ?picture .
   ?picture dc:format ?imageFormat .
}
```

friend	picture	imageFormat
nodeID://b630511	http://www.ilrt.bristol.ac.uk/people/cmdjb/events/dc7/orig/eric.png	"image/png"@en
nodeID://b630512	http://ioctl.org/jan/test/wizard.jpg	"image/jpeg"@en
nodeID://b630508	http://rdfweb.org/people/danbri/rdfweb/libby.gif	"image/gif"@en

Fig. 6.4 Result from running the query shown in List 6.6

And Fig. 6.4 shows the result.

We have seen and discussed the object-to-subject transfer in List 6.5. In List 6.6, this transfer happens at a deeper level. The graph pattern in List 6.6 tries to match

Brickley's friend, who has a `foaf:depiction` property instance defined, and this instance further has a `dc:format` property instance created, and we will like to return the value of this property instance. This chain of reference is the key to writing queries using SPARQL, and is also frequently used.

In order to construct the necessary chain of references when writing SPARQL queries, we need to understand the structure of the ontologies that the given RDF graph file has used. Sometimes, in order to confirm our understanding, we need to read the graph which we are querying against. This should not surprise you at all: if you have to write SQL queries against some database tables, the first thing is to understand the structures of these tables, including the relations between them. The table structures and the relations between these tables can in fact be viewed as the underlying ontologies for these tables.

6.2.2.3   Using **OPTIONAL** Keyword for Matches

The `optional` keyword is another frequently used SPARQL feature, and the reason why `optional` keyword is needed is largely due to the fact that an RDF data graph is only a semistructured data model. For example, two instances of the same class type in a given RDF graph may have different sets of property instances created for each one of them.

Let us take a look at Brickley's FOAF document, which has defined a number of `foaf:Person` instances. For example, one instance is created to represent Brickley himself, and quite a few others are defined to represent people he knows. Some of these `foaf:Person` instances do not have `foaf:name` property defined, and similarly, not every instance has `foaf:homepage` property instance created either.

This is perfectly legal, since there is no `owl:minCardinality` constraint defined on class `foaf:Person` regarding any of the above properties. For instance, not everyone has a homepage; it is therefore not reasonable to require each `foaf:Person` instance to have a `foaf:homepage` property value. Also, recall that `foaf:mbox` is a inverse functional property, which is used to uniquely identify a given person. As a result, having a `foaf:name` value or not for a given `foaf:Person` instance is not vital either.

This has answered the question we had in the previous section from List 6.5: not every one Brickley's friends has a name, e-mail and homepage defined. And since the query in List 6.5 works like a logical AND, it only matches a friend whom Brickley knows and has *all* these three properties defined. Obviously, this return fewer people compared to the result returned by the query in List 6.4.

Now, we can change the query in List 6.5 a little bit: find all the people known by Brickley, and show their name, e-mail and homepage if *any* of that information is available.

To accomplish this, we need the `optional` keyword, as shown in List 6.7.

List 6.7 Change List 6.5 to use the `optional` keyword

```
base <http://danbri.org/foaf.rdf>
prefix foaf: <http://xmlns.com/foaf/0.1/>

select *
from <http://danbri.org/foaf.rdf>
where
{
   <#danbri> foaf:knows ?friend .
   optional { ?friend foaf:name ?name . }
   optional { ?friend foaf:mbox ?email . }
   optional { ?friend foaf:homepage ?homepage . }
}
```

This query says, find all the people known by Brickley, and show their name, e-mail and homepage information if *any* of this information is available. Run this query, you will see the difference between this query and the one shown in List 6.5. And here is the rule about the `optional` keyword: the search will try to match all the graph patterns, but does not fail the whole query if the graph pattern modified by `optional` keyword fails.

Figure 6.5 shows the result when List 6.7 is run. Comparing Fig. 6.5 to Fig. 6.3, you will see the difference.

Note that in List 6.7, there are three different graph patterns modified by `optional` keyword, and any number of these graph patterns can fail, yet does not cause the solution to be dropped. Clearly, if a query has multiple `optional` blocks, these `optional` blocks act independently of one another; any one of them can be omitted from or present in a solution.

Also note that the graph pattern modified by an `optional` keyword can have any number of triple patterns inside it. In List 6.7, each graph pattern modified by `optional` keyword happens to contain only one triple pattern. If a graph pattern modified by `optional` keyword contains multiple triple patterns, every single triple pattern in this graph pattern has to be matched in order to include a solution in the result set. For example, consider the query in List 6.8:

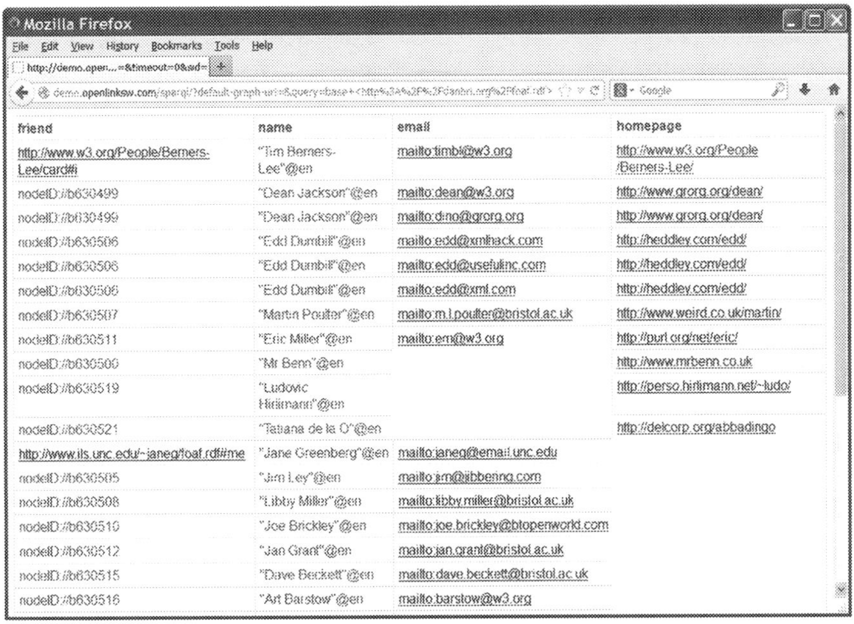

friend	name	email	homepage
http://www.w3.org/People/Berners-Lee/card#i	"Tim Berners-Lee"@en	mailto:timbl@w3.org	http://www.w3.org/People/Berners-Lee/
nodeID://b630499	"Dean Jackson"@en	mailto:dean@w3.org	http://www.grorg.org/dean/
nodeID://b630499	"Dean Jackson"@en	mailto:dino@grorg.org	http://www.grorg.org/dean/
nodeID://b630506	"Edd Dumbill"@en	mailto:edd@xmlhack.com	http://heddley.com/edd/
nodeID://b630506	"Edd Dumbill"@en	mailto:edd@usefulinc.com	http://heddley.com/edd/
nodeID://b630506	"Edd Dumbill"@en	mailto:edd@xml.com	http://heddley.com/edd/
nodeID://b630507	"Martin Poulter"@en	mailto:m.l.poulter@bristol.ac.uk	http://www.weird.co.uk/martin/
nodeID://b630511	"Eric Miller"@en	mailto:em@w3.org	http://purl.org/net/eric/
nodeID://b630509	"Mr Benn"@en		http://www.mrbenn.co.uk
nodeID://b630519	"Ludovic Hirlimann"@en		http://perso.hirlimann.net/~ludo/
nodeID://b630521	"Tatiana de la O"@en		http://delcorp.org/abbadingo
http://www.ils.unc.edu/~janeg/foaf.rdf#me	"Jane Greenberg"@en	mailto:janeg@email.unc.edu	
nodeID://b630505	"Jim Ley"@en	mailto:jim@jibbering.com	
nodeID://b630508	"Libby Miller"@en	mailto:libby.miller@bristol.ac.uk	
nodeID://b630510	"Joe Brickley"@en	mailto:joe.brickley@btopenworld.com	
nodeID://b630512	"Jan Grant"@en	mailto:jan.grant@bristol.ac.uk	
nodeID://b630515	"Dave Beckett"@en	mailto:dave.beckett@bristol.ac.uk	
nodeID://b630516	"Art Barstow"@en	mailto:barstow@w3.org	

Fig. 6.5 Result from running the query shown in List 6.7

List 6.8 Use optional keyword on the whole graph pattern (compared with List 6.7)

```
base <http://danbri.org/foaf.rdf>
prefix foaf: <http://xmlns.com/foaf/0.1/>

select *
from <http://danbri.org/foaf.rdf>
where
{
   <#danbri> foaf:knows ?friend .
   optional {
               ?friend foaf:name ?name .
               ?friend foaf:mbox ?email .
               ?friend foaf:homepage ?homepage .
            }
}
```

Figure 6.6 shows the result when runing List 6.8.

And comparing Fig. 6.6 with Fig. 6.5, you will see the difference: List 6.8 says, find all the people known by Brickley, show their name, e-mail and homepage information if *all* of this information is available, or, if *none* of this information is available.

friend	name	email	homepage
http://www.w3.org/People/Berners-Lee/card#i	"Tim Berners-Lee"@en	mailto:timbl@w3.org	http://www.w3.org/People/Berners-Lee/
nodeID://b630499	"Dean Jackson"@en	mailto:dean@w3.org	http://www.grorg.org/dean/
nodeID://b630499	"Dean Jackson"@en	mailto:dino@grorg.org	http://www.grorg.org/dean/
nodeID://b630506	"Edd Dumbill"@en	mailto:edd@usefulinc.com	http://heddley.com/edd/
nodeID://b630506	"Edd Dumbill"@en	mailto:edd@xml.com	http://heddley.com/edd/
nodeID://b630506	"Edd Dumbill"@en	mailto:edd@xmlhack.com	http://heddley.com/edd/
nodeID://b630507	"Martin Poulter"@en	mailto:m.l.poulter@bristol.ac.uk	http://www.weird.co.uk/martin/
nodeID://b630511	"Eric Miller"@en	mailto:em@w3.org	http://purl.org/net/eric/
http://mmt.me.uk/foaf.rdf#mischa			
http://www.ils.unc.edu/~janeg/foaf.rdf#me			
nodeID://b630498			
nodeID://b630500			
nodeID://b630501			
nodeID://b630502			
nodeID://b630503			

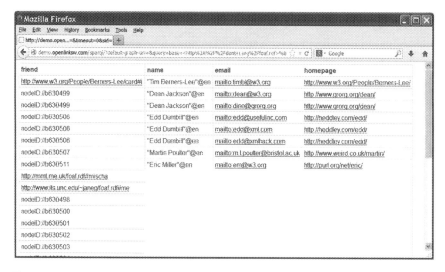

Fig. 6.6 Result from running the query shown in List 6.8

friend	email	ref
http://www.w3.org/People/Berners-Lee/card#i	mailto:timbl@w3.org	http://www.w3.org/People/Berners-Lee/card
http://www.ils.unc.edu/~janeg/foaf.rdf#me	mailto:janeg@email.unc.edu	http://www.ils.unc.edu/~janeg/foaf.rdf#me
nodeID://b630499	mailto:dean@w3.org	http://www.grorg.org/dean/foaf.rdf
nodeID://b630499	mailto:dino@grorg.org	http://www.grorg.org/dean/foaf.rdf
nodeID://b630505	mailto:jim@jibbering.com	http://jibbering.com/foaf.rdf
nodeID://b630506	mailto:edd@usefulinc.com	http://heddley.com/edd/foaf.rdf
nodeID://b630506	mailto:edd@xml.com	http://heddley.com/edd/foaf.rdf
nodeID://b630506	mailto:edd@xmlhack.com	http://heddley.com/edd/foaf.rdf
nodeID://b630507	mailto:m.l.poulter@bristol.ac.uk	http://www.weird.co.uk/martin/webwho.xrdf
nodeID://b630510	mailto:joe.brickley@btopenworld.com	http://hippvrigs.fiendsreunited.com/people/joe/foaf.rdf
nodeID://b630511	mailto:em@w3.org	http://purl.org/net/eric/webwho.xrdf
nodeID://b630512	mailto:jan.grant@bristol.ac.uk	http://ioctl.org/jan/webwho.xrdf
nodeID://b630513	mailto:michaelm@netsol.com	http://battey.dscga.com/michaelmwho.xrdf
nodeID://b630515	mailto:dave.beckett@bristol.ac.uk	http://purl.org/net/dajobe/webwho.xrdf
nodeID://b630516	mailto:barstow@w3.org	http://www.w3.org/People/Barstow/webwho.rdf

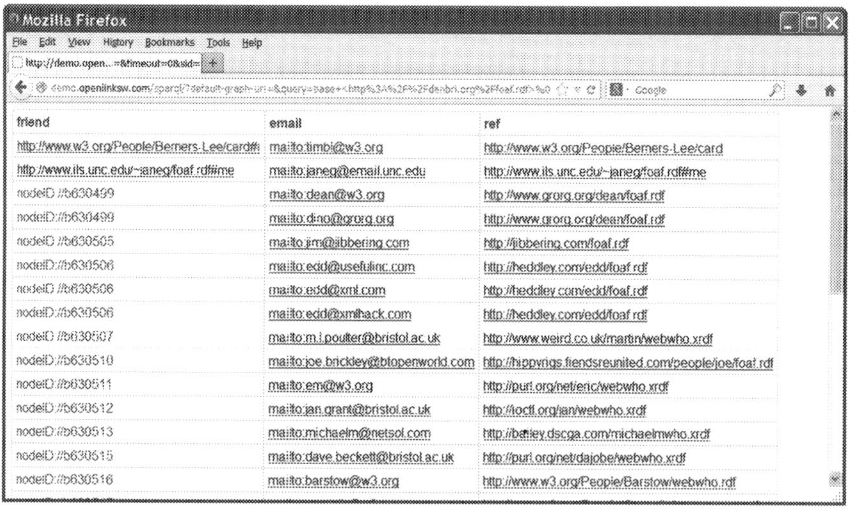

Fig. 6.7 Result from running the query shown in List 6.9

Let us look at one more example before we move on, which will be used in our later chapters: find all the people known by Brickley, for anyone of them, if she/he has e-mail address, show it, and if she/he has `rdfs:seeAlso` value, also get this value. This query is shown in List 6.9, and Fig. 6.7 shows the result.

List 6.9 Find Dan Brickley's friends, who could also have e-mail addresses and rdfs:seeAlso defined

```
base <http://danbri.org/foaf.rdf>
prefix foaf: <http://xmlns.com/foaf/0.1/>
prefix rdfs: <http://www.w3.org/2000/01/rdf-schema#>

select *
from <http://danbri.org/foaf.rdf>
where
{
   <#danbri> foaf:knows ?friend .
   optional { ?friend foaf:mbox ?email. }
   optional { ?friend rdfs:seeAlso ?ref. }
}
```

6.2.2.4 Using Solution Modifier

At this point, we know SPARQL query is about matching patterns. More specifically, the SPARQL engine tries to match the triples contained in the graph patterns against the RDF graph, which is a collection of triples. Once a match is successful, it will bind the graph pattern's variables to the graph's nodes, and one such variable binding*See* bind is called a *query solution*. Since the select clause has specified a list of variables (or all the variables, as shown in our examples so far), the values of these listed variables will be selected from the current query solution to form a row that is included in the final query result, and this row is called a *solution*. Obviously, another successful match will add another new solution, so on and so forth, thereby creating a table as the final result, with each solution presented as a row in this table.

Sometimes, it is better or even necessary for the solutions in the result table be reorganized according to our need. For this reason, SPARQL has provided several *solution modifiers*, which are the topic of this section.

The first one to look at is the distinct modifier, which eliminates duplicate solutions from the result table. Recall the query presented in List 6.3, which tries to find all the properties and their values that Brickley has used to describe himself. Now, let us change the query so only the property names are returned, as shown in List 6.10:

List 6.10 Change List 6.3 to return only one variable back

```
base <http://danbri.org/foaf.rdf>
prefix foaf: <http://xmlns.com/foaf/0.1/>

select ?property
from <http://danbri.org/foaf.rdf>
where
{
  <#danbri> ?property ?value.
}
```

run the query, and you can see a lot of repeated properties. Modify List 6.10 once more time to make it look as the query in List 6.11,

List 6.11 Use distinct keyword to eliminate repeated solutions from List 6.10

```
base <http://danbri.org/foaf.rdf>
prefix foaf: <http://xmlns.com/foaf/0.1/>

select distinct ?property
from <http://danbri.org/foaf.rdf>
where
{
  <#danbri> ?property ?value.
}
```

and you will see the difference: all the duplicated solutions are now gone.

Another frequently used solution modifier is order by, which is also quite often used together with asc() or desc(). It orders the result set based on one of the variables listed in the where clause. For example, the query in List 6.12 tries to find all the people who have even been mentioned in Brickley's FOAF file, and they are listed in a more readable way, as shown in Fig. 6.8.

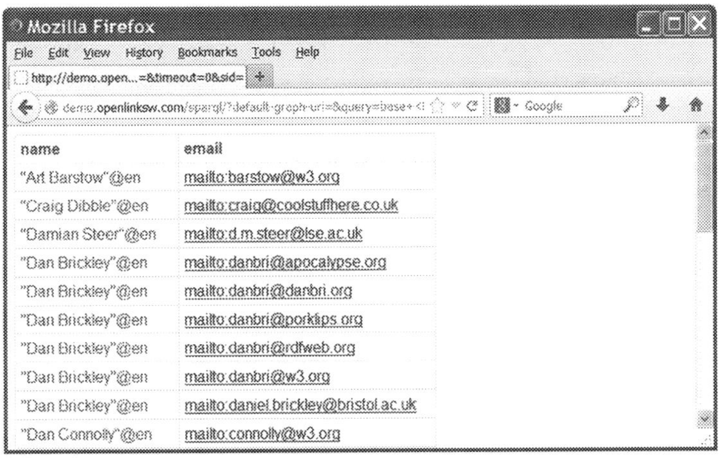

Fig. 6.8 Result from running the query shown in List 6.12

List 6.12 Use `order by` and `asc()` to modify results

```
base <http://danbri.org/foaf.rdf>
prefix foaf: <http://xmlns.com/foaf/0.1/>

select ?name ?email
from <http://danbri.org/foaf.rdf>
where
{
  ?x a foaf:Person.
  ?x foaf:name ?name.
  ?x foaf:mbox ?email.
}
order by asc(?name)
```

Note that a pair of solution modifiers, namely, `offset/limit`, is often used together with `order by`, to take a defined slice from the solution set. More specifically, `limit` sets the maximum number of solutions to be returned, and `offset` sets the number of solutions to be skipped. These modifiers can certainly be used separately; for example, using `limit` alone helps us to ensure that not too many solutions are collected. Let us modify the query in List 6.12 to make it look like the one shown in List 6.13:

List 6.13 Use `limit/offset` to modify results

```
base <http://danbri.org/foaf.rdf>
prefix foaf: <http://xmlns.com/foaf/0.1/>

select ?name ?email
from <http://danbri.org/foaf.rdf>
where
{
  ?x a foaf:Person.
  ?x foaf:name ?name.
  ?x foaf:mbox ?email.
}
order by asc(?name)
limit 10 offset 1
```

Run this query and compare with the result shown in Fig. 6.8; you will see the result from `offset/limit` clearly.

6.2.2.5   Using **FILTER** Keyword to Add Value Constraints

If you have used SQL to query a database, you know it is quite straightforward to add value constraints in SQL. For example, if you are querying against a student database system, you may want to find all the students whose GPA is within a given range. In SPARQL, you can also add values constraints to filter the solutions in the result set, and the keyword to use is called `filter`.

More specifically, value constraints specified by the `filter` keyword are logical expressions that evaluate to `boolean` values when applied on values of bound variables. Since these constraints are logical expressions, we can therefore combine them together by using logical `&&` and `||` operators. Only those solutions that are evaluated to be `true` by the given value constraints are included in the final result set. Let us take a look at some examples.

List 6.14 helps us to accomplish the following: if Tim Berners-Lee is mentioned in Brickley's FOAF file, then we want to know what has been said about him:

List 6.14 What has been said about Berners-Lee?

```
base <http://danbri.org/foaf.rdf>
prefix foaf: <http://xmlns.com/foaf/0.1/>

select distinct ?property ?propertyValue
from <http://danbri.org/foaf.rdf>
where
{
  ?person foaf:name "Tim Berners-Lee"@en .
  ?person ?property ?propertyValue .
}
```

When you run this query against Brickley's FOAF document, you will indeed see some information about Tim Berners-Lee, such as his homepage, his e-mail address, etc. However, note that this query does not use any filter keyword at all; instead, it directly adds the constraints to the triple pattern.

This is certainly fine, but with the major drawback that you have to specify the information with exact accuracy. For example, in List 6.14, if you replace the line

```
?person foaf:name "Tim Berners-Lee"@en .
```

with this line,

```
?person foaf:name "tim Berners-Lee"@en .
```

the whole query will not work at all.

A better way to put constraints on the solution is to use filter keyword. List 6.15 shows how to do this:

List 6.15 Use filter keyword to add constraints to the solution

```
1:  base <http://danbri.org/foaf.rdf>
2:  prefix foaf: <http://xmlns.com/foaf/0.1/>

3:  select distinct ?property ?propertyValue
4:  from <http://danbri.org/foaf.rdf>
5:  where
6:  {
7:    ?timB foaf:name ?y .
8:    ?timB ?property ?propertyValue .
9:    filter regex(str(?y), "tim berners-Lee", "i").
10: }
```

Line 9 uses the filter keyword to put constraints on the solution set. It uses a regular expression function called regex() to do the trick: for a given triple, its

Table 6.1 Functions and operators provided by SPARQL

Category	Functions and operators
Logical	`!, &&, ||`
Math	`+, -, *, /`
Comparison	`=, !=, >, <`
SPARQL testers	`isURL(), isBlank(), isLiteral(), bound()`
SPARQL accessors	`str(), lang(), datatype()`
Other	`sameTerm(), langMatches(), regex()`

object component is taken and converted into a string by using the `str()` function, and if this string matches the given string, "`tim berners-Lee`", this `filter` will be evaluated to be `true`, in which case, the subject of the current triple will be bound to a variable called `?timB`. Notice "`i`" means ignore the case, so the string is matched even if it starts will a lowercase `t`.

The rest of List 6.15 is easy: line 7 together with line 9 will bind variable `?timB` to the right resource, and line 8 will pick up all the properties and their related values that are ever used on this resource, which accomplishes our goal.

Run this query, and you will see it gives exactly the same result as given by List 6.14. However, it does not require us to know exactly how the desired resource is named in a given RDF file.

Note that `str()` is a function provided by SPARQL for us to use together with `filter` keyword. Table 6.1 summarizes the frequently used functions and operators; we will not go into a detailed description of each one of them, since you can easily check them out.

Let us take a look at another example of using `filter` keyword: we want to find those who are known by Brickley and are also related to W3C (note that if someone has an e-mail address such as `someone@w3.org`, we will then assume he/she is related to W3C). List 6.16 is the query we can use:

List 6.16 Find Dan Brickley's friends who are related to W3C

```
base <http://danbri.org/foaf.rdf>
prefix foaf: <http://xmlns.com/foaf/0.1/>
prefix rdfs: <http://www.w3.org/2000/01/rdf-schema#>

select ?name ?email
from <http://danbri.org/foaf.rdf>
where
{
    <#danbri> foaf:knows ?friend .
    ?friend foaf:mbox ?email.
    filter regex(str(?email), "w3.org", "i" ).
    optional { ?friend foaf:name ?name. }
}
```

Note that this query does not put e-mail address as an optional item; in other words, if someone known by Brickley is indeed related to W3C, however, without his/her `foaf:mbox` information presented in the FOAF document, this person will not be selected.

List 6.17 gives the last example of using `filter`. It tries to find all those defined in Brickley's FOAF file, and whose birthday is after the start of 1970 and before the start of 1980. It shows another flavor of `filter` keyword, and also how to do necessary data conversations for the correct comparison we need.

List 6.17 Find all the person whose birthday is within a given time frame

```
base <http://danbri.org/foaf.rdf>
prefix foaf: <http://xmlns.com/foaf/0.1/>
prefix xsd: <http://www.w3.org/2001/XMLSchema#>

select ?name ?dob
from <http://danbri.org/foaf.rdf>
where
{
   ?person a foaf:Person .
   ?person foaf:name ?name .
   ?person foaf:dateOfBirth ?dob .
   filter ( xsd:date(str(?dob)) >= "1970-01-01"^^xsd:date &&
            xsd:date(str(?dob)) < "1980-01-01"^^xsd:date )
}
```

6.2.2.6   Using **Union** Keyword for Alternative Match

Sometimes, a query needs to be expressed by multiple graph patterns that are mutually exclusive, and any solution has to match exactly one of these patterns. This situation is defined as an *alternative match* situation, and SPARQL has provided the `union` keyword for us to accomplish this.

A good example is from FOAF ontology, which provides two properties for e-mail address: `foaf:mbox` and `foaf:mbox_sha1sum`. The first one takes a readable plain text as its value, and the second one uses hash-codes of an e-mail address as its value to further protect the owner's privacy. If we want to collect all the e-mail addresses that are included in Brickley's FOAF file, we have to accept either one of these two alternative forms, as shown in List 6.18.

List 6.18 Using `union` keyword to collect e-mail information

```
base <http://danbri.org/foaf.rdf>
prefix foaf: <http://xmlns.com/foaf/0.1/>

select ?name ?mbox
from <http://danbri.org/foaf.rdf>
where
{
   ?person a foaf:Person .
   ?person foaf:name ?name .
   {
      { ?person foaf:mbox ?mbox. }
      union
      { ?person foaf:mbox_sha1sum ?mbox. }
   }
}
```

Figure 6.9 shows the query result.

Now, any solution has to match one and exactly one of the two graph patterns that are connected by the `union` keyword. If someone has both a plaintext e-mail address and a hash-coded address, then both of these addresses will be included in the solution set. This is also the difference between `union` keyword and `optional` keyword: as

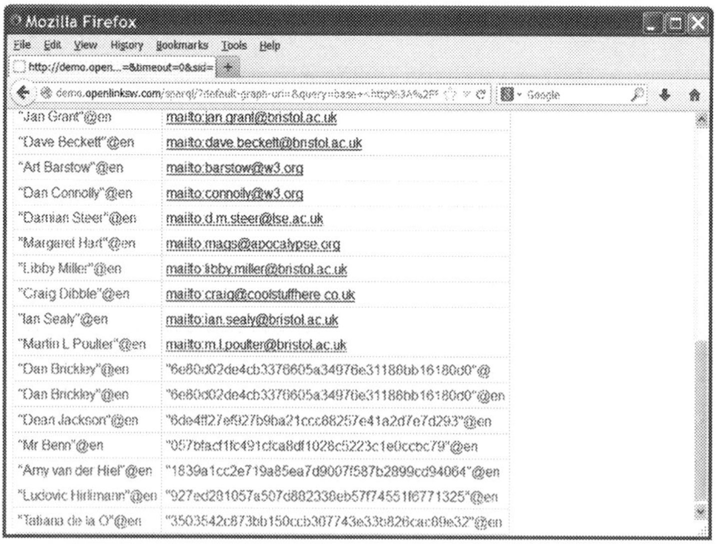

Fig. 6.9 Result from running the query shown in List 6.18

seen in List 6.19, since the `optional` keyword is used, a given solution can be included in the result set without matching any of the two graph patterns at all.

List 6.19 Using `optional` keyword is different from using `union`, as shown in List 6.18

```
base <http://danbri.org/foaf.rdf>
prefix foaf: <http://xmlns.com/foaf/0.1/>

select ?name ?mbox
from <http://danbri.org/foaf.rdf>
where
{
   ?person a foaf:Person .
   ?person foaf:name ?name .
   optional { ?person foaf:mbox ?mbox. }
   optional { ?person foaf:mbox_sha1sum ?mbox. }
}
```

After you run the query in List 6.19, you can find those solutions in the result set which do not have any e-mail address, and these solutions will for sure not be returned when the query in List 6.18 is used.

Another interesting change to List 6.18 is shown in List 6.20:

List 6.20 Another example using the `union` keyword differently from List 6.18

```
base <http://danbri.org/foaf.rdf>
prefix foaf: <http://xmlns.com/foaf/0.1/>

select ?name ?mbox ?mbox1
from <http://danbri.org/foaf.rdf>
where
{
   ?person a foaf:Person .
   ?person foaf:name ?name .
   {
      { ?person foaf:mbox ?mbox. }
      union
      { ?person foaf:mbox_sha1sum ?mbox1. }
   }
}
```

and the result is shown in Fig. 6.10. I will leave it for you to understand.

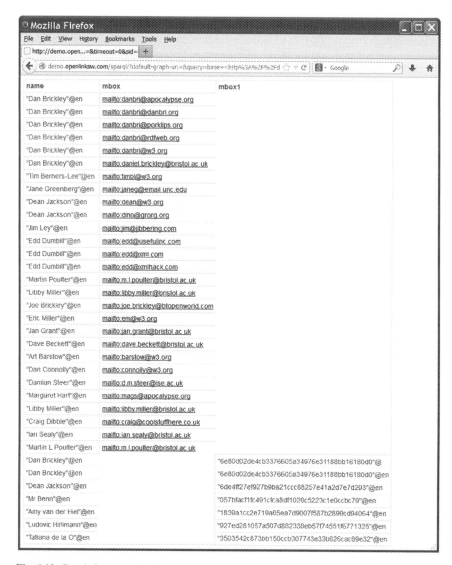

Fig. 6.10 Result from running the query shown in List 6.20

Before we move to the next section, let us take a look at one more example of
`union` keyword, and this example will be useful in a later chapter.

As we know, almost any given Web page has links to other pages, and these links
are arguably what makes the Web interesting. A FOAF file is also a Web page, with
the only difference of being a page that machines can understand. Therefore, it
should have links pointing to the outside world as well. The question is: what are
these links in a given FOAF page? (We will see how to use these links in a later
chapter.)

At this point, at least the following three links can be identified:

- `rdfs:seeAlso`
- `owl:sameAs`
- `foaf:isPrimaryTopicOf`

Since all these properties can take us to either another document or another resource on the Web, they can be understood as links to the outside world.

The query shown in List 6.21 can help us to collect all these links from Brickley's FOAF document. If you can think of more properties that can be used as links, you can easily add them into List 6.21.

List 6.21 Using `union` keyword to collection links to the outside world

```
base <http://danbri.org/foaf.rdf>
prefix foaf: <http://xmlns.com/foaf/0.1/>
prefix rdfs: <http://www.w3.org/2000/01/rdf-schema#>
prefix owl: <http://www.w3.org/2002/07/owl#>

select ?name ?seeAlso ?sameAs ?topicOf
from <http://danbri.org/foaf.rdf>
where
{
    ?person a foaf:Person .
    ?person foaf:name ?name .
    {
        { ?person rdfs:seeAlso ?seeAlso. }
        union
        { ?person owl:sameAs ?sameAs. }
        union
        { ?person foaf:isPrimaryTopicOf ?topicOf. }
    }
}
```

6.2.2.7 Working with Multiple Graphs

So far, all the queries we have seen have involved only one RDF graph, and we have specified it by using the `from` clause. This graph, in the world of SPARQL, is called a *background graph*. In fact, in addition to this background graph, SPARQL allows us to query any number of *named graphs*, which is the topic of this section.

The first thing to know is how to make a named graph available to a query. As with the background graph, named graphs can be specified by using the following format:

```
from named <uri>
```

Where `<uri>` specifies the location of the graph. Within the query itself, named graphs are used with the `graph` keyword, together with either a variable name that will bind to a named graph or the same `<uri>` for a named graph, as we will see in the examples. In addition, each named graph will have its own graph patterns to match against.

To show the examples, we need to have another RDF graph besides the FOAF file created by Brickley. For our testing purposes, we will use my own FOAF document as the second graph. You can see my FOAF file here:

```
http://iyangyu.com/foaf.rdf
```

Now, let us say that we would like to find those people who are mentioned by both Brickley and myself in our respective FOAF files. List 6.22 is our initial solution, which works with multiple graphs and uses `graph` keyword in conjunction with a variable called `graph_uri`:

List 6.22 Find those who are mentioned by both Brickley's and the author's FOAF documents

```
1:   prefix foaf: <http://xmlns.com/foaf/0.1/>
2:   select distinct ?graph_uri ?name ?email
3:   from named <http://liyangyu.com/foaf.rdf>
4:   from named <http://danbri.org/foaf.rdf>
5:   where
6:   {
7:       graph ?graph_uri
8:       {
9:           ?person a foaf:Person .
10:          ?person foaf:mbox ?email .
11:          optional { ?person foaf:name ?name . }
12:      }
13:  }
```

First of all, notice lines 3 and 4 specify the two named graphs by using `from named` keyword, and each graph is given by its own `<uri>`. As you can tell, one of the graphs is the FOAF file created by Brickley and the other one is my own FOAF document. Furthermore, lines 8–12 define a graph pattern, which will be applied to each of the named graphs available to this query.

When this query is executed by SPARQL engine, variable `graph_uri` will be bound to the URI of one of the named graphs, and the graph pattern shown from lines 8–12 will be matched against this named graph. Once this is done, variable `graph_uri` will be bound to the URI of the next name graph, and the graph pattern is again matched against this current named graph, so on and so forth, until all the named graphs are finished. If a match is found during this process, the matched person's `foaf:mbox` property value will be bound to `email` variable, and the `foaf:name` property value (if exists) will be bound to `name` variable. Finally, line 2 shows the result: it not only shows all the names and e-mails of the selected people, it also shows from which file the information is collected.

Figure 6.11 shows the result of running List 6.22. At the time you are running this query, it is possible that you may see different results, but the discussion here still applies.

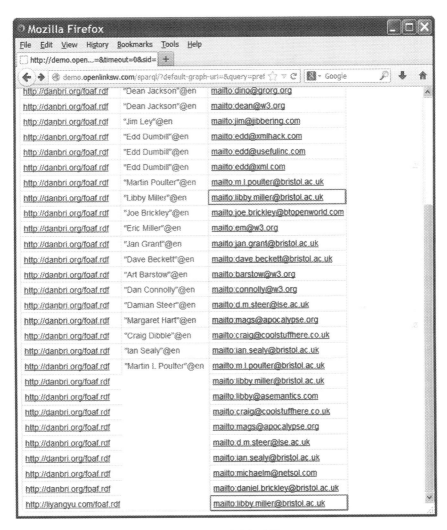

Fig. 6.11 Result from running the query shown in List 6.22

Figure 6.11 shows that both FOAF files have mentioned a person whose e-mail address is given by the following:

<mailto:libby.miller@bristol.ac.uk>

As we will see in Chap. 7, a person can be uniquely identified by her/his foaf: mbox property value, it does not matter whether we have assigned a foaf:name property value to this person or not. And to show this point, in my FOAF file, the name of the person identified by the above e-mail address is intentionally not provided.

Notice that in order to find those people who are mentioned by both FOAF documents, we have to manually read the query result shown in Fig. 6.11, i.e., to find common e-mail addresses from both files. This is certainly not the best solution for us, and we need to change our query to *directly* find those who are mentioned in both graphs.

This new query is shown in List 6.23.

List 6.23 Change List 6.22 to direct get the required result

```
1:  prefix foaf: <http://xmlns.com/foaf/0.1/>
2:  select distinct ?name ?email
3:  from named <http://liyangyu.com/foaf.rdf>
4:  from named <http://danbri.org/foaf.rdf>
5:  where
6:  {
7:      graph <http://liyangyu.com/foaf.rdf>
8:      {
9:          ?person a foaf:Person .
10:         ?person foaf:mbox ?email .
11:         optional { ?person foaf:name ?name . }
12:      } .
13:     graph <http://danbri.org/foaf.rdf>
14:     {
15:         ?person1 a foaf:Person .
16:         ?person1 foaf:mbox ?email .
17:         optional { ?person1 foaf:name ?name . }
18:     } .
19: }
```

In this query, the graph keyword is used with the URI of a named graph (lines 7, 13). The graph pattern defined in lines 8–12 will be applied on my FOAF file,

Fig. 6.12 Result from
running the query shown in
List 6.23

and if matches are found in this graph, they become part of a query solution: the
value of `foaf:mbox` property is bound to a variable named `email`, and value of
`foaf:name` property (if exists), is bound to a variable called `name`. The second
graph pattern (lines 14–18) will be matched against Brickley's FOAF graph,
and the bound variables from the previous query solution will be tested here: the
same variable `email` will have to be matched here, and if possible, the same `name`
variable should match as well. Recall the key of graph patterns: any given
variable, once bound to a value, has to bind to that value during the whole
matching process.

Note that the variable representing a person is different in two graph patterns: in the
first graph pattern it is called `person` (line 9) and in the second graph pattern, it is
called `person1` (line 15). The reason should be clear now: it does not matter whether
this variable holds the same value or not in both patterns, since the `email` value is used
to uniquely identify a person resource. Also, it is possible that a given person resource
is represented by blank nodes in both graphs, and blank nodes only have a scope that is
within the graph that contains them. Therefore, even though they represent the same
resource in the real world, it is simply impossible to match them at all.

Now by running the query in List 6.23, we will be able to find all those
people who are mentioned simultaneously in both graphs. Figure 6.12 shows the
result.

As we discussed earlier, part of the power of RDF graphs comes from data
aggregation. Since both RDF files have provided some information about Libby
Miller, it will be interesting to aggregate these two pieces of information together,
and see what has been said about Miller as a `foaf:Person` instance. List 6.24
accomplishes this.

List 6.24 Data aggregation for Libby Miller

```
1:   prefix foaf: <http://xmlns.com/foaf/0.1/>
2:   select distinct ?graph_uri ?property ?hasValue
3:   from named <http://liyangyu.com/foaf.rdf>
4:   from named <http://danbri.org/foaf.rdf>
```

```
 5:   where
 6:   {
 7:       graph <http://liyangyu.com/foaf.rdf>
 8:       {
 9:          ?person1 a foaf:Person .
10:          ?person1 foaf:mbox ?email .
11:          optional { ?person1 foaf:name ?name . }
12:       } .

13:       graph <http://danbri.org/foaf.rdf>
14:       {
15:          ?person a foaf:Person .
16:          ?person foaf:mbox ?email .
17:          optional { ?person foaf:name ?name . }
18:       } .

19:       graph ?graph_uri
20:       {
21:          ?x a foaf:Person .
22:          ?x foaf:mbox ?email .
23:          ?x ?property ?hasValue.
24:       }

25: }
```

So far, we have seen examples where the graph keyword is used together with a variable that will bind to a named graph (List 6.22), or it is used with an <uri> that represents a named graph (List 6.23). In fact, these two usage patterns can be mixed together, as shown in List 6.24. After the discussion of Lists 6.22 and 6.23, List 6.24 is quite straightforward: clearly, lines 7–18 find those who have been included in both graphs, and lines 19–24 provide graph patterns that will collect everything that has been said about those instances from all the named graphs.

Figure 6.13 shows the query result generated by List 6.24. Again, at the time you are running the query, the result could be different. Nevertheless, as shown in Fig. 6.13, statements about Miller from both FOAF files have been aggregated together. This simple example, in fact, shows the basic flow of how an aggregation agent may work by using the search capabilities provided by SPARQL endpoints.

The last example of this section is given by List 6.25, where a background graph and a named graph are used together. Read this query and try to find what it does before you read on.

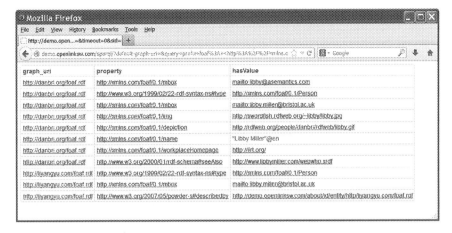

Fig. 6.13 Result from running the query shown in List 6.24

List 6.25 What does this query do? Think about it before reading on

```
 1:  prefix foaf: <http://xmlns.com/foaf/0.1/>
 2:  select distinct ?property ?hasValue
 3:  from <http://danbri.org/foaf.rdf>
 4:  from named <http://liyangyu.com/foaf.rdf>
 5:  from named <http://danbri.org/foaf.rdf>

 6:  where
 7:  {
 8:     graph <http://liyangyu.com/foaf.rdf>
 9:     {
10:        ?person1 a foaf:Person .
11:        ?person1 foaf:mbox ?email .
12:        optional { ?person1 foaf:name ?name . }
13:     } .

14:     graph <http://danbri.org/foaf.rdf>
15:     {
16:        ?person a foaf:Person .
17:        ?person foaf:mbox ?email .
18:        optional { ?person foaf:name ?name . }
19:     } .

20:     ?x a foaf:Person .
21:     ?x foaf:mbox ?email .
22:     ?x ?property ?hasValue.

23: }
```

The interesting part of this query is at lines 3–5, where a background graph is specified on line 3, and two named graphs are introduced on lines 4 and 5. Notice that lines 3 and 5 are in fact the same graph.

Now, lines 8–19 are the same as the query in List 6.24 (trying to find those who are mentioned in both graphs), and lines 20–22 are a graph pattern that does not specify any graph, so this pattern is matched against the background graph. Therefore, this query, after finding those who are the mentioned in both Brickley's file and my file, tries to collect everything that has been said about them from Brickley's file *only*. This is not a data aggregation case as shown by List 6.24, but it shows the combination usage of a background graph and a named graph. Figure 6.14 shows the query result, and comparing it to Fig. 6.13, you will see the difference.

As this point, we have covered quite a few features of SPARQL's `select` query, and the examples presented here should have given you enough to explore its other features on your own. Let us move on to SPARQL's other query styles, which we will briefly discuss in the next several sections.

6.2.3 CONSTRUCT Query

`construct` query is another query form provided by SPARQL which, instead of returning a collection of query solutions, returns a new RDF graph. Let us take a look at some examples.

List 6.26 creates a new FOAF graph, which has a collection of all the names and e-mails of those who are mentioned in Brickley's FOAF document. List 6.27 shows part of this new graph.

Fig. 6.14 Result from running the query shown in List 6.25

List 6.26 Example of a query

```
prefix foaf: <http://xmlns.com/foaf/0.1/>

construct {
   ?person a foaf:Person.
   ?person foaf:name ?name.
   ?person foaf:mbox ?email.
}
from <http://danbri.org/foaf.rdf>

where
{
   ?person a foaf:Person.
   ?person foaf:name ?name.
   ?person foaf:mbox ?email.
}
```

List 6.27 Part of the generated RDF graph

```
<?xml version="1.0"?>
<rdf:RDF
    xmlns:foaf="http://xmlns.com/foaf/0.1/"
    xmlns:rdf="http://www.w3.org/1999/02/22-rdf-syntax-ns#">
  <foaf:Person>
    <foaf:mbox rdf:resource="mailto:craig@coolstuffhere.co.uk"/>
    <foaf:name xml:lang="en">Craig Dibble</foaf:name>
  </foaf:Person>
  <foaf:Person>
    <foaf:name xml:lang="en">Joe Brickley</foaf:name>
    <foaf:mbox rdf:resource=
              "mailto:joe.brickley@btopenworld.com"/>
  </foaf:Person>
  <foaf:Person>
    <foaf:mbox rdf:resource="mailto:libby.miller@bristol.ac.uk"/>
    <foaf:name xml:lang="en">Libby Miller</foaf:name>
  </foaf:Person>
... more ...
```

This generated new graph is indeed clean and nice, but it is not that interesting. In fact, a common use of the `construct` query form is to transform a given graph to a new graph that uses a different ontology.

For example, List 6.28 will transfer FOAF data to `vCard` data, and List 6.29 shows part of the resulting graph.

List 6.28 Another `construct` query which changes FOAF document into vCard
document

```
prefix foaf: <http://xmlns.com/foaf/0.1/>
prefix vCard: <http://www.w3.org/2001/vcard-rdf/3.0#>

construct {
   ?person vCard:FN ?name.
   ?person vCard:URL ?homepage.
}
from <http://danbri.org/foaf.rdf>

where
{
   optional {
     ?person foaf:name ?name .
     filter isLiteral(?name) .
   }
   optional {
     ?person foaf:homepage ?homepage .
     filter isURI(?homepage) .
   }
}
```

List 6.29 Part of the new graph expressed as vCard data

```
<?xml version="1.0"?>
<rdf:RDF
    xmlns:foaf="http://xmlns.com/foaf/0.1/"
    xmlns:rdf="http://www.w3.org/1999/02/22-rdf-syntax-ns#"
    xmlns:vCard="http://www.w3.org/2001/vcard-rdf/3.0#">
  <rdf:Description>
    <vCard:FN xml:lang="en">Dan Connolly</vCard:FN>
  </rdf:Description>
  <rdf:Description>
    <vCard:FN xml:lang="en">Dan Brickley</vCard:FN>
  </rdf:Description>
  <rdf:Description>
    <vCard:FN xml:lang="en">Jim Ley</vCard:FN>
  </rdf:Description>
  <rdf:Description>
    <vCard:FN xml:lang="en">Eric Miller</vCard:FN>
    <vCard:URL rdf:resource="http://purl.org/net/eric/"/>
  </rdf:Description>

... more ...
```

6.2.4 *DESCRIBE Query*

At this point, every query we have constructed requires us to know something about the data graph. For example, when we are querying against a FOAF document, at least we know some frequently used FOAF terms, such as `foaf:mbox` and `foaf:name`, so we can provide search criteria to the SPARQL query processor. This is similar to writing SQL queries against a database system: we have to be familiar with the structures of the tables in order to come up with queries.

However, sometimes we just don't know much about the data graph, and we don't even know what to ask. If this is the case, we can ask a SPARQL query processor to describe the resource we want to know, and it is up to the processor to provide some useful information about the resource we have asked about.

This is the reason behind the `describe` query. After receiving the query, a SPARQL processor creates and returns an RDF graph; the content of the graph is decided by the query processor, not the query itself.

For example, List 6.30 is one such query:

List 6.30 Example of `describe` query

```
prefix foaf: <http://xmlns.com/foaf/0.1/>

describe ?x
from <http://danbri.org/foaf.rdf>
where
{
    ?x foaf:mbox <mailto:timbl@w3.org> .
}
```

In this case, the only thing we know is the e-mail address, so we provide this information and ask the SPARQL processor to tell us more about the resource whose e-mail address is given by `<mailto:timbl@w3.org>`. The query result is another RDF graph whose statements are determined by the query processor. For OpenLink's Virtuoso endpoint, Fig. 6.15 shows the result.

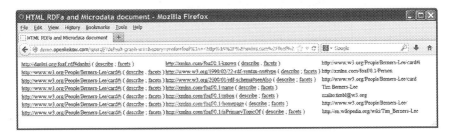

Fig. 6.15 Result from running the query shown in List 6.30

6.2.5 ASK Query

SPARQL's `ask` query is identified by the `ask` keyword, and the query processor
simply returns a `true` or `false` value, depending on whether the given graph
pattern has any matches in the dataset or not.

List 6.31 is a simple example of the `ask` query:

List 6.31 Example of using `ask` query

```
prefix foaf: <http://xmlns.com/foaf/0.1/>

ask
from <http://danbri.org/foaf.rdf>
where
{
    ?x foaf:mbox <mailto:danbri@danbri.org>.
}
```

This query has a graph pattern that is equivalent to the following question: is
there a resource whose `foaf:mbox` property uses `<mailto:danbri@danbri.`
`org>` as its value? To answer this query, the processor tries to match the graph
pattern against the FOAF data graph, and apparently, a successful match is found;
therefore, `true` is returned as the answer.

It is fun to work with the `ask` query. For example, List 6.32 tries to decide
whether it is true that Brickley was either born before January 1, 1970 or after
January 1, 1980:

List 6.32 Ask the birthday of Dan Brickley

```
base <http://danbri.org/foaf.rdf>
prefix foaf: <http://xmlns.com/foaf/0.1/>
prefix xsd: <http://www.w3.org/2001/XMLSchema#>

ask
from <http://danbri.org/foaf.rdf>
where
{
   <#danbri> foaf:dateOfBirth ?dob .
   filter ( xsd:date(str(?dob)) <= "1970-01-01"^^xsd:date ||
            xsd:date(str(?dob)) >= "1980-01-01"^^xsd:date )
}
```

And certainly, this will give `false` as the answer. Notice we should understand this answer in the following way: the processor cannot find any binding to compute a solution to the graph pattern specified in this query.

Obviously, a `true` or `false` answer depends on the given graph pattern. In fact, you can use any graph pattern together with an `ask` query. As the last example, you can ask whether Brickley's FOAF file and my own FOAF file have both described anyone in common, and this query should look very familiar, as shown in List 6.33:

List 6.33 Ask if the two FOAF documents have described anyone in common

```
prefix foaf: <http://xmlns.com/foaf/0.1/>

ask
from named <http://www.liyangyu.com/foaf.rdf>
from named <http://danbri.org/foaf.rdf>
where
{
    graph <http://liyangyu.com/foaf.rdf>
    {
        ?person a foaf:Person .
        ?person foaf:mbox ?email .
        optional { ?person foaf:name ?name . }
    } .
    graph <http://danbri.org/foaf.rdf>
    {
        ?person1 a foaf:Person .
        ?person1 foaf:mbox ?email .
        optional { ?person1 foaf:name ?name . }
    } .
}
```

If you run the query, you will get `true` as the answer, as you might have expected.

6.2.6   What Is Missing from SPARQL 1.0?

At this point, we have covered the core components of the SPARQL 1.0 standard. If you are experienced with SQL queries, you have probably realized the fact that there is something missing in SPARQL 1.0 language constructs. Let us briefly discuss these issues in this section, and in the next section we take a closer look at SPARQL 1.1, the SPARQL Working Group's latest standard.

The most obvious fact about SPARQL 1.0 is that it is read-only. In its current stage, SPARQL 1.0 is only a retrieval query language; there are no equivalents of the SQL `insert`, `update` and `delete` statements.

The second noticeable missing piece is that SPARQL 1.0 does not support any grouping capabilities or aggregate functions, such as `min`, `max`, `avg`, `sum`, just to name a few. There are some implementations of SPARQL 1.0 that provide these functionalities; yet, standardization is needed so a uniform interface can be reached.

Another important missing component is the service description. More specifically, there is no standard way for a SPARQL endpoint to advertise its capabilities and its dataset.

There are other functionalities that are missing, and we are not going to list them all there. Fortunately, these missing pieces are also the main components of the new SPARQL 1.1 standard, which is covered in detail in the next section.

6.3   SPARQL 1.1 Query Language

6.3.1   Introduction: What Is New?

As we discussed in Sect. 6.1.1, the SPARQL 1.1 Recommendations produced by the SPARQL Working Group has altogether 11 documents. These documents together define a set of specifications, as shown in Table 6.2.

It is obviously not possible to cover everything in detail. We will only focus on new SPARQL 1.1 Query Language features, SPARQL 1.1 Federated Query and

Table 6.2 SPARQL 1.1 specifications

Specification	Definitions
SPARQL 1.1 Query Language	A query language for RDF
SPARQL 1.1 Query Results JSON, CSV and TSV Formats	Besides the standard XML format, three alternative popular formats to exchange answers to SPARQL queries
SPARQL 1.1 Federated Query	An extension of SPARQL 1.1 Query Language for executing queries distributed over different SPARQL endpoints
SPARQL 1.1 Entailment Regimes	Rules for using SPARQL 1.1 in an inferencing environment such as RDFS and OWL
SPARQL 1.1 Update Language	An update language for RDF
SPARQL 1.1 Protocol for RDF	Means for conveying arbitrary SPARQL queries and update requests to a SPARQL service
SPARQL 1.1 Service Description	A method for discovering and a vocabulary for describing SPARQL services
SPARQL 1.1 Graph Store HTTP Protocol	Minimal means for managing RDF graph content directly via common HTTP operations
SPARQL 1.1 Test Cases	A suite of test cases for understanding corner cases and assessing whether a system is SPARQL 1.1 conformant

SPARQL 1.1 Update Language, because these specifications are the ones that are most relevant to our daily development work on the Semantic Web.

6.3.2 SPARQL 1.1 Query

SPARQL 1.1 Query Language offers extra features that include aggregates, subqueries, negation, property paths and assignments. We take a look at each one of these features in this section.

6.3.2.1 Aggregates

If you are experienced with SQL queries, chances are that you are familiar with aggregate functions. These functions operate over the columns of a result table, and can conduct operations such as counting, numerical averaging or selecting the maximal/minimal data element from the given column. The SPARQL 1.0 query standard does not provide these operations, and if an application needs these functions, the application has to take a SPARQL query result set and calculate the aggregate values by itself.

Enabling a SPARQL engine to calculate aggregates for the users makes the application more light-weight, since the work is done on the SPARQL engine side. In addition, this normally results in significantly smaller result sets being returned to the application. If the SPARQL endpoint is accessed over HTTP, this also help to reduce the traffic on the network.

With these considerations, SPARQL 1.1 supports aggregate functions. A query pattern yields a solution set, and from this solution set, a collection of columns is returned to the user as the query result. An aggregation function then operates on this set to create a new solution set that normally contains a single value representing the result from the aggregate function.

The following aggregate functions are currently supported by SPARQL 1.1:

- COUNT
- SUM
- MIN/MAX
- AVG
- GROUP_CONCAT
- SAMPLE

Understand that aggregates apply expressions over groups of solutions. Grouping maybe specified by using GROUP BY syntax, and by default, a solution set consists of a single group, which contains all solutions.

Fig. 6.16 Result from running the query shown in List 6.34

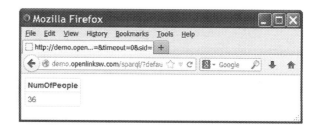

The first example queries about how many people have their e-mail addresses provided in a given FOAF document. List 6.34 shows the query itself.

List 6.34 Example of using count() aggregate function

```
prefix foaf: <http://xmlns.com/foaf/0.1/>
SELECT count(*) AS ?NumOfPeople
from <http://danbri.org/foaf.rdf>
WHERE {
    ?x a foaf:Person;
        foaf:mbox ?mbox .
}
```

This does not require much of an explanation at all. Figure 6.16 shows the result.

The following example scans a given FOAF document and tries to sum up all the ages of the people included in this document, as shown in List 6.35.

List 6.35 Example of using sum() aggregate function

```
prefix foaf: <http://xmlns.com/foaf/0.1/>
SELECT ( sum(?age) AS ?ages )
from <http://danbri.org/foaf.rdf>
WHERE {
    ?x a foaf:Person;
        foaf:age ?age.
}
```

The final result is stored in the ages variable.

The next example is taken from W3C's official SPARQL 1.1 Query Language document.[9] List 6.36 shows a simple data set:

---

[9] http://www.w3.org/TR/sparql11-query/

List 6.36 Data set taken from W3C SPARQL 1.1 Query Language document

```
@prefix : <http://books.example/> .

:org1 :affiliates :auth1, :auth2 .
:auth1 :writesBook :book1, :book2 .
:book1 :price 9 .
:book2 :price 5 .
:auth2 :writesBook :book3 .
:book3 :price 7 .
:org2 :affiliates :auth3 .
:auth3 :writesBook :book4 .
:book4 :price 7 .
```

From this simple data set, we can tell that authors from `org1` have written books that can sell for altogether $21, and the only author in `org2` has written a book that sells for $7. Our goal is to write a query to find the department that has a total book price that is more than $10.

To accomplish this, we can start from finding out the total book price of each department. List 6.37 shows the query.

List 6.37 Find the total book price for each departure

```
PREFIX : <http://books.example/>
SELECT ?org (SUM(?price) AS ?totalPrice)
WHERE {
  ?org :affiliates ?auth .
  ?auth :writesBook ?book .
  ?book :price ?price .
}
GROUP BY ?org
```

If you are familiar with database SQL, BROUG BY in SPARQL keeps the same meaning. The triples are divided into different groups based on `org`, the subject of `affiliates` property, and the prices within each group are then aggregated by using SUM function. Figure 6.17 shows the query result.

It is easy to change the aggregate function to get different matrix. For example, List 6.38 retrieves the average price of the books in each departure, and Fig. 6.18 shows the query result.

Fig. 6.17 Result from
running the query shown in
List 6.37

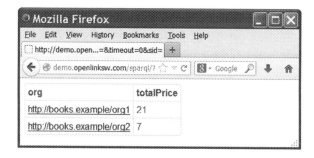

Fig. 6.18 Result from
running the query shown in
List 6.38

List 6.38 Find the average book price for each departure

```
PREFIX : <http://books.example/>
SELECT ?org (AVG(?price) AS ?averagePrice)
WHERE {
  ?org :affiliates ?auth .
  ?auth :writesBook ?book .
  ?book :price ?price .
}
GROUP BY ?org
```

Similarly, to find the most expensive book in each department, we can simply use
aggregate function MAX, as shown in List 6.39, and Fig. 6.19 shows the query result.

List 6.39 Find the most expensive book within each departure

```
PREFIX : <http://books.example/>
SELECT ?org (MAX(?price) AS ?mostExpensivePrice)
WHERE {
  ?org :affiliates ?auth .
  ?auth :writesBook ?book .
  ?book :price ?price .
}
GROUP BY ?org
```

Fig. 6.19 Result from running the query shown in List 6.39

Fig. 6.20 Result from running the query shown in List 6.40

Now, with what we have already learned, accomplishing the goal of finding the department that has a total book price greater than $10 is easy. List 6.40 shows the query, and Fig. 6.20 shows the result.

List 6.40 Find the department that has a total book price that is greater than $10

```
PREFIX : <http://books.example/>
SELECT ?org (SUM(?price) AS ?totalPrice)
WHERE {
  ?org :affiliates ?auth .
  ?auth :writesBook ?book .
  ?book :price ?price .
}
GROUP BY ?org
HAVING (SUM(?price) > 10)
```

The last example we would like to discuss here is the SAMPLE function. Let us go back to Brickley's FOAF document, and assume the goal is to pick *only one* e-mail address for those in the document who have actually provided at least one e-mail address. Note that quite a few people in the document have more than one e-mail address; so how can we make sure among multiple e-mail addresses of a person that only one is picked up?

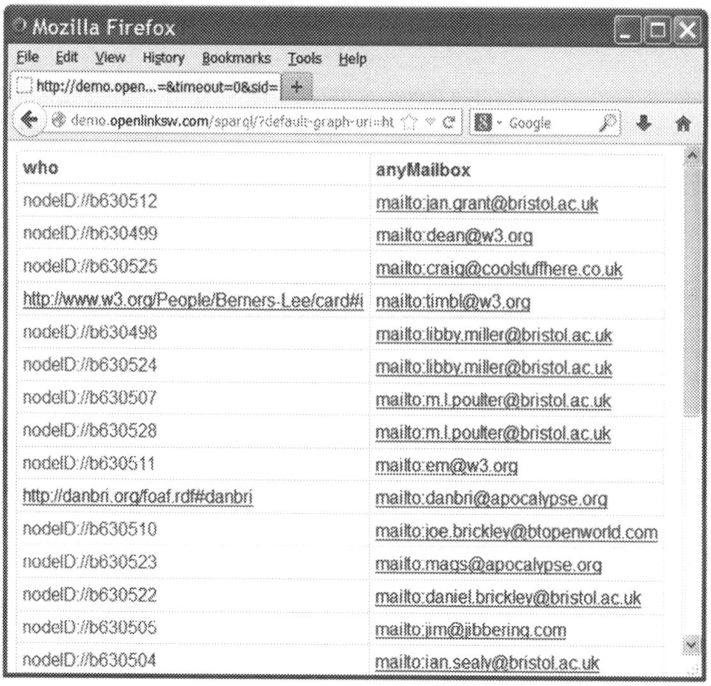

who	anyMailbox
nodeID://b630512	mailto:ian.grant@bristol.ac.uk
nodeID://b630499	mailto:dean@w3.org
nodeID://b630525	mailto:craig@coolstuffhere.co.uk
http://www.w3.org/People/Berners-Lee/card#i	mailto:timbl@w3.org
nodeID://b630498	mailto:libby.miller@bristol.ac.uk
nodeID://b630524	mailto:libby.miller@bristol.ac.uk
nodeID://b630507	mailto:m.l.poulter@bristol.ac.uk
nodeID://b630528	mailto:m.l.poulter@bristol.ac.uk
nodeID://b630511	mailto:em@w3.org
http://danbri.org/foaf.rdf#danbri	mailto:danbri@apocalypse.org
nodeID://b630510	mailto:joe.brickley@btopenworld.com
nodeID://b630523	mailto:mags@apocalypse.org
nodeID://b630522	mailto:daniel.brickley@bristol.ac.uk
nodeID://b630505	mailto:jim@jibbering.com
nodeID://b630504	mailto:ian.sealy@bristol.ac.uk

Fig. 6.21 Result from running the query shown in List 6.41

To accomplish this, we can use `GROUP BY` to group on each individual, and then use `SAMPLE` to pick just one e-mail address, regardless of how many e-mail addresses that individual actually has. List 6.41 shows the query, and Fig. 6.21 shows the query result.

List 6.41 Using `sample()` to return one and only one e-mail address

```
prefix foaf: <http://xmlns.com/foaf/0.1/>
SELECT (?subj AS ?who) (sample(?obj) AS ?anyMailbox)
from <http://danbri.org/foaf.rdf>
WHERE {
  ?subj foaf:mbox ?obj.
} group by ?subj
```

As you can see from Fig. 6.21, each person has only one e-mail address included in the query result. Run the query without `SAMPLE` operator, and you will be able to see the difference more clearly.

In addition, `SAMPLE` aggregate can also help to solve the issue where it is not possible to project a particular variable or apply functions over that variable out of a `GROUP` simply because that particular variable is not grouped upon. Now, with `sample` aggregate function, this is very easy, as shown in List 6.41.

6.3.2.2   Subqueries

Subqueries are not new in querying. In practice, it is sometimes helpful or necessary to use the result from one query to continue the next query.

For example, let us consider a simple request: assume we would like to find all the friends Brickley has, and for each one of them, we would like to know their e-mail addresses. Obviously, this task can be easily accomplished by using a single query; and there is no need to use any SPARQL 1.1 features either.

However, let us slightly change the request: find all the friends Brickley has, and for each of them, we would like to have only one e-mail address returned.

This can actually be accomplished by using SAMPLE function, as shown in List 6.42. Figure 6.22 shows the query result.

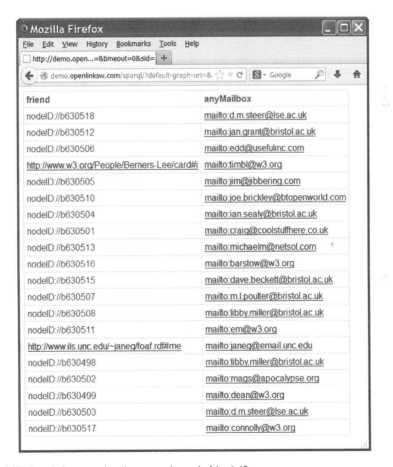

Fig. 6.22   Result from running the query shown in List 6.42

List 6.42 Using `sample()` to return one and only one e-mail address of Brickley's friends

```
prefix foaf: <http://xmlns.com/foaf/0.1/>
SELECT ?friend (sample(?email) AS ?anyMailbox)
from <http://danbri.org/foaf.rdf>
WHERE {
  <http://danbri.org/foaf.rdf#danbri> foaf:knows ?friend.
  ?friend foaf:mbox ?email.
} group by ?friend
```

Now, we can use the subquery feature provided by SPARQL 1.1 to accomplish the same goal. List 6.43 shows the query.

List 6.43 Using the subquery feature to accomplish the same as by List 6.42

```
prefix foaf: <http://xmlns.com/foaf/0.1/>
SELECT ?friend ?anyMailbox
from <http://danbri.org/foaf.rdf>
WHERE {
  <http://danbri.org/foaf.rdf#danbri> foaf:knows ?friend .
  {
    SELECT ?friend (sample(?email) AS ?anyMailbox)
    WHERE {
      ?friend foaf:mbox ?email.
    } GROUP BY ?friend
  }
}
```

If you run this query, you can see the result is the same as shown in Fig. 6.22. Understand that for subquery, the result is achieved by first evaluating the inner query:

```
SELECT ?friend (sample(?email) AS ?anyMailbox)
WHERE {
  ?friend foaf:mbox ?email.
} GROUP BY ?friend
```

which returns all the people, together with only one e-mail for each one of them. The out-query is evaluated next, which returns the people Brickley knows. The two result sets are then joined together to produce the final result by using `?friend` as the join key.

6.3.2.3   Negation

Negation can sometimes be implemented by simply using the language constructs
from SPARQL 1.0 only. Let us consider the request of finding all the people in
Brickley's FOAF document who do not have any e-mail address specified. The
query in List 6.44 will accomplish this, and note it only uses the language features
from SPARQL 1.0.

List 6.44 Find all the people who do not have any e-mail address specified

```
prefix foaf: <http://xmlns.com/foaf/0.1/>

SELECT ?name
from <http://danbri.org/foaf.rdf>
WHERE {
   ?x foaf:givenname ?name .
   OPTIONAL { ?x foaf:mbox ?mbox } .
   FILTER (!BOUND(?mbox))
}
```

List 6.44 uses the BOUND() operator. In general, the BOUND() operator is used as
follows:

```
xsd:boolean BOUND(variable var)
```

It returns `true` if *var* is bounded to a value, and returns `false` otherwise. The
BOUND() operator is quite often used to test that a graph pattern is *not* expressed by
specifying an OPTIONAL graph pattern which uses a variable, and then testing to see
that the variable is not bound, just as shown in List 6.44. This testing method is
called *negation as failure* in logic programming.

With this said, the query in List 6.44 is easy to understand: it matches the people
with a name but no expressed e-mail address. However, the negation-as-failure
method is not quite intuitive and has a somewhat convoluted syntax. To fix this,
SPARQL 1.1 has adopted several new operators to implement a better way of
negation.

One such new operator is NOT EXISTS, which is used together with filter
expression. List 6.45 shows one example, which accomplishes exactly the same
thing that List 6.44 does.

List 6.45 Find all the people who do not have any e-mail address specified by using NOT EXISTS operator

```
prefix foaf: <http://xmlns.com/foaf/0.1/>
SELECT ?name
from <http://danbri.org/foaf.rdf>
WHERE {
   ?x foaf:givenname  ?name .
   FILTER NOT EXISTS { ?x foaf:mbox ?mbox } .
}
```

SPARQL 1.1 also provides filter expression EXISTS, which tests whether a pattern can be found in the data. For example, List 6.46 tries to find all the people who have provided at least one e-mail address.

List 6.46 Find all the people who have specified at least one e-mail address by using EXISTS operator

```
prefix foaf: <http://xmlns.com/foaf/0.1/>
SELECT ?name
from <http://danbri.org/foaf.rdf>
WHERE {
   ?x foaf:name  ?name .
   FILTER EXISTS { ?x foaf:mbox ?mbox } .
}
```

Another different style of negation provided by SPARQL 1.1 is the MINUS operator. It evaluates both its arguments, then calculates solutions on the left-hand side that are not compatible with the solutions on the right-hand side. List 6.47 accomplishes exactly the same goal as List 6.45 does, but with a cleaner syntax.

List 6.47 Find all the people who do not have any e-mail address specified by using MINUS operator

```
prefix foaf: <http://xmlns.com/foaf/0.1/>
SELECT ?name
from <http://danbri.org/foaf.rdf>
WHERE {
   ?x foaf:givenName ?name .
   MINUS {
     ?x foaf:mbox ?mbox .
   }
}
```

It is important to understand the difference between NOT EXISTS and MINUS, and use them carefully. More specifically, NOT EXISTS works by testing whether a pattern exists in the data, given the bindings already determined by the query. On the other hand, MINUS tries to remove triples by evaluating the two patterns.

The following example is taken from W3C's official document. Regardless of the dataset, this query that uses NOT EXISTS should produce no solutions,

```
SELECT *

{
    ?s ?p ?o
    FILTER NOT EXISTS { ?x ?y ?z }
}
```

since {?s ?p ?o} matches everything in the dataset, and {?x ?y ?z} matches everything that {?s ?p ?o} matches, so it eliminates any solutions.

The following query that uses MINUS returns everything back,

```
SELECT *

{
    ?s ?p ?o
    MINUS { ?x ?y ?z }
}
```

because there is no shared variable between {?s ?p ?o} and {?x ?y ?z}, so no bindings are eliminated.

Furthermore, assume the following simple dataset,

```
@prefix : <http://example/> .
:a :b :c .
```

This query that uses a concrete pattern (a pattern without variables) will return no solutions:

```
SELECT *

{
    ?s ?p ?o
    FILTER NOT EXISTS { :a :b :c }
}
```

However, this query still returns everything back,

```
SELECT *

{
    ?s ?p ?o
    MINUS { :a :b :c }
}
```

because there is no match of binding, so everything solution picked by {?s ?p ?o} stays.

6.3.2.4 Property Paths

A property path is defined as a route through a graph between two graph nodes. Obviously, a triple pattern is a property path of length exactly 1.

Property path is critical in any query. If you have some experience writing SPARQL queries, you have probably seen the cases where you need to follow property paths to finish your query. More specifically, in order to find what you want, you need to construct a query that covers fixed-length paths to traverse along the hierarchical structure expressed in the given dataset. List 6.48 shows one such example. This query tries to find the name of my friend's friend:

List 6.48 Find the name of my friend's friend

```
prefix foaf:<http://xmlns.com/foaf/0.1/>
SELECT ?name
  from <http://liyangyu.com/foaf.rdf>
where {
  ?myself foaf:mbox <mailto:liyang@liyangyu.com> .
  ?myself foaf:knows ?friend .
  ?friend foaf:knows ?friendOfFriend .
  ?friendOfFriend foaf:name ?name .
}
```

As shown in List 6.48, the paths we have traversed include the following: myself, friend, friendOfFriend, name of friendOfFriend. This is quite long and cumbersome. The property paths feature provided by SPARQL 1.1 Query will make this a lot simpler for us. List 6.49 shows the new query:

List 6.49 Find the name of my friend's friend by using property path

```
prefix foaf:<http://xmlns.com/foaf/0.1/>
SELECT ?name
from <http://liyangyu.com/foaf.rdf>
where {
  ?myself foaf:mbox <mailto:liyang@liyangyu.com> .
  ?myself foaf:knows/foaf:knows/foaf:name ?name .
}
```

This accomplishes exactly the same goal as the query in List 6.48, but with a much cleaner syntax.

Quite a few operators are supported by SPARQL 1.1 in property path expressions, including the following ones:

- binary operator |
- binary operator /
- unary operators *, ? and +
- unary ^ inverse link operator

Operator | is used for *alternative* selections. For example, the query shown in List 6.50 matches all the possible names:

List 6.50 Find all the matching names for Brickley

```
prefix foaf: <http://xmlns.com/foaf/0.1/>
SELECT *
from <http://danbri.org/foaf.rdf>
WHERE {
   <http://danbri.org/foaf.rdf#danbri>
        foaf:name|foaf:givenname ?name .
}
```

This would be quite useful if it is unclear which property (foaf:name or foaf:givenname) has been used for name. Similarly, dc:title|rdfs:label could be used as the property path when trying to find the description of the subject.

Operator / is used for *sequence*, and the query shown in List 6.49 is one such example. Note the property path in List 6.49 has a fixed length, that is, one can use it to find the friend of a friend. What if we would like to trace all the way down to find all the connections by following foaf:knows relationship?

This can be solved by using unary operators *, ? and +, so that connectivity between the subject and object by a property path of arbitrary length can be created. More specifically, * represents "zero or more" property path, + represents "one or more" and ? represents "zero or one". List 6.51 shows a query that tries to find the names of the all the people that can be reached from Brickley by `foaf:knows`.

List 6.51 Find all the people that can be reached from Brickley by `foaf:knows`

```
prefix foaf:<http://xmlns.com/foaf/0.1/>
SELECT ?name
from <http://danbri.org/foaf.rdf>
where {
   <http://danbri.org/foaf.rdf#danbri>
        foaf:knows+/foaf:name ?name  .
}
```

List 6.52 shows another way of using arbitrary length path matching—it tries to find all the possible types of a resource, including all the super-types of resources.

List 6.52 Find all the possible types of a resource, including all supertypes

```
PREFIX   rdfs:     <http://www.w3.org/2000/01/rdf-schema#>
PREFIX   rdf:      <http://www.w3.org/1999/02/22-rdf-syntax-ns#>
SELECT ?resource ?type
{
   ?resource rdf:type/rdfs:subClassOf* ?type  .
}
```

Be careful when running List 6.52; it could take quite a while to check all the super-types.

It is also possible to combine these length operators with alternative selections. For example,

```
{ ?ancestor (ex:motherOf|ex:fatherOf)+ <#me> . }
```

can be used to trace all the ancestors of `<#me>`.

Finally, unary ^ inverse link operator can be very helpful in some cases. To understand this operator, let us first see a simple example. Recall that `foaf:mbox` is an inverse functional property, so the query shown in List 6.53 can be used to uniquely locate the person whose e-mail address is known.

List 6.53 Use e-mail address to uniquely locate the person

```
prefix foaf:<http://xmlns.com/foaf/0.1/>
SELECT ?who
from <http://danbri.org/foaf.rdf>
where {
    ?who foaf:mbox <mailto:danbri@w3.org> .
}
```

In other words, to identify a person instance, you don't actually have to remember the URI for that person; all you need is to include the pattern shown in List 6.53, which always locates that person correctly. This trick is also used in List 6.49, where instead of remembering my own URI, the following pattern is used to identify myself:

```
?myself foaf:mbox <mailto:liyang@liyangyu.com>
```

Now, List 6.54 is equivalent to List 6.53; the only difference is that List 6.54 uses the inverse property path, and also swaps the roles of subject and object accordingly.

List 6.54 Use e-mail address to uniquely locate the person, as in List 6.53, but with inverse property path

```
prefix foaf:<http://xmlns.com/foaf/0.1/>
SELECT ?who
from <http://danbri.org/foaf.rdf>
where {
    <mailto:danbri@w3.org> ^foaf:mbox ?who .
}
```

If you do a test run of both List 6.53 and List 6.54, you will see they both return Brickley's URI as the result.

With this in place, List 6.55 is not difficult to understand: it tries to find all the people who know someone that Brickley knows.

List 6.55 Find all the people who know someone that Brickley knows

```
prefix foaf:<http://xmlns.com/foaf/0.1/>
SELECT ?who
from <http://danbri.org/foaf.rdf>
where {
  <http://danbri.org/foaf.rdf#danbri>
        foaf:knows/^foaf:knows ?who .
  FILTER ( <http://danbri.org/foaf.rdf#danbri> != ?who )
}
```

6.3.2.5 Assignment

Sometimes it is helpful if the value of an expression can be added to a solution mapping by assigning a new variable to the value of the expression. The variable itself should also be allowed in the query and returned as part of the result if necessary. SPARQL 1.1 has added support for this functionality, which is known as assignment.

To assign the value of an expression to a variable, the following syntax should be used:

expression AS *?var*

To add the variable into the solution mapping, or to use the variable with query, the BIND keyword can be used. The following simple dataset (List 6.56) is taken from W3C's official document about SPARQL 1.1, and List 6.57 shows one example query that uses BIND keyword for assignment.

List 6.56 A small dataset from W3C's SPARQL 1.1 Query Language document: book_data.ttl

```
@prefix dc:   <http://purl.org/dc/elements/1.1/> .
@prefix :     <http://example.org/book/> .
@prefix ns:   <http://example.org/ns#> .

:book1  dc:title      "SPARQL Tutorial" .
:book1  ns:price      42 .
:book1  ns:discount   0.2 .
:book1  ns:publisher  "W3C" .
:book1  ns:pubYear    "2010" .

:book2  dc:title      "The Semantic Web" .
:book2  ns:price      23 .
:book2  ns:discount   0.25 .
:book2  ns:publisher  "Springer" .
:book2  ns:pubYear    "2011" .
```

List 6.57 Find the book with price less than $20 (after discount), and show the title and the price of the book

```
PREFIX   dc:  <http://purl.org/dc/elements/1.1/>
PREFIX   ns:  <http://example.org/ns#>

SELECT   ?title ?price
FROM <http://liyangyu.com/book_data.ttl>
{  { ?x ns:price ?p .
     ?x ns:discount ?discount
     BIND (?p*(1-?discount) AS ?price)
  }
  {?x dc:title ?title . }
  FILTER(?price < 20)
}
```

Fig. 6.23 Result from running the query shown in List 6.57

List 6.57 is straightforward: the value of expression `?p*(1-?discount)` is assigned to variable `price`, which is used in the `FILTER` and returned as part of the result. The `FILTER` applies to the whole group pattern to get the correct result (a book that costs less than $20). Figure 6.23 shows the query result.

Another useful feature we would like to discuss here is the `VALUES` keyword offered by SPARQL 1.1 Query Language. Compared to SPARQL 1.1's new `BIND` keyword, the `VALUES` keyword lets us create tables of values, offering powerful new options when filtering query results.

Let us again use the dataset in List 6.56 as the base dataset. The query shown in List 6.58 retrieves each book, with its title, year published and publisher. Obviously, since there is no filter of any kind, the two books in the dataset will all be returned in the result set.

List 6.58 Show the book title, the year published and publisher

```
PREFIX dc:    <http://purl.org/dc/elements/1.1/>
PREFIX :      <http://example.org/book/>
PREFIX ns:    <http://example.org/ns#>

SELECT distinct ?book ?title ?pyear ?publisher
FROM <http://liyangyu.com/book_data.ttl>
{
    ?book dc:title ?title ;
    ns:publisher ?publisher ;
    ns:pubYear ?pyear ;
    ns:price ?price .
}
```

The query in List 6.59 has a `VALUES` clause, indicating that we are only interested in results that have `Springer` as the value of `?publisher` variable. This `VALUES` clause acts like a new filter, and the query result is shown in Fig. 6.24. As we can see, only one book is now returned, and this book is indeed published by Springer.

Fig. 6.24 Result from
running the query shown in
List 6.59

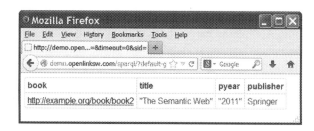

Fig. 6.25 Result from
running the query shown in
List 6.60

List 6.59 Same as List 6.58, but only pick those with the right publisher

```
PREFIX dc:    <http://purl.org/dc/elements/1.1/>
PREFIX :      <http://example.org/book/>
PREFIX ns:    <http://example.org/ns#>

SELECT distinct ?book ?title ?pyear ?publisher
FROM <http://liyangyu.com/book_data.ttl>
{
    ?book dc:title ?title ;
        ns:publisher ?publisher ;
        ns:pubYear ?pyear ;
        ns:price ?price .
    VALUES ?publisher { "Springer" }
}
```

List 6.60 goes further by having a two-dimensional table to use for filtering out
the results. After retrieving all the books, this query only passes along the results
that have either a `?publisher` value of `Springer`, or a `?pyear` value of `2010`.
Figure 6.25 shows the query result.

List 6.60 Same as List 6.58, but only pick those with the right publisher or the right published year

```
PREFIX dc:    <http://purl.org/dc/elements/1.1/>
PREFIX :      <http://example.org/book/>
PREFIX ns:    <http://example.org/ns#>

SELECT distinct ?book ?title ?pyear ?publisher
FROM <http://liyangyu.com/book_data.ttl>
{
   ?book dc:title ?title ;
        ns:publisher ?publisher ;
        ns:pubYear ?pyear ;
        ns:price ?price .
 VALUES (?pyear ?publisher ) {
      ( UNDEF "Springer" )
      ( "2010" UNDEF )
 }
}
```

Obviously, for this case, the two books in the dataset will both be picked, since one of them satisfies the publisher condition and the other one satisfies the published year condition.

Understand that when creating a data table by using VALUES keyword, it is not necessary to assign a vlue to every position in the table. The UNDEF keyword acts as a wildcard, indicating that any value at that position is acceptable, as shown in List 6.60.

It may have occured that all these query conditions could have been easily specified without VALUES keywords. This impression is easily understandable given the small toy dataset. In real practice, especially if one is working with large amounts of data together with complex filtering conditions, the VALUES keyword can offer a much cleaner and easier way of result filtering, with very little extra code in the queries.

6.3.3 SPARQL 1.1 Federated Query

For many of us, the Semantic Web is a data integration platform at a Web scale; it is all about publishing structured data on the Web and then being able to consume it at an integrated level. It is therefore important for SPARQL to provide the ability to retrieve data from multiple sources and combine it.

To accomplish this, SPARQL 1.1 defines the SERVICE keyword that can be used to create SPARQL *federated queries*. In particular, a SERVICE keyword allows us to direct a portion of a query to a remote SPARQL endpoint, just as the GRAPH keyword directs queries to a particular named graph. We cover SPARQL 1.1 federated query in detail in this section.

6.3.3.1 Simple Query to a Remote SPARQL Endpoint

List 6.61 shows the simplest form of using SERVICE keyword.

List 6.61 Simplest form of using SERVICE keyword

```
SELECT ?varibleName...
WHERE {
   SERVICE <sparql_endpoint>
  {   }
}
```

Inside the {} block that follows SERVICE keyword, one can have a collection of triple patterns or another SELECT and WHERE clause, as shown in the coming examples. When the SERVICE keyword is used, the content of {} block is sent to the remote SPARQL endpoint specified by sparql_endpoint, is then executed and the results are returned.

To see one example, let us start from my FOAF document. Inside my FOAF document, I have one such statement,

```
<foaf:topic_interest
 rdf:resource="http://dbpedia.org/resource/Semantic_Web"/>
```

and our goal is to query DBpedia to know more about http://dbpedia.org/resource/Semantic_Web. To do so, we can use the query shown in List 6.62.

List 6.62 Query a remote endpoint and combine the result with data from a local dataset

```
PREFIX foaf:   <http://xmlns.com/foaf/0.1/>
PREFIX rdfs: <http://www.w3.org/2000/01/rdf-schema#>
SELECT *
FROM <http://liyangyu.com/foaf.rdf>
WHERE
{
   <http://www.liyangyu.com/foaf.rdf#liyang>
        foaf:topic_interest ?topic .
  SERVICE <http://dbpedia.org/sparql> {
    ?topic rdfs:label ?label .
  }
}
```

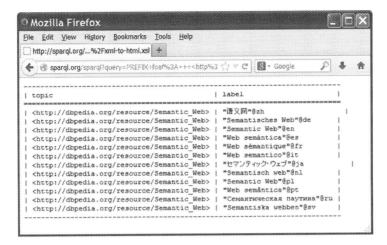

Fig. 6.26 Result from running the query shown in List 6.62

List 6.62 is the simplest form of federated query. It queries a remote SPARQL endpoint (DBpedia endpoint) and joins the returned data with the data from a local dataset (give by `http://liyangyu.com/foaf.rdf`). More specifically, `?topic`, as the binding variable from querying the local dataset, is used to query the remote DBpedia dataset, and the labels about this topic re returned so one can understand more about the topic itself.

At the time of this writing, instead of using the Virtuoso Live Demo Server endpoint, let us use SPARQLer endpoint[10] based on Jena, which seems to provide more stable support to SPARQL 1.1 federated query. Figure 6.26 shows the query result.

6.3.3.2 Federated Queries with Multiple SPARQL Endpoints

A federated query often means to access more than one remote SPARQL endpoints to retrieve the needed data. List 6.63 shows one such example. Here, we use Linked Movie Database[11] to retrieve a list of movies featuring Tom Hanks, and then we used DBpedia endpoint to retrieve information about his birthdate.

---

[10] http://sparql.org/sparql.html

[11] http://linkedmdb.org/

List 6.63 Query two remote endpoints to integrate information about Tom Hanks

```
PREFIX imdb: <http://data.linkedmdb.org/resource/movie/>
PREFIX dbpedia: <http://dbpedia.org/ontology/>
PREFIX dcterms: <http://purl.org/dc/terms/>
PREFIX rdfs: <http://www.w3.org/2000/01/rdf-schema#>

SELECT *
from <http://xmlns.com/foaf/0.1/>
{
   SERVICE <http://data.linkedmdb.org/sparql>
   {
      SELECT ?movieTitle WHERE {
         ?actor imdb:actor_name "Tom Hanks".
         ?movie imdb:actor ?actor ;
                dcterms:title ?movieTitle .
      }
   }
   SERVICE <http://dbpedia.org/sparql>
   {
      SELECT ?actor ?birth_date WHERE {
            ?actor rdfs:label "Tom Hanks"@en ;
               dbpedia:birthDate ?birth_date .
      } LIMIT 1
   }

}
```

Note that in order to make the query work, a dummy dataset has to be specified as shown by `from` clause in List 6.63 to avoid a "No dataset description for query" error message. The dummy dataset is not actually used so any dataset can be specified there.

Figure 6.27 shows the query result. The first part of the query finds all the

6.3.4 SPARQL 1.1 Update

If you are experienced with SQL queries, you know how easy it is to change the data in the database. SPARQL 1.1 Update allows an RDF graph or RDF store to be updated the same way as SQL to databases. In particular, it provides two categories of operations. The first one is called *graph update*, which is responsible for addition and removal of triples from one specific graph. The second one is called *graph management*, which is intended for creation and deletion of graphs within a given graph store.

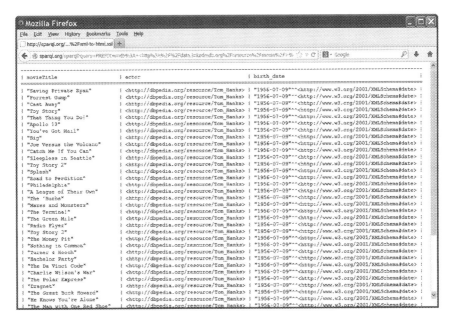

Fig. 6.27 Result from running the query shown in List 6.63

Understand that SPARQL 1.1 Update is intended to be a language for specifying and executing updates to RDF graphs in a *graph store*, which is a mutable container of RDF graphs managed by a single service. It has one (unnamed) slot holding a defect graph, and zero or more named slots holding named graphs. An operation should specify the graph it intends to update, or it will work with the default graph. Unless otherwise specified, the unnamed graph in the store will be the default graph for any operations on that store. Named graphs can be added or deleted from a graph store, so it is possible that there is one unnamed graph and no named graphs in a store.

Furthermore, SPARQL 1.1 Protocol and SPARQL 1.1 Graph Store HTTP Protocol together define how exactly a graph store should be accessed. For SPARQL users, the technical details of these protocols are often not as important as the update language itself. It is sufficient to understand that a graph store is often accessible by an *update service*, which accepts and processes update requests, and the details are hidden behind the service itself. This service can also be referred as a SPARQL endpoint, similar to the read-only query service that operates on RDF datasets.

6.3.4.1 Graph Update: `INSERT DATA` Operation

One way to add one or more RDF statements into a given graph is to use the `INSERT DATA` operation. This operation creates the graph if it does not exist. List 6.64 shows one example:

List 6.64 Use INSERT DATA to update a given graph

```
prefix foaf:<http://xmlns.com/foaf/0.1/>
prefix liyang: <http://www.liyangyu.com/foaf.rdf#>
INSERT DATA
{
  GRAPH <http://www.liyangyu.com/foaf.rdf>
  {
    liyang:liyang foaf:workplaceHomepage <http://www.delta.com> ;
                  foaf:schoolHomepage  <http://www.osu.edu> .
  }
}
```

This inserts two new statements into my personal FOAF document. And these two statements show the homepage of the company I work for, and the homepage of the school from which I graduated.

Note that any number of RDF statements can be inserted into a graph within one INSERT DATA request. In addition, the GRAPH clause is optional; an INSERT DATA request without the GRAPH clause simply operates on the default graph in the RDF store.

Also understand that variables are not allowed in INSERT DATA request. That is, an INSERT DATA statement only allows inserting ground triples. Blank nodes are assumed to be disjoint from the blank nodes in the graph store, and will be inserted with "fresh" blank nodes.

6.3.4.2   Graph Update: DELETE DATA Operation

Similar to adding statements, the DELETE DATA operation removes triples from a graph. List 6.65 shows one example:

List 6.65 Example of using DELETE DATA operation to delete triples from a graph

```
prefix foaf:<http://xmlns.com/foaf/0.1/>
prefix liyang: <http://www.liyangyu.com/foaf.rdf#>
DELETE DATA
{
  GRAPH <http://www.liyangyu.com/foaf.rdf>
  {
    liyang:liyang foaf:workplaceHomepage <http://www.delta.com> ;
                  foaf:schoolHomepage  <http://www.osu.edu> .
  }
}
```

This deletes the two statements we have just added into my FOAF document. Similarly, any number of statements can be deleted in one DELETE request, and the GRAPH clause is optional: a DELETE DATA statement without the GRAPH clause simply operates on the default graph in the RDF store.

As with INSERT DATA request, variables are not allowed in DELETE DATA request. In addition, a DELETE DATA statement cannot contain blank nodes. Furthermore, the deletion of nonexistent triples has no effect on the graph; such a request is simply ignored.

Note that there is no such operation as UPDATE in SPARQL 1.1 Update. Updating a triple in a graph actually takes two steps: the first step is to delete the current triple, and the second step is to add a new triple. List 6.66 gives one example.

List 6.66 Update a triple by using DELETE DATA and INSERT DATA operation

```
prefix foaf:<http://xmlns.com/foaf/0.1/>
prefix liyang: <http://www.liyangyu.com/foaf.rdf#>
DELETE DATA
{
  GRAPH <http://www.liyangyu.com/foaf.rdf>
  {
    liyang:liyang foaf:mbox <mailto:liyang@liyangyu.com> .
  }
};

prefix foaf:<http://xmlns.com/foaf/0.1/>
prefix liyang: <http://www.liyangyu.com/foaf.rdf#>
INSERT DATA
{
  GRAPH <http://www.liyangyu.com/foaf.rdf>
  {
    liyang:liyang foaf:mbox <mailto:liyang910@yahoo.com> .
  }
}
```

6.3.4.3 Graph Update: DELETE/INSERT Operation Based on Binding Patterns

As we have discussed in Sects. 6.3.4.1 and 6.3.4.2, both the INSERT DATA operation and the DELETE DATA operation only allow ground triples. These are useful operations, but there are indeed cases where the delete/insert operation should be carried out based on dynamic bindings for a query pattern. This requirement is covered by the DELETE/INSERT operation provided by SPARQL 1.1.

List 6.67 is an example taken from W3C's official SPARQL 1.1 Update document,[12] which shows a typical usage of this operation.

List 6.67 Update a graph using DELETE/INSERT operation

```
PREFIX foaf:  <http://xmlns.com/foaf/0.1/>

WITH <http://example/addresses>
DELETE { ?person foaf:givenName 'Bill' }
INSERT { ?person foaf:givenName 'William' }
WHERE
  { ?person foaf:givenName 'Bill'
  }
```

The WITH clause specifies the graph that will be operated upon—the subsequent clauses, including DELETE, INSERT and WHERE will all be operating on this graph. If no WITH clause is used, the default graph contained by the graph store will be the target graph.

After the WITH clause, we have DELETE, INSERT and WHERE clause. DELETE has to happen before INSERT, which should happen before the WHERE clause. The pattern in the WHERE clause is evaluated first and only once, after which the delete operation will be performed, and then the insert operation will be performed. In other words, all the solution bindings from the WHERE clause are applied to the DELETE and INSERT operation for defining the triples to be deleted from or inserted into the Graph Store.

Now, it is easy to understand List 6.67: it tries to update the graph http://example/addresses to rename all the people with the given name "Bill" to "William".

It is also possible to not have either the INSERT operation or the DELETE operation. If the DELETE clause is omitted, the operation will only INSERT data. If the INSERT clause is omitted, the operation will only DELETE data.

List 6.68 shows one example of DELETE operation only. It tries to delete everything about a person whose e-mail address is used to identify the person.

List 6.68 Update a graph using DELETE operation only

```
PREFIX foaf:  <http://xmlns.com/foaf/0.1/>

WITH <http://example/addresses>
DELETE { ?myself ?property ?value }
WHERE
{
   ?myself foaf:mbox <mailto:liyang@liyangyu.com> ;
        ?property ?value
}
```

---

[12] http://www.w3.org/TR/2013/REC-sparql11-update-20130321/

If the DELETE operation involves two graphs, the GRAPH clause should be used instead of the WITH clause, as shown in List 6.69 (this example is taken from W3C's official SPARQL 1.1 Update document).

List 6.69 Update two graphs by using DELETE operation

```
PREFIX foaf:  <http://xmlns.com/foaf/0.1/>

DELETE WHERE {
   GRAPH <http://example.com/names> {
    ?person foaf:givenName 'Fred' ;
            ?property1 ?value1
   }
  GRAPH <http://example.com/addresses> {
    ?person ?property2 ?value2
  }
}
```

List 6.69 involves two graphs: from graph http://example.com/names, it removes all the statements about a resource whose given name is Fred, and from graph http://example.com/addresses, it removes everything about the same resource as well.

List 6.70 shows the two graphs before the operation, and List 6.71 shows them after the operation.

List 6.70 The two graphs before the DELETE operation shown in List 6.69

```
# Graph: http://example.com/names
@prefix foaf:  <http://xmlns.com/foaf/0.1/> .

<http://example/william> a foaf:Person .
<http://example/william> foaf:givenName "William" .
<http://example/fred> a foaf:Person .
<http://example/fred> foaf:givenName "Fred" .

# Graph: http://example.com/addresses
@prefix foaf:  <http://xmlns.com/foaf/0.1/> .

<http://example/william> foaf:mbox  <mailto:bill@example> .
<http://example/fred> foaf:mbox  <mailto:fred@example> .
```

List 6.71 The two graphs after the DELETE operation shown in List 6.69

```
# Graph: http://example.com/names
@prefix foaf:  <http://xmlns.com/foaf/0.1/> .

<http://example/william> a foaf:Person .
<http://example/william> foaf:givenName "William" .

# Graph: http://example.com/addresses
@prefix foaf:  <http://xmlns.com/foaf/0.1/> .

<http://example/william> foaf:mbox  <mailto:bill@example> .
```

As you can tell, in the second graph, only the resource about Fred is removed. This is because ?person variable happens in *both* graph patterns (see List 6.69), therefore they are bound to the same resource. As a comparison, variable ?property1 and ?property2 are purposely made to be not the same variable in the two patterns, as are variables ?value1 and ?value2. This way, only the two resources themselves from the two graphs are bound, but not the specific properties and property values.

List 6.72 shows one example where only the INSERT operation is used (this example is taken from W3C's official SPARQL 1.1 Update document). Note since two graphs are involved in this query, the GRAPH clause is used.

List 6.72 Update one graph by using INSERT operation

```
PREFIX dc:  <http://purl.org/dc/elements/1.1/>
PREFIX xsd: <http://www.w3.org/2001/XMLSchema#>

INSERT
{ GRAPH <http://example/bookStore2> { ?book ?p ?v } }
WHERE
{ GRAPH  <http://example/bookStore>
   { ?book dc:date ?date .
     FILTER ( ?date > "1970-01-01T00:00:00-02:00"^^xsd:dateTime )
        ?book ?p ?v
   }
}
```

In List 6.72, pattern ?book ?p ?v shows up exactly the same in both patterns, making sure only the binding triples are copies from graph (http://example/bookStore) to graph (http://example/bookStore2) correctly. List 6.73 shows the two graphs before the operation, and List 6.74 shows the two graphs after the operation.

List 6.73 The two graphs before the INSERT operation shown in List 6.72

```
# Graph: http://example/bookStore
@prefix dc: <http://purl.org/dc/elements/1.1/> .
@prefix xsd: <http://www.w3.org/2001/XMLSchema#> .

<http://example/book1>
      dc:title "Fundamentals of Compiler Design" .
<http://example/book1>
      dc:date "1977-01-01T00:00:00-02:00"^^xsd:dateTime .

<http://example/book2> ns:price 42 .
<http://example/book2> dc:title "David Copperfield" .
<http://example/book2> dc:creator "Edmund Wells" .
<http://example/book2>
         dc:date "1948-01-01T00:00:00-02:00"^^xsd:dateTime .

<http://example/book3> dc:title "SPARQL 1.1 Tutorial" .

# Graph: http://example/bookStore2
@prefix dc: <http://purl.org/dc/elements/1.1/> .

<http://example/book4> dc:title "SPARQL 1.0 Tutorial" .
```

List 6.74 The two graphs after the INSERT operation shown in List 6.72

```
# Graph: http://example/bookStore
@prefix dc: <http://purl.org/dc/elements/1.1/> .
@prefix xsd: <http://www.w3.org/2001/XMLSchema#> .

<http://example/book1>
     dc:title "Fundamentals of Compiler Design" .
<http://example/book1>
     dc:date "1977-01-01T00:00:00-02:00"^^xsd:dateTime .

<http://example/book2> ns:price 42 .
<http://example/book2> dc:title "David Copperfield" .
<http://example/book2> dc:creator "Edmund Wells" .
<http://example/book2>
         dc:date "1948-01-01T00:00:00-02:00"^^xsd:dateTime .
```

```
<http://example/book3> dc:title "SPARQL 1.1 Tutorial" .

# Graph: http://example/bookStore2
@prefix dc: <http://purl.org/dc/elements/1.1/> .

<http://example/book1>
        dc:title "Fundamentals of Compiler Design" .
<http://example/book1>
        dc:date "1977-01-01T00:00:00-02:00"^^xsd:dateTime .

<http://example/book4> dc:title "SPARQL 1.0 Tutorial" .
```

As a final example, List 6.75 shows multiple operations combining an INSERT with a DELETE. Again, this example is taken from W3C's official SPARQL 1.1 Update document.

List 6.75 Multiple operations combing INSERT with DELETE

```
PREFIX dc:  <http://purl.org/dc/elements/1.1/>
PREFIX dcmitype: <http://purl.org/dc/dcmitype/>
PREFIX xsd: <http://www.w3.org/2001/XMLSchema#>

INSERT
{ GRAPH <http://example/bookStore2> { ?book ?p ?v } }
WHERE
{ GRAPH  <http://example/bookStore>
  { ?book dc:date ?date .
    FILTER ( ?date < "2000-01-01T00:00:00-02:00"^^xsd:dateTime )
    ?book ?p ?v
  }
} ;

WITH <http://example/bookStore>
DELETE
{ ?book ?p ?v }
WHERE
{ ?book dc:date ?date ;
        dc:type dcmitype:PhysicalObject .
  FILTER ( ?date < "2000-01-01T00:00:00-02:00"^^xsd:dateTime )
  ?book ?p ?v
}
```

With what we have learned so far, List 6.75 is actually easy to understand. It first copies triples from one graph to another based on a pattern (similar to List 6.72), then it removes triples from a graph by using another pattern match (similar to List

6.68). Again, note in List 6.75, both the GRAPH clause and the WITH clause are used to specify the underlying graphs, and pattern ?book ?p ?v shows up exactly the same in all patterns, making sure only the binding triples are copies or deleted.

List 6.76 shows the two graphs before the operations in List 6.75, and List 6.77 shows the two graphs after the operations shown in List 6.75.

List 6.76 The two graphs before the INSERT and DELETE operation shown in List 6.75

```
# Graph: http://example/bookStore
@prefix dc: <http://purl.org/dc/elements/1.1/> .
@prefix dcmitype: <http://purl.org/dc/dcmitype/> .


<http://example/book1>
        dc:title "Fundamentals of Compiler Design" .
<http://example/book1>
        dc:date "1996-01-01T00:00:00-02:00"^^xsd:dateTime .
<http://example/book1> a dcmitype:PhysicalObject .


<http://example/book3> dc:title "SPARQL 1.1 Tutorial" .


# Graph: http://example/bookStore2
@prefix dc: <http://purl.org/dc/elements/1.1/> .


<http://example/book4> dc:title "SPARQL 1.0 Tutorial" .
```

List 6.77 The two graphs after the INSERT and DELETE operation shown in List 6.75

```
# Graph: http://example/bookStore
@prefix dc: <http://purl.org/dc/elements/1.1/> .
@prefix dcmitype: <http://purl.org/dc/dcmitype/> .


<http://example/book3> dc:title "SPARQL 1.1 Tutorial" .


# Graph: http://example/bookStore2
@prefix dc: <http://purl.org/dc/elements/1.1/> .
@prefix dcmitype: <http://purl.org/dc/dcmitype/> .


<http://example/book1>
        dc:title "Fundamentals of Compiler Design" .
<http://example/book1>
        dc:date "1996-01-01T00:00:00-02:00"^^xsd:dateTime .
<http://example/book1> a dcmitype:PhysicalObject .


<http://example/book4> dc:title "SPARQL 1.0 Tutorial" .
```

6.3.4.4 Graph Update: **LOAD** Operation

The LOAD operation copies all the triples of a remote graph into the specified target graph in the graph store. If no target graph is specified, the defect graph will be used. If the destination graph already exists, no data from that graph will be removed.

List 6.78 loads all the statements from my FOAF document into a more general store.

List 6.78 Use LOAD operation to add my FOAF document into a graph store

```
LOAD <http://liyangyu.com/foaf.rdf>
      INTO GRAPH <http://people/liyang.rdf>
```

In fact, with what we have so far, the LOAD operation is not necessarily needed since its functionality can be implemented by simply using the INSERT operation. However, it does provide a more convenient and effective choice when needed.

6.3.4.5 Graph Update: **CLEAR** Operation

The CLEAR operation deletes all the statements from the specified graph in the graph store. Note that this operation does *not* remove the graph itself from the graph store, even the graph contains no triples after the operation. List 6.79 shows one example.

List 6.79 Use the CLEAR operator to delete all the triples from a specific graph

```
CLEAR GRAPH <http://liyangyu.com/foaf.rdf>
```

List 6.79 deletes everything from graph http://liyangyu.com/foaf.rdf contained by the graph store. List 6.80 deletes all the triples from the default graph of the graph store, and list 6.81 deletes all the triples in all named graphs contained by the graph store.

List 6.80 Use the CLEAR operator to delete all the triples in the default graph of the graph store

```
CLEAR DEFAULT
```

List 6.81 Use the CLEAR operator to delete all the triples in all named graphs contained by the graph store

```
CLEAR NAMED
```

and finally, List 6.82 deletes all triples in all graphs of the graph store.

List 6.82 Use the `CLEAR` operator to delete all the triples in all graphs contained by the store

```
CLEAR ALL
```

6.3.4.6 Graph Management: **CREATE** Operation

In SPARQL 1.1 Update, the following is used to create a new named graph:

```
CREATE (SILENT) GRAPH <uri>
```

This creates a new empty graph whose name is specified by `uri`. After the graph is created, we can manipulate its content by adding new statements into it, as we have discussed in previous sections.

Note the optional `SILENT` keyword is for error handling. For example, if the graph named `uri` already exists in the store, unless this keyword is present, the SPARQL 1.1 Update service will not flag an error message back to the user.

6.3.4.7 Graph Management: **DROP** Operation

In SPARQL 1.1 Update, the following operation will remove the specified named graphs from the graph store:

```
DROP (SILENT) ( GRAPH <uri> | DEFAULT| NAMED | ALL )
```

The `GRAPH` keyword is used to remove a graph denoted by `uri`, the `DEFAULT` keyword is used to remove the default graph from the Graph Store, the `NAMED` keyword is used to remove all the named graphs from the Graph Store, and finally, the `ALL` keyword is used to remove all graphs from the store, i.e., to reset the store.

6.3.4.8 Graph Management: **COPY** Operation

The `COPY` operation inserts all triples from an input graph into the destination graph. The content in the input graph remains the same, but the content in the destination graph, if any, is removed before insertion. The following is one simple example, which copies all the triples from the default graph to a named graph:

```
COPY DEFAULT TO <http://example.org/default_backup>
```

6.3.4.9   Graph Management: MOVE Operation

The MOVE operation is similar to the COPY operation: it inserts all triples from an input graph into the destination graph; however, the input graph is dropped after insertion. Also, the content in the destination graph, if any, is removed before insertion. The following is one simple example, which moves all the triples from the default graph to a named graph:

```
MOVE DEFAULT TO <http://example.org/default_backup>
```

Again, after the move, the default graph is dropped. In fact, right after the default graph is dropped, the graph store instantiates a brand new default graph; therefore DROP DEFAULT is equivalent to CLEAR DEFAULT.

6.3.4.10   Graph Management: ADD Operation

The ADD operation is similar to the COPY operation: it inserts all triples from an input graph into the destination graph; however, the content in the destination graph, if any, is kept intact after the insertion. Also, the content from the input graph remains the same as well. The following is one simple example, which adds all the triples from the default graph to a named graph:

```
ADD DEFAULT TO <http://example.org/all_default_backup>
```

Again, after the move, the default graph does not change, and the destination graph still has its original content before the addition.

6.3.5   Other SPARQL 1.1 Features

Up to this point, we have covered some of the most important new features offered by SPARQL 1.1. In this last section of the chapter, we cover some new SPARQL 1.1 built-in functions and operators. Table 6.3 is a brief summary of these new built-in functions and operators.

To learn and understand these new functions and operators, the best way is to try them out and see what they can accomplish. In this section, we again use OpenLink's Virtuoso Live Demo Server as the endpoint (see Fig. 6.1) for the

Table 6.3 Functions and operators provided by SPARQL 1.1

Category	Functions and operators
New string functions	`CONCAT, CONTAINS, ENCODE_FOR_URI, LCASE, STRENDS, STRLEN, STRSTARTS, SUBSTR, UCASE`
New numeric functions	`ABS, CEIL, FLOOR, ROUND`
New date/time and related functions	`NOW, DAY, HOURS, MINUTES, MONTH, SECONDS, TIMEZONE, TZ, YEAR`
Hash functions	`MD5, SHA1, SHA224, SHA256, SHA384, SHA512`
New RDF terms constructors and functions	`BNODE, IRI, URI, isNUMERIC, STRDT, STRLANG`
Others	`COALESCE, EXISTS(NOT EXISTS), IF, IN(NOT IN), RAND`

testing. It is not possible to cover every one of these functions and operators. Those that are not covered here can be tested and learned similarly.

6.3.5.1 Examples of String Functions

List 6.83 shows how to use string function CONCAT.

List 6.83 Use CONCAT operator to get the full name of a person

```
PREFIX foaf:    <http://xmlns.com/foaf/0.1/>
SELECT *
FROM <http://liyangyu.com/foaf.rdf>
WHERE
{
   ?person foaf:givenname ?firstname ;
           foaf:family_name ?lastname .
 BIND(CONCAT(?firstname, " ", ?lastname) AS ?fullname)
}
```

Clearly, the CONCAT function concatenates two input strings as a single one, as we would expect from its name. Note the BIND operator is used to assign the resulting string to a new variable called fullname. Figure 6.28 shows the query result.

In fact, to learn and understand any function or operator, we sometimes can use Virtuoso Live Demo Server's default graph, and simply add the function or operator we would like to understand. For example, List 6.84 uses a dummy query to help us understand ENCODE_FOR_URI function.

Fig. 6.28 Result from
running the query shown in
List 6.83

List 6.84 Example of using ENCODE_FOR_URI operator

```
SELECT ?s ?p ?o ENCODE_FOR_URI("Roger Federer")
WHERE
{
    ?s ?p ?o.
}
LIMIT 1
```

Obviously, the query itself does not do anything interesting, which is why we call it a dummy query. All we have done in List 6.84 is to include the ENCODE_FOR_URI operator into the query SELECT clause so we can learn what exactly it does. Figure 6.29 shows the query result.

From the above, we understand this function encodes the input string that is intended to be used in the path segment of a URI. The effect of the function is to escape reserved characters; each such character in the string is replaced with its percent-encoded form.

List 6.85 shows both STRENDS and LCASE function. STRENDS tests if the input string (the first parameter) ends with the specified string (the second parameter). LCASE changes the input string into its low case form.

List 6.85 Example of using STRENDS and LCASE operator

```
PREFIX foaf:    <http://xmlns.com/foaf/0.1/>
SELECT *
FROM <http://liyangyu.com/foaf.rdf>
WHERE
{
    ?person foaf:givenname ?firstname ;
            foaf:family_name ?lastname .
      FILTER ( STRENDS(?lastname, LCASE("Yu")) ).
}
```

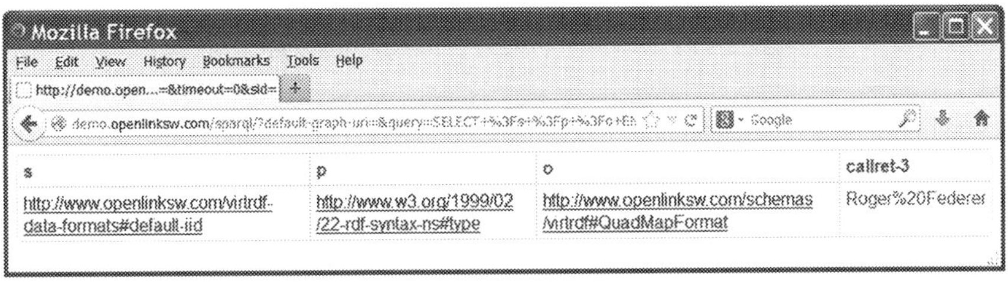

Fig. 6.29 Result from running the query shown in List 6.84

Fig. 6.30 Result from running the query shown in List 6.85

Figure 6.30 shows the query result. Note if LCASE is not used, the query will not work unless we change Yu to yu manually.

With what we have discussed so far, other string functions in Table 6.3 should be easy to understand, so we will not cover the rest of them here.

6.3.5.2 Examples of Numeric Functions

Numeric functions shown in Table 6.3 are all quite intuitive to understand. Let us see some examples to confirm our intuition.

List 6.86 shows the use of the ROUND operator. This query again uses the default graph in Virtuoso Live Demo Server, but the query itself is not a dummy query: it finds those resources that use geo:geometry and retrieves at most ten numeric object values. The values are then rounded into their closest integers. Figure 6.31 shows the query result.

List 6.86 Example of using ROUND operator

```
SELECT ?o AS ?original ROUND(?o) AS ?ROUND_value
WHERE
{
    ?s geo:geometry ?geo .
    ?s ?p ?o .
    FILTER ( isnumeric(?o) )
} LIMIT 10
```

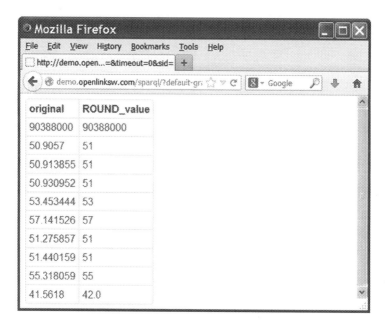

Fig. 6.31 Result from running the query shown in List 6.86

Finally, List 6.87 shows the usage of ABS operator, just by modifying the query in List 6.86. Figure 6.32 shows the query result.

List 6.87 Example of using ABS operator

```
SELECT ?o AS ?original ABS(?o) AS ?ABS_value
WHERE
{
    ?s geo:geometry ?geo .
    ?s ?p ?o .
    FILTER ( isnumeric(?o) )
} LIMIT 10
```

6.3.5.3   Examples of Date/Time and Related Functions

To test date/time and related functions, we can again use the dummy query trick that we used in Sect. 6.3.5.1. For example, List 6.88 shows the current time, as you might expect.

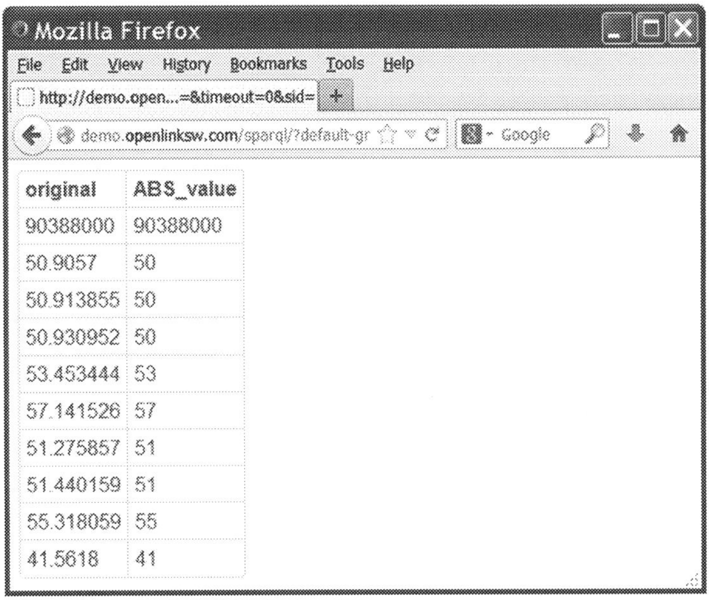

original	ABS_value
90388000	90388000
50.9057	50
50.913855	50
50.930952	50
53.453444	53
57.141526	57
51.275857	51
51.440159	51
55.318059	55
41.5618	41

Fig. 6.32 Result from running the query shown in List 6.87

List 6.88 Example of using NOW operator

```
SELECT NOW()
WHERE
{
   ?s ?p ?o.
}
LIMIT 1
```

Since this one is quite straightforward, we will not include the query result screen.

`DAY`, `HOURS`, `MINUTES`, `MONTH`, `SECONDS` and `YEAR` are work in a similar fashion: they return the corresponding part of the input argument, which has an `xsd:dateTime` type. More specifically, `DAY` returns the day part of the argument, `HOURS` returns the hours part of the argument, and `MINUTES` returns the minutes part of the argument, so on and so forth. List 6.89 shows one example of using `HOURS` operator, and this query returns `14` as the value for the variable `hour`.

Fig. 6.33 Result from running the query shown in List 6.90

List 6.89 Example of using HOURS operator

```
SELECT HOURS("2011-01-10T14:45:13.815-05:00"^^xsd:dateTime)
       AS ?hour
WHERE
{
   ?s ?p ?o.
}
LIMIT 1
```

Finally, both TIMEZONE and TZ return the time zone part of the input argument, but TIMEZONE returns the time zone as an xsd:dayTimeDuration type value, while TZ returns it as a simple literal. For example, List 6.90 uses the TIMEZONE operator, and Fig. 6.33 shows the query result.

List 6.90 Example of using TIMEZONE operator

```
SELECT TIMEZONE("2011-01-10T14:45:13.815-05:00"^^xsd:dateTime)
       AS ?timezone
WHERE
{
   ?s ?p ?o.
}
LIMIT 1
```

Note if we replace TIMEZONE with TZ, we get -05:00 as the result.

Fig. 6.34 Result from running the query shown in List 6.91

6.3.5.4   Examples of Hash Functions

First, understand that MD5 and SHA are both cryptographic hash functions, where MD stands for Message-Digest and SHA stands for Secure Hash Algorithm. SPARQL 1.1 provides these functions to return the needed checksum, as a hex-digit string. The larger the number, such as SHA384 and SHA512, the more complex the algorithms are and therefore more protection will be provided.

List 6.91 shows how SHA1 is used, and Fig. 6.34 shows the result.

List 6.91   Example of using SHA1 operator

```
SELECT SHA1('liyang@liyangyu.com')
WHERE
{
    ?s ?p ?o
}
LIMIT 1
```

And replacing SHA1 in List 6.91 with other operators (such as SHA384 and SHA512) and running the query again, you will see the checksum gets longer and longer.

6.3.5.5   Other New Functions and Operators

There are a few more new functions and operators we would like to cover in this last section of the chapter, since they act as utility functions, and can be quite useful in some cases. The first one is the COALESCE function, which returns the RDF term value of the first expression that evaluates without error. Note in SPARQL, operating on an unbound variable will raise an error. To understand what COALESCE does, consider the dataset in List 6.92.

List 6.92 Simple dataset for understanding COALESCE function

```
@prefix dc: <http://purl.org/dc/elements/1.1/> .
@prefix dcmitype: <http://purl.org/dc/dcmitype/> .

<http://example/book1> a dcmitype:PhysicalObject .
<http://example/book1> dc:title "SPARQL 1.1 Tutorial" .

<http://example/book2> a dcmitype:PhysicalObject .
```

List 6.93 shows one query that works with this simple dataset:

List 6.93 Simple query based on the dataset shown in List 6.92

```
@prefix dc: <http://purl.org/dc/elements/1.1/> .
@prefix dcmitype: <http://purl.org/dc/dcmitype/> .

SELECT ?book ?booktitle
WHERE {
?book a dcmitype:PhysicalObject .
OPTIONAL {
  ?book dc:title ?booktitle .
}
}
```

The query in List 6.93 returns the following result:

```
<http://example/book1> "SPARQL 1.1 Tutorial"
<http://example/book2>
```

This result is obviously not as nice as the following:

```
<http://example/book1> "SPARQL 1.1 Tutorial"
<http://example/book2> Not Available
```

So how could one create a custom string (Not Available) like the above?

This is exactly what the COALESCE function is designed to do. The query in List 6.94 shows the details.

List 6.94 A query uses COALESCE function to get a custom string

```
@prefix dc: <http://purl.org/dc/elements/1.1/> .
@prefix dcmitype: <http://purl.org/dc/dcmitype/> .

SELECT ?book (COALESCE(?booktitle, "Not available") AS ?bkTitle)
WHERE {
   ?book a dcmitype:PhysicalObject .
   OPTIONAL {
     ?book dc:title ?booktitle .
   }
}
```

Again, the COALESCE function returns the RDF term value of the first expression that evaluates without error. For <http://example/book1>, ?booktitle evaluates to SPARQL 1.1 Tutorial. For the second book, i.e., <http://example/book2>, ?booktitle is an unbound variable, therefore COALESCE function picks up Not available, since it is the first expression that evaluates without error. The final result is exactly what we are looking for.

Another function we would like to cover here is the STRLANG function, which constructs a literal with lexical form and language tag as specified by the argument. List 6.95 shows one example of using this function, and Fig. 6.35 shows the result.

List 6.95 Example of using STRLANG function

```
SELECT STRLANG("example", "en")
WHERE
{
   ?s ?p ?o
}
LIMIT 1
```

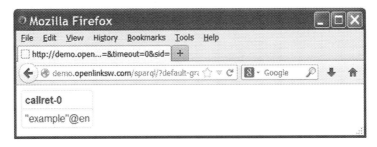

Fig. 6.35 Result from running the query shown in List 6.95

Fig. 6.36 Result from running the query shown in List 6.96

Since the same literal value can have different language tags associated with it in different dataset, it is often convenient to use STRLANG function to add the correct language tag.

Finally, let us understand the IRI function, which can be handy when a new URI is needed, for example, in a CONSTRUCT query. List 6.96 shows an example of using IRI function, and Fig. 6.36 shows the result.

List 6.96 Example of using IRI function

```
SELECT IRI("<http://dbpedia.org/resource/Roger_Federer>")
WHERE
{
    ?s ?p ?o
}
LIMIT 1
```

Obviously, the IRI function returns a fresh IRI by resolving the string argument. Note the IRI is resolved against the base IRI of the query and must result in an absolute IRI. Finally, understand that the URI function is simply a synonym for IRI.

6.4 Summary

We have covered SPRAQL in this chapter, the last core technical component of the Semantic Web.

First, understand how SPARQL fits into the technical structure of the Semantic Web, and how to set up and use a SPARQL endpoint to submit queries against RDF models.

Second, understand the following main points about SPARQL query language:

- basic SPARQL query language concepts such as triple pattern and graph pattern;
- basic SPARQL query forms such as SELECT query, ASK query, DESCRIBE query and CONSTRUCT query;
- key SPARQL language features and constructs, and use them effectively to build queries, including working with multiple graphs.

Finally, this chapter also covered SPARQL 1.1, a collection of new features added to the current SPARQL standard. Make sure you understand the following about SPARQL 1.1:

- the SPARQL 1.1 technical components;
- the language features and constructs of SPARQL 1.1 Query, including aggregate functions, subqueries, negation, assignment and property paths;
- the language features and constructs of SPARQL 1.1 Update, including inserting and deleting operations on a single graph, creating and deleting graphs from a graph store;
- SPARQL 1.1. federated queries, and other new SPARQL 1.1 features such as string operator, date/time operators, hash functions, etc.

At this point in the book, we have covered all the core technical components of the Semantic Web. The next six chapters will give you some concrete examples of the Semantic Web at work, which will further enhance your understanding about the materials presented so far in the book.

Part II
Applied Semantic Web

Chapter 7
FOAF: Friend of a Friend

At this point, we have learned the major technical components for the Semantic Web, and it is time for us to take a look at some real-world examples. Starting from *Friend of a Friend* (FOAF) is a good choice since it is simple and easy to understand, yet it does tell us a lot about what the Semantic Web looks like, especially in the area of social networking.

Studying FOAF also gives us a chance to practice what we have learned about RDF, RDFS and OWL. Another good reason is that FOAF namespace shows up in many ontology documents and in many literatures, so understanding FOAF seems to be necessary.

As usual, we first examine what exactly is FOAF, and what it accomplishes for us. Then we dive inside FOAF to see how it works. Finally, we take a look at some real examples and also come up with our own FOAF document.

Another interesting topic we cover in this chapter is semantic markup. As you will see, semantic markup is the actual implementation of the idea of adding semantics to the current Web to make it machine-readable. However, once you understand semantic markup, you will see the issues associated with it. The possible solutions to these issues are covered in later chapters, and they will give you even more opportunity to further understand the idea of the Semantic Web.

7.1 What FOAF Is and What It Does

7.1.1 FOAF in Plain English

In the early days of the Semantic Web, developers and researchers were eager to build some running examples of the Semantic Web, for the purpose of experimenting with the idea and hopefully, showing the benefits of the Semantic Web. Yet, as we saw in the previous chapters, to build applications on the Semantic Web, we must have some

© Springer-Verlag Berlin Heidelberg 2014
L. Yu, *A Developer's Guide to the Semantic Web*,
DOI 10.1007/978-3-662-43796-4_7

ontologies, and we must markup Web documents by using these ontologies so we can turn them into the documents that are machine-readable.

Obviously, in order to promptly create such an application example, it would be easier to focus on some specific domain, so the creation of the ontologies would be constrained in scope and would not be too formidably hard. In addition, to rapidly yield a large number of Web documents that would be created by using this specific ontology, it would have to involve a lot of people who were willing to participate in the effort. Therefore, a fairly straightforward project to start with would be some people-centric semantic Web application.

There are tons of millions of personal Web pages on the Web. On each such Web site, the author often provides some personal information, such as e-mails, pictures, interests, etc. The author may also include some links to his/her friends' Web sites, therefore creating a social network. And with this network, we can answer questions such as "who has the same interest as I do?", and maybe that means we can sell our old camera to him. And also, we can find someone who lives close to us and who also works at roughly the same location, so we can start to contact him and discuss the possibility of car-pooling.

All this sounds great. However, since all the personal Web sites are built for human eyes, we would have to do all the above manually, and it is very hard to create any application to do all that for us.

To make these documents understandable to an application, two major steps have to be accomplished: first, a machine-readable ontology about person has to be created, and second, each personal homepage has to be marked up, i.e., it has to be connected to some RDF statement document written by using this ontology.

This was the motivation behind the FOAF project. Founded by Dan Brickley and Libby Miller in mid-2000, FOAF is an open community-led initiative with the goal of creating a machine-readable web of data in the area of personal homepages and social networking.

It is important to understand the concept of "machine-readable web of data". Just like the HTML version of your homepage, FOAF documents can be linked together to form a web of data. The difference is that this web of data is formed with well-defined semantics, expressed in the person ontology. We will definitely come back to this point later this chapter and in the coming chapters as well.

In plain English, FOAF is simply a vocabulary (or, ontology) that includes the basic terms to describe personal information, such as who you are, what you do, and who your friends are, and so on. It serves as a standard for everyone who wants to markup their homepages and turn them into documents that can be processed by machines.

7.1.2   FOAF in Official Language

First, the official FOAF Web site is found here:

```
http://www.foaf-project.org/
```

It has an official definition of FOAF:

The *Friend of a Friend* (FOAF) project is creating a Web of machine-readable pages describing people, the links between them and the things they create and do.

This definition should be clear enough based on our discussion so far. Again, you can simply understand FOAF as a machine-readable ontology describing persons, their activities and their relations to other people. Therefore, FOAF and FOAF ontology are interchangeable concepts.

Notice that FOAF ontology is not a standard from W3C, it is managed by following the style of an Open Source[1] or Free Software[2] project standards, and is maintained by a community of developers. However, FOAF does depend on W3C standards, such as RDF and OWL. More specifically,

- FOAF ontology is written in OWL, and
- FOAF documents must be well-formed RDF documents.

FOAF ontology's official specification can be found at this location:

```
http://xmlns.com/foaf/spec/
```

New updates and related new releases can be found at this page as well. In addition, the FOAF ontology itself can be found (and downloaded) from this URL:

```
http://xmlns.com/foaf/spec/index.rdf
```

As usual, FOAF ontology is a collection of terms, and all these terms are identified by predefined URIs, which all share the following leading string:

```
http://xmlns.com/foaf/0.1/
```

By convention, this URI prefix string is associated with namespace prefix `foaf:`, and is typically used in RDF/XML format with the prefix `foaf`.

Finally, there is also a wiki site for the FOAF project, which is found at the following URL,

```
http://wiki.foaf-project.org/w/Main_Page
```

and you can use this wiki to learn more about FOAF project as well.

7.2   Core FOAF Vocabulary and Examples

With what we have learned so far, and given the fact that FOAF ontology is written in OWL, understanding FOAF ontology should not be difficult. In this section, we cover the core terms in this ontology, and also present examples to show how the FOAF ontology is used.

---

[1] http://www.opensource.org/

[2] http://www.gnu.org/philosophy/free-sw.html

7.2.1   The Big Picture: FOAF Vocabulary

FOAF terms are grouped in categories. Table 7.1 summarizes these categories and the terms in each category. Notice that FOAF is also under constant change and update; it would not be surprising if, at the time you read this book, you find more terms in some categories.

As you can see, the FOAF ontology is not a big ontology at all, and most of the terms are quite intuitive. Notice that a term starting with a capital letter identifies a class; otherwise, it identifies a property.

Table 7.1 FOAF vocabulary

Category	Terms
Basic FOAF classes and properties	`foaf:Agent`, `foaf:Person`, `foaf:name`, `foaf:nick`, `foaf:title`, `foaf:homepage`, `foaf:mbox`, `foaf:mbox_sha1sum`, `foaf:img`, `foaf:depiction`, `foaf:depict`, `foaf:surname`, `foaf:familyName`, `foaf:givenName`, `foaf:firstName`, `foaf:lastName`
Properties about personal information	`foaf:weblog`, `foaf:knows`, `foaf:interest`, `foaf:currentProject`, `foaf:pastProject`, `foaf:plan`, `foaf:based_near`, `foaf:age`, `foaf:workplaceHomepage`, `foaf:workInfoHomepage`, `foaf:schoolHomepage`, `foaf:topic_interest`, `foaf:publications`, `foaf:geekcode`, `foaf:myersBriggs`, `foaf:dnaChecksum`
Classes and properties about online accounts and instance messaging	`foaf:OnlineAccount`, `foaf:OnlineChatAccount`, `foaf:OnlineEcommerceAccount`, `foaf:OnlineGamingAccount`, `foaf:account`, `foaf:accountServiceHomepage`, `foaf:accountName`, `foaf:icqChatID`, `foaf:msnChatID`, `foaf:jabberID`, `foaf:yahooChatID`, `foaf:skypeID`
Classes and properties about projects and groups	`foaf:Project`, `foaf:Organization`, `foaf:Group`, `foaf:member`, `foaf:membershipClass`
Classes and properties about documents and images	`foaf:Document`, `foaf:Image`, `foaf:PersonalProfileDocument`, `foaf:topic`, `foaf:page`, `foaf:primaryTopic`, `foaf:primaryTopicOf`, `foaf:tipjar`, `foaf:sha1`, `foaf:made`, `foaf:maker`, `foaf:thumbnail`, `foaf:logo`

7.2.2 Core Terms and Examples

It is not possible to cover all the FOAF terms in detail. In this section, we discuss some of the most frequently used terms, and leave the rest of them for you to study.

The `foaf:Person` class is one of the core classes defined in FOAF vocabulary, and it represents people in the real world. List 7.1 is the definition of `Person` class, taken directly from the FOAF ontology:

List 7.1 Definition of `Person` class

```
<rdfs:Class rdf:about="http://xmlns.com/foaf/0.1/Person"
          rdfs:label="Person"
          rdfs:comment="A person."
          vs:term_status="stable">
  <rdf:type rdf:resource="http://www.w3.org/2002/07/owl#Class"/>
  <rdfs:subClassOf>
     <owl:Class rdf:about="http://xmlns.com/wordnet/1.6/Person"/>
  </rdfs:subClassOf>
  <rdfs:subClassOf>
     <owl:Class rdf:about="http://xmlns.com/foaf/0.1/Agent"/>
  </rdfs:subClassOf>
  <rdfs:subClassOf>
     <owl:Class rdf:about="http://xmlns.com/wordnet/1.6/Agent"/>
  </rdfs:subClassOf>
  <rdfs:subClassOf>
     <owl:Class rdf:about=
           "http://www.w3.org/2000/10/swap/pim/contact#Person"/>
  </rdfs:subClassOf>
  <rdfs:subClassOf>
     <owl:Class rdf:about=
         "http://www.w3.org/2003/01/geo/wgs84_pos#SpatialThing"/>
  </rdfs:subClassOf>
  <rdfs:isDefinedBy rdf:resource="http://xmlns.com/foaf/0.1/"/>
  <owl:disjointWith
       rdf:resource="http://xmlns.com/foaf/0.1/Document"/>
  <owl:disjointWith
       rdf:resource="http://xmlns.com/foaf/0.1/Organization"/>
  <owl:disjointWith
       rdf:resource="http://xmlns.com/foaf/0.1/Project"/>
</rdfs:Class>
```

As you can see, `foaf:Person` is defined as a subclass of the `Person` class defined in WordNet. WordNet is a semantic lexicon for the English language.

It groups English words into sets of synonyms called synsets, and provides short and general definitions, including various semantic relations between these synonym sets. Developed by the Cognitive Science Laboratory of Princeton University, WordNet has two goals: first, to produce a combination of dictionary and thesaurus that is more intuitively usable, and second, to support automatic text analysis and artificial intelligence applications.

During the past several years, WordNet has found more and more usage in the area of the Semantic Web, and FOAF class `foaf:Person` is a good example. By being a subclass of `wordNet:Person`, FOAF vocabulary can fit into a much broader picture. For example, an application which only knows WordNet can also understand `foaf:Person` even if it has never seen FOAF vocabulary before.

By the same token, `foaf:Person` is also defined to be a subclass of several outside classes defined by other ontologies, such as the following two classes:

```
http://www.w3.org/2000/10/swap/pim/contact#Person
http://www.w3.org/2003/01/geo/wgs84_pos#SpatialThing
```

Notice that `foaf:Person` is a subclass of `foaf:Agent`, which can represent a person, a group, software or some physical artifacts. A similar agent concept is also defined in WordNet. Furthermore, `foaf:Person` cannot be anything such as a `foaf:Document`, `foaf:Organization` or `foaf:Project`.

Besides `foaf:Person` class, FOAF ontology has defined quite a few other classes, with the goal to include the main concepts that can be used to describe a person as a resource. You can read these definitions just as the way we have understood `foaf:Person`'s definition. For example, `foaf:Document` represents the things that are considered to be documents used by a person, such as `foaf:Image`, which is a subclass of `foaf:Document`, since all images are indeed documents.

Properties defined by FOAF can be used to describe a person on a quite detailed level. For example, `foaf:firstName` is a property that describes the first name of a person. This property has `foaf:Person` as its domain, and `http://www.w3.org/2000/01/rdf-schema#Literal` as its value range. Similarly, `foaf:givenname` is the property describing the given name of a person, and it has the same domain and value range. Notice a simpler version of these two properties is the `foaf:name` property.

The `foaf:homepage` property relates a given resource to its homepage. Its domain is `http://www.w3.org/2002/07/owl#Thing`, and its range is `foaf:Document`. It is important to realize that this property is an inverse functional property. Therefore, a given `Thing` can have multiple homepages; however, if two `Things` have the same homepage, then these two `Things` are in fact the same `Thing`.

A similar property is the `foaf:mbox` property, which describes a relationship between the owner of a mailbox and the mailbox. This is also an inverse functional property: if two `foaf:Person` resources have the same `foaf:mbox` value, these two `foaf:Person` instances have to be exactly the same person. On the other hand, a `foaf:Person` can indeed own multiple `foaf:mbox` instances. We will come back to this important property soon.

Let us take a look at some examples, and we will also cover some other important properties in these examples.

First, List 7.2 shows a typical description of a person:

List 7.2 Example of using `foaf:Person`

```
1:  <rdf:RDF
1a:    xmlns:rdf="http://www.w3.org/1999/02/22-rdf-syntax-ns#"
2:     xmlns:foaf="http://xmlns.com/foaf/0.1/">
3:
4:  <foaf:Person>
5:     <foaf:name>Liyang Yu</foaf:name>
6:     <foaf:mbox rdf:resource="mailto:liyang@liyangyu.com"/>
7:  </foaf:Person>
8:
9:  </rdf:RDF>
```

List 7.2 simply says that there is a person, this person's name is `Liyang Yu` and the person's e-mail address is `liyang@liyangyu.com`.

The first thing to notice is that there is no URI to identify this person at all. More specifically, you don't see the following pattern where `rdf:about` attribute is used on `foaf:Person` resource:

```
<foaf:Person rdf:about="some_URI"/>
```

This seems to have broken one of the most important rules we have for the world of the Semantic Web. This rule says, whenever you decide to publish some RDF document to talk about some resource on the Web (in this case, `Liyang Yu` as a `foaf:Person` instance), you need to use a URI to represent this resource, and you should always use the existing URI for this resource if it already has one.

In fact, List 7.2 is correct, and this is done on purpose. This is also one of the important features of a FOAF document. Let us understand the reason here.

It is certainly not difficult to come up with a URI to uniquely identify a person. For example, I can use the following URI to identify myself:

```
<foaf:Person
       rdf:about="http://www.liyangyu.com/people#LiyangYu"/>
```

The difficult part is how to make sure other people know this URI and when they want to add additional information about me, they can reuse this exact URI.

One solution comes from `foaf:mbox` property. Clearly, an e-mail address is closely related to a given person, and it is also safe to assume that this person's friends should all know this e-mail address. Therefore, it is possible to use an e-mail address to uniquely identify a given person, and all we need to do is to make sure if two people have the same e-mail address, these two people are in fact the same person.

As we discussed earlier, FOAF ontology has defined the `foaf:mbox` property as an inverse functional property, as shown in List 7.3:

List 7.3 Definition of `foaf:mbox` property

```
<rdf:Property rdf:about="http://xmlns.com/foaf/0.1/mbox"
              vs:term_status="stable"
              rdfs:label="personal mailbox"
              rdfs:comment="...">

  <rdf:type rdf:resource=
      "http://www.w3.org/2002/07/owl#InverseFunctionalProperty"/>
  <rdf:type rdf:resource=
      "http://www.w3.org/2002/07/owl#ObjectProperty"/>
  <rdfs:domain rdf:resource="http://xmlns.com/foaf/0.1/Agent"/>
  <rdfs:range
        rdf:resource="http://www.w3.org/2002/07/owl#Thing"/>
  <rdfs:isDefinedBy rdf:resource="http://xmlns.com/foaf/0.1/"/>

</rdf:Property>
```

Now, if one of my friends has the following descriptions in her FOAF document:

```
<foaf:Person>
  <foaf:nick>Lao Yu</foaf:nick>
  <foaf:title>Dr</foaf:title>
  <foaf:mbox rdf:resource="mailto:liyang@liyangyu.com"/>
</foaf:Person>
```

An application that understands FOAF ontology will be able to recognize the `foaf:mbox` property and conclude that this is exactly the same person as described in List 7.2. And apparently, among other extra information, at least we now know this person has a nickname called `Lao Yu`.

Clearly, property `foaf:mbox` has solved the problem of identifying a person as a resource: when describing a person, you don't have to find the URI that identifies this person, and you certainly don't have invent your own URI either; all you need to do is to make sure you include his/her e-mail address in your description, as shown here.

`foaf:mbox_sha1sum` is another property defined by the FOAF vocabulary which functions just like the `foaf:mbox` property. You will see this property quite often in related documents and literatures, so let us talk about it here as well.

As you can tell, the value of `foaf:mbox` property is a simple textual representation of your e-mail address. In other words, after you have published your FOAF document, your e-mail address is open to the public. This may not be what you wanted. For one thing, spam can flood your mailbox within a few hours. For this reason, FOAF provides another property, `foaf:mbox_sha1sum`, which offers a different representation of your e-mail address. You can get this representation by taking your e-mail address and applying the SHA1 algorithm to it. The resulting representation is indeed long and ugly, but your privacy is well protected.

There are several different ways to generate the SHA1 sum of your e-mail address; we will not cover the details here. Remember to use `foaf:mbox_sha1sum` as much as you can, and it is also defined as an inverse functional property, so it can be used to uniquely identify a given person.

Now let us move on to another important FOAF property, `foaf:knows`. We use it to describe our relationships with other people, and it is very useful when it comes to building the social network using FOAF documents. Let us take a look at one example. Suppose part of my friend's FOAF document looks like this:

```
<foaf:Person>
    <foaf:name>Connie</foaf:name>
    <foaf:mbox rdf:resource="mailto:connie@liyangyu.com"/>
</foaf:Person>
```

If I want to indicate in my FOAF document that I know her, I can include the code in List 7.4 into my FOAF document:

List 7.4 Example of using `foaf:knows` property

```
1:   <foaf:Person>
2:     <foaf:name>Liyang Yu</foaf:name>
3:     <foaf:mbox rdf:resource="mailto:liyang@liyangyu.com"/>
4:     <foaf:knows>
5:       <foaf:Person>
6:         <foaf:mbox rdf:resource="mailto:connie@liyangyu.com"/>
7:       </foaf:Person>
8:     </foaf:knows>
9:   </foaf:Person>
```

This shows that I know a person who has an e-mail address given by connie@liyangyu.com. Again, since property `foaf:mbox` is used, a given

application will be able to understand that the person I know has a name called
Connie; notice that no URI has been used to identify her at all.

Also notice that you cannot assume that the foaf:knows property is a symmetric
property; in other words, that I know Connie does not imply that Connie knows
me. If you check the FOAF vocabulary definition, you can see foaf:knows is
indeed not defined as symmetric.

Perhaps the most important use of the foaf:knows property is to connect FOAF
files together. Often by mentioning other people (foaf:knows), and by providing a
rdfs:seeAlso property at the same time, we can link different RDF documents
together. Let us discuss this a little further at this point, and in the later chapters, we
will see applications built upon this relationships.

We saw property rdfs:seeAlso in previous chapters. It is defined in RDF
schema namespace, and it indicates that there is some additional information
about the resource this property is describing. For instance, I can add one more
line into List 7.1, as shown in List 7.5:

List 7.5 Example of using rdfs:seeAlso property

```
 1: <rdf:RDF
1a:     xmlns:rdf="http://www.w3.org/1999/02/22-rdf-syntax-ns#"
 2:     xmlns:rdfs="http://www.w3.org/2000/01/rdf-schema#"
 3:     xmlns:foaf="http://xmlns.com/foaf/0.1/">
 4:
 5: <foaf:Person>
 6:   <foaf:name>Liyang Yu</foaf:name>
 7:   <foaf:mbox rdf:resource="mailto:liyang@liyangyu.com"/>
 8:   <rdfs:seeAlso
8a:         rdf:resource="http://www.yuchen.net/liyang.rdf"/>
 9: </foaf:Person>
10:
11: </rdf:RDF>
```

Line 8 says that if you want to know more about this Person instance, you can
find it in the resource pointed to by http://www.yuchen.net/liyang.rdf.

Here, the resource pointed to by http://www.yuchen.net/liyang.rdf is an
old FOAF document that describes me, but I can, in fact, point to a friend's FOAF
document using rdfs:seeAlso, together with property foaf:knows, as shown in
List 7.6:

List 7.6 Use `foaf:knows` and `rdfs:seeAlso` to link RDF documents together

```
1:  <rdf:RDF
1a:     xmlns:rdf="http://www.w3.org/1999/02/22-rdf-syntax-ns#"
2:      xmlns:rdfs="http://www.w3.org/2000/01/rdf-schema#"
3:      xmlns:foaf="http://xmlns.com/foaf/0.1/">
4:
5:    <foaf:Person>
6:     <foaf:name>Liyang Yu</foaf:name>
7:     <foaf:mbox rdf:resource="mailto:liyang@liyangyu.com"/>
8:     <rdfs:seeAlso
8a:          rdf:resource="http://www.yuchen.net/liyang.rdf"/>
9:     <foaf:knows>
10:       <foaf:Person>
11:        <foaf:mbox rdf:resource="mailto:connie@liyangyu.com"/>
12:        <rdfs:seeAlso
12a:           rdf:resource="http://www.liyangyu.com/connie.rdf"/>
13:       </foaf:Person>
14:     </foaf:knows>
15:    </foaf:Person>
16:
17: </rdf:RDF>
```

Now, an application seeing the document shown in List 7.6 will move on to access the document identified by the following URI (line 12):

```
http://www.liyangyu.com/connie.rdf
```

and by doing so, FOAF aggregators can be built without the need for a centrally managed directory of FOAF files.

As a matter of fact, property `rdfs:seeAlso` is treated by the FOAF community as the hyperlink of FOAF documents. More specifically, one FOAF document is considered to contain a hyperlink to another document if it has included `rdfs:seeAlso` property, and the value of this property is where this hyperlink is pointing to. Here, this FOAF document can be considered as a root HTML page, and the `rdfs:seeAlso` property is just like an `<href>` tag contained in the page. It is through the `rdfs:seeAlso` property that a whole web of machine-readable metadata can be built. We will see more about this property and its important role in the chapters yet to come.

The last two FOAF terms we would like to discuss here are `foaf:depiction` and `foaf:depicts`. It is quite common that people put their pictures on their Web sites. To help us add statements about the pictures into the related FOAF document, FOAF vocabulary provides two properties to accomplish this. The first property is the `foaf:depiction` property, and second one is `foaf:depicts` property; make sure you know the difference between these two.

The `foaf:depiction` property is a relationship between a thing and an image that depicts the thing. In other words, it makes the statement such as "this person (Thing) is shown in this image". On the other hand, `foaf:depicts` is the inverse property: it is a relationship between an image and something that image depicts. Therefore, to indicate the fact that I have a picture, I should use line 9 as shown in List 7.7:

List 7.7 Example of using `foaf:depiction` property

```
1:  <rdf:RDF
1a:     xmlns:rdf="http://www.w3.org/1999/02/22-rdf-syntax-ns#"
2:      xmlns:rdfs="http://www.w3.org/2000/01/rdf-schema#"
3:      xmlns:foaf="http://xmlns.com/foaf/0.1/">
4:
5:  <foaf:Person>
6:      <foaf:name>Liyang Yu</foaf:name>
7:      <foaf:mbox rdf:resource="mailto:liyang@liyangyu.com"/>
8:      <rdfs:seeAlso
8a:          rdf:resource="http://www.yuchen.net/liyang.rdf"/>
9:      <foaf:depiction rdf:resource=
9a:                  "http://www.liyangyu.com/pictures/yu.jpg"/>
10: </foaf:Person>
11:
12: </rdf:RDF>
```

I will leave it to you to understand the usage of the `foaf:depicts` property.

Up to this point, we have talked about several classes and properties defined in the FOAF vocabulary. Again, you should have no problem reading and understanding the whole FOAF ontology. Let us move on to the topic of how to create your own FOAF document and also make sure that you know how to get into the "friend circle".

7.3   Create Your FOAF Document and Get into the Friend Circle

In this section, we talk about several issues related to creating your own FOAF document and joining the circle of friends. Before we can do all this, we need to know how FOAF project has designed the flow, as we will see in the next section.

7.3.1   How Does the Circle Work?

The circle of FOAF documents is created and maintained by the following steps.

Step 1. A user creates the FOAF document.

As a user, you create a FOAF document by using the FOAF vocabulary as we discussed in the previous section. The only thing you need to remember is that you should use `foaf:knows` property together with `rdfs:seeAlso` property to connect your document with the documents of other friends.

Step 2. Link your homepage to your FOAF document.

Once you have created your FOAF document, you should link it from your homepage. And once you have finished this step, you are done; it is now up to the FOAF project to find you.

Step 3. FOAF uses its crawler to visit the Web and collect all the FOAF documents.

In the context of FOAF project, a crawler is called a *scutter*. Its basic task is not much different from a crawler: it visits the Web and tries to find RDF files. In this case, it has to find a special kind of RDF file: a FOAF document. Once it finds one, the least it will do is to parse the document, and store the triples into its data system for later use.

An important feature about the scutter is that it has to know how to handle the `rdfs:seeAlso` property: whenever the scutter sees this, it follows the link to reach the document pointed to by `rdfs:seeAlso` property. This is the way FOAF constructs a network of FOAF documents.

Another important fact about scutter is that it has to take care of the data merging issue. To do so, the scutter has to know which FOAF properties can uniquely identify resources. More specifically, `foaf:mbox`, `foaf:mbox_sha1sum` and `foaf:homepage` are all defined as inverse functional properties; therefore, they can all uniquely identify individuals that have one of these properties. In the real operation, one solution the scutter can use is to keep a list of RDF statements which involve any of these properties, and when it is necessary, it can consult this list to merge together different triples that are in fact describing the same individuals.

Step 4. FOAF maintains a central repository and is also responsible for keeping the information up to date.

FOAF also has to maintain a centralized database to store all the triples it has collected and other relevant information. To keep this database up to date, it has to run the scutter periodically to visit the Web.

Step 5. FOFA provides a user interface so we can find our friends and conduct other interesting activities.

FOAF offers some tools one can use to view the friends in the circle, which further defines the look-and-feel of the FOAF project. Among these tools, FOAF explorer is quite popular, and you can find this tool as this location:

```
http://xml.mfd-consult.dk/foaf/explorer/
```

Figure 7.1 is an example of viewing a FOAF document using FOAF explorer. The FOAF document being viewed was created by Dan Brickley, one of the founders of the FOAF project.

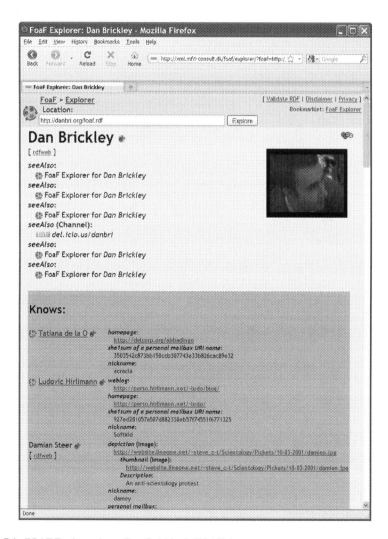

Fig. 7.1   FOAF Explorer shows Dan Brickley's FOAF document

Up to this point, we have gained understanding about how FOAF project works to build a network of FOAF documents. It is time to create our own FOAF document and join the circle.

7.3.2   Create Your FOAF Document

The most straightforward way to create a FOAF document is to use a simple text editor. This requires you to directly use the FOAF vocabulary. Given the self-explanatory nature of the FOAF ontology, this is not difficult to do. Also you need to validate the final document, just to make sure its syntax is legal.

The other choice is to use tools to create FOAF documents. The most popular one is called "FOAF-a-matic", you can find the link to this tool from the FOAF official Web site, and at the current time, its URL is given below:

```
http://www.ldodds.com/foaf/foaf-a-matic.html
```

Figure 7.2 shows the main interface of this authoring tool.

To use this form, you don't have to know any FOAF terms, you just need to follow the instructions to create your FOAF document. More specifically, this form allows you to specify your name, e-mail address, homepage, your picture and phone number and other personal information. It also allows you to enter information about your work, such as work homepage and a small page describing what you do at your work. More importantly, you will have a chance to specify your friends, and provide their FOAF documents as well. Based on what we have learned so far, this will bring both you and your friends into the FOAF network.

Notice that you can leave a lot of fields on the form empty. The only required fields are "First Name", "Last Name" and "Your Email Address". By now, you should understand the reason why you have to provide an e-mail address—FOAF does not assign an URI to you at all, and later on in life, it will use this e-mail address to uniquely identify you.

Once you have finished filling out the form, by clicking the "FOAF me!" button, you will get a RDF document which uses FOAF vocabulary to present a description about you. At this point, you need to exercise your normal "copy and paste" trick in the output window, and copy the generated statements into your favorite editor, and save it to a file so you can later on join the circle of friends, as is discussed next.

7.3.3   Get into the Circle: Publish Your FOAF Document

Once you have created your FOAF document, the next step is to publish it in a way that it can be easily harvested by the scutter (FOAF's crawler) or other applications

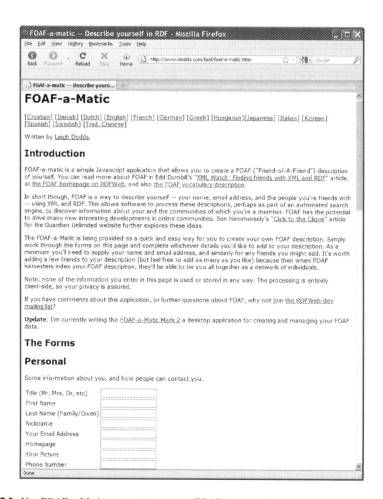

Fig. 7.2 Use FOAF-a-Matic to create your own FOAF document

that can understand FOAF documents. This is what we mean when we say "get into the circle". There are three different ways to get into the circle, and we discuss these different methods in this section.

• Add a link from you homepage to your FOAF document

The easiest solution is to link your homepage to your FOAF document. This can be done using the `<link>` element as shown in List 7.8:

List 7.8 Add a link from your homepage to your FOAF document

```
<!-- this is your homepage -->
<html>
<head>
... ...
<link rel="meta" type="application/rdf+xml" title="FOAF"
      href="http://www.liyangyu.com/foaf.rdf"/>
... ...
</head>

<body>
... ...
</body>
</html>
```

Remember to substitute `href` to point to your own FOAF document. Also notice that your FOAF file can be any name you like, but `foaf.rdf` is a common choice.

This is quite easy to implement; however, the downside is the fact that you have to wait for the crawler to visit your homepage to discover your FOAF document. Without this discovery, you will never be able to get into the circle. Given the fact that there are millions of personal Web sites out there on the Web, the FOAF scutter will have to traverse the Web for long time to find you, if it can find you at all.

To solve this problem, you can use the second solution, which makes the discovery process much more efficient.

- Ask your friend to add a `rdfs:seeAlso` link that points to your document

This is a recommended way to get your FOAF document indexed. Once your friend has added a link to your document by using `rdfs:seeAlso` in his/her document, you can rest assured that your data will appear in the network.

To implement this, your friend needs to remember that he/she has to use `foaf:knows` and `rdfs:seeAlso` together by inserting the following lines into his/her FOAF document:

```
<foaf:knows>
   <foaf:Person>
      <foaf:mbox rdf:resource="mailto:you@yourEmail.com"/>
      <rdfs:seeAlso rdf:resource="http://path_to_your_foaf.rdf"/>
   </foaf:Person>
</foaf:knows>
```

Now, the fact that your friend is already in the circle means that the FOAF scutter has visited his/her document already. Since the scutter periodically revisits the same files to pick up any updates, it will see the `rdfs:seeAlso` link and will then pick up yours. This is the reason why your FOAF document will be guaranteed to be indexed.

Obviously, this solution is feasible only when you have a friend who is already in the circle. What if you do not have anyone in the circle at all? We then need the third solution discussed next.

• Use the "FOAF Bulletin Board"

Obviously, instead of waiting for FOAF network to find you, you can report to it voluntarily. The FOAF project provides a service for you to do this, and it is the so-called FOAF Bulletin Board. To access this service, visit the FOAF Wiki site, and find the FOAF Bulletin Board page. You can also use the following URL to direct access the page:

```
http://wiki.foaf-project.org/w/FOAFBulletinBoard
```

Once you are on the page, you will see a registry of people whose FOAF documents have been collected by FOAF. To add your own FOAF document, you need to log in first. Once you log in, you will see an `Edit` tab. Click this tab, you will then be able to edit a document in the editing window. Add your name, and a link to your FOAF document; click "`save page`" when you are done, and you are then in the FOAF network.

There are other ways you can use to join the circle, but we are not going to discuss them here. A more interesting question at this point, is what does the FOAF world looks like, especially after more and more people have joined the circle? In other words, how does FOAF project change the world of personal Web pages for human eyes into a world of personal Web pages that are suitable for machine processing? Let us take a look at this interesting topic in the next section.

7.3.4   From Web Pages for Human Eyes to Web Pages for Machines

Let us take a look at the world of personal Web pages first. Assuming in my Web page, `www.liyangyu.com`, I have included links pointing to my friends' Web sites. One of my friends, on his Web site, has also included links that pointing to his friends, and so on and so forth. This has created a link of documents on the Web, just as what we have today.

Now using FOAF vocabulary, I have created a FOAF document that describing myself. Quite similar to my personal Web site, in this FOAF document, I talk about myself, such as my e-mail, my name, my interests, etc. Yet there is a fundamental difference: when I talk about myself in this FOAF document, I have used a language that machines can understand. For the machine, this FOAF document

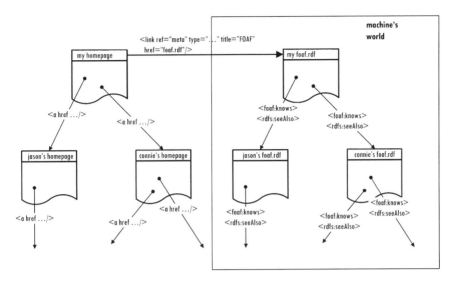

Fig. 7.3 Homepages for human eyes vs. homepages for machines

has become my new personal homepage, it might look ugly to human eyes, but it looks perfectly understandable to machines.

Now, assuming all my friends have created their machine-readable homepages, and just like what I have done in my human-readable homepage, I can now put links that point to my friends' FOAF documents in my machine-readable homepage. This is done by using `foaf:knows` together with `rdfs:seeAlso` property. Furthermore, this is also true for all my friends: in their machine-readable homepages, they can add links to their friends' machine-readable homepages, and so on and so forth.

This will then create a brand new social network on the Web, coexisting with the traditional linked documents on the current Web. This whole new network is now part of the Semantic Web, in the domain of human networks.

The above two different Web networks are shown in Fig. 7.3. By now, probably two things have become much more clear. First, the reason why FOAF is called "Friend Of A Friend" has become clearer; and second, the reason why `foaf:knows` together with `rdfs:seeAlso` is considered by the FOAF community the hyperlink of the FOAF documents has become clear as well.

7.4   Semantic Markup: A Connection Between the Two Worlds

Before we move on to continue exploring the Semantic Web world, we need to talk about one important issue: semantic markup.

7.4.1   What Is Semantic Markup?

So far in this book, we have used the phrase semantic markup quite a few times already. So, what exactly is semantic markup? How does it fit into the whole picture of the Semantic Web?

First of all, after all these chapters, we have gained a much better understanding about the Semantic Web. In fact, at this moment if we had to use one sentence to describe what exactly the Semantic Web is, it would be really simple: it is all about extending the current Web to make it more machine-understandable.

To accomplish this goal, we first need some language(s) to express meanings that machines can understand. This is one of the things we have learned the most at this point: we have covered RDF, RDFS and OWL. These languages can be used to develop a formal ontology and to create RDF documents that machines can process. And as we have learned in this chapter, we used FOAF ontology to create RDF documents that describe ourselves. Obviously, we can use other ontologies in other domains to create more and more RDF documents that describe resources in the world.

However, when we look at our goal and what we have accomplished so far, we realize the fact that there is something missing: the current Web is one world, the machine-readable semantics expressed by ontologies is another world, and where is the connection between these two? If these two worlds always stand independently with each other, there will be no way we can extend the current Web to make it more machine-readable.

Therefore, we need to build a connection between the current Web and the semantic world. This is what we call "adding semantics to the current Web".

As you might have guessed, adding semantics to the current Web is called *semantic markup*; sometimes, it is also called *semantic annotation*.

7.4.2   Semantic Markup: Procedure and Example

In general, a semantic markup file is an RDF document containing RDF statements that describe the content of a Web page by using the terms defined in one or several ontologies. For instance, suppose a Web page describes some entities in the real world, the markup document for this Web page may specify that these entities are instances of some classes defined in some ontology, and these instances have some properties and some relationships among them, and so on.

When an application reaches a Web page and somehow finds this page has a markup document (more details on this later), it reads this markup file and also loads the related ontologies into its memory. At this point, the application can act as if it understands the content of the current Web page, and it can also discover some implicit facts about this page. The final result is that the same Web page not only continues to look great to human eyes, but also makes perfect sense to machines.

More specifically, there are several steps you need to follow when semantically marking up a Web page:

Step 1. Decide which ontology or ontologies to use for semantic markup.

The first thing is to decide which ontology to use. Sometimes, you might need more than one ontology. This involves reading and understanding the ontology to decide whether the given ontology fits your need, or whether you agree with the semantics expressed by the ontology. It is possible that you have to come up with your own ontology; in that case, you need to remember the rule of always trying to reuse existing ontologies, or simply construct your new ontology by extending some given ontology.

Step 2. Markup the Web page.

Once you have decided the ontology you are going to use, you can start to markup the page. At this point, you need to decide exactly what content on your page you want to markup. Clearly, it is neither possible nor necessary to mark up everything on your page. Having some sort of application in your mind would help you to make the decision. The question you want to ask yourself is, for instance, if there were an application visiting this page, what information on this page would I want the agent to understand? Remember, your decision is also constrained by the ontology you have selected: the markup statements have to be constructed based upon the ontology; therefore, you can only markup the contents that are supported by the selected ontology.

You can elect to create you markup document by using a simple editor or by using some tools. Currently there are tools available to help you to markup your pages, as we will see in our markup examples later in this chapter. If you decide to use a simple editor to manually markup a Web page, remember to use a validator to make sure your markup document at least does not contain any syntax errors. The reason is simple: the application that reads this markup document may not be as forgiving as you are hoping; if you make some syntax mistakes, a lot of your markup statements may be totally skipped and ignored.

After you have finished creating the markup document, you need to put it somewhere on your Web server. You also need to remember to grant enough rights to it so the outside world can access it. This is also related to the last step discussed below.

Step 3. Let the world know your page has a markup document.

The last thing you need to do is to inform the world that your page has a markup document. At the time of this writing, there is no standard way of accomplishing this. A popular method is to add a link in the HTML header of the Web page, as we have seen in this chapter when we discuss the methods we can use to publish FOAF documents (see List 7.8).

With all this said, let us take a look at one example of semantic markup. My goal is to markup my own personal homepage, www.liyangyu.com, and to do so, we will follow the steps discussed earlier.

The first step is to choose an ontology for markup. Clearly, my home page is all about a person, so quite obviously we are going to use FOAF ontology. We might need other vocabularies down the road, but for now, we will stick with FOAF ontology only.

The second step is to create the markup document. With all the examples we have seen in this chapter, creating this document should not be difficult at all: it is simply an RDF document that describes me as a resource by using the terms defined in FOAF ontology.

Again, it is up to us to decide what content in the page should be semantically marked up. As a starter, List 7.9 shows a possible markup document.

List 7.9 A markup document for the author's homepage

```
1: <?xml version="1.0" encoding="UTF-8"?>
2: <rdf:RDF
2a:     xmlns:rdf="http://www.w3.org/1999/02/22-rdf-syntax-ns#"
3:      xmlns:rdfs="http://www.w3.org/2000/01/rdf-schema#"
4:      xmlns:dc="http://www.purl.org/metadata/dublin-core#"
5:      xmlns:foaf="http://xmlns.com/foaf/0.1/">
6:
7: <rdf:Description rdf:about="http://www.liyangyu.com">
8:   <rdf:type
8a:       rdf:resource="http://xmlns.com/foaf/0.1/Document"/>
9:   <dc:title>liyang yu's home page</dc:title>
10:  <dc:creator
10a:      rdf:resource="http://www.liyangyu.com/foaf.rdf#liyang"/>
11: </rdf:Description>
12:
13: <rdf:Description
13a:      rdf:about="http://www.liyangyu.com/foaf.rdf#liyang">
14:
15:   <rdf:type rdf:resource="http://xmlns.com/foaf/0.1/Person"/>
16:   <foaf:name>liyang yu</foaf:name>
17:   <foaf:title>Dr</foaf:title>
18:   <foaf:givenname>liyang</foaf:givenname>
19:   <foaf:family_name>yu</foaf:family_name>
20:   <foaf:mbox_sha1sum>
20a:     1613a9c3ec8b18271a8fe1f79537a7b08803d896
20b:  </foaf:mbox_sha1sum>
21:   <foaf:homepage rdf:resource="http://www.liyangyu.com"/>
22:
```

```
23:    <foaf:workplaceHomepage
23a:         rdf:resource="http://www.delta.com"/>
24:    <foaf:topic_interest
24a:    rdf:resource="http://dbpedia.org/resource/Semantic_Web"/>
25:    <foaf:knows>
26:     <foaf:Person>
27:       <foaf:mbox rdf:resource="mailto:connie@liyangyu.com"/>
28:       <rdfs:seeAlso rdf:resource=
28a:            "http://www.liyangyu.com/connie.rdf#connie"/>
29:     </foaf:Person>
30:    </foaf:knows>
31:
32: </rdf:Description>
33:
34: </rdf:RDF>
```

As you can tell, this document contains some basic information about me, and it also includes a link to a friend I know. With what we have learned in this chapter, this document should be fairly easy to follow, and not much explanation is needed.

Now imagine an application that comes across my home page. By reading List 7.9, it will be able to understand the following facts (not a complete list):

- The resource identified by `http://www.liyangyu.com` is a `foaf:Document` instance, and it has a `dc:title` whose value is `liyang yu's home page`, and a resource named `http://www.liyangyu.com/foaf.rdf#liyang` has created this document;
- `http://www.liyangyu.com/foaf.rdf#liyang` is a `foaf:Person` type resource; its `foaf:homepage` is identified by `http://www.liyangyu.com`.
- `http://www.liyangyu.com/foaf.rdf#liyang` has these properties defined: `foaf:name`, `foaf:title`, `foaf:mbox_sha1sum` etc.
- `http://www.liyangyu.com/foaf.rdf#liyang` also `foaf:knows` another `foaf:Person` instance, whose `foaf:mbox` property is given by the value of `connie@liyangyu.com`, etc.

Notice that Dublin Core vocabulary is used to identify the page title and page author (lines 9–10), and the URI that represents the concept of the Semantic Web is also reused (line 24). Again, this URI is coined by the DBpedia project, which is discussed in Chap. 10.

Now we are ready for the last step: explicitly indicate the fact that my personal Web page has been marked up by an RDF file. To do so, we can use the first solution presented in Sect. 7.3.3. In fact, by now you should realize that a FOAF document can be considered as a special markup to a person's homepage, and all I have done here was simply create a FOAF document for myself.

There are also tools available to help us markup a given Web page. For example, SMORE is one of the projects developed by the researchers and developers in the University of Maryland at College Park, and you can take a look at their work from their official Web page:

http://www.mindswap.org/

SMORE allows the user to markup Web documents without requiring a deep knowledge of OWL terms and syntax. You can create different instances easily by using the provided GUI, which is quite intuitive and straightforward. Also, SMORE lets you visualize your ontology; therefore it can be used as a OWL ontology validator as well.

We are not going to cover the details about how to use it; you can download it from here and experiment with it on your own:

http://www.mindswap.org/2005/SMORE/

If you use it for markup, your final result would be a generated RDF document that you can directly use as your markup document. You might want to make modification if necessary; but generally speaking, it is always a good idea to use a tool to create your markup file whenever it is possible.

7.4.3   Semantic Markup: Feasibility and Different Approaches

As we mentioned earlier, the process of marking up a document is the process of building the critical link between the current Web and the machine-readable Web. It is the actual implementation of the so-called adding semantics to the current Web. However, as you might have realized already, there are lots of unsolved issues associated with Web page markup.

The first thing you might have noticed is that no matter whether we have decided to markup a page manually or by using some tools, it seems to be quite a lot of work just to markup a simple Web page such as my personal homepage. The question then is, how do we finish all the Web pages on the Web? Given the huge number of pages on the Web, it is just not practical. Also, it is not trivial at all to implement the markup process; a page owner has to learn at least something about ontology, OWL and RDF, among other things. Even if all single-page owners agree to markup their pages, how do we make sure everyone is sharing ontologies to the maximum extent without unnecessarily inventing new ones?

These thoughts have triggered the search for the so-called killer application in the world of the Semantic Web. The idea is that if we could build a killer semantic Web application to demonstrate some significant benefit to the world, there will then be enough motivation for the page owners to markup their pages. However, without the link between the current Web and the machine-readable semantics being built, the killer application (whatever it is) simply cannot be created.

At the time of this writing, there is still no final call about this killer application. However, the good news is, there are at least some solutions to the above dilemma, and in the upcoming chapters, we will be able to see examples of these solutions. For now, let us briefly introduce some of these solutions:

- Manually markup in a much more limited domain and scope

Semantic markup by the general public on the whole Web seems to be too challenging to implement, but for a much smaller domain and scope, manual markup is feasible. For example, for a specific community or organization, their knowledge domain is much smaller, so publishing and sharing a collection of core ontologies within the community or the organization is quite possible. If a relatively easier way of manually semantic markup is provided, it is then possible to build semantic Web application for this specific community or organization.

- Machine-generated semantic markup

There has been some research in this area, and some automatic markup solutions have been proposed. However, most of these techniques are applied to technical texts. For the Web that contains highly heterogeneous text types that are mainly made up by natural languages, there seems to be no efficient solution yet.

However, some Web content already provides structured information as part of the content. Therefore, instead of parsing natural languages to produce markup files, machines can take advantage of this existing structured information, and generate markup documents based on these structured data.

We can also see one example along this line as well, and it is the popular DBpedia project. We will learn more details later on, but for now, DBpedia is completely generated by machine, and the source for these machine-readable documents all comes from the structured information contained in Wikipedia.

- Create a machine-readable Web all on its own

There seems to be one key assumption behind the previous two solutions: there have to be two formats for one piece of Web content: one for human viewing and one for machines.

In fact, do we really have to do this at all? If we start to publish machine-readable data, such as RDF documents, and somehow make all these documents connect to each other, just like what we have done when creating Web pages, then we will be creating a linked data Web! And since everything on this linked data Web is machine-readable, we should be able to develop a lot of interesting applications as well, without any need to do semantic markup. This is the idea behind the Linked Data Project, and we will study it as well in another future chapter.

At this point, we are ready to move on and to study the above three solutions in detail. The goal is twofold: first, to build more understanding about the Semantic Web; second, these solutions will be used as hints to you, and hopefully you will be able to come up and design even better solutions for the idea of the Semantic Web.

7.5   Summary

In this chapter, we have learned FOAF, an example of the Semantic Web in the domain of social networking.

The first thing we should understand from this chapter is the FOAF ontology itself. This includes its core terms and how to use these terms to describe people, their basic information, the things they do and their relationships to other people.

It is useful to have your own FOAF document created. You should understand how to create it and how to publish it on the Web, and further, how to get into the "circle of trust".

Semantic markup is an important concept. Not only you should be able to manually markup a Web document, but also you should understand the following about it:

- It provides a connection between the current Web and the collection of knowledge that is machine-understandable.
- It is the concrete implementation of so-called "adding semantics to the current Web".
- It has several issues regarding whether it is feasible in the real world. However, different solutions do exist, and these solutions have already given rise to different applications on the Semantic Web.

Chapter 8
DBpedia

At the end of Chap. 7, we discussed the topic of semantic markup. More specifically, it is possible to automatically generate markup documents for some Web content, especially when there is preexisting structured information contained in these content.

This chapter provides one such example, the popular DBpedia project. In fact, it is important to understand DBpedia, not only as an example of automatically generated markup, but also as because of its key position in the Web of Linked Data, as we will see in Chap. 9.

8.1 Introduction to DBpedia

8.1.1 From Manual Markup to Automatic Generation of Annotation

As we have learned by now, the classic view of the Semantic Web is to add semantic annotations to each page by using the RDF data model and ontologies, so that the added information can be processed by a machine.

However, in general, manually adding semantic annotations for a large-scale application is quite difficult. For instance, it requires the availability of widely accepted ontologies, and manually marking up millions of pages, which is simply not practical or at the least is formidably expensive. In addition, what about the new pages that are generated each day? How can we require an ordinary user to conquer the learning curve and go through the extra steps to markup the page?

The reason why some manual approaches have been successful is largely due to the uniqueness of the sites themselves. More specifically, these sites normally have limited scopes, and quite often are only used internally by some organization. It is therefore not necessary to have standard ontologies built beforehand, and a home-grown ontology is often good enough for the goal.

© Springer-Verlag Berlin Heidelberg 2014
L. Yu, *A Developer's Guide to the Semantic Web*,
DOI 10.1007/978-3-662-43796-4_8

Obviously, not every application can offer a favorable environment to a manual approach. To overcome this difficulty, another approach has become popular in recent years, where the semantic annotation information is automatically generated. Instead of independently adding semantic markups to the current Web document, this approach tries to derive semantic information automatically from the existing structured information contained in the Web document.

The main attraction of this automatic approach is that it does not require much manual work, and is therefore quite scalable. However, it does have to deal with the imperfection of the information on each page, and how well it works heavily depends upon how much structured information is contained in a given page.

In this chapter, we are going to study one example system that is built solely by using this automatic approach: the DBpedia project. Once you finish this chapter, you will have examples of both approaches, which should be valuable for your future development work.

Note that these two approaches can also benefit from each other. For example, the more manual annotations there are, the more precise the automatic approach will be, since it can directly take advantage of the existing structured information. Similarly, automatically generating the semantic information can minimize the need for manual approaches, and combining these two approaches can sometimes be the best solution for your project.

8.1.2   From Wikipedia to DBpedia

The most successful and popular wiki by far is probably Wikipedia, the largest online encyclopedia created and maintained by a globally distributed author community. At the time of this writing, Wikipedia appears in more than 280 different languages, with the English version containing more than 4.4 million articles. You can access Wikipedia from here:

```
http://en.wikipedia.org/wiki/Main_Page
```

and you will be amazed by how much information it provides.   ·

However, as we have discussed in the previous chapter, similar to any other traditional wiki site, using Wikipedia means reading it. It is up to you to digest all the information, and to search though pages to find what you are looking for.

The solution is probably not surprising: use the Semantic Web technologies to make better use of the vast amount of knowledge in Wikipedia. This time, however, instead of adding semantic markup to each wiki page, tools and agents have been developed to extract existing structured information from each page. And furthermore,

- The extracted information takes the form of an RDF data graph, and this graph is the corresponding machine-readable page of the original wiki page.
- Repeating this extraction process for each page in Wikipedia builds a huge collection of RDF data graphs, which form a large RDF dataset.

- This RDF dataset can be viewed as Wikipedia's machine-readable version, while the original Wikipedia remains as the human-readable one.
- Since all the RDF graphs in this RDF dataset share the same set of ontologies, they therefore share precisely defined semantics, meaning that we can query against this dataset and find what we want much more easily.

The above is the outline of an idea about how to transform Wikipedia to make it more useful. It was originally proposed by researchers and developers from University of Leipzig, Freie Universität Berlin and OpenLink Software. The initial release of this RDF dataset was in January of 2007, and the dataset is called *DBpedia*. The exact same idea has since then grown into a project called the *DBpedia Project*, as described here:

```
http://dbpedia.org/About
```

And here is the official definition of DBpedia, taken directly from the above official Web site:

DBpedia is a crowd-sourced community effort to extract structured information from Wikipedia and make this information available on the Web. DBpedia allows you to ask sophisticated queries against Wikipedia, and to link the different data sets on the Web to Wikipedia data. We hope that this work will make it easier for the huge amount of information in Wikipedia to be used in some new interesting ways. Furthermore, it might inspire new mechanisms for navigating, linking, and improving the encyclopedia itself.

The rest of this chapter presents DBpedia project in detail. Here is a quick summary of the DBpedia dataset at the time of this writing:

- Its latest release is DBpedia 3.9, extracted from Wikipedia dumps generated in late March and early April of 2013.
- It describes more than 4.0 million things, out of which 3.22 million are classified in a consistent ontology, including at least 832,000 persons, 639,000 places, 116,000 music albums, 78,000 films and 209,000 organizations, just to name a few.
- It has 27.6 million links to external Web pages, 45.0 million external links to other RDF datasets and 67.0 million links to Wikipedia categories.

At the time you are reading this chapter, the above numbers most likely will have changed. It will be interesting to make a comparison to see how fast the dataset grows. Yet, the basic techniques behind it should remain the same, and that is the topic of the rest of this chapter.

8.1.3 The Look-and-Feel of DBpedia: Page Redirect

Before we start to understand the automatic extraction of semantic information, it will be helpful to get a basic feeling of DBpedia: what does it look like and how are we going to access it?

As far as a user is concerned, DBpedia is essentially a huge RDF dataset. And there are two ways to access it:

1. Use a Web browser to view different RDF graphs contained in the DBpedia dataset.
2. Use a SPARQL endpoint to query against the DBpedia dataset with the goal of discovering information with much greater ease.

The second way of accessing DBpedia is perhaps the one that DBpedia project has intended for us to do. However, using a Web browser to access a specific RDF graph contained in the dataset feels like using DBpedia as if it were another version of the original Wikipedia, and it would be interesting to those curious minds. And by comparing the two pages—the original one from Wikipedia and the generated RDF graph from DBpedia, we can also learn a lot about DBpedia itself.

This section focuses on the first way of accessing DBpedia, and the second way is covered in detail in later sections.

Let's use Swiss tennis player Roger Federer as an example. First, let us see how he is described in Wikipedia. Open Wikipedia from this URL,

```
http://www.wikipedia.org/
```

And type *Roger Federer* in the search box; also make sure *English* is the selected language by using the language selection drop-down list. Once you click the continue button, you will be taken to the page as shown in Fig. 8.1.

And notice this page has the following URL,

```
http://en.wikipedia.org/wiki/Roger_Federer
```

Now, to get to its DBpedia equivalent page, replace the following prefix in the above URL,

```
http://en.wikipedia.org/wiki/
```

with this one,

```
http://dbpedia.org/resource/
```

and you get the following URL,

```
http://dbpedia.org/resource/Roger_Federer
```

which is the corresponding machine-readable DBpedia page for Roger Federer.

Now enter this URL into your Web browser. Instead of seeing this exciting new DBpedia equivalent page, your browser will redirect you to the following URL,

```
http://dbpedia.org/page/Roger_Federer
```

And there, you will see the corresponding RDF graph for Roger Federer displayed as an HTML page, as shown in Fig. 8.2. So what has happened?

We will cover the reason in the next chapter, but here is a quick answer to this question. The page,

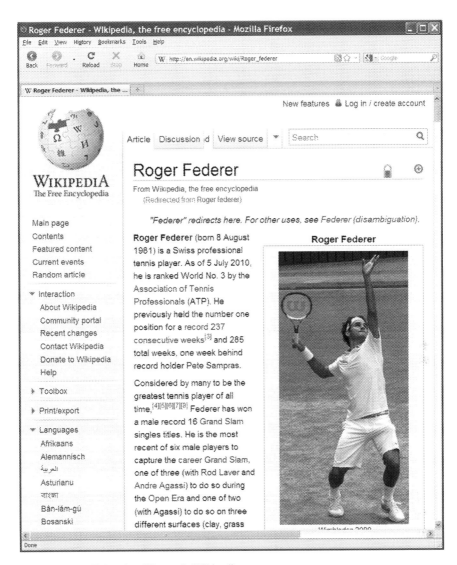

Fig. 8.1 Roger Federer's wiki page in Wikipedia

```
http://dbpedia.org/resource/Roger_Federer
```

in fact represents a generated RDF data file that is intended for machines to read, not for human eyes to enjoy. Therefore, it does not display as well as a traditional Web page in an ordinary HTML browser. Yet in order to give back what has been requested by its user, DBpedia has implemented an HTTP mechanism called *content negotiation* (details in Chap. 9) so your browser will be redirected to the following page,

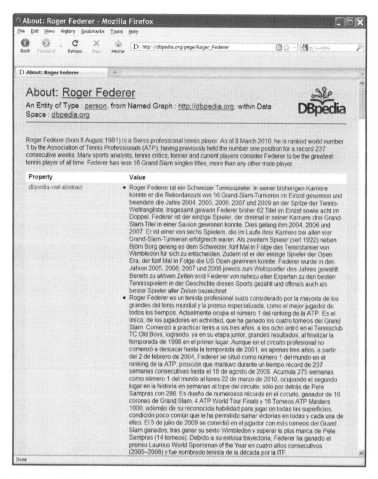

Fig. 8.2   Generated RDF graph for Roger Federer, displayed as an HTML page

```
http://dbpedia.org/page/Roger_Federer
```

which then presents the page as shown in Fig. 8.2.

As you can see, this page is mainly a long summary of property–value pairs, which are presented in a table format. You may also find this page not as readable as its original Wikipedia version. However, it is also quite amazing that everything on this page is automatically extracted from the original text. We will come back to this page again, but for now, what has been described here is the simplest way to access DBpedia.

As a summary, any page in Wikipedia has the following URL:

http://en.wikipedia.org/wiki/_Page_Name_

And you can always replace the prefix and use the follow URL to access its corresponding DBpedia equivalent page:

http://dbpedia.org/resource/*Page_Name*

8.2 Semantics in DBpedia

Before we get into the exciting world of using SPARQL to query against DBpedia, we need to understand how structured information is extracted from the corresponding Wikipedia pages, which we cover in this section.

8.2.1 *Infobox Template*

The key idea of DBpedia is to automatically extract structured information from existing wiki pages without the need to make any change to them. As we all know, a wiki page is simply a page of text. So where is the structured information?

The answer lies in a special type of templates called *infoboxes*. Let us take a look at these templates first. Notice the goal of this section is to show you that the information contained in infobox templates is the main source for structured information extraction, and not to discuss how to create and populate an infobox. If you are completely new to infobox, it might be helpful to check out its basic concept from Wikipedia's `help` page.

Templates in Wikipedia were originally introduced mainly for layout purposes, and the infobox template is one particular type of these templates. When used on a page, it provides summary information about the subject that is being discussed on the given page, and the direct benefit to the user is to save time: if you don't have time to read the long wiki page, you can simply read this infobox to get its main point.

For the wiki site itself, infobox offers several benefits. First, since it is created from a template, similar subjects on different pages all have a uniform look and a common format. Second, to change the display style and common texts in infoboxes, one does not have to go through each one of these infoboxes. Instead, one can simply modify the style and common texts from a well-controlled central place (the template page), and all the displayed infoboxes will be changed.

To see the code behind a given infobox, for example, the infobox on Roger Federer's page, you can simply click the `view source` tab on the top of the page (Fig. 8.1).

List 8.1 shows part of the code for the infobox on Roger Federer's wiki page. Notice the actual image of the infobox is not included here, since we are mainly interested in code behind the infobox. Again, remember by the time you read this chapter, this infobox may as well be changed, but the basic idea will still be the same. Also, in order for us to read it easily, List 8.1 has been edited slightly.

List 8.1 Infobox on Roger Federer's wiki page

```
{{Infobox Tennis player
|playername = Roger Federer
|image = [[File:Roger Federer (26 June 2009, Wimbledon) 2
new.jpg|200px|]]
|caption = Wimbledon 2009
|country = [[Switzerland]]
|nickname= ''Swiss Maestro''<ref>...</ref><br />
           ''Federer Express''</br>
           ''Fed Express''</br>
           ''FedEx''<ref>...</ref><br/>
|residence = [[Wollerau]], [[Switzerland]]
|datebirth = {{birth date and age|df=yes|1981|08|08}}
|placebirth = [[Basel]], [[Switzerland]]
|height = {{height|m=1.86}}
|weight = {{convert|85.0|kg|lb st|abbr=on}}<ref>...</ref>
|turnedpro = 1998<ref>...</ref>
|plays = Right-handed; one-handed backhand
|careerprizemoney = [[US$]] 53,362,068<br />* [[ATP Tour
records#Earnings|All-time leader in earnings]]
|singlesrecord = 678-161 (80.8%)<ref>...</ref>
|singlestitles = 61
|highestsinglesranking = No. '''1''' (February 2, 2004)
|currentsinglesranking = No. '''1''' (July 6, 2009)
|AustralianOpenresult = '''W''' (
   [[2004 Australian Open - Men's Singles|2004]],
   [[2006 Australian Open - Men's Singles|2006]],
   [[2007 Australian Open - Men's Singles|2007]])
|FrenchOpenresult = '''W''' (
   [[2009 French Open - Men's Singles|2009]])
|Wimbledonresult = '''W''' (
   [[2003 Wimbledon Championships - Men's Singles|2003]],
   [[2004 Wimbledon Championships - Men's Singles|2004]],
   [[2005 Wimbledon Championships - Men's Singles|2005]],
   [[2006 Wimbledon Championships - Men's Singles|2006]],
   [[2007 Wimbledon Championships - Men's Singles|2007]],
   [[2009 Wimbledon Championships - Men's Singles|2009]])
|USOpenresult = '''W''' (
   [[2004 U.S. Open - Men's Singles|2004]],
   [[2005 U.S. Open - Men's Singles|2005]],
   [[2006 U.S. Open - Men's Singles|2006]],
   [[2007 U.S. Open - Men's Singles|2007]],
   [[2008 U.S. Open - Men's Singles|2008]])
```

```
|Othertournaments = Yes
|MastersCupresult = '''W''' (
   [[2003 Tennis Masters Cup#Singles|2003]],
   [[2004 Tennis Masters Cup#Singles|2004]],
   [[2006 Tennis Masters Cup#Singles|2006]],
   [[2007 Tennis Masters Cup#Singles|2007]])
|Olympicsresult = ''SF'' (
   {{OlympicEvent|Tennis|2000 Summer|title=2000|subcategory=Men's
Singles}})
|doublesrecord = 112-72 (60.8%)
|doublestitles = 8
|OthertournamentsDoubles = yes
|grandslamsdoublesresults= yes
|AustralianOpenDoublesresult = 3R (2003)
|FrenchOpenDoublesresult = 1R (2000)
|WimbledonDoublesresult = QF (2000)
|USOpenDoublesresult = 3R (2002)
|OlympicsDoublesresult = [[Image:Gold medal.svg|20px]] '''Gold
Medal''' ({{OlympicEvent|Tennis|2008
Summer|title=2008|subcategory=Men's Doubles}})
|highestdoublesranking = No. 24 (9 June 2003)
|updated = 24 November 2009}}
```

Now, besides admiring Roger Federer's amazing career achievements, we should not miss the most important thing we see from this infobox: an infobox is simply a collection of property–value pairs.

The infobox shown in List 8.1was created by the page authors, who used an infobox template designed for athletes, which belongs to `People` category. There are infobox templates for a large number of other categories as well, for example, `Place`, `Music`, `Movie`, `Education` and `Organization`, just to name a few. All these infoboxes, although from different category templates, share the same style: each one of them is a collection of property–value pairs.

This property–value pair style should suggest the creation of RDF statements, with each statement mapping to one such pair in the infobox. More specifically, for a given pair, the property name maps to the predicate of a statement, and the property value maps to the object of that statement.

What about the subject of these RDF statements? Notice the entire collection of property–value pairs in a given infobox are together used to describe the subject of that given page. Therefore, all the RDF statements should share the exact same subject, and the subject of the current wiki page naturally becomes the resource described by the generated RDF statements.

And this is the basic idea behind DBpedia's automatic information extraction.

8.2.2   Creating DBpedia Ontology

8.2.2.1   The Need for Ontology

As we have learned, RDF statements use classes and properties to describe resources, and these classes and properties are defined in some given ontologies. It should be clear to us that when using the same set of ontologies, distributed RDF graphs are able to share the same precisely defined semantics, and when linked together, they can provide new nontrivial facts that are valuable to us. Therefore, whenever we discuss a collection of RDF documents, the first question we should ask is, what are the ontologies used by these RDF documents?

Note, however, it is perfectly legal to create RDF statements without using any ontology at all. The result is that the resources described by these statements will not have any precisely defined meanings. In addition, they will not be able to participate in any reasoning process, or take advantage of any benefit from aggregation with other resources. These RDF statements will simply remain isolated with fairly limited value.

In fact, generating RDF statements without using ontology was indeed a major drawback in the early versions of DBpedia's extractor. To have a better idea about this, let us take a look at one such example.

Again, go back to the page for Roger Federer. List 8.2 shows part of the infobox on his page in Wikipedia.

List 8.2 Name, birthday and birthplace information from Roger Federer's infobox

```
|playername = Roger Federer
|datebirth = {{birth date and age|df=yes|1981|08|08}}
|placebirth = [[Basel]], [[Switzerland]]
```

One earlier version of DBpedia's extractor, when parsing this infobox, would simply turn the attribute names contained in the infobox into the predicates of the generated RDF statements. For example, for Federer's name attribute, the predicate would have the following name:

```
dbprop:playername
```

where dbprop is the abbreviation of http://dbpedia.org/property/. For his birthdate and birthplace attributes, the corresponding RDF predicates would look like these:

```
dbprop:datebirth
dbprop:placebirth
```

Other property–value pairs would be processed similarly.

Now, take a look at the infobox of another person, Tim Berners-Lee. Part of his infobox is shown in List 8.3.

List 8.3 Name, birthday and birthplace information from Berners-Lee's infobox

```
| name        = Tim Berners-Lee
| birth_date  = {{birth date and age|1955|6|8|df=y}}
| birth_place = [[London]], [[UK]]
```

Similarly, the extractor would use the following property names as the predicates of the generated RDF statements:

```
dbprop:name
dbprop:birth_date
dbprop:birth_place
```

Since there is no formal ontology shared by these statements, there will be no way for the machine to know the following fact:

- Both Roger Federer and Tim Berners-Lee are resources whose class type is `Person`
- `dbprop:name` is the same as `dbprop:playername`.
- `dbprop:birth_date` is the same as `dbprop:datebirth`.
- `dbprop:birth_place` is the same as `dbprop:placebirth`.

And without knowing the above, as far as any application is concerned, the generated statements are just a collection of alphabetic strings.

The conclusion: whenever RDF statements are generated, ontologies should be used. And more specifically to the case of DBpedia, we need formal definitions of classes and properties. The attributes in infobox templates will be mapped to these classes and properties when RDF statements about the page subject are generated.

Fortunately, the above idea has been implemented by the new extractor in DBpedia Release 3.2. More specifically,

- It first creates an instance of some class type defined in the ontology to represent the subject of the current page.
- It then maps each attribute extracted from the infobox to a property that is defined in the ontology and that can also be used to describe the given subject instance.
- The extracted property value becomes the object of the created RDF statement.

We are going to study a real example of the generated RDF graph, but at this point, let us take a look at the ontology that is being used.

The ontology used by the new extractor is simply called *DBpedia ontology*; it is based on OWL and it forms the structural backbone of DBpedia. Its features can be summarized as follows (Jentzsch 2009):

- It is a shallow, cross-domain ontology.
- It is manually created, based on the most commonly used infobox templates within Wikipedia. More specifically,

  – from 685 most frequently used templates, 205 ontology classes are defined, and
  – from 2,800 template properties, 1,200 ontology properties are created.

Of course, as of today, DBpedia ontology has much more content compared to its earlier versions. Its 3.9 version release in mid-2013 has 529 class definitions and 2,333 property definitions. To access this ontology, you can visit DBpedia's official Web site and find the link to this ontology. At the time of this writing, this link is as follows:

```
http://wiki.dbpedia.org/Ontology
```

The rest of this section focuses on how this ontology is developed.

8.2.2.2   Mapping Infobox Templates to Classes

First, each Wikipedia's infobox template is carefully and manually mapped to a class defined in DBpedia ontology.

For example, one such infobox template is the `Tennis player` template, which has been manually mapped to the following class:

```
http://dbpedia.org/ontology/TennisPlayer
```

Currently, Wikipedia has more than 680 infobox templates, and these templates are mapped to about 529 classes defined in DBpedia ontology. Table 8.1 shows more example mappings.

The following reverse-engineering steps are used to come up with the information contained in Table 8.1, and they are listed here so you can explore the mapping on your own if you need to. Notice we have used the city of Berlin as our example to describe these steps.

Step 1. Go to the page about the city of Berlin in Wikipedia.

Table 8.1 Mapping Wikipedia's infobox templates to classes defined in DBpedia ontology

Wikipedia infobox template	DBpedia class mapping	Example page
Tennis player	dbclass:TennisPlayer	Roger Federer
Officeholder	dbclass:officeHolder	Bill Clinton
Person	dbclass:Person	Tim Berners-Lee
German State	dbclass:PopulatedPlace	Berlin
Film	dbclass:Film	Forrest Gump
Company	dbclass:Company	Ford Motor Company
University	dbclass:University	Tsinghua University

Prefix dbclass: <http://dbpedia.org/ontology/>

```
http://en.wikipedia.org/wiki/Berlin
```

Step 2. After you land on the page about Berlin, click `edit this page` link to see the infobox code.

In our example, you can see the infobox has a template called `German state`.

Step 3. Open up Berlin's corresponding page in DBpedia.

The following link will be able to take you to the DBpedia Berlin page:

```
http://dbpedia.org/resource/Berlin
```

Step 4. When you reach the DBpedia Berlin page, click the RDF icon in the upper right-hand corner, and this will take you to the RDF file generated by the extractor (more on this later).

In our example, this takes you to the following page,

```
http://dbpedia.org/data/Berlin.rdf
```

Step 5. Confirm the above file does exist at the above URL. In other words, you should be able to open the above URL without any trouble. Now open up a SPARQL endpoint, and conduct the query as shown in List 8.4:

List 8.4 SPARQL query to check the class type for city Berlin

```
select distinct ?value
from <http://dbpedia.org/data/Berlin.rdf>
where
{
   <http://dbpedia.org/resource/Berlin> rdf:type ?value .
}
order by asc(?value)
```

This will show you all the class types that Berlin as a resource belongs to. And you can see the most specific class type is the following:

```
http://dbpedia.org/ontology/PopulatedPlace
```

and this is how we know that infobox template `German state` has been mapped to class http://dbpedia.org/ontology/City as shown in Table 8.1. You can repeat the above steps for other mappings shown in Table 8.1. For a given infobox template that is not included in Table 8.1, you can find its corresponding class type by following the above steps as well.

To gain more understanding of this ontology, let us go back to Roger Federer's wiki page again. His wiki page has an infobox template called Tennis player, and as discussed earlier, this has been manually mapped to TennisPlayer class defined in DBpedia ontology. List 8.5 shows the definition:

List 8.5 Definition of TennisPlayer class in DBpedia ontology

```
<owl:Class rdf:about="http://dbpedia.org/ontology/TennisPlayer">
  <rdfs:label xml:lang="en">Tennis Player</rdfs:label>
  <rdfs:subClassOf
      rdf:resource="http://dbpedia.org/ontology/Athlete"/>
</owl:Class>
```

As shown in List 8.5, class TennisPlayer is a subclass of Athlete, whose definition is shown in List 8.6.

List 8.6 Definition of Athlete class in DBpedia ontology

```
<owl:Class rdf:about="http://dbpedia.org/ontology/Athlete">
  <rdfs:label xml:lang="en">Athlete</rdfs:label>
  <rdfs:subClassOf
      rdf:resource="http://dbpedia.org/ontology/Person"/>
</owl:Class>
```

And similarly, class Person is defined in List 8.7.

List 8.7 Definition of Person class in DBpedia ontology

```
<owl:Class rdf:about="http://dbpedia.org/ontology/Person">
  <rdfs:label xml:lang="en">Person</rdfs:label>
  <rdfs:subClassOf
      rdf:resource="http://www.w3.org/2002/07/owl#Thing"/>
</owl:Class>
```

Therefore, Person is the top-level class. By following the same route, you can get a good understanding about every class defined in DBpedia ontology.

8.2.2.3 Mapping Infobox Template Attributes to Properties

DBpedia ontology also includes a set of properties, which are created by another important mapping that is also manually implemented. More specifically, for a given Wikipedia infobox template, the attributes used in the template are carefully

mapped to a set of properties defined in DBpedia ontology, and these properties all
have the template's corresponding ontology class as their rdfs:domain. For now,
more than 2,800 template properties have been mapped to about 2,333 ontology
properties.

For example, to see the properties that can be used on TennisPlayer class, we
can start from its base class, namely Person. Since TennisPlayer is a sub-class of
Person, all the properties that can be used on a Person instance can also be used to
describe any instance of TennisPlayer.

The SPARQL query in List 8.8 can be used to find all these properties:

List 8.8 SPARQL query to find all the properties defined for Person class

```
prefix dbpediaOnt: <http://dbpedia.org/ontology/>
select distinct ?propertyName
from <http://downloads.dbpedia.org/3.4/dbpedia_3.4.owl>
where
{
  ?propertyName rdfs:domain dbpediaOnt:Person .
}
```

Note the following link in List 8.8,

```
http://downloads.dbpedia.org/3.4/dbpedia_3.4.owl
```

which is the URL location for DBpedia ontology. To get to its 3.9 version, use the
following URL,

```
http://downloads.dbpedia.org/3.9/dbpedia_3.9.owl
```

And List 8.9 shows part of the results:

List 8.9 Some of the properties defined for Person class

```
<http://dbpedia.org/ontology/Person/otherName>
<http://dbpedia.org/ontology/Person/birthName>
<http://dbpedia.org/ontology/Person/birthDate>
<http://dbpedia.org/ontology/Person/birthPlace>
<http://dbpedia.org/ontology/title>
<http://dbpedia.org/ontology/party>
<http://dbpedia.org/ontology/child>
<http://dbpedia.org/ontology/spouse>
<http://dbpedia.org/ontology/partner>
<http://dbpedia.org/ontology/father>
<http://dbpedia.org/ontology/mother>
```

Similarly, repeat the query shown in List 8.8, but change the class name to
`Athlete`, so the query tells us all the properties defined for class `Athlete`. List 8.10
shows some of the properties that can be used to describe an `Athlete` instance.

List 8.10 Some of the properties defined for `Athlete` class

```
<http://dbpedia.org/ontology/currentNumber>
<http://dbpedia.org/ontology/currentPosition>
<http://dbpedia.org/ontology/currentTeam>
<http://dbpedia.org/ontology/formerTeam>
```

And List 8.11 shows the ones for `TennisPlayer`. Again, you can obtain these
two lists by modifying the query given in List 8.8.

List 8.11 Some of the properties defined for `TennisPlayer` class

```
<http://dbpedia.org/ontology/careerprizemoney>
<http://dbpedia.org/ontology/plays>
```

Take a quick look at the properties contained in Lists 8.9, 8.10 and 8.11. We will
see some of them in use when the extractor tries to describe Roger Federer as a
resource of type `TennisPlayer` in the next section.

Now, we go back to Tim Berners-Lee's example. Without even studying the
infobox template on his wiki page, we are sure he will be another instance of class
`Person` or its subclass. Therefore, he will share lots of properties with the instance
that identifies Roger Federer. The situation where same properties have different
names, as we have described earlier, will not happen again.

Finally, you can always follow what we have done here to understand DBpedia
ontology, which will be very helpful when you need to conduct SPARQL queries,
as we will show in the sections to come.

8.2.3 Infobox Extraction Methods

Now we have reached the point where we are ready to see how the extractor works.
In general, the extractor visits a wiki page, parses the infobox template on the page
and generates an RDF document that describes the content of the given page.

In real practice, it is much more complex than this. More specifically,
Wikipedia's infobox template system has evolved over time without a centralized
coordination, and the following two situations happen quite often:

- Different communities use different templates to describe the same types of things.

For example, to describe Roger Federer, a `Tennis player` template is used. Yet to describe Pete Sampras (another famous tennis player), a `Tennis biography` template is used. We will see more about this in later sections.

- Different templates use different names for the same attribute.

For example, to describe Roger Federer, `datebirth` and `placebirth` are used, and when it comes to describing Tim Berners-Lee, `birth_date` and `birth_place` are used.

Other things similar to the above can also happen. In general, one of the main reasons for the above is that it is difficult to guarantee all the Wikipedia editors will strictly follow the recommendations given on the page that describes a template.

As a result, the DBpedia project team has decided to use two different extraction approaches in parallel: a generic approach and a mapping-based approach, which are discussed in the next two sections.

8.2.3.1 Generic Infobox Extraction Method

The generic infobox extraction method is quite straightforward, and can be described as follows:

- For a given Wikipedia page, a corresponding DBpedia URI is created, which has the following form,

  `http://dbpedia.org/resource/Page_Name`

- The above DBpedia URI will be used as the URI identifier for the subject.
- The predicate URI is created by concatenating the following namespace fragment and the name of the infobox attribute,

  `http://dbpedia.org/property/`

- An object is created from the attribute value, and will be postprocessed in order to generate a suitable URI identifier or a simple literal value;
- Repeat this for each attribute–value pair until all are processed.

The above process will be repeated for each page in Wikipedia. The advantage is that this approach can completely cover all infoboxes and their attributes. The disadvantage is that synonymous attribute names are not resolved. Therefore, some ambiguity always exists, and SPARQL queries will be difficult to construct. In addition, there is no formal ontology involved, meaning that no application can make any inferencing based on the generated RDF statements.

8.2.3.2 Mapping-Based Infobox Extraction Method

The main difference between the mapping-based extraction approach and the
generic extraction approach that we discussed above is that the mapping-based
approach makes full use of the DBpedia ontology. More specifically, two types of
mapping are included:

- Template-to-class mapping: infobox template types are mapped to classes. As
  we have discussed, at this point, more than 680 templates are mapped to
  529 ontology classes.
- Attribute-to-property mapping: properties from within the templates are mapped
  to ontology properties. At this point, more than 2,800 template properties are
  mapped to 2,333 ontology properties.

And to implement these mappings, fine-tuned rules are created to help parse the
infobox attribute names and values. The following is a rundown of the steps the
extractor uses to generate the RDF graph for a given page:

- For a given Wikipedia page, its on-page infobox template type is retrieved by the
  extractor.
- Based on the *template-to-class* mapping rule, the extractor is able to find its
  corresponding class type defined in DBpedia ontology.
- The extractor then creates an RDF resource as an instance of this class, and this
  resource will also be the subject of all the future RDF statements for this page. In
  addition, it has the following URI as its identifier,

```
http://dbpedia.org/resource/Page_Name
```

- The extractor now parses the attribute–value pairs found in the infobox on the
  current page. More specifically, the *attribute-to-property* mapping rules have to
  be applied to map each attribute to the appropriate property defined in the
  ontology. Each such mapping will create a predicate URI;
- For each attribute value, a corresponding object will be created to represent the
  value, and will be post-processed in order to generate either a suitable URI
  identifier or a simple literal value.
- Repeat this for each attribute–value pair until all are processed.

The above are the basic steps used to generate an RDF document for a given
page. Today, this extraction approach is the one that is in use, and it has been
repeated for a large portion of Wikipedia. The generated machine-readable data set
is called DBpedia, as you have known.

Notice that to save space, we are not going to include examples here and list the
generated RDF statements. If you would like to, you can go to the page and get the
generated RDF file easily. For example, the generated DBpedia page for Roger
Federer can be accessed from here,

```
http://dbpedia.org/page/Roger_Federer
```

At the bottom of the page, you will find different sterilization formats of the generated RDF document.

The advantage of this mapping-based approach is obvious: the RDF documents are based on ontologies; therefore, SPARQL queries are much easier to construct, and any given application can now conduct inference on the datasets.

The main disadvantage is that this method cannot provide complete coverage of the Wikipedia pages. For example, it can only cover the infobox templates that have been mapped to the ontology. However, with more and more mapping being built, more coverage can be easily implemented.

Finally, notice that the quality of DBpedia heavily depends on this extractor, which further depends on the mapping rules and the DBpedia ontology itself. At the time of your reading, this algorithm will almost certainly be improved, but the idea as described above will likely remain the same.

8.3   Accessing DBpedia Dataset

DBpedia is a huge collection of RDF graphs, with precisely defined semantics. And of course, there are different paths one can use when it comes to interaction with DBpedia. However, it is difficult for first-time users to use portions of this infrastructure without any guidance. Actually, given that data gathering and exposure via RDF standards is making constant progress, the related user interfaces, documentation, data presentation and general tutorials for users are still surprisingly limited.

In this section, we discuss three different methods you can use to interact with DBpedia, and they will serve as a starting point for you. With this starting point, you will find your journey with DBpedia much easier and more enjoyable.

8.3.1   Using SPARQL to Query DBpedia

8.3.1.1   SPARQL Endpoints for DBpedia

As you might has guessed, you can use SPARQL to query DBpedia. In fact, DBpedia provides a public SPARQL endpoint you can use:

```
http://dbpedia.org/sparql
```

In practice, this endpoint is generally used directly by remote agents. We therefore will access the endpoint via a SPARQL viewer, and you can find it at this place:

```
http://dbpedia.org/snorql/
```

Figure 8.3 shows the opening page of this SPARQL explorer:

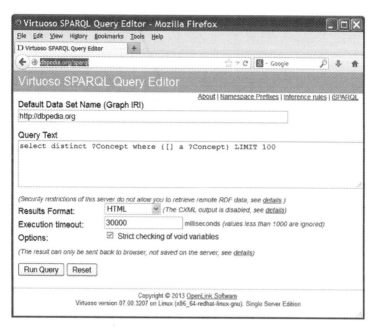

Fig. 8.3 DBpedia's SPARQL endpoint

In order to make your query construction easier, List 8.12 provides a set of namespace shortcuts,

List 8.12 Predefined namespaces that can be used in SPARQL explorer for DBpedia

```
PREFIX owl: <http://www.w3.org/2002/07/owl#>
PREFIX xsd: <http://www.w3.org/2001/XMLSchema#>
PREFIX rdfs: <http://www.w3.org/2000/01/rdf-schema#>
PREFIX rdf: <http://www.w3.org/1999/02/22-rdf-syntax-ns#>
PREFIX foaf: <http://xmlns.com/foaf/0.1/>
PREFIX dc: <http://purl.org/dc/elements/1.1/>
PREFIX : <http://dbpedia.org/resource/>
PREFIX dbpedia2: <http://dbpedia.org/property/>
PREFIX dbpedia: <http://dbpedia.org/ontology/>
PREFIX skos: <http://www.w3.org/2004/02/skos/core#>
```

For the rest of this section, all our examples should have the same prefix definitions as above, and we therefore will not include them in our queries. However, remember if you are trying the queries out, you do need to include them into your query strings.

8.3.1.2 Examples of Using SPARQL to Access DBpedia

Obviously, to start using SPARQL to query DBpedia dataset, you have to know the resource name of the subject you are interested in, its class type and some properties that can be used to describe the resource.

To get to know the subject's corresponding resource name, follow this simple rule: if the subject has the following page in Wikipedia,

http://en.wikipedia.org/wiki/_Name_

its resource name will then be given by the following URI:

http://dbpedia.org/resource/_Name_

To know which class type this resource belongs to, the easiest way is to use the query as shown in List 8.13. Again, using Roger Federer as our favorite example:

List 8.13 SPARQL query to understand the class type of the resource identifying Federer

```
SELECT * WHERE {
    :Roger_Federer a ?class_type.
}
```

Note that if you are trying out the query shown in List 8.13 (and other queries in this chapter) by using DBpedia SPARQL endpoint (Fig. 8.3), make sure you include the predefined namespaces contained by List 8.12 into your query that posted to DBpedia SPARQL endpoint. Figure 8.4 shows the result of the query in List 8.13.

Now, the query shown in List 8.13 tells us the class type of the resource that represents Roger Federer. For our immediate purpose, we will remember the most specific one: dbpedia:TennisPlayer.

List 8.14 is another simple query we can use to find what properties the extractor has used to describe Roger Federer:

List 8.14 SPARQL query to find out all the properties used to describe Federer

```
SELECT * WHERE {
    :Roger_Federer ?propertyName ?propertyValue.
}
```

With these two queries (in fact, you can use the query in List 8.14 alone), you can gain some basic knowledge about your subject of interest, and you can start more interesting queries from here.

For example, List 8.15 shows all the tennis players who are from the same country as Federer is:

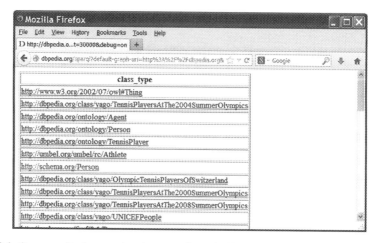

Fig. 8.4 Query result when running the query shown in List 8.13

List 8.15 Find all the tennis players who are from the same country as Federer

```
SELECT distinct ?someone ?birthPlace
WHERE {
    :Roger_Federer dbpedia:birthPlace ?birthPlace.
    ?someone a dbpedia:TennisPlayer.
    ?someone dbpedia:birthPlace ?birthPlace.
}
```

Figure 8.5 shows the query result at the time of this writing. Again, if you are trying the above query out, remember to include List 8.12 into your query string.

The query in List 8.16 tries to find those tennis players who have also won all the Grand Slams that Federer has won:

List 8.16 Find all those players who also won all the Grand Slams that Federer has won

```
SELECT distinct * WHERE {
    :Roger_Federer dbpedia2:australianopenresult ?aussie_result.
    :Roger_Federer dbpedia2:usopenresult ?us_result.
    :Roger_Federer dbpedia2:wimbledonresult ?wimbeldon_result.
    :Roger_Federer dbpedia2:frenchopenresult ?frenchopen_result.
    ?player a dbpedia:TennisPlayer.
    ?player dbpedia2:australianopenresult ?aussie_result.
    ?player dbpedia2:usopenresult ?us_result.
    ?player dbpedia2:wimbledonresult ?wimbeldon_result.
    ?player dbpedia2:frenchopenresult ?frenchopen_result.
}
```

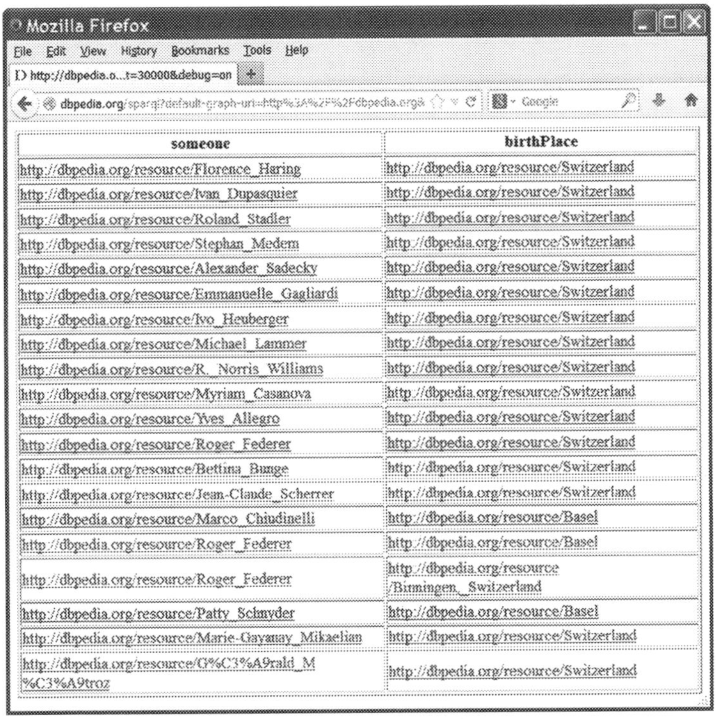

someone	birthPlace
http://dbpedia.org/resource/Florence_Haring	http://dbpedia.org/resource/Switzerland
http://dbpedia.org/resource/Ivan_Dupasquier	http://dbpedia.org/resource/Switzerland
http://dbpedia.org/resource/Roland_Stadler	http://dbpedia.org/resource/Switzerland
http://dbpedia.org/resource/Stephan_Medem	http://dbpedia.org/resource/Switzerland
http://dbpedia.org/resource/Alexander_Sadecky	http://dbpedia.org/resource/Switzerland
http://dbpedia.org/resource/Emmanuelle_Gagliardi	http://dbpedia.org/resource/Switzerland
http://dbpedia.org/resource/Ivo_Heuberger	http://dbpedia.org/resource/Switzerland
http://dbpedia.org/resource/Michael_Lammer	http://dbpedia.org/resource/Switzerland
http://dbpedia.org/resource/R._Norris_Williams	http://dbpedia.org/resource/Switzerland
http://dbpedia.org/resource/Myriam_Casanova	http://dbpedia.org/resource/Switzerland
http://dbpedia.org/resource/Yves_Allegro	http://dbpedia.org/resource/Switzerland
http://dbpedia.org/resource/Roger_Federer	http://dbpedia.org/resource/Switzerland
http://dbpedia.org/resource/Bettina_Bunge	http://dbpedia.org/resource/Switzerland
http://dbpedia.org/resource/Jean-Claude_Scherrer	http://dbpedia.org/resource/Switzerland
http://dbpedia.org/resource/Marco_Chiudinelli	http://dbpedia.org/resource/Basel
http://dbpedia.org/resource/Roger_Federer	http://dbpedia.org/resource/Basel
http://dbpedia.org/resource/Roger_Federer	http://dbpedia.org/resource/Birmingen,_Switzerland
http://dbpedia.org/resource/Patty_Schnyder	http://dbpedia.org/resource/Basel
http://dbpedia.org/resource/Marie-Gayanay_Mikaelian	http://dbpedia.org/resource/Switzerland
http://dbpedia.org/resource/G%C3%A9rald_M%C3%A9troz	http://dbpedia.org/resource/Switzerland

Fig. 8.5 Query result when running the query shown in List 8.15

As we know, so far, Federer has won all four Grand Slams in his career, and List 8.16 is looking for other players who have also won all four titles. Figure 8.6 shows the query result.

Clearly, this query does not return Pete Sampras as one of the players who have won all the Grand Slam titles that Federer has won. If you have followed the tennis world even vaguely, you might know the reason: Sampras has never won the French Open in his career; that is why he is not included in the query result.

Now, we can change the query by eliminating the French Open result, as shown in List 8.17,

List 8.17 Change the query in List 8.16 to exclude French Open results

```
SELECT distinct * WHERE {
    :Roger_Federer dbpedia2:australianopenresult ?aussie_result.
    :Roger_Federer dbpedia2:usopenresult ?us_result.
    :Roger_Federer dbpedia2:wimbledonresult ?wimbeldon_result.
    ?player a dbpedia:TennisPlayer.
    ?player dbpedia2:australianopenresult ?aussie_result.
    ?player dbpedia2:usopenresult ?us_result.
    ?player dbpedia2:wimbledonresult ?wimbeldon_result.
}
```

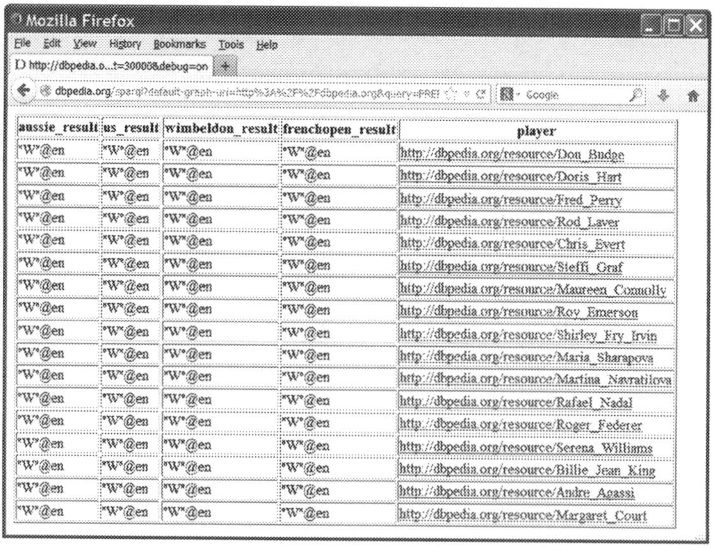

aussie_result	us_result	wimbeldon_result	frenchopen_result	player
"W"@en	"W"@en	"W"@en	"W"@en	http://dbpedia.org/resource/Don_Budge
"W"@en	"W"@en	"W"@en	"W"@en	http://dbpedia.org/resource/Doris_Hart
"W"@en	"W"@en	"W"@en	"W"@en	http://dbpedia.org/resource/Fred_Perry
"W"@en	"W"@en	"W"@en	"W"@en	http://dbpedia.org/resource/Rod_Laver
"W"@en	"W"@en	"W"@en	"W"@en	http://dbpedia.org/resource/Chris_Evert
"W"@en	"W"@en	"W"@en	"W"@en	http://dbpedia.org/resource/Steffi_Graf
"W"@en	"W"@en	"W"@en	"W"@en	http://dbpedia.org/resource/Maureen_Connolly
"W"@en	"W"@en	"W"@en	"W"@en	http://dbpedia.org/resource/Roy_Emerson
"W"@en	"W"@en	"W"@en	"W"@en	http://dbpedia.org/resource/Shirley_Fry_Irvin
"W"@en	"W"@en	"W"@en	"W"@en	http://dbpedia.org/resource/Maria_Sharapova
"W"@en	"W"@en	"W"@en	"W"@en	http://dbpedia.org/resource/Martina_Navratilova
"W"@en	"W"@en	"W"@en	"W"@en	http://dbpedia.org/resource/Rafael_Nadal
"W"@en	"W"@en	"W"@en	"W"@en	http://dbpedia.org/resource/Roger_Federer
"W"@en	"W"@en	"W"@en	"W"@en	http://dbpedia.org/resource/Serena_Williams
"W"@en	"W"@en	"W"@en	"W"@en	http://dbpedia.org/resource/Billie_Jean_King
"W"@en	"W"@en	"W"@en	"W"@en	http://dbpedia.org/resource/Andre_Agassi
"W"@en	"W"@en	"W"@en	"W"@en	http://dbpedia.org/resource/Margaret_Court

Fig. 8.6 Query result when running the query shown in List 8.16

And we do get more players back this time, but we still cannot find Pete Sampras in the result set. However, we know he did win all the other three titles. So what is wrong?

The reason is the resource that represents Pete Sampras,

```
http://dbpedia.org/resource/Pete_Sampras
```

has not been created as an instance of class `dbpedia:TennisPlayer`, since the infobox template used on his wiki page is not the tennis player template. Clearly, this is another example showing the importance of ontology.

You can further explore the DBpedia dataset by using SPARQL queries, and you can try some other areas that you like, for example, movies or music. In addition, try to think about how you can accomplish the same thing in Wikipedia. For example, try to accomplish what List 8.16 has accomplished in Wikipedia. Obviously, you have to sift through lots of pages for tennis players. It is very likely you will stop, and decide to find something better to do.

8.3.2 Direct Download of DBpedia Datasets

Another way to access DBpedia is to directly download its RDF dumps. One reason to do this is that you can then build your application on the datasets that you have downloaded. Since the datasets are on your local machine, your application will run faster, and therefore be easier to test.

To access this download page, visit the following URL:

```
http://wiki.dbpedia.org/Downloads39
```

Since currently the most recent release of DBpedia is 3.9, the download site has a 39 suffix. To access earlier datasets, use the specific version number for that dataset. For example, the following allows you to download the 3.5.1 dataset:

```
http://wiki.dbpedia.org/Downloads351
```

At the time of your reading, this will be changed for sure, so the link to the download page will also be changed. However, you can always find the latest download link on DBpedia's homepage.

8.3.2.1   The Wikipedia Datasets

The first dataset you can download contains the original Wikipedia files, i.e., a copy of all Wikipedia wikis in the form of wikitext source, and a copy of all pages from all Wikipedia wikis in HTML format. Obviously, these are the input materials for the DBpedia extractor, and they are offered here as a foundation for your own research, or for building your own applications.

8.3.2.2   DBpedia Core Datasets

The second part of the downloadable files is the so-called core datasets. They are machine-readable datasets generated by DBpedia project itself. To generate these datasets, a complete DBpedia dataset is first created by the DBpedia extractor, and it is then sliced into several parts based on triple predicate. The resulting parts are the datasets you see, and each dataset is offered in the form of N-triples. We will not be able to cover all the datasets here, but the discussion should be detailed enough for you to continue your own exploration of these datasets.

The first dataset is the DBpedia Ontology dataset. It is offered here so you can download and make use of this ontology in your own applications. The main advantage of this ontology is that it is created from a central knowledge resource, and it is not domain-specific. It is written in OWL and should be easily understood. List 8.18 shows part of this ontology:

List 8.18 A portion of the DBpedia ontology

```xml
<?xml version="1.0" encoding="UTF-8"?>
<rdf:RDF
        xmlns = "http://dbpedia.org/ontology/"
        xml:base="http://dbpedia.org/ontology/"
        xmlns:owl="http://www.w3.org/2002/07/owl#"
        xmlns:xsd="http://www.w3.org/2001/XMLSchema#"
        xmlns:rdf="http://www.w3.org/1999/02/22-rdf-syntax-ns#"
        xmlns:rdfs="http://www.w3.org/2000/01/rdf-schema#">

<owl:Ontology rdf:about="">
  <owl:versionInfo xml:lang="de">
     Version 3.4 2009-10-05
  </owl:versionInfo>
</owl:Ontology>

<owl:Class
     rdf:about="http://dbpedia.org/ontology/PopulatedPlace">
  <rdfs:label xml:lang="en">Populated Place</rdfs:label>
  <rdfs:subClassOf
       rdf:resource="http://dbpedia.org/ontology/Place"/>
</owl:Class>

<owl:Class rdf:about="http://dbpedia.org/ontology/Place">
  <rdfs:label xml:lang="en">Place</rdfs:label>
  <rdfs:subClassOf
       rdf:resource="http://www.w3.org/2002/07/owl#Thing"/>
</owl:Class>

<owl:Class rdf:about="http://dbpedia.org/ontology/Country">
  <rdfs:label xml:lang="en">Country</rdfs:label>
  <rdfs:subClassOf
     rdf:resource="http://dbpedia.org/ontology/PopulatedPlace"/>
</owl:Class>

<owl:Class rdf:about="http://dbpedia.org/ontology/Area">
  <rdfs:label xml:lang="en">Area</rdfs:label>
   <rdfs:subClassOf
     rdf:resource="http://dbpedia.org/ontology/PopulatedPlace"/>
</owl:Class>
```

The second core dataset is the Ontology Types dataset. This dataset includes all the resources covered by DBpedia and their related types. For example, List 8.19 shows two triples you will find in this file:

List 8.19 Example triples included in Ontology Types dataset

```
<http://dbpedia.org/resource/Roger_Federer>
<http://www.w3.org/1999/02/22-rdf-syntax-ns#type>
<http://dbpedia.org/ontology/TennisPlayer> .

<http://dbpedia.org/resource/Tim_Berners-Lee>
<http://www.w3.org/1999/02/22-rdf-syntax-ns#type>
<http://dbpedia.org/ontology/Person> .
```

With this dataset and the DBpedia ontology, different levels of reasoning can start to take place. For example, based on the following statements:

```
<http://dbpedia.org/resource/Roger_Federer>
<http://www.w3.org/1999/02/22-rdf-syntax-ns#type>
<http://dbpedia.org/ontology/TennisPlayer> .

<http://dbpedia.org/ontology/TennisPlayer>
<http://www.w3.org/2000/01/rdf-schema#subClassOf>
<http://dbpedia.org/ontology/Athlete> .

<http://dbpedia.org/ontology/Athlete>
<http://www.w3.org/2000/01/rdf-schema#subClassOf>
<http://dbpedia.org/ontology/Person> .
```

An application now understands that Roger Federer is not only a `TennisPlayer`, but also an `Athlete` and a `Person`. Notice the first statement above comes from the Ontology Type dataset, and the other two statements are from the DBpedia Ontology dataset.

The next dataset is the Ontology Infobox Properties dataset, where all the properties and property values of all resources are collected. List 8.20 shows some example content you will find in this dataset:

List 8.20 Example content in Ontology Infoboxes dataset

```
<http://dbpedia.org/resource/Roger_Federer>
<http://xmlns.com/foaf/0.1/homepage>
<http://www.rogerfederer.com/> .

<http://dbpedia.org/resource/Roger_Federer>
<http://dbpedia.org/ontology/country>
<http://dbpedia.org/resource/Switzerland> .

<http://dbpedia.org/resource/Roger_Federer>
<http://dbpedia.org/ontology/birthDate>
"1981-08-08"^^xsd:date .

<http://dbpedia.org/resource/Roger_Federer>
<http://dbpedia.org/ontology/plays>
"Right-handed; one-handed backhand" .
```

If you are developing your own application, this dataset will become a main source from which you will expect to get most of the machine-readable data. In fact, this dataset is further sliced into a collection of more detailed datasets based on triple predicate, and the following is a brief rundown of these generated datasets. Again, we only discuss a few, and you can understand the rest accordingly.

The `Titles` dataset is about `rdfs:label` property; therefore it contains triples as follows:

```
<http://dbpedia.org/resource/Roger_Federer>
<http://www.w3.org/2000/01/rdf-schema#label>
"Roger Federer"@en .

<http://dbpedia.org/resource/Tim_Berners-Lee>
<http://www.w3.org/2000/01/rdf-schema#label>
"Tim Berners-Lee"@en .
```

The `Homepages` dataset is about `foaf:homepage` property; therefore it contains triples as follows:

```
<http://dbpedia.org/resource/Roger_Federer>
<http://xmlns.com/foaf/0.1/homepage>
<http://www.rogerfederer.com/> .

<http://dbpedia.org/resource/Tim_Berners-Lee>
<http://xmlns.com/foaf/0.1/homepage>
<http://www.w3.org/People/Berners-Lee/> .
```

Finally, the `Persondata` dataset is all about personal information; therefore it contains predicates such as `foaf:name`, `foaf:givenname` and `foaf:surname`. The following are some triple examples from this dataset:

```
<http://dbpedia.org/resource/Roger_Federer>
<http://xmlns.com/foaf/0.1/name>
"Roger Federer" .

<http://dbpedia.org/resource/Roger_Federer>
<http://xmlns.com/foaf/0.1/givenname>
"Roger"@de .

<http://dbpedia.org/resource/Roger_Federer>
<http://xmlns.com/foaf/0.1/surname>
"Federer"@de .
```

8.3.2.3   Extended Datasets

Besides the core datasets we discussed above, DBpedia has also created a collection of extended datasets, which provide links to those datasets that are outside of DBpedia. We will have more understanding about the reasons behind these extended datasets when we finish the next chapter. For now, let us briefly examine these extended datasets to get some basic understanding. Again, we will not cover all of them, and what you learn here will be enough for you to continue on your own.

One example extended dataset is called `Links to RDF Bookmashup`. It maps DBpedia books to the books identified by the RDF Bookmashup project developed by Freie Universität Berlin.[1] RDF Bookmashup assigns URIs to books, authors, reviews, and online bookstores and purchase offers. Whenever a book title is submitted, the mashup queries Amazon API for information about the book and Google Base API for purchase offers from different bookstores that sell the book. The aggregated information is returned in RDF format and therefore can be understood by applications.

List 8.21 shows some example statements from this extended dataset:

---

[1] http://www4.wiwiss.fu-berlin.de/bizer/bookmashup/

List 8.21 Example statements from Links to RDF Bookmashup dataset

```
<http://dbpedia.org/resource/Honour_Among_Thieves>
<http://www.w3.org/2002/07/owl#sameAs>
<http://www4.wiwiss.fu-berlin.de/bookmashup/books/9780330419031>
.


<http://dbpedia.org/resource/Honour_Among_Thieves>
<http://www.w3.org/1999/02/22-rdf-syntax-ns#type>
<http://dbpedia.org/class/Book> .

<http://dbpedia.org/resource/Acquainted_With_the_Night>
<http://www.w3.org/2002/07/owl#sameAs>
<http://www4.wiwiss.fu-berlin.de/bookmashup/books/0002006391> .

<http://dbpedia.org/resource/Acquainted_With_the_Night>
<http://www.w3.org/1999/02/22-rdf-syntax-ns#type>
<http://dbpedia.org/class/Book> .
```

8.3.3 Access DBpedia as Linked Data

Finally, we can access DBpedia datasets as part of Linked Data. Linked Data is covered in the next chapter, and you will see more on this topic then. For now, understanding two important aspects of DBpedia project will prepare you well.

The first thing to understand is that DBpedia's resource identifiers are set up in such a way that DBpedia dataset server delivers different documents based on different requests. More specifically, the following URI that identifies Roger Federer,

```
http://dbpedia.org/resource/Roger_Federer
```

returns RDF descriptions when accessed by semantic Web applications, and returns HTML content for the same information if accessed by traditional Web or human users. This is the so-called content negotiation mechanism that we will discuss in detail in the next chapter.

Second, to facilitate URI reuse, DBpedia should be consulted whenever you are ready to describe a resource in the world. Since DBpedia is the machine-readable version of Wikipedia, it is therefore possible that DBpedia has already created a URI for the resource you intend to describe. For example, the Nikon D300 camera that we worked with in the earlier chapters of this book has the following DBpedia URI:

```
http://dbpedia.org/resource/Nikon_D300
```

As we will see in the next chapter, using URIs created by the DBpedia project not only promotes URI reuse, but also helps to create more linked data. In fact, Linked Data publishers often try to find DBpedia resource URIs to build more links.

In order to make it easy to discover these related URIs, DBpedia provides a lookup service that returns DBpedia URIs for a given set of keywords. This service can be accessed from the following URL,

```
http://lookup.dbpedia.org/api/search.asmx
```

and not only human users can directly access it: it can also be used as a Web service. The submitted keywords is used to compare against the `rdfs:label` property of a given resource, and the most likely matches are returned. Figure 8.7 shows the results when using "Roger Federer" as keywords.

As shown in Fig. 8.7, `http://dbpedia.org/resource/Roger_Federer` is returned as the first choice. Therefore, if you were to search for a URI that identifies Federer, you would easily find it.

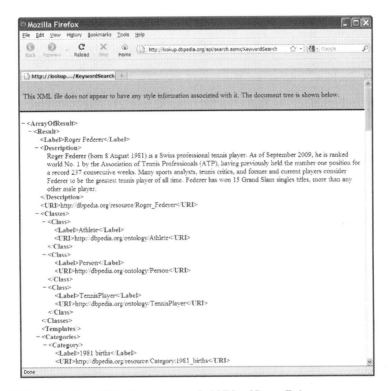

Fig. 8.7 Use DBpedia's URI lookup service to find URIs of Roger Federer

8.4   Summary

In this chapter, we learned DBpedia. It is not only another example of the Semantic Web technologies at work, but also a key component on the Web of Linked Data, as we will see in the next chapter.

First, understand the following about DBpedia:

- It is a machine-readable version of Wikipedia.
- It is automatically generated by processing the preexisting structured information on each page in Wikipedia.

Also, understand that in order to make DBpedia machine-readable, the following has been implemented by the DBpedia project team:

- A DBpedia ontology is defined by manually mapping infobox templates to classes and template attributes to properties.
- A DBpedia extractor is developed to process the infobox on a given Wikipedia page, an RDF document that represents the page is generated and terms from the DBpedia ontology are used when generating this RDF document.
- The DBpedia extractor has visited a good portion of Wikipedia, and the result is the DBpedia dataset, which is machine-readable.

Finally, understand different ways of accessing DBpedia:

- DBpedia can be accessed by using a Web browser.
- DBpedia can be accessed by using a SPARQL endpoint.
- DBpedia can be accessed as part of the Linked Data.

Reference

Jentzsch A (2009) DBpedia – extracting structured data from Wikipedia. Presentation at Semantic Web In Bibliotheken (SWIB2009), Cologne, Germany

Chapter 9
Linked Open Data

In Chap. 8, we studied the DBpedia project, where semantic documents are automatically generated. As we discussed in Chap. 7, besides annotating the pages manually or generating the markup documents automatically, there is indeed another solution: to create a machine-readable Web all from scratch.

The idea is simple: if we start to publish machine-readable data, such as RDF documents on the Web, and somehow make all these documents connected to each other, then we will be creating a Linked Data Web that can be processed by machines.

This is the idea behind the Linked Open Data (LOD) project, the topic of this chapter.

9.1 The Concept of Linked Data and Its Basic Rules

In recent years, the concept of *Linked Data*, and the so-called Web of Linked Data, has attracted tremendous attention from both the academic world and real application world. In this section, we examine the concept of Linked Data and its basic rules. What we learn here from this section will provide a solid foundation for the rest of this chapter.

9.1.1 The Concept of Linked Data

The concept of Linked Data was originally proposed by Tim Berners-Lee in his 2006 Web architecture note.[1] Technically speaking, Linked Data refers to data

---

[1] http://www.w3.org/DesignIssues/LinkedData.html

© Springer-Verlag Berlin Heidelberg 2014
L. Yu, *A Developer's Guide to the Semantic Web*,
DOI 10.1007/978-3-662-43796-4_9

published on the Web in such a way that it is machine-readable, its meaning is explicitly defined, it is linked to other external data sets, and it can in turn be linked to from external data sets as well. Conceptually, Linked Data refers to a set of best practices for publishing and connecting structured data on the Web.

The connection between Linked Data and the Semantic Web is quite obvious: publishing and consuming machine-readable data is central to both of these concepts. In fact, in recent years, Linked Data and the Semantic Web became two concepts that are interchangeable. After finishing this chapter, you can reach your own conclusion regarding the relationship between Linked Data and the Semantic Web.

In practice, the basic idea of Linked Data is quite straightforward and can be summarized as follows:

- Use the RDF data model to publish structured data on the Web.
- Use RDF links to interlink data from different data sources.

Applying these two simple tenets repeatedly leads to the creation of a Web of Data that machines can read and understand. This Web of Data, at this point, can be understood as one realization of the Semantic Web. The Semantic Web, therefore, can be viewed as created by the linked structured data on the Web.

Given that Linked Data is also referred to as the *Web of Linked Data*, it is then intuitive to believe that it must share lots of common traits exhibited by the traditional Web. This is a true intuition, yet for every single one of these traits, the Web of Linked Data is profoundly different from the Web of documents.

Let us take a look at this comparison, which will certainly give us more understanding of Linked Data and the Semantic Web. Notice that at this point, some of the comparisons may not make perfect sense to you, but rest assured that they will become clear after you have finished the whole chapter.

- On the traditional Web, anyone can publish anything at his/her will, at any time.

The same is true for the Linked Data Web: anyone, at any time, can publish anything on the Web of Linked Data, except that the published documents have to be RDF documents. In other words, these documents are for machines to use, not for human eyes.

- To access the traditional Web, we use Web browsers.

The same is true for the Web of Linked Data. However, since the Web of Linked Data is created by publishing RDF documents, we use Linked Data browsers that can understand RDF documents and can follow the RDF links to navigate between different data sources. Traditional Web browsers, on the other hand, are designed to handle HTML documents, and they are not the best choices when it comes to accessing the Web of Linked Data.

- The traditional Web is interesting since everything on the Web is linked together.

The same is true for the Web of Linked Data. An important fact, however, is that under the hood, the HTML documents contained by the traditional Web are connected by untyped hyperlinks. The Web of Linked Data, rather than simply connecting documents, uses the RDF model to make *typed links* that connect arbitrary things in the world. The result is that we can then build much smarter applications, as we will see in the later part of this chapter.

- The traditional Web can provide structured data that can be consumed by Web-based applications.

This is especially true with more and more APIs being published by major players on the Web. For example, eBay, Amazon and Google all have published their APIs. Web applications that consume these APIs are collectively named as *mashups*, and they offer quite impressive Web experiences to their users. On the other hand, under the Web of Linked Data, mashups are called *semantic mashups*, and they can be developed in a much more scalable and efficient way. More importantly, they have the ability to grow dynamically upon unbounded data sets, and that is what makes them much more useful than traditional mashups. Again, details will be covered in later sections.

Before we move on, understand that the technical foundation for the Web of Linked Data is not something we have to create from the ground up. To its very bottom, the Web of Linked Data is a big collection of RDF triples, where the subject of any triple is a URI reference in the namespace of one data set, and the object of the triple is a URI reference in the namespace of another. In addition, by employing HTTP URIs to identify resources, the HTTP protocol as retrieval mechanism and the RDF data model to represent resource descriptions, Linked Data is directly built upon the general architecture of the Web—a solid foundation that has been tested for more than 20 years.

Furthermore, what we have learned so far, such as the RDF model, RDF Schema, OWL and SPARQL, all these technical components will find their usages in the world of Linked Data.

9.1.2 How Big Are the Web of Linked Data and the LOD Project?

The most accurate way to calculate the size of the Web of Linked Data is to use a crawler to count the number of RDF triples that it has collected when traveling on the Web of Linked Data. This is quite a challenging task, and given that some of the RDF triples are generated dynamically, we therefore have to run the crawler repeatedly in order to get the most recent count.

However, the size of the Web of Data can be estimated based on the dataset statistics collected by the LOD community in the ESW wiki.[2] According to these statistics, the Web of Data, on May 4, 2010, consists of 13.1 billion RDF triples, which are interlinked by around 142 million RDF links (as of September 29, 2009). Notice the majority of these triples are generated by the so-called wrappers, which are utility applications responsible for generating RDF statements from existing relational database tables, and only a small portion of these triples are generated manually.

The Linking Open Data Community Project has been focusing on the idea and implementation of the Web of Data for the last several years. It was originally sponsored by W3C Semantic Web Education and Outreach Group, and you can find more information about this group from this URL:

```
http://www.w3.org/2001/sw/sweo/
```

For the rest of this chapter, we will mainly examine the Linked Data project from a technical perspective; you can always find more information the project from the following Web sites:

- Linking Open Data project wiki home page:

```
http://esw.w3.org/SweoIG/TaskForces/CommunityProjects/
    LinkingOpenData
```

- Linked Data at the ESW Wiki page:

```
http://esw.w3.org/topic/LinkedData
```

- Linked Data Community Web site:

```
http://linkeddata.org/
```

9.1.3   The Basic Rules of Linked Data

The basic idea of Linked Data is to use the RDF model to publish structured data on the Web, and to also use RDF links to interlink data from different data sources.

In practice, to make sure the above idea is carefully and correctly followed when constructing the Web of Linked Data, four basic rules were further proposed by Tim Berners-Lee in his 2006 Web architecture note:

Rule 1. Use URIs as names for things.
Rule 2. Use HTTP URIs so that a client (machine or human reader) can look up these names.
Rule 3. When someone looks up a URI, useful information should be provided.
Rule 4. Include links to other URIs, so that a client can discover more things.

---

[2] http://esw.w3.org/topic/TaskForces/CommunityProjects/LinkingOpenData/DataSets/Statistic,
http://esw.w3.org/topic/TaskForces/CommunityProjects/LinkingOpenData/DataSets/LinkStatistics

The first rule is obvious, and it is also what we have been doing all the time: for a given resource or concept, we should use a unique and universal name to identify it. This simple rule eliminates the following two ambiguities on the traditional Web: first, the same name (word) in different documents can refer to completely different resources or concepts, and second, a given resource or concept can be represented by different names (words) in different documents.

The second rule simply puts one more constraint on the first rule by specifying that not only should we use URIs to represent objects and concepts, we should also only use HTTP URIs.

The reason behind this rule is quite obvious. To make sure that data publishers can come up with identifiers that are indeed globally unique without involving any centralized management, the easiest way is to use HTTP URIs, since the domain part of these URIs can automatically guarantee their uniqueness. In addition, HTTP URIs naturally suggest to the clients that these URIs can be directly used as a means of accessing information about the resources over the Web.

The third rule further strengthens the second rule: if the client is dereferencing a given URI in a Web browser, there should always be some useful information returned back to the client. In fact, at the early days of the Semantic Web, this was not always true: when a given URI was used in a browser, there might or might not be any information coming back at all. We will see more details on this rule later.

The last rule is there to make sure the Linked Data world will grow into a real Web: without the links, it will not be a Web of data. In fact, the really interesting thing happens only when the data is linked together and the unexpected fact is discovered by exploring the links.

Finally, notice that the above are just the rules of the Web of Linked Data; breaking these rules does not destroy anything. However, without these rules, the data will not be able to provide anything that is interesting.

Now that we have all the background information and we have also learned all the rules, let us take a detailed look into the world of Linked Data. In the next two sections, we first study how exactly to publish RDF data on the Web, and we then explore different ways to link these data together on the Web.

9.2 Publishing RDF Data on the Web

RDF data is the building block of Linked Data. Publishing RDF data on the Web means following these steps:

- Identifying things by using URIs;
- Choosing vocabularies for RDF data;
- Producing RDF statements to described the things;
- Creating RDF links to other RDF data sets, and finally
- Serving your RDF triples on the Web.

Let us study each one of them in detail.

9.2.1 Identifying Things with URIs

9.2.1.1 Web Document, Information Resource and URI

To begin with, a URI is not something new, and for most of us, a URI represents a Web document. For example, the following URI,

```
http://www.liyangyu.com/
```

represents the front page of my personal Web site. This page, like everything else on the traditional Web, is a Web document. We often call the above URI a URL, and as far as the Web document is concerned, URL and URI are interchangeable. A URL is a special type of URI: it tells us the location of the given Web document. In other words, if a user types in the above URL (URI) into a Web browser, the front page of my Web site will be returned.

Recall that a Web document is defined as something that has a URI and can return representations of the identified resource in response to HTTP requests. The returned representations can take quite a few formats including HTML, JPEG or RDF, just to name a few.

In recent years, Web documents have a new name: *information resources*. More precisely, everything we find on the traditional document Web, such as documents, images (and other media files) are information resources. In other words, information resources are the resources that satisfy the following two conditions:

- They can be identified by URIs.
- They can return representations when the identified resources are requested by the users.

Figure 9.1 shows the above concept:

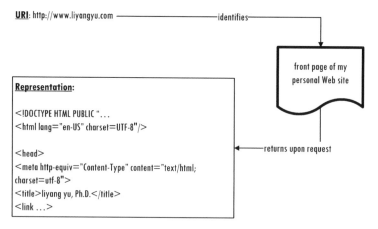

Fig. 9.1 URI/URL for information resource

Currently on the Web, to request the representations of a given Web document, clients and servers use the HTTP protocol to communicate. For example, the following could be the request sent to the server:

```
GET / HTTP/1.1
Host: www.liyangyu.com
Connection: close
User-Agent: Mozilla/4.0 (compatible; MSIE 7.0; Windows NT 5.1)
Accept-Encoding: gzip
Accept-Charset: ISO-8859-1,UTF-8;q=0.7,*;q=0.7
Cache-Control: no
Accept-Language: de,en;q=0.7,en-us;q=0.3
```

And the server will answer with a response header, which tells the client whether the request was successful, and if successful, the content (representation) will follow the response header.

Let us go back to our basic question in this section: what URIs should we use to identify things in the world? At this point, we can come up with part of the answer: for all the information resources, we can simply use the good old URLs as their URIs to uniquely identify them.

Now, what URIs should we use for the rest of the things (resources) in the world?

9.2.1.2 Non-information Resources and Their URIs

Except for the information resources, the rest of the resources in the world are called *non-information resources*. In general, non-information resources include all the real-world objects that exist outside the Web, such as people, places, concepts, ideas, anything you can imagine and anything you want to talk about.

To come up with URIs that can be used to identify these non-information resources, there are two important rules proposed by W3C Interest Group.[3] Let us use some examples to understand them.

Let us say I want to come up with a URI to represent myself (a non-information resource). Since I already have a personal Web site, www.liyangyu.com, could I then use the following URI to identify myself?

```
http://www.liyangyu.com/
```

This idea is quite intuitive, given that the Web document at the above location describes me and the URI itself is also unique. However, this clearly confuses a person with a Web document. For any user, the first question that comes to mind will be, does this URI represent this person's homepage, or does it represent him as a person?

---

[3] "Cool URIs for the Semantic Web", W3C Interest Group Note 03 December 2008 (http://www.w3.org/TR/cooluris/)

If we use the above URI to identify me, it is then likely that part of my FOAF file would look like the following:

```
<rdf:Description rdf:about="http://www.liyangyu.com/">
  <foaf:name>liyang yu</foaf:name>
  <foaf:title>Dr</foaf:title>
  <foaf:givenname>liyang</foaf:givenname>
  <foaf:family_name>yu</foaf:family_name>
  <foaf:mbox rdf:resource="liyang@liyangyu.com"/>
```

Now, if this URI represents my homepage, then how could a homepage have `foaf:name`, and how could it also have a `foaf:mbox`? On the other hand, if this URI represents a person named Liyang Yu, the above FOAF document in general seems to be describing a homepage which has a Web address given by www. liyangyu.com.

Having all this said, it seems to be clear that I need another unambiguous URI to represent myself. And this gives the first rule summarized by W3C Interest Group:

Be unambiguous: There should be no confusion between identifiers for Web documents and identifiers for other resources. URIs are meant to identify only one of them, so one URI cannot stand for both a Web and a real-world object.

Now let us say I have already come up with a URI to represent myself, for example,

```
http://www.liyangyu.com/foaf.rdf#liyang
```

then what happens if the above URI is dereferenced in a browser—do we get anything back at all? If yes, what do we get back?

For information resources, we get one possible form of representation back, which could be an HTML page, for example. For non-information resources, based on the following rule proposed by W3C Interest Group, when their URIs are used in a browser, related information should be retrieved as follows:

Be on the Web: Given only a URI, machines and people should be able to retrieve a description about the resource identified by the URI from the Web. Such a look-up mechanism is important to establish shared understanding of what a URI identifies. Machines should get RDF data and humans should get a readable representation, such as HTML. The standard Web transfer protocol, HTTP, should be used.

This rule makes it clear that for URIs identifying non-information resources, some descriptions should be returned to the clients. However, it does not specify any details for implementation purpose.

It turns out in the world of Linked Data, the implementation of this rule also dictates how the URIs for non-information resources are constructed. Let us cover the details next.

9.2.1.3 URIs for Non-information Resources: 303 URIs and Content Negotiation

The first solution is to use the so-called *303 URIs* to represent non-information resources. The basic idea is to create a URI for a given non-information resource, and when a client posts a request using this URI, the server will return the special HTTP status code `303 See Other`. This not only indicates that the requested resource is not a regular Web document, but also further redirects the client to some other document which provides information about the thing identified by this URI. By doing so, we will be able to satisfy the above two rules and also avoid the ambiguity between the real-world object and the non-information resource that represents it.

As a side note, if the server answers the request using a status code in the 200 range, such as `200 OK`, it is then clear that the given URI represents a normal Web document, or, information resource.

Now, in the case where a `303 See Other` status code is returned, which document should the server redirect its client to? This depends on the request from the client. If the client is an RDF-enabled browser (or some applications that understands RDF model), it will more likely prefer a URI which points to an RDF document. If the browser is a traditional HTML browser (or the client is a human reader), it will then more likely prefer a URI that points to an HTML document. In other words, when sending the request, the client will include information in the HTTP header to indicate what type of representation it prefers. The server will inspect this header to return a new URI that links to the appropriate response. This process is called *content negotiation*.

It is now a common practice that for a given real-world resource, we can often have three URIs for it. For example, for myself as a non-information resource, the following three URIs could be in use:

- a URI that identifies me as a non-information resource:

  `http://www.liyangyu.com/resource/liyang`

- a URI that identifies a Web document which has an RDF/XML representation describing me. This URI will be returned when a client prefers an RDF description:

  `http://www.liyangyu.com/data/liyang`

- a URI that identifies a Web document that has an HTML representation describing me. This URI will be returned when a client prefers an HTML document:

  `http://www.liyangyu.com/page/liyang`

And the first URI,

`http://www.liyangyu.com/resource/liyang`

is often the one that is seen by the outside world as my URI.

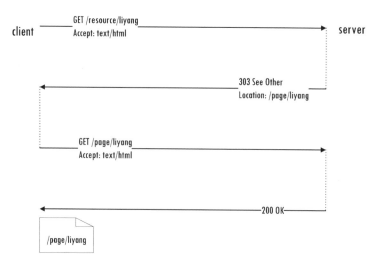

Fig. 9.2 Example of content negotiation

The above schema for constructing URIs for non-information resources is also viewed as the best practice by the Linked Data community. Another example is the following three URIs about Berlin, as seen in DBpedia project:

- a URI that is used as the identifier for Berlin:

```
http://dbpedia.org/resource/Berlin
```

- a URI that identifies a representation in HTML format (for human readers):

```
http://dbpedia.org/page/Berlin
```

- a URI that identifies a representation in RDF/XML format (for machines):

```
http://dbpedia.org/data/Berlin
```

It is now clear that for a given resource, there could be multiple content types for its representation, such as HTML format and RDF/XML format, as seen above. Figure 9.2 shows the process of content negotiation, using my own URI as an example:

The following steps show the interaction between the server and a client:

- The client requests an HTML Web document:

```
GET /resource/liyang HTTP/1.1
Host: www.liyangyu.com
Accept: text/html
```

- The server's response header should include the following fields:

```
HTTP/1.1 303 See Other
Location: http://www.liyangyu.com/page/liyang
```

- The client requests a machine-readable document for the resource:

```
GET /resource/liyang HTTP/1.1
Host: www.liyangyu.com
Accept: application/rdf+xml
```

- The server's response header should include the following fields:

```
HTTP/1.1 303 See Other
Location: http://www.liyangyu.com/data/liyang
```

As a summary, 303 URIs require content negotiation when they are used in a browser to retrieve their descriptions. Furthermore, content negotiation requires at least two HTTP round-trips to the server to retrieve the desired document. However, 303 URIs eliminate the ambiguity between information and non-information resources; therefore they provide a uniform and consistent way of representing resources in the real world.

9.2.1.4 URIs for Non-information Resources: Hash URIs

A *hash URI* is a URI that contains a fragment, i.e., the part that is separated from the rest of the URI by a hash symbol ("#"). For example, the following is a hash URI to identify me as a resource:

```
http://www.liyangyu.com/foaf.rdf#liyang
```

and liyang (to the right of #) is the fragment part of this URI.

Hash URI provides an alternative choice when it comes to identifying non-information resources. The reason behind this solution is related to the HTTP protocol itself.

More specifically, when a hash URI is used in a browser, the HTTP protocol requires the fragment part to be stripped off before sending the URI to the server. For example, if you dereference the above URI into a Web browser and also monitor the request sent out to the server, you will see the following lines in the request:

```
GET /foaf.rdf HTTP/1.1
Host: www.liyangyu.com
```

Clearly, the fragment part is gone. Instead of retrieving this URI,

```
http://www.liyangyu.com/foaf.rdf#liyang
```

the client is in fact requesting this one:

```
http://www.liyangyu.com/foaf.rdf
```

In other words, a URI that includes a hash fragment cannot be retrieved directly; therefore it does not identify a Web document at all. As a result, any URI including a fragment part is a URI that identifies a non-information resource; thus the ambiguity is avoided.

Now that there is no ambiguity associated with a hash URI, what should be served if the URI is dereferenced in a browser? Since we know the fragment part will be taken off by the browser, we can simply serve a document (either human-readable or machine-readable) at the resulting URI which does not have the fragment part. Again using the following as the example,

```
http://www.liyangyu.com/foaf.rdf#liyang
```

we can then serve an RDF document identified by the this URI:

```
http://www.liyangyu.com/foaf.rdf
```

Notice there is no need for any content negotiation, which is probably the main reason why hash URIs look attractive to us.

Hash URIs do have a downside. Consider the following three URIs:

```
http://www.liyangyu.com/foaf.rdf#liyang
http://www.liyangyu.com/foaf.rdf#connie
http://www.liyangyu.com/foaf.rdf#ding
```

which represent three different resources. However, using any one of them in a browser will send a single request to this common URI:

```
http://www.liyangyu.com/foaf.rdf
```

and if someone is only interested in #connie, the whole document will still have to be returned. Obviously, using hash URIs lacks the flexibility of configuring a response for each individual resource.

It is also worth mentioning that even when hash URIs are used, we can still use content negotiation if we want to serve both HTML and RDF representations for the resources identified by the URIs. For example,

- The client requests an HTML Web document for the following resource,

```
http://www.liyangyu.com/foaf.rdf#liyang
```

and you will see these lines in the request:

```
GET /roaf.rdf HTTP/1.1
Host: www.liyangyu.com
Accept: text/html
```

- The response header from the server should include the following fields:

```
HTTP/1.1 303 See Other
Location: http://www.liyangyu.com/foaf.html
```

Notice we assume there is an HTML file called foaf.html which includes some HTML representations of the given resource.

- Now the client requests a machine-readable document for the resource:

```
GET /roaf.rdf HTTP/1.1
Host: www.liyangyu.com
Accept: application/rdf+xml
```

- The response header from the server should include the following fields:

```
HTTP/1.1 303 See Other
Location: http://www.liyangyu.com/foaf.rdf
```

And similarly, the following two hash URIs,

```
http://www.liyangyu.com/foaf.rdf#connie
http://www.liyangyu.com/foaf.rdf#ding
```

will have exactly the same content negotiation process, since their fragment parts will be taken off by the browser before sending them out to the server.

9.2.1.5 URIs for Non-information Resources: 303 URIs vs. Hash URIs

Now that we have introduced both 303 URIs and hash URIs, the next question is about when should a 303 URI be used and when should a hash URI be used. Table 9.1 briefly summarizes the advantages and disadvantages of both URIs.

The following are simple guidelines. Once you have more experience working with the linked data and the Semantic Web, you will be able to add more to them:

- For ontologies that are created by using RDF Schema and OWL, it is preferred to use hash URIs to represent all the terms defined in the ontology, and frequent access of this ontology will not generate lots of network redirects.
- If you need a quicker and easier way of publishing linked data or small and stable datasets of RDF resource files, hash URI should be the choice.
- Other than the above, 303 URIs should be used to identify non-information resources, if possible.

Table 9.1 303 URI vs. Hash URI: advantages and disadvantages

	303 URI	Hash URI
Advantages	Provides the flexibility of configuring redirect targets for each resource; Provides the flexibility of changing/ updating these targets easily and freely, at any given time.	Does not require content negotiation, therefore reduces the number of HTTP round-trips; Since content negotiation is not required, publishing linked data is easier and quicker.
Disadvantages	Requires two round-trips for each use of a given URI.	All the resource descriptions have to be collected in one file.

9.2.1.6 URI Aliases

When it comes to identifying things with URIs, one obvious fact we have noticed so far is the lack of centralized control of any kind. In fact, anyone can talk about any resource, and come up with a URI to represent that resource. It is therefore quite possible that different users happen to talk about the same non-information resource. Furthermore, since they are not aware of each other's work, they create different URIs to identity the same resource or concept. Since all these URIs are created to identify the same resource or concept, they are called *URI aliases*.

It is commonly suggested that when you plan to publish RDF statements about a given resource, you should try to find at least some of the URI aliases for this resource first. If you can find one or multiple URIs for the resource, by all means reuse one of them; create your own only if you have very strong reason to do so. And in which case, you should use `owl:sameAs` to link it to at least one existing URI. Certainly, you can create your own URI if you cannot find any existing ones at all.

Now, how do you find the URI aliases for the given resource? At the time of this writing, there are some tools available on the Web. Let us use one example to see how these tools can help us.

Assume that we want to publish some RDF statements about Roger Federer, the tennis player who holds the most Grand Slam titles at the current time. Since he is such a well-known figure, it is safe to assume that we are not the first ones who would like to say something about him. Therefore, there should be at least one URI identifying him, if not more.

A good starting place where we can search for these URI aliases is the *Sindice* Web site. You can access this Web site here,

```
http://sindice.com/
```

More specifically, Sindice can be viewed as a Semantic Web search engine, and it was originally created at the Digital Enterprise Research Institute (DERI) as a research project. Its main idea is to index the Semantic Web documents over the Web; so for a given URI, it can search its datasets and further tell us which dataset has mentioned this given URI.

To us, a more useful feature of Sindice is when searching its datasets, Sindice not only accepts URIs, but also takes keywords. When it accepts keywords, it will find all the URIs that either describe or closely match the given keywords first, then it will locate all the datasets that contain these URIs. This is what we need when we want to know if there are any existing URIs identifying Roger Federer. Figure 9.3 shows the query session:

And Fig. 9.4 shows the Sindice search result:

The first result in Fig. 9.4 shows a URI identifying Roger Federer (we know this by noticing the file type of this result, i.e., an RDF document), and this URI is given as follows:

```
http://dbpedia.org/resource/Roger_Federer
```

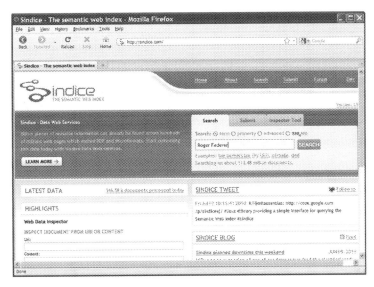

Fig. 9.3   A Sindice search session (search for Roger Federer)

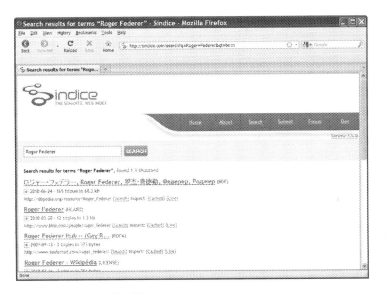

Fig. 9.4   Search results from Fig. 9.3

To collect other URI aliases identifying Roger Federer, we can continue to use Sindice. However, another tool, called *sameAs*, can also be very helpful. You can find sameAs by accessing its Web site:

```
http://www.sameas.org/
```

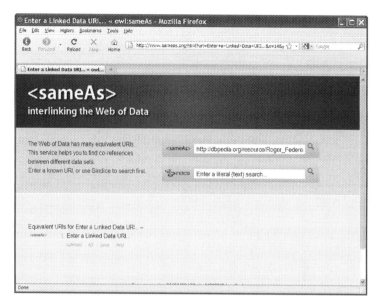

Fig. 9.5 Use sameAs to find URI aliases

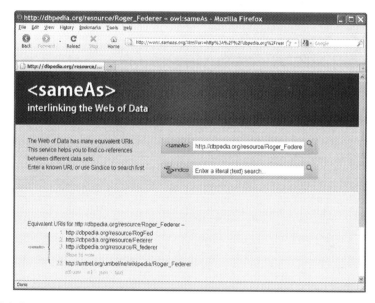

Fig. 9.6 SameAs search result

It will help us to find the URI aliases for a given URI. In our case, our search is shown in Fig. 9.5,
and Fig. 9.6 shows the result:

Clearly, at the time of this writing, there are about 23 URIs identifying Roger Federer, as shown in Fig. 9.6. It is now up to us to pick one of these URIs so we can publish something about Roger Federer.

As you can tell, these two Web sites are very helpful on finding existing URIs. In fact, `www.sameas.org` even provides a link to `www.sindice.com`, as shown in Fig. 9.5. You can either directly enter a URI in the `<sameAs>` box to search for its URI aliases, or, you can use Sindice first by entering the keywords in the `Sindice` box.

Recall the lookup service we discussed in Chap. 8 about DBpedia—it is another service we can use to locate URIs that are created by DBpedia for a given resource. See Fig. 8.4 and Sect. 8.3.3 for details.

At this point, we have briefly discussed URI aliases. With the development of the Semantic Web, let us hope that there will better and better solutions out there, which will greatly facilitate the reuse of URIs.

9.2.2 Choosing Vocabularies for RDF Data

By now, you should understand that when publishing RDF statements, you should always try to use terms defined in one or more ontologies. For example, the predicate of an RDF statement should always be a URI that comes from the ontologies you are using. In addition, it is recommended that instead of inventing your own ontology, you should always use the terms from well-known existing ontologies. Reusing ontologies will make it possible for clients to understand your data and further process your data; therefore the data you have published can easily become part of the Web of Linked Data.

At this point, there is already a good collection of some well-known ontologies covering multiple application domains. You can find this collection at the Linking Open Data project wiki homepage (see Sect. 9.1.2), and make sure to check back often for updates. The following is a short list, just to name a few:

- Friend-of-a-Friend (FOAF): terms for describing people;
- Dublin Core (DC): terms for general metadata attributes;
- Semantically-Interlinked Online Communities (SIOC): terms for describing online communities;
- Description of a Project (DOAP): terms for describing projects;
- Music Ontology: terms for describing artists, albums and tracks;
- Review Vocabulary: terms for representing reviews.

In case you do need to create your own ontology, it is still important to make use of the terms that are defined in these well-known ontologies. In fact, some of the ontologies given above, such as the Music Ontology, make use of the terms defined in other ontologies. For example, List 9.1 is taken from the Music Ontology, and it shows the definition of class `SoloMusicArtist`.

List 9.1 Part of the Music ontology

```
<?xml version='1.0' encoding='UTF-8'?>
<!DOCTYPE rdf:RDF [
    <!ENTITY dc 'http://purl.org/dc/elements/1.1/'>
    <!ENTITY mo 'http://purl.org/ontology/mo/'>
    <!ENTITY ns1 'http://www.w3.org/2003/06/sw-vocab-status/ns#'>
    <!ENTITY owl 'http://www.w3.org/2002/07/owl#'>
    <!ENTITY rdf 'http://www.w3.org/1999/02/22-rdf-syntax-ns#'>
    <!ENTITY rdfs 'http://www.w3.org/2000/01/rdf-schema#'>
    <!ENTITY xsd 'http://www.w3.org/2001/XMLSchema#'>
]>

<rdf:RDF
    xmlns:dc="&dc;"
    xmlns:mo="&mo;"
    xmlns:ns1="&ns1;"
    xmlns:owl="&owl;"
    xmlns:rdf="&rdf;"
    xmlns:rdfs="&rdfs;"
    xmlns:xsd="&xsd;"
>

...

<rdfs:Class rdf:about="&mo;SoloMusicArtist"
    mo:level="1"
    rdfs:label="SoloMusicArtist"
    ns1:term_status="stable">
  <rdfs:subClassOf rdf:resource="&mo;MusicArtist"/>
  <rdfs:subClassOf
        rdf:resource="http://xmlns.com/foaf/0.1/Person"/>
  <rdf:type rdf:resource="&owl;Class"/>
  <rdfs:comment>Single person whose musical creative work shows
sensitivity and imagination.
  </rdfs:comment>
  <rdfs:isDefinedBy rdf:resource="&mo;"/>
</rdfs:Class>
...
```

Notice SoloMusicArtist is defined as a subclass of foaf:Person. Therefore, if a given client sees the following:

```
<rdf:Description
   rdf:about="http://zitgist.com/music/artist/79239441-bfd5-4981-
   a70c-55c3f15c1287">
   <rdf:type
     rdf:resource="http://purl.org/ontology/mo/SoloMusicArtist"/>
</rdf:Description>
```

It will know the real-world resource identified by this URI,

```
http://zitgist.com/music/artist/79239441-bfd5-4981-a70c-
   55c3f15c1287
```

must be an instance of `foaf:Person`. If this client is not interested in any instance of `foaf:Person`, it can safely disregard any RDF statements that are related to this resource. Clearly, this reasoning is possible only when the authors of the Music Ontology have decided to make use of the terms defined in the FOAF ontology.

Creating ontologies, like any other design work, requires not only knowledge, but also experience. It is always helpful to learn how other ontologies are created, so check out the ontologies listed above. After reading and understanding how these ontologies are designed and coded, you will be surprised to see how much you have learned. Also, with the knowledge you have gained, it is more likely that you will be doing a solid job when creating your own.

9.2.3 Creating Links to Other RDF Data

Now that you have come up with the URIs, and you have the terms from the ontologies to use, you can go ahead make your statements about the world. There is only one thing you need to remember: you need to make links to other RDF datasets so your statements can participate in the Linked Data cloud.

In this section, we discuss the basic language constructs and ways you can use to add these links.

9.2.3.1 Basic Language Constructs to Create Links

Let us start with a simpler case: you are creating a FOAF document. The easiest way to make links in this case is to use `foaf:knows`, as we have shown in Chap. 7. Using `foaf:knows` will not only make sure you can join the "circle of trust", but also it will put your data into the Linked Data cloud.

In fact, besides `foaf:knows`, there are couple other FOAF terms you can use to create links. Let us take a look at some examples:

- use `foaf:interest` to show your interest:

For example,

```
<rdf:RDF
   xmlns:dc="http://purl.org/dc/terms/"
   xmlns:foaf=http://xmlns.com/foaf/0.1/"
   <!- other namespace definitions ->
>
<foaf:interest>
   <rdf:Description
       rdf:about="http://dbpedia.org/resource/Photography">
      <dc:title>photography</dc:title>
   </rdf:Description>
</foaf:interest>
```

This will link you to the world of photography as defined in DBpedia. And as you know, DBpedia is a major component of the Linked Data cloud.

- use `foaf:base_near` to show where you are located:

For example,

```
<rdf:RDF
      xmlns:foaf="http://xmlns.com/foaf/0.1/"
      <!- other namespace definitons ->
>
   <rdf:Description
       rdf:about="http://www.liyangyu.com/foaf.rdf#liyang">
      <foaf:name>liyang yu</foaf:name>
      <foaf:based_near
           rdf:resource="http://dbpedia.org/resource/Beijing"/>
      <!- other descriptions I may want ->
   </rdf:Description>
</rdf:RDF>
```

This will link you to Beijing, the capital city of China, which is represented by DBpedia as `http://dbpedia.org/resource/Beijing`. Again, this is good enough for putting you into the Linked Data cloud.

With the above two examples, you understand that there are different FOAF terms you can use to link to the Web of Linked Data. We will leave it to you to discover other FOAF terms that can be used besides the above two examples.

For a more general case, at least two properties should be considered when making links: `rdfs:seeAlso` and `owl:sameAs`.

`rdfs:seeAlso` is defined in W3C's RDFS vocabulary, and it is used to indicate that another resource might provide additional information about the subject resource. It therefore can be used to link the current RDF document into the Linked Data world.

In addition, notice that `rdfs:domain` of `rdfs:seeAlso` is `rdfs:Resource`, and `rdfs:range` of `rdfs:seeAlso` is also `rdfs:Resource`. As a result, this property is entirely domain-neutral, and works for people, companies, documents, etc.

List 9.2 shows one simple example of using `rdfs:seeAlso`.

List 9.2 Use `rdfs:seeAlso` to create link

```
<rdf:Description
     rdf:about="http://www.liyangyu.com/foaf.rdf#liyang">
  <foaf:name>liyang yu</foaf:name>
  <foaf:title>Dr</foaf:title>
  <foaf:givenname>liyang</foaf:givenname>
  <!-- other descriptions here -->
  <rdfs:seeAlso>
    <rdf:Description
      rdf:about="http://www.liyangyu.com/people/connie.rdf">
    </rdf:Description>
  </rdfs:seeAlso>
</rdf:Description>
</rdf:RDF>
```

`rdfs:seeAlso` property in List 9.2 says that you can find more information about resource `http://www.liyangyu.com/foaf.rdf#liyang` from anther RDF document (`connie.rdf`). A given client can follow this link to download `connie.rdf` and expect to be able to parse this file and collect more information about the current resource.

This simple example in fact raises a very interesting question: when we build our application, is it safe to assume that the value of `rdfs:seeAlso` property will always be a document that can be parsed as RDF/XML?

Unfortunately, the answer is no. As we have discussed, the formal definition of `rdfs:seeAlso` is couched in very neutral terms, allowing a wide variety of document types. You could certainly reference a JPEG or PDF or HTML document with `rdfs:seeAlso`, which are not RDF documents at all. Therefore, an application should always account for all these possibilities when following the `rdfs:seeAlso` link.

Sometimes, it is a good idea to explicitly indicate that `rdfs:seeAlso` property is indeed used to reference a document that is in RDF/XML format. List 9.3 shows how this can be implemented:

List 9.3 Use `rdfs:seeAlso` together with `dc:format` to provide more information

```
<rdf:Description
      rdf:about="http://www.liyangyu.com/foaf.rdf#liyang">
  <foaf:name>liyang yu</foaf:name>
  <foaf:title>Dr</foaf:title>
  <foaf:givenname>liyang</foaf:givenname>
  <!-- other descriptions here -->
  <rdfs:seeAlso>
    <rdf:Description
        rdf:about="http://www.liyangyu.com/people/connie.rdf">
       <dc:format>application/rdf+xml</dc:format>
    </rdf:Description>
  </rdfs:seeAlso>
</rdf:Description>
</rdf:RDF>
```

Another useful feature about `rdfs:seeAlso` is that it is often used as a typed link, which can be very helpful to clients. List 9.4 shows one example of a typed link specified using `rdfs:seeAlso`:

List 9.4 `rdfs:seeAlso` used with typed link

```
<rdf:Description
      rdf:about="http://www.liyangyu.com/foaf.rdf#liyang">
  <foaf:name>liyang yu</foaf:name>
  <foaf:title>Dr</foaf:title>
  <foaf:givenname>liyang</foaf:givenname>
  <!-- other descriptions here -->
  <rdfs:seeAlso>
     <rdf:Description
         rdf:about="http://www.liyangyu.com/publication/liyang">
        <rdf:type
   rdf:resource="http://example.org/someAuthorClassDefinition"/>
        <dc:format>application/rdf+xml</dc:format>
     </rdf:Description>
  </rdfs:seeAlso>
  <rdfs:seeAlso>
     <rdf:Description
       rdf:about="http://www.liyangyu.com/publication/yu_cv.rdf">
        <rdf:type
   rdf:resource="http://example.org/someResumeClassDefinition"/>
        <dc:format>application/rdf+xml</dc:format>
     </rdf:Description>
  </rdfs:seeAlso>
</rdf:Description>
</rdf:RDF>
```

Imagine an application that is only interested in publications (not CVs). This typed link will help the application to eliminate the second `rdfs:seeAlso`, and only concentrate on the first one.

`owl:sameAs` is also nothing new. It is defined by OWL to state that two URI references refer to the same individual. It is now frequently used by Linked Data publishers to create links between datasets. For example, Tim Berners-Lee, in his own FOAF file, has been using the following URI to identify himself:

```
http://www.w3.org/People/Berners-Lee/card#i
```

and he also uses the following four `owl:sameAs` properties to state that the individual identified by the above URI is the same individual as identified by these URIs:

```
<owl:sameAs rdf:resource="http://identi.ca/user/45563"/>
<owl:sameAs
rdf:resource="http://www.advogato.org/person/timbl/foaf.rdf#me"/>
<owl:sameAs rdf:resource=
"http://www4.wiwiss.fu-berlin.de/bookmashup/persons/Tim+Berners-
Lee"/>
<owl:sameAs rdf:resource=
"http://www4.wiwiss.fu-berlin.de/dblp/resource/person/100007"/>
```

and clearly, some of these URIs can be used to link his FOAF document into the Linked Data cloud. In fact, at this point, the last two URIs are indeed used for this purpose.

`owl:sameAs` can certainly be used in other RDF documents. Generally speaking, when instances of different classes refer to the same individual, these instances can be identified and linked together by using `owl:sameAs` property. This directly supports the idea that the same individual can be seen in different contexts as entirely different entities, and by linking these entities together, we can discover the unexpected facts that are both interesting and helpful to us.

The above discussion has listed some basic language constructs we can use to create links. In practice, when it comes to creating links in RDF documents, there are two methods: creating the links manually or generating the links automatically. Let us briefly discuss these two methods before we close this section.

9.2.3.2 Creating Links Manually

Manually creating links is quite intuitive, yet it does require you be familiar with the published and well-known linked datasets out there, therefore you can pick your linking targets. In particular, the following steps are normally followed when creating links manually in your RDF document:

- Understand the available linked datasets

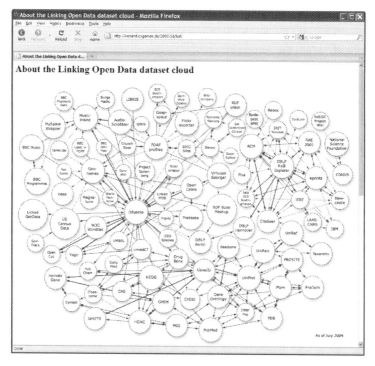

Fig. 9.7 Richard Cyganiak's clickable version of LOD Cloud as of July 2009

This can be done by studying the currently available datasets published and organized by experts in the field. For example, as of July 2009, Richard Cyganiak has published the *LOD Cloud* as shown in Fig. 9.7. The updated version can be accessed from this location:

```
http://linkeddata.org/images-and-posters
```

And if you access this Linked Data collection at the above location, you can actually click each dataset and start to explore that particular dataset. This will help you to get an overview of all the datasets that are available today, and you can also select the dataset(s) that you wish to link into.

• Find the URIs as your linking targets

Once you have selected the datasets to link into, you can then search in these datasets to find the URIs to which you want to link. Most datasets provide a search interface, such as a SPARQL endpoint, so you can locate the appropriate URI references for your purpose. If there is no search interface provided, you can always use Linked Data browsers to explore the dataset, as we will discuss in a later section.

With the above two steps, you can successfully create your links. Let us take a look at a simple example.

Assume I have created my own FOAF document, and I am ready to create some links that point into some available linked dataset. The first step is to choose such a dataset. Let us say I would like to express that I am interested in the Semantic Web, and I need to find a dataset that describes the concept of the Semantic Web. Since DBpedia is machine-readable version of Wikipedia, it is safe to assume that DBpedia might already have included the concept of the Semantic Web. Therefore, DBpedia is currently chosen as the target dataset.

The second step is to search in DBpedia datasets for the URI that represents the Semantic Web. In fact, I have found the following URI that describes this concept:

```
http://dbpedia.org/resource/Semantic_Web
```

and with this, the I can add the following link into my own FOAF:

```
<http://www.liyangyu.com/foaf.rdf#liyang>
foaf:topic_interest <http://dbpedia.org/resource/Semantic_Web> .
```

This will successfully put my own small FOAF document into the Web of Linked Data.

In some cases, you can use a relatively direct way to find the URI reference that you can use to create your links. For example, without selecting any datasets, we can directly search the phrase "the Semantic Web" in Sindice.com. We can easily find a list of URIs that have been created to identify this concept, including the URI coined by DBpedia.

9.2.3.3 Creating Links Automatically

Compared to manually creating links, generating links automatically is certainly more efficient and more scalable, and it is always the preferred method if possible. However, at the time of this writing, there is still a lack of good and easy-to-use tools to automatically generate RDF links. In most cases, dataset-specific algorithms have to be designed to accomplish the task. In this section, we briefly discuss this topic so as to give you some basic idea along this direction.

A collection of often-used algorithms is the so-called *pattern-based algorithms*. This group of algorithms takes advantage of the fact that for a specific domain, there may exist some generally accepted naming pattern, which could be useful for generating links.

For example, in the publication domain, if the ISBN is included as part of the URI that used to identify a book, as in the case of the RDF Book Mashup dataset, then a link can be created with ease. More specifically, DBpedia can locate all the wiki pages for books, and if a given wiki page has an ISBN number included, this number is used to search among the URIs used by the RDF Book Mashup dataset. When a match is found, an `owl:sameAs` link is created to link the URI of the book in DBpedia to the corresponding RDF Book Mashup URI. This algorithm has helped to generate at least 9,000 links between DBpedia and RDF Book Mashup dataset.

In cases where no common identifiers can be found across datasets, more complex algorithms have to be designed based on the characteristics of the given datasets. For example, many geographic places appear in both the Geonames[4] dataset as well as in the DBpedia dataset. To make the two sets of URIs representing these places link together, the Geonames team has designed a property-based algorithm to automatically generate links. More specifically, properties such as latitude, longitude, country, population, etc., are taken into account, and a link will be created if all these properties show some similarity as defined by the team. This algorithm has generated about 70,500 links between the datasets.

In summary, automatic generation of links is possible for some specific domain, or with a specifically designed algorithm. When it is used properly, it is much more scalable then the manual method.

9.2.4 Serving Information as Linked Data

9.2.4.1 Minimum Requirements for Being Linked Open Data

Before we can put our data onto the Web, we need to make sure it satisfies some minimal requirements in order to be qualified as "Linked Data on the Web":

1. If you have created any new URI representing a non-information resource, this new URI has to be dereferenceable in the following sense:

   - Your Web server must be able to recognize the MIME-type `application/rdf+xml`.
   - Your Web server has to implement the 303 redirect as described in Sect. 9.2.1.3. In other words, your Web server should be able to return an HTTP response containing an HTTP redirect to a document that satisfies the client's need (either an `rdf+xml` document or an `html+text` document, for example).
   - If implementing 303 redirect on your Web server is not your plan, your new URIs have to be hash URIs, as we have discussed in Sect. 9.2.1.5.

2. You should include links to other data sources, so a client can continue its navigation when it visits your data file. These links can be viewed as outbound links.

---

[4] http://www.geonames.org/ontology/

3. You should also make sure there are external RDF links pointing at URIs contained in your data file, so the open Linked Data cloud can find your data. These links can be viewed as the inbound links.

At this point, these requirements should look fairly straightforward. The following includes some technical details that you should be aware of.

First, you need to make sure your Web server is able to recognize the rdf+xml as a MIME type. Obviously, this is necessary since once you have published your data into the link data cloud, different clients will start to ask for rdf+xml files from your server. In addition, this is a must if you are using hash URIs to identify real world resources.

A popular tool we can use for this purpose is cURL,[5] which provides a command-line HTTP client that communicates with a given server. It is therefore able to help us to check whether a URI supports some given requirements, such as understanding rdf+xml as a MIME type, supporting 303 redirects and content negotiation, just to name a few.

To get this free tool, visit:

```
http://curl.haxx.se/download.html
```

On this page, you will find different packages for different platforms. MS Windows users can find the download here:

```
http://curl.haxx.se/download.html#Win32
```

Once you have downloaded the package, you can extract it to a location of your choice, and you should be able to find curl.exe in that location. You can then start to test whether a given server is able to recognize the rdf+xml MIME type.

For testing purposes, we can request a URI for my FOAF as follows:

```
curl -I http://www.liyangyu.com/foaf.rdf#liyang
```

Notice the -I parameter has to be used here (refer to cURL's documentation for details). Once we submit the above line, the server sends back the content type and other HTTP headers along with the response. For this example, the following is part of the result:

```
HTTP/1.1 200 OK
Last-Modified: Tue, 11 Aug 2009 02:49:10 GMT
Accept-Ranges: bytes
Content-Length: 1152
Content-Type: application/rdf+xml
Connection: close
```

---

[5] http://curl.haxx.se/

The important line is the `Content-Type` header. We see the file is served as `application/rdf+xml`, just as it should be. If we were to see `text/plain` here, or if the `Content-Type` header was missing, the server configuration would have to be changed.

When it comes to fixing the problem, it does depend on the server. Using Apache as an example, the fix is simple: just add the following line to `httpd.conf` file, or to an `.htaccess` file in the Web server's directory where the RDF files are located:

```
AddType application/rdf+xml.rdf
```

That is it. And since you are on it, you might as well go ahead add the following two lines to make sure your Web server can recognize two more RDF syntaxes, i.e., N3 and Turtle:

```
AddType text/rdf+n3;charset=utf-8.n3
AddType application/x-turtle.ttl
```

Now, when it comes to configuring your Web server to implement 303 redirect and furthermore content negotiation, it is unfortunately not all that easy. This process depends heavily on your particular Web server and its local configuration; it is sometimes quite common that you may not even have the access rights that are needed to make the configuration changes. Therefore, we will not cover this in detail, but remember, this is one step that is needed to publish Linked Data on the Web and it is not hard at all if you have the full access to your server.

With all this said, let us take a look at an example showing how to publish Linked Data on the Web.

9.2.4.2 Example: Publishing Linked Data on the Web

A good starting point is to publish our own FOAF files as linked data on the Web. Let us start with my own FOAF file. To satisfy the minimal requirements that we have discussed above, we can follow these steps:

Step 1. Check whether our Web server is configured to return the correct MIME type when serving `rdf/xml` files.

Let us assume this step has been done correctly, or, you can always follow the previous discussion to make sure your Web server is configured properly.

Step 2. Since we are not going to configure our Web server to implement 303 redirect and content negotiation, we decide to use Hash URI to identify our FOAF files:

```
http://www.liyangyu.com/foaf.rdf#liyang
```

Again, when a client attempts to dereference this URI, the hash fragment (#liyang) will be taken off by the client before it sends the URI to the server. The resulting URI is therefore given by the following:

```
http://www.liyangyu.com/foaf.rdf
```

Now, all we need to do is to make sure that we put the RDF file, foaf.rdf, at the right location on the server, so a client submitting the above URI will be able to look into the response and find the RDF file successfully.

In this example, foaf.rdf file should be located in the root directory on our server, and it could look like something as shown in List 9.5:

List 9.5 The author's FOAF document

```
1: <?xml version="1.0" encoding="UTF-8"?>
2: <rdf:RDF
3:      xml:lang="en"
4:      xmlns:rdf="http://www.w3.org/1999/02/22-rdf-syntax-ns#"
5:      xmlns:rdfs="http://www.w3.org/2000/01/rdf-schema#"
6:      xmlns:foaf="http://xmlns.com/foaf/0.1/">
7:
8: <rdf:Description
8a:     rdf:about="http://www.liyangyu.com/foaf.rdf#liyang">
9:   <foaf:name>liyang yu</foaf:name>
10:   <foaf:title>Dr</foaf:title>
11:   <foaf:givenname>liyang</foaf:givenname>
12:   <foaf:family_name>yu</foaf:family_name>
13:   <foaf:mbox_sha1sum>1613a9c3ec8b18271a8fe1f79537a7b08803d896
13a: </foaf:mbox_sha1sum>
14:   <foaf:homepage rdf:resource="http://www.liyangyu.com"/>
15:   <foaf:workplaceHomepage
15a:        rdf:resource="http://www.delta.com"/>
16:   <rdf:type rdf:resource="http://xmlns.com/foaf/0.1/Person"/>
17: </rdf:Description>
18: </rdf:RDF>
```

Step 3. Make sure you have outbound links.

We can add some outbound links to the existing linked datasets. As shown in List 9.6, properties <foaf:knows> (lines 18–24) and <foaf:topic_interest> (line 26) are used to add two outbound links. This ensures that any client visiting my FOAF document can continue its journey into the Linked Data cloud:

List 9.6 FOAF document with outbound links

```
1: <?xml version="1.0" encoding="UTF-8"?>
2: <rdf:RDF
3:        xml:lang="en"
4:        xmlns:rdf="http://www.w3.org/1999/02/22-rdf-syntax-ns#"
5:        xmlns:rdfs="http://www.w3.org/2000/01/rdf-schema#"
6:        xmlns:foaf="http://xmlns.com/foaf/0.1/">
7:
8: <rdf:Description
8a:      rdf:about="http://www.liyangyu.com/foaf.rdf#liyang">
9:    <foaf:name>liyang yu</foaf:name>
10:   <foaf:title>Dr</foaf:title>
11:   <foaf:givenname>liyang</foaf:givenname>
12:   <foaf:family_name>yu</foaf:family_name>
13:   <foaf:mbox_sha1sum>1613a9c3ec8b18271a8fe1f79537a7b08803d896
13a:  </foaf:mbox_sha1sum>
14:   <foaf:homepage rdf:resource="http://www.liyangyu.com"/>
15:   <foaf:workplaceHomepage
15a:        rdf:resource="http://www.delta.com"/>
16:   <rdf:type rdf:resource="http://xmlns.com/foaf/0.1/Person"/>
17:
18:   <foaf:knows>
19:     <!-- the following is for testing purpose -->
20:     <foaf:Person>
21:        <foaf:mbox
21a:            rdf:resource="mailto:libby.miller@bristol.ac.uk"/>
22:        <foaf:homepage
22a:            rdf:resource="http://www.ilrt.bris.ac.uk/~ecemm/"/>
23:     </foaf:Person>
24:   </foaf:knows>
25:
26:   <foaf:topic_interest
26a:      rdf:resource="http://dbpedia.org/resource/Semantic_Web"/>
27:
28: </rdf:Description>
29: </rdf:RDF>
```

Step 4. Make sure you have inbound links.

This step is to make sure my FOAF document can be discovered by the outside world. The details about this can be found in Chap. 7; refer back to that chapter if you need to.

After these four steps, we are ready to upload my FOAF document onto the server at the right location and claim success. However, for those with curious minds, how do we know it is published as linked data correctly based on the given standards? Is there a way to check this?

The answer is yes. Let us now take a look at how to make sure we have done everything correctly.

9.2.4.3 Make Sure You Have Done It Right

Just as we have validators for checking RDF documents, including RDF instance files and OWL ontologies, we also have Linked Data validators which can be used to confirm whether some structured data is published correctly as linked data, based on the current best practices as we have been discussing in this chapter.

Here is one such tool you can use. It is called Vapour, and you can access this service from this location:

```
http://vapour.sourceforge.net/
```

Figure 9.8 shows this page.

Let us again use my own FOAF document as shown in List 9.6 as the example, and we will validate whether this FOAF document is published correctly as linked data. To do so, click the `try our public service` link in Fig. 9.8, and enter the following URI as shown in Fig. 9.9,

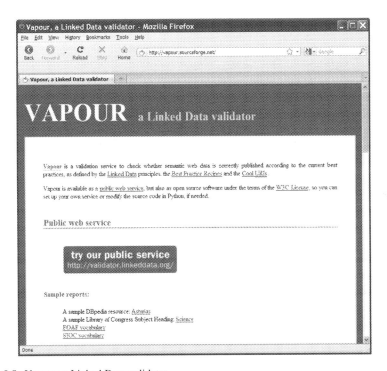

Fig. 9.8 Vapour: a Linked Data validator

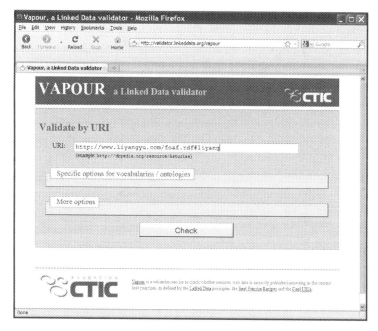

Fig. 9.9 Check our URI to make sure it is published correctly as Linked Data

```
http://www.liyangyu.com/foaf.rdf#liyang
```

Once we click `Check` button, we get the result as shown in Fig. 9.10. Clearly, all tests are passed, meaning that my FOAF document is indeed published correctly as linked data.

You can also see more details on the same page if you try this test out, including dereferencing resource URI with and without content negotiation. As a summary, it is always a good idea to use a validation service when you publish linked data on the Web, to make sure your data participates into the loop successfully.

9.3 The Consumption of Linked Data

Now that we understand how the Web of Lined Data is built, the next step is to study what to do with it. In general, this involves discovering linked data, accessing linked data and building applications that run on top of the Web of Linked Data, as summarized below.

- Discovery of Linked Data

For a given resource in the world, for example, a city or a tennis player, how do we know this resource has already been a subject of Linked Data? Is there any

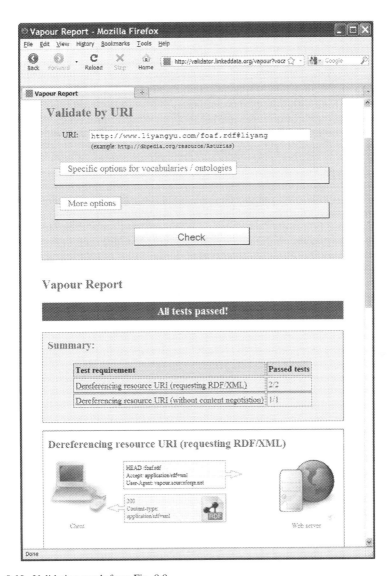

Fig. 9.10 Validating result from Fig. 9.9

Linked Data search engine that crawls the Web of Linked Data by following links between data sources, and therefore provides answers to our questions?

- Accessing Linked Data

We use Web browsers to access our current Web, the Web of documents. For the Web of Linked Data, do we have similar Linked Data browsers that we can use to access the Web of Linked Data? If we have indeed discovered some linked data that we are interested in, how can we start from there? And by using a Linked Data browser, can we start browsing in one data source and then navigate along links into related data sources?

- Applications built upon Linked Data

Given that the Web of Linked Data is built for machines to read and understand, we can go beyond discovery and accessing the Web of Linked Data and create new applications built upon the Web of Linked Data. Compared to Web 2.0 mashups, Linked Data applications offer much more flexibility and completeness in their operations, as we will see later in this chapter.

9.3.1 Discover Specific Targets on the Linked Data Web

In the world of the traditional hypertext Web, discovery almost exclusively means using one of the major search engines to find the information you are interested in. Search engines are therefore the places where the navigation process begins.

For the Web of Linked Data, the same is true: we need search engines that can work on the Web of Linked Data and therefore that can provide us with a tool to make our discovery.

It will not be too surprising if you are seeing a different look-and-feel from the search engines that work on the Web of Linked Data. After all, the Web of Linked Data is quite different from our traditional Web of documents. In fact, semantic Web search engines are mostly geared toward the needs of applications, not that of human eyes. Nevertheless, some researchers and developers have designed search engines that have a similar look-and-feel as the traditional search engines, and this breed of search engines can be very useful to at least some user groups.

In this section, we cover both of these two types, with the goal of discovering linked data on the Web. To make things easier, we start from those Semantic Web search engines that look familiar to our human eyes.

9.3.1.1 Semantic Web Search Engine for Human Eyes

First, remember that search engines of this kind are Semantic Web search engines from their roots. Instead of crawling the Web of documents and indexing each document, these search engines crawl the Web of Linked Data by following their RDF links, and prepare their indexes based on the Web of Linked Data.

Falcons is a good example of this type of search engine. Falcons represents "Finding, aligning and learning ontologies, ultimately for capturing knowledge via ontology-driven approaches", and it was developed by Institute of Web Science (IWS), Southeast University of China. You can access it from the following link:

```
http://iws.seu.edu.cn/services/falcons/
```

The first thing to notice about Falcons is that it provides a keyword-based search service, i.e., the user is presented with a search box, where keywords related to the topics in mind can be entered. Falcons then reacts by returning a list of results that may be related to the topic. Clearly, this closely mimics the same look-and-feel offered by current market leaders such as Google and Yahoo!

Let us say we want to discover if there is any linked data about tennis player Roger Federer. Obviously, if Roger Federer is indeed mentioned in the Web of Linked Data, he has to be some instance of a given class. For example, he could be an instance of some class such as `Person` defined in some ontology. With this in mind, we should use the `Object` search in Falcons, and enter Roger Federer in the search box. This will tell Falcons that the results we are searching for have to contain "Roger Federer" as keywords and should be coming from some instance data, not class or type definitions.

Once we submit this query, Falcons responds by returning a list of results. When presenting the results, for each object (instance data), Falcons shows its title, label, comment, image, page, type and URI, if applicable. Clearly, for the Web of Linked Data, type and URI are all important since type identifies the class of this instance data, and URI uniquely identifies the instance. For our example, the first result is a good hit: the URI is given by

```
http://dbpedia.org/resource/Roger_Federer
```

and its type is `Person`. Clearly, the above URI comes from DBpedia, and we know already that DBpedia is a key component of Linked Data. Therefore, just based on the very first result, we know we have discovered some linked data for tennis player Roger Federer, which can be a good start point for whatever we plan to do next.

Notice that Falcons also provides a `Type` pane together with the search result, and this is, in fact, a very useful feature. Recall that when we first started our search for any linked data related to Roger Federer, we could only say that if this data exists, it has to be some instance data of some class type. However, we don't really know what exactly this class type is, except that the correct type should be something like `Person` or `Athlete`.

Now, the `Type` pane on the result page shows all the types that are found in the results. Notice that the initial search focuses on "Any type"; therefore it does not put any further constraints on the type at all. Once we have the initial results back, we can further narrow down the type by clicking a specific type in the `Type` pane. For example, we can click `Person` in the `Type` pane, telling Falcons that we believe Roger Federer should be an instance of some `Person` class. Once we do this, all the subclasses of type `Person` are now summarized in `Type` pane, and you can continue to narrow down your search. Therefore, `Object` search can be guided by recommended concepts, and we can further refine search results by selecting object types.

Besides `Object` search tab as we have discussed above, Falcons provides two more search tabs: `Concept` and `Document`. `Concept` search is not much related to discovering linked data on the Web; it is more suited for locating classes and properties defined in ontologies that are published on the Web. It is quite useful if you want to find classes and properties that you can reuse, instead of inventing them again.

`Document` search gives you a more traditional search engine experience, especially the look-and-feel of the search results. If you search for Roger Federer, any RDF document that contains these words will be returned as part of the result list, be these search items in the instance data or the class or property definitions. Although not quite efficient, this search can also be used to discover linked data on the Web.

9.3.1.2 Semantic Web Search Engine for Applications

We have made use of the Sindice search engine in previous sections, with the goal of discovering if there is any URI existing for some real-world object that we would like to talk about. For example, if we want to say something about Roger Federer, we can use Sindice to discover the URI for him, as shown in Figs. 9.3 and 9.4.

The Sindice search engine therefore can also be used as a tool to discover linked data on the Web. When used by human users, it has a similar look-and-feel to that of Falcons: a certain number of keywords can be provided to Sindice, and Sindice will return RDF documents on the Web which contains these keywords.

Furthermore, if you know the URI for some real world object, you can search it in Sindice, and Sindice will return all the RDF documents on the Web that contain this given URI. For example, Fig. 9.11 shows the result from Sindice when we search for the URI of Roger Federer:

Clearly, these RDF documents are all linked to some extent since they all have the URI of Roger Federer in their triples.

Certainly, Sindice feels much like Falcons. As human users, we can use both to discover linked data on the Web. However, there is more to Sindice: it can be used by applications as well.

We have not yet discussed Linked Data applications at this point. However, it is quite intuitive to realize that the first thing each Linked Data application will have to do is to somehow harvest some linked data before it can do anything interesting with the data. As a result, each Linked Data application will have to implement its own crawling and indexing component, just to find the linked data of interest. Clearly, moving this common infrastructure for crawling and indexing the Web of Linked Data to a search engine that each individual Linked Data application can then use is a much better and cleaner design.

This is the rationale behind the design and implementation of Sindice's Data Web Services API, and also the reason why we claim Sindice can be a search engine used by applications. More specifically, each application, by using the Sindice API, can query Sindice's collection and receive a set of links that point to those potentially relevant RDF documents, which can then be processed by the application to create other interesting results.

At the time of this writing, the Sindice API is still in early beta version, and is experiencing rapid changes and development. Therefore, we are not going to show

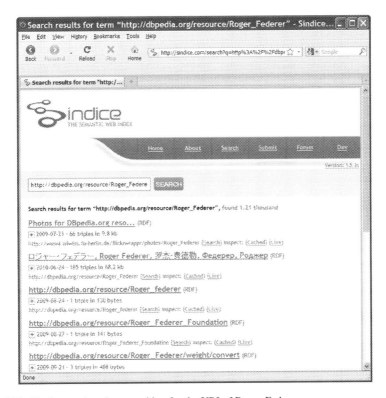

Fig. 9.11 Sindice results when searching for the URI of Roger Federer

any concrete examples here, but the basic idea as we have discussed above will not change.

Before we conclude this section, let us very briefly discuss two more semantic Web search engines, just to give you a flavor of other choices when it comes to discovering linked data on the Web:

• Semantic Web Search Engine (SWSE)

SWSE is developed by DERI Ireland, and can provide search capabilities more suitable toward human users. It accepts keyword-based search, and further offers access to its underlying data store via SPARQL query language. At this point, you can access SWSE from this URL:

```
http://swse.deri.org/
```

Also, notice that, similar to Sindice, SWSE is more related to search for instance data, not types and properties.

• Swoogle

Swoogle was developed by UMBC Ebiquity Research group, which consists of faculty and students from the Department of Computer Science and Electrical

Engineering (CSEE) of University of Maryland, Baltimore County (UMBC). Unlike Sindice or SWSE, Swoogle is designed to search ontologies that relate to the concepts provided by its users. Swoogle also provides Web services to the public users, which can be used by applications that are built on top of the Linked Data Web. At this point, Swoogle can be accessed at this location:

```
http://swoogle.umbc.edu/
```

9.3.2 Accessing the Web of Linked Data

Accessing the Web of Linked Data has two different meanings. First, human users can access it in a way that is similar to what has been done in the traditional Web of documents, i.e., Linked Data browsers can be used to manually navigate from one data source to another. Second, applications that are built to understand linked data can access the Linked Data Web and further accomplish requirements that differ from ours. For example, the so-called Follow-Your-Nose method can be used by applications to browse the Web of Linked Data. In this section, we take a closer look at both of these methods.

9.3.2.1 Using a Linked Data Browser

As human users, we can access the Web of Linked Data manually. This normally requires us to discover a specific piece of linked data on the Web first, which is then used as the starting point for further navigation on the Web of Linked Data.

As traditional Web browsers allow us to access the Web by following hypertext links, their counterparts in the Web of Linked Data, the so-called Linked Data browsers, allows us to navigate from the starting data source to the next data source. This process can go on by following links that are expressed and coded as RDF triples, and that is all there is to it when it comes to manually accessing the Web of Linked Data.

Therefore, the key component in this process is the Linked Data browser. To learn how to manually access the Linked Data Web is to learn how to use one of these browsers.

In recent years, quite a few browsers have been developed and deployed for public use. To find a list of these browsers, you can visit the W3C's ESW Wiki page,[6] which is also updated quite frequently.

In this section, we take the Sig.ma browser as an example to show you how Linked Data browsers can be used to access the Web of Linked Data. Sig.ma is built

---

[6] http://esw.w3.org/topic/TaskForces/CommunityProjects/LinkingOpenData/SemWebClients

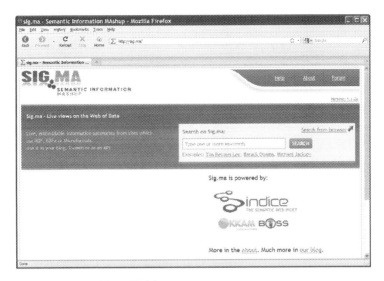

Fig. 9.12 Sig.ma: a Linked Data Web browser

on top of Sindice, which provides the data needs for Sig.ma. To some extent, Sig. ma acts much like Sindice's front-end GUI. You can access Sig.ma at:

```
http://sig.ma/
```

And its main page is shown in Fig. 9.12.

To start using Sig.ma, simply enter the keywords you want to search in the input box and hit the SEARCH button, quite like using Sindice as a search engine. Obviously, this step is to find some entry point to access the Web of Linked Data.

Once you hit the SEARCH button, Sig.ma starts its work by doing the following:

1. Selects 20 data sources from the Web of Linked Data based on the keywords you have entered;
2. Aggregates the information contained in these data sources, and
3. Presents the aggregated information and the data sources back to the user.

Notice the first step is accomplished by using the underlying Sindice search engine to carry out a keyword-based search in the Web of Linked Data to select the relevant data sources. If there are fewer than 20 data sources that are considered to be relevant to the given keywords, then whatever sources are available will be included in the result set. If there are more than 20 data sources that are relevant, you can add the other data sources later on, as will be discussed soon.

Aggregating over the selected data sources essentially means collecting everything each data source says about the resource or concept represented by the keywords you have provided. And since the data sources are all taken from the Web of Linked Data, aggregating different data sources can be done easily.

Once the first two steps are done, Sig.ma presents the results back to the user by dividing the screen into the left pane and the right pane. The left pane shows the

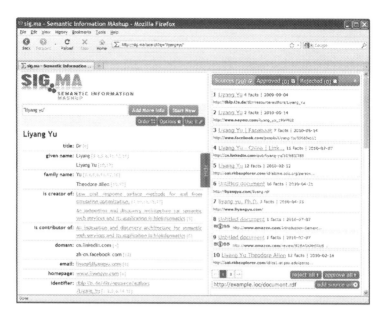

Fig. 9.13 Using Sig.ma to search for "liyang yu"

aggregated information, which is called the "sigma" for this search. The right pane
shows the data source base on which the sigma is obtained.

Let us use one example to see how it works. This time, instead of searching for
Roger Federer, I will search for myself. The reason being that if we were to search
Roger Federer, too many datasets would be included. To show you how to use Sig.
ma, a search that does not yield too many results is better.

Now, enter the keywords "liyang yu" in the search box (remember to include
them in a pair of double quotes). Once you hit the SEARCH button, you will be
presented with the result page as shown in Fig. 9.13 (note that if you are trying this,
it is likely that what you see is not the same as what we printed here, and the reason
is obvious).

Let us first take a look at the left pane, i.e., the sigma of this search. It is quite
different from what you would have seen had you used a Google search. More
specifically, Google search simply gives you back a list of links that point to a
collection of Web pages, with each one of them contains the keywords "liyang yu".
Google itself is not able to tell you facts such as, on a given Web page, the word
Liyang shows up as a given name, and on some other page, the word Yu shows up
as a family name, so on and so forth.

For Sig.ma, however, this is not difficult at all. Not only does it know the word
Liyang is a given name and the word Yu is a family name, it knows quite a lot more.
For example, it can tell the string liyang@liyangyu.com represents my e-mail
address. Clearly, since Sig.ma is built upon a Web of Linked Data, it is therefore
able to present the result in a way that seems like the machine is able to understand
all the data sources it has encountered during its search.

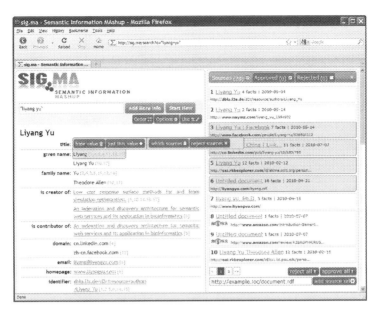

Fig. 9.14 Hovering the mouse over Liyang shows the data sources from which this information is obtained

Now since the sigma pane shows the result of data aggregation, it is certainly useful to include the data sources that have been used to obtain the current sigma. This is the right pane, as shown in the Fig. 9.13. For discussion purpose, let us call it the source pane.

It is very easy for Sig.ma to trace the data source for each information segment in the sigma. For example, if you hover your mouse over the given name "Liyang", at least four data sources in the source pane will be highlighted, telling us that this information is included in all four of these data sources, as shown in Fig. 9.14.

In fact, each data source in the source pane has a number associated with it, indicating how many facts are collected from this particular data source. For example, data source number 4,

```
http://www.liyangyu.com/
```

has contributed three facts to the current sigma, as shown in Fig. 9.13. To see a detailed list of these three facts, hover your mouse over this document. The facts from this document will be highlighted in the sigma pane, as shown in Fig. 9.15:

Notice there is a pop-up menu showing up when you hover the mouse over data source number 4 (Fig. 9.15). The first selection in this pop-up menu is called solo, which is a very useful tool: if you click solo, the current sigma will show only the facts that are collected from this data source, as seen in Fig. 9.16:

To go back to the complete list of facts, simply click unsolo, as you can easily tell.

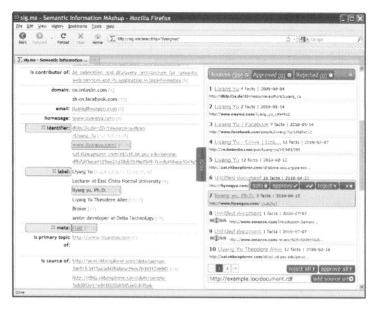

Fig. 9.15 Hover mouse over a data source document, and all the facts from this document are highlighted

Fig. 9.16 Clicking `solo` only shows the facts collected from the selected data source in the Sigma pane

Another useful feature of Sig.ma is the ability to approve and reject data sources. Recall the fact that search in Sig.ma is based on keyword-matching, i.e., when it scans a given RDF data source, it looks for the keywords in that document. The keywords themselves can appear in a comment, a label or the string value of a given subject. They can also show up in a URI that identifies a subject, a predicate or an object. As the developers of Sig.ma have pointed out, since very simple strategies have been purposely chosen at this stage to filter data source candidates, it is quite possible that a given data source is, in fact, not the data source you are looking for.

In the case where a given data source should not be included in the sigma, you can simply click the `reject` button from the pop-up menu in the source pane (you need to hover the mouse over the selected source data document). Once this is done, all the facts in the current sigma will be removed and the data source will be removed as well. For example, go back to Fig. 9.13; we can reject document number 4 by easily following these steps.

It is now easy to understand the `approve` selection. Clicking `approve` for a given data resource means that this data source is highly relevant to the search, and should stay in the source pane at all time.

Besides rejecting and/or approving the data source files contained in the current source pane, I can click the `Add More Info` button in the sigma pane to ask Sig.ma to search more datasets. Once more data sources have been added, I can start to filter them again by applying the same reject/approve process until all the data sources are stable in the source pane.

Figure 9.17 shows my final sigma. As you can tell, I have rejected altogether 12 data sources to reach this sigma:

In fact, my final sigma presents a set of entry points to the Web of Linked Data, since each one of the corresponding data sources in the source pane contains links to the Web of Linked Data. It is now time to start our navigation by following these links.

Let us go back to Fig. 9.17. Notice the label `topic interest:` and its value `Semantic Web`. Clicking this link brings us to a brand new sigma (Fig. 9.18).

As you can tell, the sigma about Semantic Web opens another new entry to the Linked Data Web for you to explore. For example, you can do the following:

• You can start to explore Jena Semantic Web Framework,
• You can start to read more about Resource Description Framework (RDF)
• You can start to understand OWL, and more.

Sig.ma is an excellent tool to search and access the Web of Linked Data; I will leave this to you to continue.

Finally, notice that we have only covered some basic functionality provided by Sig.ma. Sig.ma was first released on July 22, 2009, and given that it is under constant development and improvement, at the time when you are reading this book, you will likely see a different version of Sig.ma. However, the basics should remain the same.

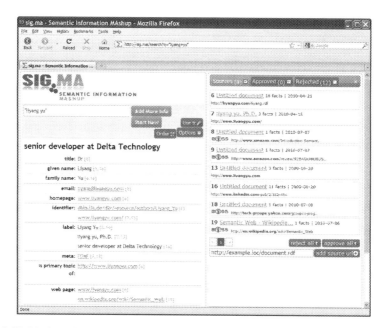

Fig. 9.17   My final sigma after rejecting 12 data sources

9.3.2.2   Using SPARQL Endpoints

We have discussed how to use Linked Data browsers to access the Web of Linked Data manually in the previous section. While it is a useful way to explore the Linked Data, it does not take full advantage of the fact that the Web of Linked Data contains structured data, which means that we can actually access the Linked Data by using a query language.

In this section, we use SPARQL to access the Web of Linked Data. In fact, this is not something completely new to us. In Chap. 8, we discussed how to use SPARQL to access DBpedia. We will expand on the same idea and show you how to use SPARQL to access the Web of Linked Data in general.

A good starting point is the current Linked Data cloud presented in Fig. 9.7. Again, the benefit of accessing it online is that you can get the version that is clickable: when you click a data set, it directly takes you to the home site of that data set.

Now, let us say that we want to understand more about Musicbrainz, which at this point we know nothing about. Click this data set takes us to the home site of Musicbrainz. On its home site, we can find the following SPARQL endpoint (notice that not all the datasets provide SPARQL endpoints):

```
http://dbtune.org/musicbrainz/snorql/
```

and opening this endpoint gives us the query interface supported by the dataset.

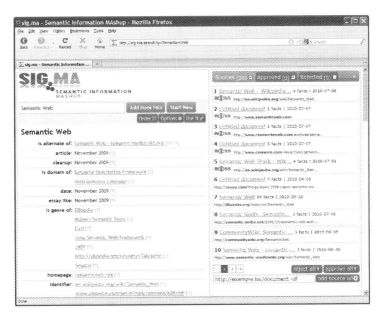

Fig. 9.18 Clicking Semantic Web from Fig. 9.17 takes us to this new sigma

Now, to explore this data set, or rather, to explore any given data set, we can always start from two general queries. The first query is given below:

```
SELECT DISTINCT ?concept
WHERE
{[] a ?concept}
```

This shows all classes that are used in a given dataset. Notice that there might be a large number of classes used, and some of them might look unfamiliar to you. However, this query can give you some feeling about what the given data set is all about.

Let us try this query on the Musicbrainz dataset. Enter the above query in the query box, but change the query so it looks like this:

```
SELECT DISTINCT ?concept
WHERE
{[] a ?concept}
LIMIT 10
```

Adding LIMIT 10 is to make sure the query can be executed in a reasonable amount of time. You can change it to another integer number if you prefer, such as 20, etc.

Once you submit the query, you should get some results back. For example, part of the classes I got are shown as follows:

```
bio:Birth
bio:Death
db:vocab/puidjoin
db:vocab/l_label_track
db:vocab/lt_artist_label
db:vocab/lt_artist_artist
lingvoj:LinguisticSystem
mo:MusicArtist
mo:Performance
mo:Release
mo:Record
```

Again, by the time you are reading this book, you could get different results back.

Now, the above class list gives us some basic idea about what is covered in this dataset. For example, this data set is more about some music artists, their albums, their performance, and so on.

The second useful query is similar to the first one. It asks about all the properties that are included in a given data set:

```
SELECT DISTINCT ?property
WHERE
{?sub ?property ?obj}
```

Again, you might want to use it together with the LIMIT 10 constraint, just to make sure the performance of the endpoint is acceptable:

```
SELECT DISTINCT ?property
WHERE
{?sub ?property ?obj}
LIMIT 10
```

The following is the result:

```
rdfs:label
db:vocab/puidjoin_puid
db:vocab/puidjoin_usecount
db:vocab/puidjoin_id
db:vocab/puidjoin_track
rdf:type
db:vocab/l_label_track_enddate
db:vocab/l_label_track_link_type
db:vocab/l_label_track_begindate
db:vocab/l_label_track_modpending
```

As you can tell, the above two queries are very useful when you know nothing about the data set. In fact, some SPARQL endpoints have included these two queries for you as your default starting point.

After these two general queries, it is up to you to continue your exploration. In most cases, what you will be doing depends on the results from these two queries. For example, for the Musicbrainz dataset, I am interested in `mo:MusicArtist` class, and I want to find who are the members of this class. To do so, I will use the following query:

```
SELECT ?artist
WHERE
{?artist a <http://purl.org/ontology/mo/MusicArtist> }
LIMIT 10
```

And I got ten instances of `mo:MusicArtist` back. One of them is the following:

```
db:artist/0002260a-b298-48cc-9895-52c9425796b7
```

To know more about this instance, I continue to execute the following query:

```
SELECT ?property ?hasValue ?isValueOf
WHERE {
    {       <http://dbtune.org/musicbrainz/resource/artist/0002260a-
b298-48cc-9895-52c9425796b7> ?property ?hasValue }
    UNION
    { ?isValueOf ?property
      <http://dbtune.org/musicbrainz/resource/artist/0002260a-
b298-48cc-9895-52c9425796b7> }
}
```

This query finds everything has been said about this artist. Once you execute the query, you will get the name of the artist, the record label, etc. Obviously, we can continue like this by following a number of different directions, and at some point, we will find ourselves moving on to explore other data sets.

The point is clear: besides using Semantic Web browsers or Semantic Web search engines to access the Web of Linked Data, it is also very useful and efficient to access it by using SPARQL queries. After all, search engines will point you to a set of documents that might contain the answer, but SPARQL queries can directly give you the answer you need.

9.3.2.3   Accessing the Linked Data Web Programmatically

The most significant difference between our current Web and the Web of Linked Data is that the Web of Linked Data can be processed by machines. Given this, it is certainly possible to access the Web of Linked Data programmatically, and it is already the backbone of many Linked Data applications (as we will see in the next section).

Different applications may implement different ways of accessing the Web of Linked Data. However, two basic methods of accessing the Linked Data Web should be understood: one is referred to as the Follow-Your-Nose method, and the other is about issuing SPARQL queries within your application by using supporting tools.

The best way to learn these two methods is by going through some examples. Since these two methods are quite generic, they are discussed in Chap. 16, and you can find working examples for each method there. For now, we will move on with the discussion of Linked Data applications.

9.4 Linked Data Application

Discovering and accessing linked data is only the first step, our ultimate goal is to build applications that make use of linked data. In this section, we present one popular example to show you how linked data can be used.

9.4.1 *Linked Data Application Example: Revyu*

9.4.1.1 Revyu: An Overview

Revyu is a Web site that everyone can login to review and rate anything in the world. However, it is not just another review site; it is developed by using the Semantic Web technologies and standards, and by following Linked Data principles and best practices. More importantly, it also consumes linked data from the Web to enhance its user experience.

Revyu is implemented in PHP, and runs on a regular Apache Web server. It can be accessed at this location:

```
http://revyu.com/
```

A registered user can review and rate things by filling out a Web form, which does not require any knowledge of the Semantic Web. Once finished, the user can submit this review form and the review will show up at the site.

This does not sound too different from other review sites at all. However, lots of things then happen inside Revyu. To understand all these, we first need to

Fig. 9.19 Review page for the movie *Broken Flowers*

understand one fact: every review created in Revyu is also expressed as an RDF graph, besides its normal look-and-feel on the Web.

Let us look at one example. From the Revyu homepage, click the `Search Things` link to search for the movie *Broken Flowers*, for which a review has been created as an example by Tom Heath, the creator of Revyu. Figure 9.19 shows the review page of the movie Broken Flowers.

On this page, click the link that identifies the reviewer. In this case, the link reads as `by tom on 30 Jan 2007`. Once you click this link, you will land on the page as shown in Fig. 9.20.

On the right side of the page, you will find a link called `RDF Metadata for this Review of Broken Flowers` (the right-hand side of Fig. 9.20). Clicking this link takes us to the RDF format of this review.

With the understanding that every review in Revyu has its RDF representation, let us now take a look at what happens inside Revyu when a review is submitted by a user.

• All things represented in Revyu are assigned with URIs.

At the moment a review is submitted, the reviewer (i.e., the user), the review the user creates and the resource being reviewed are all assigned with URIs. Also, the

Fig. 9.20 Reviewer page of tom

tags used when reviewing the resource are assigned with URIs as well (we will discuss tags later this section).

Notice that Revyu is designed to follow the four basic principles of Linked Data discussed early in this chapter. To see this, we can open the RDF document which represents the review of *Broken Flowers*, and locate the URI Revyu has assigned to Tom Heath:

```
http://revyu.com/people/tom
```

Since this URI represents a non-information resource, if it is dereferenced, our Internet browser should receive an HTTP 303 See Other response. Furthermore, our browser should also receive a URL pointing to a document that describes the resource, in this case, Tom Heath.

To test this, let us paste the above URI into our Web browser, and we will be taken to another URL given as below,

```
http://revyu.com/people/tom/about/html
```

which contains an HTML description about Tom.

In fact, content negotiation is also supported by Revyu: if a user agent asks for HTML format, it will receive an HTML document located at the above URL, and if it asks for an RDF format, it will receive an RDF description located at this URL:

```
http://revyu.com/people/tom/about/rdf
```

- Tags are used to create links to the datasets on the Web of Linked Data.

Obviously, the collection of reviewed items is at the center of any review site. As we have discussed, every item in this collection has been assigned a URI by Revyu. However, an isolated URI is not of much value unless one of the following two (or both) things can happen:

- It is associated with another resource URI contained in another data set, by using `owl:sameAs` or `rdfs:seeAlso` property;
- It is associated with a type information (a class defined in an ontology), so some application can performance reasoning on this URI.

Clearly, asking the user of Revyu to accomplish either one of these conditions is not feasible: not only does the user have to understand the Semantic Web technologies and standards, but also there must be ontologies readily available that can provide sufficient coverage to any arbitrary item that may receive a review.

The solution taken by the Revyu designers is to use tags. In particular, it is up to the user to associate keyword tags to the item being reviewed. With this tag information, Revyu is then responsible for deriving type information and linking the item to a certain resource described by another dataset.

Currently two domains are covered by Revyu: books and films. More specifically, when Revyu recognizes that a new item is tagged as book, it will examine every Web link provided by the reviewer at the time the review is submitted. For example, the reviewer may have provided a link from Amazon that contains some information about the book. When examining this link, Revyu parses the Web document downloaded from the link and attempts to extract an ISBN number embedded in the document. If Revyu can find an ISBN number, it concludes that the reviewed item is indeed a book, and it asserts a corresponding `rdf:type` statement in the generated RDF statements.

As one example, List 9.7 shows some generated RDF statements for the reviewed book titled *The Unwritten Rules of Ph.D. Research*. The reviewer has provided the related link from Amazon, which contains the ISBN number (line 23). Based on this information, line 26 has been added by Revyu to establish the type information for this item.

List 9.7 RDF statements generated by Revyu (a book review)

```
1: <?xml version="1.0" encoding="UTF-8" ?>
2: <rdf:RDF
3:    xml:base="http://revyu.com/"
4:    xmlns:rdf="http://www.w3.org/1999/02/22-rdf-syntax-ns#"
5:    xmlns:rdfs="http://www.w3.org/2000/01/rdf-schema#"
6:    xmlns:xsd="http://www.w3.org/2001/XMLSchema#"
7:    xmlns:owl="http://www.w3.org/2002/07/owl#"
8:    xmlns:dc="http://purl.org/dc/elements/1.1/"
9:    xmlns:dcterms="http://purl.org/dc/terms/"
10:    xmlns:vcard="http://www.w3.org/2001/vcard-rdf/3.0#"
11:    xmlns:foaf="http://xmlns.com/foaf/0.1/"
12:    xmlns:rev="http://purl.org/stuff/rev#"
13:    xmlns:tag=
13a:        "http://www.holygoat.co.uk/owl/redwood/0.1/tags/"
14:    xmlns:ns1="http://www.hackcraft.net/bookrdf/vocab/0_1/">
15:
16: <rdf:Description
16a:      rdf:about="things/the-unwritten-rules-of-phd-research">
17:    <rev:hasReview rdf:resource=
17a:        "reviews/82825d6cec2a2267c541848397e1605ab0042af0"/>
18:    <tag:tag rdf:resource=
18a:        "taggings/82825d6cec2a2267c541848397e1605ab0042af0"/>
19: </rdf:Description>
20:
21: <owl:Thing rdf:about=
21a:      "things/the-unwritten-rules-of-phd-research">
22:    <rdfs:label>The Unwritten Rules of Phd Research, by Gordon
22a:                Rugg and Marian Petre </rdfs:label>
23:    <rdfs:seeAlso rdf:resource=
23a:                  "http://www.amazon.co.uk/Unwritten-Rules-Phd-
23b:                  Research/dp/0335213448/"/>
24:    <foaf:homepage rdf:resource=
24a:          "http://mcgraw-hill.co.uk/openup/unwrittenrules/"/>
25:    <owl:sameAs rdf:resource=
25a:        "http://www4.wiwiss.fu-berlin.de/bookmashup/
25b:         books/0335213448"/>
26:    <rdf:type rdf:resource=
26a:        "http://www.hackcraft.net/bookrdf/vocab/0_1/Book"/>
27: </owl:Thing>
28:
29: <rdf:Description rdf:about=
29a:      "taggings/82825d6cec2a2267c541848397e1605ab0042af0">
```

```
30:    <rdfs:label>A bundle of Tags associated with this Thing, de
30a:           fining when they were added and by whom</rdfs:label>
31: </rdf:Description>
32:
33: </rdf:RDF>
```

If a reviewed item is tagged as a movie or film, Revyu issues a query against DBpedia's SPARQL endpoint with the goal of finding any instance data whose type is given by `yago:Film` and that also has the same name as the reviewed item. If this is successful, Revyu will conclude that the reviewed item is indeed a movie, and an `rdf:type` statement will be generated. For example, once the review for movie *Broken Flowers* is submitted, Revyu is able to confirm that this item is the movie named *Broken Flowers*, and List 9.8 shows the RDF statements generated for the item:

List 9.8 RDF statements generated by Revyu (a movie review)

```
1: <?xml version="1.0" encoding="UTF-8" ?>
2: <rdf:RDF
3:    xml:base="http://revyu.com/"
4:    xmlns:rdf="http://www.w3.org/1999/02/22-rdf-syntax-ns#"
5:    xmlns:rdfs="http://www.w3.org/2000/01/rdf-schema#"
6:    xmlns:xsd="http://www.w3.org/2001/XMLSchema#"
7:    xmlns:owl="http://www.w3.org/2002/07/owl#"
8:    xmlns:dc="http://purl.org/dc/elements/1.1/"
9:    xmlns:dcterms="http://purl.org/dc/terms/"
10:    xmlns:vcard="http://www.w3.org/2001/vcard-rdf/3.0#"
11:    xmlns:foaf="http://xmlns.com/foaf/0.1/"
12:    xmlns:rev="http://purl.org/stuff/rev#"
13:    xmlns:tag=
13a:        "http://www.holygoat.co.uk/owl/redwood/0.1/tags/"
14:    xmlns:ns1=
14a:        "http://www.csd.abdn.ac.uk/~ggrimnes/dev/imdb/IMDB#">
15:
16: <rdf:Description rdf:about=
16a:    "things/broken-flowers-film-movie-bill-murray-jim-jarmusch-
16b:    sharon">
17:    <rev:hasReview rdf:resource=
17a:        "reviews/8b9c45cfecb7087430daa963cd6bcd51d2fce30d"/>
18:    <tag:tag rdf:resource=
18a:        "taggings/8b9c45cfecb7087430daa963cd6bcd51d2fce30d"/>
19: </rdf:Description>
```

```
20:
21: <owl:Thing rdf:about=
21a:    "things/broken-flowers-film-movie-bill-murray-
21b:     jim-jarmusch-sharon">
22:    <rdfs:label>Broken Flowers</rdfs:label>
23:    <rdfs:seeAlso rdf:resource=
23a:        "http://en.wikipedia.org/wiki/Broken_flowers"/>
24:    <foaf:homepage rdf:resource=
24a:        "http://www.brokenflowersmovie.com/"/>
25:
26:    <owl:sameAs rdf:resource=
26a:        "http://dbpedia.org/resource/Broken_Flowers"/>
27:    <rdf:type rdf:resource=
27a:    "http://www.csd.abdn.ac.uk/~ggrimnes/dev/imdb/IMDB#Movie"/>
28: </owl:Thing>
29:
30: <rdf:Description rdf:about=
30a:    "taggings/8b9c45cfecb7087430daa963cd6bcd51d2fce30d">
31:    <rdfs:label>A bundle of Tags associated with this Thing,
31a:                defining when they were added and
31b:                by whom</rdfs:label>
32: </rdf:Description>
33:
34: </rdf:RDF>
```

As you can see, line 27 is added to identify the type of the reviewed item.

9.4.1.2 Revyu: Why It Is Different

Revyu is different from other review sites. For books and movies, Revyu assigns a URI to the item being reviewed and also generates an RDF document to represent the review itself. Furthermore, Revyu searches against existing linked datasets and automatically creates links to these external datasets whenever possible. For example, line 25 of List 9.7 and line 26 of List 9.8 are the links to other datasets. As a result, these links have turned both these two RDF documents into newly produced linked data on the Linked Data Web.

In fact, changing the submitted review into structured data not only adds new elements to the Linked Data Web, but also makes it much easier for any application that attempts to consume the review results.

For example, to get the review for a given item, all the application has to do is to query the Revyu dataset by issuing SPARQL query via Revyu's SPARQL interface, and the result is an RDF document that can be easily processed. Compared to Amazon, where the review data has to be obtained by using its own APIs (Amazon

Web services), the benefit is quite obvious. We will come back to this point later this chapter.

Besides producing new linked data, Revyu also consumes existing linked data on the Web to enhance its user experience.

To see this, let us go back to line 25 of List 9.7 and line 26 of List 9.8. Since these statements are links that point to other linked datasets, one can simply apply the Follow-Your-Nose method to retrieve additional information about the reviewed item. In fact, this is exactly what Revyu has done. For example, by following the link on line 26 of List 9.8, Revyu was able to obtain this movie's entry in DBpedia, which contains the URI of the film's promotional poster, and the name of the director, etc. All this additional information is displayed on the page about this film, as shown in Fig. 9.19.

Clearly, this automatic consumption of the existing linked data has greatly enhanced the value of the whole site, without requiring this information to be manually entered by the reviewer.

Similarly, Revyu can fetch more information about the book from RDF Book Mashup dataset (line 25 of List 9.7), such as the book cover and author information, which is also displayed on the Revyu page about the book. Again, all this does not require any extra work from the reviewer, but it is very valuable to anyone who is reading these reviews.

Furthermore, the same idea can be applied to a reviewer. Recall that each reviewer is assigned a URI, and a simple RDF document is created for this reviewer. If a given reviewer has an existing FOAF document, an `rdfs:seeAlso` statement will be included in the RDF description. For example, List 9.9 shows the RDF document created for me by Revyu:

List 9.9 RDF statements generated by Revyu for a reviewer

```
1:  <?xml version="1.0" encoding="UTF-8" ?>
2:  <rdf:RDF
3:     xml:base="http://revyu.com/"
4:     xmlns:rdf="http://www.w3.org/1999/02/22-rdf-syntax-ns#"
5:     xmlns:rdfs="http://www.w3.org/2000/01/rdf-schema#"
6:     xmlns:xsd="http://www.w3.org/2001/XMLSchema#"
7:     xmlns:owl="http://www.w3.org/2002/07/owl#"
8:     xmlns:dc="http://purl.org/dc/elements/1.1/"
9:     xmlns:dcterms="http://purl.org/dc/terms/"
10:    xmlns:vcard="http://www.w3.org/2001/vcard-rdf/3.0#"
11:    xmlns:foaf="http://xmlns.com/foaf/0.1/"
12:    xmlns:rev="http://purl.org/stuff/rev#"
13:    xmlns:tag=
13a:        "http://www.holygoat.co.uk/owl/redwood/0.1/tags/">
14:
```

```
15:  <foaf:Person rdf:about="people/liyang">
16:    <foaf:mbox_sha1sum>
16a:       1613a9c3ec8b18271a8fe1f79537a7b08803d896
16b:   </foaf:mbox_sha1sum>
17:    <foaf:nick>liyang</foaf:nick>
18:    <foaf:made rdf:resource=
18a:        "reviews/cbe1fd43cf7de69ee0530fe65593d6d77d03daed"/>
19:    <foaf:made rdf:resource=
19a:        "reviews/436f699d347d433315507923664cf567fe872a59"/>
20:    <rdfs:seeAlso
20a:         rdf:resource="http://www.liyangyu.com/foaf.rdf"/>
21:  </foaf:Person>
22:
23:  </rdf:RDF>
```

Revyu will dereference the URI on line 20 and query the resulting FOAF document for information such as my photo, location, home page, interests, etc. This information then automatically shows up at my profile page without me entering them at all.

As a summary, Revyu is a simple and elegant application that makes use of existing linked data to enhance its user experience without asking for extra work from its users. Although it is not a large-scale linked data application, it does show us the benefits offered by the Web of Linked Data.

9.4.2   Web 2.0 Mashups vs. Linked Data Mashups

In the previous section, you saw an interesting application that consumes linked data on the Web. However, up to now, consuming linked data on the Web on a large scale still remains as an open question, and the business value of the Linked Data Web can be better appreciated only through these large-scale applications.

However, researchers and developers in the field of the Semantic Web are still very optimistic about its future, and one of the reasons is based on the comparison of the so-called Web 2.0 mashup to semantic mashup. In fact, if Web 2.0 mashups can continue to remain in high demand in the environment of the traditional Web, semantic mashups under the concept of the Semantic Web will sooner or later be the real data mashup tool that everyone will use, simply because it is much easier, much more efficient and much more scalable. The rest of this section explains this conclusion in detail.

Exactly what is a mashup? In a very simple sentence, a *mashup* is a Web application that collects structured data produced by third parties through APIs offered by these parties, and processes the data in some way and then represents the data back to users in a form that differs from its original look-and-feel. Normally, a mashup application either enhances the visual presentation of the data, or offers added value to its users by combining the data from different sources, or both. This concept is more related to Web 2.0, where more and more Web sites expose their data via their APIs.

A typical mashup could be something like this: a shopbot can be coded to retrieve the price of a given product (such as a camera with a specific make and model number) from Amazon.com by accessing its published APIs. At the same time, the same shopbot can also retrieve the price of the same product from BestBuy.com (assuming BestBuy has also published their APIs), and these two prices can be compared and returned to the user so the user can decide where to buy the product. The shopbot can even retrieve the prices from these two vendors periodically, so the user can see the change in these prices over a certain amount of time, and therefore can buy the product when its price has gone down and reached a relatively stable stage. Here the added value is obvious, and we can expand this shopbot in many ways, such as including more vendors and more products, etc.

This all sounds correct and feasible. However, when you really set off to construct such a shopbot, you will soon discover its limitations:

• Poor scalability of the method itself

Since different vendors publish different APIs, this is a constant learning process. You will have to learn each set of APIs, and once a new vendor is available, you will have to learn a new set of APIs again. Therefore, the construction of such a mashup is not scalable and its maintenance will be quite expensive as well.

• Limited coverage at most

Obviously, the shopbot only understands the APIs that you have coded for it to understand; it cannot do any simple exploration on its own. The data coverage is therefore very limited and, any decision based on this shopbot will probably not be optimal either.

• Lost links to channel back to the data providers

Once the data is retrieved and consumed by the shopbot, the link between the shopbot and the original data provider is lost; a user cannot link back to the original data-providing site. Even in the case where we have decided to put some links channeling back to the data providers, these are shallow links at best, and they will not be able to link back to the precise locations of those particular data components. In addition, a mashup site supported by this shopbot only shows the price, and what if the original site offers some free gifts if you buy it now? If there were a link back to this particular product, the user might be able to catch this offer. Even more importantly, the links that channel back to the original data provider mean more incoming traffic, which means significant chances for some potential business value.

Now, with all the above being said, let us take a look at what would be the case if a mashup application were developed under the environment of Linked Data Web.

In fact, Revyu is such a mashup: it retrieves data from external Web sites (DBpedia, RDF Book Mashup, etc.) to enhance its user experience, a typical way that a mashup should work. More specifically,

• Good scalability of the method itself

Under the Web of Linked Data, structured data is expressed by using RDF graphs and standards, which is the only set of standards across all the sites, and there are no specific APIs for each site to expose its structure data. Therefore, constructing the mashup and maintaining the mashup is quite scalable; there is no need to constantly learn new APIs.

• Unbounded coverage of datasets

Obviously, Web 2.0 mashups work against a fixed set of data sources, while Linked Data applications operate on top of an unbounded, global data space. This enables them to deliver more complete answers as new data sources appear on the Web.

• Crucial links to channel back to the data providers

In Linked Data mashups, all the items (resources) are identified by URIs, each of which may be minted and controlled by the data provider. If a user looks up one of these URIs, the user may be channeled back to the original data provider; it is then up to the data provider to publish appropriate content to further direct the incoming traffic. This linking-back capability is a key difference between Web 2.0 mashups and Linked Data mashups, and this is where the potential business value could be.

Besides the above, Linked Data mashups also offers their users a chance to chain up almost unlimited resources. More specifically, each item in the mashup is identified by a URI, which can be linked to other resources in other datasets, and the links themselves are also typed. As a result, you can choose to follow a specific link and visit a specific resource, which further takes you to other resources in other datasets, and so on. As this point, you should be able to appreciate the value of this unlimited linkage, without the need of much explanation at all.

9.5 Summary

In this chapter, we learned about Linked Open Data. It is another example of the Semantic Web technologies at work, and it is quite different from other examples we have learned. Instead of adding semantics to the current Web (either manually or automatically), its idea is to create a machine-readable Web from scratch. It is therefore also called the Web of Linked Data, or the Linked Data Web.

First, understand the following about Linked Open Data:

• Its basic concept and basic principles;
• Its relationship to the classic view of the Semantic Web, i.e., it can be viewed as an implementation of the vision of the Semantic Web.

Second, understand the two major topics about Linked Open Data: how to publish linked data on the Web and how to consume linked data on the Web.

You need to understand the following about how to publish linked data on the Web:

- How to mint URIs for resources, and the difference between 303 URIs and Hash URIs;
- How to create links to other datasets, and how to make sure your data is published as linked data, i.e., the minimal requirements for linked data on the Web;
- Remember to use a validator to make sure you have done everything correctly.

You need to understand the following about how to consume the linked data:

- Consuming linked data means discovering linked data on the Web, accessing the Web of Linked Data and building applications on top of the Web of Linked Data.
- There are semantic Web search engines you can use to discover linked data on the Web.
- There are Semantic Web browsers you can used to access the Web of Linked Data manually.
- You can also use SPARQL endpoints to access the Web of Linked Data, and in addition, you can programmatically access the Web of Linked Data from within your applications.
- The ultimate goal is to create powerful applications that make use of the Web of Linked Data.

Finally, to show you how to build applications on top of the Web of Linked Data, we have included Revyu as one such example. Make sure you understand how Revyu makes use of the linked data on the Web, and more importantly, let this serve as a hint to you, so you can come up with possible applications of your own to show the power of the Web of Linked Data.

Chapter 10
schema.org and Semantic Markup

Since schema.org is a joint effort by Google, Bing and Yahoo!, it has been viewed as a signal of mainstream support for the idea of the Semantic Web. As a well-accepted ontology for common things in life, since its first release in June 2011, it has been constantly making a significant difference in the application world. What does this mean to developers who work on the Semantic Web? What possibilities are now open for new applications and new ideas?

We briefly covered the topic of semantic markup in Chap. 7. Without the added structured data, the Semantic Web lacks the necessary component to go far.

In this chapter, schema.org, together with semantic markup, are discussed in depth. This will not only provide you with a sound understanding about schema.org and semantic markup, but will also show you again, the benefits and possibilities offered by Semantic Web technologies.

10.1 Introduction to schema.org

10.1.1 What Is schema.org?

By now, you understand that the Semantic Web world has only two founding components: the RDF data model and ontology. Once these two components are implemented, you will have a running version of the Semantic Web, or, a Web of Data.

RDF is important because it provides us with a model we can use to represent structured data in such a way that machines can mechanically operate on this data, to the extent that it gives us the feeling that machines can actually *understand* the

© Springer-Verlag Berlin Heidelberg 2014
L. Yu, *A Developer's Guide to the Semantic Web*,
DOI 10.1007/978-3-662-43796-4_10

data they are working with. At the current stage, for the implementation of the Semantic Web, the RDF data model and its implementation (RDF triples, RDF triplestores) are no longer a hurdle: billions of RDF triples exist in the real application world already, and the number is growing.

Ontology is important because it provides a set of *shared terms* that one actually needs to create RDF triples. Without ontology, RDF triples cannot be created with clearly defined meanings, and RDF triples cannot be integrated together to form a Web of Data. To see this, recall the FOAF ontology that we discussed in Chap. 7. Using the terms defined by FOAF ontology, anyone can create an RDF graph (of any size) to describe anyone, at any time. Without any further agreement, these distributed RDF graphs not only share the same clearly defined meanings, but can also be easily integrated together to discover facts that none of the single RDF graphs would be able to unveil.

However, as important as it is, the implementation of ontology, compared to the implementation of the RDF model, has not been smooth. There are simply too many issues to address. For example, who is responsible for creating these ontologies? How do we make sure a published ontology is acceptable to everyone? More importantly, how do we make sure the *mainstream* application world can accept and support these ontologies?

It might be helpful to take one step back and think about the reason why the current Web is such a success. It is actually quite simple: the current Web is successful because anyone, at any time, from anywhere, can publish anything on the Web, without much else needed. To see this, simply think about the popularity enjoyed by social networking sites today.

By the same token, for the Semantic Web to be a success, would it be nice, or almost necessary, that we could have just one single ontology, which actually covers all the common things in life? So anyone, at any time, from anywhere, can publish structured data about a movie, a tennis event, a place, a person, a recipe, a company, etc.? Would it be even nicer if the mainstream application world, at the same time, would accept this one single ontology, and actually support it?

To turn the idea of the Semantic Web into solid reality, this indeed might be the way to go. In other words, instead of focusing on domain-specific ontologies and trying to come up with the so-called killer applications, it might be much easier to create one such *common thing vocabulary* that everyone can understand and use, so that the benefits of the Semantic Web can be finally understood and appreciated by the general public.

On June 2, 2011, one such general vocabulary was announced and released. It is called *schema.org*,[1] and it was a joint effort by Google, Bing and Yahoo! On

---

[1] http://schema.org/

November 1, 2011, Yandex,[2] the largest search engine in Russia, also joined the effort.

From Google, Bing and Yahoo!'s point of view, schema.org is created as a vocabulary for structured data markup on Web pages. It can be understood as a centralized solution in the sense that content page authors just need to learn one such vocabulary, and major search engines just need to support one such vocabulary. The goal is to make sure search engines can start to understand the page content, and therefore can deliver better search performance. For example, search engines should be able to at least improve how these pages are presented in the search results.

From the Semantic Web's point of view, schema.org is an ontology that covers the general aspects of day-to-day life, and it is supported by the mainstream application world. This not only shows the fact that the Semantic Web idea is starting to get into the mainstream, but also that it offers more chances for further developments that are not limited to the search result presentations (for example, the LRMI project discussed in this chapter).

In this chapter, we first discuss the details of schema.org, and we then use two examples to show how schema.org is used in real-world applications. Again, it is important that these examples not only teach you more about the vision of the Semantic Web, but that they also serve as inspirations to your own ideas for applications on the Semantic Web.

10.1.2   Understanding the schema.org Vocabulary

First, everything about schema.org is in its official Website, which is given by the following URL,

http://schema.org

Also understand schema.org's core is its vocabulary, normally referred to as schema.org. When it comes to content markup, different syntaxes (or markup languages) can be selected and used, as discussed in details in Sect. 10.2.

As we discussed in Sect. 10.1.1, the goal of the schema.org vocabulary is to provide terms for all common aspects of our daily life, therefore it is not surprising that it tries to cover everything. More specifically, at this point, it has more than 100 categories, such as movies, music, TV shows, places, products and organizations, etc., covered by altogether about 350 classes. For this reason, the schema.org

---

vocabulary can also be understood as a broad, entry-level schema for the basics of many domains.

In fact, schema.org also grows by absorbing other ontologies. For example, on November 8, 2012, the GoodRelations[3] ontology was integrated into schema.org. More specifically, this means that the terms from GoodRelations ontology[4] are directly available from within schema.org, and one can therefore use all GoodRelations types and properties directly from the schema.org namespace in the markups.

With what we have learned from this book, understanding the schema.org vocabulary is quite straightforward. One way to study this ontology is that you can browse it on the schema.org Website, which provides two ways to look at it. One way is to view one class per page; the other is a full list of types (together with the properties for each type), on a single page.[5]

For developers who work in the Semantic Web development area, it is always more satisfactory to study the ontology in a more formal form, such as an OWL document. In fact, the whole schema.org vocabulary can be downloaded as an OWL document from this URL,

http://schema.org/docs/schemaorg.owl

Let us download the document and open it. As an example, List 10.1 shows the definition of the Event class.

List 10.1 Event class definition in schema.owl ontology

```
<owl:Class rdf:about="http://schema.org/Event">
   <rdfs:label xml:lang="en">Event</rdfs:label>
 <rdfs:subClassOf rdf:resource="http://schema.org/Thing"/>
 <rdfs:comment xml:lang="en">An event happening at a
   certain time at a certain location.</rdfs:comment>
 </owl:Class>
```

And List 10.2 shows the definition of property location, which can be used to describe an Event instance.

List 10.2 location property definition in schema.owl ontology

```
<owl:ObjectProperty rdf:about="http://schema.org/location">
   <rdfs:label xml:lang="en">location</rdfs:label>
   <rdfs:comment xml:lang="en">The location of the event or
                          organization.</rdfs:comment>
   <rdfs:range>
      <owl:Class>
         <owl:unionOf rdf:parseType="Collection">
           <rdf:Description rdf:about="http://schema.org/Place"/>
           <rdf:Description
                rdf:about="http://schema.org/PostalAddress"/>
         </owl:unionOf>
      </owl:Class>
   </rdfs:range>
   <rdfs:domain>
      <owl:Class>
         <owl:unionOf rdf:parseType="Collection">
            <rdf:Description
                rdf:about="http://schema.org/Event"/>
            <rdf:Description
                rdf:about="http://schema.org/Organization"/>
         </owl:unionOf>
      </owl:Class>
   </rdfs:domain>
</owl:ObjectProperty>
```

List 10.2 should look straightforward to you. Based on this definition, the location property can be used to describe an Event instance or an Organization instance, and its value has to be either a Place instance or a PostalAddress instance.

10.2   Content Markup Using schema.org

10.2.1   RDFa 1.1 Lite: A Simple Subset of RDFa

As we discussed in Sect. 10.1.2, schema.org only provides the terms (types and properties, to be more precise) one can use to mark up the page content document; it is yet another decision when it comes to what language to use to do the actual markup.

At this point, three different markup formats are supported: microformats, microdata and RDFa. We have covered microformats and RDFa in detail in Chap. 3, and microdata has been used and explained extensively as the example format at both schema.org's official site and Google's rich snippets help page (see Sect. 10.2.3). In this section, let us cover RDFa 1.1 *Lite* in more details, so your understanding of available markup formats will be complete.

Recall RDFa has been a W3C standard since October 2008, and it has been quite successful as a system for annotating HTML content on the Web (see Sect. 3.3 for full coverage of RDFa as a W3C standard). RDFa is also supported by Google and other search engines as one of the accepted formats for generating rich snippets.

Since the emergence of the schema.org initiative, especially due to the simplicity of microdata, there was a need to simplify RDFa even further for easy content markup. W3C took action and produced a simplified version for RDFa and called this *RDFa 1.1 Lite*.

RDFa Lite 1.1 became a W3C standard on June 7, 2012. You can find its standard document on the W3C official Web site.[6] In general, RDFa 1.1 Lite is a minimal subset of RDFa; it consists of a few attributes that may be used to express machine-readable data in Web content pages. It is probably the simplest standard that W3C has ever created.

Before we study the details of RDFa 1.1 Lite, understand that it is completely upwards compatible with the full set of RDFa 1.1 attributes. This means that if one finds that RDFa 1.1 Lite isn't powerful enough, transitioning to the full version of RDFa is just a matter of adding the more powerful RDFa attributes into the existing RDFa Lite markup.

RDFa 1.1 Lite has only five attributes: vocab, typeof, property, resource and prefix. Let us look at one markup example to see how these attributes should be used. List 10.3 shows a code snippet from my personal page, and will be used as the base HTML code for markup.

List 10.3 HTML code for markup examples

```
<!-- myself -->
<div>
<p>My name is Liyang Yu, I live in Atlanta, Georgia. I am
currently working as a software engineer at <a
href="http://www.delta.com">Delta Air Lines</a>, and I also work
with Carmen Hetrea on several Semantic Web issues for <a
href="http://www.britannica.com/">Encyclopedia Britannica</a>. We
both like photography as well.
</p>
</div>
```

---

[6] http://www.w3.org/TR/rdfa-lite/

For now, we would like to markup only the first half of the page. More specifically, we would like to say this is a person, his name is Liyang Yu, he lives in Atlanta, Georgia, and he works for Delta Air Lines as a software engineer.

The first step of the markup process is to choose a vocabulary to use. Theoretically speaking, to markup a Web content page, any ontology can be selected and used. However, since schema.org is supported by Google, Bing, Yahoo! and Yandex, and at least the immediate benefit is the rich snippets generated in the search result page, schema.org seems to be the first choice, if possible.

For our purpose, at least for now, schema.org is good enough. To indicate that schema.org is the vocabulary we will be using, we use the `vocab` attribute as follows, which also sets the stage in RDFa Lite:

```
<div vocab="http://schema.org/">
...
</div>
```

Note the `vocab` attribute is applicable to the whole `<div>` block. It is not necessary to use `<div>` all the time, for example, `<body>` is used often as well. Either way, an element that wraps all the markups should be selected and used.

Now, once we have specified the vocabulary, we need to specify the type of resource that is being marked up. In our case, we are talking about a person, and schema.org provides one such type, namely, `Person`. Therefore, we use `typeof` attribute as follows to tell search engines (or any other soft agent) that all the markups in this `<div>` block are about an instance whose type is `Person`,

```
<div vocab="http://schema.org/" typeof="Person">
...
</div>
```

With the above in place, all we need now is to use `property` attribute to add all the specific markups we would like to add. This is also the time to check schema.org to find all the attributes and types that you will need to use to markup a `Person` instance.

Figure 10.1 shows how schema.org defines `Person` and its properties (see http://schema.org/Person).

With help from Fig. 10.1, we understand that we will be using the `name`, `address`, `affiliation` and `jobTitle` (not included in Fig. 10.1) properties to finish our markup. Also note that both `name` and `jobTitle` are expecting simple text strings as values, while `address` and `affiliation` are expecting another type as values. More specifically, `address` takes a `PostalAddress` instance as its value, and `affiliation` takes an `Organization` instance as its value. In what follows, we will implement the markup by creating a `PostalAddress` instance as required by schema.org, however, we will use a simple text string as the value for `affiliation` property. We discuss why this is done in Sect. 10.2.3.

List 10.4 shows the markup we have.

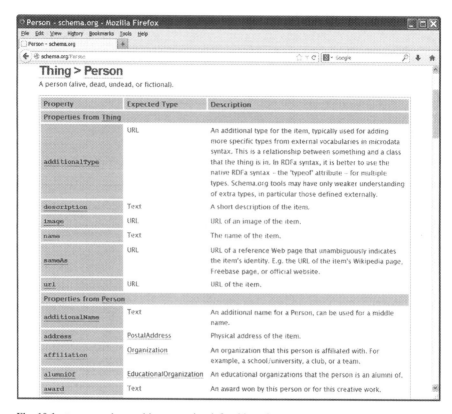

Fig. 10.1 Person class and its properties defined by schema.org

List 10.4 RDFa markup of List 10.3

```
<!-- myself -->
<div vocab="http://schema.org/" typeof="Person">
<p>My name is <span property="name">Liyang Yu</span>, I live in
<span rel="address">
   <span typeof="PostalAddress">
      <span property="addressLocality">Atlanta</span>,
      <span property="addressRegion">Georgia</span>.
   </span>
</span> I am currently working as a <span
property="jobTitle">software engineer</span> at
<a property="affiliation" href="http://www.delta.com">Delta Air
Lines</a>, and I also work with Carmen Hetrea on several Semantic
Web issues for <a href="http://www.britannica.com/">Encyclopedia
Britannica</a>. We both like photography as well.
</p>
</div>
```

With all that we have learned and said, List 10.4 does not need much explanation. Note that the <span> element is often used to add the markup, and it does not change the look-and-feel of the HTML page. Also, for a property that takes a text string as its value, @property is used (for example, name, jobTitle and affiliation). For the address property, @rel is used since it takes an instance of PostalAddress as its value. Again, you need to check schema.org page to know that to describe a PostalAddress instance, addressLocality and addressRegion can be used.

List 10.4 has quite a lot of markup data at this point. If you study the markups between <div> and </div>, you will realize that all the added markups are actually describing one *anonymous* resource—we don't know what this resource is, we only know it has name, jobTitle, address and affiliation. However, sometimes, it is important to explicitly name the resource, so the added markup data can be harvested and further integrated together with other markup data collected from other Web sites. This, of course, is vital for the Linked Data idea.

To explicitly name the resource, resource attribute is used, as shown in List 10.5.

List 10.5 RDFa markup of List 10.3 with resource attribute

```
<!-- myself -->
<div vocab="http://schema.org/"
resource="http://www.liyangyu.com/foaf.rdf#liyang" typeof="Person">
<p>My name is <span property="name">Liyang Yu</span>, I live in
<span rel="address">
  <span typeof="PostalAddress">
    <span property="addressLocality">Atlanta</span>,
    <span property="addressRegion">Georgia</span>.
  </span>
</span> I am currently working as a <span
property="jobTitle">software engineer</span> at
<a property="affiliation" href="http://www.delta.com">Delta Air
Lines</a>, and I also work with Carmen Hetrea on several Semantic
Web issues for <a href="http://www.britannica.com/">Encyclopedia
Britannica</a>. We both like photography as well.
</p>
</div>
```

This is the reason why RDFa 1.1 Lite provides the resource attribute. Note that for Google rich snippets, explicitly naming the underlying resource does not make any difference, as far as the generated rich snippets is concerned.

The last attribute we need to cover in RDFa 1.1 Lite is the prefix attribute, which is specifically designed for when we need to use more than one vocabulary in the markup.

Let us look at List 10.3 again. Understand that so far, we have added the markup for only the first half of the page. For second half of List 10.3, let us say we also would like to markup the fact that Liyang knows Carmen, whose workplace homepage is given by `http://www.britannica.com/`.

To accomplish this, schema.org is not enough. We would like to use FOAF (see Chap. 7) ontology, since it gives us enough terms to accomplish what we want to do. List 10.6 shows the new markup.

List 10.6 RDFa markup of List 10.3 with the added FOAF ontology

```
<!-- myself -->
<div vocab="http://schema.org/"
prefix="foaf:http://xmlns.com/foaf/0.1/"
resource="http://www.liyangyu.com/foaf.rdf#liyang"
typeof="Person">
<p>My name is <span property="name">Liyang Yu</span>, I live in
<span rel="address">
   <span typeof="PostalAddress">
      <span property="addressLocality">Atlanta</span>,
      <span property="addressRegion">Georgia</span>.
   </span>
</span> I am currently working as a <span
property="jobTitle">software engineer</span> at
<a property="affiliation" href="http://www.delta.com">Delta Air
Lines</a>, and I also work with
<span rel="foaf:knows">
   <span typeof="foaf:Person">
      <span property="foaf:name">Carmen Hetrea</span> on several
Semantic Web issues for <a property="foaf:workplaceHomepage"
href="http://www.britannica.com/">Encyclopedia Britannica</a>.
   </span>
</span> We both like photography as well.
</p>
</div>
```

List 10.6 does not require much explanation either. As usual, the `vocab` attribute specifies schema.org; meanwhile, the `prefix` attribute is used to introduce FOAF ontology, and prefix `foaf` is used as the shortcut for the FOAF ontology. Furthermore, `foaf:knows`, `foaf:Person`, `foaf:name` and `foaf:workplaceHomepage` are used to finish the markup.

In fact, List 10.6 can enjoy a little improvement: there is no need to use the `vocab` attribute at all; one can simply use the `prefix` attribute to register all the needed ontologies (there can be more than two if needed), and then use their respective prefixes to make reference to each vocabulary as needed. This is shown in List 10.7.

List 10.7 Final RDFa markup of List 10.3

```
<!-- myself -->
<div prefix="schema:http://schema.org/
foaf:http://xmlns.com/foaf/0.1/"
resource="http://www.liyangyu.com/foaf.rdf#liyang"
typeof="schema:Person">
<p>My name is <span property="schema:name">Liyang Yu</span>, I
live in
<span rel="schema:address">
   <span typeof="schema:PostalAddress">
      <span property="schema:addressLocality">Atlanta</span>,
      <span property="schema:addressRegion">Georgia</span>.
   </span>
</span> I am currently working as a <span
property="schema:jobTitle">software engineer</span> at
<a property="schema:affiliation"
href="http://www.delta.com">Delta Air Lines</a>, and I also work
with
<span rel="foaf:knows">
   <span typeof="foaf:Person">
      <span property="foaf:name">Carmen Hetrea</span> on several
Semantic Web issues for
      <a property="foaf:workplaceHomepage"
href="http://www.britannica.com/">Encyclopedia Britannica</a>.
   </span>
</span> We both like photography as well.
</p>
</div>
```

At this point, we have finished our coverage of RDFa Lite. In the next section, let us discuss another important issue: which markup format should one use for the markup task?

10.2.2   What Markup Format to Use?

There has been a long debate over the issue of which format to use for content markup: microdata or RDFa. It might be fair to say that microdata and RDFa will coexist for a long time yet to come. However, for developers who are interested in the development work on the Semantic Web, this section attempts to offer some considerations about what would be a better choice in the long run.

Google's recommendation has been microdata, largely due to the fact that RDFa is not as simple as microdata for content developers to grasp. As we discussed in Sect. 10.2.1, W3C greatly simplified RDFa; its much simpler version, RDFa 1.1 Lite was released as a W3C standard on June 7, 2012. In fact, on the same day, Google announced that besides RDFa, they would support RDFa Lite for schema. org as well.[7] A recent study by Mika and Potter (2012) showed that RDFa has been growing quite steadily and significantly among the three markup formats.

For semantic Web developers, we recommend RDFa, and this recommendation is based on the following considerations.

First and foremost, RDFa is compatible with all the other RDF-based standards. This is extremely important if the goal is to develop applications on the Semantic Web, which goes far beyond the scope of search result enhancement such as rich snippets.

Second, RDFa and RDFa 1.1 Lite are both W3C standards, while microdata is still a working draft,[8] dated October 25, 2012. And finally, RDFa and RDFa 1.1 Lite make it very easy to work with multiple ontologies, and they offer better support for datatypes as well.

The considerations listed above sometimes could imply a better environment for further application development on the Semantic Web. For example, BestBuy has been using RDFa to add semantic data into their page content, and Facebook only supports RDFa, not microdata.

10.2.3   Type Checking and Other Issues

Before we move on to the more exciting application examples of schema.org and semantic markup, we need to discuss several issues that one should be aware of. Having a clear understanding of these issues will certainly help us to create structured data that is more likely to be useful, and not simply ignored.

- Value type checking

The first of these issues is type checking. Let us take Fig. 10.1 as one such example, where class `Person` is shown in detail. As we discussed in Sect. 10.2.1, property `address` takes an instance whose type is `PostalAddress` as its value, and property `affiliation` takes an instance whose type is `Organization` as its value. With the understanding of these required types, one should expect to see an `Organization` instance being used in List 10.7 for `affiliation`, just as a

---

[7] http://blog.schema.org/2012/06/semtech-rdfa-microdata-and-more.html

[8] http://www.w3.org/TR/microdata/

`PostalAddress` instance has been used for `address`. However, a simple text string has been provided for the `affiliation` property instead.

This is indeed an error in List 10.7. Theoretically, all the markups should follow the schema as we have just discussed. However, in real practice, by the spirit of "some data is better than none", this kind of violation is expected and even accepted. For developers like you and me, we should always do our best to study the ontology and understand the required types, and implement the markup as best as we can.

- What to markup, and how much is enough?

If you study schema.org, you will find that for each class, there are often quite a few properties used to describe it. For example, class `Person` has more than 50 properties. So how many properties should you use when marking up content? What we have done in List 10.7 seems to be quite arbitrary—there are still things we can markup, yet we have not.

Markup is not an all-or-nothing choice, and what to markup and what not to markup heavily depends on the purpose of the markup. More specifically, if the goal is to make sure those major search engines can generate rich snippets for your page, then for each content type (such as people, review, event, etc.), you will have to make sure you have at least marked up the required properties (see more detailed discussion in Sect. 10.3.2.3). Once you have marked up all the required properties, it is then up to you to decide whether to markup the nonrequired properties or not.

On the other hand, if your markup is more geared toward your own specific application running on the Semantic Web, then the decision of what to markup heavily depends on the requirements and the goal of your specific application. For one such example, see Chap. 17.

- Visible content vs. nonvisible content

If you are marking up content for those major search engines to read (for example, to generate rich snippets), a general rule is that you should mark up only the content that is visible to people who visit the Web and page, and not the content in hidden `div`'s or other hidden page elements.

As a matter of fact, coding markup data into existing HTML elements can be very complicated, and often cannot be done automatically. Therefore, creating additional blocks with pure, invisible RDFa or microdata markup (so-called *invisible markup*) has many advantages, and can be a very attractive solution to many of us. For a detailed discussion, see Hepp et al. (2009).

Major search engine companies are aware of the advantages offered by invisible markup. The reason why invisible markup is forbidden is mainly because of the potential risk of spam. For now, we should follow this rule and avoid invisible content markup.

There are indeed some exceptions to this rule. For example, Geographic information, such as latitude and longitude of an event location, can be marked up using invisible content. In general, this kind of information is not visible on a Web page about an event, but providing it helps to ensure the location of the event can be accurately mapped. More specifically, this is often implemented by using `<span typeof="Geo">`, and `content` attributes are then used to specify the latitude and longitude information. For more detailed discussion of these exceptions, check Google's rich snippet help page, as discussed in Sect. 10.3.2.3.

• Marking up dates and time

The final issue we want to discuss here is about the markup of dates and times. More specifically, dates and times can be difficult for machines to understand. For example, 01/11/2013—does this mean January 11, 2013, or does this mean November 1, 2013? To avoid this ambiguity, we should also use the `content` attribute to clearly markup the date, as shown by the following example:

```
<span property="v:startDate" content="2014-08-25">
         <time datetime="2014-08-25">August 25, 2014</time>
```

Obviously, marking up content pages can be quite complex and can have many issues in practice. It is not quite possible for us to cover all the potential issues one might encounter in real life. Again, it is always helpful to check the related documents on Web sites, as shown in Sect. 10.3.2.3.

10.2.4 Validating Your Markup

In Sect. 10.2.1, we discussed semantic markup using RDFa 1.1 Lite with schema.org in great detail, and we used one example to show the markup process. The final finished content page is shown in List 10.7. The question is, how do we make sure our markup is correct and the added structured data can be successfully picked by Web applications?

Ideally, one would hope that there are tools that can help us to validate our markup. One such validation tool was developed by Ivan Herman and is hosted by W3C, and can be accessed by using the following URL,

http://www.w3.org/2012/pyRdfa/

It is called *RDFa 1.1 Distiller and Parser*, and keep in mind, it is only capable of extracting RDFa markups from the submitted content page.

Figure 10.2 shows the look-and-feel of this validation tool. To use it, simply provide the URL of the content page, or use Direct Text Input, as shown in Fig. 10.2.

To run the validator, List 10.7 is uploaded to the author's Web server, as shown in Fig. 10.2. Keep all the values at their default values and click `Go!`, and a file named `extract` will be generated. This file contains all the RDF triples that are successfully extracted from the content page submitted, and these triples should be presented in Turtle format, as specified by the Output Format option (Fig. 10.2).

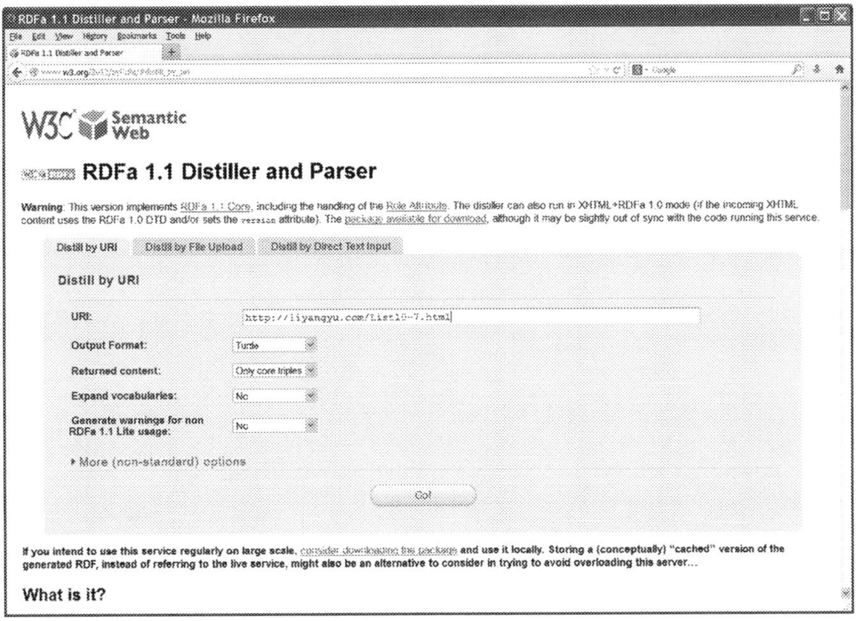

Fig. 10.2 RDFa 1.1 distiller and parser

To validate whether the markup is correctly done, we need to inspect the generated file to see if it has all the triples that we expect to see. List 10.8 shows the content of `extract` file:

List 10.8 Extracted RDF triples in Turtle format, by RDFa 1.1 distiller and parser

```
@prefix foaf: <http://xmlns.com/foaf/0.1/> .
@prefix schema: <http://schema.org/> .

<http://www.liyangyu.com/foaf.rdf#liyang> a schema:Person;
    schema:address [ a schema:PostalAddress;
            schema:addressLocality "Atlanta";
            schema:addressRegion "Georgia" ];
    schema:affiliation <http://www.delta.com>;
    schema:jobTitle "software engineer";
    schema:name "Liyang Yu";
    foaf:knows [ a foaf:Person;
                foaf:name "Carmen Hetrea";
                foaf:workplaceHomepage
                    <http://www.britannica.com/> ] .
```

The triples shown in List 10.8 are indeed what we expected to see, and our markup is successfully done.

Again, it is always a good idea to run your markup against a validation tool like this; that way, you can rest assured that everything is done correctly on your side, and it is now up to the applications to pick up the structured data correctly.

10.3   Content Markup Example 1: Google Rich Snippets

Schema.org, as we have discussed, is proposed as an ontology that can be used for Web page content markup. Its advantage over other ontologies lies in the fact that the structured markup data created by using schema.org is guaranteed to be recognizable by all major search engines.

Based on the research conducted by Bizer et al. (2013), schema.org has gained significant popularity, even just 6 months after its release. More specifically, Bizer et al. crawled 3 billion Web pages during the first half of 2012, and found 369 million out of the 3 billion pages (about 12.3 %) contained structured markup data, and schema.org was widely adopted as the vocabulary used for the markup.

For Semantic Web developers, the really interesting question is, how is the added markup information being used? In the next two sections of this chapter, we study two examples, namely, Google's rich snippets and the LRMI project. These examples will not only answer the question well, but also can hopefully be the inspiration for more interesting ideas from you.

10.3.1   What Is Rich Snippets: An Example

A user's direct experience with any search engine comes from the search result page. This not only includes how relevant the results are to the submitted query, but also the search result presentation. As far as the search result presentation is concerned, the goal is to summarize and describe each individual result page in such a way that it gives the user a clear indication of how relevant this current page is to the original search.

For a user-submitted query, Google returns the search result in the form of a collection of pages. In order to help the user to locate the result quickly and easily, for each page in this collection, Google shows a small sample of the page content. This small sample is often called a *page snippet*.

Google introduced the so-called *Rich Snippets* to the world on May 12, 2009. This is a new presentation of the snippets resulting from using the related Semantic Web technology, as we will see in the next section. For now, let us take a look at one such example.

If you search for "singin in the rain" using Google, you will get the result as shown in Fig. 10.3:

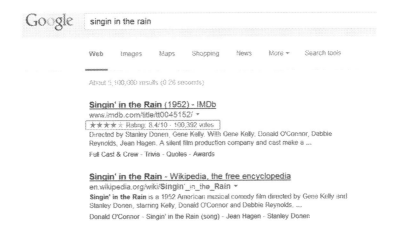

Fig. 10.3 Rich snippets example when searching for "singin in the rain"

In Fig. 10.3, the rating stars, the actual rating (8.4/10) and the number of votes (100,392), as shown in the red box, are together the rich snippet. As a comparison, the next result, i.e., the one from the Wikipedia, does not contain any rich snippet. To put it more formally, rich snippets are the lines of additional information that appear under a search result, and are designed to give users a sense of what's on the page and why it is relevant to their query.

If you are following along, you can actually click the first result, and land on the IMDB page (in this case, the page is given by URL http://www.imdb.com/title/tt0045152/). Place your mouse in the page, right click, and then select View Page Source; you will be able to see the code behind this page. Note the following lines in the code,

```
<div    class="star-box-details"    itemtype="http://schema.org/
AggregateRating" itemscope itemprop="aggregateRating">
Ratings:
<strong><span  itemprop="ratingValue">8.4</span></strong><span
class="mellow">/<span itemprop="bestRating">10</span></span>
```

This is what has made all the difference. If you check the related Wikipedia page in Fig. 10.3, you will not find the same markup as above. For now, do not worry about these lines; you will understand them completely when you finish this chapter.

Obviously, the rich snippets in Fig. 10.3 give a user a more convenient summary of information about the search results at a glance. More specifically in this case, the review rating and the number of votes are clearly shown, which are the most important information a user needs when deciding about the quality of a movie.

Figure 10.4 shows another example of rich snippets. Again, the information in the red box is the rich snippets.

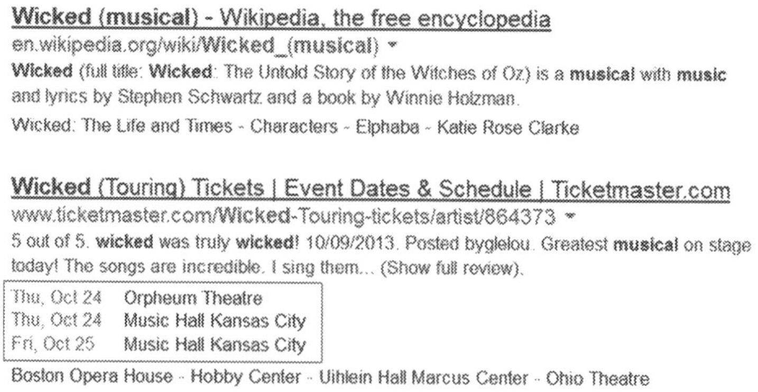

Wicked (musical) - Wikipedia, the free encyclopedia
en.wikipedia.org/wiki/Wicked_(musical) ▾
Wicked (full title: **Wicked**: The Untold Story of the Witches of Oz) is a **musical** with **music**
and lyrics by Stephen Schwartz and a book by Winnie Holzman.
Wicked: The Life and Times - Characters - Elphaba - Katie Rose Clarke

Wicked (Touring) Tickets | Event Dates & Schedule | Ticketmaster.com
www.ticketmaster.com/Wicked-Touring-tickets/artist/864373 ▾
5 out of 5. **wicked** was truly **wicked**! 10/09/2013. Posted by glelou. Greatest **musical** on stage
today! The songs are incredible. I sing them... (Show full review).

Thu, Oct 24	Orpheum Theatre
Thu, Oct 24	Music Hall Kansas City
Fri, Oct 25	Music Hall Kansas City

Boston Opera House - Hobby Center - Uihlein Hall Marcus Center - Ohio Theatre

Fig. 10.4   Rich snippets example when search for "wicked the musical"

If you are curious enough to check the code behind the page, you will see
`http://schema.org/Event` is used.

The benefit of having rich snippets in the Search Engine Results Pages (SERPs) is quite straightforward to understand. In fact, high ranking along in SERPs are no longer enough. Rich snippets are part of increasingly enhanced SERPs designed to help people make decisions before they click. It has been working quite well since it draws a user's attention to your relevant result, and it also provides instant information; therefore the user knows what to expect before accessing the site. These two together imply more click-throughs to the sites with rich snippets and more qualified visitors who are likely to stay on the site longer.

In fact, many companies have seen a 20–30 % increase in click-through rates (CTR) when using rich snippets.[9] For example, Jay Myers, Lead Web Development Engineer at BestBuy.com, has reported a 30 % increase in search traffic.[10]

Now, how are rich snippets related to the Semantic Web? And how does Google gather the information to create rich snippets? Let us answer these questions in the next section.

10.3.2   Google Rich Snippets: Semantic Markup Using schema.org

10.3.2.1   The Basic Flow of Rich Snippets

To fully understand how rich snippets work and how they fit into the search world, some understanding of the basic flow of a search engine is needed. Chapter 17 of this book describes a project that creates a search engine, which further supports

---

[9] http://yoast.com/rich-snippets-everywhere/

[10] http://www.slideshare.net/jaymmyers/myers-jay-rev

rich snippets. If you don't have much background in search engines, now is a good time to review the first few sections of Chap. 17, just to understand how a search engine works.

With that knowledge, it is not hard to realize that improving the quality of search result presentation is not an easy task. In general, an automatically generated abstract for a given page often provides a poor overview of the page. More specifically, when a search engine indexes the words contained in a page, it normally picks up the text contained in the immediate area where the query keywords are found, and returns this text as the page summary. This obviously is not always a reliable way to describe an individual page. In addition, tables or images have to be removed from the page summary, due to the fact that there are no reliable algorithms to automatically recognize and select the appropriate images or tables. The end result is that the page summaries on the SERPs are often not much help to the end users.

The idea of rich snippets is therefore suggested to enhance the presentation of the search results: a few lines of information are added on the result page. They not only show the core information about the page, but also tell the user why the content of the page is relevant to the submitted query. The implementation of rich snippets is quite straightforward as well: they are created by using the structured data embedded in Web pages, and the structured data is added by content authors like you and me, by using the process known as semantic markup.

More specifically, the crawler stills work as usual, i.e., traveling from page to page and downloading the page content along its way. However, the indexer's work has changed quite a bit: when indexing a given page, it also looks for the markup formats the search engine supports. Once some embedded markups are found, they will be collected and will be used to generate the rich snippets later at the search time.

To generate the rich snippets, a presentation format that will be helpful to its users has to be decided. For example, what information should be included and shown in the snippets? In what order should this information be shown?

What a search engine has is the collected markups. In general, the final format a search engine uses to store these markups remains unknown to the outside world. These collected markups can be expressed in RDF statements, or some other format that a particular search engine has invented and used internally. However, no matter what the format is, these structured data can always be expressed in the form of name–value pairs.

Obviously, these name–value pairs are ultimately created by millions of Web page authors all over the world. Therefore, there is very little consistency exhibited by these pairs. For example, some of these pairs are reviews of a product, some are about people, some are about a trip to Shanghai and some are about a tennis match, just to name a few. Thus, if all these pairs were to be considered, it would be very difficult to find a uniform way to present the information, i.e., generate the rich snippets.

In general, two solutions can be considered to solve this problem. The first solution is to limit the *type*s of markups a user can add; therefore the variety of the name–value pairs is limited. This implies that a more uniform and consistent snippet can be created automatically by the search engine itself.

The second option is to allow the markup of any type of item a user would like to markup. However, the user also has to tell the search engine how to use the embedded structure data to generate a presentation format for the rich snippet.

These two are obviously quite different solutions. Google has decided to use the first solution, and that is the reason why Google has to limit the content types it supports. For example, at the time of this writing, Google supports the markup of event, people, products and a few others. For a complete list, see Sect. 10.3.2.2. In addition, for each content type, there is a list of required fields. For example, if an event is the item that is being marked up, then the name of the event and the starting date of the event are among those fields that are required. Again, see Sect. 10.3.2.2 for more details. The benefit of these limitations, as we have discussed, is that a user only has to add the markup information, and does not have to do anything regarding the presentation at all.

10.3.2.2   Markup for Rich Snippets: Basic Steps

There are several steps to take when you decide to markup content for Google rich snippets. These steps are:

- Decide if Google is currently supporting the items you would like to markup.
- Decide which markup format you would like to use (microdata, microformats and RDFa).
- Implement the actual markup for your content.
- Test it using Google's testing tool.

When you are done with the above, it will be Google's turn—when Google discovers the new markup on your site, it will begin reading the markup tags and displaying the rich snippets for your site within the SERPs. For the rest of this section, we discuss the above steps in detail.

First off, you need to decide for your specific topic, whether Google has a rich snippet support for it or not. At the time of this writing, Google supports rich snippets for these content types:

- reviews
- people
- products
- business and organizations
- recipes
- events
- music

For examples of reviews and events, see Sect. 10.2.1. If your content type does not belong the above list, you will have to wait for Google to support it, hopefully at a later time.

When it comes to markup format, Google supports microdata, microformats and RDFa. Google suggests using microdata, but any of the three is acceptable. For example, BestBuy's rich snippet markup is all done by using RDFa. For this book, we will be mainly using RDFa. For a comprehensive comparison and discussion, see Tennison (2012).

The last two steps, i.e., markup the content and test the markup by using Google's structured testing tool, are discussed in the next section by using examples. For now, let us discuss one very important issue: what ontology should we use when marking up the content for rich snippets?

If microformats is used for the markup, there is indeed a limitation about what vocabularies you can use. You will have to use only the ontologies supported by the language constructs of microformats. On the other hand, if microdata or RDFa markup language is selected, any ontology can be used, due to the fact that both RDFa and microdata have a unified parsing model. This can be easily tested by using Google's rich snippet testing tool—you will see the structured information created by the markup is always correctly extracted, regardless of what underlying vocabulary is being used.

Although Google is able to parse microdata or RDFa markup for any ontology, it still simply bases its rich snippets only on schema.org. For example, no matter how well the FOAF markup is created in your content page, Google will not produce a rich snippet for it. Therefore, in real practice, at least at this stage, always use schema.org, which is guaranteed to be recognizable by Google, Bing and Yahoo. Looking into the future, it is more likely that schema.org will grow to fit more content topics than the possibility that more ontologies will be adopted and supported.

Finally, understand rdf.data-vocabulary.org is recognized by Google as well, but schema.org is simply a more current version and should replace rdf.data-vocabulary.org whenever possible.

10.3.2.3   Markup for Rich Snippets: Examples by RDFa

Let us use one example in this section to demonstrate the markup process. We will be using RDFa to markup an event content type; all the important issues for creating a correct markup are discussed in detail. The guidelines here are equally applicable when marking up a different content type by using a different markup formats.

List 10.9 shows the simple content page, which describes the 2014 US Open Tennis Championship, in New York City.

List 10.9 A simple content page for US Open Tennis Championships event

```
<!DOCTYPE html>
  <head>
    <title>2014 US Open Tennis Championships - A USTA
Event</title>
  </head>
  <body id="doc">
    <h1>US Open 2014</h1>

    <!-- Event: US Open 2014 -->
    <div>
      <h2><a href="http://www.usopen.org/index.html">2014 US Open
Tennis Championships</a></h2>
      <p>The United States Open Tennis Championships is a
hardcourt tennis tournament which is the modern iteration of one
of the oldest tennis championships in the world, the U.S.
National Championship, for which men's singles was first
contested in 1881.</p>
      <div>
        BJK Tennis Center, New York City, New York
      </div>
      <div>
        <time datetime="2014-08-25">August 25, 2014</time>
&ndash;
        <time datetime="2014-09-08">September 8, 2014</time>
      </div>
    </div>

  </body>
</html>
```

As simple as it is, this content page describes the name of the event, the location and time of the event, for the year of 2014.

Now we are ready to add the markup using RDFa. We know we will use the terms from schema.org, and `http://schema.org/Event` will be the class type. Let us open schema.org and check out all the properties that can be used to describe an event instance.

At the time of this writing, there are 18 properties one can use to describe an event instance. For example, `url`, `name`, `location`, `startDate`, just to name a few. Obviously, it is neither necessary nor possible to use every one of these properties.

Therefore, the first thing to do, is to decide which properties we would like to use for the markup, and this decision has to be made by looking at the content page as well—whatever properties we select to use, the content page has to have the information for those selected properties.

In fact, for any content type (certainly including event type), it is always the case that some properties are simply *required* by Google for the rich snippets to be generated. In other words, regardless of the content type being considered, it is always necessary to check out the Google rich snippets guideline page, to find out what the required properties are for the content type at hand.

To do so, let us go to Google's rich snippet starting page, given by the following URL,

https://support.google.com/webmasters/answer/99170

On the left pane of the page, you will see `Rich snippets types` link. Clicking this link takes you to the next page, which lists all the supported types. Since we are marking up an event content type, find the event type, and click it. This takes you to the rich snippet *event* guideline page.

Note that the page links and content we have just described are all part of Google's `Webmaster Tools`. Google constantly updates the content in its `Webmaster Tools` page; therefore at the time you are reading this, you might have to probe around to find the correct link and content.

Once we are on the event guideline page, we can find out the required properties for marking up an event content type. More specifically, these properties are:

- `summary`
- `url`
- `location`
- `startDate`

Understand these property names are microdata property names, which could be different from those in schema.org. In fact, for event type, there is no property named `summary` in schema.org; the corresponding property in schema.org is called `name`.

At this point, let us first add the markup that uses `name`, `url`, `location` and `startDate`, since these are the required properties for the rich snippet to be generated. List 10.10 shows the detailed markup.

List 10.10 Markup of the content page shown in List 10.9 (first cut, *added markup in bold*)

```
<!DOCTYPE html>
  <head>
    <title>2014 US Open Tennis Championships - A USTA
Event</title>
  </head>
  <body id="doc">
    <h1>US Open 2014</h1>

    <!-- Event: US Open 2014 -->
    <div xmlns:schema="http://schema.org/" typeof="schema:Event">
      <h2><a href="http://example.com/usopen.org/index.html"
rel="schema:url"><span property="schema:name">2014 US Open Tennis
Championships</span></a></h2>
      <p>The United States Open Tennis Championships is a
hardcourt tennis tournament which is the modern iteration of one
of the oldest tennis championships in the world, the U.S.
National Championship, for which men's singles was first
contested in 1881.</p>
      <div property="schema:location">
        BJK Tennis Center, New York City, New York
      </div>
      <div>
       <span property="schema:startDate" content="2014-08-25">
        <time datetime="2014-08-25">August 25, 2014</time>
&ndash;
       </span>
       <span property="schema:endDate" content="2014-09-08">
        <time datetime="2014-09-08">September 8, 2014</time>
       </span>
      </div>
    </div>

  </body>
</html>
```

Note we first use the xmlns attribute to declare a namespace, which indicates the namespace where the ontology is specified. More specifically, this specifies that schema.org is the vocabulary that is in use. Also, schema is used as the abbreviation (prefix) for this vocabulary; any term with the format of schema:termName is therefore known to be a term taken from schema.org. In addition, typeof attribute is used to indicate that the marked-up content describes an event.

It is totally acceptable to begin the markup by using this line,

```
<div vocab="http://schema.org/" typeof="Event">
```

This uses the `vocab` attribute to specify the ontology being used, and since there is no prefix for the namespace, the term taken from schema.org has no prefix attached. We recommend the markup in List 10.10 since it is more readable and clearer: anyone reading this markup will be able to easily understand which term is taken from where.

Another important issue is about the value type of the markup. Recall in an RDF statement, we have subject, predicate and object. The value of the object could be either a simple value, or another resource. For a given property used in the markup, if the value of the property is a simple value, attribute `property` should be used in the markup; otherwise, attribute `rel` should be used, indicating the value of the property is another resource.

An example of attribute `rel` is seen from `schema:url` property. Since the value of this property is another resource (identified by URL `http://example.com/usopen.org/index.html`), `rel` is used. For all the other markups, since the property values are all simple text strings, attribute `property` is used. For example, the event name, 2014 US Open Tennis Championships, is marked up by using `schema:name`, and the location of the event is marked by using `schema:location` property.

In general, when adding the markup, we should try to reuse the content existing in the page as much as possible. For example, `schema:name` and `schema:location` are all reusing the existing content on the page. If the existing content on the page does not fulfill the needs, we must use the `content` attribute to specify the needed value in the markup. For example, for `schema:startDate` and `schema:endDate`, we must use the `content` attribute to specify the date in the format that Google rich snippets can accept (see Sect. 10.2.3).

Another interesting piece is the URL given by `http://example.com/usopen.org/index.html`. Yes, it should be `http://usopen.org/index.html`, and we will explain this in the next section. For now, simply take the value as it is.

At this point, we have added all the required properties (with `schema:endDate` as any extra property). We also decided not to use any other properties from schema.org, so we can therefore claim we have finished the first cut of the markup.

In fact, reading the Google event guideline, you will find that `schema:location` property may need some extra work. More specifically, it is acceptable to use a text string as the value of this property (as seen in List 10.10), but it is recommended that a resource of type `Organization` should be used to specify a venue name and address. For a better rich snippet presentation in the final search result page, let us further accomplish this requirement.

However, as specified by schema.org, `schema:location` can accept two values: an instance whose type is `schema:Place`, or an instance with type `schema:PostalAddress`, and `schema:Organization` should not be its type. So why is there this discrepancy?

Actually, this guideline is referring to rdf.data-vocabulary.org as the vocabulary, which can be considered as an earlier version of schema.org, but not to schema.org itself. We should always go with schema.org if possible. We have modified List 10.10, and its newer version is now shown in List 10.11.

List 10.11 Markup of the content page shown in List 10.9 (newer version, *added markup in bold*)

```
<!DOCTYPE html>
  <head>
    <title>2014 US Open Tennis Championships - A USTA
Event</title>
  </head>
  <body id="doc">
    <h1>US Open 2014</h1>

    <!-- Event: US Open 2014 -->
    <div xmlns:schema="http://schema.org/" typeof="schema:Event">
      <h2><a href="http://example.com/usopen.org/index.html"
rel="schema:url"><span property="schema:name">2014 US Open Tennis
Championships</span></a></h2>
      <p>The United States Open Tennis Championships is a
hardcourt tennis tournament which is the modern iteration of one
of the oldest tennis championships in the world, the U.S.
National Championship, for which men's singles was first
contested in 1881.</p>
        <div rel="schema:location">
          <span typeof="schema:Place">
            <span property="schema:name">BJK Tennis Center</span>
            <span rel="schema:address">
              <span typeof="schema:PostalAddress">
                <span property="schema:addressLocality">New York
City</span>,
                <span property="schema:addressRegion">New
York</span>
              </span>
            </span>
          </span>
        </div>
        <div>
         <span property="schema:startDate" content="2014-08-25">
         <time datetime="2014-08-25">August 25, 2014</time> -
         </span>
         <span property="schema:endDate" content="2014-09-08">
         <time datetime="2014-09-08">September 8, 2014</time>
         </span>
        </div>
    </div>

  </body>
</html>
```

With the discussion about List 10.10 in place, it is fairly straightforward to understand List 10.11. Note the new vocabulary and its new namespace; also note how v:Organization is used to specify a venue name (v:name) and address (v: Address) for the given event. Finally, understand v:summary has replaced v:name, since in rdf.data-vocabulary.org, there is a v:summary property for the type v: Event, but not v:name.

At this point, we have finished the markup for our simple 2014 US Open Tennis Championships content page. The process we have discussed here is applicable to other content types, and it is always a good idea to check on the Google rich snippet guideline page, as we have shown here.

The last step of the markup process is to run the markup against Google's snippet testing tool, just to make sure the markup can be generated successfully. Let us cover this topic in the next section.

10.3.3   Using Google Rich Snippets Testing Tool

Now that we have finished marking up our content, we are ready for the last step— test it by using Google's rich snippet testing tool.

At the time of this writing, this testing tool is hosted at this URL,

http://www.google.com/webmasters/tools/richsnippets

Figure 10.5 shows the look-and-feel of this tool.

There are two ways to specify the source content page. One is to use the URL of the content file, and the other is to directly paste the content into the HTML textbox.

To specify the URL of the content file actually requires your content document to have been published on a server already. As one such example, let us use the "singin in the rain" page, which has the following URL, http://www.imdb.com/title/ tt0045152/. Enter this URL into the URL textbox, then hit PREVIEW, and you will see the screen as shown in Fig. 10.6.

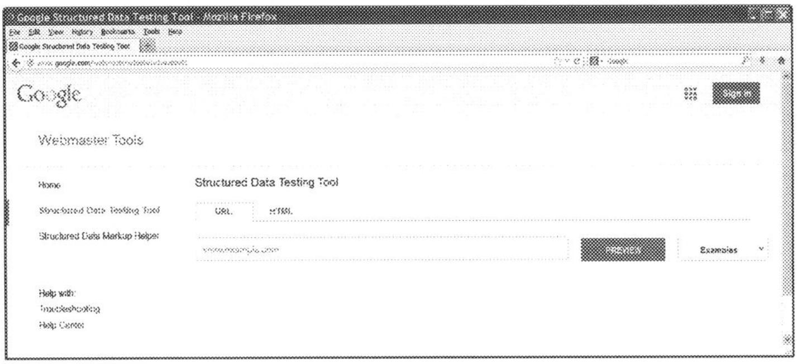

Fig. 10.5 Rich snippets testing tool provided by Google

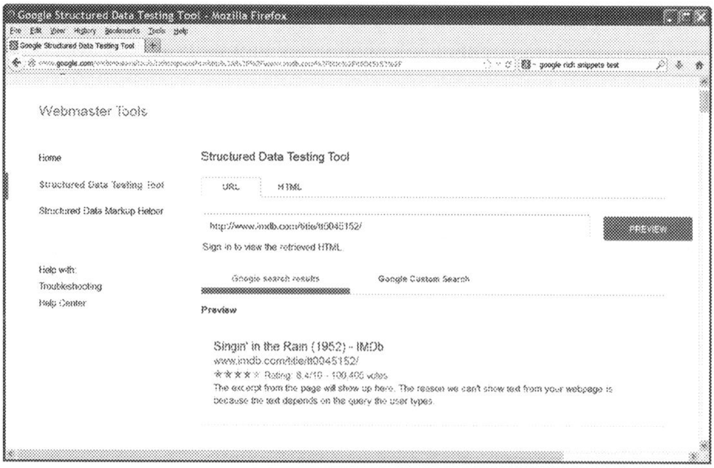

Fig. 10.6 Rich snippets preview of "singin in the rain" on imdb.com

As shown in Fig. 10.6, the rich snippet preview is exactly what is shown today on the search result page (compare this to Fig. 10.3). Also, take a look at the structured data extracted from the page by the testing tool (under the `Extracted structured data` section), and you will see schema.org is used for all the markups.

Another way to test is to simply paste your document into the HTML textbox. This is quite useful, especially when the content document has not been published on a server yet. To see one such example, let us paste the markup we have just finished (as shown in List 10.11), and hit the `PREVIEW` button. Figure 10.7 shows the result.

The last line, where the date of the event (Aug 25, 2014–Sept 8, 2014), the venue (BJK Tennis Center) and the location (New York City, New York) is shown, is the generated rich snippet. Figure 10.7 confirms the markup information we have added is correct and can be used to generate rich snippets successfully, and that is what Google will show when the page is included in a search result.

Of course, the reason why we have accomplished a successful test in just one run is because we have avoided all the possible problems at the time the markup was created (see Sect. 10.3.2.3). In real life, however, it is possible that we will see some warnings and errors when testing our markups. When warnings/errors are encountered, it is always helpful to check the Google rich snippet supporting page as discussed in Sect. 10.3.2.3. More specifically, you need to locate the guideline page for your content type and understand what might be the problem by reading the guidance and tips on the page.

Here, as one example, let us discuss the top two errors that developers normally encounter so that you will be well prepared when you see these errors.

The first error normally reads "Error: Event urls are pointing to a different domain than the base url." This message in most cases can be ignored. The base URL refers to the URL of the document that is being tested. For example, `http://www.imdb.com/title/tt0045152/` is the base URL of the document

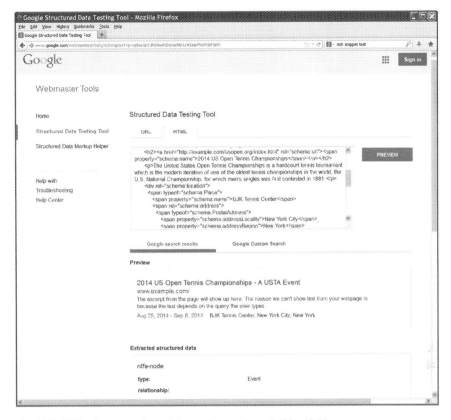

Fig. 10.7 Rich snippets preview of the markup as shown in List 10.11

on dmdb.com, which describes the movie "Singin in the Rain". Google requires that links contained by the markup can only point to pages (resources) within the same domain (imdb.com is the domain for this example). This requirement is designed to prevent possible spamming practices.

In the cases where the markup document is directly pasted into the textbox of the testing tool, it does not really have a base URL. Therefore Google assigns one to it. Normally, this assigned URL defaults to be www.example.com/. This also implies the domain is now example.com. If the markup has a URL that points to something other than example.com, you will get this error message.

This also explains why in List 10.10 and List 10.11, `http://example.com/usopen.org/index.html` is used to replace `http://www.usopen.org/index.html`. Had this not been done, we would have received the same error message.

The second error message often reads "Error: Incomplete rdfa with schema.org." It happens most likely because the markup does not have all the required fields. This has been discussed in the previous section in detail. Again, it is your responsibility to check the related Google rich snippet guideline document, and make sure that for the specific content type you are marking up, you have all the required properties covered.

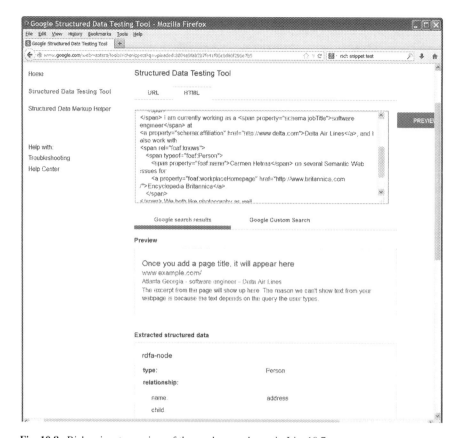

Fig. 10.8 Rich snippets preview of the markup as shown in List 10.7

In general, remember there is a guideline page for each specific content type, for example, a guideline page for event, a guideline page for product, a guideline page for review, so on and so forth. Therefore, make sure the correct guideline is checked and followed. Finally, besides the guideline page for each content type, Google has also provided a troubleshooting page, which has the following URL,

https://support.google.com/webmasters/answer/1093493

This page also includes a detailed checklist for you to make sure you have done your markup right. Usually, reading through this checklist will help you to troubleshoot your problem as well.

Before we move on to the next topic, let us answer one last leftover question from Sect. 10.3.2.2: what if, besides schema.org, another ontology not currently supported by Google rich snippets is used in the markup? Will the extracted structured data contain the entire markup? Will the rich snippet still show?

List 10.7 offers one such example, where terms from FOAF and schema.org are used for the markup. Let us paste List 10.7 into the Google rich snippet testing tool and observe what will happen. Figure 10.8 shows the result.

From Fig. 10.8, one can confirm things are working as expected: the rich snippet is generated correctly, and the extracted structured data includes everything we have added.

10.4   Content Markup Example 2: LRMI Project

The Learning Resource Metadata Initiative (LRMI)[11] is a project co-led by the Association of Educational Publishers[12] and Creative Commons, and funded by the Bill & Melinda Gates Foundation and the William and Flora Hewlett Foundation. The LRMI project was announced on June 7, 2011, and has been growing steadily together with schema.org. For Semantic Web developers, it is yet another example of semantic markup at work.

10.4.1   The Idea of LRMI

Educators often conduct searches to find their own resources to support student learning. In recent years, the ways that educators seek and find learning resources have changed dramatically. For instance, searches that used to be conducted in libraries are now often done on the Internet, which takes only seconds to finish. A recent survey[13] conducted by LRMI project found nearly three in four educators conduct online searches for educational materials at least several times a week, and one in four educators conduct search on a daily basis.

While the Internet makes searching for learning resources easy, the sheer vastness of material available makes it extremely challenging to find just the right learning resources to address specific student needs. For instance, survey participants complained that there were "too many irrelevant results" and that the process of sifting through thousands (or sometimes millions) of potential resources to find the ones that met their specific needs was "too time consuming."

Let us look at one such example[14] described by Dave Gladney, project manager of the LRMI for the Association of Educational Publishers. The example being discussed is about a fourth-grade teacher who is trying to help several students with the following Common Core Reading Standard for International Text K-5:

---

[11] http://www.lrmi.net/

[12] The 501(c)(3) division of the Association of American Publishers, to be more precise.

[13] http://www.lrmi.net/survey-results-show-need-for-more-targeted-results-when-searching-online-for-learning-resources

[14] http://edtechdigest.wordpress.com/2012/12/14/the-lrmi-a-common-sense-method-for-finding-common-core-resources/

Craft and Structure 4 – Determine the meaning of general academic and domain-specific words or phrases in a text relevant to grade 4 topic or subject area.

Let us say global warming is the specific topic that is under consideration, and the teacher would like to find an article that fits the particular standard, and also has comprehension questions and related writing activities. The material should also be appropriate for a small-group work and designed to be completed within an hour.

For this example, a search for "global warming lesson plans" returns more than 1 million pages. Finding an educational resource that matches the grade level and also accommodates all of the requirements that aligns to the specific standard is simply too time-consuming to do.

The LRMI project is created to directly address these concerns. It focuses on educational resources on the Web, and its goal is to make it easier and more convenient to find learning resources that meet specific student and class needs.

To reach its goal, the LRMI project elected to first establish a common vocabulary for describing learning resources, and then to promote the markup of educational content on the Web. Once a specialized schema about educational resources is developed and once a critical mass of educational content has been marked up by using this schema, it will then become much easier to parse and filter that content; therefore Web search will return much more relevant results.

This idea is feasible since it provides a win–win solution for all the participants. More specifically,

- Publishers of learning resources can have their pages surface above the mass of other Web pages (better discoverability), and therefore can promote their own market share significantly.
- Learners and educators can enjoy a much more efficient and fruitful search experience, and they can find the correct learning resources with much ease.
- Education technology developers can build applications that further leverage the structured data contained by this well-described universe of learning materials, further increasing the value of these materials to all participants, including learners, publishers, schools, governments and the general public.

Let us consider again the example we have just discussed. With the LRMI markup in place, the potentially matching articles now have sufficient structured data to make them identifiable to the search engines. Using the LRMI search criteria outlined above, in just a few clicks, the targeted resources meeting the exact specifications should be easily located.

The LRMI schema was inspired by schema.org, which creates a common vocabulary for marking up content pages on the Web. If a common vocabulary can be created, it is also possible for specialized communities and industries to extend it to meet their own needs.

This educational-specific vocabulary that the LRMI project proposed is also called *the LRMI specification*. Version 1.0 of this specification was released on May 14, 2012. At the time of this writing, the latest specification is version 1.1, released on February 7, 2013.

In April of 2013, the LRMI specification was adopted by schema.org. Therefore, publishers of educational resources can now use LRMI markup to provide rich, educational-specific structured data about their resources, with the confidence that this structured information will be recognized by major search engines.

Understand that even after the adaptation of LRMI types and properties by schema.org, it is for now unclear how or when search engines will use the LRMI specification. However, the adoption itself should give content publishers confidence that marking up using LRMI terms is a worthwhile investment for tomorrow at least.

To better follow the progress of the LRMI project, it is useful to understand the timeframe for it:

* Phase I: June 2011–March 2012

This phase has been completed. During this phase, the LRMI specification draft version (see Sect. 10.4.2) was created and submitted to schema.org for consideration for adoption as the standard online markup schema for learning resources. Also, another main effort was to promote the public awareness of the LRMI project, especially among the educational resource community.

* Phase II: March 2012–April 2013

This phase has also been completed. One major accomplishment is the adoption of LRMI specification into the vocabulary of schema.org. Others include the proof-of-concept markup of learning resources, the continuation of awareness building and hands-on publisher marking up support.

* Phase III: May 2013–April 2014

This phase is currently an ongoing effort. Among others, one of the main goals is to promote publishers' willingness to markup their learning resources by demonstrating the value of the LRMI properties in a search environment. Supporting tools and sandboxes for publishers are being built actively in order to accomplish this.

At the time of this writing, we are in the middle of the third phase. In the next two sections, we will first introduce the LRMI specification, and then we will look at examples of LRMI markup in action.

10.4.2   LRMI Specification

In this section, we take a closer look at the LRMI specification. To understand this specification, it is important to know what potential searching criteria educators often use to locate educational resources. In general, educators can search for materials using the following criteria:

* subject/area
* age range

- standards alignments
- media type
- interactive type (such as active, mixed)
- time required
- usage type (such as assignment or group work)
- resource type (such as handout or presentation)
- copyright/licensing information

The LRMI specification,[15] together with some existing schema.org properties, is designed and outlined to match these criteria, as shown in Table 10.1.

Obviously, if an existing schema.org property can adequately describe a certain aspect of the learning resources as required, it is simply better to reuse the term, instead of inventing a new one in the LRMI project. In Table 10.1, those terms that have a prefix `schema`, for example, `schema:about`, are the terms that currently exist in schema.org.

The LRMI specification shown in Table 10.1 is all about properties. Obviously, properties have to be used together with a specific type (class). When the LRMI specification was adopted by schema.org, it was decided that these new properties should go under `schema:CreativeWork` type. Therefore, every educational resource on the Web is now an instance of `schema:CreativeWork`. To confirm this, as described in Sect. 10.1.2, you can open schema.org vocabulary and find all the properties in Table 10.1 under `schema:CreativeWork`.

Note that the LRMI project has also added one new class into schema.org (which is not shown in Table 10.1). This new class is called `EducationalAudience`; it is a subclass of `schema:Audience`. A single new property, namely, `educationalRole`, is added for this new class, representing the role that describes the target audience of the content.

Before we move on to the next section, let us discuss the `educationalAlignment` property in more detail. This property is considered a "killer feature" since it provides the opportunity for content publishers to indicate how materials align with educational standards such as the Common Core State Standards (CCSS).[16] Obviously, this alignment is often one of the key search criteria used by educators.

As we discussed earlier, checking with schema.org vocabulary will tell you how to use this property. More specifically, this property takes an instance of type `AlignmentObject` as its value. Furthermore, `targetUrl` property under `AlignmentObject` should be used to point to the desired level in an established educational framework. Note the alignment itself is often coded as an URL node, as shown in List 10.12.

---

[15] http://www.lrmi.net/the-specification

[16] http://www.corestandards.org/

Table 10.1 LRMI specification

Search criteria	Property	Description
Subject/area	schema:about	The subject of the content.
Age range	typicalAgeRange	The typical range of ages the content's intended end user.
Standards alignments	educationalAlignment	An alignment to an established educational framework.
Media type	schema: associatedMedia	The media type of the educational resource.
Interactive type	interactiveType	The predominant mode of learning supported by the learning resource. Acceptable values are active, expositive, or mixed. • Ex: active • Ex: mixed
Time required	timeRequired	Approximate or typical time it takes to work with or through this learning resource for the typical intended target audience. • Ex: P30M • Ex: P1H25M
Usage type	educationalUse	The purpose of the work in the context of education. • Ex: assignment • Ex: group work
Resource type	learningResourceType	The predominant type or kind characterizing the learning resource. • Ex: presentation • Ex: handout
Copyright/ licensing information	useRightsUrl	The URL where the owner specifies permissions for using the resource. • Ex: http://creativecommons.org/ licenses/by/3.0/ • Ex: http://publisher.com/content-use-description
Others	isBasedOnUrl	A resource that was used in the creation of this resource. This term can be repeated for multiple sources.
	schema:name	The title of the resource.
	schema:dateCreated	The date on which the resource was created.
	schema:author	The individual credited with the creation of the resource.
	schema:publisher	The organization credited with publishing the resource.
	schema:inLanguage	The primary language of the resource.

List 10.12 Example of using `educationalAlignment` to map core academic standard

```
<li itemprop="educationalAlignment" itemscope
itemtype="http://schema.org/AlignmentObject"><meta
itemprop="targetUrl"
content="http://corestandards.org/2010/math/content/6/RP/1"
/><span itemprop="targetDescription">6.RP.1: 1. Understand the
concept of a ratio and use ratio language to describe a ratio
relationship between two quantities.</span>
```

The markup in List 10.12 indicates the underlying educational resource should be mapped to the following node in an established educational framework,

```
http://corestandards.org/2010/math/content/6/RP/1
```

If expressed in plain English, it means to "understand the concept of a ratio and use ratio language to describe a ratio relationship between two quantities." The advantage of expressing an academic standard as a URL node is quite intuitive: by doing so, both the content publishers and educators can now share a common language to describe a given academic standard, and any ambiguity along this line can be avoided.

Other properties in the LRMI specification do not need too much explanation. There are two user guides published on the LRMI official Web site (http://www.lrmi.net/),

- The Content Developer's Guide to the Learning Resource Metadata Initiative and Learning Registry[17]
- The Smart Publisher's Guide to LRMI Tagging[18]

The information provided by these two guides should be quite adequate to get you started on your own markup.

10.4.3 LRMI Implementation Examples

10.4.3.1 LRMI Markup Example

At the time of this writing, about 5,000 educational resources have been marked up using LRMI specification (as part of the proof-of-concept phase). The LRMI project's official Web site has collected some examples[19] of these markups, providing a good reference point for your own markup work.

---

[17] http://www.lrmi.net/wp-content/uploads/2013/03/lrmi_lr_guide.pdf

[18] http://www.lrmi.net/wp-content/uploads/2013/03/LRMI_tagging_Guide.pdf

[19] http://www.lrmi.net/the-specification/examples

Note that, for some of these examples, the LRMI markup was not added to the original page (hosted at the content publisher's domain); as a proof of concept, the markup was implemented on a simulated page hosted by LRMI domain. This way, both the original page and the LRMI version can be viewed side by side for comparison. As one would expect, the two versions do not exhibit any dramatic difference, since the added structured information is intended for machines, and should not change the look-and-feel of the page to human eyes.

To actually see the markup in LRMI terms, one can use the Google rich snippet testing tool as we discussed in Sect. 10.3.3. For example, one example markup page hosted by LRMI project domain is about a page called "Learning About Ratios: A Sandwich Study", and the markup page itself is given by the following URL:

http://lrmi.net/examples/nsdl20110414163807295T.htm

Provide this URL to the Google rich snippet testing tool, and you will be able to see the structured data extracted by the tool. List 10.13 shows part of the extracted information.

List 10.13 Part of extracted markups from page http://lrmi.net/examples/ nsdl20110414163807295T.htm

```
type:  http://schema.org/alignmentobject
property:
   targeturl: http://corestandards.org/2010/math/content/6/RP/1
   targetdescription: 6.RP.1: 1. Understand the concept of a
ratio and use ratio language to describe a ratio relationship
between two quantities.
```

Of course, this will not allow you to see the actual markup itself. For that purpose, one can simply use View Page Source selection on the page and look for key terms such as educationalAlignment. List 10.14 shows the markup used to generate the structured data shown in List 10.13.

List 10.14 Actual LRMI markups that generate structured data shown in List 10.13

```
<li itemprop="educationalAlignment" itemscope
itemtype="http://schema.org/AlignmentObject"><meta
itemprop="targetUrl"
content="http://corestandards.org/2010/math/content/6/RP/1"
/><span itemprop="targetDescription">6.RP.1: 1. Understand the
concept of a ratio and use ratio language to describe a ratio
relationship between two quantities.</span>
```

10.4.3.2   Customized Searching and Filtering Based on LRMI Markup

Marking up a content page only adds structured data into the page; it does not put the information to any use. It is up to a specific application to pick up this information and find a use for it.

One such application is from the major search engines—rich snippets are generated by leveraging some of the schema.org markups. However, as we discussed in Sect. 10.4.1, at this point, major search engines are not supporting the LRMI part of schema.org just yet. In other words, the added LRMI markups will not produce any rich snippets.

However, instead of waiting for support from major search engines, one can actually make use of the LRMI markups in many other possible ways. For instance, a customized search engine can be developed to use the LRMI markup to effectively filter the search results—much in the same way the LRMI specification was originally designed.

More specifically, for a Web site that has control over a large body of learning resources, and if these resources have already been marked up using LRMI specification, a customized search engine can then be developed to offer much more efficient search within the site itself. With a powerful search engine in place, one should be confident that the site would be able to attract and retain more and more visitors.

Understand that it is not a must that one has to use LRMI specification to markup the resources. Any schema can be used, as long as the search engine is accordingly developed to recognize these markups. In fact, one can even invent a new schema and use it to accomplish all this. However, using a well-accepted vocabulary such as schema.org will ensure that the added structured information can be widely recognized by many other applications, including applications we cannot even imagine today. This also implies that the marked up learning resources can have a chance to participate in some larger circle, for example, linked by many other resources. And finally, if standards are followed, there will also be more tools available for use, not only improving the quality of the system, but also saving valuable development time and effort.

One example Web site is the Illinois Shared Learning Environment (ISLE) site.[20] In a nutshell, ISLE has access to a large collection of learning resources, and since these resources are all marked up using LRMI specification, ISLE's own customized search engine can read the structured data in the markups and make use of it to offer a much more efficient search experience to the user. Figure 10.9 shows the look and feel of the site.

Now, let us say a teacher is searching for course material about *fractions*, for grade 4 students. Simply typing *fraction* in the search yields about 2,366 results, as shown in Fig. 10.10.

---

[20] http://ioer.ilsharedlearning.org

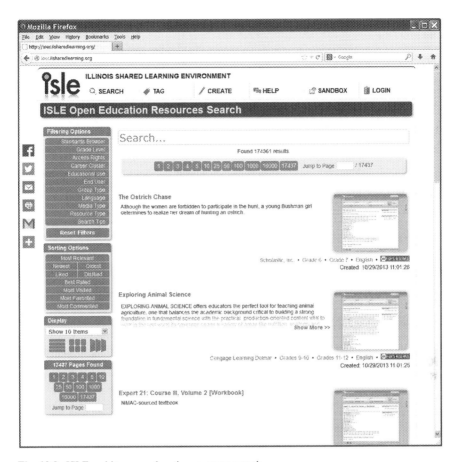

Fig. 10.9 ISLE and its open education resource search

Now, using the *Filtering Options* in the left pane, let us check Grade 4 in *Grade Level* filter, Teacher/Education Specialist in *End User* filter and finally, Course in *Resource Type* filter. Once this is done, we have only two results left, as shown in Fig. 10.11, and these two are quite satisfactory results indeed.

In fact, with the addition of each filter, you can see the resulting page body getting smaller and smaller.

I hope by now, this excellent example has successfully demonstrated the benefits of having semantic markups in the content pages. Even without the immediate support from major search engines, the added structured information can still make a difference.

Finally, note that ISLE also provides an online tool to help content publishers mark up their content pages. To start this tool, simply click the *TAG* menu at the top portion of the page (Fig. 10.9). It is quite a friendly tool to publishers—one can add structured data by simply answering questions, and there is no need to get familiar

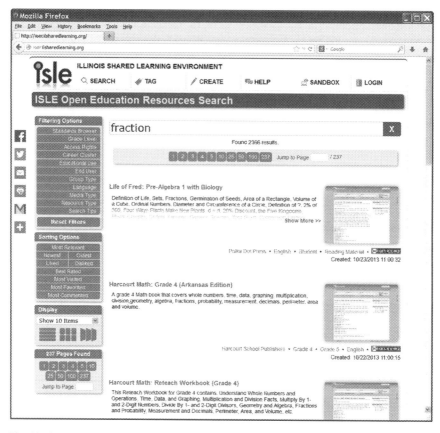

Fig. 10.10   Search for *fraction* in ISLE returns 2,366 pages

with LRMI specifications. Tools like this are indeed very helpful when it comes to promoting semantic markups.

10.5   Summary

This chapter covers the main components of schema.org, including the vocabulary itself, and the markup languages that are recommended. It also uses two examples to showcase the real-world applications of schema.org.

One such example is Google rich snippets. You should be able to understand why rich snippets can help search and how schema.org helps to make rich snippets possible, on a global scale.

The second example is the Learning Resource MetaData Initiative (LRMI), which uses schema.org as it underlying ontology. This is another great example

Fig. 10.11 Search for *fraction* in ISLE with filter options returns two highly relevant pages

to show how semantic markup and the related Semantic Web technologies work in real applications.

References

Bizer C, Eckert K, Meusel R, Mühleisen H, Schuhmacher M, Völker J (2013) Deployment of RDFa, microdata, and microformats on the web – a quantitative analysis. 12th International Semantic Web Conference (ISWC2013), Proceedings Part II, Sydney, Australia, October 2013. pp 17–32

Hepp M, Roberto G, Andreas R (2009) RDF2RDFa: turning RDF into snippets for copy-and-paste. Technical Report TR-2009-01. PDF at http://www.heppnetz.de/files/RDF2RDFa-TR.pdf

Mika P, Potter T (2012) Metadata statistics for a large web corpus, vol 937. CEUR Workshop Proceedings. CEUR-WS.org

Tennison J (2012) HTML data guide. W3C Interest Group Note 08 March 2012. http://www.w3.org/TR/html-data-guide/

Chapter 11
Social Networks and the Semantic Web

In recent years, social networking sites have grown with amazing speed. They are not only the source of vast amounts of user-generated data, but they are also changing our lives in almost every aspect, such as finding old friends, sharing pictures, discussing hot topics and finding jobs, just to name a few.

For us, this presents an interesting question: how are social networking sites related to the Semantic Web? Can the Semantic Web idea help social networking sites in any way? Indeed, with help from the Semantic Web standards and technologies, social networking websites have been operating with new meaning, and as a result, users and content publishers are interacting with each other at much more meaningful levels than have been thought of before.

In this chapter, three major social networking sites are discussed as case studies. We will see how the Semantic Web is changing them, and we will evaluate how close each of them is to the Semantic Web realization. For us, this not only shows the power of the Semantic Web idea, but also can be used as a springboard for ideas for our own development work on the Semantic Web.

This chapter can also be viewed as an extension to Chap. 10. Again, it shows the basic flow of the Semantic Web: to publish structured data on the Web and to make sense out of the published data. We will once again see examples of how semantic markup, even just a little, can take us far.

11.1 Overview of Social Networking Websites

Social networking websites often refer to online communities of people who share interests, activities, backgrounds or real-life connections. Users of social networking websites are often represented by their public profiles, and they interact with

© Springer-Verlag Berlin Heidelberg 2014   517
L. Yu, *A Developer's Guide to the Semantic Web*,
DOI 10.1007/978-3-662-43796-4_11

each other through chat, message, e-mail, video, video-chat, file-sharing, blogging and discussion groups.

The following are some examples of popular social networking websites:

- Facebook

Facebook[1] is an online social networking service founded in February 2004. Users participate in Facebook by creating personal profiles, adding other users as friends, exchanging messages and receiving automatic notifications when profiles are updated. In addition, users may join common-interest user groups, organized based on workplace, school or other characteristics.

- Google+

Google+[2] is an online social networking service owned and operated by Google. It was first launched in June 2011, and now it is the second-largest social networking site after Facebook. Users participate in Google+ by making connections to other people, and by having these connections in different circles or categories. For example, friends, family and acquaintances are all different circles. Users can share updates, photos, links, videos, etc., within a circle.

- Twitter

Twitter[3] is an online social networking and microblogging service founded in March 2006. Users participate in Twitter by registering on the site, and then sending and reading short messages limited to 140 characters, which are also called *Tweets*. Tweets are displayed on the user's profile page, and users may subscribe to other users' Tweets, which is often called "following someone on Twitter".

- LinkedIn

LinkedIn[4] is an online social networking service founded in December 2002. It is for people in professional occupations. Users participate in LinkedIn by creating their profiles, and by accepting and sending invitations to other users in order to build connections. Those users who are connected often share similar professional interests or backgrounds. The connections can be used to build up a contact network, possibly for job hunting and business opportunities.

- Pinterest

Pinterest[5] is an online social networking service founded in December 2009. By December 2011, it had become one of the top ten largest social networking

---

[1] https://www.facebook.com/

[2] https://plus.google.com

[3] https://twitter.com/

[4] https://www.linkedin.com/

[5] https://www.pinterest.com/

services,[6] with 11 million total visits per week. Users participate in Pinterest by creating profiles, saving images and categorizing them on different pinboards. They can also follow other user's boards if they have similar tastes. Popular categories include travel, cars, food, film, humor, home design, art, sports and fashion.

There are other popular social networking websites on the Internet that cannot be covered one by one here. In fact, not all of the social networking website are clones of each other. Each one offers a unique user experience from a different perspective, and does what it does better than any other site.

Users of social networking websites join the sites to keep in touch with their old friends, and to create new online friendships with people who share similar interests and backgrounds. Some social networking websites even offer the opportunity to establish and expand business contacts to find a job.

For the rest of this chapter, we will look at social networking websites from a different perspective: we will study how the Semantic Web technologies can help these sites to work and operate with different meanings. To follow the content of this chapter, it is not necessary that you are active on social networking sites. All you need is your understanding about the idea of the Semantic Web.

11.2 Facebook's Open Graph Protocol

Search engine companies and social networking companies always have a need to understand the content of a Web page. For Google this is important because if the content of a Web page is understood (at least to some extent), more relevant search results can be returned so more traffic will stay with Google. For social networking companies such as Facebook, if the content behind the Web pages you are liking or sharing is better understood, you will be served better, and your needs will be understood better.

One way to achieve this is to add semantic markup to the Web pages. As we saw in Chap.10, if Web content is marked up by using schema.org, Google will be able to extract structured data from the markup and to further generate rich snippets. Rich snippets can help users to understand why a page is included in the result and why it is relevant to the search.

For Facebook, this basic idea remains the same. However, the page content is marked up by using Open Graph Protocol (OGP) terms rather than terms from schema.org, and the extracted structured data is used to understand the specific *kind* of thing that is being liked, and to create a *typed* link back to the content page.

In this section, we start from Open Graph Protocol, and our goal is to understand how Facebook uses the markup, and how this whole idea is related to the Semantic Web.

---

[6] Sloan, Paul (December 22, 2011). "Pinterest: Crazy growth lands it as top 10 social site". CNET News. Retrieved February 2, 2012.

11.2.1 Open Graph Protocol

Open Graph Protocol (OGP) is a simple and compact schema (a collection of types and properties) that one can use to markup a Web page. It was originally announced by Facebook in April 2010, and currently it supports RDFa as the markup language. It is widely used by IMDB, Microsoft, NHL, Posterous, Rotten Tomatoes, TIME, Yelp and many others, as reported by OGP's official Web site.

Let us focus on the basic types and properties of Open Graph schema in this section. With all these technical details in place, we will be ready to move on to examples and applications.

First, understand that when terms (such as types and properties) from OGP are used to markup a Web page, the markup itself has to be placed by using <meta> tags in the <head> section of the Web page, and RDFa has to be the markup language. This is actually simpler than the markup for generating rich snippets, where the markup can be embedded everywhere in the page. In addition, the OGP schema itself is also a much smaller set when compared to schema.org (and other possible ontologies).

When marking up the page, the first thing required is to specify the type of object that is being described. This is done by using the og:type property. Note og is the namespace prefix, which represents the overall OGP namespace given by the following URL,

```
http://ogp.me/ns#
```

In fact, RDFa property typeof could have been selected to accomplish the same thing, yet the OGP design team decided to use a property of their own.

Following the Semantic Web standards, the value of *type* property (such as rdf:type or RDFa's typeof) should be specified by a URI that represents a class defined in some ontology. For example, schema:Place defined in schema.org, or foaf:Person defined in FOAF ontology.

However, in OGP, og:type only takes string as its value, and the available types represented by strings are those that are agreed upon by the community. More specifically, when the community agrees on a specific type, it is added to the so-called *list of global types*. For example, the following statement says the current Web page that is being marked up is about a book:

```
<meta property="og:type" content="book" />
```

Note the content attribute is used to indicate that the value of og:type will be a simple text string. Table 11.1 summarizes all the global types OGP currently supports.

Note that any non-marked up Web page should be treated as using website as its default og:type.

Once a type is specified, properties can be added to describe the type. Regardless of the specific type, three properties are required, as summarized in Table 11.2.

Table 11.1 Global types currently supported by OGP schema

Category	og:type value	OGP namespace URI
Music	music.song music.album music.playlist music.radio_station	http://ogp.me/ns/music#
Video	video.movie video.episode video.tv_show video.other	http://ogp.me/ns/video#
Article	article	http://ogp.me/ns/article#
Book	book	http://ogp.me/ns/book#
Profile	profile	http://ogp.me/ns/profile#
Website	website	http://ogp.me/ns/website#

Table 11.2 Required properties for all types

Property	Property meaning
og:title	The title of the rich object as it should appear within the social graph, can be anything you want
og:image	An image URL that should represent the rich object within the graph social graph, can be anything you want
og:url	The canonical URL of the rich object, and will be used as its permanent ID in the graph, e.g., http://www.imdb.com/title/tt0117500/ is one such URL

Table 11.3 Optional properties for all types

Property	Property meaning
og:audio	A URL to an audio file to accompany the rich object
og:description	A short description of the rich object; will be shown inside the rich object
og:determiner	The word that appears before the rich object's title in a sentence. Possible choices are a, an, the, "" and auto. If auto is chosen, the consumer of the data should choose between a or an. The default is "" (blank)
og:locale	The locale these tags are marked up in. Its format should be language_TERRITORY. The default is en_US
og:locale: alternate	An array of other locales this page is available in
og:site_name	If the object is part of a larger website, the name that should be displayed for the overall site
og:video	A URL to a video file that complements the rich object

In addition, Table 11.3 shows the properties that can be used for any type, and they are optional.

There are also properties that are applicable for only a specific type. For example, a book has an author, an isbn number, a release_date and a tag.

These properties are written using an extra : in the markup. For example, `book:author`, `book:isbn`. Some other examples are `profile:first_name`, `profile:last_name`, `article:author`, etc.

We will not cover all the details about OGP schema, and what we have learned so far is good enough for us to focus on our main goal in this section: to understand how OGP is helping Facebook and how it is related to the idea of the Semantic Web. If you need to understand more about OGP schema, the online documentation is always a good place to go.

Understand that there is an OGP ontology that formally defines all the types and properties. List 11.1 shows part of this ontology.

List 11.1 Part of the OGP ontology

```
@prefix rdf: <http://www.w3.org/1999/02/22-rdf-syntax-ns#> .
@prefix rdfs: <http://www.w3.org/2000/01/rdf-schema#> .
@prefix owl: <http://www.w3.org/2002/07/owl#> .
@prefix og: <http://ogp.me/ns#> .
@prefix ogc: <http://ogp.me/ns/class#> .
@prefix bibo: <http://purl.org/ontology/bibo/> .
@prefix dc: <http://purl.org/dc/elements/1.1/> .
@prefix foaf: <http://xmlns.com/foaf/0.1/> .
@prefix geo: <http://www.w3.org/2003/01/geo/wgs84_pos#> .
@prefix gr: <http://purl.org/goodrelations/v1#> .
@prefix vcard: <http://www.w3.org/2006/vcard/ns#> .
@prefix xsd: <http://www.w3.org/2001/XMLSchema#> .


##### PROPERTIES #####

og:url a rdf:Property ;
  rdfs:label "url"@en-US ;
  rdfs:comment "The canonical URL of your object that will be
               used as its permanent ID in the graph, e.g.,
               \"http://www.imdb.com/title/tt0117500/\"."@en-US ;
  rdfs:seeAlso dc:identifier, foaf:homepage ;
  rdfs:isDefinedBy og: ;
  rdfs:range ogc:url .
og:type a rdf:Property ;
  rdfs:label "type"@en-US ;
  rdfs:comment "The type of your object, e.g., \"movie\".
               Depending on the type you specify, other
               properties may also be required."@en-US ;
  rdfs:seeAlso rdf:type ;
  rdfs:isDefinedBy og: ;
  rdfs:range ogc:string .
og:title a rdf:Property ;
```

```
    rdfs:label "title"@en-US ;
    rdfs:comment "The title of the object as it should appear
                  within the graph, e.g.,  \"The Rock\"."@en-US ;
    rdfs:subPropertyOf rdfs:label ;
    rdfs:isDefinedBy og: ;
    rdfs:range ogc:string .
......


##### DATATYPES #####

ogc:mime_type_str a rdfs:Datatype ;
  rdfs:label "mime type string"@en-US ;
  rdfs:comment "Valid mime type strings (e.g.,
                \"application/mp3\")."@en-US ;
  rdfs:isDefinedBy og: ;
  rdfs:subClassOf xsd:string .
ogc:boolean_str a rdfs:Datatype ;
  rdfs:label "boolean string"@en-US ;
  rdfs:comment "A string representation of a true or false value.
                The lexical space contains: \"true\", \"false\",
                \"1\", and \"0\"."@en-US ;
  rdfs:isDefinedBy ogc: ;
  rdfs:subClassOf xsd:string .
ogc:date_time_str a rdfs:Datatype ;
  rdfs:label "date/time string"@en-US ;
  rdfs:comment "A string representation of a temporal value
                composed of a date (year, month, day) and an
                optional time component (hours, minutes).  The
                lexical space is defined by ISO 8601."@en-US ;
  rdfs:isDefinedBy ogc: ;
  rdfs:subClassOf xsd:string .
......
```

This is actually a very compact and intuitive ontology. The most noticeable feature is that there is no class definition included in the ontology, and that is also the reason why `rdfs:range` is used and `rdfs:domain` is never in use. This agrees with the fact that in OGP, `og:type` only takes strings as its values, as we have discussed earlier. We discuss this again in Sect. 11.2.2.3.

11.2.2 How Does It Work: Creating Typed Links Using OGP

11.2.2.1 The Basic Idea and Process

As we just discussed in Sect. 11.2.1, the Facebook OGP schema is a set of types and properties that one can use to markup a Web page. With the markup in place, the Web page can become part of the Facebook experience, and more importantly, Facebook is now able to tell what specific kind of thing is being liked. Let us take a look at how this is actually implemented.

Let us say a Web page has been marked up using OGP types and properties. In addition, a Facebook "Like" button has also been placed on the same page.

Now a visitor is looking at the page and decides to click the `Like` button. The moment the `Like` button is clicked, Facebook will create a connection between the visitor and the Web page. The web page will show up in the "Likes and Interests" area of that user's Facebook profile, and it will appear as a *rich* object in Facebook's social graph. The richness of the object depends on how much markup has been added. The object that represents the Web page can now be referenced and connected across social network user profiles, blog posts, search results, Facebook's news feed and more.

For Facebook, an even more important result from the added markup is that it is able to tell what exactly is being liked. To see this, consider the case where there is only a `Like` button on the page, and page itself does not contain any OGP markup at all. A visitor can still click the `Like` button; however, all Facebook knows in this case is that a link is liked and nothing further. Unfortunately, for Facebook, all these links are created equal, and there is nothing more exciting that Facebook can offer.

On the other hand, with the OGP markup, Facebook can parse the required `og:type` property from the markup, and comes to the realization that, for example, a book is being liked. It can therefore go out to find others who liked the same book, and may even recommend more books.

What if it is a movie that is being liked? Or, what if it is a song that is being liked? One can easily imagine these similar scenarios. The important fact is, for Facebook, these Web pages are still just links. However, with the added OGP markup, these links have transformed from *untyped* links to *typed* ones, and that is the reason behind all the exciting things Facebook can offer.

11.2.2.2 Open Graph Markup Examples

Before we move on to see what Facebook can do with the added markup, let us first look at one example to understand what we have discussed so far. List 11.2 shows a markup for a book.

List 11.2 Example OGP markup for a book object

```
<html xmlns="http://www.w3.org/1999/xhtml"
      xmlns:og="http://ogp.me/ns#"
      xmlns:book="http://ogp.me/ns/book#"
      xmlns:fb="https://www.facebook.com/2008/fbml">

<head>
<meta property="og:type" content="book" />
<meta property="og:title" content="A Developer's Guide to the Se-
mantic Web" />
<meta property="og:site_name" content="Amazon.com" />
<meta property="og:description" content="this is a book about the
Semantic Web" />
<meta property="og:locale" content="en_US" />
<meta property="og:url"
      content="http://liyangyu.com/book_test0.html" />
<meta property="og:image"
      content="http://www.liyangyu.com/image/devGuide.jpg" />
<meta property="book:author" content="http://liyangyu.com" />
<meta property="book:isbn" content="978-3642159695" />
<meta property="book:release_date" content="2011-01-05" />
<meta property="book:tag" content="the Semantic Web" />
<meta property="book:tag" content="deveoper's guide" />
</head>

<body>
<div id="fb-root"></div>
<script>(function(d, s, id) {
  var js, fjs = d.getElementsByTagName(s)[0];
  if (d.getElementById(id)) return;
  js = d.createElement(s); js.id = id;
  js.src = "//connect.facebook.net/en_US/all.js#xfbml=1";
  fjs.parentNode.insertBefore(js, fjs);
}(document, 'script', 'facebook-jssdk'));</script>

<!-- other content are not included here -->

</body>

<div class="fb-like"
    data-href="http://liyangyu.com/book_test0.html"
    data-layout="standard" data-action="like"
    data-show-faces="true" data-share="true"></div>
```

Fig. 11.1 A page shows up
in Facebook space as a rich
object

Note the content on the page (in between <body> tag) is not included, since they
are irrelevant to the markup, which can only exist in <head> section. The markup
includes the required properties as shown by the bold lines, together with some
optional ones and properties related to book type. The <script> tag and <div>
tag are responsible for the Like button on the page.

To test this, a public Web server is needed, and you should at least have the right to
push static content pages such as the one shown in List 11.2 to the server. The author
was able to test this by using his own domain, liyangyu.com. Once this page was
published on the server, a browser was used to access the page. The moment the Like
button was clicked, a link was created between the Facebook profile and the page. The
page itself then shows up as a rich object in Facebook page, as shown in Fig. 11.1.

It is obvious how the properties are mapped to the GUI elements in Fig. 11.1. For
example, og:title is mapped to the title of the book, and book:author is mapped
to the link text under the title.

Meanwhile, the key information is at the top, which says "Liyang Yu likes a
book." book is the typed link we are interested in, and it tells Facebook, it is a book
that we like, not anything else.

For comparison, we can remove all the markups in <head> section (keep
everything else the same) and test it again. Figure 11.2 shows how it looks in
Facebook after the markups are removed.

As shown in Fig. 11.2, although Facebook is able to retrieve some existing
markup from the main page and use that information to show the picture and the
title of the page, it can only say "Liyang Yu likes a link." This is what is called an
untyped link—it does not tell Facebook anything specific, because a link could be a
link to a book, to a movie, to an event, to a place, and so on. We will come back to
this topic in the next section.

Finally, understand that one can always check the OGP markup by using the
debugger[7] provided by Facebook. The URL of the page is needed to run the tool.
For example, Fig. 11.3 shows the debug information for List 11.2.

---

[7] https://developers.facebook.com/tools/debug/

Fig. 11.2 A page shows up in Facebook space as an untyped link

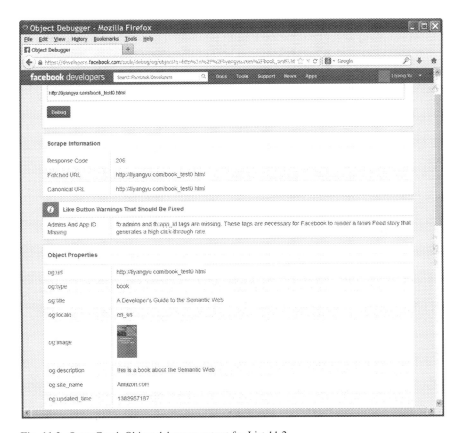

Fig. 11.3 Open Graph Object debugger output for List 11.2

11.2.2.3 Open Graph Issues

At this point, we have learned how semantic markup is added to a Web page for a typed link to be created by Facebook. Based on what we have learned about the Semantic Web, we should be able to identify several issues with this approach.

Facebook supports RDFa as the markup format. However, Facebook's usage of RDFa does not fully agree with the W3C's RDFa guideline. List 11.3 shows what the Facebook design team tried to use.

List 11.3 OGP markup that Facebook design team tried to use

```
<html xmlns="http://www.w3.org/1999/xhtml"
      xmlns:og="http://ogp.me/ns#"
      xmlns:dc=" http://purl.org/dc/elements/1.1/"
      xmlns:foaf=" http://xmlns.com/foaf/0.1/"
      xmlns:fb="https://www.facebook.com/2008/fbml">

<head>
  <meta property="og:type" content="book" />
  <meta property="dc:title"
        content="A Developer's Guide to the Semantic Web" />
  <meta property="foaf:logo"
        content="http://www.liyangyu.com/image/devGuide.jpg" />
</head>
```

List 11.3 was believed to be too complex for content developers. For instance, to follow List 11.3, one has to learn FOAF ontology and Dublin Core, at a minimum. The decision then was to follow what we saw in List 11.2, which is also known as the *minimal form* of RDFa.

Perhaps the most surprising fact is that OGP ontology (Sect. 11.2.1) does not define any class, and property og:type always has to use a text string to represent the class type. Since there is no class defined, there is no such thing as class hierarchy, and there is no such concept as domain of a property.

This is probably acceptable for the immediate goal set by Facebook. However, moving forward, semantic markup from each page can be gathered together and interesting applications can be built on top of these structured data. When this comes into the plan, the lack of class and class hierarchy can hurt these applications and can greatly limit the possibility of reasoning on the gathered structured data.

For example, movies, books and songs can all be considered as creative work. Assuming there is a need to understand how many users have liked creative work, an application based on OGP schema has to hard-code the fact that liking creative work means to like movies, or books or songs. On the other hand, if the ontology had specified the fact that book, movie and song are all subclasses of creative work, the same application would be able to easily understand how to obtain the requested information without the need to hard-code anything. In addition, new types as subclasses of creative work can be added to the ontology at any time, and new markups can be added to the page freely; the application itself does not need any change.

Another consequence of not having class definition in OGP ontology is that this has practically made it a fact that the added structured data using OGP schema will only be recognized and understood by Facebook itself, not by any other application. For example, an application outside of Facebook can recognize `schema:book` easily, but it will not be able to understand `content="book"` actually means the object on the page is also an instance of `schema:book`.

Besides the above issues, there are other issues with the approach Facebook has taken. For example, there is only one object allowed on each page, which is again a rather surprising limitation. Another consideration is the true openness of OGP schema itself—for it to be qualified as *open* protocol, it should be developed in an open collaboration with the Web. More specifically, Google, Yahoo! and W3C would have valuable contributions to make.

Overall speaking, at this stage, following W3C standards and getting the related Semantic Web elements correct does not seem to be the highest priority for Facebook. Instead, the priority is to make this as simple as possible so content publishers can participate without too much of a learning curve to conquer.

Although this is only a "limited version of the Semantic Web" implemented by Facebook, it is yet another example of how a little semantics can get us far, as is discussed in the next section.

11.2.3 Implications for the Semantic Web

To put it simply, Facebook, at least within its own domain, has implemented its own version of the Semantic Web. The added markup using OGP schema maps to semantics, that is, the knowledge that the user is not just interacting with a Web page, but is liking a specific kind of thing. Furthermore, the things being liked can be bucketed into categorizes such as books, movies, music, etc. This simple and somewhat flawed (Sect. 11.2.2.3) semantic layer can then give rise to all sorts of applications that are far from simple and ordinary.

The most recent application based directly on the structured data generated by parsing the added markup is Facebook's new *Graph Search*,[8] introduced in January 2013. More specifically, since the added markup, Facebook now knows *who* likes *what*. It is then easy to answer questions such as "my friends who like books," or even "my friends who like books and also live in Atlanta". These are just some example questions that can be easily answered by Graph Search.

---

[8] https://www.facebook.com/about/graphsearch

Based what we have learned already, the magic behind Graph Search is clear. When a query such as "friends who like book and live in Atlanta" is submitted by a user, Graph Search traverses all of the user's relationships and find his friends who like books, and then filters them by checking whether they are currently living in Atlanta or not. By applying the same graph traversal algorithms, one can see how even more complex questions can easily be answered. To eliminate the confusion of how to perform such complicated searches, Facebook offers a set of drop-lists and controls that are useful to make refinements to the questions one might ask.

The release of Graph Search has triggered quite a bit of discussion around key issues such as privacy, implications for users and publishers, etc. These topics are outside the scope of this book. For us, Graph Search is at least a great example of how added semantic markup can help us to accomplish functionalities that would not be possible otherwise. At this point, we do not know exactly what other applications will be built on top of Facebook's data repository, but we know for sure they will be even more powerful and impressive.

Perhaps the most important takeaway from what Facebook has accomplished should be the following: Facebook has successfully provided a strong incentive for content publishers and Web sites to finally add more markups in their sites. For the world of the Semantic Web, the more markup data that exists, the better the applications one can build.

11.3   Twitter Cards for Structured Information

With what we have learned about Facebook's Open Graph Protocol, it is not difficult to understand Twitter Cards. Again, the basic idea remains the same: add semantic markups into the Web pages. With the added markup, users who tweet links to this content will have a "card" added to the Tweet. This not only means one can control how the content is displayed with Tweets, it also drives more engaged traffic to the site. From this perspective, Twitter Cards is similar to Google's rich snippets.

In this section, we study the details of Twitter Cards. Our goal is to understand how Twitter uses the markup to generate Twitter Cards, and how this whole idea is related to the Semantic Web.

11.3.1   Twitter Cards Overview

In early 2012, Twitter started to experiment with new ways for users to interact with Twitter. The solution Twitter decided upon was to give website owners the option to add markups into their page contents, and when users expand Tweets containing links to these sites, they will see content previews, images, video and more, extending beyond the normal limit of 140 characters.

Table 11.4 Card types supported by Twitter

Card type	Purpose
Summary Card	Summary Card is the default card, which can be used for many kinds of Web content, such as blog posts, news articles, products and restaurants. It includes title, description, and a small image, which are often sufficient enough to provide a helpful description
Summary Card with large image	Similar to the Summary Card, but offers a larger image
Photo Card	Photo card is designed to allow an image to be at the center of a Tweet, implementing the idea of "a picture is worth of a thousand words"
Gallery Card	A Gallery Card can represent collections of photos within a Tweet. This is designed to let the user know that there is more than just a single image at the URL shared, but rather a gallery of related images
App Card	App Card is designed to provide a profile of an application, including name, description and icon. It can also highlight attributes such as the rating and the price
App Installs and Deep-Linking	This is to allow users to download the app (if they don't already have it installed), or deep-link into the app (if the app is ready installed on the user's mobile device)
Player Card	Player Card is designed for steaming media experiences such as audio, video or slideshows. It allows content publishers to present their content inside of an iFrame within the Tweet
Product Card	Product Card is designed to represent retail items on Twitter, and to drive sales. It can showcase a product via an image or a description. It also allows the content publisher to highlight two other key details about the product

Twitter named the technology behind this feature Twitter Cards,[9] and it was first released in mid-2012. At the time of this writing, Twitter supports eight different types of cards, as show in Table 11.4.

When a Tweet links to a content page, if the page has been marked up by using Twitter properties, the Tweet will have a card inside it. The specific type of card depends on the markup in the content page.

Let us use Summary Card as an example to gain more understanding about Twitter property markup. For other card types, the markup process remains the same, with the only difference being the specific card type and related properties for the selected type.

First, understand that all the Twitter properties should be placed inside the <head> section of the page, by using <meta> tag. Each card type supports and requires a specific set of properties, but all cards share one basic property in common, and that is the card type property, identified by twitter:card. And it is always necessary to specify the type of the card. For example, the following markup says the card type is a Summary Card:

```
<meta name="twitter:card" value="summary">
```

---

[9] https://dev.twitter.com/blog/twitter-cards

Table 11.5 Required properties for Summary Card

Property name	Purpose
`twitter:title`	Title should be concise and will be truncated at 70 characters
`twitter:` `description`	A description of the page content, as appropriate for presentation within a Tweet. Should not be the same as the title, and should not be used for describing the services provided by the Website
`twitter:image`	An image represents the content of the page, and should be specific to the content, not a generic image such as the logo of the Website

Other possible type values include summary_large_image, photo, gallery, product, app or player. In addition, if no `twitter:card` value is set, Summary Card is the default card type.

For a Summary Card, the required properties are shown in Table 11.5. If any of these required properties are not included in the markup, the card may not be shown in the Tweet.

Other Twitter properties can be used when adding the markup, but they are not required and may be ignored by the Twitter crawler. For other type of Twitter Cards, one can check the online Twitter developer document[10] to find the required properties.

Note Twitter markups are simple key–value pairs, or property–value pairs. The combined collection of property–value pairs defines the overall card experience on Twitter. These simple key–value pairs do not even require a namespace prefix declaration. More specifically, Open Graph markup requires specifying `og` prefix via `<html prefix="og:http://ogp.me/ns#">`; however, no such markup is required for Twitter cards or the `"twitter:"` prefix. Also, note Open Graph markup is implemented by using `property` and `content` attributes, while Twitter cards use `name` and `value` attributes.

In fact, Twitter markup and Open Graph markup are closely related. When checking the page content, Twitter Card processor first looks for markup using Twitter properties, and if none are present, it falls back to the supported Open Graph properties. Besides the `name` and `value` attributes, the Twitter processor can understand `property` and `content` attributes as well.

For example, consider a content page that has been marked up to generate a Summary Card in Tweets. For this purpose, `twitter:description` is a required property. However, if the Twitter processor cannot find this property, it falls back to `og:description` property. Similarly, if it cannot find the required `twitter:title` property, it falls back to `og:title` property. For more examples, Twitter's online markup reference document[11] shows a more complete list of Twitter properties and their corresponding Open Graph Fallbacks.

---

[10] https://dev.twitter.com/docs/cards

[11] https://dev.twitter.com/docs/cards/markup-reference

11.3.2 How Does It Work: Structured Information for Rich Tweets

11.3.2.1 The Basic Idea and Process

At this point, the basic idea behind Twitter Cards is very clear. A content publisher can add markups by using the Twitter properties, and Twitter will work out the rest. More specifically, any Tweet that includes a link to the page will automatically have a Twitter Card inside it. This gives the reader a preview of the content before clicking through to the website.

Four steps are needed to accomplish this.

- Select the card type.

The currently supported card types were discussed in Sect. 11.3.1, and related details can also be found at Twitter's developer support site. It is the content publisher's responsibility to review the supported card type and decide which one is the best choice for representing the page content.

- Add the pertinent markup to the page content.

The specific markup that is needed in the page depends on the selected card type. Summary Card is used as one example in Sect. 11.3.1 to show the required properties that one has to use. Implementations of other card types can be done similarly. Again, Twitter's online developer document is the best resource to check out the latest properties that Twitter supports.

- Test the markup and submit application.

To make sure the added markup can be recognized by the Twitter processor, Twitter provides a Card Validator[12] for content publishers to check their markup. Content publishers enter the URL of a page that contains markup to start the test. Once the page has been validated, the content publisher can request final approval for the card.

- Tweet the URL and see the card.

After receiving the approval notice from Twitter, the content publisher can Tweet the URL, and should see the card appear below within the Tweet.

11.3.2.2 Twitter Card Markup Examples

Since the potentially long turnover time of application for final approval from Twitter, we will not create Twitter Card markup from the scratch; instead, we will use existing production content page to show markup examples.

---

[12] https://dev.twitter.com/docs/cards/validation/validator

The existing content page is from the *New York Times*.[13] On the *New York Times'* home page, enter "Roger Federer" in the search box. Click the Search button, and you will find a link in the search result page pointing to an article named *Why Roger Federer is the Greatest of All Time*.

Click the link to open the article.[14] After you enjoy reading this nice piece published on September 10, 2013 by Michael Steinberger, open the page source of this article. On the page source, you will find the Twitter markups. List 11.4 shows part of it.

List 11.4 Twitter markup on one *New York Times* article

```
<meta property="og:type" content="article" />
<meta property="og:url" con-
tent="http://6thfloor.blogs.nytimes.com/2013/09/10/why-roger-
federer-is-the-greatest-of-all-time/" />
<meta property="og:site_name" content="The 6th Floor Blog" />
<meta property="og:description" content="Yes, he has a lousy rec-
ord against Nadal. But he&amp;#8217;s displayed a consistency and
durability at a time when the competition is deeper than it has
ever been." />
<meta property="og:image"
con-
tent="http://graphics8.nytimes.com/images/2013/08/21/magazine/21-
federer-steinberger/21-federer-steinberger-superJumbo.jpg"/>
<meta name="twitter:card" value="summary">
<meta property="twitter:title"
      content="Why Roger Federer Is the Greatest of All Time " />
<meta property="twitter:url"
      content="http://6thfloor.blogs.nytimes.com/2013/09/10/why-
roger-federer-is-the-greatest-of-all-time/" />
<meta property="twitter:description" content="Yes, he has a lousy
record against Nadal. But he&amp;#8217;s displayed a consistency
and durability at a time when the competition is deeper than it
has ever been." />
<meta name="twitter:image"
con-
tent="http://graphics8.nytimes.com/images/2013/08/21/magazine/21-
federer-steinberger/21-federer-steinberger-thumbLarge-v2.jpg"/>
<meta name="twitter:site" value="@nytmag"><meta name="PT" con-
tent="Blogs" />
```

---

[13] http://www.nytimes.com/

[14] http://6thfloor.blogs.nytimes.com/2013/09/10/why-roger-federer-is-the-greatest-of-all-time/

List 11.4 actually serves as a good example of having both Open Graph Protocol markup and Twitter Card markup on the same page. It is indeed encouraging to see content publishers at the *New York Times* are willing to take the time and effort to learn about markup and have also implemented the markup nicely.

With what we have learned from Sect. 11.3.1, List 11.4 does not need too much explanation. Note the Twitter processor is quite tolerant as far as the syntax is concerned. More specifically, one can use the `name` attribute together with the `value` attribute (as recommended by Twitter's developer site), or the `property` attribute together with the `content` attribute. In fact, even the `name` attribute together with the `content` attribute is allowed. The Twitter processor is implemented this way to make sure as many content publishers as possible can participate in marking up their pages without worrying too much about the correct syntax.

Let us now use the Twitter debugger (its URL was given in Sect. 11.3.2.1) to test the article about Roger Federer. Open the validator for Summary Card, click the `Validate & Apply` tab, paste the URL of the page into the text box and click the `go!` button. Figure 11.4 shows part of the validation result.

Note the validator not only collects the markup that it can recognize, but also shows a preview of the card, indicating what it will look like when opened in a Tweet. To include this preview in the validator, a WebKit-based browser has to be used. More specifically, Internet Explorer and Firefox will not work because they

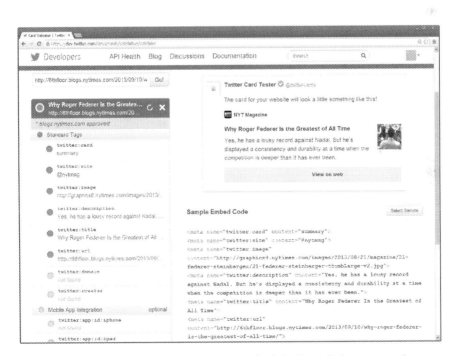

Fig. 11.4 Use Twitter's Summary Card validator to check the Roger Federer page markup

are not WebKit-based, but Apple's Safari[15] browser and Google's Chrome[16] browser will work. Figure 11.4 is based on Chrome browser.

In real practice, after the validation is successfully finished, the next and last step is to apply for the final approval from Twitter. Since we are looking at a production content page that has the markup already and we are also not the owner of the site, it is not possible for us to practice this step. We will therefore simply move on to the next step: Tweet the URL and check the result.

To do so, move to the end of the article. You will find several social media logos, including Facebook, Twitter and Google+. Click the Twitter icon, which will enable us to Tweet the link to this article and share it with our followers.

After creating the Tweet, let us check and see it in my Twitter account. Indeed, there is a new Tweet in my account that reads, "Why Roger Federer Is the Greatest of All Time." Besides the conventional choices such as `Reply`, `Delete` and `Favorite`, the Tweet offers a new choice called `View summary`, with a little card icon attached to it.

This is what Twitter has done on our behalf. More specifically, the Twitter processor has picked up the added markup and it understands these markup are there for a Summary Card. It therefore uses the markup to create a Summary Card attached to the Tweet. Figure 11.5 shows what you will see after clicking `View summary`.

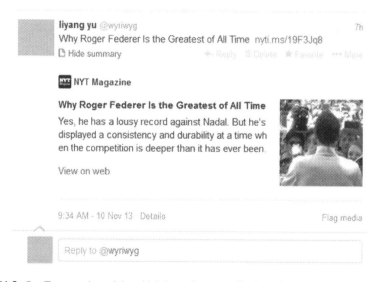

Fig. 11.5 Our Tweet to the article, which has a Summary Card attached to it

---

[15] www.apple.com/safari/

[16] www.google.com/chrome

Other card types follow the same pattern. For example, if a content page contains Twitter markup for a Photo Card, one will find a `View photo` link under the Tweet that points to this page. Clicking this link opens the Photo Card.

In fact, check your Twitter account and go through the Tweets you have received. It is likely that you will see quite a few different Twitter Card types attached to your Tweets. And now, you understand what is behind all these cards.

11.3.2.3 Twitter Card Issues

We have discussed issues about Open Graph Protocol in Sect. 11.2.2.2. Compared to Facebook's Open Graph, Twitter's Twitter Card idea, as far as its implementation is concerned, is even further away from the Semantic Web standards.

Twitter's markup does not follow any of the popular formats, such as microformats, microdata or RDFa/RDFa Lite. As shown in List 11.4, the markup format is simply a collection of name–value pairs, which at best remotely resembles the minimal form of RDFa. In addition, only one card type can be specified per content page.

Twitter does not have any ontology of its own. The card types, such as Summary Card, Player Card, Photo Card, etc., are created based on the recommendation from the community. Besides a set of common properties that all card types share, there are some specific properties associated with each card type. Similarly, these properties are specified in related developer documentation, and not expressed in the form of a formal ontology. In addition, there is no such concept as URI; thus there is no way to uniquely identify a resource in the real world.

Twitter understands the value of sharing vocabularies. Effort is put into maximizing the interoperability by making the Twitter processor understand at least Open Graph Protocol. In fact, a better choice could have been schema.org from the beginning—the entire Twitter markup needs so far can all be accomplished by using terms from schema.org. As we will see in the next section, Pinterest has decided to use schema.org, which works quite well for their needs.

In fact, because of Google rich snippets (Chap. 10) and some other applications such as LRMI (Chap. 10), Best Buy and Pinterest's rich pins, schema.org has gained great popularity among content publishers. It could have been quite an easy task for publishers to accept schema.org as the markup terms for Twitter Cards as well.

It is probably obvious by now that all the limitations faced by Facebook are also applicable to Twitter Cards. For instance, if new applications were to be developed based on the collected structured data (for marketing and related purposes, for example), these applications would have to be coupled quite tightly with the types and properties defined by Twitter at that particular time point. Future changes to the types and properties would likely force the applications to be changed dramatically, or even to be rewritten. Another example is that the added structured data for Twitter Cards cannot be reused by other applications, unless those applications are modified and coded so they are able to understand Twitter-specific types and properties.

In summary, as far as the Twitter design team is concerned, the more content publishers who are willing to participate in the Twitter Card markup, the better. Again, simplicity has a higher priority than strictly following the related W3C Semantic Web standards.

11.3.3   Structured Information, But Not Semantic Web Yet

The idea behind Twitter Cards is similar to the idea behind Google's rich snippets: users can get a preview of the content before clicking through to the website. This not only helps the user to understand the content better, but also attracts more engaged traffic to the website.

However, apart from the idea of adding markups to the content, what Twitter has implemented at this point is not the Semantic Web yet, as we discussed in Sect. 11.3.2.3. A good example that can be considered part of the Semantic Web is Best Buy's markup using RDFa.

In fact, it is quite easy to do a comparison. Let us take a Best Buy page, say, http://stores.bestbuy.com/516/, and use `View Page Source` to examine the markup contained in the page. You will find that RDFa standard is strictly followed, and all the terms used are taken from existing ontologies such as schema.org, FOAF, SKOS, vCards, etc. To see the RDF statements that can be extracted from the on page markup, simply paste the page URL into W3C's RDFa 1.1 Distiller and Parser.[17] List 11.5 shows part of these statements.

---

[17] http://www.w3.org/2012/pyRdfa/

List 11.5 Extracted RDF statements based on the Best Buy page markup

```
@prefix foaf: <http://xmlns.com/foaf/0.1/> .
@prefix geo: <http://www.w3.org/2003/01/geo/wgs84_pos#> .
@prefix gr: <http://purl.org/goodrelations/v1#> .
@prefix r: <http://rdf.data-vocabulary.org/#> .
@prefix rdfs: <http://www.w3.org/2000/01/rdf-schema#> .
@prefix skos: <http://www.w3.org/2004/02/skos/core#> .
@prefix v: <http://www.w3.org/2006/vcard/ns#> .
@prefix xsd: <http://www.w3.org/2001/XMLSchema#> .


<http://stores.bestbuy.com/516/#pagesections> a skos:Concept;
    skos:narrower <http://stores.bestbuy.com/516/announcements/>,
        <http://stores.bestbuy.com/516/clearance/>,
        <http://stores.bestbuy.com/516/details/> .


<http://stores.bestbuy.com/516/#store_516> a
gr:LocationOfSalesOrServiceProvisioning;
    gr:hasOpeningHoursSpecification
<http://stores.bestbuy.com/516/#storehours_fri>,
        <http://stores.bestbuy.com/516/#storehours_mon>,
        <http://stores.bestbuy.com/516/#storehours_sat>,
        <http://stores.bestbuy.com/516/#storehours_sun>,
        <http://stores.bestbuy.com/516/#storehours_thu>,
        <http://stores.bestbuy.com/516/#storehours_tue>,
        <http://stores.bestbuy.com/516/#storehours_wed>,
        <http://stores.bestbuy.com/516/details/>;
    rdfs:seeAlso <http://stores.bestbuy.com/wp-content/store-
images/516/medium.jpg>;
    geo:lat_long "34.051708, -84.284645";
    v:adr [ v:geo [ v:latitude "34.051708";
                    v:longitude "-84.284645" ] ],
        [ a v:Address,
              v:Work;
            v:email <mailto:Stmgrs000516@bestbuy.com>;
            v:locality "Alpharetta, ";
            v:postal-code "30022";
            v:region "GA";
            v:street-address "975 N Point Dr";
            v:tel "678-339-1321" ],
        <http://deals.bestbuy.com/>,
        <http://stores.bestbuy.com/516/details/>,
```

```
<http://www.bestbuy.com/site/olspage.jsp?id=cat12091&type=page&al
lstores=no&mode=fromResult&storeId=516>;
    foaf:depiction <http://stores.bestbuy.com/wp-content/store-
images/516/medium.jpg> .
<http://stores.bestbuy.com/516/#store_review_516> a r:Review-
aggregate;
    r:itemreviewed [ a r:Organization;
            r:name "Best Buy - Alpharetta";
            r:rating <http://stores.bestbuy.com/516/wp-
content/themes/localstores-
specialselections/images/bazaarvoice/transparent-stars/rating-
4.gif> ] .


<http://stores.bestbuy.com/516/reviews/> r:count "240" .


<http://stores.bestbuy.com/516/#storehours_fri> a
gr:OpeningHoursSpecification;
    gr:closes "22:00"^^xsd:time;
    gr:hasOpeningHoursDayOfWeek gr:Friday;
    gr:opens "10:00"^^xsd:time .

……
```

As a comparison, using the same tool on the URL that points to the *New York Times* article about Roger Federer will not extract any structured information at all.

The basic idea of the Semantic Web is to publish structured data on the Web and to make sense out of it. To accomplish this, ideally, data should be published by using W3C standards such as RDF/RDFa, OWL, etc., and ideally should follow the Linked Data principles, such as dereferenceable URIs that return RDF data and link to other data.

However, at this stage of the Semantic Web idea, structured data in any form is better than no structured data at all. Twitter at least has shown another great example of how important it is to publish structured data on the Web, and more importantly, it has successfully provided enough motivation for content publishers to do so.

If more and more companies can follow what Twitter has accomplished, content publishers will eventually understand the importance of adding semantic markups to the content, and will eventually make this a necessary step of the whole publishing process. That will eventually offer a solid foundation for the full implementation of the Semantic Web idea.

11.4 Rich Pins for Structured Information

Pinterest's rich pins remind us of Google's rich snippets. Indeed, just like rich snippets, rich pins allow the consumers to know more about the item on the pin and to further make a decision about it without ever leaving the pin itself.

Again, the added semantic markups on the Web pages are what make this possible. In this section, we study the details of rich pins. Our goal is to understand how rich pins are generated by using the markups on the page, and how the idea and implementation of rich pins is related to the Semantic Web.

11.4.1 Rich Pin Overview

Pinterest is currently the most popular social scrapbooking tool on the Web. To make it more interesting and attractive to users, Pinterest has decided to allow publishers to attach structured data to their content, so the pins can be generated with more relevant information, such as where to actually purchase the product, and whether the movie is suitable for children to view, etc.

The technology behind this feature is known as rich pins, and was first released in May 2013.[18] In this section, we focus on the basic pin types and their properties, and exactly what markup is needed to generate rich pins. With all these technical details in place, we will be able to understand examples and its applications.

At the time of this writing, Pinterest supports four different types of rich pins, as shown in Table 11.6.

Let us use product rich pin as an example to see the detailed markup that is needed for Pinterest to generate a product rich pin. For other rich pin types, one can check the online developer guide[19] to finish the markup similarly.

First, note that to create product rich pin, both schema.org and Open Graph Protocol can be used to implement the markup. If Open Graph Protocol is selected as the vocabulary, the entire markup should be placed inside the `<head>` section of the page, by using `<meta>` tag. On the other hand, if the markup uses terms from schema.org, the markup itself cannot be placed inside `<head>` section, but has to be added inside the `<body>` section, together with the real content. In addition, microdata is the markup format that is currently supported when schema.org is used.

Using terms from schema.org to implement markup is slightly more complex than using terms from Open Graph Protocol. However, schema.org markup supports multiple products on the same page, while using Open Graph Protocol means only one product markup per page is allowed. For this reason, let us focus on the markup using schema.org.

---

[18] http://blog.pinterest.com/post/50883178638/introducing-more-useful-pins

[19] http://developers.pinterest.com/rich_pins/

Table 11.6 Currently supported rich pin types

Rich pin type	Purpose	Supported vocabularies
Product	Product rich pin includes key product information such as product description, price, availability and where to purchase the product	schema.org, Open Graph Protocol
Recipe	Recipe rich pin includes key recipe information such as ingredients, preparation time	schema.org, hRecipe formats
Movie	Movie rich pin includes key movie information such as release date, director, actor(s), content rating (such as PG-13) and review information	schema.org
Article	Article rich pin includes related information about an article, such as title, description of the article and author	Open Graph Protocol

Table 11.7 Required properties for product rich pin

Property name	Purpose
schema:url	Canonical URL for the page, where the markup is added
schema:name	Product name
schema:price	Offer price. Note this property uses class schema:Offer as its domain
schema: priceCurrency	Currency code for the price. Note this property uses class schema: Offer as its domain

Similar to Twitter Cards, each pin type supports and requires a specific set of properties. However, type property is required for all pin types. For example, the following markup,

```
<div itemscope itemtype="http://schema.org/Product">
```

tells Pinterest parser the related markups are here for a product type rich pin.

For a product rich pin, the required properties are shown in Table 11.7.

Other properties can be used when adding the markup, but are not required. These include schema:description, schema:brand, schema:availability, just to name a few.

It is actually important to include property schema:availability, because it tells the consumers whether the product is still available for purchasing. Note property schema:availability uses class schema:Offer as its domain, and its value range is class schema:ItemAvailability. Class schema: ItemAvailability is defined by enumeration, and its instances are summarized in Table 11.8.

Another important tip to remember is to include the site name by using Open Graph term og:site_name, since schema.org does not have a site name property. Having the site name showing on the rich pin lets consumers remember your site, and has the potential to attract more traffic to your site as well.

With the understanding of the product rich pin, other types of rich pins can be similarly studied.

Table 11.8 Possible values for product availability

Instance of schema: Item Availability	Indication
http://schema.org/InStock	Indicates the item for sale is in stock
http://schema.org/OnlineOnly	Indicates the item for sale is available only online
http://schema.org/InStoreOnly	Indicates the item for sale is available only in stores
http://schema.org/OutOfStock	Indicates the item for sale is out of stock
http://schema.org/PreOrder	Indicates the item for sale is available for preorder
http://schema.org/Discontinued	Indicates the item for sale has been discontinued

11.4.2 How Does It Work: Generating Rich Pins Using schema.org

11.4.2.1 The Basic Idea and Process

The creation of rich pins is similar to that of Twitter cards. A publisher first adds rich pin markups to the page content, where a Pin it button is also offered. When a consumer clicks the Pin it button on the page, Pinterest's processor reads the added structured data inside the page and uses it to attach some extra information to the pin it creates, thus turning it into a rich pin. For instance, for a product pin, the extra information includes price, availability and store URL. For a recipe pin, the extra information would be ingredient lists and the time it takes to prepare the food.

Four steps are needed to accomplish this whole process.

• Select the pin type.

The currently supported rich pin types were discussed in Sect. 11.4.1. The idea of rich pin is relatively new compared to Twitter Cards; thus only four different types are supported. It is expected that more and more rich pin types will be released by Pinterest soon. It is again the content publisher's responsibility to review the supported pin types and decide which one is the best choice for representing the page content.

• Add the pertinent markup to the page content.

Each rich pin type has its own set of properties. Some of them are required, and the others are nice to have. Product rich pin is used as one example in Sect. 11.4.1 to show the markup requirements. Implementations of other rich pins can be done similarly. Again, Pinterest's online developer document is able provide all the details that are needed.

- Test the markup and submit application.

Similar to other social networking sites, Pinterest provides a Rich Pin Validator[20] for content publishers to check their markup. Once the markup has been validated, content publishers can request final approval from Pinterest for processing and generating the rich pins.

- Consumers click Pin it button, and more incoming traffic to be expected.

Once the approval is granted, you will soon notice the richness of the created pin. This is also where change is expected: with the rich pin, consumers can gain more understanding about the item on the pin without even leaving the pin, and more engaged traffic will lead to more successful business transactions.

11.4.2.2 Rich Pin Markup Examples

We will again use an existing production page as one example to show the markup of rich pin. It is the wall clock[21] example that is also used in Pinterest's online developer guide.

On the product page, again use View Page Source to open the page source. On the page source, you will find rich pin markups. List 11.6 shows part of it.

List 11.6 Part of the markup in the wall clock product page (edited for formatting purposes)

```
<div id="review_totals" class="pdreview_sidebar fl "
    itemscope=""
    itemtype="http://schema.org/Product">
  <meta itemprop="manufacturer" content="Bai Design"
        itemtype="http://schema.org/Organization">
  <meta itemprop="brand" content="Bai Design"
        itemtype="http://schema.org/Organization">

  <div itemscope=""
       itemtype="http://schema.org/PriceSpecification">
    <meta itemprop="price" content="25.51">
    <meta itemprop="priceCurrency" content="USD" >
  </div>

  <meta itemprop="name" content="Landmark Studio Wall Clock">
```

---

[20] http://developers.pinterest.com/rich_pins/validator/

[21] http://www.wayfair.com/Bai-Design-Landmark-Studio-Wall-Clock-715.LA-BAI1296.html

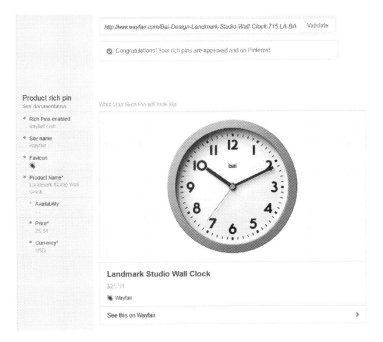

Fig. 11.6 Use Pinterest's rich pin validator to check the wall clock page markup

With what we have learned so far, List 11.6 does not need too much explanation. Note the markup shown in List 11.6 is implemented by using microdata and schema.org. In fact, the same markup is repeated on the same page by using terms from Open Graph Protocol (in the `<head>` section), with `og:url` and `og:site_name` being the extra properties included.

Let us now use the rich pin validator to test the page. Paste the URL of the page into the validator textbox, and click the Validate button to test it. Figure 11.6 shows the validation result.

Note the validator not only shows some of the markup values on the left pane, but also shows a preview of the rich pin. The price, the currency and the store name are the "richness" of this pin. Note the product availability is not included in the markup.

Remember the article in *The New York Times* about Roger Federer (Sect. 11.3.2.2)? In fact, *The New York Times* is one of the partners that Pinterest had when testing the rich pin idea. We can therefore expect to see lots of rich pin markups in their articles. List 11.7 shows the markup for article type rich pin in this Roger Federer article.

List 11.7 Part of the markup in the Roger Federer article in *The New York Times*

```
<meta property="og:type" content="article" />
<meta property="og:url"
content="http://6thfloor.blogs.nytimes.com/2013/09/10/why-roger-
federer-is-the-greatest-of-all-time/" />
<meta property="og:site_name" content="The 6th Floor Blog" />
<meta property="og:description" content="Yes, he has a lousy rec-
ord against Nadal. But he&#8217;s displayed a consistency and du-
rability at a time when the competition is deeper than it has ev-
er been." />
<meta property="og:image" con-
tent="http://graphics8.nytimes.com/images/2013/08/21/magazine/21-
federer-steinberger/21-federer-steinberger-superJumbo.jpg"/>
```

And Fig. 11.7 shows how the article looks in my Pinterest account.

Fig. 11.7 How the article looks after using rich pin markup

Compared to a simple link, this article rich pin tells a lot more about the article itself, without the need to click through it.

11.4.2.3   Rich Pin Issues

Compared to Open Graph Protocol and Twitter Cards, Pinterest's rich pin idea is the closest to the Semantic Web platform—if more restrictions are added.

One of these restrictions is to use schema.org as the *only* markup vocabulary. For now, besides schema.org, Pinterest supports Open Graph Protocol as well. The reason why Pinterest supports Open Graph Protocol is likely because of the consideration of reusing as much existing markups as possible, and also making the markup process as smooth as possible for the content publishers.

However, using Open Graph Protocol terms is a questionable choice, as we have discussed in Sect.11.2.2.3. To position the content well and eventually participate in the Semantic Web global implementation, it is always a good idea to use a true ontology, preferably also a widely accepted one. schema.org, at least at this point, is a far better choice. In addition, because of the fast-growing popularity of schema. org, it is in fact not too much to expect content publishers to become more and more comfortable with schema.org.

Another restriction is to move toward RDFa. Pinterest currently supports microdata, and there is no mention of RDFa or RDFa Lite in their online technical documentation. Again, this is done purposely to avoid any confusion for the content publishers. In Sect. 10.2.2 we discussed the choice between microdata and RDFa, and it is likely that RDFa and RDFa Lite, which are both W3C standards, will offer a smoother transition to the full version of the Semantic Web.

If Pinterest's design team would consider these changes, there would be no other immediate issues that could block Pinterest's great potential.

11.4.3   Semantic Markup at Work

As we have discussed, the idea behind rich pins is similar to the idea behind Google's rich snippets: rich pins let consumers understand the content and the key information before clicking through to the website. This not only helps them to make further decisions, but can also attract more engaged traffic to the website.

More importantly, what Pinterest has implemented so far has positioned itself well for the Semantic Web idea, and the simple implementation of "schema.org + semantic markup" can indeed go quite far. Let us take a look at some examples.

Recall the price information on a product rich pin. What if the price has dropped recently? Similarly, there is also the availability status on the rich pin, whose value can change from "preorder" to "in stock". If you are experienced with rich pins, you probably have noticed that these important information can actually change automatically to reflect the latest updates.

In fact, these automatic updates on the rich pins could be more important then at first glance. Those consumers who have pinned a lamp from a store probably have never shopped at that store, and these pins are often just a wish list for them—they aspire to acquire but are not quite ready to purchase yet. The automatic price drop on the rich pins might just be the push a consumer needs to make the final purchase.

So how does the price and other related information (such as availability status) get automatically updated on rich pins? This is actually the work of the Pinterest crawler: it checks the sites on a daily basis, and it collects the updates to make sure the next time a rich pin is retrieved, the information on that pin will be accordingly updated. The reason why this can be accomplished in a scalable and maintainable fashion is because of the semantic markups contained by the content pages, obviously.

What if the consumer has not recently returned to his pin boards for a while, so he is unaware of the price drop? Pinterest recently released the automatic notification service,[22] where an e-mail will be sent to alert the customer if the price drops. This, again, depends on the fact that Pinterest is able to check and capture the updates in the first place.

For content publishers, the whole process works quite like magic. For those customers who have never shopped at their store and merely pinned a product from the store, the store cannot reach them in any way. However, just because those customers have pinned a product from the store, Pinterest will now be able to reach them and tell them the price change and other related information that can very possibly get them to come to the store.

For a second example, let us consider adding some more information for product rich pin. This is particularly useful for a category such as jewelry, where there is understandably lots of skepticism when it comes to buying online. Without seeing the product in person, consumers often have concerns about the quality and value. If customer reviews from the product page can be added to the markup information, it could be of great help to the potential buyers.

This again is quite feasible for Pinterest, as long as schema.org is used as the underlying vocabulary, which has plenty of terms to describe customer reviews. In fact, one of the rich snippets Google generates has customer review information embedded. It is thus likely to be the case that customer review markups are already readily available on many pages today.

The last example will not be as easy as the previous one and may require more work. More specifically, on a product rich pin, it would nice if *multiple* available prices could be displayed, or, the lowest price and the store that offers this lowest price can be displayed.

Imagine exactly the same product, such as a digital camera, which has a unique model number, is offered by multiple stores, possibly with different prices. Consumers have also pinned the product, each from the web site of a different store.

---

[22] http://blog.pinterest.com/post/57057851300/pin-a-little-save-a-little

To collect all these available prices and show them on a single rich pin, Pinterest has to be able to identify the fact that these product pins, although created from different store sites, are actually referring to exactly the same item.

What Pinterest currently has in place will not be enough to accomplish this requirement. There are different solutions one could evaluate and use. Whatever the solution is, the idea of using URI to uniquely identify a resource in the world may likely come into play, which is probably why URI is one of the core concepts in the Semantic Web.

Regardless of the detailed solution, it is important to understand that since Pinterest has schema.org and hopefully RDFa as its tool, the following markup would be a good start to address the need:

```
<p    vocab="http://schema.org/"    resource=URI_of_the_product
Typeof="Product">
```

The same markup, on the other hand, seems to be not quite possible for Facebook and Twitter, at least at this stage.

Without going into any further details, it is not difficult to foresee other examples that can make rich pin experiences even better. It is probably also fair to say, if one follows the Semantic Web standards and tries their best to reuse existing and widely accepted ontologies, there will then be endless possibilities to create enhancements and applications that will bring the user experience to a better and higher level altogether.

11.5 Summary

In this chapter, we focus on how semantic markup (using schema.org and others) can help to change the way social networking sites work. More specifically, we use three most popular social networking sites, namely, Facebook, Twitter and Pinterest as examples, and discuss their related semantic components one by one.

For Facebook, we take a look at the Open Graph protocol; for Twitter, we study Twitter cards, and for Pinterest, we focus on rich pins. These not only show how the Semantic Web can help social networking sites, but also serve as examples to us as developers, so we can draw inspiration and come up with our own applications.

Chapter 12
Other Recent Applications: data.gov and Wikidata

In this chapter, we study two recent applications, namely, data.gov and Wikidata project. Unlike the applications we studied in the previous two chapters, where the structured information are created by semantic markup, these two applications focus more on the collection and manipulation of structured datasets themselves. With this chapter in place, you will gain a more complete understanding about the Semantic Web standards at work.

The Web site data.gov has attracted more and more attention in the recent years. Based on the visitor metrics collected,[1] the daily visitor numbers have doubled within less than 2 years. Understanding the vast amount of structured data gathered by data.gov and how these datasets are related to the Semantic Web concepts and standards is vital for developing applications, especially applications based on the government data.

The Wikidata project started in 2012 and was the first new Wikimedia project since 2006. Its core data repository was created with full compliance to the Semantic Web standards. Although the full potential of the data repository itself has yet to be accomplished, the benefits of having a centralized semantic data core are clearly revealed by the project itself.

12.1 Data.gov and the Semantic Web

12.1.1 Understanding Data.gov

The site data.gov[2] is a US government Web site that was first launched in May 2009. The purpose is to increase the ability of the public to easily find, download

---

[1] http://www.data.gov/metric/visitorstats/dailyvisitorstatistics

[2] http://www.data.gov/

© Springer-Verlag Berlin Heidelberg 2014
L. Yu, *A Developer's Guide to the Semantic Web*,
DOI 10.1007/978-3-662-43796-4_12

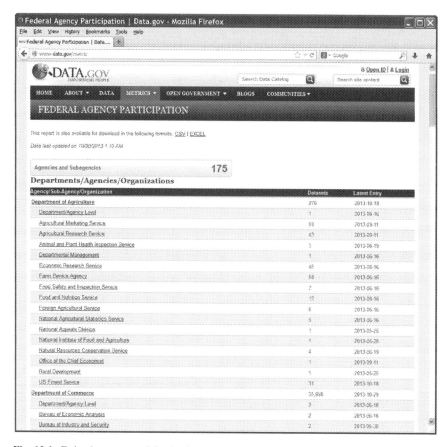

Fig. 12.1 Federal agency participation in open government data, from October 30, 2013

and use datasets that are generated and held by the federal Government. Data.gov, as a gateway to these datasets, provides a descriptions of the datasets, information about how to access the datasets and tools that leverage these datasets.

At the time of this writing, data.gov contains 91,034 datasets, originating from 175 government agencies and subagencies.[3] Figure 12.1 shows the current federal agency participation.

For example, a recently released dataset is called the Medicare Provider Charge Data,[4] which includes information comparing the charges for the 100 most common inpatient services and 30 common outpatient services. The dataset actually shows

---

[3] http://www.data.gov/metric

[4] http://www.cms.gov/Research-Statistics-Data-and-Systems/Statistics-Trends-and-Reports/Medi
care-Provider-Charge-Data/index.html

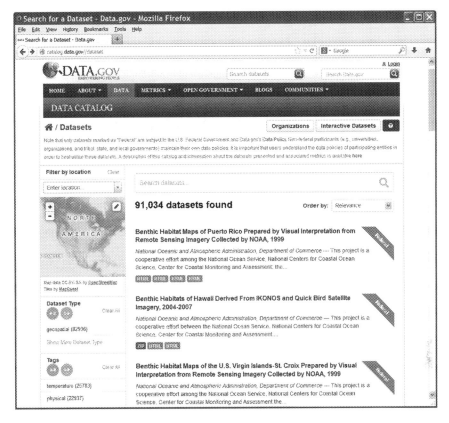

Fig. 12.2 Data catalog for searching datasets on data.gov

significant variation across the country and within communities in what providers charge for these common services. This dataset was released as part of the Obama administration's work to make the US health care system more affordable and accountable.

To search for the datasets you are interested in, you first need to go to the *data catalog*. The data catalog is given by:

```
http://catalog.data.gov//dataset
```

Figure 12.2 shows the search interface.

The easiest way to search for datasets is to simply enter some keyword(s) into the search box that has says "Search datasets..." (Fig. 12.2). Let us again use the Medicare Provider Charge Data as an example. Simply enter "Medicare Provider Charge Data" into the search box and start the search. You should be able to get search results back that look similar to what is shown in Fig. 12.3.

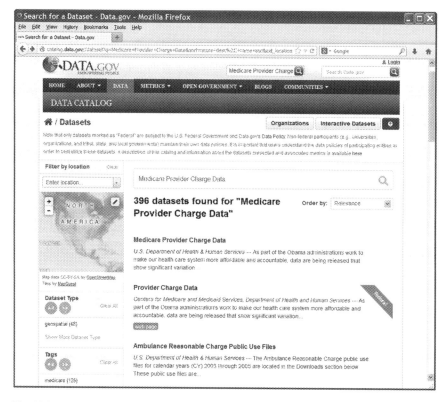

Fig. 12.3   Search results when searching by "Medicare Provider Charge Data"

As shown in Fig. 12.3, the first item in the result page is what we are looking for. Click the name of the dataset, and you will land on the page that describes the actual dataset, which also provides link(s) you can follow to actually download the dataset.

In order to facilitate the search, the data catalog actually provides filters one can use to narrow down the search. The left pane (Fig. 12.2) includes different filters one can select from. One of these filters is a *Format* filter, and one can find the RDF format as one of the available formats.

Let us use the same search as our example. Clicking the "+" sign attached to the RDF format selection selects all the datasets that offer the content in RDF format. Once this filter is used, out of the original 396 datasets (Fig. 12.2), only 25 datasets are left, as shown in Fig. 12.4.

To actually download the dataset, simply click the desired format logo. For instance, clicking the RDF logo under the name Medicare Spending Per Patient (the first resulting dataset shown in Fig. 12.4) downloads the dataset in RDF format. For curious minds, part of the downloaded content is given in List 12.1.

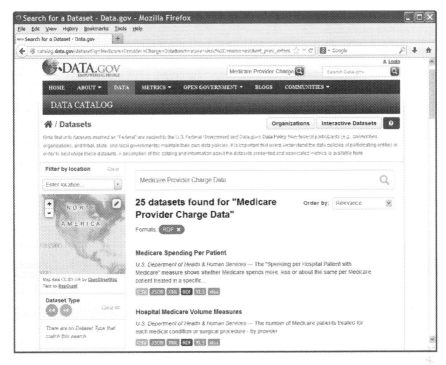

Fig. 12.4 Narrow the search in Fig. 12.3 by using RDF format as a filter

List 12.1 Part of the downloaded Medicare Spending Per Patient in RDF format

```
<rdf:RDF xmlns:rdf="http://www.w3.org/1999/02/22-rdf-syntax-ns#"
         xmlns:rdfs="http://www.w3.org/2000/01/rdf-schema#"
         xmlns:socrata="http://www.socrata.com/rdf/terms#"
         xmlns:dcat="http://www.w3.org/ns/dcat#"
         xmlns:ods="http://open-data-
                standards.github.com/2012/01/open-data-standards#"
         xmlns:dcterm="http://purl.org/dc/terms/"
         xmlns:geo="http://www.w3.org/2003/01/geo/wgs84_pos#"
         xmlns:skos="http://www.w3.org/2004/02/skos/core#"
         xmlns:foaf="http://xmlns.com/foaf/0.1/"
         xmlns:dsbase="http://data.medicare.gov/resource/"
         xmlns:ds="http://data.medicare.gov/resource/fhse-gisv/">
```

```
<rdf:Description
    rdf:about="http://data.medicare.gov/resource/fhse-gisv/1">
  <socrata:rowID>1</socrata:rowID>
  <rdfs:member
    rdf:resource="http://data.medicare.gov/resource/fhse-gisv"/>
  <ds:provider_id>100007</ds:provider_id>
  <ds:hospital_name>FLORIDA HOSPITAL</ds:hospital_name>
  <ds:address_1>601 E ROLLINS ST</ds:address_1>
  <ds:city>ORLANDO</ds:city>
  <ds:state>FL</ds:state>
  <ds:zip_code>32803</ds:zip_code>
  <ds:county_name>ORANGE</ds:county_name>
  <foaf:phone rdf:resource="tel:4073031976"/>
  <ds:measure>Spending per Hospital Patient with
             Medicare</ds:measure>
  <ds:spending_per_hospital_patient_with_medicare>1.06
  </ds:spending_per_hospital_patient_with_medicare
</rdf:Description>


<rdf:Description
    rdf:about="http://data.medicare.gov/resource/fhse-gisv/2">
  <socrata:rowID>2</socrata:rowID>
  <rdfs:member
    rdf:resource="http://data.medicare.gov/resource/fhse-gisv"/>
  <ds:provider_id>330101</ds:provider_id>
  <ds:hospital_name>NEW YORK-PRESBYTERIAN
                  HOSPITAL</ds:hospital_name>
  <ds:address_1>525 EAST 68TH STREET</ds:address_1>
  <ds:city>NEW YORK</ds:city>
  <ds:state>NY</ds:state>
  <ds:zip_code>10021</ds:zip_code>
  <ds:county_name>NEW YORK</ds:county_name>
  <foaf:phone rdf:resource="tel:2127464189"/>
  <ds:measure>Spending per Hospital Patient with
             Medicare</ds:measure>
  <ds:spending_per_hospital_patient_with_medicare>0.95
  </ds:spending_per_hospital_patient_with_medicare>
</rdf:Description>
```

You can see quite a few ontologies have been used to create the RDF content, with each resource representing one provider. The RDF triples describing each provider all use the same properties (from different ontologies); therefore understanding one resource is enough to understand the rest of the dataset.

What is more interesting from this example is that quite a few datasets actually include RDF as their format. This means data.gov is closely related to the idea of the Semantic Web. In fact, a recent statement[5] issued by the US White House indicates that additional efforts have been taken to help Federal agencies to make more data open and available in machine-readable formats. This again shows close relationship between data.gov and the Semantic Web. Let us take a closer look at this topic in the next section.

12.1.2 How Is Data.gov Related to the Semantic Web?

Data.gov should have everything to do with the idea of the Semantic Web. In fact, now that you have reached this far in this book, you should be able to identify some possible areas within data.gov that could benefit tremendously from the Semantic Web standards and related technologies. Let us discuss some of these areas in this section.

First, there is a W3C eGovernment Interest Group,[6] among several other W3C groups that are related to eGov; this interest group has been quite active. The goal of this group is to use or promote the use of W3C technologies to improve government services and operations. This group has also been working together with the Government Linked Data (GLD) Working Group[7] to develop standards that help governments publish their data as effective and usable Linked Data, using the Semantic Web Technologies.

In a recent meeting sponsored by eGovernment Interest Group (April 2013), a presentation[8] by the data.gov team proposed the idea of creating a *Data Ecosystem*, which includes key phases such as gathering data, connecting the community, providing an infrastructure, encouraging technology developers and finally, gathering more data and connecting more people. Among these phases, providing an infrastructure is more important than ever. With this infrastructure in place, the whole data ecosystem will be built on standards and interoperability, which is the also the key goal of Linked Data activity.

How far are we from this infrastructure regarding today's datasets released by data.gov? Let us again go back to List 12.1 as one example to gain some understanding on this.

In List 12.1, URI `http://data.medicare.gov/resource/fhse-gisv/1` is used to identify a resource. Dereferencing this URI, however, will not generate any useful information about the resource it identifies. In other words, this dataset was not created by following Linked Data principles. In fact, by sampling other datasets that have used the RDF data format, one can quickly discover that it is likely that none of the datasets was created by following the Linked Data principles.

---

[5] http://www.whitehouse.gov/sites/default/files/microsites/ostp/2013opendata.pdf

[6] http://www.w3.org/egov/wiki/Main_Page

[7] http://www.w3.org/2011/gld/wiki/Main_Page

[8] http://www.w3.org/egov/wiki/images/8/8f/DataGov_April_2013.pdf

There is, of course, more room for improvements for these datasets. For example, List 12.1 mentioned a hospital named Florida Hospital, and it has used several more RDF triples to describe some related facts of this hospital, including its address, the city it is located in and its phone number, etc. In fact, Florida Hospital does have its own entry in DBpedia, and the following is the URI used to identify this resource,

```
http://dbpedia.org/resource/Florida_Hospital_Orlando
```

Dereferencing this URI shows you more information about the resource. In fact, the entry of Florida Hospital in DBpedia not only has significant overlap with List 12.1, it also offers quite some extra data, such as specifying the resource is of a type given by schema:Hospital.

It is therefore a better idea to simply make a link into the related DBpedia entry, as shown in List 12.2:

List 12.2 An improved version of List 12.1 (with a link pointing to DBpedia data)

```
<rdf:Description
    rdf:about="http://data.medicare.gov/resource/fhse-gisv/1">
  <owl:sameAs rdf:resource=
      "http://dbpedia.org/resource/Florida_Hospital_Orlando">
  <socrata:rowID>1</socrata:rowID>
  <rdfs:member rdf:resource=
              "http://data.medicare.gov/resource/fhse-gisv"/>
  <ds:provider_id>100007</ds:provider_id>
  <ds:measure>Spending per Hospital Patient with
              Medicare</ds:measure>
  <ds:spending_per_hospital_patient_with_medicare>1.06
  </ds:spending_per_hospital_patient_with_medicare>
</rdf:Description>
```

By reusing the structured information from DBpedia, we can actually enjoy one extra benefit: any structured data about Florida Hospital that is newly added into DBpedia will be automatically collected by any application that reads the data shown in List 12.2.

This is also related to another issue that one has to be careful about. Imagine a use case where Florida Hospital is included in multiple datasets, and it will have to be described in detail in each of these datasets. If the pattern shown in List 12.1 is used and followed, one has to repeatedly recode the same information about Florida Hospital. This not only inflates the size of the datasets unnecessarily, but is also very error prone—how does one make sure the telephone number of the hospital is always correctly coded?

Besides all of the above, there is yet another important issue to be considered. As you have learned in this book, each time you look at RDF graphs, there is one single question that you always have to ask: what is the ontology used in the RDF statements?

Again let us use List 12.1 as the example dataset. As shown in List 12.1, there are quite a few ontologies used, with most of the terms taken from the following ontology,

```
http://data.medicare.gov/resource/fhse-gisv/
```

This is obviously an ontology coded by the data.gov team specialized in the medicare branch. It is again worth considering whether existing ontologies can fulfill the goal without us inventing any new ones.

The goal of data.gov is to empower people. Perhaps it is safe to assume that the majority of the datasets are simply data that can be used with common sense and that do not require a background in some specialized field. It is therefore possible that schema.org, an ontology that describes the common things in life (Chap. 10), should be good enough for most of the datasets. List 12.3 shows how List 12.1 looks if schema.org is used.

List 12.3 Another version of List 12.1, made by using schema.org

```
<rdf:Description
    rdf:about="http://data.medicare.gov/resource/fhse-gisv/1">

  <rdf:type rdf:resource="schema:Hospital"/>
  <schema:name>FLORIDA HOSPITAL</schema:name>
  <schema:telephone>4073031976</schema:telephone>
  <schema:naics>100007</schema:naics>
  <schema:description>Spending per Hospital Patient with
                     Medicare</schema:description>
  <schema:address>
    <rdf:Description>
       <rdf:type rdf:resource="schema:PostalAddress"/>
       <schema:streetAddress>601 E ROLLINS ST
       </schema:streetAddress>
       <schema:addressLocality>ORLANDO
       </schema:addressLocality>
       <schema:addressRegion>FL</schema:addressRegion>
       <schema:postalCode>32803</schema:postalCode>
    </rdf:Description>
  </schema:address>

  <socrata:rowID>1</socrata:rowID>
    <rdfs:member rdf:resource=
              "http://data.medicare.gov/resource/fhse-gisv"/>
    <ds:spending_per_hospital_patient_with_medicare>1.06
    </ds:spending_per_hospital_patient_with_medicare>

</rdf:Description>
```

As shown in List 12.3, only a few properties cannot be fully modeled by schema. org. These unmapped properties could be modeled by using existing ontologies after a careful study of the dataset, and without the need to necessarily invent a new ontology.

Again, reusing URIs/ontologies and linking into the Linked Data cloud whenever possible are the core concepts in the Semantic Web world. For the datasets on data.gov to be used efficiently and effectively by the public, these concepts remain vital. This is indeed the key relationship between data.gov and the world of the Semantic Web.

Data.gov's official Web site has a section[9] for the Semantic Web. At the time of this writing, this section is mainly about creating mashup applications by using the datasets gathered by data.gov. We will take a closer look at these mashups and their related issues in the next section.

In summary, there is still quite a bit of work to be done when it comes to introducing the Semantic Web standards and technologies into data.gov. More specifically,

- Develop URI naming schema for use when converting government datasets to RDF

   In fact, not only is a widely accepted naming schema needed to coin URIs for resources, it is also necessary to facilitate the reuse of these URIs across the datasets. For instance, one dataset refers to the city of Atlanta from the energy consumption perspective, and yet another dataset includes the city of Atlanta for education-related data. For both these datasets, the same URI for the city of Atlanta should be used, for obvious reasons.
- Ensure the datasets are published by following Linked Data principles

   The goal of data.gov is to increase the ability of the public to easily find, download and use datasets that are generated and held by the US federal Government. Linked Data principles are at this time the best practice guide to ensure the accomplishment of these goals.
- Develop standard ontologies so datasets can share the same terms

   Reusing existing ontologies within a dataset makes sure the dataset can be recognized and analyzed by as many applications as possible. It also promotes the idea of Linked Data and the Semantic Web. Of course, for the needs that are not covered by existing ontologies, new ontologies simply have to be defined. However, new ontologies should be defined and released as standards, so that they can be reused as much as possible.

These considerations are also at the core of the infrastructure that is currently needed for data.gov. Fortunately, the W3C Government Linked Data (GLD) Working Group is actively working on this; we will take a look at their work in the next section.

---

[9] http://www.data.gov/developers/page/semantic-web

12.1.3   Potential eGov Standards: Breaking the Boundaries of Datasets

The goal of the GLD Working Group is to provide standards and other information that help governments around the world publish their data as effective and usable Linked Data using the Semantic Web technologies, so that the published structured content can be readily found, accessed, shared and re-used with others. This is indeed a big challenge. Based on a report[10] released by the GLD Working Group in April 2013, there are more than one million government datasets published on the Web, in nearly 200 catalogues, published by 43 countries, in 24 languages. And yet it is a fact that they are often hard to find and require considerable programming effort to use. For example, human health and environmental scientists have reported that they often spend over 50 % of their time manipulating the data so they can be interlinked.[11]

The deliverables from the GLD Working Group are directed toward promoting information sharing and interoperability among multiple, distributed and heterogeneous datasets. More specifically, some main deliverables include the following:

- Best practices for publishing linked data
- Standard vocabularies
- Procurement, vocabulary selection, URI construction, versioning, stability, legacy data issues
- Cookbook for linked open data
- Community directory

At the time of this writing, there has not yet been any standard released. However, quite a few of them are in the "working draft (i.e., work in progress)" status. In this section, we take a look at one of these working draft documents in order to obtain some basic understanding of these efforts. Note that since they are not W3C standards yet, we will not study them in much detail at this point. It is always a good idea to check back often to follow the work of the GLD Working Group, especially if you are doing development work using datasets published by government agencies.

One example deliverable document is called the Data Catalog Vocabulary (DCAT).[12] It is an ontology designed to facilitate interoperability between data catalogs published on the Web. By using DCAT terms to describe datasets in data catalogs, publishers increase discoverability and enable applications to easily consume metadata from multiple catalogs.

---

[10] http://www.w3.org/2011/gld/wiki/images/3/3e/W3C_GLD_WG_at_EU_Data_Forum_2013_-_BHyland_20130410_NOTES.pdf

[11] Source: RPI IODGS Data Analytics Project Statistics as of 2013 see http://logd.tw.rpi.edu/iogds_data_analytics

[12] http://www.w3.org/TR/vocab-dcat/

Table 12.1 Main classes defined by DCAT ontology

Class	Definition and usage note	Main properties
dcat:Catalog	Represents a catalog. Typically, a web-based data catalog is represented as a single instance of this class.	dc:title, dc:description, dc:issued, dc:modified, dc:language, dc:license, dc:rights, dc:spatial, dcat:dataset, foaf:homepage
dcat:Dataset	Represents a collection of data, published by a single agent, and available for access or download in one or more formats.	dc:title, dc:description, dc:issued, dc:modified, dc:identifier, dcat:keyword, dc:language, dcat:contactPoint, dcat:distribution, dcat:landingPage
dcat:Distribution	Represents an accessible form of a dataset. For example, a download-able file, or the API that is used to access the dataset should also be defined as an instance of this class.	dc:title, dc:description, dc:issued, dc:modified, dc:license, dc:rights, dc:format, dcat:accessURL, dcat:mediaType, dcat:byteSize

Based on this working draft, the URIs in DCAT ontology all share the following lead string,

```
http://www.w3.org/ns/dcat#
```

and this URI prefix string is associated with namespace prefix dcat. There are three main classes defined in this ontology, as shown in Table 12.1. Note that DCAT ontology makes extensive use of terms from other vocabularies, in particular Dublin Core (see Sect. 2.6.1 for more details about Dublin Core). Again, Dublin Core often has dc as its namespace prefix.

Table 12.1 is quite intuitive and not much explanation is needed. The following example definitions that use the terms defined by DCAT are all taken from the working draft document with minor modifications. More specifically, List 12.4 shows an example description of a data catalog by using the terms defined in DCAT.

List 12.4 An example catalog description using the terms defined in DCAT

```
:catalog
  a dcat:Catalog ;
  dc:title "example Catalog" ;
  rdfs:label "Example Catalog" ;
  foaf:homepage <http://example.org/catalog> ;
  dc:publisher :agent-Office ;
  dc:language <http://id.loc.gov/vocabulary/iso639-1/en> ;
  dcat:dataset :dataset-001 , :dataset-002 , :dataset-003 ;
  .
```

In List 12.4, the catalog instance includes three datasets (represented by relative URI `dataset-001`, `dataset-002` and `dataset-003`), and it lists each of its datasets using the `dcat:dataset` property. List 12.5 shows the definition of `dataset-001`.

List 12.5 Definition of `dataset-001` using the terms defined in DCAT

```
:dataset-001
  a dcat:Dataset ;
  dc:title "Example dataset 001" ;
  dcat:keyword "keyword1","keyword2" ,"keyword3" ;
  dc:issued "2011-12-05"^^xsd:date ;
  dc:modified "2011-12-05"^^xsd:date ;
  dc:publisher :some-agent-office ;
  dc:language <http://id.loc.gov/vocabulary/iso639-1/en>  ;
  dcat:distribution :dataset-001-csv ;

  .
```

List 12.5 shows the basic information about dataset `dataset-001`, including how the dataset should be accessed (as specified by `dcat:distribution` property). List 12.6 shows the details of this access method.

List 12.6 Definition of `dataset-001-csv` using the terms defined in DCAT

```
:dataset-001-csv
  a dcat:Distribution ;
  dcat:downloadURL <http://www.example.org/files/001.csv> ;
  dc:title "CSV distribution of example dataset 001" ;
  dcat:mediaType "text/csv" ;
  dcat:byteSize "5120"^^xsd:decimal ;

  .
```

These examples show the main features of DCAT ontology, and should also provide you with a good start if you need to study and understand more about the deliverables from the GLD Working Group.

Let us move on to the next section, where we see some applications showcased by data.gov. This again will help us understand the importance of publishing government data as Linked Data and following the Semantic Web standards.

12.1.4 Example Data.gov Applications

At this point, there is still a key question that we have not answered yet: what is the purpose of all these published datasets? Exactly what can one do with them?

The answer is simple: these datasets should be used to promote information sharing and to create different applications. For example, one possible kind of applications are those built upon multiple datasets, which can provide decision support in a way that none of the datasets can accomplish *alone*.

As we mentioned in Sect. 12.1.1, the data.gov Web site has a section featuring the Semantic Web.[13] This section is also the only place in the whole portal where applications based on the published datasets are showcased. Figure 12.5 shows one such example.[14]

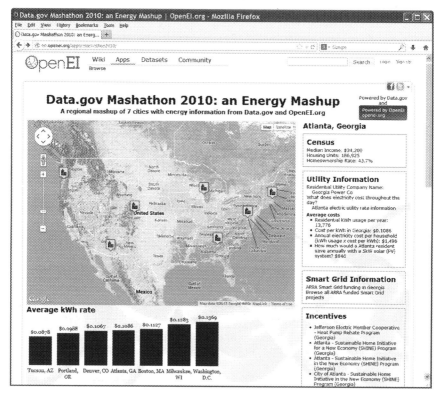

Fig. 12.5 An energy data mashup created by using datasets gathered on data.gov

---

[13] http://www.data.gov/developers/page/semantic-web

[14] http://en.openei.org/apps/mashathon2010/

This is a typical mashup application. It combines data from the Energy Information Administration (EIA) on data.gov with data from Open Energy Information (OpenEI), the US Census and SmartGrid.gov, and provides a comparison of seven cities with populations of roughly half a million people.

The city in Fig. 12.5 is Atlanta, Georgia. By click on a city on the map, one can view some basic statistics about the city, the local utility company, rates, rebates, financial incentive programs and up-to-date information about local Smart Grid projects. Clicking on different cities enables one to compare and contrast the cities to see how local utility rates, median income and other regional factors relate to average annual electricity use.

Although this application shows the power of the published datasets, it is not yet a Linked Data mashup (for discussion of mashup vs. Linked Data mashup, see Sect. 11.4.2). In other words, it is created by studying specific APIs, which are applicable only for the datasets that are involved. If other mashups were to be created based on a new set of datasets, the related new APIs for those datasets would have to be studied, and new code would have to be written to interact with these new APIs.

In fact, other applications showcased by the data.gov page are all of the same type, and are therefore are not covered in more detail. The key here is that they result from interacting with different APIs, which are in front of different datasets.

At the time of this writing, data.gov claims 295 APIs have been created and released, and there is also a page[15] where developers can request APIs for those datasets that have not yet offered APIs.

This, unfortunately, shows the gap between what we have now and an expected data.gov built upon the Semantic Web standards and the Linked Data principles. More specifically, if all the datasets were to be published by following the Semantic Web standards, all these datasets would have a *uniform* API, and there would be no need to request an API for a dataset. Furthermore, developers would have to just learn one *single* API that would work for all the datasets.

Obviously, with the current Semantic Web standards in place, a SPARQL interface could be a candidate for this API. As long as a dataset is published by following the Semantic Web standards, a SPARQL endpoint is all it needs to become open to the outside world. Furthermore, if there are only a handful ontologies used by all the datasets, it would be even easier for developers to query the SPARQL endpoints.

This is the beauty of the idea of the Semantic Web. And in fact, once the Semantic Web standards are followed when publishing all the datasets, the possibilities of new applications will only be limited by our imaginations.

---

[15] https://explore.data.gov/nominate

12.2   Wikidata and the Semantic Web

12.2.1   From Wikipedia to Wikidata

Wikidata[16] is a project led by the German chapter of Wikimedia,[17] and it is run in close cooperation with the Wikimedia Foundation,[18] which operates several online collaborative wiki projects, including Wikipedia. The Wikidata project was launched on October 30, 2012 and it was the first new project of the Wikimedia Foundation since 2006. The project is being funded through a donation of 1.3 million Euros, half of which was granted by the Allen Institute for Artificial Intelligence,[19] an organization established by Microsoft cofounder Paul Allen. Another quarter of the funding comes from the Gordon and Betty Moore Foundation,[20] and the final quarter comes from Google.

The main goal of the Wikidata project is to collect data in a structured form, so that the collected data is reusable and machine-readable. More specifically, reusable means the collected data can be shared at least by Wikimedia projects and possibly third parties, and machine-readable means that computers will be able to easily process and "understand" it.

It is not easy to fully appreciate the goal of the Wikidata project without understanding what a challenge it actually is to run and maintain an online collaborative wiki project such as Wikipedia. In this section, we start with this challenge, so as to gain more understanding of the value of the Wikidata project.

One more piece of background knowledge one has to know: at the time of this writing, Wikipedia supports more than 280 languages; therefore there are altogether more than 280 different language versions of Wikipedia.

12.2.1.1   Are All the Infoboxes the Same?

We discussed infoboxes in Sect. 8.2. Again, an infobox appears on the right side of a Wikipedia page (part of the reason it is called an infobox is because it is in a text box). Figure 12.6 shows part of the infobox on Roger Federer's Wikipedia page.

Figure 12.6 shows some basic information about Federer as a tennis player; such as the year he turned pro, his current ranking in the world, his total prize money, and so on. The most obvious fact about the infobox is that it takes a table form, and it contains seemingly structured information.

---

[16] http://www.wikidata.org/wiki/Wikidata:Main_Page

[17] Wikimedia Deutschland, http://www.wikimedia.de/wiki/Hauptseite

[18] http://wikimediafoundation.org/wiki/Home

[19] http://www.projecthalo.com/

[20] http://www.moore.org/

Fig. 12.6 Part of the infobox on Roger Federer's Wikipedia page

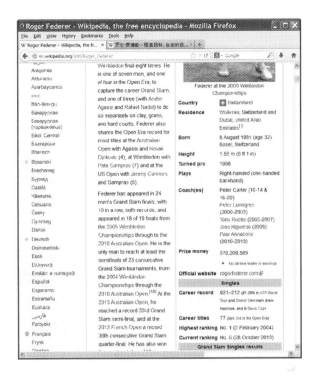

In addition, since these are all basic facts and should not change from one language version of Wikipedia to another language version of Wikipedia, it is therefore completely understandable if one assumes that these facts are all collected at a centralized database, and are shared across all language versions. In fact, this is not the case. The infobox shown in Fig. 12.6 was created by text editing, which uses a markup format that is not quite friendly to all users. List 8.1 shows part of this markup, for example.

Since these basic facts are not shared across all the language versions of Wikipedia, it is possible that the same infobox in another language version may contain different facts. Figure 12.7 shows the infobox in the Chinese version of Roger Federer's Wikipedia page.

One can right away tell the discrepancies between the infobox in the English version and the one in the Chinese version. For example, Career record and Prize money both have different figures. In fact, the mechanisms used to maintain the two infoboxes are also different—different templates, different formatting and different conventions, etc.

In addition, what if a new fact is available and has to be populated to all the infoboxes in all the language versions, for example, Roger Federer has a new ranking? Unfortunately, this has to be done on each and every single infobox, for all the language versions.

Fig. 12.7 Part of the infobox on Roger Federer's Wikipedia page (Chinese version)

One of the goals of Wikidata project is to solve this problem once and for all. In other words, for all the different language versions of Wikipedia, Wikidata should be a *data repository*, where the basic facts are centralized, shared and reused by the all the infoboxes on the same topic, across all the language versions.

12.2.1.2 Are All the Language Links the Same?

Now assume a data repository that houses all the structured information is available, so one can extract the necessary facts from this data repository to populate all the infoboxes in all the language versions. To actually accomplish this, we need to solve one issue first: if we have pages about Roger Federer in different languages, we need to know that these pages are all referring to the *same* topic, or the *same* resource.

This is not a big issue for the Roger Federer topic as a specific example, but it could be an issue for other topics. For example, if the centralized structured data is about Washington as the first President of the United States, once a topic page is reached in a specific language version, how does one know this topic page is about President Washington, and not Washington, DC as the capital city of the United States, or even the state of Washington?

This issue is currently handled by the *links* on the left side of the article (see Fig. 12.6, for example), which list all the languages in which there is also an article about this *same* topic. These links are called *interlanguage* links (or, *interwiki* links). If one has updated the infobox in the English version, one can simply find all the other infoboxes to update by following these links. Understand that although Wikipedia supports more than 280 languages, it does not mean a specific topic (and its page) can be found in all these language versions.

This current implementation, however, has one issue: every article in every language has to explicitly link to all the others, which can quickly produce a messy graph. In addition, the link list has to be manually maintained and the editing tool looks very similar to the one shown in List 8.1. In fact, if one randomly selects a wiki page and checks the editing history on this page, it could be the case that all the recent editing was simply done to maintain these language links. It is also not surprising that on some topic pages, there were more characters needed for the language links than for the actual content!

Another goal of the Wikidata project is to solve this issue, again, by having a data repository. More specifically, the centralized store maintains a list of all the wiki pages that cover the respective topic. On a specific language page where this topic is covered, the language links as shown in Fig. 12.6 will be populated by this centralized list instead of being created and maintained locally.

12.2.1.3 What About Fact Lists?

Wikipedia is a collection of human knowledge. It is expected to have answers to lots of questions, and in most cases, it does.

For example, one can ask the questions such as follows:

- List all the presidents of the United States, in chronological order
- List all the cities that have hosted at least one summer Olympic Games, and currently have a female mayor
- List the top 20 countries, in term of their current population
- List all the tennis players who have ranked as the world number one for at least 100 weeks

The truth is, Wikipedia does not have a *direct* answer to any of these questions, and one has to read through quite a lot Wikipedia pages in order to have the answer. For example, in order to find all the tennis players who have ranked as the world number one for at least 100 weeks, one has to read all the pages about tennis players (such as the Roger Federer page) and manually write down the qualified players.

Fig. 12.8 List of US presidents in Wikipedia

One way to address this issue is to use the so-called Wikipedia *lists*. A Wikipedia list is a special page consisting of a lead section followed by a list of items, which are often collected for a specific purpose. The items on the list include links to articles in a particular subject area, and may include additional information about the listed items.

For instance, to answer the first question as listed above, one can create a list page that lists all the presidents of the United States, in chronological order. In fact, a list like this does exist,[21] as shown in Fig. 12.8.

This way, if someone else has the same question, this list will give the answer.

Note it is often the case that the same list is available in multiple language versions of Wikipedia. For instance, the list shown in Fig. 12.8 has about 106 language versions. Figure 12.9 shows the Chinese version of the same list.

It may be surprising to understand that the English version and the Chinese version of the same list were actually created separately and manually. In fact, all the other language versions were also created separately.

The issues with this solution are obvious. Since the same information is repeatedly and manually edited, there is a good chance for errors. Second, if some new information becomes available (for instance, there will be a new president at least every 8 years), the new information has to be added to all the lists, manually and repeatedly for each language version.

Fortunately, Wikidata project also addresses this issue by having a data repository. More specifically, based on the collected data, Wikidata will be able to create and update list articles automatically. In fact, instead of creating list articles to provide answers to common questions, Wikidata should even have the ability to answer questions directly (see Sect. 12.2.4).

---

[21] http://en.wikipedia.org/wiki/List_of_Presidents_of_the_United_States

Fig. 12.9 List of US presidents in Wikipedia (Chinese version)

12.2.2   Three Phases of the Wikidata Project

We discussed three major issues in today's Wikipedia in Sect. 12.2.1. These major issues have been targeted by the Wikidata project separately, and therefore became the three phases of the Wikidata project. Based on what we discussed in Sect. 12.2.1, these phases are quite easily understood.

- Phase I: Centralize Language Links

Based on the official status update,[22] this phase has been completed for all versions of Wikipedia as of March 2013. Let us again use the Roger Federer as our example to see how this is implemented in Wikidata.

To reach Federer's Wikidata page, we first land on his page in Wikipedia. From his page, on the left side pane, you will find the links to his other pages in all the different language versions. Move to the bottom of these links, and you will find one clickable link that reads `Edit links`. Click this link to go to the Wikidata page where all the facts about Federer are collected, including all the links to other language versions. In fact, you can also directly access the page by using this URL,

http://www.wikidata.org/wiki/Q1426

as we discuss in the next section.

Figure 12.10 shows part of the centralized links. The language link on each specific language version page is now populated by this centralized list instead of being created and maintained locally. Since the implementation of this phase, on

---

[22] http://meta.wikimedia.org/wiki/Wikidata/Status_updates/2013_03_01

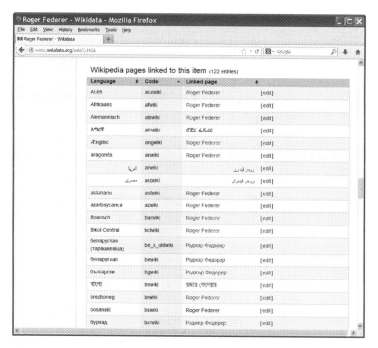

Fig. 12.10 The centralized language links for Roger Federer

average, the size of each wiki page has shrunk by 50 % just due to the removal of the local language links.

If Federer's page later becomes available in a new language, this new language link can be added on the same page shown in Fig. 12.10. In addition, existing links can be edited as well, as shown in Fig. 12.11. In Fig. 12.11, the add link at the last line is where a new language link can be added.

- Phase II: Provide a central repository for infobox data for all Wikipedia pages

According to the official Wikidata site, the first software version of Phase 2 was deployed to Wikidata on February 2013, and some elements have not yet been rolled out. In fact, checking out Federer's page on Wikidata again, one can see the collected statements about Federer, as shown in Fig. 12.12.

These centralized facts should be used to autogenerate the infobox on Wikipedia pages. However, at the time of this writing, not all the data elements on each individual infobox have been collected yet (prize money is one such example), and it is unclear when this phase will be finalized.

- Phase III: Automatically update and translate list articles

Based on the information published at the official Wikidata site, this phase will happen in late 2013. In fact, if you open up a list contained by Wikipedia and check

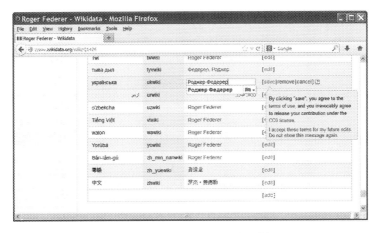

Fig. 12.11 Existing links can be edited and new links can be adde

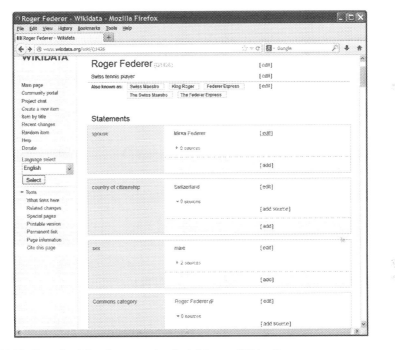

Fig. 12.12 Centralized data for generating the infobox on Wikipedia pages

its different language versions, you can find discrepancies among these versions, which confirms the fact that the source data for these different language versions are not from a centralized location.

12.2.3 *Wikidata as a Data Repository*

At this point, the problems with the current Wikipedia pages are fully discussed, and the goal of the Wikidata project is also clear. We, however, have not yet had a chance to look into the Wikidata project so as to understand its semantic flavor. This is what we now focus on.

12.2.3.1 Wikidata URI Schema

*Item*s are the way Wikidata refers to anything of interest, and they are usually the things that Wikipedia articles are about. One page in Wikidata describes one item. For example, Roger Federer is an item contained in Wikidata.

In Wikidata, not surprisingly, items are identified by URIs. Wikidata has published a document discussing the URI schema[23] it uses. Since understanding these URIs is the first step, let us focus on Wikidata URI schema in this section.

Recall the URI schema used by DBpedia:

- `http://dbpedia.org/resource/Roger_Federer` is the URI for the item Roger Federer;
- `http://dbpedia.org/page/Roger_Federer` is the HTML representation of the description about Roger Federer, and finally,
- `http://dbpedia.org/data/Roger_Federer` offers the machine-readable data about Roger Federer.

By default, dereferencing `http://dbpedia.org/data/Roger_Federer` gives back the RDF model in RDF/XML format. Using `http://dbpedia.org/data/Roger_Federer.ttl` returns the RDF model in Turtle format. Other possible suffixes include `json`, `rdf`, `ntriples`, etc.

The schema used by Wikidata at the current stage focuses on the item ID itself. More specifically, each item has an item ID, in the form of `Q{id}`. For example, Roger Federer has an item ID given by `Q1426`. The persistent URI for Roger Federer is then the following,

`http://www.wikidata.org/entity/`**`Q1426`**

which is also used for linked data as the canonical URI. If dereferenced, it rewrites to the following,

`http://www.wikidata.org/wiki/Special:EntityData/`**`Q1426`**

---

[23] http://meta.wikimedia.org/wiki/Wikidata/Notes/URI_scheme

which then implements content negotiation and redirects to the correct page. For example,

```
https://www.wikidata.org/wiki/Q1426
```

points to the Wikidata HTML page that describes the item, and dereferencing the following URL,

```
http://www.wikidata.org/wiki/Special:EntityData/Q1426.ttl
```

returns the RDF triples in Turtle format. Other suffixes include rdf, nt, json, just to name a few. For those with curious minds, List 12.7 shows part of the Turtle statements one obtains.

List 12.7 Part of the statements when dereferencing using

```
http://www.wikidata.org/wiki/Special:EntityData/Q1426.ttl

@prefix entity: <http://www.wikidata.org/entity/> .
@prefix wikibase: <http://www.wikidata.org/ontology#> .
@prefix rdfs: <http://www.w3.org/2000/01/rdf-schema#> .
@prefix skos: <http://www.w3.org/2004/02/skos/core#> .
@prefix schema: <http://schema.org/> .
@prefix data: <http://www.wikidata.org/wiki/Special:EntityData/>
.
@prefix cc: <http://creativecommons.org/ns#> .
@prefix xsd: <http://www.w3.org/2001/XMLSchema#> .

entity:Q1426
    a wikibase:Item ;
    rdfs:label "Roger Federer"@en, "Roger Federer"@it, ..., ;
    skos:prefLabel "Roger Federer"@en, "Roger Federer"@it, ..., ;
    schema:name "Roger Federer"@en, "Roger Federer"@it,..., ;
    schema:description "Swiss tennis player"@en,
                       "tennista svizzero"@it,...,;
    skos:altLabel "Swiss Maestro"@en, "King Roger"@en, ...,
                "The Federer Express"@en .
...

data:Q1426
    a schema:Dataset ;
    schema:about entity:Q1426 ;
    cc:license <http://creativecommons.org/publicdomain/zero/1.0/>;
    schema:version 82598255 ;
    schema:dateModified "2013-10-29T21:37:47Z"^^xsd:dateTime .
...
```

```
<http://en.wikipedia.org/wiki/Roger_Federer>
  a schema:Article ;
  schema:about entity:Q1426 ;
  schema:inLanguage "en" .

<http://br.wikipedia.org/wiki/Roger_Federer>
  a schema:Article ;
  schema:about entity:Q1426 ;
  schema:inLanguage "br" .

...
```

Note that dereferencing the following URL,

```
http://www.wikidata.org/entity/Q1426.ttl
```

returns the same content as shown in List 12.7.

Finally, understand that for other items, one can simply replace Q1426 with the corresponding ID number to get the correct URIs.

12.2.3.2   DBpedia Vs. Wikidata

When discussing the Wikidata data repository, one would naturally make a connection to another data repository that is also closely related to Wikipedia, and that data repository is DBpedia.

We have covered DBpedia in detail in Chap. 8. DBpedia is fundamentally different from Wikidata. It extracts structured data from the infoboxes in Wikipedia, and publishes them as linked data. Applications can access the data by using a SPARQL endpoint, and DBpedia data sets have been one of the core components of the linked data cloud.

Wikidata, on the other hand, does not extract any structured data from the infoboxes. On the contrary, as a centralized data repository, it allows infoboxes to be populated based on its datasets. The Wikidata datasets themselves are created through its interfaces, and can be maintained and edited by anyone.

With the full implementation of the Wikidata project, the infoboxes in Wikipedia will be much more structured and uniform across different language versions of Wikipedia. This means that the algorithms used by DBpedia to extract structured data from those infoboxes can be made much less complex, and additionally can be run with more efficiency. The DBpedia development team can further concentrate on the tasks that make the DBpedia datasets more accessible and more open, for instance, enhanced SPARQL endpoints and more links to the linked data cloud.

Finally, data in the Wikidata project will be further annotated with provenance information. This is discussed in more detail in the next section, but in a nutshell,

RDF statements in Wikidata not only record the property–value pair, but also include the related information about the sources of the property–value pair.

12.2.4 Wikidata and the Semantic Web

12.2.4.1 Wikidata Data Model and Its Ontology

One of Wikidata project's goals is to make sure the collected data is machine-readable. To accomplish this, the Wikidata project team decided from the very beginning that the collected data would be published by following the related W3C Semantic Web standards. More specifically, this means topics on Wikipedia pages will have their own URIs, they will be described by RDF statements, and terms from selected ontologies will be used when creating these RDF statements.

To describe this formally, Wikidata has proposed a *Data Model*[24] to define what structured information Wikidata attempts to capture. It is not possible to capture all statements that one could make about a resource in the world. A balance must be found between expressive power and complexity/usability. Also understand that the data model is only conceptual and its core focus is about "which information do we have to support", and it does not specify how the data should be represented technically or syntactically. Separate documents are used to specify these issues. For example, there is a further document[25] describing the serialization of the Wikidata data model in RDF.

To increase understanding of the data model, Wikidata also published a simpler version of the proposed data model, called the Data Model Primer.[26] For the rest of this section, we will take a look at this data model, including the Wikidata ontology. We will then look at some real RDF triples extracted from Wikidata's data repository. This will give you a solid foundation for developing applications built upon Wikidata data repository.

The Wikidata data model starts from *Item*. As we discussed in Sect. 12.2.3.1, item represents a resource (a "thing") in the real world, and there are articles in different language versions in Wikipedia describing the same resource. As shown in List 12.7, an item often has a label (a name) and a description identified in each language version. Also, an item has a link pointing to the specific Wikipedia page in a specific language, and if an item is described in multiple language versions, it will have more than one language link.

Besides storing this basic information about an item, there is also a list of *Statement*s that users have entered about the item. Statements are the main approach of representing factual data, such as the current ranking of Roger

---

[24] http://meta.wikimedia.org/wiki/Wikidata/Data_model

[25] http://meta.wikimedia.org/wiki/Wikidata/Development/RDF

[26] http://meta.wikimedia.org/wiki/Wikidata/Notes/Data_model_primer

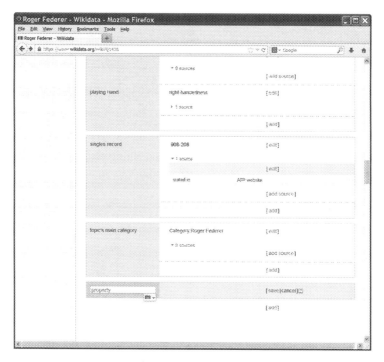

Fig. 12.13 Add a new property for Roger Federer on Wikidata item page

Federer. A statement consists of three parts: a *claim*, a list of *reference*s for the claim and a list of *qualifier*s for the claim. The claim part of a statement is actually a traditional RDF statement, i.e., with subject, property and property value, where the property can again take another item as its value. The reference list and the qualifier list of a statement are new concepts in Wikidata, and they are also optional.

Let us use Roger Federer as one example. As shown in Fig. 12.13, one property is called `singles record`, and it has a string, `908-208`, as its value. This says that up to this point during his tennis career, for single's matches, Federer has won 908 times and has lost 208 times. The `source` for this claim, as shown in Fig. 12.13, is from the `ATP website`,[27] and this is a reference for this claim. In addition, note that Federer is still quite active in his career; therefore one might want to add the fact that "as of August 2013, 908–208 is valid". This new information is a qualifier. Obviously, references and qualifiers are important in Wikipedia, as stated by the Wikidata design team—this is one way to model *disagreement*.

---

[27] http://www.atpworldtour.com, Association of Tennis Professionals (ATP).

The concept of *Property* in Wikidata is quite interesting. Properties are defined by the users; therefore any property can be created. For example, Fig. 12.13 shows how to add a new property for Roger Federer on the Wikidata item page.

As opposed to items, properties do not refer to Wikipedia pages. However, a property in Wikidata has its own page in the namespace `Properties`, and it often uses a property identifier prefixed with letter `P`, in the form of `P{id}`. In addition, property also has a data type associated with it, and the data type is described on the property's Wikidata page.

To see the list of all properties in Wikidata, visit this page,

https://www.wikidata.org/wiki/Wikidata:List_of_properties

On this page, the properties are divided by topic, such as properties for person, properties for organizations, properties for events, properties for place and so on. The properties can also be listed as a summary table,[28] which could be more easily understood.

Any property has a URI to identify itself, and the URI has the following form,

`http://www.wikidata.org/entity/`**`P{id}`**

For example, property `place of birth` has `P19` as its property ID; its URI is therefore given by

`http://www.wikidata.org/entity/`**`P19`**

Dereferencing it goes to the following URL:

`https://www.wikidata.org/wiki/Property:P19`

which is the page in Wikidata for this property (Fig. 12.14).

With an understanding of the data model in place, we can take a look at Wikidata's own ontology, which has the following namespace:

`wikibase: <http://www.wikidata.org/ontology#>`

as shown in List 12.7.

The Wikidata ontology is surprisingly small (to download this ontology, see Sect. 12.2.4.2). It has defined only five basic classes, as well as a handful of data types and data values. It is quite straightforward, except for the handling of properties.

More specifically, as we have discussed, properties are created and edited by Wikidata editors. The number of properties grows dynamically, and their definitions also change. Therefore it is not possible to hard-code these properties in an

---

[28] https://www.wikidata.org/wiki/Wikidata:List_of_properties/Summary_table

Fig. 12.14 Wikidata page for property `place of birth` (P19)

ontology beforehand, as one normally does. To see this, take FOAF ontology as an example, where all the properties that use `Person` as their domain are predefined and cannot be added or modified once the FOAF ontology is created.

To solve this issue, the Wikidata design team decided to model properties as OWL individuals, instead of being subclasses of `rdfs:Property`, as shown in List 12.8.

List 12.8 Definition of Wikidata `Property` class (excerpt from Wikidata ontology, edited for display purpose)

```
<owl:Class rdf:about="&wikibase;Property">
  <rdfs:label>item</rdfs:label>
  <rdfs:comment>The class of Wikibase properties.</rdfs:comment>
  <rdfs:subClassOf rdf:about="&wikibase;Entity"/>
</owl:Class>
```

Now, any newly added property just needs to be a member of the `wikibase:Property` class. Note the `wikibase:Property` class is a subclass of the `wikibase:Entity` class. List 12.9 shows the definitions of all the five basic classes used in Wikidata.

List 12.9 Definition of all five Wikidata classes (excerpt from Wikidata ontology, edited for display purpose)

```
<!-- Basic classes -->

<owl:Class rdf:about="&wikibase;Entity">
   <rdfs:label>item</rdfs:label>
   <rdfs:comment>The class of Wikibase entities.</rdfs:comment>
</owl:Class>

<owl:Class rdf:about="&wikibase;Item">
   <rdfs:label>item</rdfs:label>
   <rdfs:comment>The class of Wikibase items.</rdfs:comment>
   <rdfs:subClassOf rdf:about="&wikibase;Entity"/>
</owl:Class>

<owl:Class rdf:about="&wikibase;Property">
   <rdfs:label>item</rdfs:label>
   <rdfs:comment>The class of Wikibase properties.</rdfs:comment>
   <rdfs:subClassOf rdf:about="&wikibase;Entity"/>
</owl:Class>

<owl:Class rdf:about="&wikibase;Statement">
   <rdfs:label>statement</rdfs:label>
   <rdfs:comment>The class of (reified)
                 statements.</rdfs:comment>
</owl:Class>

<owl:Class rdf:about="&wikibase;Reference">
   <rdfs:label>reference</rdfs:label>
   <rdfs:comment>The class of (reified)
                 references.</rdfs:comment>
</owl:Class>
```

Finally, to understand more about properties in Wikidata, let us go back to property P19. Dereferencing this URL,

```
http://www.wikidata.org/entity/P19.ttl
```

returns the statements shown in List 12.10.

List 12.10 Definition of property P19 (edited for display purpose)

```
@prefix entity: <http://www.wikidata.org/entity/> .
@prefix wikibase: <http://www.wikidata.org/ontology#> .
@prefix rdfs: <http://www.w3.org/2000/01/rdf-schema#> .
@prefix skos: <http://www.w3.org/2004/02/skos/core#> .
@prefix schema: <http://schema.org/> .
@prefix data: <http://www.wikidata.org/wiki/Special:EntityData/>
 .
@prefix cc: <http://creativecommons.org/ns#> .
@prefix xsd: <http://www.w3.org/2001/XMLSchema#> .

entity:P19
 a wikibase:Property ;
 rdfs:label "place of birth"@en, … ;
 skos:prefLabel "place of birth"@en, … ;
 schema:name "place of birth"@en, … ;
 schema:description "the most specific known (e.g. city instead
                     of country)"@en, … ;
 skos:altLabel "birthplace"@en, …  .

data:P19
 a schema:Dataset ;
 schema:about entity:P19 ;
 cc:license <http://creativecommons.org/publicdomain/zero/1.0/> ;
 schema:version 83234203 ;
 schema:dateModified "2013-11-02T10:48:10Z"^^xsd:dateTime .
```

Any application that encounters P19 will be able to receive the definition shown
in List 12.10 and understand it.

12.2.4.2   Example Wikidata Datasets

With our understanding about Wikidata data model and its ontology, it is time for us
to take a look at some datasets generated by the Wikidata project.

At the time of this writing, the official Wikidata dumps can be found at this URL,

http://dumps.wikimedia.org/wikidatawiki/

There are several scripts[29] one can use to analyze Wikidata datasets. These
scripts download the recent Wikidata dumps and process them to create RDF/Turtle

---

[29] https://github.com/mkroetzsch/wda

files. There are options available when running these scripts so as to customize the output (for example, only create claim statements but not reference statements, or to export only texts in English, etc.). It could take several hours to finish the process.

Some example exports can be found at this URL,

http://semanticweb.org/RDF/Wikidata/

which includes four Turtle files: language links only, labels only, statements only and the Wikidata ontology that we have discussed in Sect. 12.2.4.1.

Among these four Turtle files, we have studied the ontology file already. The language links file and the labels file are both quite simple. They contain the exact statements as shown in List 12.7; more specifically the statements involve schema: inLanguage and rdfs:label properties.

Let us again use Roger Federer as an example to study the statements file. Note even for one single item, there are quite some statements describing it—several hundreds at the time of this writing. List 12.11 therefore only includes a few statements describing Federer as an item, but it is good enough for one to follow the pattern in the dataset.

List 12.11 Some statements describing Federer as an Item

```
@@prefix w: <http://www.wikidata.org/entity/> .
@prefix wo: <http://www.wikidata.org/ontology#> .
@prefix r: <http://www.w3.org/1999/02/22-rdf-syntax-ns#> .
@prefix rs: <http://www.w3.org/2000/01/rdf-schema#> .
@prefix o: <http://www.w3.org/2002/07/owl#> .
@prefix x: <http://www.w3.org/2001/XMLSchema#> .
@prefix so: <http://schema.org/> .
@prefix sk: <http://www.w3.org/2004/02/skos/core#> .
@prefix pv: <http://www.w3.org/ns/prov#> .

. . .

Q1426
   a    wo:Item ;
   w:P26s    w:Q1426S53EC49AB-9F46-4FD4-9AAE-C6342CAEDEE9 ;
   w:P27s    w:Q1426SA2132D11-FBBD-44BE-8807-D792797A0F75 ;
   . . . .

w:Q1426S53EC49AB-9F46-4FD4-9AAE-C6342CAEDEE9
   a    wo:Statement ;
   w:P26v    w:Q233306 .

w:Q1426SA2132D11-FBBD-44BE-8807-D792797A0F75
   a    wo:Statement ;
   w:P27v    w:Q39 .

. . .
```

The first statement about Q1426 simply says its type is a Wikidata item. To understand the second statement, keep in mind that the following long string,

```
w:Q1426S53EC49AB-9F46-4FD4-9AAE-C6342CAEDEE9
```

is simply a statement ID and acts like a blank node that has a node ID. We can actually rewrite all the statements that involve P26 in a simpler way as shown in List 12.12:

List 12.12 Property P26 is used to describe Federer

```
Q1426 w:P26s _nodeId .
_nodeId rdf:type wo:Statement .
_nodeId w:P26v w:Q233306 .
```

To understand what P26 stands for, dereference the following URL:

```
http://www.wikidata.org/entity/P26
```

and similarly, to understand what Q233306 is, dereference this URL:

```
http://www.wikidata.org/entity/Q233306
```

Once this dereferencing is done, List 12.12 can be written as List 12.13:

List 12.13 Property P26 is used to describe Federer (List 12.12 rewritten)

```
Q1426 w:spouse(P26) _nodeId .
_nodeId rdf:type wo:Statement .
_nodeId w:spouse(P26) Mirka Federer(Q233306).
```

Similarly, the same translation can be done for all the statements involving P26 in List 12.11, and the result is shown in List 12.14.

List 12.14 Property P27 is used to describe Federer (List 12.12 rewritten)

```
Q1426 w:country of citizenship(P27) _nodeId .
_nodeId rdf:type wo:Statement .
_nodeId w:country of citizenship(P27)  Switzerland(Q39) .
```

By following the same pattern, one can easily understand the statements in the statement dataset. Note the reason why Wikidata uses wo:Statement is because of the reference list and the qualifier list. `wo:Statement` provides an easier way to model these two lists, as one can find in the statement file.

In addition, note that property name often has a letter attached to it, indicating the type of the resource used as the value of the property. For instance, in List 12.12, in `w:P26s`, letter `s` is used to indicate the value of this property is an instance of `wikibase:Statement`. While in `w:P26v`, letter `v` is used to indicate the value of this property is an instance of `wikibase:Item`, a real *value* to some extent.

Finally, understand that this part of the Wikidata project is still in a very early stage; therefore changes are expected. The Wikidata project provides a data access page,[30] and one can check back to this page often to keep up with the updates.

At this point, we have a solid understanding about how Wikidata uses the Semantic Web standards to create its data repository. Obviously, with the structured data in place, Wikidata can support projects well beyond Wikipedia and the like. Everyone will be able to use Wikidata for a variety of different services—again, the data is there, and it is up to us to find the best use for it.

12.3 Summary

This chapter uses two more recent developments to show how the idea of the Semantic Web can be applied to real-world applications. The first example is data.gov. We discussed the background of data.gov, and how it is related to the Semantic Web. Examples are used to show the benefits of using Semantic Web technologies on government open data.

The second example is Wikidata. The relationship between Wikipedia, DBpedia and Wikidata was discussed, and how the Semantic Web fits into the picture was further presented in great detail. Again, this interesting and inspiring project can be used as the basis for us to come up with ideas of our own.

---

[30] https://www.wikidata.org/wiki/Wikidata:Data_access

Part III
Building Your Own Applications
on the Semantic Web

Chapter 13
Getting Started: Change Your Data into Structured Data

Starting with this chapter, we will focus on building our own applications on the Semantic Web. And indeed, before any application can be created, we have to have data first. While it is not hard to find large amounts of structured data on the Web (for example, from the open data cloud), it is also important to understand how to create your *own* RDF data. Therefore your application has a starting point, and your domain can eventually become part of the Semantic Web.

Creating RDF content is a nontrivial task. Issues such as what format to use and what ontologies to adopt require careful planning. In addition, if most of the structured data are stored in relational database tables, how should we convert them into RDF content? These interesting topics are discussed in this chapter, with the goal of building a solid starting point so you can start your own work on the Semantic Web.

13.1 RDF Data in General

In this section, we take a look at RDF data in general. Creating RDF data starts from modeling your data needs. For example, if the goal is to describe the products you provide, data modeling work will focus on identifying those attributes (properties) that are most relevant when it comes to describing these products. These properties and their possible values will then become the main content of the RDF data. Obviously, a schema or vocabulary has to be defined as well so that the terms in this schema can be used to represent the properties themselves. This schema is also known as ontology in the world of the Semantic Web, and every effort should be made to reuse existing ontologies, instead of inventing your own.

In this chapter, we assume all the above modeling work has been finished, and the next step is to create concrete RDF content based on these modeling results.

© Springer-Verlag Berlin Heidelberg 2014
L. Yu, *A Developer's Guide to the Semantic Web*,
DOI 10.1007/978-3-662-43796-4_13

589

The focus of this chapter is how to create the RDF data, although some discussion about ontology selection is also included.

13.1.1 What Does RDF Data Refer to?

Before we start, it is important to understand what exactly we are referring to when we say RDF data. As we now know, an ontology contains terms and the relationships between these terms, often for a specific domain. Terms are often called classes or concepts (class and concept are interchangeable words in the world of ontology). The relationships between these classes can be expressed by using a hierarchical structure: super-classes represent higher-level concepts, and subclasses represent finer concepts. The finer concepts shall have all the attributes and features that those higher-level concepts have.

Besides the relationships between concepts, there is another level of relationship expressed by using a special group of terms: properties. These property terms describe various features and attributes of the concepts, and they can be used to associate different classes together. Therefore, the relationships between classes are not only super-class or subclass relationships, but also relationships expressed in terms of properties. Classes and class hierarchies, together with properties, are the core components of an ontology.

From the perspective of description logic, the above understanding of an ontology maps to the concept of *TBox* data. Once a TBox is applied to a certain real application, there will be its corresponding *ABox* data to make it complete. For example, `foaf:Person` is a class contained by FOAF ontology, and if we say `http://dbpedia.org/data/Roger_Federer` is a member of `foaf:Person` class, we start to get into ABox data. This very statement (assertion) is often considered as part of the ABox data, instead of TBox.

In description logic, although there is a clear distinction between TBox assertions and ABox assertions, they together belong to the underlying knowledge base. In the world of the Semantic Web, any ontology *can* contain any amount of instance data. However, it is a common practice to group TBox data together and separately from its ABox data. The resulting TBox data is the ontology, and the ABox data is also called *instance data* of the ontology.

This pattern is actually more intuitive and easier to understand. For instance, there is only one FOAF ontology, but these are many instance data documents: one such data document represents Roger Federer, another document describes Tim Berners-Lee, and even ordinary people like you and me can have our own FOAF instance documents, and so on. Notice all these instance documents make no modifications to the original FOAF ontology.

For the rest of this book, we will follow this pattern. Furthermore, these instance documents are also referred to as *RDF data*, or simply *structured data*. And by *creating* RDF data, we refer to the activity that uses the terms from (mostly) existing ontologies to describe certain resources in a certain application domain, by following the RDF model specified by W3C.

13.1.2 Decide in Which Format to Publish Your RDF Data

The Semantic Web uses a *graph data model* to store its data, and RDF is the format in which this model is written. Meanwhile, RDF data itself has different serialization formats that one can choose from. Therefore, to create RDF data, the first decision is in which serialization format the RDF data should be coded. Popular choices include RDF/XML, Notation 3, Turtle, N-triples and TriG/N-Quads.

We briefly discussed some of these formats in Chap. 2. In this section, we cover these formats again, so a complete comparison and understanding can be reached.

13.1.2.1 RDF/XML

At the time of this writing, RDF/XML is still the only W3C standard syntax for the RDF model. RDF/XML was originally proposed and used due to the existence of mature and efficient tools that can parse and store XML files. Today, RDF/XML can be recognized and processed by just about any RDF tool one can find. However, it is usually not the best sterilization format to use mainly because it is quite verbose and somewhat difficult for human eyes to read and write.

Without much of an explanation, List 13.1 shows a very simple RDF/XML data file.

List 13.1 A simple example RDF data file in RDF/XML format

```
1:   <?xml version="1.0" encoding="UTF-8"?>
2:   <rdf:RDF
3:       xmlns:rdf="http://www.w3.org/1999/02/22-rdf-syntax-ns#"
4:       xmlns:rdfs="http://www.w3.org/2000/01/rdf-schema#"
5:       xmlns:dc="http://purl.org/dc/elements/1.1/"
6:       xmlns:owl="http://www.w3.org/2002/07/owl#"
7:       xmlns:foaf="http://xmlns.com/foaf/0.1/">
8:
9:   <rdf:Description
9a:      rdf:about="http://www.liyangyu.com/foaf.rdf#liyang">
10:     <rdf:type
10a:        rdf:resource="http://xmlns.com/foaf/0.1/Person"/>
11:  </rdf:Description>
12:
13:
```

```
14: <rdf:Description
14a:      rdf:about="http://www.liyangyu.com/foaf.rdf#liyang">
15:    <foaf:name>liyang yu</foaf:name>
16: </rdf:Description>
17:
18: <rdf:Description
18a:      rdf:about="http://www.liyangyu.com/foaf.rdf#liyang">
19:    <foaf:title>Ph.D.</foaf:title>
20: </rdf:Description>
21:
22:
23: </rdf:RDF>
```

There are only three RDF statements in this RDF data file, and it takes about 20 lines to include them all. A simpler version is given in List 13.2, but it is not as readable as List 13.1: you have to break it down in your mind to realize that it actually represents three different RDF statements.

List 13.2 A simpler version of List 13.1

```
1: <?xml version="1.0" encoding="UTF-8"?>
2: <rdf:RDF
3:       xmlns:rdf="http://www.w3.org/1999/02/22-rdf-syntax-ns#"
4:       xmlns:rdfs="http://www.w3.org/2000/01/rdf-schema#"
5:       xmlns:dc="http://purl.org/dc/elements/1.1/"
6:       xmlns:owl="http://www.w3.org/2002/07/owl#"
7:       xmlns:foaf="http://xmlns.com/foaf/0.1/">
8:
9: <rdf:Description
9a:      rdf:about="http://www.liyangyu.com/foaf.rdf#liyang">
10:    <rdf:type
10a:        rdf:resource="http://xmlns.com/foaf/0.1/Person"/>
11:    <foaf:name>liyang yu</foaf:name>
12:    <foaf:title>Ph.D.</foaf:title>
13: </rdf:Description>
14:
15: </rdf:RDF>
```

13.1.2.2   Turtle

At the time of this writing, *Turtle* is in *Candidate Recommendation*[1] status and will soon become a new W3C standard syntax for RDF data. Turtle is very popular

---

[1] http://www.w3.org/TR/turtle/

among developers, especially when there is a need to write RDF data manually. Turtle is significantly more compact than RDF/XML, and much more readable to human eyes. In addition, SPARQL query language constructs its RDF queries by using almost exactly the same syntax as Turtle.

As an example, List 13.3 is in Turtle syntax and is equivalent to List 13.1:

List 13.3 Turtle version of List 13.1

```
1:    @prefix rdfs: <http://www.w3.org/2000/01/rdf-schema#>.
2:    @prefix foaf: <http://xmlns.com/foaf/0.1/>.
3:    @prefix dc: <http://purl.org/dc/elements/1.1/>.
4:    @prefix owl: <http://www.w3.org/2002/07/owl#>.
5:    @prefix rdf: <http://www.w3.org/1999/02/22-rdf-syntax-ns#>.
6:    <http://www.liyangyu.com/foaf.rdf#liyang> a foaf:Person;
7:      foaf:name "liyang yu";
8:      foaf:title "Ph.D.".
```

Obviously, Turtle feels like a natural representation of RDF. Note that letter a is the shorthand for rdf:type, and ";" is used to specify different predicates applied to a single subject. These are just some examples of the shorthand expressions offered by Turtle; for more examples, see Sect. 2.4.2.

Turtle is a subset of *Notation 3* (N3 for short). Notation 3 is a serialization format originally proposed by Tim Berners-Lee in 1998. It has a compact syntax for writing RDF, but it also extends RDF with features from first-order logic. Notation 3 was never very popular among developers, and it is now considered largely a legacy format. To this extent, Turtle can be roughly viewed as Notation 3 without the first-order logic extensions.

Finally, understand that it is typical for a Turtle document to start with many prefix declarations (see lines 1–5 in List 13.3). Those who write a lot of RDF documents normally have a saved block of such declarations that are often simply copied and pasted into every RDF document for convenience. List 13.4 shows a set of frequently used prefixes.

List 13.4 Commonly used namespace declarations

```
@prefix owl:  <http://www.w3.org/2002/07/owl#> .
@prefix xsd:  <http://www.w3.org/2001/XMLSchema#> .
@prefix rdfs: <http://www.w3.org/2000/01/rdf-schema#> .
@prefix rdf:  <http://www.w3.org/1999/02/22-rdf-syntax-ns#> .
@prefix foaf: <http://xmlns.com/foaf/0.1/> .
@prefix dc:   <http://purl.org/dc/elements/1.1/> .
@prefix dbp:  <http://dbpedia.org/> .
@prefix dbpr: <http://dbpedia.org/resource/> .
@prefix dbpp: <http://dbpedia.org/property/> .
@prefix skos: <http://www.w3.org/2004/02/skos/core#> .
```

To look up popular namespaces and their declarations, a useful resource for RDF developers is `prefix.cc`, found at `http://prefix.cc/`.

13.1.2.3 N-triples

If most of the shorthand expressions are removed from Turtle, a simpler version of Turtle is obtained. N-triples can be understood as one such simplified version of Turtle. N-triples' basic feature is that only one RDF triple exists per line. Although it makes N-triples more verbose than Turtle, this feature, however, implies that N-triples documents can be quickly parsed and can be more conveniently processed by Unix command-line tools. N-triples documents are also highly compressible; therefore large RDF sources such as DBpedia often publish RDF data in N-triples format.

List 13.5 shows the same statements from List 13.1 in N-triples format.

List 13.5 The statements from List 13.1 in N-triples format

```
<http://www.liyangyu.com/foaf.rdf#liyang>
    <http://www.w3.org/1999/02/22-rdf-syntax-ns#type>
    <http://xmlns.com/foaf/0.1/Person>.

<http://www.liyangyu.com/foaf.rdf#liyang>
    <http://xmlns.com/foaf/0.1/name> "liyang yu".

<http://www.liyangyu.com/foaf.rdf#liyang>
    <http://xmlns.com/foaf/0.1/title> "Ph.D.".
```

Note that new lines within the triples in List 13.5 are added due to the page width. When reading them, keep in mind that one single triple should occupy one single line, and should end with a period at the end of the line.

13.1.2.4 TriG and NQuads

RDF data usually takes the form of a set of RDF triples, also known as a *triplestore*. In reality, RDF triples are often collected from different sources; therefore those triples that are harvested from a single source can be viewed as a subset of the whole triplestore. However, for each subset of triples, once collected into the triplestore, the information about its source of origin is lost.

In other words, the "boundaries" of these subsets in the triplestore disappear, and the ability to identify each subset is also lost. Furthermore, the information about whether a single triple was asserted once or multiple times, e.g., by separate distinct sources, is also lost.

The solution to this problem is the TriG notation and the NQuads notation. TriG notation can be simply understood as "Turtle plus graphs", and NQuads notation can be understood as "N-Triples plus graphs".

TriG and NQuads are closely related to the concept of *named graph*. A named graph is an RDF graph which is assigned a name in the form of a URL. The idea of extending a triple into a quad by adding a URI that represents the source graph has been around for quite a few years. The most commonly used quad syntaxes are TriG and NQuads, and when using named graphs, TriG is the *de facto* sterilization format. List 13.6 shows an example RDF graph using TriG notation:

List 13.6 The same statements in TriG format

```
@prefix rdfs: <http://www.w3.org/2000/01/rdf-schema#>.
@prefix foaf: <http://xmlns.com/foaf/0.1/>.
@prefix dc: <http://purl.org/dc/elements/1.1/>.
@prefix owl: <http://www.w3.org/2002/07/owl#>.
@prefix rdf: <http://www.w3.org/1999/02/22-rdf-syntax-ns#>.

<http://www.liyangyu.com/rdf/1> {
    <http://www.liyangyu.com/foaf.rdf#liyang> a foaf:Person;
        foaf:name "liyang yu";
        foaf:title "Ph.D."
}
```

Obviously, TriG is the same as Turtle except that statements in a single graph are grouped within { }. Graph URL <http://www.liyangyu.com/rdf/1> In List 13.6 represents the source graph from which the statements within { } are collected.

NQuads extends N-Triples by adding a graph URL at the end of each triple, therefore assuming the following format:

<subject> <predicate> <object> <**context**> .

where <context> is the placeholder for the graph URL. List 13.7 shows the same triples as in List 13.6, but in NQuads format.

List 13.7 The same statements in NQuads format

```
@prefix rdfs: <http://www.w3.org/2000/01/rdf-schema#>.
@prefix foaf: <http://xmlns.com/foaf/0.1/>.
@prefix dc: <http://purl.org/dc/elements/1.1/>.
@prefix owl: <http://www.w3.org/2002/07/owl#>.
@prefix rdf: <http://www.w3.org/1999/02/22-rdf-syntax-ns#>.

<http://www.liyangyu.com/foaf.rdf#liyang>
   <http://www.w3.org/1999/02/22-rdf-syntax-ns#type>
   <http://xmlns.com/foaf/0.1/Person>
<http://www.liyangyu.com/rdf/1> .

<http://www.liyangyu.com/foaf.rdf#liyang>
   <http://xmlns.com/foaf/0.1/name> "liyang yu"
<http://www.liyangyu.com/rdf/1> .

<http://www.liyangyu.com/foaf.rdf#liyang>
   <http://xmlns.com/foaf/0.1/title> "Ph.D."

<http://www.liyangyu.com/rdf/1> .
```

By extending the core RDF model from a triple to a quad, named graphs provide an extra degree of freedom when managing an RDF dataset. Some benefits include:

- Tracking the provenance of RDF data. The graph URL can be used to track the source of the data.
- Replication of RDF graphs. The RDF triples identified by the graph URL can be separately exchanged and replicated.
- Flexible queries can be implemented. Name graphs allow queries to be addressed to an individual name graph or a collection of graphs.

Finally, as a simple summary, Turtle is the preferred format if you want to write a few hundred triples by hand, and N-Triples is used to publish large RDF data sets like DBpedia.

13.1.3   Decide Which Ontology to Use to Publish Your Data

13.1.3.1   Discovering Ontologies

First, understand that creating RDF data almost always means the involvement of some kind of vocabulary. More specifically, to make a resource interesting and useful, its types and/or properties have to be described. And once you start to describe the type and properties of a particular resource, you have to use some terms, and these terms have to be either coined by yourself, or to be taken from some existing vocabulary, also known as an ontology.

It is widely recommended that if possible, existing ontologies should be used, instead of inventing new ones. Obviously, the key question is how to discover and examine those existing ontologies so as to decide which ones to use.

It is probably not feasible or practical to present a full list of existing ontologies, given the dynamic nature of the Semantic Web world. Table 13.1 shows some well-known examples, which perhaps each developer should be aware of.

It is always a good idea to closely follow the latest development in the Semantic Web community[2] and check back with online resources[3] to find the ontology that might be suitable for your needs. In addition, there are also several helpful search

Table 13.1 Well-known ontologies

Ontology	Brief description
schema.org	Written in OWL, created by Google, Microsoft and Yahoo!. See Sect. 10.1
Dublin Core	Written in RDFS, offers terms for describing documents
FOAF	Written in OWL, offers terms for describing persons and their social network, and their relations to other related objects
Basic Geo	Written in RDFS, offers terms for representing latitude, longitude and altitude information about spatially-located objects
BIO	Written in RDFS, offers terms for describing biographical information about people, both living and dead. It is used often in FOAF documents
vCard RDF	Original vCard format's RDFS version
Creative Commons metadata	Semantically-Interlinked Online Communities Project, written in OWL, offers terms for interconnecting discussion methods such as blogs, forums and mailing lists
SIOC	Minimal means for managing RDF graph content directly via common HTTP operations
GoodRelations	Written in OWL, offers terms for specifying offerings and other relevant aspects of e-commerce on the Web
DOAP	Description of a Project, written in RDFS, offers terms for describing software projects similar to using FOAF to describe people
Music Ontology	Written in OWL, offers terms for describing music, such as the artists, albums, tracks, performances and arrangements
Programmes Ontology	Written in OWL, offers terms for describing brands, series (seasons), episodes, broadcast events and broadcast services, etc.

---

[2] http://semanticweb.org/wiki/Ontology

[3] http://www.w3.org/wiki/Good_Ontologies

tools one can use to discover reusable ontologies. Some of them are briefly discussed here.

- Linked Open Vocabularies (LOV)[4]

This is an online search tool that allows you to search for ontologies that are used in the Linked Data Cloud. The search can be conducted either at the ontology level or at the element level, and the result also includes metrics about the usage of the ontologies in the Semantic Web.

- vocab.cc[5]

This is also an online tool that searches for ontologies based on user queries, which could be arbitrary queries or a specific URI. To help the decision for a specific ontology, information about the usage in the Billion Triple Challenge Dataset[6] (BTCD) of a given property or class is also provided. More specifically, this includes the number of overall appearances of the given URI in the BTCD, as well as the number of documents within the BTCD that contain the given URI.

- Falcons[7]

Falcons is another online search tool which offers four different ways of search, i.e., by object, by concept, by ontology and by document. It also allows users to filter the search results by limiting the search to class or property, or even to a specific Web site. The GUI design for Falcons is quite useful when it comes to ontology search: the fragment of the ontology that is related to the search keyword (s) is presented in a graph model that clearly shows the relevance of the keyword(s).

Besides what we have discussed above, it is important that one follows the development of the Semantic Web and keep a close watch for possible ontology and ontology updates.

Note that it is not always easy to understand ontologies, especially those complex ones. Compared to the FOAF ontology, which only has a handful of classes, schema.org may require careful study and research work. Without fully understanding the ontology at hand, one cannot make a reliable decision about whether this ontology is usable for the specific needs.

It is therefore important for developers to have an efficient and effective way to study a given ontology at hand. In the next section, we use schema.org as one example to see what kind of tools one can use to help us in this regard.

---

[4] http://lov.okfn.org/dataset/lov/index.html

[5] http://vocab.cc/

[6] http://km.aifb.kit.edu/projects/btc-2012/

[7] http://ws.nju.edu.cn/falcons/ontologysearch/index.jsp

13.1.3.2   Understanding a New Ontology

First, make sure you have downloaded schema.org ontology.[8] After downloading, you should get a file named `schema.owl` or `schemaorg.owl`; either would be fine.

To study this ontology, an obvious first step is to examine it by using a simple text editor. However, you would quickly find that this way of studying an ontology is not efficient at all. Some better tools are definitely needed. Fortunately, there are quite a few OWL ontology editors and engineering tools available in the market. A brief discussion of these tools is presented in Chap. 14. For our immediate purpose, we will use TopBraid Composer[9] and show how it can help us understand schema. org more efficiently.

TopBraid Composer offers a free edition, which would be sufficient for this section. For detailed downloading and installing instructions, see TopBraid Composer's Web site. The rest of this section assumes you have TopBraid Composer downloaded and installed successfully on your local machine.

Let us start TopBraid Composer by going into the installation directory and double-clicking the TopBraid Composer executable file. Once it starts, an initial view is presented, depending on local settings. Regardless of how this view looks, the following operations should all work.

To open schema.org ontology, click `File` from the top menu bar, select `New` from the drop-down list and then select `Project...`. When the `New Project` window shows up, click `General`, then highlight `Project`, and click the `Next` button. When the `Project Name` text box is shown, enter a name for this project, for example, `schema_ontology`. Keep everything else as the default values, and click `Finish`.

Now you have a new project called `schema_ontology` in your Navigator window. If you don't see the Navigator window, you can bring it up by using the following procedure. First, click `Window` from the top menu bar, and move the cursor to `Show View`. Wait a moment, and a list of view names will show up; simply find Navigator and click it, and this will bring Navigator window up if it has not been up yet. In what follows, this is the procedure we will use to open other views as well.

Obviously, our `schema_ontology` project is simply an empty project. Highlight it in the Navigator window, and right-click on it to bring up a menu list. From this pop-up list, select `Import...`, which brings up the `Import` window. Expand the `General` node, and highlight `File System`, then click `Next`. When the `From directory:` text box is shown, use the `Browser` button to navigate to the directory where your downloaded `schema.owl` is saved. Open this directory, which will

---

[8] http://schema.org/docs/schemaorg.owl

[9] http://www.topquadrant.com/products/TB_Composer.html

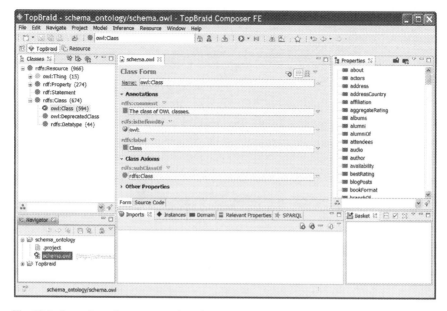

Fig. 13.1 Importing schema.org ontology into the project

show up on the left side, and check `schema.owl` file in the right side, then click the `Finish` button.

Once this is done, go back to the Navigator window, where you will see that the `schema.owl` file is now part of our `schema_ontology` project. Double-click on the `schema.owl` file, and it will be physically imported into the project. This takes a few seconds, and about 6700 lines are imported. Once this process is done, we are ready to explore the `schema.owl` ontology. At this point, your project view should be similar to what is shown in Fig. 13.1.

Let us start from the `Classes` view in the upper-left section of Fig. 13.1. Expand the `owl:Thing` node, and you will see all the classes defined in `schema.owl`, since all classes are subclasses of `owl:Thing`. This is already a much easier way to view all the defined classes, which are arranged based on their names, in alphabetical order. `schema.owl` contains classes for creative work, events, organizations, persons, places, etc.

Most classes defined in the `schema.owl` ontology have subclasses, which in turn have their own subclasses. Let us use class `NewsArticle` as one such example, and Fig. 13.2 shows what you should see about it.

Obviously, `NewsArticle` is a subclass of `Article`, which is a subclass of `CreativeWork`. Figure 13.2 also shows some useful details about class `NewsArticle`. For example, the middle window, called `Class Form`, shows its label in multiple languages, its direct base class, and all the properties that are related to this class. You can also click the `Source Code` tab to show the source code for its class definition.

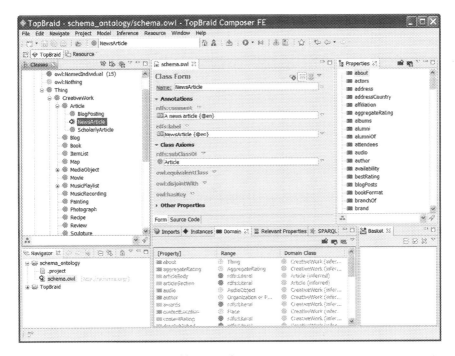

Fig. 13.2 Class `NewsArticle` and its properties

A sound understanding about a class and its hierarchy is just a start. To be able to decide whether an ontology is reusable for any class in this ontology, it is also important to understand what properties are defined for this class, i.e., what properties use this class as their domain. This can be easily accomplished in TopBraid Composer. As shown in Fig. 13.2, `Domain` view is used for this purpose. Again, if `Domain` view does not show up in your project, you can add it by using the open view procedure we discussed earlier.

More specifically, using `NewsArticle` as example, `Domain` view shows all the properties that can be used to describe instances of the `NewsArticle` class. Note that those properties shown in lighter font are defined for the base classes of `NewsArticle`, which will be inherited by `NewsArticle` class. Those properties shown in normal font are specifically defined for the `NewsArticle` class.

Once we obtain an understanding about all the classes and their properties, we have reached a fairly detailed view of the underlying ontology. The last step is to see some instance examples, thereby to reach a complete understanding of the ontology. This again can be done in TopBraid Composer. More specifically, the `Instances` view shows all the instances that are defined for the class that is being shown in `Class Form`. For our example, since schema.org does not contain any instance data, we will not be able to see the instances. However, in your own development work, this is an important step to complete.

13.2   Creating RDF Data Manually

In most cases, it is probably not a good idea to create RDF data manually. First, this method is quite error-prone, given how "ugly" an RDF document is. A small typo will cause a big chunk of the RDF document to be completely ignored by the RDF parsing tool that is being used. Second, it is not a scalable solution: manually creating RDF data will likely not be fast enough for any real and practical application.

Therefore, the majority of the rest of this chapter focuses on how to create RDF content automatically, most often from some existing structured data. However, from time to time, there might be some need to create RDF data manually. For example, a small RDF document may be needed just to test some idea out. This section focuses on how to manually create RDF data. Some popular RDF editors and validators are introduced; TopBraid Composer is then used as example to show how RDF documents can be created. The goal is to make sure, as a developer, you understand how to quickly create and validate some small RDF documents.

13.2.1   Popular Editors and Validators

When manually creating RDF documents, you can simply open your favorite text editor and start to add, line-by-line, from scratch. If you have indeed tried this already, you probably still remember how much you had wished you had some kind of editing support so it could be done more easily.

Our recommendation: unless you enjoy creating RDF statements using a simple text editor, use an RDF editor and remember to do some validation as well.

There are quite a few RDF editors available, ranging from commercially supported software suites to light-weight editors created by individual developers. For those commercially supported software suites, editing RDF documents is only part of their overall functionality. Some example packages include TopBraid Composer, Protégé and Neon Toolkit. For more details about these packages, see Sect. 14.1.

Additionally, there are several choices for validation of RDF documents. First off, note that if you start your work using one of the editors mentioned here, it is guaranteed that when you are done with your RDF document, it will be valid. The reason is quite obvious: the editor itself guides you through the editing process, and it will not allow any invalid entries into the RDF document.

If you have already created your RDF document by other means, you can use TopBraid Composer or Protégé as validators. For example, to use TopBraid Composer as a validator, you can create a new and empty RDF document, and then try to import the RDF document you want to validate. When TopBraid Composer imports the document, the first thing it does is to validate that the document being imported is a valid RDF document. If it is not, TopBraid Composer shows the error information in its `Error Log` window and will not import it (see more details in the next section).

The second choice is to use one of the light-weight validators. One of these validators is the W3C RDF Validation Service from W3C's official site, which was discussed in detail in Sect. 2.6.3. One limitation of this service is that it only accepts the RDF/XML format, so it is necessary to first convert the document from other formats to the RDF/XML format.

Another light-weight tool is the validator[10] maintained by the rdf:about site. This validator accepts RDF/XML, Notation 3, N-triples and Turtle as input formats, and it can convert documents into formats other than the format used by the input.

With all this in place, let us move on to a concrete example. We will see how we can use TopBraid Composer to manually create a new RDF file, and this will also allow us to get more familiar with TopBraid Composer, a popular tool among Semantic Web developers.

13.2.2   Examples: Using TopBraid to Create RDF Data

We saw TopBraid Composer at work in Sect. 13.1.3.2. In this section, we cover more details about this tool. Our goal now is to create a simple RDF document, and we would expect to see a much easier way to do this, compared to using a simple text editor.

To start, click `File` from the top menu bar, select `New` from the drop-down list and then select `RDF/OWL File`. A window named `Create RDF/OWL File` appears, and several details about this new RDF/OWL file have to be specified first.

Let us say we would like to create a simple RDF document to describe Roger Federer, the tennis player. For now, use `http://example/` as the `Base URI` prompted by the `Create RDF/OWL File` window. Also, use `federer` as the file name, and keep `ttl` as the file type.

Note that `Create RDF/OWL File` window also offers a few initial imports, which include some of the frequently used ontologies we have discussed. For now, leave these unchecked, and click `Finish`. You should see something like Fig. 13.3. Again, if you are following along and if some views are not shown in your project, you can open the needed views by following the opening view procedure we discussed in Sect. 13.1.3.2.

As shown in Fig. 13.3, TopBraid Composer created a prefix named `example` to represent the base URI that we entered. Also, TopBraid Composer added some useful namespaces for us, as shown in the `Ontology Overview` window. These useful namespaces include `owl`, `rdf`, `rdfs` and `xsd`. New namespaces can be added by using the `Add` button in that window.

As we have discussed throughout the book, to describe resources in real world, we will always need to think about what ontology to use. For our purpose here, let us say we have decided to use terms from schema.org to describe Federer.

---

[10] http://www.rdfabout.com/demo/validator/

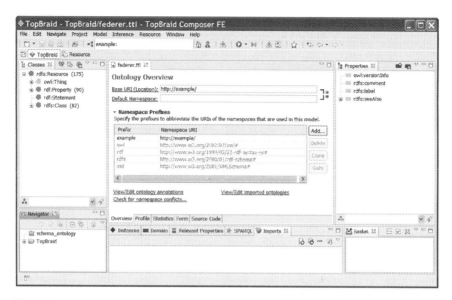

Fig. 13.3 Initial view when trying to create an RDF document about Roger Federer

To use schema.org, we first need to import it into our RDF document. To do so, first select `Imports` tab, then open the project named `schema_ontology` that we created in Sect. 13.1.3.2. Now, highlight `schema.owl` under the `schema_ontology` project, and drag it into the window belonging to the `Imports` tab. TopBraid Composer will then import `schema.owl`; once this is done, your workspace should look like something like that shown in Fig. 13.4.

Note that since `schema.owl` is now imported, you will see many more items in both the `Classes` window and the `Properties` window. This is because every class and property defined in `schema.owl` are now included in these two windows.

It is now time for us to add more RDF statements to describe Federer. First, we would like to say Federer is a `schema:Person` instance. To do so, find the `owl:Thing` node in the `Classes` window, expand this node and find the `schema.org:Thing` node under it. Expand this node again and find `schema.org:Person`. Highlight `schema.org:Person`, and right-click on it, then select `Create instance...` from the pop-up menu. This brings up a new dialog window.

Inside this window, you can specify the name of the new resource. For now, let us name this resource `example:Roger_Federer`, and then click `OK` button. A new instance of class `schema.org:Person` is now created, and your workspace should look like the one shown in Fig. 13.5.

First note in `Classes` window, right behind `schema.org:Person` class, there is now are parentheses with number 1 inside. This means a new instance of this class has been created. Similarly, there are parentheses with number 1 for class `schema.org:Thing`. Since `schema.org:Person` is subclass of `schema.`

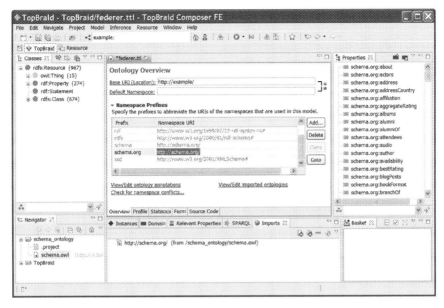

Fig. 13.4 Importing `schema.owl` into your RDF document view

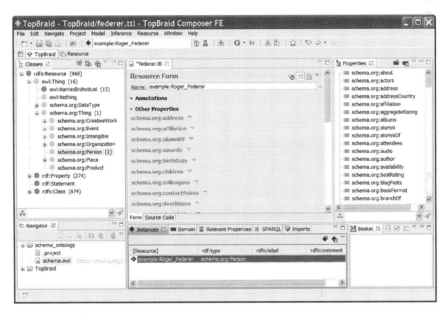

Fig. 13.5 Specifying Federer as a `schema:Person` instance

`org:Thing`, an instance of `schema.org:Person` is also an instance of the parent class.

Another feature to notice is the `Resource Form` in the middle of the workspace. This form shows all the properties that one can use to describe this resource. Obviously, since TopBraid Composer knows the type of this resource, it is then quite straightforward to gather all the properties that can be used to describe this resource, including those properties that use the parent class as the domain. For example, `schema.org:birthDate`, `schema.org:children` and `schema.org:address`, etc.

Finally, note the `Instances` window at the bottom part of the workspace. It should show the current instance that is being worked on. If you highlight this instance and right-click on it, a pop-up menu provides several things you can do, such as rename or delete this instance, just to name a few.

The `Resource Form` area is where we will spend most of our time to add more statements about Federer. Use the vertical bar in the window to find `schema.org:name`, click the white arrow beside it and select `Add empty row`, which brings up a text area below property `schema.org:name`. Enter `roger federer` and click `OK`, which adds a value of property `schema.org:name` to the resource. Similarly, repeat the same steps for property `schema.org:jobTitle`, and add `Swiss Tennis Player` as the value to this property. If you have been following along, your workspace should look like the one shown in Fig. 13.6.

Now, at the top right of `Resource Form`, find the "`Add widget for property...`" button, and click it to bring up a list of properties. From this list, find `owl:sameAs`,

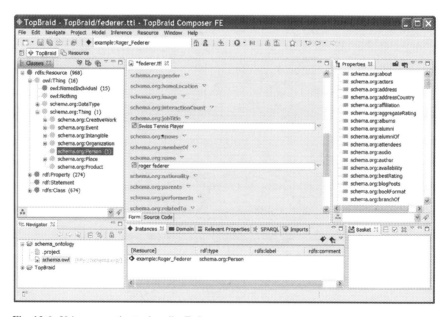

Fig. 13.6 Using properties to describe Federer

highlight it and click OK. This adds it to the property list that can be used to describe
Federer. Add the following value to this property,

<http://dbpedia.org/resource/Roger_Federer>.

Obviously, more properties can be used to describe Federer, depending on our
specific needs. This is much easier than using a simple text editor, and should be
your choice when you have to create RDF documents manually.

To locate the created RDF document, navigate to the local workspace on your
computer, and you will find a TopBraid directory, under which you will also find a
file named federer.ttl. Its content should look like the one shown in List 13.8.

List 13.8 RDF document created by TopBraid Composer

```
1:   # baseURI: http://example/
2:   # imports: http://schema.org/
3:
4:   @prefix example:  <http://example/> .
5:   @prefix owl: <http://www.w3.org/2002/07/owl#> .
6:   @prefix rdf: <http://www.w3.org/1999/02/22-rdf-syntax-ns#> .
7:   @prefix rdfs:     <http://www.w3.org/2000/01/rdf-schema#> .
8:   @prefix schema:   <http://schema.org/> .
9:   @prefix xsd:      <http://www.w3.org/2001/XMLSchema#> .
10:
11:  example:
12:     rdf:type owl:Ontology ;
13:     owl:imports <http://schema.org/> ;
14:     owl:versionInfo "Created with TopBraid
14a:                    Composer"^^xsd:string .
15:
16:  example:Roger_Federer
17:     rdf:type <http://schema.org/Person> ;
18:     <http://schema.org/jobTitle>
19:         "Swiss Tennis Player"^^xsd:string ;
20:     <http://schema.org/name>
21:         "roger federer"^^xsd:string ;
22:     owl:sameAs <http://dbpedia.org/resource/Roger_Federer> .
```

You can manually remove lines 11–14. As a matter of fact, TopBraid Composer
treats any OWL/RDF document as an ontology. This, in general, is correct. However,
as we discussed earlier, RDF data is considered as an ABox instance, while ontology
is an instance of TBox. Manually removing lines 11–14 does not hurt anything; it
only makes the resulting RDF statements more like an ABox instance.

At this point, we have seen the process of manually creating RDF documents.
Even with the support from a powerful tool such as TopBraid Composer, it is still
quite a tedious process. To create RDF content more efficiently, a better approach
has to be implemented.

13.3 RDB2RDF: W3C's Standard for Converting DB Content to RDF Triples

13.3.1 RDB2RDF: General Background

Before we set off to explore other possible approaches to creating RDF content, it might be a good idea to first understand where the vast quantities of data actually stays in real-world applications.

For obvious reasons, we will take Web-based applications as examples. Regardless of whether Web-based applications are offering products or services, they are often backed up by a backend database system, and most likely they share the following workflow:

- Relevant data is typically stored in backend relational database.
- User queries are submitted through Web forms and then translated into SQL queries.
- SQL queries are executed against database tables, and results are sent back to Web browsers as tables or simply as unstructured text.

This general flow can take a variety of different forms. For instance, instead of querying their own backend databases, some applications accept the user query and then use it to consume Web service(s), which in turn are backed up by its own database systems.

Obviously, a more efficient and scalable approach is to directly create RDF data from the content of these relational databases. Since the content in the relational database systems is also structured data, transforming this content into another structured data content (RDF dataset) is therefore easy to implement. In fact, the detailed mapping from relational database to RDF content has been the focus of a large body of research work in diverse domains. This research work has recently led to the implementation of generic mapping tools as well as domain-specific ones.

It is therefore necessary to have a standard that all the implementations of such mappings could follow. To facilitate this effort, the W3C established the Relational Database to RDF (RDB2RDF) Working Group in late 2009. The RDB2RDF working group started the process of standardizing a mapping language called *R2RML* and an automatic default mapping language called *Direct Mapping*. On September 27, 2012, their work became the latest standard released by W3C; it is known as the RDB2RDF standard.

Currently, the RDB2RDF standard has the following two main components:

- R2RML: RDB to RDF Mapping Language,[11] and
- Direct mapping of relational data to RDF.[12]

---

[11] http://www.w3.org/TR/r2rml/

[12] http://www.w3.org/TR/rdb-direct-mapping/

We take a closer look at these new standards for the rest of this section. We then present examples that focus on the implementation aspect, so you can see how to create RDF content of your own.

13.3.2   Direct Mapping from RDB to RDF

The *direct mapping* takes as input a relational database, including its schema and instance data, and generates an RDF representation of the same data. The resulting RDF graph is also called the *direct graph*. The direct mapping defines a simple transformation, providing a basis for defining and comparing more intricate transformations. Before looking into any example, let us discuss the basic idea of this mapping first.

In general, a database has multiple tables, with each table representing one entity. The attributes of an entity are represented by the columns in the table. Therefore, if one entity is mapped to a class type, each column can then be mapped to a property used to describe the class. Also, each row in the table represents one instance of the class type, and can be uniquely identified by a primary key. Therefore, using RDF terminology, one table in a database can be understood as follows:

- The whole table can be mapped to one specific RDFS/OWL class.
- Each row represents one instance of this class.
- Each row key represents an RDF subject.
- Each column in the table is an RDF predicate.
- Each column value is an RDF object.
- Each row is represented in RDF by a set of triples with a common subject, identified by the row key.

Relationships between entities (tables) are modeled by the foreign keys in the tables. For a relational schema, a direct graph can be generated by using the following basic rules:

- Create/identify an RDFS/OWL class for each database table; usually, the table name is used as the class name.
- Each row in the given table is represented by one RDF resource, and to identify this RDF resource, the primary key(s) and the value(s) of the primary key(s) are used as part of its IRI, and this IRI is called the subject IRI.
- Assign an `rdf:type` predicate for each row (using the subject IRI as the subject), identifying it as an instance of the corresponding RDFS/OWL class.
- For each column, construct a triple containing the subject IRI as its subject, the column IRI as its predicate and the column's value as its object. The column IRI should use the column name as part of its IRI.

Table 13.2 `People` table

ID	fname	addr
INTEGER PRIMARY KEY	VARCHAR(20)	INTERGE REFERENCES Address(ID)
7	Bob	18
8	Sue	null

Table 13.3 `Address` table

ID	City	State
INTEGER PRIMARY KEY	VARCHAR(30)	VARCHAR(2)
18	Cambridge	MA

Let us take a look at one simple example to understand this direct mapping. We will use the tables from W3C's office RDB2RDF document in this example. Tables 13.2 and 13.3 show the original database tables.

Direct mapping of this database produces a direct graph as shown in List 13.9.

List 13.9 Direct graph generated by applying the direct mapping rules

```
1:   @base <http://foo.example/DB/> .
2:   @prefix rdf: <http://www.w3.org/1999/02/22-rdf-syntax-ns#> .
3:   @prefix xsd: <http://www.w3.org/2001/XMLSchema#> .
4:
5:   <People/ID=7> rdf:type <People> .
6:   <People/ID=7> <People#ID> 7 .
7:   <People/ID=7> <People#fname> "Bob" .
8:   <People/ID=7> <People#addr> 18 .
9:   <People/ID=7> <People#ref-addr> <Addresses/ID=18> .
10:  <People/ID=8> rdf:type <People> .
11:  <People/ID=8> <People#ID> 8 .
12:  <People/ID=8> <People#fname> "Sue" .
13:
14:  <Addresses/ID=18> rdf:type <Addresses> .
15:  <Addresses/ID=18> <Addresses#ID> 18 .
16:  <Addresses/ID=18> <Addresses#city> "Cambridge" .
17:  <Addresses/ID=18> <Addresses#state> "MA" .
```

First, since there are two tables in this database, two classes are needed, with each one of them representing each of the two tables. More specifically, the class URI is formed from the concatenation of the base URI and the table name. Given the base URI, `http://foo.example/DB/`, the two class URIs are:

```
http://foo.example/DB/People
http://foo.example/DB/Addresses
```

Note that depending on the implementation of the mapping rules, the base URI can be automatically generated or named by the users.

Second, each row is represented by one RDF resource, whose URI should be formed from the concatenation of the base URI, table name, primary key column name and primary key value. For example, the RDF resource that represents row (7, "Bob", 18) should have the following URI,

```
http://foo.example/DB/People/ID=7
```

And the RDF resource that represents row (17, "Cambridage", "MA") should have the following URI:

```
http://foo.example/DB/Addresses/ID=18.
```

The third step is to assign an rdf:type to each RDF resource. Lines 5 and 14 in List 13.9 show this assignment. Note because of the usage of the base URI (line 1), List 13.9 has a more concise format. Its "long format" can be expressed as follows:

```
<http://foo.example/DB/People/ID=7> rdf:type
    <http://foo.example/DB/People>.
<http://foo.example/DB/Addresses/ID=18> rdf:type
    <http://foo.example/DB/Addresses>.
```

The final step is to handle each row individually. For example, row (7, "Bob", 18) produces a set of triples with a common subject, whose URI was created to represent the entire row as a single RDF resource. The predicate for each column is a URI formed from the concatenation of the base URI, the table name and the column name. The object values are RDF literals formed from the lexical form of the column value. See lines 6–8, 10–12 and 15–17 for examples.

Finally, each foreign key produces a triple with a predicate composed from the foreign key column name, together with the "ref-" string. The object of these triples is the row identifier (<Addresses/ID=18>) for the referenced triple. Note that these reference row identifiers must coincide with the subject used for the triples generated from the referenced row. See line 9 as one such example.

Real-world applications often have more complex database schema. Let us look at one more example before we finish this section. Tables 13.4 and 13.5 show the database schema in this example.

Note the Department table has a composite primary key, i.e., column name and column city together are used as the primary key for the whole table. This also means the People table now has a compound foreign key to Department table. More specifically, as shown by Tables 13.4 and 13.5, the columns deptName and deptCity in the People table reference name and city in the Department table. Since the People table uses a single column as its primary key, the Department table does not have a compound foreign key reference.

List 13.10 shows the triples generated by the direct mapping.

Table 13.4 People table

ID	fname	deptName	deptCity
INTEGER PRIMARY KEY	VARCHAR (20)	VARCHAR REFERENCES Department(name)	VARCHAR REFERENCES Department(city)
7	Bob	Accounting	Cambridge
8	Sue		null

Table 13.5 Department table

name	city	manager
VARCHAR(30) PRIMARY KEY	VARCHAR(30) PRIMARY KEY	INTEGER REFERENCES People(ID)
Accounting	Cambridge	8

List 13.10 RDF triples generated by applying the direct mapping rules

```
1:    @base <http://foo.example/DB/> .
2:    @prefix rdf: <http://www.w3.org/1999/02/22-rdf-syntax-ns#> .
3:    @prefix xsd: <http://www.w3.org/2001/XMLSchema#> .
4:
5:    <People/ID=7> rdf:type <People> .
6:    <People/ID=7> <People#ID> 7 .
7:    <People/ID=7> <People#fname> "Bob" .
8:    <People/ID=7> <People#deptName> "accounting" .
9:    <People/ID=7> <People#deptCity> "Cambridge" .
10:   <People/ID=7> <People#ref-deptName;deptCity>
10a:               <Department/name=accounting;city=Cambridge> .
11:   <People/ID=8> rdf:type <People> .
12:   <People/ID=8> <People#ID> 8 .
13:   <People/ID=8> <People#fname> "Sue" .
14:
15:   <Department/name=accounting;city=Cambridge> rdf:type
15a:                                   <Department> .
16:   <Department/name=accounting;city=Cambridge>
16a:                       <Department#name> "accounting" .
17:   <Department/name=accounting;city=Cambridge>
17a:                       <Department#city> "Cambridge" .
18:   <Department/name=accounting;city=Cambridge>
18a:                       <Department#manager> 8 .
19:   <Department/name=accounting;city=Cambridge>
19a:        <Department#ref-manager> <People/ID=8> .
```

The first interesting point from List 13.10 is the URI used to represent the RDF resource in the Department table. Since Department has a composite primary key, each column contained by its primary has to be included in the URI, as shown by List 13.10. Using the long format, the row contained by the `Department` table has the following URI:

```
http://foo.example/DB/Department/name=accounting;city=Cambridge
```

Second, note how the foreign key reference is made from the `People` table to the `Department` table (line 10). Again, the following shows the long format of this mapping:

```
<http://foo.example/DB/People/ID=7>
  <http://foo.example/DB/People#ref-deptName;deptCity>
  <http://foo.example/DB/Department/name=accounting;
    city=Cambridge>.
```

The rest of List 13.10 should be quite straightforward to follow.

Obviously, this direct mapping process can be done fairly automatically, and therefore can often be generated by a software system that implements the RDB2RDF specification discussed in this section. The generated direct mapping is often in the form of an R2RML mapping document (see next section), which can then be used as the starting point for further customization. Such a generated direct mapping is also called a *default mapping*.

13.3.3   R2RML: RDB to RDF Mapping You Can Control

13.3.3.1   R2RML Mapping Language

In the direct mapping of a database, the structure of the resulting RDF graph directly reflects the structure of the database, the target RDF vocabulary directly reflects the names of database schema elements, and neither structure nor target vocabulary can be changed. This implies that each mapping actually produces its own terms, and no existing ontologies can be reused. In order to correct this, the RDB2RDF standard has defined a mapping language, which uses a separate mapping vocabulary, called *R2RML vocabulary*. To understand this vocabulary and the mapping language, we need to start from several important concepts.

First, the actual mapping is accomplished on a row-by-row basis, i.e., a row in a given table is mapped to zero or more RDF triples. A *triples map* therefore specifies a rule for translating each row of a database table to zero or more RDF triples. An *R2RML mapping* defines a mapping from a relational database to RDF, and it has one or more triples maps.

As you might have expected, an R2RML mapping itself is expressed as an RDF graph and written down in Turtle format. More formally, an RDF graph that represents an R2RML mapping is called an *R2RML mapping graph*. The R2RML vocabulary is a set of terms that are defined by RDB2RDF specification and is used to create one such mapping graph. Furthermore, the terms in this vocabulary all share the following leading string:

```
http://www.w3.org/ns/r2rml#
```

which, based on the RDB2RDF specification, should be associated with the namespace prefix `rr:`, and is typically used in RDF document with the prefix `rr`.

We will not be able to cover all the terms contained by the R2RML vocabulary, but we will focus on some important ones throughout this section so that one can at least understand how the basic mapping is accomplished.

Let us start from class `rr:TriplesMap`, which represents a set of rules specifying how to map each row in a given database table to zero or more RDF triples. Obviously, any such set of rules should be an instance of this class. Furthermore, these rules should specify the following in order for a concrete mapping to happen:

- To which database table these rules should be applied,
- How to generate a subject URI for each row contained by the database table, and
- How to generate a predicate–object pair for each column in the table.

For the table information, property `rr:logicalTable` should be used, and the value for this property should be an instance of class `rr:LogicalTable`. Property `rr:tableName` can be used on class `rr:LogicalTable` to specify the name of the database table. For example, the following RDF statement in Turtle format specifies a table whose name is `Dept`:

```
[] rr:tableName "Dept".
```

Note a blank node is created as the instance that represents the table itself. This is often seen in R2RML mapping documents; since the table instance is only used here and locally, there is not much a need to create a specific URI just to represent the table.

The following statement specifies a triples map that should be used on table `Dept`:

```
[] rr:logicalTable [ rr:tableName "Dept" ].
```

As you can see, the triples map instance itself is represented by a blank node.

Property `rr:subjectMap` should be used to generate a subject for each row in a table. The value for this property can be an instance of class `rr:SubjectMap`, which specifies how the subject should be created. More specifically, property `rr:template` can be used on class `rr:SubjectMap` to specify how the URI for the subject should be coined.

For example, the following RDF statement defines a subject map that generates the subjects' URIs from `DeptNo` column of the given table:

```
[] rr:subjectMap
 [rr:template http://data.example.com/department/{DeptNo}"].
```

Again, the triples map instance itself is represented by a blank node. Also note that {} acts as a placeholder – a column name from the database table is included inside it, but the *value* of that particular column is used to replace the column name. This is also why the property name is called rr:template.

Generating a predicate–object pair for each column in the table follows a similar pattern, but it is a little bit more complex. More specifically, property rr:predicateObjectMap should be used on the triples map instance; the value for this property must be an instance of class rr:PredicateObjectMap, which has at least two properties one can use to specify the predicate and object, respectively.

To specify the predicate, property rr:predicateMap should be used on the predicate–object map instance. There are two different possible values for this property. One is to use the *constant shortcut property* such as rr:predicate; the other choice is to use an instance of the rr:PredicateMap class. We will see more information on this later.

Similarly, to specify the object, property rr:objectMap should be used on the predicate–object map instance. Again, there are two different possible values for this property. One is to use the constant shortcut property such as rr:object, and the other choice is to use an instance of rr:ObjectMap class. Again, we will see more information on this later.

Let us summarize what we have learned at this point before we move on to examples. In general, each database table is mapped to RDF statements by using a triples map, whose rules have two main components:

- A subject map is used to generate the subjects of all RDF triples from the rows in the table. The subjects are URIs that are generated by using the primary key column(s) of the table, and
- Multiple predicate–object maps that in turn contains predicate maps and object maps.

RDF triples are produced by combining the subject map with a predicate map and object map, and applying these three to each row in the table. In general, if a table has m rows and n non-key columns, there will be at least $m \times n$ RDF triples generated.

Let us see some examples. We will again use the tables from W3C's official RDB2RDF document. The two database tables are shown in Tables 13.6 and 13.7.

Table 13.6 EMP table

EMPNO	ENAME	JOB	DEPTNO
INTEGER PRIMARY KEY	VARCHAR (100)	VARCHAR (20)	INTERGE REFERENCES DEPT (DEPTNO)
7369	SMITH	CLEAK	10

Table 13.7 DEPT table

DEPTNO	DNAME	LOC
INTEGER PRIMARY KEY	VARCHAR(30)	VARCHAR(100)
10	APPSERVER	NEW YORK

The mapping file shown in List 13.11 should be straightforward to follow.

List 13.11 A simple R2RML mapping for EMP table

```
@prefix rr: <http://www.w3.org/ns/r2rml#>.
@prefix ex: <http://example.com/ns#>.

[]
   a rr:TriplesMap;
   rr:logicalTable [ rr:tableName "EMP" ];
   rr:subjectMap [
      rr:template "http://data.ex.com/employee/{EMPNO}";
      rr:class ex:Employee;
   ];
   rr:predicateObjectMap [
      rr:predicate ex:name;
      rr:objectMap [ rr:column "ENAME" ];
   ].
```

List 13.11 creates following two RDF statements:

```
<http://data.ex.com/employee/7369> rdf:type ex:Employee.
<http://data.ex.com/employee/7369> ex:name "SMITH".
```

Let us explain more about the `rr:ObjectMap` class here. An instance of this class can be used to represent the object part of a generated RDF statement. Since the object value is often take from a particular column contained by the underlying database table, property `rr:column` is therefore often used to map a given column to the object value; in this case, ENAME is the column we use. We will see other ways to specify object value soon.

In addition, property `rr:class` and constant shortcut property `rr:predicate` may need more explanation. Since at this point they don't prevent us from understanding the mapping in general, we will discuss them in the next section.

Note the primary key in the table is used to generate the URI that represents the subject of one generated RDF statement (in this case, the primary key is EMPNO). As we discussed earlier, the intuition behind this is quite obvious. Recall each row in the given database table is viewed as one RDF resource, and since the primary key can uniquely identify each row, it is then quite natural to reuse this primary key to uniquely identify each resource.

Finally, note that only the ENAME column is used in this example to create the mapping. It is easy to add more columns, as we will see in the next few examples.

Obviously, adding the mapping for column JOB can be accomplished by following what we have done for column ENAME. However, adding the mapping for column DEPTNO takes some extra work, given that DEPTNO in the EMP table is a foreign key that links to column DETPNO in the DEPT table. Since foreign keys are ubiquitous in probably any database application, let us take a look in detail how to accomplish this mapping.

The idea itself is straightforward. Say a triples map for EMP table is called #TriplesMap_EMP, and a triples map for DEPT table is called #TriplesMap_DEPT. For predicate ex:department, its subject should come from #TriplesMap_EMP, and its object should come from #TriplesMap_DEPT. This way the link established by the foreign key can be modeled and maintained.

Let us first modify the mapping document in List 13.11. The triples map shown in List 13.11 now is not represented by a blank node, but with name #TriplesMap_EMP, as shown in List 13.12. Besides this added map name, nothing else is changed.

List 13.12 Map name is added to List 13.11

```
@prefix rr: <http://www.w3.org/ns/r2rml#>.
@prefix ex: <http://example.com/ns#>.

<#TriplesMap_EMP>
  a rr:TriplesMap;
  rr:logicalTable [ rr:tableName "EMP" ];
  rr:subjectMap [
      rr:template "http://data.ex.com/employee/{EMPNO}";
      rr:class ex:Employee;
  ];
  rr:predicateObjectMap [
      rr:predicate ex:name;
      rr:objectMap [ rr:column "ENAME" ];
  ].
```

List 13.13 shows the triples map for table DEPT.

List 13.13 A simple R2RML mapping for DEPT table

List 13.13 does not require much of an explanation. The following statements should be generated by List 13.13:

```
<http://data.ex.com/department/10> rdf:type ex:Department.
<http://data.ex.com/department/10> ex:name "APPSERVER".
<http://data.ex.com/department/10> ex:location "NEW YORK".
```

Now, to accomplish the foreign key link as we discussed earlier, we need to modify the mapping document shown by List 13.12. More specifically, we need to add another rr:predicateObjectMap property, which uses triples map <#TriplesMap_DEPT> as a parent triples map. This is shown in List 13.14.

List 13.14 Handling the foreign key in EMP table

```
 1: @prefix rr: <http://www.w3.org/ns/r2rml#>.
 2: @prefix ex: <http://example.com/ns#>.
 3:
 4: <#TriplesMap_EMP>
 5:     a rr:TriplesMap;
 6:     rr:logicalTable [ rr:tableName "EMP" ];
 7:     rr:subjectMap [
 8:         rr:template "http://data.ex.com/employee/{EMPNO}";
 9:         rr:class ex:Employee;
10:     ];
11:     rr:predicateObjectMap [
12:         rr:predicate ex:name;
13:         rr:objectMap [ rr:column "ENAME" ];
14:     ];
15:     rr:predicateObjectMap [
16:         rr:predicate ex:job;
17:         rr:objectMap [ rr:column "JOB" ];
18:     ];
19:     rr:predicateObjectMap [
20:         rr:predicate ex:department;
21:         rr:objectMap [
22:             rr:parentTriplesMap <#TriplesMap_DEPT>;
23:             rr:joinCondition [
24:                 rr:child "DEPTNO";
25:                 rr:parent "DEPTNO";
26:             ];
27:         ];
28:     ].
```

Lines 19–26 in List 13.14 perform a join between the EMP and DEPT tables, on the DEPTNO column. The object of ex:department property is generated from the subject map of the parent triples map, and therefore gives the desired result. Note several new R2RML mapping terms are used here, such as rr:joinCondition, rr:child and rr:parent. Their meanings and the way of using them are quite clear from the context, so not much explanation is needed. In addition, the map of JOB column is also added into List 13.14.

The following RDF statements are the expected results:

```
<http://data.ex.com/employee/7369> rdf:type ex:Employee.
<http://data.ex.com/employee/7369> ex:name "SMITH".
```

```
<http://data.ex.com/employee/7369> ex:job "CLERK".
<http://data.ex.com/employee/7369> ex:department
<http://data.ex.com/department/10>.
```

At this point, we have studied keys RDB2RDF language constructs that are enough to get you started with your own development work. There are other language features that we have not covered here, but with what you have learned so far, you should be able to understand them easily. Again, W3C's official Web site is always the best place to go to understand more about RDB2RDF specifications.

13.3.3.2   R2RML Mapping Customization

So far, there is still one important piece missing from the mapping document, which is, how do we customize the mapping itself so the generated RDF dataset can be recognized and processed by a much wider range of applications? Perhaps the most effective way to accomplish this goal is to use existing ontologies when the RDF statements are generated.

In this section, we focus on the language features from RDB2RDF specifications that can help us in this regard. We start from adding customized types to RDF resources.

- Add customized types to RDF resources

As we saw in the previous section, a row in a given database table is mapped to a single RDF resource, and a subject URI is generated to represent this resource. In fact, a subject URI can have one or more customized types. More specifically, property rr:class can be used on an instance of the rr:SubjectMap class. Furthermore, multiple rr:class properties can be used on one single rr:SubjectMap instance, and the values of these rr:class properties must be *class URIs* (URIs that represent an owl:class).

The basic rule of rr:class is also quite straightforward: using rr:class properties on an rr:SubjectMap instance results in the following generated RDF statements: for each RDF term generated by the subject map, an RDF triple with predicate rdf:type and the class IRI as its object is generated.

Let us see how we can use this to customize the mapping document shown in List 13.14. As line 9 in List 13.14 shows, the employee subject has a type ex:Employee. Let us customize this by using FOAF ontology, which can be easily done as shown in List 13.15.

List 13.15 Change List 13.14 so FOAF ontology is used

```
@prefix rr: <http://www.w3.org/ns/r2rml#>.
@prefix ex: <http://example.com/ns#>.
@prefix foaf: <http://xmlns.com/foaf/0.1/> .

<#TriplesMap_EMP>
  a rr:TriplesMap;
  rr:logicalTable [ rr:tableName "EMP" ];
  rr:subjectMap [
      rr:template "http://data.ex.com/employee/{EMPNO}";
      rr:class foaf:Person;
  ];
rr:predicateObjectMap [
    rr:predicate ex:name;
    rr:objectMap [ rr:column "ENAME" ];
];
rr:predicateObjectMap [
    rr:predicate ex:job;
    rr:objectMap [ rr:column "JOB" ];
];
rr:predicateObjectMap [
    rr:predicate ex:department;
    rr:objectMap [
        rr:parentTriplesMap <#TriplesMap_DEPT>;
        rr:joinCondition [
            rr:child "DEPTNO";
            rr:parent "DEPTNO";
        ];
    ];
].
```

The following statements are the expected output:

```
<http://data.ex.com/employee/7369> rdf:type foaf:Person.
<http://data.ex.com/employee/7369> ex:name "SMITH".
<http://data.ex.com/employee/7369> ex:job "CLERK".
<http://data.ex.com/employee/7369> ex:department
<http://data.ex.com/department/10>.
```

- Add customized predicates to RDF resources

To add customized predicates to the generated RDF resources, one needs to use *constant RDF terms*. If a constant RDF term is used in the mapping document, the row in the database table is ignored and a constant value is always generated.

A constant RDF term is represented by property `rr:constant`, and the value of this property is the constant value that is generated.

Property `rr:constant` can be used on different mapping instances. More specifically, if it is used on an instance of `rr:SubjectMap` or `rr:PredicateMap`, a URI must be its value. If it is used on an instance of `rr:ObjectMap`, either a URI or a literal can be used as its value.

Let us take a look at one example. List 13.16 shows one such usage of `rr:constant` property.

List 13.16 Example of using `rr:constant` property

```
[] rr:predicateMap [ rr:constant rdf:type ];
   rr:objectMap [ rr:constant foaf:Person ].
```

If List 13.16 is added to a triples map, this predicate–object map would add the following triple to *all* resources `?x` generated by the triples map:

```
?x rdf:type foaf:Person.
```

Note List 13.16 uses constant RDF terms on both predicate and object; it is perfectly valid to use a constant RDF term only on predicate or object. List 13.17 shows one such example.

List 13.17 Example of using `rr:constant` property on predicate map

```
[] rr:predicateMap [ rr:constant foaf:name ];
   rr:objectMap [ rr:column "ENAME" ].
```

If List 13.17 is added to a triples map, this predicate–object map would add the following triple to *all* resources `?x` generated by the triples map:

```
?x foaf:name "?y".
```

where `?y` represents the particular value taken from the ENAME column in the database table.

In fact, Lists 13.16 and 13.17 can be expressed more concisely by using *constant shortcut properties* `rr:subject`, `rr:predicate`, `rr:object` and `rr:graph`. Occurrences of these properties must be treated exactly as if the triples in Table 13.8 were present in the mapping document.

Given the information in Table 13.8, List 13.18 is equivalent to the following mapping statement:

```
[] rr:predicate rdf:type;
   rr:object foaf:Person.
```

Table 13.8 Constant shortcut properties and their replacement triples

Triples involving constant shortcut property	Replacement triples
?x rr:subject "?y".	?x rr:subjectMap [rr:constant ?y].
?x rr:predicate "?y".	?x rr:predicateMap [rr:constant ?y].
?x rr:object "?y".	?x rr:objectMap [rr:constant ?y].
?x rr:graph "?y".	?x rr:graphMap [rr:constant ?y].

With all we have learned here so far, we can now easily add more customized mapping into List 13.15. List 13.18 shows the new mapping document.

List 13.18 Change List 13.15 so more customized mapping is added

```
@prefix rr: <http://www.w3.org/ns/r2rml#>.
@prefix ex: <http://example.com/ns#>.
@prefix foaf: <http://xmlns.com/foaf/0.1/> .

<#TriplesMap_EMP>
  a rr:TriplesMap;
  rr:logicalTable [ rr:tableName "EMP" ];
  rr:subjectMap [
      rr:temlate "http://data.ex.com/employee/{EMPNO}";
      rr:class foaf:Person;
  ];
  rr:predicateObjectMap [
      rr:predicate foaf:name;
      rr:objectMap [ rr:column "ENAME" ];
  ];
  rr:predicateObjectMap [
      rr:predicate foaf:currentProject;
      rr:objectMap [ rr:column "JOB" ];
  ];
  rr:predicateObjectMap [
      rr:predicate ex:department;
      rr:objectMap [
         rr:parentTriplesMap <#TriplesMap_DEPT>;
         rr:joinCondition [
            rr:child "DEPTNO";
            rr:parent "DEPTNO";
         ];
      ];
  ].
```

And List 13.18 produces the following RDF statements:

```
<http://data.ex.com/employee/7369> rdf:type foaf:Person.
<http://data.ex.com/employee/7369> foaf:name "SMITH".
<http://data.ex.com/employee/7369> foaf:currentProject
"CLERK".
<http://data.ex.com/employee/7369> ex:department
<http://data.ex.com/department/10>.
```

These examples illustrate the main method used by R2RML mapping to add more customized information to the generated RDF dataset. Again, it is always helpful to refer back to W3C's official RDB2RDF specification site for more discussion and examples.

Now we are ready to move on to some real-life examples. A software system that has implemented this RDB2RDF specification is qualified as a *R2RML processor*. A R2RML processor is a system that takes R2RML mapping documents and database tables as its input, and provides access to the output RDF dataset.

Note that the RDB2RDF specification does not put any constraint on the method of access to the output dataset generated by a conforming R2RML processor. A R2RML processor may choose to materialize the generated RDF dataset into a file, or to offer virtual access through an interface that supports SPARQL, or to provide any other means of accessing the dataset.

13.4 RDB2RDF Example Implementation

13.4.1 RDB2RDF Direct Mapping

Direct mapping, as we discussed, has the drawback of lacking the control of the terms being used. Each direct mapping has to practically invent its own terms, and no existing ontologies can be used. For this reason, it is not that popular in real development. As a result, we won't spend much time on this topic. There are several tools one can use for direct mapping if needed. One such example is D2RQ Platform,[13] which is not discussed in detail here.

On the other hand, R2RML gives much more control to the user, and existing ontologies can be used in the mapping. For the rest of this section, we focus on one such example by using Virtuoso.

---

[13] http://d2rq.org/

13.4.2   Step-by-Step R2RML Example: Virtuoso

13.4.2.1   Installing and Configuring Virtuoso Open Source Edition

Virtuoso[14] provides a sound implementation of the R2RML specification. It is available in both open source and commercial editions. The open source edition is also known as *OpenLink Virtuoso*. Everything in this section can be accomplished by using the open source edition.

First, let us go through the installation and configuration of the Virtuoso system. At the time of this writing, the latest downloadable version can be found at,

```
http://sourceforge.net/projects/virtuoso/
```

You may need to navigate around to find the version that works the best for your machine. This example uses version is 6.1.6, released on August 2, 2012. The downloaded file itself is named `virtuoso-opensource-win32-20120802.zip`.

Once you download this file, the next step is to unzip it to the directory of your choice. Let us call this path `%VIRTUOSO_HOME%`, which also acts as a generic placeholder and represents whatever path you have used when you installed your version.

To start the Virtuoso server, it has to be registered as a Windows service, and the service first has to be started. To do so, a configuration file is needed. Virtuoso provides a default configuration file at this location,

```
C:\%VIRTUOSO_HOME%\database\virtuoso.ini
```

This configuration file can be edited to fit your specific needs. For now, accept the default settings in this file and move on to the step of registering a service for Virtuoso server. To do so, the following path needs to be appended to the PATH variable:

```
%VIRTUOSO_HOME%\bin;%VIRTUOSO_HOME%\lib
```

More specifically, you need to open your control panel, select system to open System Properties window. Once you reach System Properties window, click Advanced tab, and then click Environment Variables button. This is where you can append the above path to the current PATH variable (note this should be the PATH variable in System variables section). In addition, a new variable named VIRTUOSO_HOME should also be added, and its value should be the location where you have installed your virtuoso package.

---

[14] http://www.openlinksw.com/dataspace/doc/dav/wiki/Main/

Once you have finished, open a Windows command window, navigate to `%VIRTUOSO_HOME%\database` directory, and issue the following command:

```
virtuoso-t -?
```

If everything is setup correctly, you should see the Virtuoso version number and some help and use information. If not, you need to check to make sure your path was set up correctly.

If all is working well, you can move on to register Virtuoso server as a Windows service. Again, in a Windows command window, under `%VIRTUOSO_HOME%\database` directory, type the following command,

```
virtuoso-t +service screate +instance "myVirtuosoInstance" +configfile
virtuoso.ini
```

and you should see the following screen response,

```
[Using virtuoso.ini in {%VIRTUOSO_HOME%}\database]

The Virtuoso_myVirtuosoInstance service has been registered and is
associated with the executable {%VIRTUOSO_HOME%}\bin\virtuoso-t.exe
```

which indicates that you have successfully registered the service, named `MyVirtuosoInstance`, as shown above. You can certainly name your instance differently, but you need to remember this instance name and use it consistently. Also, understand again that `{%VIRTUOSO_HOME%}` is simply a placeholder; you should see your real path when you try the above commend on your computer.

Now, verify the service has been created and registered with Windows system by issuing the command:

```
virtuoso-t +service list
```

and your screen response should be looking like this,

```
myVirtuosoInstance Stopped
```

To start the service, type this command,

```
virtuoso-t -I "myVirtuosoInstance" +service start
```

If you have done everything correctly, `myVirtuosoInstance` service should be started successfully, and your screen response should be this,

```
The Virtuoso_myVirtuosoInstance service is being started
```

It might take a little bit time for the service to start. To confirm it has been started, you can issue this command again,

```
virtuoso-t +service list
```

and you should see screen response as follows,

```
myVirtuosoInstance Running
```

Now, your Virtuoso server is up and running on your Windows machine, and you should be able to fire up Virtuoso's starting page and begin your work.

To get to Virtuoso's starting page, first examine the configuration file to get the port number. To do so, open this configuration file at `C:\%VIRTUOSO_HOME%\database\virtuoso.ini`, and look for the `ServerPort` parameter. For example,

```
[HTTPServer]
```

```
ServerPort = 8890
```

Now, point your Web browser to `http://localhost:8890/` to get to Virtuoso's starting page, as shown in Fig. 13.7.

which indicates that you have successfully installed Virtuoso server.

The following command can be used to shutdown the server:

```
virtuoso-t -I "myVirtuosoInstance" +service stop
```

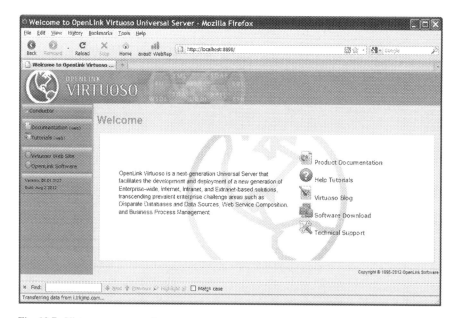

Fig. 13.7 Virtuoso server starting page

The registered service can be deleted by using the following command:

```
virtuoso-t +service delete +instance "myVirtuosoInstance".
```

13.4.2.2 Creating Database Tables and Loading Table Contents

Before we can start anything, we need to have database tables we can work on. To be more consistent with Virtuoso's documentation, we will use the Product Catalog database mentioned in the Virtuoso official document[15] as the example database tables.

The schema of the Product Catalog is given Tables 13.9, 13.10 and 13.11, as shown below.

To create new database tables and to load relational contents into these tables, one can use Virtuoso `Conductor` as shown in this section. There are other ways to accomplish the same thing, for example, by using the `isql` command line utility. However, Virtuoso `Conductor` is the easiest.

Let us start the Virtuoso service as described above and point a Web browser to `http://localhost:8890/`. Click `Conductor` from the left menu pane, and you will be asked for login account and password. At the time of this writing, the

Table 13.9 Product table

Field	Type	Key
PRODUCT_ID	VARCHAR(25)	PRIMARY KEY
PRODUCT_DESCRIPTION	VARCHAR(125)	
PRODUCT_CAT_ID	INTEGER	(FK)
PRODCUT_FORMAT_ID	INTEGER	(FK)

Table 13.10 Product Category table

Field	Type	Key
PRODUCT_CAT_ID	INTEGER	PRIMARY KEY
PRODUCT_CATEGORY_DESCRIPTION	VARCHAR(50)	

Table 13.11 Product Format table

Field	Type	Key
PRODUCT_FORMAT_ID	INTEGER	PRIMARY KEY
PRODUCT_FORMAT_DESCRIPTION	VARCHAR(75)	

---

[15] http://virtuoso.openlinksw.com/whitepapers/relational%20rdf%20views%20mapping.html

Table 13.12 Virtuoso user names and passwords

User name	Default password	Usage
dba	dba	Default Database Administrator account.
dav	dav	WebDAV Administrator account.
vad	vad	WebDAV account for internal usage in VAD (disabled by default).
demo	demo	Default demo user for the demo database. This user is the owner of the Demo catalogue of the demo database.
soap	soap	SQL User for demonstrating SOAP services.
fori	fori	SQL user account for 'Forums' tutorial application demonstration in the Demo database.

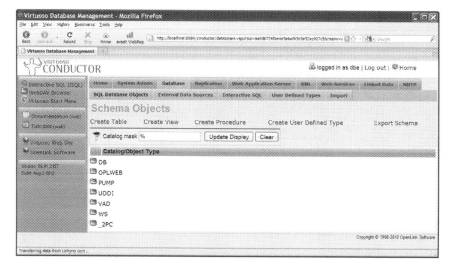

Fig. 13.8 Conductor's Database session

Virtuoso documentation[16] shows a collection of default passwords, as shown in Table 13.12.

We can use dba as our login account and dba as our password as well at this point.

Once we are in Conductor session, click the Database link to bring up the screen as shown in Fig. 13.8.

---

[16] http://docs.openlinksw.com/virtuoso/newadminui.html#defpasschange

This shows a list of databases that are already loaded.

To create the PRODUCT database, click the Interactive SQL link, and enter the SQL script shown in List 13.19 into the text area to create our first table:

List 13.19 SQL script to create PRODUCT table

```
create table DB.DBA.PRODUCT (
    PRODUCT_ID VARCHAR(25),
    PRODUCT_DESCRIPTION VARCHAR(125),
    PRODUCT_CAT_ID INTEGER,
    PRODUCT_FORMAT_ID INTEGER,
    PRIMARY KEY (PRODUCT_ID)
);
```

Figure 13.9 shows your current screen.

Click the Execute button, and a result window shows as in Fig. 13.10, indicating the script was successfully executed.

Click Return, then execute the SQL scripts shown in List 13.20 by following the same steps.

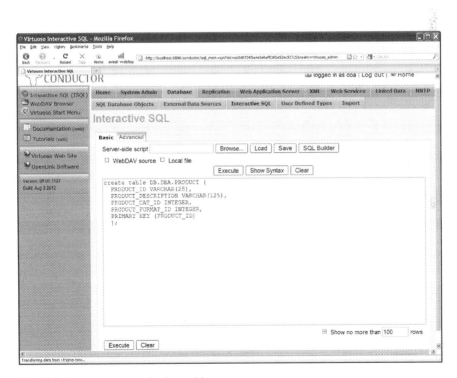

Fig. 13.9 Create PRODUCT database table

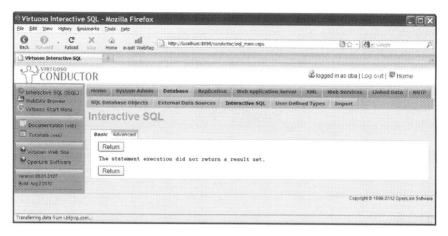

Fig. 13.10 Successfully create PRODUCT database table

List 13.20 SQL scripts to create PRODUCT_CATEGORY and PRODUCT_FORMAT table

```
create table DB.DBA.PRODUCT_CATEGORY (
    PRODUCT_CAT_ID INTEGER,
    PRODUCT_CATEGORY_DESCRIPTION VARCHAR(50),
    PRIMARY KEY (PRODUCT_CAT_ID)
    );

create table DB.DBA.PRODUCT_FORMAT (
    PRODUCT_FORMAT_ID INTEGER,
    PRODUCT_FORMAT_DESCRIPTION VARCHAR(75),
    PRIMARY KEY (PRODUCT_FORMAT_ID)
    );
```

After executing List 13.20, all the three tables should be created successfully. To see this, click the Database link again, and you should see the new database list now includes DB, as shown in Fig. 13.11.

Click on DB to show the tables we have just created. Now, run the SQL script shown in List 13.21 to add content into these new tables:

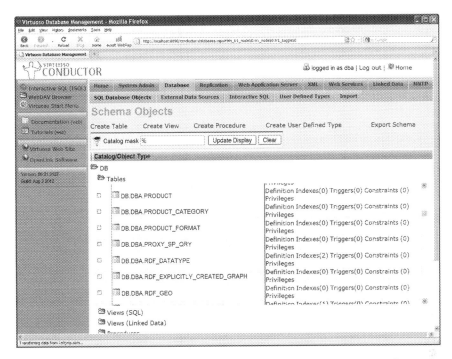

Fig. 13.11 PRODUCT, PRODUCT_CATEGORY and PRODUCT_FORMAT tables are all created

List 13.21 SQL scripts to add sample data into three tables

```
insert into DB.DBA.PRODUCT values ( 'odbc-informix-ee',
                          'ODBC Drivers for Informix', 1, 4);
insert into DB.DBA.PRODUCT values ( 'odbc-informix-mt',
                          'ODBC Driver for Informix', 1, 3);
insert into DB.DBA.PRODUCT values ( 'odbc-informix-st',
                          'ODBC Driver for Informix', 1, 2);
insert into DB.DBA.PRODUCT values ( 'jdbc-ingres-mt',
                          'JDBC Driver for Ingres', 2, 3);
insert into DB.DBA.PRODUCT values ( 'oledb-odbc-st',
                          'OLE DB Provider for ODBC', 3, 2);
insert into DB.DBA.PRODUCT values ( 'dotnet-postgres-mt',
                      '.NET Data Provider for PostgreSQL', 4, 3);

insert into DB.DBA.PRODUCT_CATEGORY values (1, 'ODBC Drivers');
insert into DB.DBA.PRODUCT_CATEGORY values (2, 'JDBC Drivers');
insert into DB.DBA.PRODUCT_CATEGORY values (3,
                                  'OLEDB Data Providers');
insert into DB.DBA.PRODUCT_CATEGORY values (4,
                                  'ADO.NET Data Providers');
```

```
insert into DB.DBA.PRODUCT_FORMAT values (1, 'Enterprise');
insert into DB.DBA.PRODUCT_FORMAT values (2,
                              'Single-Tier (Lite Edition)');
insert into DB.DBA.PRODUCT_FORMAT values (3,
                          'Multi-Tier (Enterprise Edition)');
insert into DB.DBA.PRODUCT_FORMAT values (4,
                           'Single-Tier (Express Edition)');
```

To run this script, again click the `Interactive SQL` link, enter the script into the text area, and click `Execute`. To make sure the tables are correctly filled, use `Interactive SQL` to execute the following simple query to confirm:

```
select * from DB.DBA.PRODUCT;
```

All the rows in the PRODUCT table are returned successfully.

13.4.2.3   Loading Ontology

Before we can start with our mapping, we need to load the ontology we are going to use. The role of this ontology will become clear when the mapping is created. For our purpose, we will use GoodRelations,[17] which is written in OWL, and it provides a vocabulary that one can use to describe product, price and related company data.

To make our work simpler, let us first download the ontology to our local machine. At the time of this writing, the GoodRelations ontology can be downloaded from this URL:

```
http://www.heppnetz.de/ontologies/goodrelations/v1.owl
```

and `v1.owl` is the file name of this ontology.

Once we have this ontology on our local machine, we need to make it visible to our Virtuoso server. To do so, first create a directory called `user_data` (or any name you like) under `%VIRTUOSO_HOME%`. Change the Virtuoso configuration file `virtuoso.ini` to make this directory visible to the Virtuoso system (note `virtuoso.ini` locates at `%VIRTUOSO_HOME%\database`). More specifically, add the directory to `DirsAllowed` variable as follows (again, note this shows what the author has on his PC. For your case, you need to use your path as defined by `%VIRTUOSO_HOME%`):

```
DirsAllowed = ., ../vad, C:/liyang/DevApp/virtuoso-opensource/
user_data
```

Start the Virtuoso server as we described earlier. Once the server has started successfully, start the `isql` utility on a command window:

---

[17] http://purl.org/goodrelations/

```
%VIRTUOSO_HOME%\bin>isql
OpenLink Interactive SQL (Virtuoso), version 0.9849b.
Type HELP; for help and EXIT; to exit.
SQL>
```

and use the following command to load the GoodRelations ontology into Virtuoso server:

```
DB.DBA.RDF_LOAD_RDFXML(file_to_string('C:/liyang/DevApp/virtuoso-
opensource/user_data/v1.owl'), '', 'http://purl.org/goodrelations/
v1#');
```

Again, note this shows what the author has on his PC. For your case, you need to use your path to specify the ontology. You will see the following if the load is successful:

```
SQL> DB.DBA.RDF_LOAD_RDFXML(file_to_string('C:/liyang/DevApp/vir-
tuoso-opensource/user_data/v1.owl'), '', 'http://purl.org/
goodrelations/v1#');
Connected to OpenLink Virtuoso
Driver: 06.01.3127 OpenLink Virtuoso ODBC Driver
Done. - 1094 msec.
SQL>
```

To confirm it is indeed loaded, use the following simple SPARQL query:

```
SQL>sparql select * from <http://purl.org/goodrelations/v1#> where
{?s ?p ?o};
```

and all the RDF statements (about 1200) in the ontology should be returned.

13.4.2.4 Creating R2RML Mapping Document

Before coding the R2RML document needed for this exercise, we need to understand how exactly the chosen ontology can be used on the database content. Tables 13.13, 13.14 and 13.15 together show some sample data.

Based on the sample content and GoodRelations ontology, possible mappings between the relational content and the classes/properties described by the GoodRelations ontology can be summarized as follows:

- Table `PRODUCT` can be mapped to class `gr:ActualProductOrServiceInstance`.
- `PRODUCT.PRODUCT_DESCRIPTION` can be mapped to property `gr:description`, and values under column `PRODUCT.PRODUCT_DESCRIPTION` can be directly used as the object values.

Table 13.13 Sample data in PRODUCT table

PRODUCT_ID	PRODUCT_ DESCRIPTION	PRODUCT_ CAT_ID	PRODUCT_ FORMAT_ID
odbc- informix-ee	ODBC Drivers for Informix	1	4
odbc- informix-mt	ODBC Driver for Informix	1	3
odbc- informix-st	ODBC Driver for Informix	1	2
jdbc- ingres-mt	JDBC Driver for Ingres	2	3
oledb- odbc-st	OLE DB Provider for ODBC	3	2
dotnet- postgres-mt	.NET Data provider for PostgreSQL	4	3

Table 13.14 Sample data in PRODUCT_CATEGORY table

PRODUCT_CAT_ID	PRODUCT_CATEGORY_DESCRIPTION
1	ODBC Drivers
2	JDBC Drivers
3	OLE DB Data Providers
4	ADO.NET Data Providers

Table 13.15 Sample data in PRODUCT_FORMAT table

PRODUCT_FORMAT_ID	PRODUCT_FORMAT_DESCRIPTION
1	Enterprise
2	Single-Tier (Lite Edition)
3	Multi-Tier (Enterprise Edition)
4	Single-Tier (Express Edition)

- Table PRODUCT_CATEGORY can be mapped to class gr: ProductOrServiceModel.
- PRODUCT_CATEGORY.PRODUCT_CATEGORY_DESCRIPTION can be mapped to property gr:category, and values under PRODUCT_CATEGORY.PRODUCT_CATE-GORY_DESCRIPTION column can be directly used as the object values.
- Property gr:hasMakeAndModel will be used to connect table PRODUCT and table PRODUCT_CATEGORY.
- Table PRODUCT_FORMAT can be mapped to class gr:QuantitativeValue.
- PRODUCT_FORMAT.PRODUCT_FORMAT_DESCRIPTION can be mapped to property gr:hasValue, and values under column PRODUCT_FORMAT.PRODUCT_FOR-MAT_DESCRIPTION can be directly used as the object values.
- The gr:quantitativeProductOrServiceProperty will be used to connect table PRODUCT and PRODUCT_FORMAT.

With all these mapping decisions in place, List 13.22 shows the R2RML document we obtain.

List 13.22 R2RML mapping document `product.n3`

```
@prefix rr: <http://www.w3.org/ns/r2rml#> .
@prefix rdf: <http://www.w3.org/1999/02/22-rdf-syntax-ns#> .
@prefix gr: <http://purl.org/goodrelations/v1#> .
<#TriplesMapProduct>
   a rr:TriplesMap;
   rr:logicalTable [  rr:tableName "PRODUCT" ];
   rr:subjectMap [
      rr:template
         "http://liyangyu.com/data/test/product/{PRODUCT_ID}";
      rr:class gr:ActualProductOrServiceInstance
];
rr:predicateObjectMap [
   rr:predicateMap [ rr:constant gr:description ];
   rr:objectMap [ rr:column "PRODUCT_DESCRIPTION" ];
];
rr:predicateObjectMap [
   rr:predicateMap [ rr:constant
                   gr:quantitativeProductOrServiceProperty ];
   rr:objectMap [
      rr:parentTriplesMap <#TriplesMapFormat>;
      rr:joinCondition [
         rr:child "PRODUCT_FORMAT_ID";
         rr:parent "PRODUCT_FORMAT_ID"
      ];
   ];
];
rr:predicateObjectMap [
   rr:predicateMap [ rr:constant gr:hasMakeAndModel ];
   rr:objectMap [
      rr:parentTriplesMap <#TriplesMapCategory>;
      rr:joinCondition [ rr:child "PRODUCT_CAT_ID";
                        rr:parent "PRODUCT_CAT_ID" ];
   ];
] .
<#TriplesMapCategory> a rr:TriplesMap;
   rr:logicalTable [ rr:tableName "PRODUCT_CATEGORY" ];
   rr:subjectMap [
      rr:template
         "http://liyangyu.com/data/test/product/{PRODUCT_CAT_ID}";
      rr:class gr:ProductOrServiceModel
```

```
    ];
    rr:predicateObjectMap [
       rr:predicateMap [ rr:constant gr:category ];
       rr:objectMap [ rr:column "PRODUCT_CATEGORY_DESCRIPTION" ];
    ] .

<#TriplesMapFormat> a rr:TriplesMap;
    rr:logicalTable [ rr:tableName "PRODUCT_FORMAT" ];
    rr:subjectMap [
       rr:template
       "http://liyangyu.com/data/test/product/{PRODUCT_FORMAT_ID}";
       rr:class gr:QuantitativeValue
    ];
    rr:predicateObjectMap [
       rr:predicateMap [ rr:constant gr:hasValue ];
       rr:objectMap [ rr:column "PRODUCT_FORMAT_DESCRIPTION" ];
    ].
```

Note that Virtuoso accepts file extension as n3, not ttl.

Now, we have everything we need. Our next step is to use Virtuoso to process this mapping document and generate the RDF view we need, as shown in the next section.

13.4.2.5 Exposing the Database Tables as RDF Dataset

Before we can actually start to use Virtuoso to process our mapping document, we first need to make sure the necessary component, rdb2rdf_dav, has been installed. To check this, fire up the Virtuoso server, and point your Web browser to http:// localhost:8890/. Again, click Conductor, and log in by using dba as both the user ID and password.

Once you have logged in, click Database, then Linked Data. If you see the R2RML tab under Linked Data, rdb2rdf_dav has already been installed.

If you don't see the R2RML tab under Linked Data, you need to install component rdb2rdf_dav first. To do so, start isql utility on a command window, and use the following command in isql:

```
SQL>    DB.DBA.VAD_INSTALL('C:/liyang/DevApp/virtuoso-opensource/
vad/rdb2rdf_dav.vad',0);
```

Of course, remember to use your own installation path in the above command. If everything is correct, you will see the following result:

```
SQL_STATE SQL_MESSAGE
VARCHAR VARCHAR
```

Fig. 13.12 Validate mapping file `product.n3`

```
00000 No errors detected
00000 Installation of "RDB2RDF support" is complete.
00000 Now making a final checkpoint.
00000 Final checkpoint is made.
00000 SUCCESS
6 Rows. - 7610 msec.
SQL>
```

And you should also see the `R2RML` tab under `Linked Data` now.

Now, we are ready to run our mapping document (`product.n3`) and see how an RDF view is created based on the given relational data.

First, click the `R2RML` tab, and you will see the `R2RML Upload` window. Use the `Browse` button to locate the mapping file, and click `Validate` so the mapping file can first be validated. Meanwhile, keep all the other choices as default, as shown in Fig. 13.12.

If everything works as expected, you will see a window with a message saying "No errs or warnings found".

Now, on the same message window, click `Generate` button, and Virtuoso will generate its own mapping language, which you should not change.

To continue, in the resulting window, click the `Execute` button, which will process the mapping document and generate the RDF view we need. If everything goes well, in the resulting window, you should see system messages and an `OK` message indicating the work is finished.

Up to now, we have instructed Virtuoso to process our mapping document and an RDF view for the `PRODUCT` database has been created. To confirm this, we can issue SPARQL queries against the generated view to make sure everything is right.

Before issuing SPARQL queries, there is one more preparation we have to go through: we must make sure we have enough privilege to do that. From `Conductor`

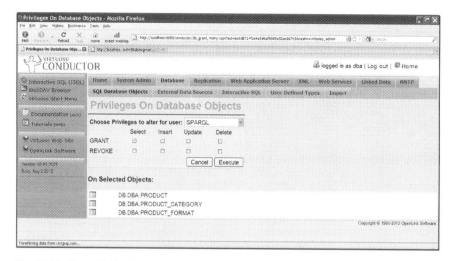

Fig. 13.13 Grant SPARQL SELECT rights to current logged in user for the three tables

screen, click the Database tab, then select DB, and open the Tables link. Find the
three tables, DB.DBA.PRODUCT, DB.DBA.PRODUCT_CATEGORY and DB.DBA.
PRODUCT_FORMAT. Check the check boxes for these three tables, then move on to
the very end of the table list, and click Privileges On Selected link, which will
open Privileges on Database Object session. Change the user to SPARQL, and
grant SELECT privilege to this user, as shown in Fig. 13.13.

Now that we have an RDF view of the PRODUCT database and we have the right
privilege assigned, we can start to issue SPARQL queries to get useful information.
To do so, we need a SPARQL query interface. The following URL points to a
SPARQL interface supported by Virtuoso:

```
http://localhost:8890/sparql
```

It is a simple SPARQL endpoint that is quite convenient to use. In fact, the same
text area provided by Interactive SQL tab can also be used to conduct SPARQL
queries against the generated RDF view. For our purpose here, we will use the
above SPARQL interface.

Figure 13.14 shows the query window. Note that the following,

```
http://liyangyu.com/r2rml#
```

is used as the default graph name, since that is what we have specified in the process
of generating the RDF view (see Fig. 13.12, Target graph IRI). To simply get
everything back, a simple query select * where {?s ?p ?o} is used, as shown in
Fig. 13.14.

Figure 13.15 shows the query result. As you can see, the data in database tables is
now changed as RDF data. We have therefore accomplished our goal.

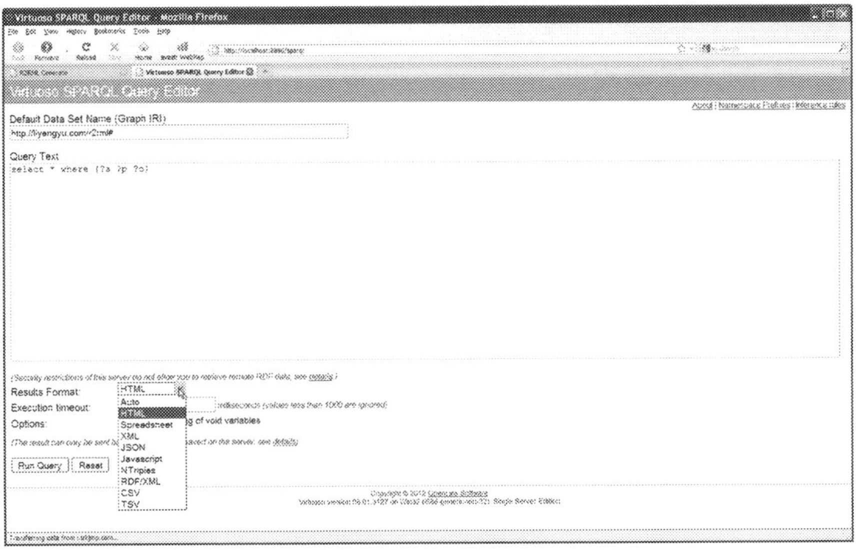

Fig. 13.14 Virtuoso SPARQL query endpoint

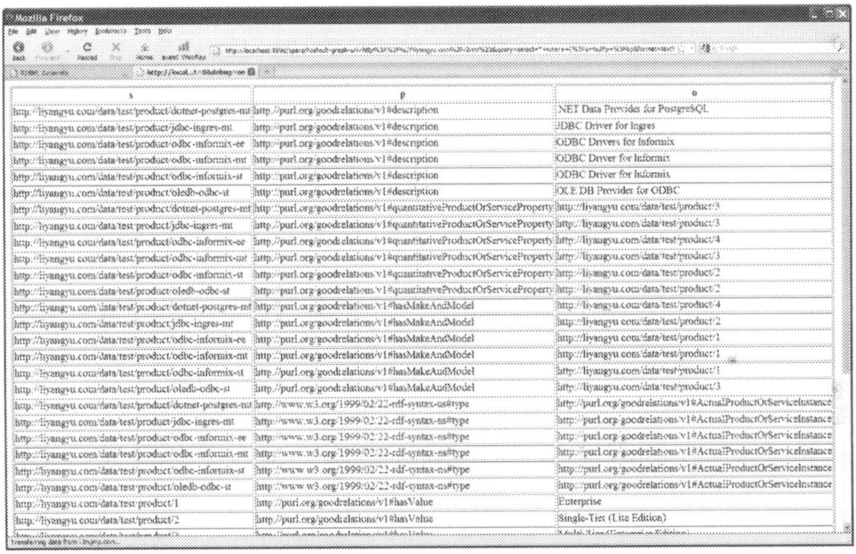

Fig. 13.15 PRODUCT database has been successfully converted into RDF statements

More useful queries can certainly be used. List 13.23 shows another query example. This query links all three tables together, therefore the product, the product description, format description and category description are much easier to read. This also confirms the mapping from relational content to RDF dataset is correctly done.

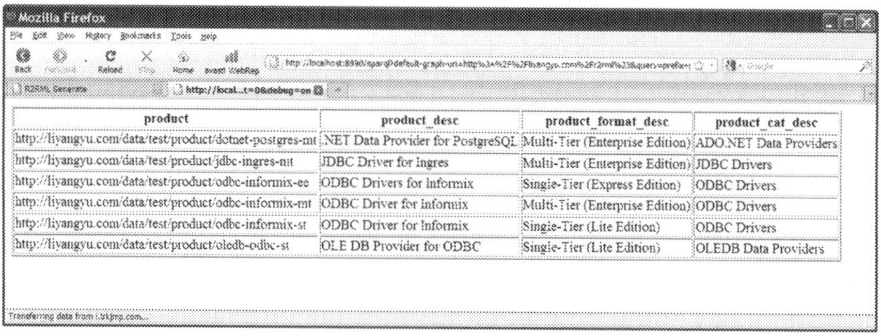

product	product_desc	product_format_desc	product_cat_desc
http://liyangyu.com/data/test/product/dotnet-postgres-mt	.NET Data Provider for PostgreSQL	Multi-Tier (Enterprise Edition)	ADO.NET Data Providers
http://liyangyu.com/data/test/product/jdbc-ingres-mt	JDBC Driver for Ingres	Multi-Tier (Enterprise Edition)	JDBC Drivers
http://liyangyu.com/data/test/product/odbc-informix-ee	ODBC Drivers for Informix	Single-Tier (Express Edition)	ODBC Drivers
http://liyangyu.com/data/test/product/odbc-informix-mt	ODBC Driver for Informix	Multi-Tier (Enterprise Edition)	ODBC Drivers
http://liyangyu.com/data/test/product/odbc-informix-st	ODBC Driver for Informix	Single-Tier (Lite Edition)	ODBC Drivers
http://liyangyu.com/data/test/product/oledb-odbc-st	OLE DB Provider for ODBC	Single-Tier (Lite Edition)	OLEDB Data Providers

Fig. 13.16 Result of executing the query shown in List 13.23

List 13.23 Another query to show the mapping is done correctly

```
prefix gr: <http://purl.org/goodrelations/v1#>
select ?product ?product_desc ?product_format_desc
       ?product_cat_desc
WHERE {
  ?product gr:description ?product_desc .
  ?product gr:hasMakeAndModel ?_product_category .
  ?product gr:quantitativeProductOrServiceProperty
           ?_product_format .
  ?_product_format gr:hasValue ?product_format_desc .
  ?_product_category gr:category ?product_cat_desc .
}
```

Figure 13.16 shows the result.

13.4.2.6 Creating the Physical Dump of the Generated RDF View

The last piece of the puzzle is how to obtain a physical dump of the generated RDF view, since it is sometimes useful to actually get the persistent RDF content.

Virtuoso offers a procedure called RDF_QM_TREE_DUMP (and its associated procedures) to dump one or more RDF view graphs in a Virtuoso server to a set of Turtle (in `.ttl` file extension) dataset files in a specified dump directory. The dump generation is made as fast as possible by grouping mappings based on underlying tables so many properties from neighbor database columns can be extracted in one table scan. The size of the generated files is limited to 5 MB; therefore, you will most likely see multiple generated RDF files.

To use this procedure, it again requires some setup work. Access the Virtuoso server by pointing a Web browser to `http://localhost:8890/`. Click `Conductor` and log in. Once you are in the `Conductor` session, click the `Database` link, and then the DB link. Under DB, look for the Procedures link and click on this link. A list of existing procedures will be shown.

Look for the following three procedures in this procedure list:

```
RDF_QM_TREE_DUMP
RDF_QM_CONTENT_OF_QM_TREE
RDF_QM_GROUP_BY_SOURCE_TABLES
```

If you can find all these procedures, you can continue to the description about how to use the procedure; otherwise, you will need to add these procedures as described below.

To add these procedures, from the same existing procedures window, look for the link called Create Procedure. Click this link, and you will see a text area under Create New Procedure/Module. Now, from the downloaded code, find the file called rdf_qm_group_by_source_tables.sql, and then cut-and-paste the content of this file into the text area. Once you are finished, click the Save button that sits below the text area. You should not see any error message, the server should automatically goes back to the procedure view, and you should see that this new procedure has been added.

Now, repeat the same exact steps as described above for (1) rdf_qm_content_of_qm_tree.sql and (2) rdf_qm_tree_dump.sql. Again, you should be able to find these files from the downloaded code package. Note that you will have to follow the correct order of adding them to the procedure list.

Once you are done adding these procedure files, you should be able to find them in the procedure list, and you should be able to run the procedure now to generate the dump of the RDF view.

To do so, start isql utility on a command window, and use the following command in isql:

```
SQL>          DB.DBA.RDF_QM_TREE_DUMP('C:/liyang/DevApp/virtuoso-
opensource/user_data', 'http://liyangyu.com/r2rml#', NULL, NULL);
Done. - 312 msec.
SQL>
```

The first parameter here is a path, representing the destination directory where the physical dump should be placed. You can use any directory you want, but remember to make sure the dump directory you use is included in the DirsAllowed parameter of the configuration file.

The second parameter represents the graph to be dumped. In our case, our graph is called http://liyangyu.com/r2rml#. The last two parameters are more about the mapping language that Virtuoso had before the RDB2RDF standard; usually using NULL is good enough.

If everything goes well, there will be no specific message when the dumping process finishes. Go to the dump directory and you will see a collection of Turtle documents that were generated, and in these documents are the "raw" RDF statements you need. List 13.24 shows one small part of these files.

List 13.24 Generated RDF dump from the RDF view

```
#2 quad maps on join of "DB"."DBA"."PRODUCT_CATEGORY"
@prefix rdf:  <http://www.w3.org/1999/02/22-rdf-syntax-ns#> .
@prefix ns1:  <http://purl.org/goodrelations/v1#> .

<http://liyangyu.com/data/test/product/1> rdf:type
      ns1:ProductOrServiceModel .
<http://liyangyu.com/data/test/product/2> rdf:type
      ns1:ProductOrServiceModel .
<http://liyangyu.com/data/test/product/3> rdf:type
      ns1:ProductOrServiceModel .
<http://liyangyu.com/data/test/product/4> rdf:type
      ns1:ProductOrServiceModel .
<http://liyangyu.com/data/test/product/1> ns1:category
      "ODBC Drivers" .
<http://liyangyu.com/data/test/product/2> ns1:category
      "JDBC Drivers" .
<http://liyangyu.com/data/test/product/3> ns1:category
      "OLEDB Data Providers" .
<http://liyangyu.com/data/test/product/4> ns1:category
      "ADO.NET Data Providers" .
```

13.5   Summary

Before starting a new development on the Semantic Web, quite a few questions
have to be answered. For example, if we are not consuming public RDF data, how
should we create our own RDF content? If we already have database tables, how
should we convert this structured information into RDF content? Which ontology
should we use? How can we start to understand a complex ontology that was
created by someone else?

This chapter provided answers to these questions. A main focus of this chapter is
the RDB2RDF W3C standard, which was discussed in great detail. Implementation
examples were also represented in a way that you could directly follow in your own
development work.

Chapter 14
Building the Foundation for Development on the Semantic Web

Finally, with what you have learned from this book, you are now ready to start your own development on the Semantic Web. To better prepare you for this work, we present an overview in this chapter that covers two major topics. With the knowledge presented in this chapter, your future development work will start with a solid foundation.

The first topic is about available development tools for the Semantic Web, including frameworks, reasoners, ontology engineering environments and other related tools. As a developer who works on the Semantic Web, understanding the available tools is simply a must.

The second topic covers some guidelines about the development methodologies. In general, building applications on the Semantic Web is different from building applications that run on the traditional Web, and this work requires its own development strategies. With a clear understanding of the methodologies, your design and development work will be more productive, and your applications will be more scalable and more maintainable.

14.1 Development Tools for the Semantic Web

14.1.1 Frameworks for the Semantic Web Applications

14.1.1.1 What Is a Framework and Why Do We Need It?

A *framework* in general can be understood as a software environment designed to support future development work. It is often created for a specific development domains, and normally contains a set of common and reusable building blocks so developers can use, extend or customize for their specific business logic. With the help from such a framework, developers do not have to start from scratch each time an application is developed.

© Springer-Verlag Berlin Heidelberg 2014
L. Yu, *A Developer's Guide to the Semantic Web*,
DOI 10.1007/978-3-662-43796-4_14

More specifically, for development work on the Semantic Web, the main features of a framework may include the following:

- Core support for RDF, RDFS and OWL;
- Inference capabilities for both RDFS ontologies and OWL ontologies;
- Support for SPARQL query;
- Handling of persistent RDF models, with the ability to scale efficiently to large datasets.

This list continues to grow as more and more development frameworks become available. For developers, a Semantic Web development framework can at least provide the following benefits:

- Frameworks provide developers with the implementation of common tasks in the form of reusable code, therefore reducing both repeated work and numbers of bugs.

For example, there is a set of common operations that have to be implemented for probably every single application on the Semantic Web. These common tasks include reading/parsing a given RDF model, understanding an RDF model and inferencing based on ontology model handling, just to name a few. Since a framework provides the support for these common tasks, developers can focus on the specific business logic, and it is more likely that they can deliver more reliable code.

- Frameworks make it easier to work with complex technologies such as the Semantic Web technologies.

By now, you have seen all the major technical components for the Semantic Web. Clearly, there is a lot to learn even before you can get started with your own development. With help from a development framework, it is not only easier to put what you have learned into practice, but you will also gain deeper understanding about the technology itself. You will get a better feeling for this when you finish the last several chapters of this book—for those chapters, you will have a chance to use a concrete framework to develop several semantic Web applications.

- Frameworks force consistency within the team, even across platforms.

This directly follows from the fact that quite a lot of the common tasks are built by reusable code and are accessed through a set of common "wrappers". This not only forces consistency, but also makes testing and debugging tasks much easier, even if you did not write the code at the first place.

Frameworks promote design patterns, standards and policies.

- This may not seem quite obvious at this point, but you will see more on this in Sect. 14.2.1.3.

With this being said, let us take a look at some popular frameworks. Notice we are not going to cover the usage details of these frameworks, since each one of them would require a separate chapter to cover. We will, however, give you an overview of each framework so you have a set of choices when it comes to your own development work.

14.1.1.2   Jena

Jena (http://jena.apache.org/) is a free, open source Java platform for applications on the Semantic Web. It was originally developed by Brian McBride from Hewlett-Packard Laboratories (HPL). Jena 1 was originally released in 2001, and Jena 2 was released in August 2003. The latest version, Jena 2.11.0, was released in September 2013.

Jena is now believed to be the most used Java toolkit for building applications on the Semantic Web. It is also the leading Java toolkit referenced in academic papers and conferences.

Jena's comprehensive support for semantic Web application development is quite obvious, given its following components:

- An RDF API;
- An OWL API, which can also be used as an RDFS API;
- Reading and writing RDF in RDF/XML, N3 and N-triples formats;
- In-memory and persistent storage of RDF models;
- SPARQL query engine, and a
- Rule-based inference engine.

Through out this book, Jena is used as our example development framework. A detailed description of Jena can be found in Chap. 15 as well.

14.1.1.3   Sesame

Sesame (http://www.openrdf.org/) is an open source Java framework for storage and querying of RDF datasets. Sesame was originally developed as a research prototype for an EU research project called On-To-Knowledge, and it is currently developed as a community project with developers participating from around the globe. Its latest version, Sesame 2.7.9, was released in December 2013.

Sesame has the following components:

- The *RDF Model*, which defines interfaces and implementation for all basic RDF entities;
- The *Repository API* (built upon the RDF Model), a higher-level API that offers a large number of developer-oriented methods for handling RDF data, including RDFS reasoning support;
- An *HTTP server* (built on top of Repository API), which consists of a number of Java Servlets that implement a protocol for accessing Sesame repositories over HTTP.

In general, Sesame's focus is on RDF data storage and query, but without much support for OWL and related inferencing tools.

14.1.1.4   Virtuoso

Virtuoso (`http://virtuoso.openlinksw.com/`) is also called *Virtuoso Universal Server*. Essentially, it is a database engine that combines the functionality of traditional RDBMS, ORDBMS, RDF, XML, free-text, Web application server and file server into a single server product package. Its latest version, V7.0, was released in April 2013, and it can be downloaded freely for Linux and various Unix platforms. A Windows binary distribution is also available. Notice there are also commercial editions of Virtuoso, with Virtual Database Engine and Data Clustering as their extra contents.

As far as the Semantic Web is concerned, Virtuoso has the following support:

- It can be used as an RDF Triple Store. One can load N3, Turtle and RDF/XML files into a Virtuoso-hosted named graph using Virtuoso SQL functions.
- It includes a number of metadata extractors for a range of known data formats, such as microformats. These metadata extractors enable automatic triple generation, and storage in its own RDF Triple Store;
- It supports SPARQL statements, and these SPARQL statements can be written inside SQL statements. In other words, any ODBC, JDBC, .net or OLE/DB application can simply make SPARQL queries just as if they were all SQL queries.
- It supports reasoning based on RDFS and OWL. Notice there are differences between the open source versions and closed source ones; you need to check the documents for more details.
- Its API support includes Jena, Sesame and Redland; all are available via the Client Connectivity Kit in the form of Virtuoso libraries.
- It supports Java, .NET bound languages, C/C++, PHP, Python and Perl.

As you can tell, Virtuoso is a product with a very board scope, not only in the Semantic Wed world, but also in data management in general. Although this book focuses on Jena, Virtuoso can be another good choice for development work on the Semantic Web.

14.1.1.5   Redland

Redland (`http://librdf.org/`) is a set of free C libraries that provide support for RDF. Its latest release was in December 2013. Redland offers the following support:

- Redland RDF library provides a C API that works with client application.

- *Raptor* as the RDF parser library, deals with reading RDF/XML and N-triples into RDF triples. It is an independent piece from Redland, but is required by Redland.
- *Rasqal* (pronounced *rascal*) as the RDF Syntax and Query Library for Redland, is responsible for executing RDF queries with SPARQL.
- Redland Language Bindings for APIs support C#, Java, Objective-C, Perl, PHP, Python, Ruby and Tcl.

Although Redland does not provide a strong support for reasoning and inferencing, it does work with C language. When speed is a major concern, Redland framework can be the choice.

14.1.2 Reasoners for the Semantic Web Applications

14.1.2.1 What Is a Reasoner and Why Do We Need It?

To put it simply, a Semantic Web *reasoner* is software that can perform reasoning tasks for applications on the Semantic Web, typically based on RDFS or OWL ontologies.

Notice reasoning refers to the process of deriving facts that are not explicitly expressed by the given ontology documents and the instance documents. In Chaps. 4 and 5, we saw quite a few examples of the reasoning power provided by RDFS and OWL ontologies. The inferencing process implemented in those examples is the work done by a reasoner.

Without touching the theoretical details of the reasoning process, Fig. 14.1 shows the basic structure of the inference process:

As Fig. 14.1 shows, a reasoner is used to derive additional RDF statements that are entailed from the given base RDF graph together with any optional ontology information. The reasoner works by employing its own rules, axioms and appropriate chaining methods (forward/backward chaining, for example).

When a given application on the Semantic Web needs a reasoner, it is usually not the best choice to write one by yourself. You should take advantage of an existing reasoner to accomplish your task. In fact, some popular development frameworks have already included reasoners for us to use, and there are also standalones reasoners that can be easily plugged into our applications. Let us take a look these choices in the next few sections.

14.1.2.2 Pellet

Pellet (http://clarkparsia.com/pellet) is an OWL 2 reasoner for Java. It is freely downloadable, and its latest release, Pellet 2.3.1, was announced in May 2013. It supports the following main reasoning functionalities:

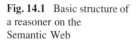

Fig. 14.1 Basic structure of a reasoner on the Semantic Web

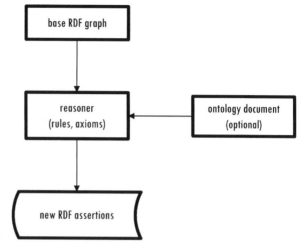

- Qualified cardinality restrictions;
- Complex subproperty axioms (between a property chain and a property);
- Local reflexivity restrictions;
- Reflexive, irreflexive, symmetric, and antisymmetric properties;
- Disjoint properties;
- Negative property assertions;
- Vocabulary sharing (punning) between individuals, classes, and properties;
- User-defined data ranges.

Besides the above, Pellet provides all the standard inference services that you can find from a traditional OWL DL reasoner, such as ontology consistency checking, classification and realization (finding the most specific classes that an individual belongs to).

Pellet itself is not embedded in any development framework. The following are some of the common ways to access Pellet's reasoning capabilities:

- As a Web-based demonstration page called OWLSight[1];
- As a command line program (included in the distribution package);
- As a set of programmatic API that can be used in a standalone application;
- The reasoner interfaces with the Manchester OWL-API and Jena. Therefore, you can use Pellet in your applications developed by Jena;
- By direct integration with the Protégé ontology editor.

---

[1] You can find this page at http://pellet.owldl.com/owlsight/

14.1.2.3 RacerPro

RacerPro (`http://www.racer-systems.com/`) is an OWL reasoner and inference server for the Semantic Web. RACER stands for Renamed ABox and Concept Expression Reasoner. RacerPro is the commercial name of the software. At this point, RacerPro 2.0 is the latest release.

RacerPro can process OWL Lite as well as OWL DL documents. Some major reasoning capabilities supported by RacerPro include the following:

- Check the consistency of an OWL ontology and a set of data descriptions;
- Find implicit subclass relationships induced by the declaration in the ontology;
- Find synonyms for resources (including both classes and instance names).

As a query server, RacerPro supports *incremental query answering* for information retrieval tasks (retrieve the next n results of a query). In addition, it supports the adaptive use of computational resources: answers that require few computational resources are delivered first, and user applications can decide whether computing all answers is worth the effort.

RacerPro is not embedded in any development framework. It offers the following deployment options a given application can choose from:

- Back-end network server application;
- File processor launched from command line interface;
- When loaded as object code, it can be part of a user application as well (Java API provided).

14.1.2.4 Jena

We have discussed Jena as a development framework in Sect. 14.1.1.2. In fact, the Jena framework also has several reasoners embedded:

- Jena's RDFS reasoner. This reasoner supports most of the RDFS entailments described by the RDFS standard (see Chap. 4).
- Jena's OWL reasoner. This is the second major set of reasoners supplied with Jena. This set includes a default OWL reasoner and two smaller/faster configurations. Each of the configurations is intended to be a sound implementation of a subset of OWL Full, but none of them is complete.

To use the complete OWL reasoning, an external reasoner such as Pellet can be used, as we described earlier.

14.1.2.5 Virtuoso

Finally, we would like to mention Virtuoso again, which also offers an OWL Reasoner. Based on its official document,

- It supports `owl:sameAs`, `rdfs:subClassOf`, and `rdfs:subPropertyOf`, which are sufficient for many purposes;
- `owl:sameAs`, `owl:equivalentClass` and `owl:equivalentProperty` are considered when determining subclass or subproperty relations;
- For version 6.1.0, `owl:TransitiveProperty`, `owl:SymmetricalProperty` and `owl:inverseOf` have also been added.

Finally, Virtuoso defaults to using backward-chaining, but if desired, forward-chaining may be forced.

14.1.3 Ontology Engineering Environments

14.1.3.1 What Is an Ontology Engineering Environment and Why Do We Need It?

The vision of the Semantic Web and its applications is characterized by a large number of ontologies. Without ontology, the Semantic Web would not exist.

However, ontology creation and development is never an easy task, mostly due to the following facts:

- A given ontology often aims to cover a whole domain by using a set of classes and properties and by summarizing their relationships. Since the domain knowledge is often complex, the resulting ontology is also complex and large in scale.
- Ontology designers/developers have different skill levels, different cultural and social backgrounds, and different understanding of the needs from potential applications.
- Ontology development requires the knowledge of ontology presentation languages (such as RDFS and OWL), which can be difficult to grasp for many domain experts, who are the main drivers behind a given ontology.
- The real world changes quickly, and ontologies that representing knowledge in the real world also have to be dynamically updated to keep up with the changes and new requirements. This makes ontology development/maintenance harder as well.

To make ontology development easier, a special group of support tools have been created, and they can be used to build a new ontology from scratch. In addition to their common editing and browsing functions, they also provide support to ontology documentation, ontology export (to different formats, and different ontology languages), ontology import (from different formats and different languages). Some tools even have some inferencing capabilities. This group of tools is often referred to as *Ontology Engineering Environment*.

The benefits offered by an ontology engineering environment are quite obvious. For example, as a basic component of any given ontology engineering environment, a graphical ontology editor can make the common tasks easy to accomplish. For any given ontology, either new or existing, these common tasks include adding new concepts, properties, relations and constraints. With help from an ontology editor's graphical user interface, domain experts will not have to be efficient in a given ontology representation language. In addition, a graphical ontology editor can help the developer to visualize and organize the overall conceptual structure of the ontology. With this help, designers and developers can discover logical inconsistencies or potential problems with the given ontology, such as not being able to fully cover the needs of foreseeable applications in the specific domain. In fact, some graphical ontology editors do have the ability to help developers and designers to reconcile logical or semantic inconsistencies among the concepts and properties defined in the ontology.

Other functions offered by an ontology engineering environment can also be very useful. For example, inferencing capability is offered to help the ontology evaluation and refinement phase. Another example is annotation using the ontology. For this function, usually a graphical user interface is provided to facilitate the annotation process. This is not only used to markup a given document, but also can be used to examine the completeness of a given ontology. Notice these functionalities are provided by employing the so-called plug-in architecture to make the tool easily extensible and customizable by the users, as we will see in the coming discussions.

Ontology engineering and development is a complex topic, and there are in fact many books available just to cover this area. With the basic knowledge we have, together with OWL/RDFS as ontology language choices, you can explore more on your own. For now, let us look at some example environments we can use in our own development work.

14.1.3.2 Protégé

Protégé (`http://protege.stanford.edu/`) is currently the leading environment for ontology development. It is a free, open source ontology editor and knowledge-based framework written in Java.

Protégé was originally developed at Stanford University; it is now supported by a community of developers and academic, government and corporate users. Its latest release was Protégé 4.3 in March 2013.

Protégé supports two main ways of modeling ontologies: the Protégé-OWL editor and the Protégé-Frames editor. The Protégé-Frames editor enables users to build ontologies in accordance with the Open Knowledge Base Connectivity protocol (OKBC), while the Protégé-OWL editor enables users to build ontologies for the Semantic Web, in particular by using the W3C standards such as RDFS and OWL. Therefore, we will focus more on its Protégé-OWL editor in this section.

It is important to notice that Protégé-OWL editors in Protégé 4.x versions only support OWL 2.0. If OWL 1.0 and RDFS are needed, Protégé-OWL editors from Protégé 3.x versions should be selected. The following main features are therefore a combination of all these previous versions:

- Create ontologies by using RDFS and OWL 1.0 (version 3.x only);
- Create ontologies by using OWL 2.0 (version 4.x only);
- Load and save OWL and RDFS ontologies. With version 3.x, OWL and RDFS files are accessible via Protégé-OWL API. However, with version 4.x, only OWL files are accessible by using OWL-API, developed by the University of Manchester, and this API is different from the Protégé-OWL API;
- Edit and visualize classes, properties and relations;
- Define logical class characteristics as OWL expressions;
- Edit OWL individuals for semantic markup;
- Execute reasoners via direct access. For example, with version 3.x, direct connection to Pellet reasoner can be established. With version 4.x, direct connection to other DL reasoners besides Pellet can also be used.

Besides the above main features, Protégé can be extended by way of a *plug-in architecture*. More specifically, plug-ins can be used to change and extend the behavior of Protégé, and, in fact, Protégé itself is written as a collection of plug-ins. The advantage is that these plug-ins can be replaced individually or as a whole to completely alter the interface and behavior of Protégé.

For developers, the Protégé Programming Development Kit (PDK) is a set of documentation and examples that describes and explains how to develop and install plug-in extensions for Protégé. If you need to use plug-ins to change Protégé, the PDK document is where you should start. Also, notice that from version 4.x, Protégé's plug-in framework has been switched to the more industry-standard technology, OSGi,[2] which allows for any type of plug-in extension. Currently, a large set of plug-ins is available; these were mainly developed either in-house or by the Protégé community.

Finally, Protégé supports a Java-based API for building applications on the Semantic Web. This Protégé API is often referred to as Protégé-OWL API; it is an open-source Java library for OWL and RDFS. More specifically, this API provides classes and methods to load and save OWL files, to query and manipulate OWL data models and to conduct reasonings. It can either be use to develop components that are executed inside Protégé-OWL editor's user interface as plug-ins, or can be used to develop external stand-alone applications.

14.1.3.3   NeOn

NeOn is a project involving 14 European partners that was cofunded by the European Commission's Sixty Framework Program. It started in March 2006 and had a duration of 4 years.[3] The goal of this project was to advance the state of the art in using ontologies for large-scale semantic applications, and the NeOn Toolkit,[4] an

---

[2] http://www.osgi.org/Main/HomePage

[3] http://www.neon-project.org

[4] http://www.neon-toolkit.org/

ontology engineering environment, is one of the core outcomes of the NeOn project.

At this point, the NeOn Toolkit is available for download from its community Web site, and its latest major version, v2.5.2, was released on December 2011. Its main features include the following:

- Supports OWL 2 specification;
- Provides NeOn OWL Editor, which can be used for creating and maintaining ontologies written in OWL.

The NeOn OWL Editor has three components: Ontology Navigator, Individual panel and Entity Properties panel. Using these components, a user can accomplish common ontology development tasks such as defining, creating and modifying classes, properties and their relationships in a given ontology. In addition, users can use these components as an ontology management tool, and tasks such as navigating between ontologies, visualizing a given ontology, inspecting related instances of a given class, etc., can also be accomplished.

Notice that the NeOn Toolkit is implemented as a set of Eclipse plug-ins. Similar to Protégé, it has a large user base. With its foundation on the Eclipse plug-in architecture, developers can build additional services and components and add them into the current NeOn Toolkit.

14.1.3.4 TopBraid Composer

TopBraid Composer (`http://www.topquadrant.com/index.html`) is a visual modeling environment for creating and managing ontologies using the Semantic Web standards such as RDFS and OWL.

TopBraid Composer has three versions available: Free Edition, Standard Edition and Maestro Edition. They each offer different packages of support, and you can visit the official Web site to check out the details to see which one fits your needs.

TopBraid Composer is implemented as an Eclipse plug-in, and it is built by using Jena API. It has four major functions: ontology editing, ontology refactoring, ontology reasoning and ontology visualization. Its main features can be summarized as follows:

- Overall features: TopBraid Composer supports both RDFS and OWL (configurable as RDFS only and/or OWL only), and supports SPARQL queries as well. It can import from or export to a variety of data formats including RDBs, XML and Excel. It also offers published APIs for custom extensions and building of Eclipse-based applications on the Semantic Web.
- Ontology editing: users can create classes and define the relationships between classes. Similarly, users can define properties and relationships between

properties. Furthermore, users can create instances based on the specified ontology. These common tasks can be accomplished by using either a form-based editor or an editor with graphical user interface.

- Ontology refactoring: users can move classes, properties and instances between models, and clone classes, properties and instances. TopBraid Composer can synchronize name changes across multiple imported models; it also has a complete log of all changes and can roll-back changes if necessary. It supports the conversion between RDFS and OWL.
- Ontology reasoning: TopBraid Composer interfaces with a collection of inference engines, including Pellet and the Jena Rule Engine. It provides the ability to convert the inferred statements into assertions, and also supports debugging of inferences with explanations.
- Ontology visualization: TopBraid Composer offers UML-like graphical notations, as well as graph visualization and editing. It also provides tree-like views describing relationships between classes and properties.

As you can tell, as an ontology engineering environment, TopBraid Composer offers relatively complete and impressive support.

14.1.4   Other Tools: Search Engines for the Semantic Web

Before we move to the next section, let us talk about search engines on the Semantic Web. They are important for your development for a variety of reasons. For example, you might want to check if there are existing ontologies that may satisfy your needs. And again, it is always good to reuse any existing URIs for the resources your development work might involve, and a search engine for the Semantic Web will help to find these URIs.

When it comes to discovering resources on the Semantic Web, Sindice, Falcon and Sig.ma are all quite useful. We have presented detailed descriptions for all three of these search engines in this book, and you can find more about each one of them in Chap. 9. More specifically, Sect. 9.3.2.1 covers Sig.ma, Sect. 9.2.1.6 covers Sindice and finally, Sect. 9.3.1.1 covers Falcon.

14.1.5   Where to Find More?

With the rapid development around the Semantic Web, it is not easy to keep up with the latest releases and new arrivals. To find more, the W3C Semantic Web wiki is a good starting place:

```
http://www.w3.org/2001/sw/wiki/Tools
```

It also has links to other useful resources online. You should check back to this page for updates and more information frequently.

14.2 Semantic Web Application Development Methodology

In this section, we discuss another important topic: methodological guidelines for building semantic Web applications.

Applications on the Semantic Web, after all, are Web applications. Therefore, existing software engineering methodologies and well-known design patterns for Web application development are still applicable. However, considering the uniqueness of semantic Web applications, such as the fact that they are built upon ontologies and the concept of linked data, what changes should be made to the existing methodologies? What are the new or improved design patterns that developers should be aware of? In this section, we answer these questions, so when it comes to your own development work, you have the necessary methodological support available.

14.2.1 From Domain Models to Ontology-Driven Architecture

14.2.1.1 Domain Models and MVC Architecture

In our daily life as software developers, whether we are working on standalone systems or Web-based applications, we all have more or less heard and used the word *model*, and quite often, we use it in the context of *domain models*. For a software system, a domain model represents the related concepts and data structures from an application domain. It also encodes the knowledge that is driving the application's behavior. To successfully complete a given application development project, developers quite often have to spend long hours working with domain experts to learn and understand the underlying domain model. They will express the domain model by using a set of classes and a description of the interactions among these classes, for example, by means of a collection of UML design diagrams.

After a few iterations with the domain experts, developers will settle down with their view of the domain model, which becomes the centerpiece of the application system. At this point, developers may have also started the design of the user interface components, which not only validate the fulfillment of the user requirements, but can also reinforce the correct understanding about the domain model.

It is certainly possible that the domain model can change. In which case, the data structure may have to be updated, which may or may not trigger a change of the implementation of those user interface components.

Finally at some point, the domain model becomes relatively stable and does not change much. It is then desirable that we can somehow reuse it in our later development work. For example, we might want to grow the system so it can offer more functionalities to the user, or somehow make part of the domain model available to other systems so some of the data elements can be accessed by the outside world.

To address all these issues, a well-known architecture is proposed. It is the so-called *Model-View-Controller* (MVC) architecture. More specifically,

- Model: the model represents domain-specific data and the business rules that specify how the data should be accessed and updated.
- View: the view renders the contents of the model to the end user, in the form of user interface elements. It is possible that for a single model component, there are multiple views (for different level of users, for example).
- Controller: the controller acts like a broker between the model and the view. For example, it accepts the user inputs from the view and translates the user requests into appropriate calls to the business objects in the model.

The controller is the key component that separates the domain model from the view. More specifically, in a standalone application, user interactions can be button clicks or menu selections, and in a Web-based application, the user requests are mapped to GET and POST HTTP requests. Once the user request is submitted by the controller, the actions performed by the model include activating business processes which result in state change of the model. Finally, based on the user requests and the outcome of the model actions, the controller responds by selecting an appropriate view to the user.

It is important to notice that both the view and the controller depend on the model; however, the model depends on none of them. This is the key benefit of the MVC architecture, and it allows us to accomplish the following:

- The model can be built and tested independent of the visual presentation.
- If there is a change in the domain model, such as a change in the business logic, the change can be easily implemented and can be transparent to the end users if necessary.
- Any change in the user interface does not generally affect the model implementation.
- The model can be reused and shared for other applications and target platforms.

For these reasons, MVC architecture is quite successful and has been widely accepted. Today, most Web-based applications are built by employing this architecture.

And how is this related to building applications on the Semantic Web? As we pointed out earlier, applications on the Semantic Web are after all, still Web-based applications. Therefore, MVC architecture remains a good choice. However, given the uniqueness of Semantic Web applications, a mere MVC solution might not be enough. Let us talk about this more in the next two sections.

14.2.1.2   The Uniqueness of Semantic Web Application Development

The most obvious uniqueness about applications on the Semantic Web is that they are using ontologies and RDF models. With the help from ontologies and RDF models, the level of efficiency and scalability that can be reached by semantic Web applications cannot be matched by traditional Web applications.

Let us go back to our task of collecting reviews about digital SLR cameras on the Web (see Chap. 2). We hope to have a soft agent to do this for us, so we don't have to read the reviews one by one. Furthermore, we would like to have the report automatically generated based on the collected reviews, so we can run this application and produce an updated report as often as we want.

Although we have not discussed this task more since Chap. 2, from what you have learned, the solution should be clear. Let us take a look at some details here.

During the course of this book, we have developed a small camera ontology, which is mainly for illustration purpose and is far from being of any practical value. Let us assume a real camera ontology has been defined by some standardization group of the camera industry, and it is widely accepted and also published at a fixed URL as an OWL file.

A camera ontology like this allows reviewers all over the world to publish metadata about their reviews, and this metadata is exactly what a soft agent collects. The collected metadata information can later be used to make conclusions about a given camera.

More specifically, a reviewer can take one of the following two alternatives:

- A reviewer can publish metadata using RDFa.

In this case, a reviewer continues to write his/her review via an HTML page, but he/she will also markup the content by using RDFa, with the terms defined in the camera ontology. This is a simpler choice since the reviewer does not have to generate another separate page for the review.

- A reviewer can publish the metadata using an RDF document.

In this case, a reviewer publishes the review via an HTML page, meanwhile, he/she also releases an RDF document that expresses the same review. Again, this RDF document is created by using the terms contained in the camera ontology.

Now, our agent can go out and collect all the available reviews. It is able to understand both RDFa markups and separate RDF documents. The final result is a set of collected RDF statements stored in an RDF data store that we have chosen to use.

Once the collection process is finished, we can start to issue SPARQL queries against the RDF data store to get the report we want. For example, our report can have the answers to the following questions:

- What is the most often used performance measurement?
- What is the average rating for a given camera model?
- What is the most popular camera model being reviewed?

This step is quite flexible and sometimes even requires some imagination. For instance, if a reviewer has included personal information in the published metadata (such as his/her location, contact information, profession, etc.), we can even start to understand the customer group for each camera model.

Clearly, all the components we have mentioned above, the agent, and the SPARQL query interface, can be packaged together into a Web-based application. With this application, one simple button click will activate the agent so it can start the collecting process, and other GUI components can be used to generate the report.

A user of this Web application does not have to know the technologies that make it possible. However, as developers, we understand how important the camera ontology is in this whole process.

In fact, for any application on the Semantic Web, the ontology *is* the domain model. In addition, understand that for a traditional Web application based on MVC architecture, the domain model maps to a set of classes that are used to code the domain knowledge, and quite often it is expressed in UML format. For an application built on the Semantic Web, the domain model maps to an ontology that is domain-specific, and there is no direct map to a set of classes established yet (more on this in the next section).

Another important fact is that if the domain model is expressed as an ontology, it can be more easily shared and reused. For example, the camera ontology we discuss above can be easily reused in a totally different application.

To see this, imagine we are building a ShopBot that can help a user to buy cameras. If camera retailers can markup their catalogs by using the same camera ontology and publish the markup on their own Web sites, our ShopBot will be able to collect them. Once the collection is done, our ShopBot could easily find a retailer who offers a camera that satisfies the user's requirement. Furthermore, with the help from the reasoning power offered by the camera ontology, our ShopBot can automatically suggest potential choices that are not obvious at first glance. You will see such a ShopBot example in the last chapter of this book.

Obviously, collecting the reviews and shopping for a camera are quite different applications, however, they are sharing and reusing the same camera ontology. In fact, they can start to share data with each other, and by aggregating the shared data elements, we can start to understand how the reviews can affect the sales of cameras.

To some extent, application development on the Semantic Web is getting easier: developers first discover sharable ontologies as the domain model, and then wire the ontologies together with remaining object-oriented components for user interface and control components.

In fact, this design concept has been taking shape for the last several years, and it is now being recognized as *Ontology Driven Architecture*. We take a closer look at this architecture in the next section.

14.2.1.3   Ontology-Driven Software Development

As we discussed earlier, a traditional application based on MVC architecture normally has its domain model mapped to classes that are defined by mainstream programming languages such as Java or C#. The related domain knowledge is coded into these classes, which are also responsible for common tasks such as communicating with databases and other resources.

For an application that runs on the Semantic Web, its domain model is expressed by ontologies. Could we again simply map all the RDFS or OWL classes into object-oriented classes and continue to build the system as we would have done traditionally? The answer is no.

The key to understand ontology-driven design is to understand the following facts about a given ontology:

- Properties in ontology are independent from specific classes.
- Instances can have multiple types, and they can change their types as a result of classification.
- Classes can be dynamically defined at run time as well.

These key differences tell us, in order to fully exploit the weak typing and flexibility offered by the RDFS/OWL ontology, we have to map RDFS/OWL classes into runtime objects, so that classes defined in the ontology become instances of some object-oriented classes. This is the key idea of the ontology-driven software development method.

For example, Fig. 14.2 shows one such mapping:

As shown in Fig. 14.2, the object-oriented model that represents ontologies in our code is designed to contain classes that represent RDFS/OWL classes, RDFS/OWL properties and RDF individuals separately, where RDF individuals are instances of the RDFS/OWL classes or RDFS/OWL properties. And obviously, all three of these classes, namely, OWLClass, OWLProperty and RDFIndividual, are subclasses of class Resource.

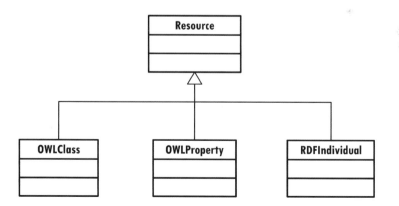

Fig. 14.2 A simple mapping of RDFS/OWL classes to runtime objects

With this design, our application can load the ontology into this object model and start to build logic on top of it. For example,

- Since RDFS/OWL classes are now instances of the class `OWLClass`, it is possible to add and modify RDFS/OWL classes at the run time.
- Since RDFS/OWL properties are now instances of the class `OWLProperty`, it is possible to assign property values to any resource dynamically, and also possible to query any property value for any resource dynamically.
- Since individuals are now instances of the class `RDFIndividual`, it is possible to change their types dynamically.

Obviously, the key is to represent the object types as objects, which provides the flexibility we need. For those of you who are familiar with design patterns, you probably have recognized this pattern already: it is known as the *Dynamic Object Model* pattern.

Now, when it comes to real development work, how do we implement the dynamic object model pattern? In fact, as developers, you don't have to worry about this. Most application development frameworks for the Semantic Web have implemented this pattern for you already, and clearly, this is one of the benefits offered by using a development framework (see Sect. 14.1.1.1).

For example, Jena provides a dynamic object model in which OWL classes, properties and individuals are stored using generic Java classes such as `OntClass` and `Individual`. If you are using other development frameworks, you will be able to see similar patterns implemented for you by the framework.

Notice that there are also some disadvantages associated with dynamic object model pattern. For instance, references to ontology objects are established only through names (i.e., strings), making code hard to maintain and test. In addition, as the ontology may change at design time, existing code may become inconsistent with the changing ontology.

One solution is to reflect the ontology concepts with custom classes, so that the ontological structure is exploited at compile-time. This also allows developers to attach access methods to these classes, leading to cleaner object-oriented design patterns. We will not go into details at this point, but in your development work, if you see reflect used, you should be able to understand the reason behind it.

14.2.1.4 Further Discussions

By this point in this book, it is probably obvious to you that lots of effort has been devoted to defining standards (earlier standards such as RDF, RDFS and OWL 1, and later standards such as OWL 2 and SPARQL 1.1, for example) and creating appropriate tool support. Work on development methodologies for semantic Web applications is still in its infancy, probably due to the fact that this field is rather new, and few people have experience in the development of real-world applications.

This is, of course, going to change. With more and more real-world applications emerge on the Web, there will be more experience gathered, and developers will be offered more guidelines. What we have presented here in this section is only a start, and only serves as a basic guideline to your development work. It is up to you to discover more and share more with your fellow developers.

14.2.2   An Ontology Development Methodology Proposed by Noy and McGuinness

It is obvious from the previous discussion how important ontologies are for any given application on the Semantic Web. In fact, when developing applications on the Semantic Web, a significant portion of the effort has to be spent on developing ontologies. These ontologies must be consistent, generally useful and formally correct. In addition, they must be extensible and may become very large.

In this section, we present a summary of an ontology development method proposed by Noy and McGuinness (2001). Over the years, these steps have been followed by many applications and research projects, and they are widely referenced in a variety of research papers as well.

Understand that there is no single correct ontology design methodology that everyone can use, and it is also impossible to cover all the issues that an ontology developer may need to consider. In most cases, it is up to you to come up with the best solution for your specific application domain.

14.2.2.1   Basic Tasks and Fundamental Rules

According to Noy and McGuinness, the basic task of developing an ontology includes the following:

- Define classes;
- Arrange the classes into a class hierarchy;
- Define properties and allowed values for the properties;
- Create instances, and specify values for the properties for the instances.

In essence, Noy and McGuinness propose an iterative approach to ontology development. More specifically, an initial ontology is created in a rough first pass. It is then revised and refined, with details provided and filled in. They summarize the fundamental rules of ontology development as follows:

- There is no such thing as the "correct way to model a domain". The solution almost always depends on the application that we have in mind and extensions we can anticipate.
- Ontology development should be an iterative process.

- Concepts in the ontology should be close to objects and relationships, where objects can be either physical or logical. Also, these are likely to be nouns (objects) or verbs (relationships) in sentences that describe the domain.

Noy and McGuinness emphasize that ontology development is iterative. The initial version of the ontology should be tested and evaluated in applications, and should be discussed with domain experts. Similarly, the revised version should be put back to the cycle for more fine-tuning.

With this in mind, let us now take a look at the basic development steps proposed by Noy and McGuinness.

14.2.2.2 Basic Steps of Ontology Development

Noy and McGuinness suggest that ontology development follow these steps:

Step 1. Determine the Domain and Scope of the Ontology

To effectively accomplish this step, developers should answer these basic questions:

- What is the domain the ontology will cover?
- For what purpose is the ontology going to be used?
- For what types of questions should the ontology be able to provide answers?
- Who will use and maintain the ontology?

Take our camera ontology as one example. If the ontology is going to be used by camera retailers, pricing information should be included. On the other hand, if the ontology is only used for performance reviews, pricing information could be optional. Therefore, understanding the application we have in mind, and anticipating what kinds of questions should be answered by using the ontology are quite important questions to answer.

Step 2. Consider Reusing Existing Ontologies

As we have discussed throughout the book, reusing existing ontology is always a good choice when it is appropriate to do so. And as pointed out by Noy and McGuinness, if one of the requirements is to make sure our system can communicate with other applications that have already committed to particular ontologies, reusing these ontologies is a must.

Step 3. Enumerate Important Terms in the Ontology

This is the step before defining classes and class hierarchy. Noy and McGuinness suggest that one create a comprehensive list of the terms in the given domain, without worrying about overlap between the concepts they represent, relations among the terms, or any properties that the concepts may have. The goal is to make sure all the important terms are included, since once we get into the details of defining classes and class hierarchy, it is easier to focus on the details and overlook the overall completeness of the ontology.

Step 4. Define Classes and the Class Hierarchy

In general, three approaches can be used when defining classes and class hierarchy.

The first one is called the *top-down* approach, where the definition process starts with the definition of the most general classes and continues to the subsequent specialization of the classes.

The second one is the *bottom-up* approach, which is the exact opposite of the top-down approach. When using this approach, developers start with the most specific classes and move on to more general ones.

The last approach is the *combination* approach. As its name suggests, it combines the above two approaches, and developers can switch between the two approaches when defining classes and class hierarchy.

Whichever approach is chosen, it is important to understand that none of these three methods is inherently better than any of the others. The choice depends strongly on the personal view of the domain. In reality, the combination approach is often the easiest for many ontology developers.

Step 5. Define the Properties of Classes

To define properties, Noy and McGuinness suggest that the developer consider the following types of properties:

- "Intrinsic" properties, which represent those inherent characteristics of a given class. For example, in camera ontology, `shutter speed` would be an intrinsic property of a given camera.
- "Extrinsic" properties, which represent those characteristics that are not inherent. For instance, the `model` of a given camera would be an extrinsic property.
- Parts, for example, a camera has a `body` and a `lens`.
- Relationships to other individuals, for example, the `manufacturer` of a given camera, the `owner` of a given camera, etc.

Step 6. Add Constraints to the Properties

First, notice that when Noy and McGuinness published their paper in 2001, properties were called slots and property constraints were called facets. You may still see these terminologies today in some of the literature.

Once we finish adding properties to the ontology, we need to consider property constraints such as cardinality constraints and value type constraints, just to name a few. The constraints you can use and add also depend on the ontology language you use. For example, OWL 2 offers many more constraint constructs than RDFS, as you have learned in this book.

Notice that for a given property, its domain and range information is also defined in this step.

Step 7. Create Instances

This step last step is also an optional step. In other words, an ontology document does not have to include instance definition. For instance, FOAF ontology does not have any instances defined.

In case you would like to include instances in the ontology document, the procedure of creating instances normally has these steps:

- Choose a class;
- Create an individual instance of that class, and
- Define values for its properties.

At this point, we have summarized the basic steps when it comes to ontology development. Obviously, steps 4 and 5 are the most important steps as well as the most flexible ones. In the next two sections, we discuss more about these two steps.

14.2.2.3   Other Considerations

Noy and McGuinness also discussed things to look out for and errors that are easy to make when defining classes and a class hierarchy. In this section, we summarize their findings, which are quite useful in real work.

- A class hierarchy represents an *is-a* relation.

To decide whether your class hierarchy is correct, an easy way is to see if a given subclass and its root class have an is-a relation. For example, a `Digital` camera is a `Camera`, therefore, `Digital` class is a subclass of `Camera` class. Also, once you have this is-a relation in your mind, you will be able to avoid some common mistakes, such as specifying a single camera as a subclass of all cameras. Obviously, a `Camera` is not a `Cameras`.

- A subclass relationship is transitive.

Another way to validate your class hierarchy is to remember that a subclass relationship is transitive. In other words, if A is a subclass of B and B is subclass of C, A is a subclass of C. You can always apply this rule to check if your class hierarchy is correct.

- How many subclasses should a class have?

First, notice that a class does not have to have subclass at all. In case it does, there are no hard rules specifying how many direct subclasses it should have. However, many well-structured ontologies have between two and a dozen direct subclasses. The two guidelines are (1) If a class has only one direct subclass, there may be a modeling problem or the ontology is not complete. (2) If there are more than a dozen subclasses for a given class, then additional intermediate categories may be necessary.

- When should we introduce a new class?

During ontology modeling, to represent some knowledge, we sometimes have to decide whether to introduce a new class, or to add a new property to an existing class. The rules of thumb summarized by Noy and McGuinness can be stated as this: a new subclass should have additional properties that its super-class does not have, or have a new property value defined for a given property, or participate in different relationships than its super-class.

Notice that in practice, the decision of whether to model a specific distinction as a property value or as a new class also depends on the scope of the domain and the task at hand.

For example, in our camera ontology, we can introduce a new class called `Digital` to represent digital cameras and also a new class called `Film` to represent film cameras. Furthermore, these two classes are subclasses of the `Camera` class. Another solution is to add a new property called `cameraMedia`, which can have values such as `digital` and `film`. Which one is a good solution for us?

The answer usually depends on the scope of the ontology and the potential applications that we have in mind. More specifically, if `Digital` and `Film` classes are very important in our domain and they play significant roles in our future applications, it is a good idea to make these separate classes instead of a single property value on their super-class. This is especially true when it is likely that we will need to specify new properties for each one of these classes.

On the other hand, if a camera only has marginal importance in our domain and whether or not the camera is a digital camera or a traditional film camera does not have any significant implications, it is then a good choice to add a new property to the `Camera` class.

- For a given concept, when should we model it as a class, and when should we model it as an instance?

This is a very common question in real development work. For example, the Nikon D200 is a digital camera made by Nikon. If we have a class named `Digital` representing digital cameras, we can now either model Nikon D200 as a subclass of `Digital`, or as an individual instance of `Digital`.

To make this decision, we need to decide the lowest level of granularity in our design. This decision is in turn determined by the potential applications of the ontology. For example, if we model Nikon D200 as a subclass of `Digital` class (and name it `Nikon_D200`), we can then model one particular Nikon D200 camera offered by a specific retailer as an instance of the `Nikon_D200` class. If we model Nikon D200 as an instance of `Digital` class, this instance will represent all the Nikon D200 cameras in the world, and any particular Nikon D200 camera will not be identified (if we want to, we need to add some property, such as `retailer`, for example). As you can tell, different design decisions have a direct impact on our future applications.

The bottom line: individual instances are the most specific concepts represented in a given ontology.

- If possible, we should always specify disjoint classes.

It is possible that in a given domain, several given classes are disjoint. For example, the `Digital` class represents the collection of all digital cameras, and the `Film` class represents all traditional film cameras. These two classes are disjoint. In other words, a given camera cannot be both a digital camera and a film camera.

Ontology language such as OWL allows us to specify that several classes are disjoint. In real practice, we should always do so for the disjointed classes. This enables the system to better validate the ontology. For example, if we create a new class that is subclass of both `Digital` and `Film`, a modeling error can be flagged by the system.

At this point, we have covered the main ontology design guidelines proposed by Noy and McGuinness. For more details, you can find their original paper to continue your study. The main point to remember: ontology design is a creative process and there is no single correct ontology for any domain. Also, the potential applications have a direct impact on ontology design, and only by using the ontology in the related applications can we further assess the quality of the ontology.

14.3   Summary

In this chapter, we presented an overview about development on the Semantic Web. This overview covered two major topics: the development tools and development methodologies you can use.

Understand the following about the development tools:

- There is a collection of development tools you can use for your development work on the Semantic Web.
- This collection includes development frameworks, ontology reasoners, ontology engineering environments and other related tools.
- Understand different tools, for example, their functionalities and their limitations, so you will be able to pick the most suitable tools for your specific application.

Understand the following about development methodologies:

- The uniqueness of development work on the Semantic Web;
- The so-called ontology-driven development methodology, and why it is suitable for the development work on the Semantic Web;
- The ontology development method proposed by Noy and McGuinness, including the basic rules, basic steps and related considerations.

Reference

Noy NF, McGuinness DL (2001) Ontology development 101: a guide to creating your first ontology. Stanford knowledge systems laboratory technical report KSL-01-05 and stanford medical informatics technical report SMI-2001-0880

Chapter 15
Example: Using Jena for Development on the Semantic Web

Part of the previous chapter presented an overview of available development frameworks you can use. This chapter focuses on Jena as a concrete example as well as our main development environment.

In this chapter, we provide quite a few examples, starting from `Hello World`, to a set of basic tasks that you will likely encounter for any of your applications on the Semantic Web, including RDF model operations, persistent RDF graph handling and inferencing capabilities. The goal is not only to show you how to use Jena as a development framework, but also to add some working Java classes into your own tool collection so you can reuse them in your future development work.

Notice Jena is a programmer's API for Java semantic Web applications. This chapter therefore assumes you are familiar with the Java programming language.

15.1 Jena: A Semantic Web Framework for Java

15.1.1 What Is Jena and What Can It Do for Us?

At this point, we have not yet developed any applications on the Semantic Web. However, based on what we learned about the Semantic Web, it is not difficult for us to realize that any Semantic Web application probably has to be able to handle the following common tasks:

- Read/parse RDF documents
- Write/create RDF documents
- Navigate/search through an RDF graph
- Query an RDF dataset by using SPARQL
- Inference using OWL ontologies

This is certainly not a complete list, but these are probably needed to make even a simple application work. Fortunately, these standard items can be developed and

© Springer-Verlag Berlin Heidelberg 2014

L. Yu, *A Developer's Guide to the Semantic Web*,
DOI 10.1007/978-3-662-43796-4_15

assembled into a library that we can use, so we can focus our attention on the business logic when developing specific Semantic Web applications.

As we discussed in Chap. 14, there are quite a few such development tools available for us to use. In this book, we use Jena as our development tool. If you are using other frameworks, what you learn here will also be helpful.

There are two steps we have to cover in order to use Jena API in our development. The first step is to download the Jena package, and the second step is to set up a Java development environment that can make use of the Jena package. These two steps are covered in detail in this section.

In this book, we use Eclipse as our Java development environment. Other environments are available and can also be selected based on your needs. Also, notice the version numbers of Jena and Eclipse in this book will probably be different from the ones you have, but again this does not matter, since the basic steps of setting up the development environment should remain the same.

15.1.2   Getting the Jena Package

To access Jena, go to the following page,

`http://jena.apache.org/`

which links to the Jena home page. To download the Jena package, click the `download` link on the page, and follow the instructions. Notice in this book, we use Jena 2.6.0 as our example package, and as far as our applications are concerned, other versions should work. You can therefore choose to download Jena 2.6.0 or any version that is higher.

Once the download is done, you will find a zip file named `Jena-2.x.x` on your local hard drive. Unzip this file to create a Jena package directory on your hard drive. Note that Jena is a library for writing applications based on RDF and OWL documents. It is only used in your application code as a collection of APIs, and there is no GUI of any kind for Jena. The core components of Jena are stored in its `\lib` directory, as you should be able to see.

To make use of the Jena library, it is important to add all the related `.jar` files to your `classpath` variable.

Using Windows XP as an example, the `classpath` variable is contained in two categories: the `System Variables` category and the `User Variables` category. It is normally enough that you make changes to the one contained in the `User Variables` category.

To do so, right-click the `My Computer` icon on your desktop, and then click `Properties`, which brings up the `System Properties` window. In this window, click the `Advanced` tab, and then click the `Environment Variables` button, which brings you to the window where you can edit the `classpath` variable contained in `User Variables` category.

15.1.3 *Using Jena in Your Projects*

Just setting up the Jena environment is not sufficient; your project has to make use of the Jena package. This section assumes you are using Eclipse as your Java development tool and shows you how to use the Jena framework in your Eclipse projects.

15.1.3.1 Using Jena in Eclipse

As far as Eclipse is concerned, the difference between a plain Java project and a Java project that uses the Jena library is that Eclipse has to know where to find the Jena library files to which the project refers. Once it locates the library files, it can load the related class definitions from the library as the necessary supporting code to our project.

One way to accomplish this is to create a lib directory in our project workspace, copy Jena-related library files to this lib directory and then add this lib directory into our project's build path. This will work; however, a user library is a better solution to use.

In Eclipse, a user library is a user-defined library (a collection of jar files) that one can reference from any project. In other words, once we have configured a user library, we can use it in multiple different projects. Furthermore, if Jena releases a new updated version, updating the user library once will guarantee that all the projects using this library will see the newly updated version. If we had created a library under each specific project workspace, we would have to copy the new version to every workspace that makes use of Jena.

To configure a user library, open up Eclipse and select Window from the menu bar. From the drop-down menu list, select preferences, which brings up the Preferences dialogue window. In this window, open Java on the left navigation tree, and then open Build Path. Once Build Path is open, select User Libraries as shown in Fig. 15.1.

Now click New to create a new user library. To do so, in the pop-up window, enter jena as the library name, and click OK to close this window. At this point, clicking Add JARs... brings up a JAR Selection window. You can then navigate to the location where you have installed Jena, and select all of the .jar files in the lib directory, which will be enough for our project. Once you click Open, you should see the user library is correctly created, as shown in Fig. 15.2 (note that you might have downloaded different Jena version, so you might see different jars):

This is quite similar to the concept of symbolic link that we are familiar with when using the Unix platform. The user library we just created simply contains a collection of links that points to those *.jar files in the lib/ directory under my Jena install directory; nothing is copied to my Eclipse workspace at all.

Now that we have configured a user library, we can start to use it in our project by adding this library to the build path of our project. To show how to do this, we need to create a new project, and since it will be our very first real programming project in this book, we will call it the Hello World project; we cover the details in the next section.

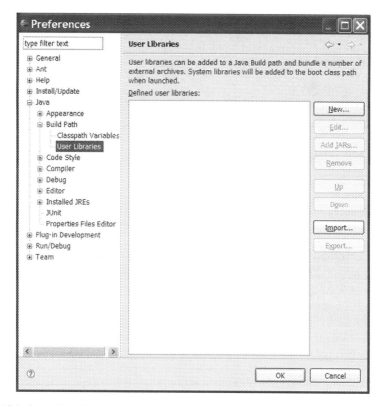

Fig. 15.1 Set up Jena framework as a user library in Eclipse

15.1.3.2 `Hello World!` from a Semantic Web Application

We all know the importance of the `Hello World` example, and we add it here so you can see how to build a project that makes use of the Jena Semantic Web framework.

Our `Hello World` example works like this: we will create a simple RDF document which contains only one RDF statement, and this statement has the following subject, property and object:

```
subject: http://example.org/test/message
property: http://example.org/test/says
object: Hello World!
```

Let us fire up Eclipse, create a new project called `HelloWorld`, and also define an empty class called `HelloWorld.java`.

Now, enter the class definition as shown in List 15.1, and it is fine if you currently don't understand the code at all.

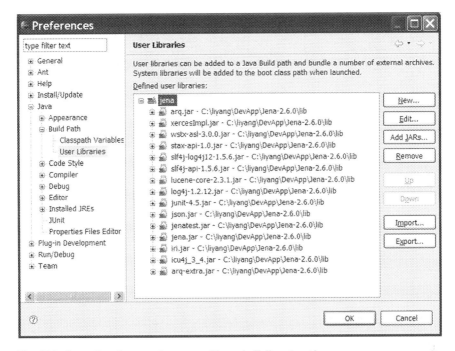

Fig. 15.2 Set up Jena framework as a user library in Eclipse (*cont.*)

List 15.1 `HelloWorld.java`

```
1: public class HelloWorld {
2:
3:   static private String nameSpace = "http://example.org/test/";
4:
5:   public static void main(String[] args) {
6:     Model model = ModelFactory.createDefaultModel();
7:
8:     Resource subject =
8a:              model.createResource(nameSpace + "message");
9:     Property property =
9a:              model.createProperty(nameSpace + "says");
10:    subject.addProperty(property,
10a:                    "Hello World!",XSDDatatype.XSDstring);
11:
12:    model.write(System.out);
13: }
14:
15:}
```

Once you have entered the definition shown in List 15.1, Eclipse shows all the error signals. For example, it does not recognize `Model`, `ModelFactory`, `Resource`

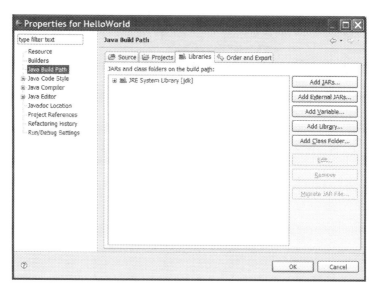

Fig. 15.3 Using Jena framework as a user library

and `Property`. Clearly, these definitions are provided by the Jena package that we would like to use, and they are currently not visible to Eclipse. We now need to tell Eclipse that the user library we just created contains the definitions that it needs; we do this by adding the user library to the build path of our project.

To do so, right-click the `HelloWorld` project node in the `Project Explorer` window to bring up the project's pop-up menu. From this menu, select `Proper-ties`, which brings up the `Properties for HelloWorld` window. In this window, navigate to the `Java Build Path` and select the `Libraries` tab (Fig. 15.3).

In this window, clicking `Add Library` brings up the dialog window, as shown in Fig. 15.4.

Highlight `User Library`, and click `Next`; select `jena` as the user library to be added, and click `Finish` to add the user library into the build path, as shown in Fig. 15.5.

Click `OK` in the `Properties for HelloWorld` window to finish this task. You should also notice that the `jena` user library shows up in the `Project Explorer` window correctly.

However, the error signals still do not disappear. In fact, Eclipse is now waiting for us to use the appropriate `import` statements so it can find the definitions for class `Model`, `ModelFactory`, `Resource` and `Property`.

In fact, this could be fairly difficult for us: as beginners, we don't know where these definitions can be found in the library either. Yet the good news is, since we have used the correct user library, all we need to do is click the error symbol (the red x in the left margin), and Eclipse shows us the right `import` statement to use. Try this out, and if you have done everything correctly, all the errors should be gone, and you should find the following `import` statements are being used, as shown in List 15.2:

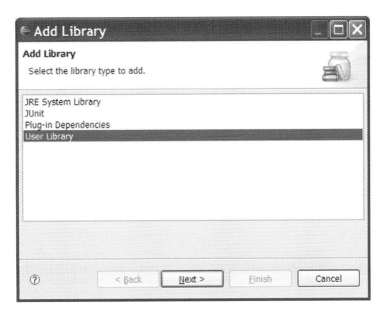

Fig. 15.4 Using Jena framework as a user library (*cont.*)

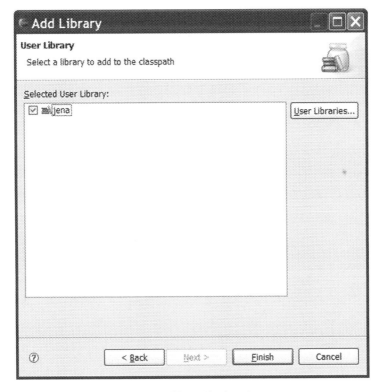

Fig. 15.5 Using Jena framework as a user library (final step)

List 15.2 `Import` statements in our `HelloWorld` project

```
import com.hp.hpl.jena.datatypes.xsd.XSDDatatype;
import com.hp.hpl.jena.rdf.model.Model;
import com.hp.hpl.jena.rdf.model.ModelFactory;
import com.hp.hpl.jena.rdf.model.Property;
import com.hp.hpl.jena.rdf.model.Resource;
```

Now, run the project, and you should be able to see the result as shown in List 15.3.

List 15.3 `HelloWorld` output

```
<rdf:RDF
    xmlns:j.0="http://example.org/test/"
    xmlns:rdf="http://www.w3.org/1999/02/22-rdf-syntax-ns#" >
  <rdf:Description rdf:about="http://example.org/test/message">
    <j.0:says rdf:datatype=
                "http://www.w3.org/2001/XMLSchema#string">
      Hello World!
    </j.0:says>
  </rdf:Description>
</rdf:RDF>
```

And congratulations—this is your first Semantic Web application developed using Jena.

One last thing before we move on: the above RDF model has only one statement, and we can make it look much better: change line 12 in List 15.1 to make it look like this:

```
12: model.write(System.out,"Turtle");
```

and run the project again. You will get a better output as shown in List 15.4.

List 15.4 A better output from `HelloWorld` project

```
<http://example.org/test/message>
  <http://example.org/test/says>
    "Hello World!"^^<http://www.w3.org/2001/XMLSchema#string> .
```

15.2   Basic RDF Model Operations

In this section, we use Jena to accomplish some basic functionalities. The goal is to get you familiar with Jena. To make things simpler, we will be using in-memory RDF models in this section, meaning that we will either create the RDF model in memory, or we will read it into memory from a given URL or a file system. Persistent RDF models are covered in the next section.

15.2.1 Creating an RDF Model

In this section, we create an empty RDF model from scratch and then add RDF statements to it. For the purpose of testing, we are going to create a model that represents my own FOAF document as shown in List 15.5 (notice that it has been changed a little bit to make it easier to work with).

List 15.5 The author's FOAF document

```
1: <?xml version="1.0" encoding="UTF-8"?>
2: <rdf:RDF
3:      xmlns:rdf="http://www.w3.org/1999/02/22-rdf-syntax-ns#"
4:      xmlns:rdfs="http://www.w3.org/2000/01/rdf-schema#"
5:      xmlns:foaf="http://xmlns.com/foaf/0.1/">
6:
7:   <rdf:Description
7a:       rdf:about="http://www.liyangyu.com/foaf.rdf#liyang">
8:     <foaf:name>liyang yu</foaf:name>
9:     <foaf:title>Dr</foaf:title>
10:    <foaf:givenname>liyang</foaf:givenname>
11:    <foaf:family_name>yu</foaf:family_name>
12:    <foaf:mbox rdf:resource="mailto:liyang@liyangyu.com"/>
13:    <foaf:homepage rdf:resource="http://www.liyangyu.com"/>
14:    <foaf:workplaceHomepage
14a:                   rdf:resource="http://www.delta.com"/>
15:    <rdf:type
15a:        rdf:resource="http://xmlns.com/foaf/0.1/Person"/>
16:
17:    <foaf:knows>
18:      <!-- the following is for testing purpose -->
19:      <foaf:Person>
20:        <foaf:mbox
20a:          rdf:resource="mailto:libby.miller@bristol.ac.uk"/>
21:        <foaf:homepage
21a:          rdf:resource="http://www.ilrt.bris.ac.uk/~ecemm/"/>
22:      </foaf:Person>
23:    </foaf:knows>
24:
25:    <foaf:topic_interest
25a:    rdf:resource="http://dbpedia.org/resource/Semantic_Web"/>
26:
27: </rdf:Description>
28: </rdf:RDF>
```

And the source code to accomplish this is shown in List 15.6.

List 15.6 Create a new RDF model and add statements to it

```
1: import java.io.PrintWriter;
2: import com.hp.hpl.jena.rdf.model.Model;
3: import com.hp.hpl.jena.rdf.model.ModelFactory;
4: import com.hp.hpl.jena.rdf.model.Resource;
5: import com.hp.hpl.jena.sparql.vocabulary.FOAF;
6: import com.hp.hpl.jena.vocabulary.RDF;
7: import com.hp.hpl.jena.vocabulary.RDFS;
8:
9:  public class MyFOAFModel {
10:
11:    public static void main(String[] args) {
12:
13:        Model model = ModelFactory.createDefaultModel();
14:        model.setNsPrefix("rdfs",RDFS.getURI());
15:        model.setNsPrefix("foaf",FOAF.getURI());
16:
17:        Resource subject = model.createResource
17a:                 ("http://www.liyangyu.com/foaf.rdf#liyang");
18:
19:        subject.addProperty(FOAF.name,"liyang yu");
20:        subject.addProperty(FOAF.title,"Dr");
21:        subject.addProperty(FOAF.givenname,"liyang");
22:        subject.addProperty(FOAF.family_name,"yu");
23:        subject.addProperty(FOAF.mbox,
23a:         model.createResource("mailto:liyang@liyangyu.com"));
24:        subject.addProperty(FOAF.homepage,
24a:         model.createResource("http://www.liyangyu.com"));
25:        subject.addProperty(FOAF.workplaceHomepage,
25a:         model.createResource("http://www.delta.com"));
26:        subject.addProperty(FOAF.topic_interest,
26a:                      model.createResource
26b:             ("http://dbpedia.org/resource/Semantic_Web"));
27:        subject.addProperty(RDF.type,FOAF.Person);
28:
29:        Resource blankSubject = model.createResource();
30:        blankSubject.addProperty(RDF.type,FOAF.Person);
31:        blankSubject.addProperty(FOAF.mbox,
31a:                      model.createResource
31b:             ("mailto:libby.miller@bristol.ac.uk"));
32:        blankSubject.addProperty(FOAF.homepage,
32a:                      model.createResource
32b:             ("http://www.ilrt.bris.ac.uk/~ecemm/"));
```

```
33:          subject.addProperty(FOAF.knows,blankSubject);
34:
35:          model.write(System.out);
36:    }
37:
38: }
```

The first thing to remember is that in Jena's world, ModelFactory class is the preferred way when it comes to creating different types of RDF models. For our purpose in this example, we want an empty, in-memory model; therefore ModelFactory.createDefaultModel() is the method to call, as shown on line 13 of List 15.6. This method returns an instance of class Model, which represents the empty RDF model we just created. At this point, we can start to add statements into this model.

To add a statement into an RDF model, the first thing to do is to create a statement. In Jena, the subject of a statement is always represented by an instance of Resource class, the predicate is represented by an instance of Property class, and the object is either a Resource instance or a literal value, which is represented by an instance of the Literal class. All of these classes, namely, Resource class, Property class and Literal class, share a common interface called RDFNode. At this point, you should be able tell how Jena's class hierarchy maps to the related concepts in RDF world.

Now, to create a statement, we create the subject first. One way to do this is to call the createResource() method provided by Model class, as shown on line 17. We pass in the URI of the subject so it can be created with the given URI as its identifier.

Once we have the subject, we can create a statement by calling method Resource.addProperty(). This method directly creates a statement in the model with the Resource as its subject. The method takes two parameters, a Property instance representing the predicate of the statement, and the statement's object. Notice the addProperty() method is overloaded in multiple forms, and one overload takes an RDFNode as its object, so a Resource or Literal can be used. There are also other overloads that take a literal represented by a Java primitive or a string, as we will see next.

With this said, line 19 should be easy to understand: it directly inserts a statement into the model with subject as its subject, foaf:name as its property and string literal "liyang yu" as its object. Notice Jena provides support for some popular vocabularies, and FOAF ontology is one of these ontologies. In this case, FOAF.name returns a Property instance that represents the foaf:name property.

As a side note, if Jena did not support FOAF ontology, line 19 could have been written as two separate lines as given below:

```
Property nameProperty =
        model.createProperty("http://xmlns.com/foaf/0.1/name");
subject.addProperty(nameProperty,"liyang yu");
```

or, a more concise form would look like this:

```
subject.addProperty
(model.createProperty("http://xmlns.com/foaf/0.1/name"),
                      "liyang yu");
```

Similarly, lines 20, 21 and 22 are all easy to understand. Line 20 inserts a statement saying our `subject` has a `foaf:title` property whose value is "`Dr`", line 21 adds a statement saying our `subject` has a `foaf:givenname` property whose value is "`liyang`" and line 22 maps to a statement saying our `subject` has a `foaf:family_name` property whose value is "`yu`". And obviously, the statements created by lines 19–22 correspond to lines 8–11 in List 15.5.

Notice that lines 19–22 all add statements whose objects have string literals as their values. Lines 23–26, on the other hand, use resources as the values of their objects. For example, line 23 inserts a statement which has another resource as its object, and again, `createResource()` is called to create this resource. Also, statements created by lines 23–26 map to lines 12, 13, 14 and 25 in List 15.5.

Line 27 is also quite straightforward: it creates a statement that maps to line 15 in List 15.5. Again, since Jena supports FOAF and the RDF vocabulary, `RDF.type` returns `rdf:type` property and `FOAF.Person` returns `foaf:Person` resource.

Lines 29–32 can be understood together with lines 19–22 in List 15.5, which define a blank node that represents an instance of `foaf:Person` class. To create this blank node, the `createResource()` method is called without any parameters being passed in, as shown on line 29.

Once this blank resource is created, we can add statements that use this resource as their subject: line 30 inserts a statement saying this blank resource is an instance of `foaf:Person`, and line 31 says this blank node has a `foaf:mbox` property that uses another resource as its value. Finally, line 32 adds a statement about its `foaf:homepage` property. Again, lines 29–32 map to lines 19–22 in List 15.5. Line 33 in List 15.6 inserts into our model the last statement which expresses the fact that the subject `foaf:know` the above blank node, and at this point, it should be quite easy to understand as well.

Now, we have finished creating a simple in-memory RDF model that represents the document shown in List 15.5. To see this model, line 35 is used, which simply prints out the model on the screen so we can take a look.

If you run the java class shown in List 15.6, you should get the output as shown in List 15.7.

List 15.7 Output generated by List 15.6

```
1:  <rdf:RDF
2:      xmlns:foaf="http://xmlns.com/foaf/0.1/"
3:      xmlns:rdf="http://www.w3.org/1999/02/22-rdf-syntax-ns#"
4:      xmlns:rdfs="http://www.w3.org/2000/01/rdf-schema#" >
5:   <rdf:Description
5a:         rdf:about="http://www.liyangyu.com/foaf.rdf#liyang">
6:      <foaf:name>liyang yu</foaf:name>
7:      <foaf:mbox rdf:resource="mailto:liyang@liyangyu.com"/>
8:      <rdf:type
8a:          rdf:resource="http://xmlns.com/foaf/0.1/Person"/>
9:      <foaf:family_name>yu</foaf:family_name>
10:      <foaf:knows rdf:nodeID="A0"/>
11:      <foaf:givenname>liyang</foaf:givenname>
12:      <foaf:title>Dr</foaf:title>
13:      <foaf:topic_interest rdf:resource=
13a:                   "http://dbpedia.org/resource/Semantic_Web"/>
14:      <foaf:homepage rdf:resource="http://www.liyangyu.com"/>
15:      <foaf:workplaceHomepage
15a:          rdf:resource="http://www.delta.com"/>
16:   </rdf:Description>
17:   <rdf:Description rdf:nodeID="A0">
18:      <foaf:homepage
18a:          rdf:resource="http://www.ilrt.bris.ac.uk/~ecemm/"/>
19:      <foaf:mbox
19a:          rdf:resource="mailto:libby.miller@bristol.ac.uk"/>
20:      <rdf:type
20a:          rdf:resource="http://xmlns.com/foaf/0.1/Person"/>
21:   </rdf:Description>
22: </rdf:RDF>
```

Notice that List 15.7 is not the best output that we can have. For one thing, the blank node has been assigned a node ID (line 17), so it is not blank anymore. In fact, a better output can be obtained by replacing line 35 with the following line, which makes use of RDF/XML-ABBR parameter:

```
model.write(new PrintWriter(System.out), "RDF/XML-ABBREV");
```

And now, run the code again, and you will see the output as shown in List 15.8.

List 15.8 A better output generated from List 15.6

```
1: <rdf:RDF
2:     xmlns:foaf="http://xmlns.com/foaf/0.1/"
3:     xmlns:rdf="http://www.w3.org/1999/02/22-rdf-syntax-ns#"
4:     xmlns:rdfs="http://www.w3.org/2000/01/rdf-schema#">
5:    <foaf:Person
5a:         rdf:about="http://www.liyangyu.com/foaf.rdf#liyang">
6:      <foaf:name>liyang yu</foaf:name>
7:      <foaf:mbox rdf:resource="mailto:liyang@liyangyu.com"/>
8:      <foaf:knows>
9:        <foaf:Person>
10:          <foaf:homepage
10a:             rdf:resource="http://www.ilrt.bris.ac.uk/~ecemm/"/>
11:          <foaf:mbox
11a:             rdf:resource="mailto:libby.miller@bristol.ac.uk"/>
12:        </foaf:Person>
13:      </foaf:knows>
14:      <foaf:family_name>yu</foaf:family_name>
15:      <foaf:givenname>liyang</foaf:givenname>
16:      <foaf:title>Dr</foaf:title>
17:      <foaf:topic_interest
17a:      rdf:resource="http://dbpedia.org/resource/Semantic_Web"/>
18:      <foaf:homepage rdf:resource="http://www.liyangyu.com"/>
19:      <foaf:workplaceHomepage
19a:         rdf:resource="http://www.delta.com"/>
20:    </foaf:Person>
21: </rdf:RDF>
```

Before we move on, notice we have been using the `addProperty()` method to create statements. In fact, statements can also be created directly on the model by calling `Model.createStatement()` with the subject, predicate, and object of the triple. For example,

```
Statement statement =
            model.createStatement(mySubject,myProperty,myObject);
```

However, a main difference between these two methods of creating statements is that creating a statement in this way doesn't add it into the model. If you want to add it into the model, call `Model.add()` with the created statement:

```
// but remember to add the created statement to the model
model.add(statement);
```

At this point, we are done using Jena to create a simple RDF model. We have seen the use of important classes such as `ModelFactory`, `Model`, `Resource` and

`Property`. We have also seen how to create resources and properties and how to insert statements into an existing RDF model.

Obviously, creating RDF models like what we have done here is not quite scalable. A large RDF model simply requires too much coding and maintenance work; there have to be other ways to build RDF models.

In real practice, most RDF documents are generated automatically, from a given database table, for instance. The generated RDF documents can then be read into memory for more processing work. Therefore, learning how to read in an RDF model is also important, and we cover this in the next section.

15.2.2 Reading an RDF Model

Compared to creating an RDF model as we have discussed in the previous section, reading a given RDF document into memory is probably a more frequently used operation. As we will see in the coming sections and chapters of this book, for many applications, we often need to read a certain RDF document located at a given URL into memory before we can do anything about it. This can be understood as downloading a machine-readable document from the Web.

In the case where no state persistence is necessary, implementing this download action is quite straightforward. List 15.9 shows how to read my FOAF document from this URL,

`http://liyangyu.com/foaf.rdf`

and to show we have correctly read the document, we also write it out in Turtle format.

List 15.9 Reading an RDF document from a given URL

```
 1: package test;
 2:
 3: import com.hp.hpl.jena.rdf.model.Model;
 4: import com.hp.hpl.jena.rdf.model.ModelFactory;
 5: import com.hp.hpl.jena.util.FileManager;
 6:
 7: public class ReadRDFModel {
 8:
 9: public static final String MY_FOAF_FILE =
 9a:         "http://liyangyu.com/foaf.rdf";
10:
11:    public static void main( String[] args ) {
12:
13:        Model model = ModelFactory.createDefaultModel();
14:        model.read(MY_FOAF_FILE);
15:        model.write(System.out,"N3");
16:    }
17: }
```

List 15.9 makes use of a basic `Model` form that is created by calling the `createDefaultModel()` method. This model uses an in-memory storage model and has no inference or any other reasoning power. In the case where we need to have inferencing capabilities, we will have to create the model in some other ways, as we will see in a later section. Also notice line 15 uses `N3` as the format parameter since Turtle is a subset of Notation 3 (N3). List 15.10 shows the output from List 15.9.

List 15.10 Output generated from List 15.9

```
@prefix rdfs:     <http://www.w3.org/2000/01/rdf-schema#> .
@prefix rdf:      <http://www.w3.org/1999/02/22-rdf-syntax-ns#> .
@prefix foaf:     <http://xmlns.com/foaf/0.1/> .

<http://www.liyangyu.com/foaf.rdf#liyang>
      a foaf:Person ;
      foaf:family_name "yu"@en ;
      foaf:givenname "liyang"@en ;
      foaf:homepage <http://www.liyangyu.com> ;
      foaf:knows
          [ a foaf:Person ;
            foaf:homepage <http://www.ilrt.bris.ac.uk/~ecemm/> ;
            foaf:mbox <mailto:libby.miller@bristol.ac.uk>
          ] ;
      foaf:mbox_sha1sum
          "1613a9c3ec8b18271a8fe1f79537a7b08803d896"@en ;
      foaf:name "liyang yu"@en ;
      foaf:title "Dr"@en ;
      foaf:topic_interest
          <http://dbpedia.org/resource/Semantic_Web> ;
      foaf:workplaceHomepage
             <http://www.delta.com> .
```

It is also possible to load an RDF document into memory from a local file system. As shown by line 15 of List 15.11, the `FileManager` class is used to finish the task.

List 15.11 Read an RDF document from local file system

```
1: package test;
2:
3: import com.hp.hpl.jena.rdf.model.Model;
4: import com.hp.hpl.jena.rdf.model.ModelFactory;
5: import com.hp.hpl.jena.util.FileManager;
6:
7: public class ReadRDFModel {
8:
9:     public static final String MY_FOAF_FILE =
9a:          "c:/liyang/myWebsite/currentPage/foaf.rdf";
10:    // public static final String MY_FOAF_FILE =
10a:   //    "http://liyangyu.com/foaf.rdf";
11:
12:    public static void main( String[] args ) {
13:
14:        Model model = ModelFactory.createDefaultModel();
15:        FileManager.get().readModel(model,MY_FOAF_FILE);
16:        // model.read(MY_FOAF_FILE);
17:        model.write(System.out,"N3");
18:    }
19: }
```

15.2.3 Understanding an RDF Model

Now that we have an RDF model in memory, we can continue to use Jena's library to know more about it. For example, knowing the answers to the following questions can be helpful:

- What types (classes) are used in this model?
- For each type used, what instances are created/included in this model?
- What are the namespaces used in this model?

You can probably list more questions here. For now, List 15.12 shows the code we can use to understand a given RDF document.

List 15.12 Understanding an RDF document

```
1: package test;
2:
3: import java.util.Iterator;
4: import java.util.Map;
5:
6: import com.hp.hpl.jena.rdf.model.Model;
7: import com.hp.hpl.jena.rdf.model.ModelFactory;
8: import com.hp.hpl.jena.rdf.model.NodeIterator;
9: import com.hp.hpl.jena.rdf.model.ResIterator;
10: import com.hp.hpl.jena.rdf.model.Resource;
11: import com.hp.hpl.jena.vocabulary.RDF;
12:
13: public class ReadRDFModel {
14:
15:     public static final String RDF_FILE =
15a:                       "http://liyangyu.com/foaf.rdf";
16:
17:     public static void main( String[] args ) {
18:
19:         Model model = ModelFactory.createDefaultModel();
20:         model.read(RDF_FILE);
21:         // model.write(System.out,"N3");
22:
23:         // show all the namespaces in the model
24:         Iterator prefixNsPairs =
24a:                  model.getNsPrefixMap().entrySet().iterator();
25:         while ( prefixNsPairs.hasNext() ) {
26:           Map.Entryentry = (Map.Entry)(prefixNsPairs.next());
27:           System.out.print("prefix:" + entry.getKey());
28:           System.out.println(", namespace:" + entry.getValue());
29:         }
30:
31:         // show all the classes and their instances
32:         System.out.println("the following types/classes have
32a:         been used in this RDF document(with their instances):");
33:         NodeIterator classes =
33a:                     model.listObjectsOfProperty(RDF.type);
34:         while ( classes.hasNext() ) {
35:           Resource typeRes = (Resource)(classes.next());
36:           System.out.println("(class/type)" + typeRes.getURI());
37:           ResIterator resources =
37a:               model.listResourcesWithProperty(RDF.type,typeRes);
38:           while ( resources.hasNext() ) {
```

```
39:              Resource instanceRes = resources.nextResource();
40:              if ( instanceRes.isAnon() ) {
41:                System.out.println(" [anonymous instance] " +
41a:                                   instanceRes.getId());
42:              } else {
43:                System.out.println(" [instance] " +
43a:                                   instanceRes.getURI());
44:              }
45:            }
46:          }
47:
48:      }
49: }
```

Line 15 specifies the RDF document we want to read, and lines 19 and 20 actually read the RDF document into our in-memory model. Lines 23–29 show a summary of the namespaces (and their prefixes) that have been used in this document. Method `getNsPrefixMap()` (line 24) is the key when it comes to namespaces. This method returns a collection of key–value pairs; for each of these pairs, the key is the prefix and the value is the namespace. As you see, line 27 retrieves the prefix and line 28 retrieves the namespace itself.

To find all the types/classes that are referenced in this model, method `listObjectsOfProperty()` is used (line 33). This method takes a property as its input parameter (in this case, this property is given by `RDF.type`) and it visits all the statements in the model and tries to match this pattern:

```
subject rdf:type object
```

Obviously, any statement following this pattern is there to assert the type of a given resource (represented by `subject`), so the `object` component must represent a class definition.

Once executed, method `listObjectsOfProperty()` returns a group of types (this group will have only one member if only one class is ever used in the whole model). For each class in this group, we try to find all the resources that are instances of this class. This is done by calling the `listResourcesWithProperty ()` method on line 37. This method takes a property instance and object type as its input parameters, and in our case, `RDF.type` is the property instance and `typeRes` represents the object type. It then tries to match all the statements that have the following pattern:

```
subject rdf:type typeRes
```

Once a match is found, the `subject` is collected and becomes one of the returned resources when the call is finished. Our code then lists out all these resources, together with their type information (lines 38–44).

Notice it could be true that a given resource is represented by a blank node, yet it is still an instance of a given type. To take this into account, we use the `isAnon()` method to test if a given resource is a blank node (line 40). If a resource is represented by a blank node, method `getId()` is called to get its identifier; otherwise, method `getURI()` is used (line 43).

Now, let us run this code against my FOAF document, and List 15.13 shows the result.

List 15.13 Output generated from List 15.12 with the author's FOAF document

```
1: prefix:rdfs, namespace:http://www.w3.org/2000/01/rdf-schema#
2: prefix:rdf,
2a:        namespace:http://www.w3.org/1999/02/22-rdf-syntax-ns#
3: prefix:foaf, namespace:http://xmlns.com/foaf/0.1/
4: the following types/classes have been used in this RDF
4a:    document (with their instances):
5: (class/type) http://xmlns.com/foaf/0.1/Person
6:    [anonymous instance] -6aa9a0b:12454881133:-8000
7:    [instance] http://www.liyangyu.com/foaf.rdf#liyang
```

As you can see, lines 1–3 show the namespaces and their prefixes that are referenced by my FOAF document, line 5 shows the only class (`foaf:Person`) used in this document, and lines 6 and 7 list the two instances that actually have the type `foaf:Person`. Therefore, we have now learned that this document describes some instances whose type is `foaf:Person`, and it has also included two such instances.

Let us try some other file that has more content than my simple FOAF document. The following RDF document seems to be a good choice,

```
http://dbpedia.org/data/Roger_Federer.rdf
```

You need to change line 15 of List 15.12 to make it looks like this:

```
public static final String RDF_FILE =
            "http://dbpedia.org/data/Roger_Federer.rdf";
```

And List 15.14 shows part of the result.

List 15.14 Understanding Federer's RDF document generated by DBpedia

```
prefix:dbpprop, namespace:http://dbpedia.org/property/
prefix:dbpedia-owl, namespace:http://dbpedia.org/ontology/
prefix:dc, namespace:http://purl.org/dc/elements/1.1/
prefix:rdfs, namespace:http://www.w3.org/2000/01/rdf-schema#
prefix:rdf, namespace:http://www.w3.org/1999/02/22-rdf-syntax-ns#
prefix:foaf, namespace:http://xmlns.com/foaf/0.1/
prefix:owl, namespace:http://www.w3.org/2002/07/owl#
prefix:skos, namespace:http://www.w3.org/2004/02/skos/core#
the following types/classes have been used in this RDF document
(with their instances):
(class/type) http://dbpedia.org/ontology/Person
  [instance] http://dbpedia.org/resource/Roger_Federer
(class/type) http://dbpedia.org/class/yago/USOpenChampions
  [instance] http://dbpedia.org/resource/Roger_Federer
(class/type)
http://dbpedia.org/class/yago/AustralianOpenChampions
  [instance] http://dbpedia.org/resource/Roger_Federer
(class/type) http://dbpedia.org/ontology/Athlete
  [instance] http://dbpedia.org/resource/Roger_Federer
(class/type) http://dbpedia.org/ontology/TennisPlayer
  [instance] http://dbpedia.org/resource/Roger_Federer
(class/type) http://dbpedia.org/class/yago/LivingPeople
  [instance] http://dbpedia.org/resource/Roger_Federer
(class/type) http://xmlns.com/foaf/0.1/Person
  [instance] http://dbpedia.org/resource/Roger_Federer
```

Based on this output, without reading the RDF document itself, we have obtained quite a bit of information about it already.

Besides understanding the type information for the resources, we can also inspect the properties defined for them. Among all the properties, the following three are of particular interest to us:

```
owl:sameAs
rdfs:seeAlso
rdfs:isDefinedBy
```

since we can follow these properties to find more about their subjects. In fact, this is the idea behind the Follow-Your-Nose algorithm, which we will see again in the next chapter. Notice that other properties can also be used in Follow-Your-Nose search, so the above list can grow, but for now, these three are the most obvious ones.

Based on the above discussion, our last query is to find all the resources that have the above properties. List 15.15 uses `owl:sameAs` as an example to show how the search is done:

List 15.15 Use `owl:sameAs` to find links

```
1: package test;
2:
3: import java.util.Iterator;
4: import java.util.Map;
5:
6: import com.hp.hpl.jena.rdf.model.Model;
7: import com.hp.hpl.jena.rdf.model.ModelFactory;
8: import com.hp.hpl.jena.rdf.model.NodeIterator;
9: import com.hp.hpl.jena.rdf.model.RDFNode;
10: import com.hp.hpl.jena.rdf.model.ResIterator;
11: import com.hp.hpl.jena.rdf.model.Resource;
12: import com.hp.hpl.jena.rdf.model.Statement;
13: import com.hp.hpl.jena.rdf.model.StmtIterator;
14: import com.hp.hpl.jena.vocabulary.OWL;
15: import com.hp.hpl.jena.vocabulary.RDF;
16:
17: public class ReadRDFModel {
18:
19:     public static final String RDF_FILE =
19a:                 "http://dbpedia.org/data/Roger_Federer.rdf";
20:
21:     public static void main( String[] args ) {
22:
23:         Model model = ModelFactory.createDefaultModel();
24:         model.read(RDF_FILE);
25:        // model.write(System.out,"N3");
26:
27:        // show all the namespaces in the model
...
34:
35:        // show all the classes and their instances
...
51:
52:        // show all instances that have a owl:sameAs property
53:        System.out.println("\nfollowing instances have
53a:                            owl:sameAs property:");
54:        StmtIterator statements = model.listStatements
54a:                        ((Resource)null,OWL.sameAs,(RDFNode)null);
55:        while ( statements.hasNext() ) {
56:            Statement statement = statements.nextStatement();
57:            Resource subject = statement.getSubject();
58:            if ( subject.isAnon() ) {
59:                System.out.print("  (" + subject.getId() + ")");
```

```
60:              } else {
61:                  System.out.print("  (" + subject.getURI() + ")");
62:              }
63:              System.out.print(" OWL.sameAs ");
64:              Resource object = (Resource)(statement.getObject());
65:              if ( object.isAnon() ) {
66:                  System.out.print("(" + object + ")");
67:              } else if ( object.isLiteral() ) {
68:                  System.out.print("(" + object.toString() + ")");
69:              } else if ( object.isResource() ) {
70:                  System.out.print("(" + object.getURI() + ")");
71:              }
72:              System.out.println();
73:          }
74:
75:      }
76: }
```

And the related code is from lines 52–72 (the rest is the same as in List 15.12). The key method to call is `listStatements()` as on line 54. Since we pass in `null` value for both the subject and object, the method tries to find all the statements that use `owl:sameAs` as the property, and the subjects and objects of these statements can be anything. This way, we will be able to find all the subjects and objects that are linked together by `owl:sameAs`. Lines 57–72 print the result in a more readable way.

Now run the code against Roger Federer's RDF document, and we should see the result as shown in List 15.16.

List 15.16 Part of the output from List 15.15

```
the following instance(s) has/have owl:sameAs property:
  (http://dbpedia.org/resource/Roger_Federer) OWL.sameAs
(http://rdf.freebase.com/ns/guid.9202a8c04000641f800000000019f52)
  (http://mpii.de/yago/resource/Roger_Federer) OWL.sameAs
(http://dbpedia.org/resource/Roger_Federer)
```

We can get more understanding about a given RDF model by inspecting other properties that we are interested in, and with what you have learned here, it should be a fairly straightforward process.

Meanwhile, understand that accessing and querying a given RDF model as we have done here is considered to be a fairly low-level view of the RDF graph. Other query techniques, such as SPARQL query language, can provide more compact and powerful results, as we show you in the next chapter. However, what you have learned here will help you to understand Jena better, and will also give you some light-weight querying methods without using SPARQL.

15.3   Handling Persistent RDF Models

15.3.1   From In-Memory Model to Persistent Model

So far to this point, we have been working with in-memory models. These models are either created from scratch, or are populated from existing files. The files can be located in a local file system, or can be downloaded from given URLs.

Although in-memory models are quite useful, they do have some disadvantages. To name a few,

- The RDF model has to be repopulated from scratch each time the application launches, thus requires a longer startup time.
- Any change made to the in-memory model will be lost when the application is shut down.
- Applications based upon in-memory models will not scale as we start to work with larger models.

A better solution is to store ontology and instance models in a database-backed RDF store, and then operate on the models just as we have discussed so far. This solution is called the *persistent model* solution, where the models are continually and transparently persisted to the backing store.

Jena is shipped with support for a collection of standard database systems, including MySQL, PostgresQL, SQL Server, Oracle and Derby. In addition, Jena's database adapters use standard Java Database Connectivity (JDBC) drivers to manage these database engines as triple stores, and Jena will create and manage its own table layout in the database systems, the details are hidden from the applications.

For developers like us, this means we can select one of the above database systems as the data store, and Jena hides the variations of SQL syntax in different databases by offering related APIs that we can use. For example, when we call listStatements() on a database-backed model, Jena will construct the appropriate SQL query, execute it through the underlying database engine, and translate the query results into a ResultSet object that our application can manipulate to retrieve each Statement object.

With this solution, our RDF models will stay in the database regardless of whether the application is on or not, and the application accesses these models via Jena APIs without loading the models into the memory. In addition, whatever the application has changed will stay in the models, and the next time that application starts, we will see the changes we have made from last time.

We will see the details of this solution in the next section. We also need to choose a database management system. In our case, we will go with MySQL, mainly due to the fact that it is freely available for different platforms.

15.3.2 Setting up MySQL

In this section, we will setup MySQL on your machine. If you have MySQL already, you can skip this section and move on to the next section.

To setup MySQL, the first step is to download the MySQL software and the JDBC driver. At this point, you should be able to find the downloadable files from this URL:

```
http://www.mysql.com/downloads/
```

If this URL does not exist at the time you are reading the book, go to MySQL's Web site,

```
http://www.mysql.com/
```

and try to find the download link from this official homepage.

At this point, the freely downloadable version is called MySQL Community Server, and that is the one you should download. After the download is completed, you can double-click the downloaded package to start installation on your machine.

Once the installation is finished, you will be asked to configure MySQL server. For example, here you have a chance to configure the port number, which is defaulted to be 3306. You can either keep the default number, or use another number, but make sure the number you are using is not in use by other server software on your machine.

Another configuration task is to specify the user ID and user password. For me, I used the given `root` user as my user name, and I entered `passwd` as my password. You can choose your combination, but you need to remember them, since they will be needed in your Java code.

Once you are done with the configuration step, you need to continue downloading the JDBC driver that goes together with MySQL. To do so, click `Connectors` link on the same download page, and you will be presented with a page that includes a list of connectors. Within these connectors, you should download `Connector/J`, the driver for Java platform. This connector is a jar file that you need to use in your Java code, and you can simply add it to your user library as we have discussed early this chapter.

Now, MySQL has been set up on your machine. To make sure MySQL database engine is working fine, you can fire up *MySQL Command Line Client*, and after

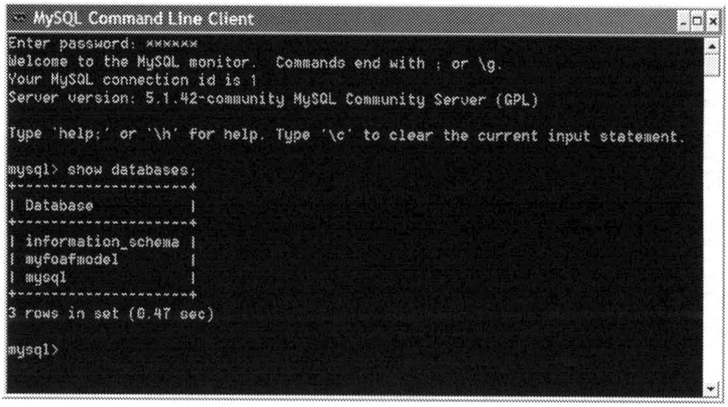

Fig. 15.6 Make sure MySQL is correctly set up

entering the password, try to issue some SQL commands, as shown in Fig. 15.6. If you can do all this successfully, MySQL is correctly set up and running, and we are ready to move on.

15.3.3   Database-Backed RDF Models

15.3.3.1   Single Persistent RDF Model

By now, we know the `Model` interface is a key abstraction in Jena. It represents an RDF model, which has a collection of statements. There are several implementations of the `Model` interface, and each one of them is for a different type of model, such as an in-memory model, a file-based model, an inferencing model and a database-backed model.

For our purpose, we need the implementation for the database-backed model. This is the class called `ModelRDB`, and `createModelRDBMaker()` method call on `ModelFactory` class can answer a `ModelMaker` object that understands how to handle `ModelRDB` object.

List 15.17 shows the code we can use to make my own FOAF document into a persistent RDF model in MySQL.

List 15.17 Load the author's FOAF document and make it a persistent RDF model in MySQL

```
1: import com.hp.hpl.jena.db.DBConnection;
2: import com.hp.hpl.jena.db.IDBConnection;
3: import com.hp.hpl.jena.rdf.model.Model;
4: import com.hp.hpl.jena.rdf.model.ModelFactory;
5: import com.hp.hpl.jena.rdf.model.ModelMaker;
6: import com.hp.hpl.jena.rdf.model.Property;
7: import com.hp.hpl.jena.rdf.model.Resource;
8: import com.hp.hpl.jena.rdf.model.Statement;
9: import com.hp.hpl.jena.rdf.model.StmtIterator;
10: import com.hp.hpl.jena.util.FileManager;
11: import com.hp.hpl.jena.util.PrintUtil;
12:
13: public class DBModelTester {
14:
15:     public static final String RDF_FILE =
15a:                    "http://www.liyangyu.com/foaf.rdf";
16:     public static final String ONTOLOGY_FILE =
16a:                    "http://xmlns.com/foaf/0.1/";
17:
18:     private static String className =
18a:                             "com.mysql.jdbc.Driver";
19:     private static String DB_URL =
19a:           "jdbc:mysql://localhost:3306/myFoafModel";
20:     private static String DB_USER = "root";
21:     private static String DB_PASSWD = "passwd";
22:     private static String DB_TYPE = "MySQL";
23:     private static String DOCUMENT_NAME = "myFoafRDF";
24:     private static String ONTOLOGY_NAME = "foaf.owl";
25:
26:     public static void main( String[] args ) {
27:
28:       IDBConnection conn = null;
29:       ModelMaker maker = null;
30:
31:       try {
32:         Class.forName(className);
33:         conn =
33a:           new DBConnection(DB_URL,DB_USER,DB_PASSWD,DB_TYPE);
34:       } catch (Exception e) { e.printStackTrace(); }
35:
36:       maker = ModelFactory.createModelRDBMaker(conn);
37:       Model m = null;
38:
```

```
39:        if ( !maker.hasModel(DOCUMENT_NAME) == true ) {
40:          System.out.println( "Loading instance
40a:                             document - one time only" );
41:          m = maker.createModel(DOCUMENT_NAME);
42:          FileManager.get().readModel(m,RDF_FILE);
43:        } else {
44:          m = maker.getModel(DOCUMENT_NAME);
45:        }
46:        printStatements(m, null, null, null);
47:
48:        // close the connection
49:        try {
50:          conn.close();
51:        } catch(Exception e) { e.printStackTrace(); }
52:
53:      }
54:
55:    private static void printStatements(Model m, Resource s,
55a:                              Property p, Resource o) {
56:        for (StmtIterator I = m.listStatements(s,p,o);
56a:                         i.hasNext(); ) {
57:          Statement stmt = i.nextStatement();
58:          System.out.println("- " + PrintUtil.print(stmt));
59:        }
60:      }
61: }
```

The interesting lines in List 15.17 start from line 18, where the driver for MySQL is specified. If you have the experience of connecting to a backend database using Java platform, this line and the next couple of lines will look familiar to you. Line 19 specifies the database URL, which uses 3306 as the default port number. If you have specified another port number during the configuration process, you should use that port number instead of 3306. Also, myFoafModel is the name of the database we are going to create, and my FOAF document will stay in this database. You can certainly choose a name you like for your database.

Lines 20–22 specify the user name, the password and the database type in order to create a connection to MySQL database engine. The user name and password we have selected at setup will be used here. Notice you have to use MySQL for DB_TYPE, since we have MySQL database as our backend database system.

Lines 23 and 24 define the names of two RDF models we are going to load into our database: myFoafRDF is the name of the model that represents my own FOAF document, and foaf.owl is the name of the model that represents the FOAF ontology. List 15.17 will only load my own FOAF document into database, and the FOAF ontology will be handled later in the next section.

Lines 31–34 create the connection to MySQL backend database, and this is fairly standard code you should use.

Line 36 is the key line. The `createModelRDBMaker()` method call on `ModelFactory` class answers a `ModelMaker` object that understands how to handle RDF models and further change them into persistent graphs in the database. Notice we need to pass the database connection we created on lines 31–34 to `createModelRDBMaker()` method, so the created `ModelMaker` object can operate in the database we have specified.

Once a `ModelMaker` object that connects to the backend database has been created, we can use it to load my FOAF document and make it a persistent RDF graph. To do so, line 39 checks if my FOAF document is already loaded into the database; if not, the `createModel()` method on the `ModelMaker` object is called to create a model that has the name specified by DOCUMENT_NAME string (line 41). This model is then populated by reading my FOAF file (line 42); in this case, this file can be obtained from the path given by line 15.

Notice this model creation and population process is executed only once (line 40). The second time you run the same code, my FOAF document is already in the database, and it will be mapped to a model directly (line 44). Clearly, this is the reason why we say my FOAF document now becomes a persistent model.

Once we reach line 46, we have an RDF model on hand, and we can do anything with it, as if it were an in-memory RDF model that we are familiar with from the previous sections. In our case, we simply print out all the statements contained in this model.

Lines 49–51 are some routine housekeeping work, and it is necessary to ensure a clean database shutdown which also helps to release system resources.

Now, what exactly is inside the backend database? To understand more about how this works, before you run the code in List 15.17, fire up the MySQL Command Line Client as shown in Fig. 15.6, and list all the databases that are currently in MySQL. For me, here is what I have:

```
mysql> show databases;

+--------------------+
| Database           |
+--------------------+
| information_schema |
| mysql              |
+--------------------+
```

and now, run the code in List 15.17. And if you running it for the first time, you should see some output such as the following:

```
Loading instance document - one time only

- (http://www.liyangyu.com/foaf.rdf#liyang
   http://xmlns.com/foaf/0.1/name 'liyang yu')
- (http://www.liyangyu.com/foaf.rdf#liyang
   http://xmlns.com/foaf/0.1/title 'Dr')
```

```
- (http://www.liyangyu.com/foaf.rdf#liyang
    http://xmlns.com/foaf/0.1/givenname 'liyang')
...
```

Once the run is successfully finished, we can go back to MySQL Command Line Client window, and list all the databases again:

```
mysql> show databases;
+--------------------+
| Database           |
+--------------------+
| information_schema|
| myfoafmodel        |
| mysql              |
+--------------------+
```

As you can see, myfoafmodel is now included in the database list. To see more about it, let us check out all the tables in this database:

```
mysql> show tables from myfoafmodel;

+--------------------+
| Tables_in_myfoafmodel|
+--------------------+
| jena_g1t0_reif     |
| jena_g1t1_stmt     |
| jena_graph         |
| jena_long_lit      |
| jena_long_uri      |
| jena_prefix        |
| jena_sys_stmt      |
+--------------------+
```

Clearly, this is all created by the Jena framework, and there is no need for us to do anything with them. However, out of curiosity, we can always check out each one of them. If we do so, we will discover the following:

- Table jena_g1t1_stmt holds all the statements contained in my FOAF document.
- Table jena_graph holds all the models in the database.

For example, to inspect what is inside `jena_graph` table, we can do the following:

```
mysql> select * from myfoafmodel.jena_graph;

+---+-----------+
| ID | Name     |
+---+-----------+
| 1 | myFoafRDF|
+---+-----------+
```

As you see, my FOAF document is currently the only model in the database, and we will see how to add another model into the database in the next section.

Before we move on, let us do an exercise to gain more understanding about persistent models. First, add the following lines into the code shown in List 15.17, and make sure you add these lines after line 46 in List 15.17:

```
// update the model
m.getResource("http://www.liyangyu.com/foaf.rdf#liyang").
addProperty(FOAF.nick, "laoyu");
```

Run the code again with the above lines added, and then shut down your application. Now, the above update you have made to the model is saved in the database. To see this, use MySQL Command Line Client to inspect the `jena_g1t1_stmt` table, and you will see the update you made to model does stay in the database.

15.3.3.2   Multiple Persistent RDF Models

In the previous section, we learned how to load a single RDF document into a backend database to make it a persistent RDF model. However, a real application often involves a number of RDF documents, including both instance and ontology files. To handle this situation, a Jena database can store multiple models, and typically, each model is represented by its own set of tables in the database.

Let us again use my FOAF document as our example. We have loaded it into the database in the previous section, and in this section, we will load the FOAF ontology into the same database. Therefore, a single database will hold two models. List 15.18 shows how this is done.

List 15.18 Load the author's FOAF document and FOAF ontology to make them persistent models

```
1: import com.hp.hpl.jena.db.DBConnection;
2: import com.hp.hpl.jena.db.IDBConnection;
3: import com.hp.hpl.jena.rdf.model.Model;
4: import com.hp.hpl.jena.rdf.model.ModelFactory;
5: import com.hp.hpl.jena.rdf.model.ModelMaker;
6: import com.hp.hpl.jena.rdf.model.Property;
7: import com.hp.hpl.jena.rdf.model.Resource;
8: import com.hp.hpl.jena.rdf.model.Statement;
9: import com.hp.hpl.jena.rdf.model.StmtIterator;
10: import com.hp.hpl.jena.util.FileManager;
11: import com.hp.hpl.jena.util.PrintUtil;
12:
13: public class DBModelTester {
14:
15:     public static final String RDF_FILE =
15a:                 "http://www.liyangyu.com/foaf.rdf";
16:     public static final String ONTOLOGY_FILE =
16a:                 "http://xmlns.com/foaf/0.1/";
17:
18:     private       static       String       className       =
"com.mysql.jdbc.Driver";
19:     private static String DB_URL =
19a:                  "jdbc:mysql://localhost:3306/myFoafModel";
20:     private static String DB_USER = "root";
21:     private static String DB_PASSWD = "passwd";
22:     private static String DB_TYPE = "MySQL";
23:     private static String DOCUMENT_NAME = "myFoafRDF";
24:     private static String ONTOLOGY_NAME = "foaf.owl";
25:
26:     public static void main( String[] args ) {
27:
28:       IDBConnection conn = null;
29:       ModelMaker maker = null;
30:
31:       try {
32:         Class.forName(className);
33:         conn = new
33a:                 DBConnection(DB_URL,DB_USER,DB_PASSWD,DB_TYPE);
34:       } catch (Exception e) { e.printStackTrace(); }
35:
36:       maker = ModelFactory.createModelRDBMaker(conn);
37:       Model m = null;
38:
39:       if ( !maker.hasModel(DOCUMENT_NAME) == true ) {
```

```
40:          System.out.println( "Loading instance document -
40a:                            one time only" );
41:        m = maker.createModel(DOCUMENT_NAME);
42:        FileManager.get().readModel(m,RDF_FILE);
43:      } else {
44:        m = maker.getModel(DOCUMENT_NAME);
45:      }
46:      printStatements(m, null, null, null);
47:
48:      if ( !maker.hasModel(ONTOLOGY_NAME) ) {
49:        System.out.println( "Loading ontology document -
49a:                            one time only" );
50:        m = maker.createModel(ONTOLOGY_NAME);
51:        FileManager.get().readModel(m,ONTOLOGY_FILE);
52:      } else {
53:        m = maker.getModel(ONTOLOGY_NAME);
54:      }
55:      printStatements(m, null, null, null);
56:
57:      try {
58:        conn.close();
59:      } catch(Exception e) { e.printStackTrace(); }
60:
61:    }
62:
63:    private static void printStatements(Model m, Resource s,
63a:                                   Property p, Resource o) {
64:      for (StmtIterator i = m.listStatements(s,p,o);
64a:                       i.hasNext(); ) {
65:        Statement stmt = i.nextStatement();
66:        System.out.println(" - " + PrintUtil.print(stmt));
67:      }
68:    }
69: }
```

Based on what we learned from List 15.17, List 15.18 does not require too much explanation. Lines 48–55 are the new lines added; they first check whether the FOAF ontology already exists in the database, and if yes, load it into the model. Otherwise, they create a persistent model representing this ontology in the database.

After you have run the code in List 15.18, we can again use MySQL Command
Line Client to check the result. First, you will see there are now more tables in the
database:

```
mysql> show tables from myfoafmodel;
+——————————————+
| Tables_in_myfoafmodel |
+——————————————+
| jena_g1t0_reif        |
| jena_g1t1_stmt        |
| jena_g2t0_reif        |
| jena_g2t1_stmt        |
| jena_graph            |
| jena_long_lit         |
| jena_long_uri         |
| jena_prefix           |
| jena_sys_stmt         |
+——————————————+
```

And since table `jena_graph` holds all the models in the database, we can take a
look at its content:

```
mysql> select * from myfoafmodel.jena_graph;
+——+—————————+
| ID | Name      |
+——+—————————+
| 1  | myFoafRDF |
| 2  | foaf.owl  |
+——+—————————+
```

Clearly, a new model, `foaf.owl`, is now added into the database.

You can continue to check other tables one by one to confirm that we have
successfully created two persistent models in our database system, which we will
not cover in detail. In general, if your application operates on large RDF documents,
persistent models should always be considered, and quite often, they may be the
best solution to your application.

15.4 Inferencing Using Jena

15.4.1 Jena Inferencing Model

In Jena's world, inferencing or reasoning refers to the process of deriving additional
facts that are not explicitly expressed by the instance documents or the ontology

documents. The term reasoner is used to refer to a specific code object that actually performs the derivation. Sometimes, a reasoner is also called an inference engine.

Jena provides a number of reasoners for us to use. The following is a list of frequently used reasoners:

- RDFS rule reasoner: an inference engine that supports almost all of the RDFS entailments.
- OWL 1 reasoner: the default reasoner that supports most of the frequently used OWL 1 constructs. In practice, this reasoner is considered to be a "full" one, and details can be found at Jena's official Web site.
- OWL 1 Mini reasoner: a slightly cut down version of the "full" OWL 1 reasoner;
- OWL 1 Micro reasoner: a smaller but faster one.

To find the supported RDFS and OWL 1 constructs for each reasoner, refer to Jena's official Web site, which provides the most up-to-date information. This section shows you the basics of using a reasoner.

The steps needed to use a reasoner for inferencing are quite standard, as summarized here:

1. Choose a reasoner: we use this step to notify the Jena system which reasoner we wish to use. One way to do this is to use `ReasonerRgistry` class;
2. Load the ontology document and bind it with the reasoner we have chosen, so the reasoner knows all the facts expressed in the ontology document. One way to do this is to use the `bindSchema()` method provided by the reasoner object.
3. Load the instance RDF document, and together with the reasoner, we can use the `ModelFactory` class to create an inference model, which contains not only the loaded instance data, but also the inferred statements.

Notice that the inference model created at step 3 not only contains all the original facts from the instance document and ontology document, but also has all the derived statements that represent the additional facts found by the reasoner. In other words, except for the steps listed above, we never have to explicitly invoke any reasoner, and once we have the inference model built, we have it all.

15.4.2 Jena Inferencing Examples

For the code examples in this section, we will continue using my FOAF document, together with the FOAF ontology. However, in order to make things a little more interesting, some change has been made to my FOAF document, as shown in List 15.19.

List 15.19 The author's FOAF document with some change for testing inference in Jena

```
 1: <?xml version="1.0" encoding="UTF-8"?>
 2: <rdf:RDF
 3:       xml:lang="en"
 4:       xmlns:rdf="http://www.w3.org/1999/02/22-rdf-syntax-ns#"
 5:       xmlns:rdfs="http://www.w3.org/2000/01/rdf-schema#"
 6:       xmlns:foaf="http://xmlns.com/foaf/0.1/">
 7:
 8:   <rdf:Description
 8a:       rdf:about="http://www.liyangyu.com/foaf.rdf#liyang">
 9:       <foaf:name>liyang yu</foaf:name>
10:       <foaf:title>Dr</foaf:title>
11:       <foaf:givenname>liyang</foaf:givenname>
12:       <foaf:family_name>yu</foaf:family_name>
13:       <foaf:mbox_sha1sum>
13a:         1613a9c3ec8b18271a8fe1f79537a7b08803d896
13b:       </foaf:mbox_sha1sum>
14:       <foaf:homepage rdf:resource="http://www.liyangyu.com"/>
15:       <foaf:workplaceHomepage
15a:          rdf:resource="http://www.delta.com"/>
16:       <rdf:type
16a:          rdf:resource="http://xmlns.com/foaf/0.1/Person"/>
17:
18:       <foaf:knows>
19:         <!-- the following is for testing purpose -->
20:         <foaf:Person>
21:           <foaf:mbox
21a:             rdf:resource="mailto:libby.miller@bristol.ac.uk"/>
22:           <foaf:homepage
22a:             rdf:resource="http://www.ilrt.bris.ac.uk/~ecemm/"/>
23:         </foaf:Person>
24:       </foaf:knows>
25:
26:       <foaf:topic_interest
26a:      rdf:resource="http://dbpedia.org/resource/Semantic_Web"/>
27:
28:  </rdf:Description>
29:
30:
31: <rdf:Description
31a:       rdf:about="http://www.liyangyu.com/foaf.rdf#yiding">
32:     <foaf:mbox_sha1sum>
32a:       1613a9c3ec8b18271a8fe1f79537a7b08803d896
32b:     </foaf:mbox_sha1sum>
33: </rdf:Description>
34:
35: </rdf:RDF>
```

Notice that the only change is in lines 31–33: a new resource is added, with resource URI given by the following:

```
http://www.liyangyu.com/foaf.rdf#yiding
```

Also notice that we have not made any statement about its type and its properties except that we have specified its `foaf:mbox_sha1sum` property (line 32), which assumes the same value as on line 13.

In fact, line 32 is the key to this new resource. Based on FOAF ontology, `foaf:mbox_sha1sum` is an inverse functional property; in other words, if two resources hold the same value on this property, these two resources, although identified by two different URIs, are actually the same thing.

As a result, we expect to see the following facts be added into the inference model created by Jena:

- The following two URIs, `http://www.liyangyu.com/foaf.rdf#yiding` and `http://www.liyangyu.com/foaf.rdf#liyang`, represent the same resource in the world.
- Therefore, `http://www.liyangyu.com/foaf.rdf#yiding` is also a `foaf:Person`, and all the properties (and their values) owned by `http://www.liyangyu.com/foaf.rdf#liyang` should also be true for `http://www.liyangyu.com/foaf.rdf#yiding`. For example, it also has the `foaf:title` property with the same value, the `foaf:name` property with the same value, so on and so forth.

List 15.20 shows how the inference model is created.

List 15.20 Example to show Jena inferencing capability

```
1: package test;
2:
3: import java.util.Iterator;
4: import com.hp.hpl.jena.rdf.model.InfModel;
5: import com.hp.hpl.jena.rdf.model.Model;
6: import com.hp.hpl.jena.rdf.model.ModelFactory;
7: import com.hp.hpl.jena.rdf.model.Property;
8: import com.hp.hpl.jena.rdf.model.Resource;
9: import com.hp.hpl.jena.rdf.model.Statement;
10: import com.hp.hpl.jena.rdf.model.StmtIterator;
11: import com.hp.hpl.jena.reasoner.Reasoner;
12: import com.hp.hpl.jena.reasoner.ReasonerRegistry;
13: import com.hp.hpl.jena.reasoner.ValidityReport;
14: import com.hp.hpl.jena.util.FileManager;
```

```
15: import com.hp.hpl.jena.util.PrintUtil;
16:
17: public class InfModelTester {
18:
19:   public static final String RDF_FILE =
19a:                  "c:/liyang/myWebsite/currentPage/foaf.rdf";
20:   public static final String OWL_FILE =
20a:                  "http://xmlns.com/foaf/0.1/";
21:
22:   public static void main( String[] args ) {
23:
24:     // load instance data
25:     Model data = ModelFactory.createDefaultModel();
26:     FileManager.get().readModel(data,RDF_FILE);
27:     // use data.read() if reading from Web URL
28:
29:     // load the ontology document
30:     Model ontology = ModelFactory.createDefaultModel();
31:     ontology.read(OWL_FILE);
32:
33:     // get the reasoner
34:     Reasoner owlReasoner = ReasonerRegistry.getOWLReasoner();
35:     owlReasoner = owlReasoner.bindSchema(ontology);
36:
37:     // use the reasoner and instance data to create
37a:    // an inference model
38:     InfModel infModel =
38a:            ModelFactory.createInfModel(owlReasoner,data);
39:
40:     // some validation to make us happy
41:     ValidityReport vr = infModel.validate();
42:     if ( vr.isValid() == false ) {
43:       System.out.print("ontology model validation failed.");
44:       for (Iterator i = vr.getReports(); i.hasNext(); ) {
45:         System.out.println(" - " + i.next());
46:       }
47:       return;
48:     }
49:
50:     Resource yu = infModel.getResource
50a:                  ("http://www.liyangyu.com/foaf.rdf#yiding");
51:     System.out.println("yu *:");
52:     printStatements(infModel, yu, null, null);
53:
54:   }
```

```
55:
56:    private static void printStatements(Model m,Resource
56a:                          s,Property p,Resource o) {
57:      for (StmtIterator i = m.listStatements(s,p,o);
57a:                        i.hasNext(); ) {
58:        Statement stmt = i.nextStatement();
59:        System.out.println(" - " + PrintUtil.print(stmt));
60:      }
61:    }
62: }
```

List 15.20 should be fairly easy to follow if we map it to the steps that are needed to create an inference model using Jena (see Sect. 15.4.1). More specifically, line 34 maps to step 1, lines 30–31 and line 35 implement step 2, and lines 25–26 and line 38 are the last step. Again, once line 38 is executed, inference model infModel holds both the original facts and the newly derived facts.

To see the derived facts, we can ask all the facts about the resource identified by http://www.liyangyu.com/foaf.rdf#yiding, and we expect to see lots of new facts added about this resource. This is done on lines 50–52, with the help from a simple private helper method call printStatements() (line 56–61), which does not require too much explanation.

Now, run the code in List 15.20. List 15.21 shows some of the newly derived facts (line numbers are added for explanation purposes).

List 15.21 Derived facts about resource yiding

```
 1:  - (http://www.liyangyu.com/foaf.rdf#yiding owl:sameAs
          http://www.liyangyu.com/foaf.rdf#liyang)
 2:  - (http://www.liyangyu.com/foaf.rdf#yiding rdf:type
          http://xmlns.com/foaf/0.1/Person)
 3:  - (http://www.liyangyu.com/foaf.rdf#yiding rdfs:label
          'liyang yu')
 4:  - (http://www.liyangyu.com/foaf.rdf#yiding foaf:name
          'liyang yu')
 5:  - (http://www.liyangyu.com/foaf.rdf#yiding
          foaf:knows 3550803e:1245b5759eb:-8000)
 6:  - (http://www.liyangyu.com/foaf.rdf#yiding
          foaf:family_name 'yu')
 7:  - (http://www.liyangyu.com/foaf.rdf#yiding
          foaf:givenname 'liyang')
 8:  - (http://www.liyangyu.com/foaf.rdf#yiding foaf:title 'Dr')
 9:  - (http://www.liyangyu.com/foaf.rdf#yiding
          foaf:topic_interest
          http://dbpedia.org/resource/Semantic_Web)
10:  - (http://www.liyangyu.com/foaf.rdf#yiding
          foaf:homepage http://www.liyangyu.com)
11:  - (http://www.liyangyu.com/foaf.rdf#yiding
          foaf:workplaceHomepage http://www.delta.com)
```

Table 15.1 Reasoner configuration using `OntModelSpec`

OntModelSpec	Language profile	Storage model	Reasoner
OWL_MEM	OWL 1 full	In-memory	None
OWL_MEM_RULE_INF	OWL 1 full	In-memory	Rule-based reasoner with OWL rules
OWL_DL_MEM_RULE_INF	OWL 1 DL	In-memory	Rule-based reasoner with OWL rules
RDFS_MEM_RDFS_INF	RDFS	In-memory	Rule reasoner with RDFS-level rules

Clearly, the inference engine has successfully recognized that these two resources are the same object in the real world (line 1), and it has also assigned all the properties owned by `http://www.liyangyu.com/foaf.rdf#liyang` to the resource identified by `http://www.liyangyu.com/foaf.rdf#yiding`, as shown by lines 2–11.

Understand that besides these basic steps of using the inference engine, we can in fact make a choice among different reasoner configurations. For example, line 34 of List 15.20 asks an OWL 1 reasoner from Jena, and since no parameter is passed on to the call, the default OWL 1 reasoner ("full" version) is returned back.

To require an OWL 1 reasoner rather than the default one, you need the help of another important class called `OntModelSpec`, which hides the complexities of configuring the inference model. More specifically, a number of common objects that represent different configurations have been predeclared as constants in `OntModelSpec`. Table 15.1 shows some of these configurations (for the complete list, refer to official Jena document).

To create an inference model with a desired specification, class `ModelFactory` should be used, with the predeclared configuration and the instance document, as shown in List 15.22. Again, List 15.22 accomplishes exactly the same thing as List 15.20 does, but with the flexibility of making your own choice of reasoner configuration.

List 15.22 Using `ontModelSpec` to create ontology model

```
1: package test;
2:
3: import java.util.Iterator;
4: import com.hp.hpl.jena.ontology.OntModel;
5: import com.hp.hpl.jena.ontology.OntModelSpec;
6: import com.hp.hpl.jena.rdf.model.Model;
7: import com.hp.hpl.jena.rdf.model.ModelFactory;
8: import com.hp.hpl.jena.rdf.model.Property;
9: import com.hp.hpl.jena.rdf.model.Resource;
10: import com.hp.hpl.jena.rdf.model.Statement;
11: import com.hp.hpl.jena.rdf.model.StmtIterator;
12: import com.hp.hpl.jena.reasoner.ValidityReport;
13: import com.hp.hpl.jena.util.FileManager;
```

```
14: import com.hp.hpl.jena.util.PrintUtil;
15:
16: public class InfModelTester {
17:
18:     public static final String RDF_FILE =
18a:                    "c:/liyang/myWebsite/currentPage/foaf.rdf";
19:     public static final String OWL_FILE =
19a:                    "http://xmlns.com/foaf/0.1/";
20:
21:     public static void main( String[] args ) {
22:
23:        // load instance data
24:        Model data = ModelFactory.createDefaultModel();
25:        FileManager.get().readModel(data,RDF_FILE);
26:        // use data.read() if reading from Web URL
27:
28:        // create my ontology model
29:        OntModel ontModel = ModelFactory.createOntologyModel
29a:                       (OntModelSpec.OWL_MEM_RULE_INF,data);
30:        ontModel.read(OWL_FILE);
31:
32:        // some validation to make us happy
33:        ValidityReport vr = ontModel.validate();
34:        if ( vr.isValid() == false ) {
...
40:        }
41:
42:        Resource yu = ontModel.getResource
42a:                   ("http://www.liyangyu.com/foaf.rdf#yiding");
43:        System.out.println("yu *:");

44:        printStatements(ontModel, yu, null, null);
45:
46:     }
47:
48:     private static void printStatements(Model m,Resource s,
48a:                                Property p,Resource o) {
...
53:     }
54: }
```

As you can tell, this is a slightly different approach compared to the one shown in List 15.20. Instead of using ModelFactory.createDefaultModel(), line 29 creates an ontology model, which uses the OntModelSpec. OWL_MEM_RULE_INF configuration together with the instance document. After line 30 is executed, a complete ontology model that consists of the desired reasoner, the ontology file itself and the instance data for the reasoner to work on is created. Compared to the basic model created by the `ModelFactory.` `createDefaultModel()` method, this ontology model has all the derived statements.

As a little experiment, we can try the `RDFS_MEM_RDFS_INF` configuration: change line 29 in List 15.22 to the following:

```
OntModel ontModel = ModelFactory.createOntologyModel
                    (OntModelSpec.RDFS_MEM_RDFS_INF,data);
```

and run the code, you will see the difference. Since RDFS is not able to handle inverse functional properties, most of the inferred facts are gone. In fact, none of the statements in List 15.21 will show up.

15.5 Summary

In this chapter, we have presented Jena as an example framework for application development on the Semantic Web. After finishing this chapter, you should be able to work effectively with the Jena library. More specifically, you should

- Understand how to set up Jena as your development framework;
- Understand how to use the Jena library to conduct basic RDF model operations, such as reading an RDF model, creating an RDF model and interrogating an RDF model;
- Understand why persistent RDF models are important, how to use Jena library to create persistent models and how to inspect these persistent models in the selected database system;
- Understand the concept of inference model and its different configurations, how to use the Jena library to create an inference model with a specific configuration and also understand how to retrieve the derived statements from the inference model.

You will see more features offered by the Jena library in the next two chapters, and with what you have learned here, you should be able to explore the Jena library on your own as well.

Chapter 16
Follow Your Nose: A Basic Semantic Web Agent

Developing applications on the Semantic Web requires a set of complex skills, yet this skill set does depend on some basic techniques. In the previous chapter, we learned some basics, and in this chapter, we continue to learn some more techniques.

The Follow-Your-Nose method is one such basic technique you want to master. It can be quite useful in many cases. This chapter focuses on this method and its related issues.

16.1 The Principle of Follow-Your-Nose Method

16.1.1 What Is the Follow-Your-Nose Method?

Follow-Your-Nose is not something new to us at all: when you are surfing on the Web, quite often, your strategy is to "follow your nose". For example, the current page you are reading normally contains links to other pages that might be interesting to you, and clicking one of these links takes you to the next page. Similarly, the next page will again contain links to other pages, which you can click to go further, and so on.

The Follow-Your-Nose policy is not only used by human readers, it is also used by soft agents. Perhaps the most obvious example is the crawler used by search engines. We discuss the workflow of search engines in Chap. 17, and we will see that Follow-Your-Nose method is the main strategy used by a crawler.

Let us go back to the Web of Linked Data, a practical version of the Semantic Web. Obviously, the most distinguished feature of the Web of Linked Data is the fact that there exists a fairly large number of links among different datasets.

© Springer-Verlag Berlin Heidelberg 2014
L. Yu, *A Developer's Guide to the Semantic Web*,
DOI 10.1007/978-3-662-43796-4_16

This feature provides us with a chance to apply the Follow-Your-Nose method. In other words, one can make data discovery by following these links and navigating from one dataset to another, so on and so forth, until the stop criteria are met. This is the concept of Follow-Your-Nose in the world of the Semantic Web.

For example, let us say we want to know more about the tennis player Roger Federer. We can dereference this URI,

http://dbpedia.org/resource/Roger_Federer

Part of the returned RDF document is shown in List 16.1:

List 16.1 owl:sameAs links defined in Federer's RDF document

```
1: <rdf:Description
1a:     rdf:about="http://dbpedia.org/resource/Roger_Federer">
2:   <owl:sameAs rdf:resource= "http://rdf.freebase.com/ns/
2a:                         guid.9202a8c04000641f800000000019f525"/>
3: </rdf:Description>
4: <rdf:Description
4a:     rdf:about="http://mpii.de/yago/resource/Roger_Federer">
5:   <owl:sameAs
5a:     rdf:resource="http://dbpedia.org/resource/Roger_Federer"/>
6: </rdf:Description>
```

Now, we can dereference the links on line 2, which will take us to another RDF document that contains more facts about Roger Federer. Furthermore, once you have landed on this new document, you can repeat this Follow-Your-Nose procedure and discover new data about him, and so on.

Notice that we don't have to concentrate only on owl:sameAs links; we can follow any links that might be interesting to us. For example, we can follow the link to know more about Switzerland, the country where he was born.

What about the second link shown on line 4 of List 16.1? We can certainly follow that as well. In general, if we have more than one link to follow, we face a situation that actually asks for a decision from us: the so-called depth-first search vs. the breadth-first search.

More specifically, by using the depth-first search, we will first ignore the second link on line 4 and only follow the link on line 2 to reach a new document. In addition, we will follow any new links found on this new document to reach another new document, so on and so forth. We will continue to reach deeper until there is nothing to follow or the stopping criteria have been met. At that point, we go back one level to follow one link on that level. Only when there are no more links to follow at all do we go all the way back to follow the link shown on line 4. As you can tell, we go deeper first before we explore any link on the same level; for this reason we call this the depth-first Follow-Your-Nose method.

The breadth-first search works in the opposite way: after following the first link on line 2, even we have found new links on the new document, we will go back to follow the link on line 4. In other words, we always try to cover the same level links before we go any deeper.

In practice, whether to use depth-first search or breadth-first search is a decision that depends on the specific application and its domain. We will come back to this decision later. For now, understanding the idea of Follow-Your-Nose is the goal.

16.1.2 URI Declarations, Open Linked Data and Follow-Your-Nose Method

Before we move on to build a Follow-Your-Nose agent, there is one important issue to understand: on the Web of Linked Data, what makes this Follow-Your-Nose policy possible? Is it safe to believe dereferencing any given link will lead us to a new data file?

The answer is yes, the Follow-Your-Nose method on the Web of Linked Data should be able to accomplish its goal. This is due to the following two facts:

- The links are typed links, i.e., they have clearly defined semantics that enable us to know which links to follow.
- The basic principles of Linked Data.

The first reason is obvious. For example, the following two properties:

```
rdfs:seeAlso
owl:sameAs
```

have clearly defined semantics, and they are considered as links between different datasets. Any application understands that by following these links, it can gather more facts about the subject resource.

Depending on different application scenarios, there may be more properties that can be considered as links, but the above two are the most obvious ones. Furthermore, with help from ontology documents, a soft agent can decide on the fly which links should be followed and which links should be ignored based on the main goal of the application. This is possible since the links can be typed links and their types (classes) are clearly defined in the ontology file.

A good example is shown in List 9.4 (Sect. 9.2.3.1). The two rdfs:seeAlso links in List 9.4 are all typed links. If our agent is trying to use the Follow-Your-

Nose method to gather information about my publications (not CVs), it can easily decide which one of those two links should be followed.

In fact, this is also one of the reasons why the Follow-Your-Nose method can work well on the Semantic Web. On our traditional Web, all the links (identified by `<a href>` tag) are untyped links; there is simply no scalable and reliable way for a soft agent to tell which one to follow and which one to avoid.

The second reason is less obvious but it is equally important. More specifically, the action of Follow-Your-Nose by a soft agent is to dereference a given URI. If the given URI cannot be dereferenced, there will be no way to carry out the policy successfully.

Fortunately, based on the Linked Data principle that we discussed in Chap. 9, the following is true:

- If the URI contains a fragment identifier (Hash URI), the part of the URI before the "#" sign should lead to a URI declaration page that is served with an RDF document.
- If the URI does not contain a fragment identifier, an attempt to dereference the URI should be answered with a 303-redirect that leads to a URI declaration page served with an RDF document as well.

In other words, the use of URIs as names, and in particular that URIs can be dereferenced using the HTTP protocol, is a critical enabling factor for the Follow-Your-Nose approach.

Finally, understand that the Follow-Your-Nose method is not an optional extra; on the contrary, it is fundamentally necessary in order to support the highly devolved, loosely coupled nature of the Linked Data Web.

In the next section, let us take a look at a real example showing you the Follow-Your-Nose method it can be implemented with help from the Jena package.

16.2   A Follow-Your-Nose Agent in Java

16.2.1   Building the Agent

In this section we code a simple agent that implements the idea of Follow-Your-Nose, and we use it to collect everything that has been said about tennis player Roger Federer on the Web of Linked Data.

To do so, we start from DBpedia. And again, here is the URI that represents Roger Federer in DBpedia:

```
http://dbpedia.org/resource/Roger_Federer
```

Starting from this seed URI, we carry out the following three steps:

1. Dereference the seed URI to get an RDF document that describes Roger Federer.
2. To collect the facts about Roger Federer, harvest all the statements that satisfy the following pattern:

```
<http://dbpedia.org/resource/Roger_Federer>
<someProperty> <someValue> .
```

3. To gather the links to follow, find all the statements that satisfy the following two patterns, and the collection of *subjectResource* and *objectResource* is the links to follow:

```
   <http://dbpedia.org/resource/Roger_Federer>
      owl:sameAs <objectResource> .
   <subjectResource>
      owl:sameAs <http://dbpedia.org/resource/Roger_Federer> .
```

The first step does not need much explanation. Based on what we learned from Chap. 15, we also know how to dereference a given URI by using the Jena library.

The second step is data discovery. In this example, the agent collects all the facts about the resource identified by the given URI. Obviously, the given statement pattern in step 2 will accomplish the goal.

The third step is where the idea of Follow-Your-Nose is implemented. Specifically, property `owl:sameAs` is used to find the links. As a result, these links are all URI aliases which all represent Roger Federer. Whichever link we follow, we are only collecting facts about Roger Federer. Notice that Roger Federer's URI can be either the subject or the object: if it appears as the object, the subject URI is the link to follow, and if it assumes the role of subject, the object URI is the link to follow. This is why we have two statement patterns to consider in step 3.

Once these steps are done on a given dataset, the agent not only has collected some facts about Federer, but also has discovered a set of links to follow. The next action is to repeat these steps by selecting a link from the collected link set, and dereferencing it to collect more data and more links.

This process is repeatedly executed until there are no more links to follow, at which point, we declare success: on the Web of Linked Data, anyone from anywhere can say something about Roger Federer, and whatever has been said, we have them all.

Lists 16.2–16.4 show the classes which implement this agent.

List 16.2 `FollowYourNose.java` class definition

```
1: package test;
2:
3: import com.hp.hpl.jena.rdf.model.Model;
4: import com.hp.hpl.jena.rdf.model.ModelFactory;
5: import com.hp.hpl.jena.rdf.model.NodeIterator;
6: import com.hp.hpl.jena.rdf.model.Property;
7: import com.hp.hpl.jena.rdf.model.RDFNode;
8: import com.hp.hpl.jena.rdf.model.ResIterator;
9: import com.hp.hpl.jena.rdf.model.Resource;
10: import com.hp.hpl.jena.rdf.model.Statement;
11: import com.hp.hpl.jena.rdf.model.StmtIterator;
12: import com.hp.hpl.jena.vocabulary.OWL;
13:
14: public class FollowYourNose {
15:
16:    private URICollection sameAsURIs = null;
17:
18:    public FollowYourNose(String uri) {
19:      sameAsURIs = new URICollection();
20:      sameAsURIs.addNewURI(uri);
21:    }
22:
23:    public void work() {
24:
25:      // get the next link to follow
26:      String currentURI = sameAsURIs.getNextURI();
27:      if ( currentURI == null ) {
28:        return;
29:      }
30:
31:      try {
32:
33:        // de-reference this link
34:        Model instanceDocument =
34a:            ModelFactory.createDefaultModel();
35:        instanceDocument.read(currentURI);
36:
37:        // do the data collection
38:        collectData(instanceDocument,currentURI);
39:
40:        // find the next links to follow
41:        updateURICollection(sameAsURIs,currentURI,
41a:                            instanceDocument,OWL.sameAs);
```

```
42:
43:      } catch (Exception e) {
44:        System.out.println("*** errors when handling (" +
44a:                                currentURI + ") ***");
45:      }
46:
47:      System.out.println("\n---- these links are yet
47a:                                to follow ---- ");
48:      sameAsURIs.showAll();
49:      System.out.println("------------------------------ ");
50:
51:      // following our nose
52:      work();
53:
54:    }
55:
56:    private void collectData(Model model, String uri) {
57:      if ( uri == null ) {
58:        return;
59:      }
60:      int factCounter = 0;
61:      System.out.println("Facts about <" + uri + ">:");
62:      for (StmtIterator si = model.listStatements();
62a:                      si.hasNext(); ) {
63:        Statement statement = si.nextStatement();
64:        if ( uri.equalsIgnoreCase(
64a:             statement.getSubject().getURI()) == true ) {
65:          factCounter ++;
66:          System.out.print(" - <" +
66a:                statement.getPredicate().toString() + "> : <");
67:          System.out.println(statement.getObject().toString()
67a:                            + ">");
68:          if ( factCounter >= 10 ) {
69:            return;
70:          }
71:        }
72:      }
73:    }
74:
75:    private void updateURICollection(
75a:               URICollection uriCollection,String uri,
76:               Model model,Property property) {
77:      if ( uri == null ) {
78:        return;
```

```
79:    }
80:    // check object
81:    Resource resource = model.getResource(uri);
82:    NodeIterator objects =
82a:               model.listObjectsOfProperty(resource,property);
83:    while ( objects.hasNext() ) {
84:      RDFNode object = objects.next();
85:      if ( object.isResource() ) {
86:        Resource tmpResource = (Resource)object;
87:        uriCollection.addNewURI(tmpResource.getURI());
88:      }
89:    }
90:    // check the subject
91:    ResIterator subjects =
91a:               model.listSubjectsWithProperty(property,resource);
92:    while ( subjects.hasNext() ) {
93:      Resource subject = subjects.nextResource();
94:      uriCollection.addNewURI(subject.getURI());
95:    }
96:  }
97:
98: }
```

List 16.3 URICollection.java definition

```
1: package test;
2:
3: import java.net.URI;
4: import java.util.HashSet;
5: import java.util.Iterator;
6: import java.util.Stack;
7:
8: public class URICollection {
9:
10:  private Stack URIs = null;
11:  private HashSet domainCollection = null;
12:
13:  public URICollection() {
14:    URIs = new Stack();
15:    domainCollection = new HashSet();
16:  }
17:
18:  public void addNewURI(String uri) {
```

```
19:     if ( uri == null ) {
20:        return;
21:     }
22:     try {
23:        URI thisURI = new URI(uri);
24:        if ( domainCollection.contains(thisURI.getHost())
24a:                                          == false ) {
25:           domainCollection.add(thisURI.getHost());
26:           URIs.push(uri);
27:        }
28:     } catch(Exception e) {};
29:   }
30:
31:   public String getNextURI() {
32:     if ( URIs.empty() == true ) {
33:        return null;
34:     }
35:     return (String)(URIs.pop());
36:   }
37:
38:   public void showAll() {
39:     for ( int i = 0; i < URIs.size(); i ++ ) {
40:        System.out.println(URIs.elementAt(i).toString());
41:     }
42:   }
43:
44: }
```

List 16.4 `FollowYourNoseTester.java` definition

```
1: package test;
2:
3: public class FollowYourNoseTester {
4:
5:  public static final String startURI =
5a:              "http://dbpedia.org/resource/Roger_Federer";
6:
7:  public static void main(String[] args) {
8:
9:     FollowYourNose fyn = new FollowYourNose(startURI);
10:    fyn.work();
11:
12: }
13:
14: }
```

The key class is `FollowYourNose.java`, defined in List 16.2. Given our earlier explanation, understanding this class is straightforward. It has one private member variable, called `sameAsURIs`, which holds all the links yet to follow (we will get to the management of these links shortly). Lines 18–21 show its constructor, a starting URI is passed in and added into `sameAsURIs`; therefore initially, there is only one link to explore.

The key member function is `work()`, defined in lines 23–54. It first checks the `sameAsURIs` link set to get the next link to follow. If there is none left, the whole process is done (line 26–29). If there is indeed one link to follow, it then implements the three steps we discussed earlier: lines 34–35 implement step 1, line 38 implements step 2 and line 41 implements step 3.

Notice that to finish steps 2 and 3, some helper functions are created. Lines 56–73 are a private member function called `collectData()`, which defines the details of step 2. Similarly, lines 75–96 create another private member function called `updateURICollection()`, which defines the details of step 3. With our earlier description about these steps, understanding these two functions should be fairly easy. We will discuss them more after we finish discussing the `work()` method.

Once all these steps are finished, `work()` shows the links yet to follow (lines 47–49) and then calls itself recursively (line 52) to follow these links. By doing so, the process of discovering data, collecting links and following links continues and finally comes to a stop when there are no more links to follow. Notice this recursive style is quite often seen in crawler-like agents like this; using this recursive calling will make your coding easier and cleaner.

Let us now go back to its two private methods, `collectData()` and `updateUR-ICollection()`. As far as this example agent is concerned, collecting data simply means to print them out, and this is the main workflow implemented by the `collectData()` method. More specifically, a `for` loop is used to iterate on each statement in the current RDF model (line 62): for the current statement, if the subject happens to be the URI that represents Federer (line 64), we print out its property name and the value of the property (lines 66–67).

Notice that `model.listStatements()` is the key Jena API call used by the `collectData()` method, which lists all the statements contained in the model. Since we are examining RDF documents in DBpedia or other datasets contained in the Web of Linked Data, if we print out everything we have collected, in most cases it will be a long list of facts. Therefore, we print only the first ten facts (lines 60, 65, 68–70) from each RDF document.

The `updateURICollection()` method also makes use of several useful Jena API calls. First, `model.getResource()` (line 81) takes Federer's URI as its input parameter and returns the corresponding resource object that represents Federer. This resource object is then used in two other API calls, namely `model.listObjectsOfProperty()` and `model.listSubjectsWithProperty()` (lines 82 and 91), which examine the two statement patterns as discussed in step 3. Once the patterns are matched, the corresponding URIs are added to our link collection (lines 87 and 94). Notice that `updateURICollection()` is called with `owl:sameAs` as one of the input parameters (line 41); therefore, only `owl:sameAs` links are considered by the agent.

At this point, we have a good understand about this key class. You can modify its two private methods, `collectData()` and `updateURICollection()`, accordingly to make the agent fit your own need. For example, instead of printing out all the facts, `collectData()` can create a persistent RDF model using a backend database, so that later on we can query the facts using SPARQL.

Finally, before we move on, let us discuss the other two helper classes briefly. Class `URICollection.java` (List 16.3) is created to hold the links yet to follow. When the agent first starts, this collection only holds the initial URI that represents Federer. More links are added to it during the work course of the agent, and finally, there should be none left and therefore the agent stops.

There are two things to notice about this collection class. First, its underlying data structure is a stack (lines 10, 14), so it implements a depth-first Follow-Your-Nose policy, rather than breadth-first. Second, on the Web of Linked Data, it is often true that links are two-way ones, i.e., dataset A has a link to dataset B, and B has a link back to A. As a result, if we collect every URI on the link, we may get into an infinite loop. To take this into account, we want to avoid adding the same URI back to the collection. Lines 24–26 of List 16.3 implement this idea: for each incoming new URI, we check its domain, and if this domain has been added before, this incoming URI is considered as previously processed and is not added to the link collection.

Class `FollowYourNoseTester.java` (List 16.4) does not require any explanation; it is a simple driver class to start your agent. Notice that the initial URI is specified at line 5, and if you want to try some other URIs, this is the line you can change.

16.2.2 Running the Agent

List 16.5 shows part of the result when using Roger Federer's URI as the seed URI.

List 16.5 Result when using Federer's URI (line numbers added for explanation purposes)

```
1: Facts about <http://dbpedia.org/resource/Roger_Federer>:
2:  - <http://dbpedia.org/property/redirect> :
       <http://dbpedia.org/resource/Roger_Federer>
3:  - <http://dbpedia.org/property/doublestitles> :
       <8^^http://www.w3.org/2001/XMLSchema#integer>
4:  - <http://dbpedia.org/property/careerprizemoney> :
       <US$45,790,270@en>
5:  - <http://dbpedia.org/property/olympicsdoublesresult> :
       <http://dbpedia.org/resource/Roger_Federer/
             olympicsdoublesresult/OlympicEvent>
```

```
 6:  - <http://dbpedia.org/property/relatedInstance> :
       <http://dbpedia.org/resource/Roger_Federer/succession_box1>
 7:  - <http://www.w3.org/1999/02/22-rdf-syntax-ns#type> :
       <http://dbpedia.org/ontology/TennisPlayer>
 8:  - <http://dbpedia.org/ontology/residence> :
       <http://dbpedia.org/resource/Switzerland>
 9:  - <http://dbpedia.org/property/abstract> :
       <Roger Federer ... >
10:  - <http://www.w3.org/2000/01/rdf-schema#comment> :
       <Roger Federer ... >
11:  - <http://dbpedia.org/property/country> :
       <http://dbpedia.org/resource/Switzerland>
12:
13:  ---- these links are yet to follow ----
14:  http://rdf.freebase.com/ns/guid.
14a:                    9202a8c04000641f800000000019f525
15:  http://mpii.de/yago/resource/Roger_Federer
16:  ------------------------------------
17:  Facts about <http://mpii.de/yago/resource/Roger_Federer>:
18:
19:  ---- these links are yet to follow ----
20:  http://rdf.freebase.com/ns/guid.
20a:                    9202a8c04000641f800000000019f525
21:  ------------------------------------
22:  Facts about <http://rdf.freebase.com/ns/guid.
22a:                    9202a8c04000641f800000000019f525>:
23:  - <http://rdf.freebase.com/ns/tennis.tennis_player.
23a:                          highest_singles_ranking> :
       <http://rdf.freebase.com/ns/guid.
23b:                    9202a8c04000641f8000000004fba118>
24:  - <http://www.w3.org/1999/02/22-rdf-syntax-ns#type> :
       <http://rdf.freebase.com/ns/base.popstra.celebrity>
25:  - <http://rdf.freebase.com/ns/type.object.key> :.
25a:  <234daeea:1246364ddc3:-7ff0>
26:  - <http://rdf.freebase.com/ns/common.topic.article> :
       <http://rdf.freebase.com/ns/guid.
26a:                    9202a8c04000641f800000000019f52f>
27:  - <http://rdf.freebase.com/ns/type.object.key> :
       <234daeea:1246364ddc3:-8000>
28:  - <http://rdf.freebase.com/ns/type.object.key> :
       <234daeea:1246364ddc3:-7ff8>
29:  - <http://rdf.freebase.com/ns/type.object.key> :
       <234daeea:1246364ddc3:-7fed>
```

```
30:   - <http://rdf.freebase.com/ns/type.object.name> :
        <??????? ??????@uk>
31:   - <http://www.w3.org/1999/02/22-rdf-syntax-ns#type> :
        <http://rdf.freebase.com/ns/base.rogerfederer.topic>
32:   - <http://rdf.freebase.com/ns/base.popstra.
32a:                                 celebrity.friendship> :
        <http://rdf.freebase.com/ns/guid.
32b:                        9202a8c04000641f800000000c5ab937>
```

Some explanation about this result will help you understand more about the Follow-Your-Nose policy.

First, lines 2–11 in List 16.5 show the first ten facts the agent has collected from dereferencing the seed URI. At the time of this writing, the RDF document retrieved from the seed URI contains the following two statements:

```
<rdf:Description
rdf:about="http://mpii.de/yago/resource/Roger_Federer">
<owl:sameAs
rdf:resource="http://dbpedia.org/resource/Roger_Federer"/>
</rdf:Description>
<rdf:Description
rdf:about="http://dbpedia.org/resource/Roger_Federer">
<owl:sameAs rdf:resource="http://rdf.freebase.com/ns/guid.
9202a8c04000641f800000000019f525"/>
</rdf:Description>
```

Our agent has detected this, and following the `owl:sameAs` link means dereferencing these two URIs:

```
http://mpii.de/yago/resource/Roger_Federer
http://rdf.freebase.com/ns/guid.
9202a8c04000641f800000000019f525
```

And these are the URI aliases you see on lines 14–15 in List 16.5.

URI `http://mpii.de/yago/resour-ce/Roger_Federer` is dereferenced next by the agent. However, no facts were collected there (lines 17, 18). The agent then moves on to dereference the next URI (line 20). It is able to collect some more facts about Roger Federer from the retrieved RDF document, as shown by lines 22–32 of List 16.5. Similarly, the agent then looks for the property `owl:sameAs` in this RDF document to continue its journey in the Linked Data Web, and so on.

To get more familiar with this example, you can use some of your favorite URIs as the seeds to see how the Follow-Your-Nose policy works in the real world. It is a simple idea; however, it does tell us a lot about the Linked Data Web.

The following list contains some suggested URIs you can try:

```
http://dbpedia.org/resource/Tim_Berners-Lee
http://dbpedia.org/resource/Semantic_Web
http://dbpedia.org/resource/Beijing
http://dbpedia.org/resource/Nikon_D300
```

16.2.3   More Clues for Follow-Your-Nose

So far at this point, we have been using the `owl:sameAs` as the only link when implementing our Follow-Your-Nose agent. In fact, there are more clues we can use.

Another obvious one is the `rdfs:seeAlso` property. However, we need to be careful when following `rdfs:seeAlso` links. More specifically, based on the Open Linked Data principle, we will be able to retrieve representations of objects from the Web, however, no constraints are placed on the format of those representations. This is especially true with the `rdfs:seeAlso` property: the response could be a JPEG file instead of an RDF document.

In general, when coding a Fellow-Your-Nose agent, we may have to use a content negotiation process and may also have to implement more protections around this to make the agent more robust.

Another similar property is `rdfs:isDefinedBy`, which is a subproperty of `rdfs:seeAlso`. Our discussion about `rdfs:seeAlso` is applicable to this property as well, and it is another link that a Fellow-Your-Nose agent should consider.

Coding a Follow-Your-Nose agent is sometimes more of an art than a science, and it requires creative heuristics to make the collected facts more complete. For a given resource, different Follow-Your-Nose agents can very possibly deliver different fact sets. A key factor, again, is about how to find clues to discover more facts.

Besides using more properties as links as we have discussed above, sometimes it may be good idea to take into the consideration of your specific resource the related properties from popular ontologies. For example, given the fact that Roger Federer is an instance of `foaf:Person`, another FOAF property, `foaf:knows`, could be something we want to consider. More specifically, if Roger Federer `foaf:knows` another resource R, then it is likely resource R also `foaf:knows` Roger Federer, and it is also possible that resource R has said something about Federer. Therefore, dereferencing the URI of resource R and scanning the retrieved RDF document to find facts about Federer is another action the agent can take.

Another FOAF property is `foaf:primaryTopicOf`. A statement such as this,

```
<http://dbpedia.org/resource/Roger_Federer>
foaf:isPrimaryTopicOf object .
```

means the resource identified by the `object` URI is mainly about Roger Federer. Therefore, dereferencing the URI of the `object` and trying to find more facts there about Federer is a good direction to pursue.

By now, you should have gotten the point. The key is to discover and examine every potential link when implementing a Fellow-Your-Nose agent. What you have learned here should be a good starting point, and now it is up to you to make it smarter.

16.2.4 Can You Follow Your Nose on Traditional Web?

Now that we have finished a Follow-Your-Nose agent on the Semantic Web, we can continue on with an interesting comparison: can we do the same on the traditional document Web? That is, can we find everything that people have said about Federer on the Web?

To get started, we first have to design a heuristic that is similar to the algorithm used by our Follow-Your-Nose agent. A possible solution is to start from Federer's own homepage. Once we download the page, we can collect everything about him from that page, including address, phone numbers, e-mail addresses, etc.

It is safe to assume that his homepage has links (`<a href=.../>`tags) that point to other Web sites. These Web sites may describe different tennis events, including the four Grand Slams, and in addition, they may include Web sites that are related to different tennis organizations, and so on. We can also make the assumption that if Roger Federer is talking about these resources on his homepage, these resources will also be likely to talk about him. Therefore, we can follow these links to check out each Web site individually, with the goal of finding information about him from these pages.

As the first glance, this sounds like a plan. However, once you begin to put it into action, you will see the problems right away. The first major hurdle comes from the fact that we probably have to do screen-scraping in order to obtain the information we want. Given that information on each page is not structured data, but is instead simple text for human eyes, you can easily imagine how difficult this screen-scraping process can be, if not totally impossible.

In fact, even if screen-scraping each page is possible, the maintenance of our agent could be very costly. Each Web site is always under active change, and a successful parsing today does not mean another successful one a certain amount of time later. For example, the "indicators/flags" that have been used to locate particular information blocks might not exist anymore. Our agent has to be constantly modified in order to process the updated Web documents.

The second major hurdle is related to the fact that there is not a unique identifier our agent can use to identify Roger Federer on each Web page. For example, one page might refer him by his full name, another page might call him the *Swiss Maestro*, and a Web page created by his funs may address him as *Fed Express*. As a result, our agent, once finished downloading a given page, will find it difficult to determine if the page has any description about Federer at all. In the worst case, even matching on the name does not necessarily mean the page is about him.

Now let us assume all the above steps are feasible and doable, and we can indeed gather something about Roger Federer. The question then is what to do with the gathered information?

Obviously, the facts are collected from different source pages, which do not offer any structured data, and also do not share any common vocabularies or any common data models (such as RDF). As a result, the collected information will be most likely unusable when it comes to supporting the following capabilities:

• Reasoning on the collected information to discover new facts

This is one of the major motivations for Follow-Your-Nose data aggregation: with help from ontologies, based on the aggregated information, we can discover facts that are not presented in any of the source documents. And clearly, the page content we have harvested from the traditional Web cannot be used for this purpose at all.

• Structured query language to answer questions

Another important operation on the collected dataset is to execute SPARQL queries so as to get direct answers to many questions. We can certainly make queries against one single RDF source file; however, only after Follow-Your-Nose data aggregation is implemented, will we be confident that the answer is complete and correct. Furthermore, since we can run our Follow-Your-Nose agent at any time, the query result may therefore include newly discovered facts. Clearly, data collected from the traditional Web cannot be easily used for any query, and including new results normally means new development and costly maintenance.

The conclusion: a simple task like this can be prohibitively difficult under the current Web environment, and even it is feasible, the result may be quite difficult to use.

In the meantime, this task can be easily accomplished under the Semantic Web, as we have seen already. In addition, the collected facts can be used for further reasoning and can be queried by language such as SPARQL.

Besides the above, our Follow-Your-Nose agent also enjoys the following benefits provided directly by the structured data on the Semantic Web:

• Easy to maintain

In fact, there is no need to maintain anything. Any source RDF document can be modified to add new facts at any time, and the same agent can again harvest all these related descriptions with the same ease without making any code changes.

• Dynamic and up to date

This is a natural extension of the maintainability of the agent: you can run it at any time to update the collected data set. The owners of data sources do not have to tell you anything or notify you whens one of them has published some new facts. Again, dynamic and distributed data aggregation is one of many benefits provided by the vision of the Semantic Web.

16.3   A Better Implementation of Follow-Your-Nose Agent: Using SPARQL Queries

So far in this chapter, we have done quite a few queries against RDF models. Some of the key methods we have been using include the following:

```
model.listStatements();
model.listSubjectsWithProperty();
model.listObjectsOfProperty();
```

And we were able to locate the specific information we needed from the model.

However, as we discussed, this type of model interrogation is often considered as a method that provides a low-level view of the model. Query languages such as SPARQL, on the other hand, can offer a more compact and powerful query notation for the same results. Therefore, when it comes to building agents such as our Fellow-Your-Nose agent, it is sometimes more compact and more efficient to use SPARQL queries.

To help when using SPARQL in applications, Jena provides a query engine called ARQ that supports SPARQL query language. ARQ includes a set of powerful APIs that we can use in our applications.

In this section, we rewrite our Follow-Your-Nose agent so SPARQL queries are used instead of simple model interrogation. By doing so, not only can we have a better agent, but we can also show you how to submit and execute SPARQL queries by using Jena APIs.

16.3.1   In-Memory SPARQL Operation

Before we start, understand that the Follow-Your-Nose agent developed in the previous section had all the data models in memory, and all the model interrogation was also executed against these in-memory models. In this section, this continues to be the case. The SPARQL queries we are going to use are therefore executed locally in memory. It is certainly possible to execute a SPARQL query remotely, with the query result returned back to the client. We cover this in the next section.

Let us start with our rewrite. A review of our Follow-Your-Nose agent indicates that the only Java class we need to change is the `FollowYourNose.java` in List 16.2. More specifically, we need to replace the query part in these two methods:

```
collectData()
updateURICollection()
```

The query used in `collectData()` method is fairly simple: all it does is try to find everything that has been said about Roger Federer. The SPARQL query shown in List 16.6 accomplishes exactly the same thing.

List 16.6 SPARQL query to find everything that has been said about Roger Federer

```
SELECT ?propertyValue ?propertyName
WHERE {
   <http://dbpedia.org/resource/Roger_Federer>
   ?propertyName ?propertyValue.
}
```

The query used in `updateURICollection()` is not difficult either. Again, it tries to find all the statements that have the following pattern:

```
<http://dbpedia.org/resource/Roger_Federer>
owl:sameAs <objectResource>
```

```
<subjustResource> owl:sameAs
<http://dbpedia.org/resource/Roger_Federer>
```

And the SPARQL query in List 16.7 exactly accomplishes the same goal:

List 16.7 SPARQL query to find those resources that `owl:sameAs` Roger Federer

```
SELECT ?aliasURI WHERE {
   { <http://dbpedia.org/resource/Roger_Federer>
     <http://www.w3.org/2002/07/owl#sameAs>  ?aliasURI.
   }
   union
   { ?aliasURI <http://www.w3.org/2002/07/owl#sameAs>
     <http://dbpedia.org/resource/Roger_Federer>.
   }
}
```

With all the correct SPARQL queries established, let us now take a look at the steps that are need to execute SPARQL queries in our application. Notice that the steps we discuss next are applicable for SELECT queries. For CONSTRUCT queries, DESCRIBE queries and ASK queries, the steps are slightly different. If you are not familiar with these queries, review Chap. 6 to get up to speed.

1. Prepare the query string, which represents the SPARQL query that you want to use to get information from the RDF model or RDF dataset. Lists 16.6 and 16.7 are examples of query strings.
2. Create a Query object by using the QueryFactory.create() method, with the query string as the input parameter.
3. Create a QueryExecution object by calling method QueryExecutionFatory. create(), the Query object you just created and the RDF model are passed in as parameters.

4. Call the `execSelect()` method on the `QueryExecution` object to execute the query, which returns the query results.
5. Handle the query results in a loop to get the needed information.
6. Call the `close()` method on the `QueryExecution` object to release system resources.

List 16.8 shows the new version of the `collectData()` method, which implements the above steps.

List 16.8 `collectData()` method is now implemented by using SPARQL query

```
1:   private void collectData(Model model, String uri) {
2:
3:     if ( uri == null ) {
4:         return;
5:     }
6:
7:     int factCounter = 0;
8:
9:     String queryString =
10:           "SELECT ?propertyName ?propertyValue " +
11:           "WHERE {" +
12:           "   <" + uri + "> ?propertyName ?propertyValue." +
13:           "}";
14:
15:    Query query = QueryFactory.create(queryString);
16:    QueryExecution qe =
16a:                   QueryExecutionFactory.create(query,model);
17:
18:    try {
19:      ResultSet results = qe.execSelect();
20:      while ( results.hasNext() ) {
21:        QuerySolution soln = results.nextSolution() ;
22:        factCounter ++;
23:        Resource res = (Resource)(soln.get("propertyName"));
24:        System.out.print(" - <" + res.getURI() + "> : ");
25:        RDFNode node = soln.get("propertyValue");
26:        if ( node.isLiteral() ) {
27:          System.out.println(((Literal)node).getLexicalForm());
28:        } else if ( node.isResource() ) {
29:          res = (Resource)node;
30:          if ( res.isAnon() == true ) {
31:            System.out.println("<" + res.getLocalName() + ">");
32:          } else {
```

```
33:                System.out.println( "<" + res.getURI() + ">");
34:            }
35:          }
36:        if ( factCounter >= 10 ) {
37:           break;
38:        }
39:      }
40:    }
41:    catch(Exception e) {
42:      // doing nothing for now
43:    }
44:    finally {
45:        qe.close();
46:    }
47:
48: }
```

With the discussion of the general steps, List 16.8 is fairly straightforward. Line 9 prepares the query string as shown in List 9.6, which also implements step 1 as discussed above. Line 15 maps to step 2, and line 16 is step 3. Line 19 is the execution of the query, and results are also returned (step 4).

The code segment that needs some explanation is in lines 20–39, the loop that handles the query result (step 5). Recall that in Chap. 6 we learned that a given query returns a set of statements as result, and each one of these statements is called a solution. In Jena SPARQL API, one such solution is represented by an instance of QuerySolution class (line 21), and to get what we are looking for from each solution, we need to use the same variable name as we used in the query string.

For example, line 23 tries to get the property name. Therefore, propertyName as the variable name has to be used, since that variable name is also used in the query string of line 9. Similarly, line 25 tries to get the property value by using the propertyValue variable.

Once we get the property value back, a little more work is needed. In general, since a property value is always on the object position, it can be either a literal or a resource. If the property value is a simple literal value, we just print it out (lines 26–27). If it is a resource, it can further be a blank node or a named resource, and we have handle them differently (lines 28–35).

Finally, line 45 implements step 6, where the query is closed so all system related resources are released.

This is the general process of executing a SPARQL query by using Jena SPARQL APIs. You will find yourself using these APIs quite often, and your code should also follow the same pattern as shown here.

List 16.9 shows the new version of the updateURICollection() method. With we have learned so far, you should be able to understand it easily.

List 16.9 `udpateURICollection()` method is now implemented by using SPARQL query

```
1:  private void updateURICollection(URICollection uriCollection,
1:a                String uri,
2:                Model model,Property property) {
3:    if ( uri == null ) {
4:      return;
5:    }
6:
7:    String queryString =
8:       "SELECT ?aliasURI " +
9:       "WHERE {" +
10:      "  { <" + uri + "> <" + OWL.sameAs + "> ?aliasURI. } " +
11:      " union " +
12:      "  { ?aliasURI <" + OWL.sameAs + "> <" + uri + ">. } " +
13:      "}";
14:
15:    Query query = QueryFactory.create(queryString);
16:    QueryExecution qe =
16a:               QueryExecutionFactory.create(query,model);
17:
18:    try {
19:      ResultSet results = qe.execSelect();
20:      while ( results.hasNext() ) {
21:        QuerySolution soln = results.nextSolution() ;
22:        RDFNode node = soln.get("aliasURI");
23:        if ( node.isResource() ) {
24:          Resource res = (Resource)node;
25:          if ( res.isAnon() == false ) {
26:             uriCollection.addNewURI(res.getURI());
27:          }
28:        }
29:      }
30:    }
31:    catch(Exception e) {
32:      // doing nothing for now
33:    }
34:    finally {
35:      qe.close();
36:    }
37: }
```

Now we have a Follow-Your-Nose agent that is completely written by using SPARQL queries. Run it, and you should see exactly the same result.

16.3.2 Using SPARQL Endpoints Remotely

Notice that so far in this chapter, we have been downloading the RDF models or datasets into our local memory and then processing them in our memory. The problem associated with this approach is quite obvious: downloading a large data file is always time consuming, and sometimes the file could be too large for our limited memory to handle, as we also discussed in the previous chapter.

A more practical way, especially when you are developing large-scale real applications, is to submit the query across the Internet and post it to the SPARQL endpoint offered by the underlying dataset. The query is then executed on that remote site, and the final result is returned back to the application for processing. By doing so, no downloading is needed, the network bandwidth is free for other use, and only the request and response are being interchanged.

This kind of remote SPARQL query can also be implemented programmatically. For example, Jena's SPARQL API provides remote query request/response processing, as we will see shortly. Also, notice that remote dataset access over the SPARQL protocol requires the underlying dataset to provide a SPARQL endpoint that supports remote data access.

At the time of this writing, some datasets on the Linked Data Web support SPARQL endpoints, and some don't. For this reason, rewriting our Follow-Your-Nose agent to make it use remote data access is not quite possible, simply because we don't know which datasets offer remote SPRAQL endpoints.

In this section, we therefore simply use one example dataset to show how remote dataset access is implemented. It is my hope that, by the time you read this book, most datasets on the Linked Data Web support SPARQL endpoints.

The example data set we are going to use is the DBpedia dataset, and here is the SPARQL endpoint it supports:

```
http://dbpedia.org/sparql
```

List 16.10 shows the code that remotely accesses this data set. Again, the submitted query is shown in List 16.6.

List 16.10 Example of accessing DBpedia remotely

```
1: package test;
2:
3: import com.hp.hpl.jena.query.Query;
4: import com.hp.hpl.jena.query.QueryExecution;
5: import com.hp.hpl.jena.query.QueryExecutionFactory;
6: import com.hp.hpl.jena.query.QueryFactory;
7: import com.hp.hpl.jena.query.QuerySolution;
8: import com.hp.hpl.jena.query.ResultSet;
9: import com.hp.hpl.jena.rdf.model.Literal;
10: import com.hp.hpl.jena.rdf.model.RDFNode;
11: import com.hp.hpl.jena.rdf.model.Resource;
12:
```

```
13: public class RemoteSPARQLAccess {
14:
15:   final static String resourceURI =
15a:               "http://dbpedia.org/resource/Roger_Federer";
16:   final static String DBpediaSPARQLEndpoint =
16a:               "http://dbpedia.org/sparql";
17:
18:   public static void main(String[] args) {
19:
20:     String queryString =
21:     "SELECT ?propertyName ?propertyValue " +
22:     "WHERE {" +
23:     "  <" + resourceURI + "> ?propertyName ?propertyValue." +
24:     "}";
25:
26:     Query query = QueryFactory.create(queryString);
27:     QueryExecution qe = QueryExecutionFactory.sparqlService
27a:                     (DBpediaSPARQLEndpoint,query);
28:
29:     try {
30:       ResultSet results = qe.execSelect();
31:       while ( results.hasNext() ) {
32:         QuerySolution soln = results.nextSolution() ;
33:         Resource res = (Resource)(soln.get("propertyName"));
34:         System.out.print(" - <" + res.getURI() + "> : ");
35:         RDFNode node = soln.get("propertyValue");
36:         if ( node.isLiteral() ) {
37:           System.out.println(((Literal)node.
37a:                             getLexicalForm());
38:         } else if ( node.isResource() ) {
39:           res = (Resource)node;
40:           if ( res.isAnon() == true ) {
41:             System.out.println( "<" +
41a:                             res.getLocalName() + ">");
42:           } else {
43:             System.out.println( "<" + res.getURI() + ">");
44:           }
45:         }
46:       }
47:     }
48:     catch(Exception e) {
49:       // doing nothing for now
50:     }
```

```
51:      finally {
52:         qe.close();
53:      }
54:   }
55:
56: }
```

Compared to List 16.8, the only difference is on line 27: the `QueryExecution` instance is created by calling `QueryExecutionFactory.sparqlService()` method, and not `QueryExecutionFactory.create()` method any longer. Also, instead of passing in the model to the method (line 16 of List 16.8), the SPARQL endpoint provided by DBpedia is passed.

The above is all that we need to do when accessing a remote SPARQL endpoint; the rest is taken care of for us by Jena. As you can tell, we then receive and process the results as if we were querying an in-memory dataset.

Finally, List 16.11 shows part of the query result.

List 16.11 Part of the result generated by List 16.10

```
- <http://www.w3.org/1999/02/22-rdf-syntax-ns#type> :
  <http://dbpedia.org/ontology/Athlete>
- <http://www.w3.org/1999/02/22-rdf-syntax-ns#type> :
  <http://dbpedia.org/ontology/Person>
- <http://www.w3.org/1999/02/22-rdf-syntax-ns#type> :
  <http://dbpedia.org/ontology/Resource>
- <http://www.w3.org/1999/02/22-rdf-syntax-ns#type> :
  <http://dbpedia.org/ontology/TennisPlayer>
- <http://www.w3.org/1999/02/22-rdf-syntax-ns#type> :
  <http://dbpedia.org/class/yago/AustralianOpenChampions>
- <http://www.w3.org/1999/02/22-rdf-syntax-ns#type> :
  <http://dbpedia.org/class/yago/USOpenChampions>
- <http://www.w3.org/1999/02/22-rdf-syntax-ns#type> :
  <http://dbpedia.org/class/yago/
                    TennisPlayersAtThe2000SummerOlympics>
- <http://www.w3.org/1999/02/22-rdf-syntax-ns#type> :
  <http://dbpedia.org/class/yago/
                    OlympicTennisPlayersOfSwitzerland>
- <http://www.w3.org/1999/02/22-rdf-syntax-ns#type> :
  <http://xmlns.com/foaf/0.1/Person>
- <http://www.w3.org/1999/02/22-rdf-syntax-ns#type> :
  <http://dbpedia.org/class/yago/
                    TennisPlayersAtThe2004SummerOlympics>
- <http://www.w3.org/1999/02/22-rdf-syntax-ns#type> :
  <http://dbpedia.org/class/yago/LivingPeople>
```

```
- <http://www.w3.org/1999/02/22-rdf-syntax-ns#type> :
  <http://dbpedia.org/class/yago/WimbledonChampions>
- <http://www.w3.org/1999/02/22-rdf-syntax-ns#type> :
  <http://dbpedia.org/class/yago/TennisPlayer110701180>
- <http://www.w3.org/1999/02/22-rdf-syntax-ns#type> :
  <http://dbpedia.org/class/yago/PeopleFromBasel(city)>
- <http://www.w3.org/1999/02/22-rdf-syntax-ns#type> :
  <http://dbpedia.org/class/yago/Person100007846>
- <http://www.w3.org/1999/02/22-rdf-syntax-ns#type> :
  <http://dbpedia.org/class/yago/SwissTennisPlayers>
- <http://dbpedia.org/property/doublesrecord> : 112-72
- <http://dbpedia.org/property/doublestitles> : 8
- <http://dbpedia.org/ontology/plays> :
  Right-handed; one-handed backhand
```

16.4 Summary

In this chapter, we created a Follow-Your-Nose agent in Java. It is our first project in this book, and not only does it further show the benefits of the Semantic Web, it also provides us with some frequently used programming techniques for our future development work.

Make sure you understand the following about the Follow-Your-Nose method and its Java implementation:

- Its basic concept and steps;
- Some technical details about Follow-Your-Nose agents, such as finding the properties that can be used as links, depth-first search vs. breadth-first search, error protection when it comes to dereferencing a given URI, etc.;
- Possible changes you can make to its current implementation to make it smarter and more efficient.

Besides the technical aspects of a Follow-Your-Nose agent, you should be able to appreciate more about the vision of the Semantic Web. For example,

- Using URI names for resources, and following the open linked data principles; these two together make it possible for the Follow-Your-Nose method to work on the Web of Linked Data;
- It is extremely difficult to implement a Follow-Your-Nose agent with good scalability on the traditional document Web, and you should understand the reason;

- Not only it is easy to build a scalable Follow-Your-Nose agent on the Semantic Web, but also it is almost effortless to maintain such an agent;
- The facts collected by a Follow-Your-Nose agent can also be easily queried by using a query language such as SPARQL.

Finally, this chapter also shows some useful details about issuing SPARQL queries programmatically. More specifically,

- Understand the basic steps of issuing SPARQL queries and retrieving the query result in your Java project;
- Understand the benefit of remotely querying datasets using SPARQL endpoints, and finally,
- Understand the language constructs to create the remote access.

Chapter 17
A Search Engine That Supports Rich Snippets

The more application examples you see, the better you understand the Semantic Web, and the easier you will find inspiration for your own applications. In this chapter, we build a search engine that supports rich snippets. After all, improving the performance of search engines was one of the main reasons why the Semantic Web was proposed. The search engine we build here serves as one of the possible answers in this direction.

This chapter gives us yet another chance to see how to use Jena to read and understand semantic markup documents. You may again realize that with the W3C standards in place, there are quite a few powerful tools you can use to build your applications on the Semantic Web.

Finally, this chapter requires some basic knowledge about how search engines work, which is covered in the first few sections. It is also assumed that you are familiar with Web application development. But if you are not, rest assured and read along, this chapter will still be useful to you.

17.1 Why This Is an Interesting Project

We saw Google's rich snippets in detail in Chap.10. There are indeed quite a few limitations associated with this rich snippets solution. For example, rich snippets are only generated for limited types of entities, such as events, recipes and people, just to name a few. In addition, the generated rich snippets are sometimes quite "lean"—a good example is given in Fig. 10.8.

Unfortunately, to see improved versions of these rich snippets, we have to wait for Google to make the next move. However, there is also some good news for us. More specifically, we quite often have full control of a specific domain, such as a Web site for a retailer, a Web site for a school, and so on. Within these much smaller domains, we can modify the search engine so our *own* rich snippets can be generated to help our users. This could be very helpful, especially when the Web

© Springer-Verlag Berlin Heidelberg 2014
L. Yu, *A Developer's Guide to the Semantic Web*,
DOI 10.1007/978-3-662-43796-4_17

site provides a search function and this search function is also the key for the whole Web site.

This is the main motivation for this chapter. Instead of waiting for the large environment to improve, we will create our own search engine that supports rich snippets for a specific domain. We will also show how easy it is to create such a search engine—it is actually much easier than you might have thought.

Finally, as always, this project can become a foundation and inspiration for more interesting applications. Again, the more you see, the more you will be convinced that in the world of the Semantic Web, we are only limited by our own imaginations.

17.2   Introduction to Lucene

17.2.1   Lucene and Our Own Customized Search Engine

Lucene[1] is a powerful Java search library that enables us to easily add search to *any* application that we might have. In recent years Lucene has become exceptionally popular and is now the most widely used search library in the world. It powers the search features behind many Web sites and desktop applications. Some of the Web sites include Apple, Comcast, Disney, Eclipse, IBM, LinkedIn, MusicBrainz, SnipSnap, etc. For a more complete list, check out Apache's Lucene PoweredBy list.[2] In fact, Twitter has also switched to a new backend search engine based on Lucene starting in October of 2010.[3]

A common reason why a Web site or an application might want its own search functionality is often because the Web site or application has some special needs so that a customized search engine is simply a must. For example, for Twitter, one of the search requirements is to support extremely low indexing latencies of less than 10 seconds, where indexing latency is defined as the time it takes between when a Tweet is just tweeted and when it becomes searchable.

For us, as we discussed in Sect. 17.1, our goal is to provide a Web site with search functionalities, which should leverage the added structured information contained by the searchable documents in the site. To accommodate this requirement, the Lucene search library is our best choice. We will use its fundamental framework together with our modifications to its indexer and searcher, so the semantic markups in the documents are taken into account when the search is conducted.

Understand that it is not our purpose to study how to use Lucene to create search engines. We will cover some basic components contained by the Lucene package,

---

[1] http://lucene.apache.org/

[2] http://wiki.apache.org/lucene-java/PoweredBy

[3] https://blog.twitter.com/2010/twitters-new-search-architecture

so that we can fulfill our goal. It is up to you to study more about Lucene if you are interested to do so. Also, if you don't have any background about Lucene, you should still be able to follow this chapter without too much difficulty.

17.2.2 Core Components of Lucene

Before we start to get into details about Lucene, we need to understand that Lucene itself is not a search engine. It simply provides the basic functionalities that are needed to build a search engine, and these basic functionalities are implemented by Lucene's core components such as indexer and searcher.

17.2.2.1 Lucene Document

To understand Lucene's indexer and searcher, we have to start with Lucene's fundamental units of indexing and searching: documents and fields.

Lucene's approach to model content focuses on the concept of *document*. A document is Lucene's atomic unit of indexing and searching. To index a raw content source, it must be first translated into Lucene's document. For our purpose in this chapter, a content page will be represented as a document in Lucene.

A document itself contains one or more *field*s, which in turn contain the "real" content. Each field has a name to identify itself, a value of the field and a series of detailed options that describe what Lucene should do with the field when it is added to the document.

How a source content page is mapped to a document instance is a pure design decision that is application-dependent. For example, to create a document instance to represent *The New York Times* article,[4] "Why Roger Federer Is the Greatest of All Time", one possible design could look like the one shown in Table 17.1.

Understand that at search time, it is the field values that are searched. For example, one could search for title:Federer to find all the documents whose title field value contains the term Federer. In addition, a field must be indexed in order for it to be searched.

In Table 17.1, field title will be indexed, which means search can be performed on title. It will be stored in the document, so in the search result page, the full title can be included. Similarly, field URL will not be indexed; therefore one cannot search articles by URL. However, it will be stored in the index; again, this means in the search result page, the full URL of the article can be shown.

---

[4] http://6thfloor.blogs.nytimes.com/2013/09/10/why-roger-federer-is-the-greatest-of-all-time/?_r=0

Table 17.1 Design of document instance representing a content page (article)

Field name	Field option: should be indexed?	Field option: should be stored?
title	Yes	Yes
author	No	Yes
date	No	Yes
URL	No	Yes
abstract	Yes	Yes
content	Yes	No
keywords	Yes	Yes

Finally, the field option about field content can also be easily understood. More specifically, we certainly want to index it, since it will for sure be searched, but there is no need to store it. If the article shows up in the search result page, one can always click its URL to reach the original article for its full content. Obviously, not storing the content of each article will also make sure the index does not grow too large.

Other fields contained in Table 17.1 can be understood similarly, and we will not cover them one by one. Again, it is a design decision, and it is driven by the requirements of each specific application.

17.2.2.2   Lucene Indexer

Lucene index is quite straightforward: it is a collection of documents, where each document is a container that holds fields, as we described in Sect. 17.2.2.1.

To create one such index, plain text is extracted first from the original content, since it is the only format Lucene can digest. The plain text is then used to create an instance of Document class, which in turn contains one or more instances of Field class, where the real content is held.

Understand the content in a field is not stored as it is in the index. For example, In Table 17.1, when field title is added to the index, its text content, "Why Roger Federer Is the Greatest of All Time", is not added into the index as it is. Instead, this text content is analyzed to produce a stream of *tokens*, and those tokens are what is actually added to the index.

A token is formally defined as an occurrence of a term from the text of a field. It consists of a term's text, the start and end offset of the term in the field and a type string. For us, it can be simply understood as a term from the text. However, the tokens generated from the original text content in the field are often different from the original text content. For example, field title, after being analyzed, may have the following tokens:

why, roger, federer, great, all, time

which are then added into the index file.

The above tokens are the result of three actions. The first action is to remove all the *stop words*, which are the frequent but meaningless tokens, from the text content. The second action is to lowercase all the terms, and the last action is to process the terms to reduce them to their roots.

Actions such as these are called *analyzing* the text field, and the related Java classes that implement these actions are called *analyzers*. Lucene offers quite a few analyzers; each one of them implements different actions. We will not go into the details about these analyzers. To create tokens from text fields, an analyzer is a must.

The Java class that actually combines all the above steps together and finally creates a Lucene index file is called a Lucene *indexer*. And it is our responsibility to create one, based on the requirements defined by our application. List 17.1 shows one simple indexer.

List 17.1 A simple Lucene indexer

```
1:   private void createIndex() throws IOException {
2:
3:      List<File> results = new ArrayList<File>();
4:      findFiles(results, new File(dataDir));
5:      System.out.println(results.size() + "articles to index");
6:
7:      // create index writer
8:      Directory directory = FSDirectory.open(new
8a:                                 File(indexDir));
9:      IndexWriterConfig iwconf = new
9a:        IndexWriterConfig(Version.LUCENE_43,
9b:                      new StandardAnalyzer(Version.LUCENE_43));
10:     iwconf.setOpenMode(IndexWriterConfig.OpenMode.CREATE);
11:     IndexWriter indexWriter = new
11a:                      IndexWriter(directory, iwconf);
12:
13:     // add documents to the index
14:     for(File file : results) {
15:        Document doc = getDocument(file);
16:        indexWriter.addDocument(doc);
17:     }
18:
19:     indexWriter.close();
20:     directory.close();
21:
22: }
```

To make everything simple, this indexer works on files that reside on the local hard drive (lines 3–5), instead of those harvested from the Web. The path to these articles is represented by dataDir, and all the articles are collected into results by using a utility call findFiles().

The index itself is created on local hard disk as well (lines 8–11). The path to the index file is identified by `indexDir`, and a standard analyzer is used to produce tokens. Also note that Lucene version 4.3 is used. The index writer is created by using the path to the index file and the index writer configuration together (line 11). Note both `IndexWriterConfig` and `IndexWriter` are Lucene classes.

Lines 14–17 actually create the index: for every article in `results`, a `Document` instance is created by using the `getDocument()` utility call, and then written to the index by calling the `addDocument()` method provided by the `IndexWriter` class.

List 17.2 shows the details of utility method `getDocument()`.

List 17.2 Create `Document` instance based on a simple article

```
1:     public static Document getDocument(File file) throws
1a:    IOException {
2:
3:         Properties props = new Properties();
4:         props.load(new FileInputStream(file));
5:
6:         Document doc = new Document();
7:
8:         // build fields
9:         String title = props.getProperty("title");
10:        String url = props.getProperty("url");
11:        String author = props.getProperty("author");
12:        String content = props.getProperty("content");
13:
14:
15:        // specify some field type: no indexing, but storing
16:        FieldType fieldType = new FieldType();
17:        fieldType.setIndexed(false);
18:        fieldType.setStored(true);
19:
20:        doc.add(new TextField("title", title,
20a:       Field.Store.YES));
21:        doc.add(new Field("url", url, fieldType));
22:        doc.add(new Field("author", author, fieldType));
23:        doc.add(new
23a:             TextField("content", content, Field.Store.NO));
24:
25:    return doc;
26:  }
```

Understand that `Document`, `TextField` and `Field` are all Lucene classes. `getDocument()` first reads the article file (lines 3–4). To make it simple, the content in the article file is organized as property–value pairs; therefore complex parsing is not needed. An example of one such article file is shown in List 17.3.

List 17.3 Example of one article file

```
title= Why Roger Federer Is the Greatest of All Time
url= http://6thfloor.blogs.nytimes.com/2013/09/10/why-roger-
federer-is-the-greatest-of-all-time/?_r=0
author=MICHAEL STEINBERGER
content=Yes, Roger Federer has a lousy record against Nadal. But
he's displayed a consistency and durability at a time when the
competition is deeper than it has ever been…
```

Once the article is read into memory, an instance of `Document` is created (line 6), and all the fields are extracted from the article file (lines 8–11). Each field is then mapped to a Lucene `Field` class and added to the document. For example, `title` is mapped to a `TextField` class instance, where indexing will be done and the text itself will also be stored (line 20). Note `TextField` class is a subclass of `Field` class.

For article `url`, a `Field` class instance is created, which also uses a `FieldType` instance in its constructor (line 21). Several options have been set with the `FieldType` instance as shown by lines 16–18. More specifically, no indexing will be done, but the text itself will again be stored. Since `url` is mapped with such a `FieldType` instance, it will therefore not be indexed, but will still be stored.

This simple indexer is good enough for our purpose. We will see it again in this chapter, and it will be changed with the ability to handle rich snippets. To understand the examples better, you can always check Lucene's online documentation for more details.[5]

17.2.2.3   Lucene Searcher

The last component we need is a searcher. A Lucene searcher is a complex topic by itself. For our purpose, it actually seems to be simpler than the indexer, at least at this point.

---

[5] http://lucene.apache.org/core/4_3_1/

List 17.4 shows a simple searcher based on the index we created in Sect. 17.2.2.2.

List 17.4 A simple searcher based on the index created by List 17.1

```
1:   private static void queryParserSearch(String fieldName,
1a:                String queryString) throws IOException,
1b:       org.apache.lucene.queryparser.classic.ParseException {
2:
3:     DirectoryReader ireader = DirectoryReader.open(
3a:                      FSDirectory.open(new File(indexDir)));
4:     IndexSearcher indexSearcher = new IndexSearcher(ireader);
5:
6:     QueryParser queryParser = new
6a:                QueryParser(Version.LUCENE_43, fieldName, new
6b:                      StandardAnalyzer(Version.LUCENE_43));
7:     Query query = queryParser.parse(queryString);
8:     TopDocs hits = indexSearcher.search(query,10);
9:
10:    System.out.println("searching for [" + queryString + "]:");
11:    System.out.println("the total number of hits = " +
11a:                      hits.totalHits);
12:    showQueryResult(indexSearcher,hits);
13:    ireader.close();
14: }
```

It is probably surprising to see how simple it is to actually do the search. Indeed, most of the heavy-lifting is done by Lucene's classes such as `IndexSearcher`, `QueryParser`, `Query` and `TopDocs`, as shown in List 17.4.

More specifically, the first step is to prepare the searcher. To do so, a `DirectoryReader` instance is used to open the index file on a local drive whose path is given by `indexDir`. An `IndexSearcher` instance is then created and linked together with the index file (line 4).

The second step is to parse the search string provided by the user. For example, "Roger Federer is the greatest", as the original search string, will have to be parsed into a string that looks like "roger federer great". Again, the string is lowercased, the stop words are removed, and *greatest* is reduced to its root *great*. Note the same analyzer is used here in the searcher as in the indexer so that the tokens will be produced in exactly the same way (lines 6–7).

The last step is the real search, which is actually quite straightforward: `search ()` method on `IndexSearcher` class is called (line 8), with the query created in the second step as one of its parameters. The other parameter, 10, specifies that the first ten hits should be returned.

The rest of the work depends on the specific needs of an application. For example, the search results can be simply shown by using some utility call (line

12). To get the total number of matching documents, `TopDocs.totalHits` is used (line 11).

Finally, a field name is needed to parse the search string (line 6). For our example here, the `fieldName` is `content`; therefore, the full search string looks like the following:

```
content: Roger Federer is the greatest
```

In real applications, the user is not aware of any field name, so it is up to you to attach the correct field name. It is often useful to create a so-called *catchAll* field, which combines all text into a single field for searching. This way, there is no need to decide on-the-fly which field should be searched against.

17.2.3   Use Lucene in Your Development Environment

Before you can use the Lucene Java library in your project, you must download it. Starting from Apache Lucene's download page,[6] you should be able to find the version you want. At the time of this writing, the latest version of Lucene is Lucene 4.5.1, and the code in this chapter uses Lucene 4.3.1. Besides Lucene 4.3.1, any version that is more recent than 4.3.1 can be used. However, understand that using a version other than 4.3.1 may force the code to be changed, since some classes and their method signatures do change.

To find Lucene's earlier version (such as Lucene 4.3.1), go to Lucene's archive page,[7] where earlier releases (as early as 2004) are listed, including Lucene 4.3.1.[8]

Assuming a Windows PC is used, downloading the zip file is the easiest thing to do. For example, for version 4.3.1, the file `lucene-4.3.1.zip` should be downloaded. Once the download is finished, unzip it to a location on your local drive.

Similar to Jena (see Chap. 15 for details), Lucene is a Java library, it does not have any GUI one can start and play with, and it is meant to be used together with the host Java code. To use the Lucene java library in your project, simply create a user library where useful Lucene library jars can be added, and the library itself should be included into your application project. Section 15.1.3.1 discussed how to create a user library in Eclipse using Jena library jars; the same steps described in Sect. 15.1.3.1 can be followed to create this user library of Lucene jars.

Figure 17.1 shows the user library that should be used for our project in this chapter. The name of the library is called `lucene`, but you can use any name of your choice.

---

[6] http://lucene.apache.org/core/downloads.html

[7] http://archive.apache.org/dist/lucene/java/

[8] http://archive.apache.org/dist/lucene/java/4.3.1/

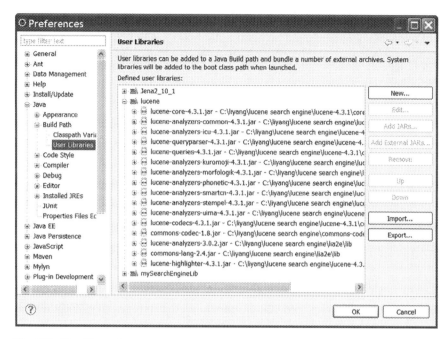

Fig. 17.1 User library `lucene`

17.3   Preparing the Semantic Markups

With the basic tutorial about Lucene Java library in place, we are ready to move on to our project. The first step of the project is to prepare the semantic markup. Recall for Google to generate rich snippets in the search result page, content publishers have to mark up their pages first. The same is true for Facebook, Twitter and Pinterest. In this section, our goal is the same: to prepare the content markup so our own rich snippets can be generated.

17.3.1   From Semantic Markup to Rich Snippets

We have discussed Google's rich snippets in great detail in Chap. 10. As great as Google's rich snippets are, they have several limitations.

First, Google supports only limited content types for generating rich snippets. For example, the supported content types include reviews, people, products, businesses/organizations, recipes, events and music. There is no compelling reason why others cannot be supported. For example, how about articles? Quite a lot of searches are conducted to find articles on a specific topic, and if rich snippets about articles could be created, they could save lots of time sifting through irrelevant results so the correct ones are reached with more easily. Similar examples can be easily found for other types.

Second, Google only supports markup by using terms from schema.org. While this does promote schema.org as a shared and more widely accepted ontology, it can limit expressiveness in some cases. There could be more flexibility for content publishers if some other popular ontologies were also supported. Some example ontologies may include FOAF, Dublin Core and Basic Geo.[9] In addition, some key terms from `owl` and `rdfs` namespaces should also be allowed; for example, `owl:sameAs` and `rdfs:seeAlso` are also very useful terms.

Third, some rich snippets generated by Google sometimes simply have too little information in them. A typical example is seen in Fig. 10.8, where a rich snippet is generated based on the markup for a person type. The rich snippet only shows location, job title and the company name. The actual markup behind Fig. 10.8 in fact provides more information than that shown in Fig. 10.8. As far as helping users is concerned, more information is nearly always more helpful.

One reason why Google has to limit the scope as discussed above may be because Google is working on the entire Web at a global scale, with simply too many content publishers, from all sorts of domains. It is therefore more important to keep it simple and easy, at least at the initial stage where the primary goal is to promote awareness of the technology itself. Once the number of marked up content pages has reached a critical mass, it could then be a better time to add more support.

On the other hand, for our project, we assume we will be working within a specific domain instead of the whole Web. The domain itself could be a government Web site where government documentations on a variety of topics are collected, and searching for the right document effectively and efficiently is always the main goal. Another possible domain could be an online retailer such as Amazon,[10] where a large number of different products are offered, and one critical requirement is to provide users with a powerful search tool that helps them to find what they are looking for quickly and easily. In general, any domain where searching is a critical piece of the functionality would be our main concern.

Since we are working within a specific domain, we will assume that we have full control. Therefore, we will support other popular ontologies besides just schema. org, and we will generate rich snippets that have more information that the ones generated by Google. This is the main idea behind this project.

17.3.2 Different Deployment Models of the Markup

Deployment of markup refers to how exactly semantic markup should be connected to the original content. There are at least two possible deployment

---

[9] http://www.w3.org/2003/01/geo/

[10] http://www.amazon.com/

models one can use. The one that we are familiar with is to have the semantic markup directly embedded into content pages. Examples include content markup for generating Google's rich snippets, content markup for Facebook's typed links, content markup for Twitter's rich cards and finally, content markup for Pinterest's rich pins.

Simplicity is one of the main advantages of the embedded deployment strategy. Information for both machines and human eyes is on the same page, and there is no need to create separate documents for the added markup. The workload on the server is therefore lighter, for obvious reasons.

Another advantage is the ability to share or reuse the same page content. List 10.7 is one good example. In List 10.7, all the added markup reuses the information that would be shown on the page. Again, this is accomplished by using the $<$span$>$ tag and the property attribute, without changing the look-and-feel of the page itself.

The second deployment choice is to collect the entire semantic markup for the original content into a separate document, and create a link between the original content and the markup document. The link itself can be either physical or logical. For example, if a content document has the following path,

```
webapps\examples\instructions.pdf
```

its semantic markup document will have this path,

```
webapps\examples\instructions.ttl
```

With this logical link, an application knows how to locate the markup file for any given content document.

It is sometimes helpful to have this second deployment model in place. For example, for an original document that is in PDF or MS Word format, it would be quite difficult to embed the markup into the document, and creating a separate markup file is a much easier solution. Also, applications can read the separate markup file directly, instead of parsing the original document to extract all the markup.

The disadvantages of using such a deployment model are also obvious: some standard about how to locate this separate markup file has to be created, and sometimes information has to be repeated in both documents, which could become a reason for inconsistent content.

In fact, for any application that recognizes the added semantic markup, regardless of whether the markup is embedded in the page or contained in a separate file, it is likely that the markup information will eventually be treated as if they were coming from a separate document: the application has to extract the markup from the original document and handle them separately.

17.3.3   Examples of Markup

Let us say we are hired by an imaginary tennis Web site, which offers tennis news, latest commentary, instructions, blogs and discussion groups. A search function is required so that readers can locate the resource they are looking for. It is our goal to provide a search engine to this imaginary Web site, and the search result page presented by this search engine shall include Google-style rich snippets for each link.

Building a full-fledged search engine is obviously a significant undertaking. Just to start, a crawler will be needed to visit this imaginary Web site to collect all the content pages within the domain. For each content page, semantic markup contained by the page has to be extracted and collected.

To focus more on the core components of the search engine and generating rich snippets, we will assume a much simpler environment. More specifically, instead of crawling any Web site, we will place some content pages into a centralized location (on a hard drive locally), and the index used by the search engine will be built from these content pages. In addition, these content pages will be simple text files, therefore avoiding the work of extracting real content from HTML pages. Finally, since the content pages are text files, separate files will be created as their corresponding markup documents, instead of embedding markup into the pages themselves.

To turn this into a practical project, it is clear which components need to be expanded. In fact, in real practice, for a Web page, before anything can be done, both the real text content and the added semantic markup have to be extracted independently from the page. The technique used to accomplish this is not closely related to the Semantic Web standards. Therefore, having organized text contents and their related markup files as existing input to our system is quite acceptable for our purpose.

Now, let us see some examples of underlying content pages and their related markup documents. List 17.3 is one good example of a content page. Note that to make it easy, not only simple text files are used, but also the content of each file is organized into property and value pairs, and therefore could be easily read and parsed by the indexer.

In general, markup should be created in such a way that it can describe the most key aspects of the page content, and the rich snippet generated based on the markup should be able to provide enough information about the content. Just by reading the rich snippet, the user should understand why the page is relevant to the original search without evening clicking through to the page itself.

To accomplish this, some basic design decisions should be made about creating markup contents. For example, Google specifies a different set of required properties for each different type. The same is true for Facebook, Twitter and Pinterest markup.

There are no required properties specified for this project. More specifically, List 17.5 shows the markup for List 17.3.

List 17.5 Markup for the content page shown in List 17.3

```
1: @prefix schema: <http://schema.org/>.
2:
3: [] a schema:Article;
4:    schema:description "an article about Roger Federer, the
4a:                       greatest of all time.";
5:    schema:about [
6:       a schema:Person;
7:       schema:familyName "Federer";
8:       schema:givenName "Roger";
9:       schema:alternateName "the Greatest of All Time";
10:      schema:jobTitle "swiss professional tennis player";
11:      schema:award "a record of 17 majors"
12:   ].
```

As shown in List 17.5, lines 3–6 say this basic fact: *this page is a* schema:
article *about a* schema:Person. Lines 7–12 express additional facts about this
person. Note the blank node (identified by []) on line 3 represents the content page;
and in general, there is no need to create a URI to uniquely represent the content
page itself. Also note that the entire person instance is represented by an anonymous
resource, again denoted by [] from lines 6–12. It is certainly fine if one wants to use
a URI to represent this person instance, but it is not a must, since it is not practical to
require content publishers to come up with URIs for their resources. Nevertheless,
List 17.6 shows the markup when a URI is used for the person instance.

List 17.6 Markup for the content page shown in List 17.3, but with a URI for the
schema:Person instance

```
1: @prefix schema: <http://schema.org/>.
2:
3: [] a schema:Article;
4:    schema:description "an article about Roger Federer, the
4a:                       greatest of all time.";
5:    schema:about <http://dbpedia.org/resource/Roger_Federer> .
6:    <http://dbpedia.org/resource/Roger_Federer> a schema:Person;
7:       schema:familyName "Federer";
8:       schema:givenName "Roger";
9:       schema:alternateName "the Greatest of All Time";
10:      schema:jobTitle "swiss professional tennis player";
11:      schema:award "a record of 17 majors" .
```

Regardless of whether a URI is used to identify the instance, the markup for each content page should always follow this basic pattern:

this page is a `class/type` *about a* `class/type`

List 17.7 shows another simple content page.

List 17.7 Another content page about a tennis event in Shanghai, China

```
title=2013 Shanghai Rolex Masters Details
url=http://en.shanghairolexmasters.com/event/details.aspx
author=unknown
content=Welcome to the 4th Edition of the Shanghai Rolex Masters,
one of the world's biggest tennis tournaments and the only such
tournament to be staged outside North America and Europe. The
Shanghai Rolex Masters is one of only nine ATP Masters 1000
tournaments in the world and is the culmination and feature event
of the Asian Swing. The Shanghai Rolex Masters was named ATP
Masters 1000 Tournament of the Year for 2009, 2010 and 2011. 2013
will also welcomes Roger Federer to play in Shanghai.
```

And List 17.8 shows the markup for this content page.

List 17.8 Markup file for List 17.7

```
1: @prefix schema: <http://schema.org/>.
2:
3: [] a schema:NewsArticle;
4:    schema:description "2013 Shanghai Rolex Masters Details.";
5:    schema:about [
6:        a schema:SportsEvent;
7:        schema:description "Shanghai Rolex Masters";
8:        schema:startDate "2013-10-5";
9:        schema:endData "2013-10-13";
10:       schema:location [
11:           a schema:Place;
12:           schema:description: "Shanghai, China"
13:       ]
14:  ].
```

Again, following the basic pattern, this markup says this page is a `schema:NewsArticle` about a `schema:SportsEvent`. Lines 7–14 simply add more details about this event.

17.4   Building the Search Engine

First off, understand the entire source code for the search engine can be found at the author's Web site. The following components should be included:

- `Chap17SearchEngineIndexer`
- `Chap17SearchEngineSearcher`
- `Chap17SearchEngineTester`
- `Chap17SearchEngineWeb`

The tester (`Chap17SearchEngineTester`) contains code that starts the indexer (`Chap17SearchEngineIndexer`), which has to be run first so an index can be created on a local hard drive. This obviously has to be done before anything else can happen. The tester also contains code to test the searcher (`Chap17SearchEngine-Searcher`), so we can make sure the searcher runs correctly before it is used in the search engine Web app. The search engine (`Chap17SearchEngineWeb`) itself is implemented by using the searcher as a one-user dependency jar, and it actually does not need to include the indexer component.

To use the source code, you will have to do some adjustments, such as configuring the path to the index file, creating related user libraries and changing package names, etc. You should be familiar with Web application development and deployment, and you will need a Web server as well.

17.4.1   Creating the Indexer

17.4.1.1   The Updated Flow of the Indexing Process

The indexer component needed by this search engine is implemented by `Indexer.java`, which can be found in the `Chap17SearchEngineIndexer` package. The `Indexer` class constructor accepts two parameters, representing two different paths. The first one points to the index file that will be created, and it should reside somewhere on your local hard drive. The second path also points to a data source directory on your hard drive, and it is the location where the indexer can find all the source documents to index, together with their markup files. As we discussed in Sect. 17.3.3, the indexer will not crawl the Web; it will simply index documents and process the related markup files from this centralized data source.

These two paths should be specified first. The following `Indexer` constructor should be used to accomplish this:

```
public Indexer(String indexPath, String dataSource) {
    indexDir = indexPath;
    dataDir = dataSource;
}
```

Some example documents and their markup files can be found from the downloaded source code. Copy these documents and their markup files to the specified data source so they become the initial files the indexer can work with. More documents and markup files should be added into this data source for more experimental runs.

The following code is used to build the index:

```
Indexer indexer = new Indexer(indexPath, dataSource);
indexer.createIndex();
```

createIndex() method actually looks a lot like List 17.1, and will not be discussed in details.

It is important to understand that for the speed of search, rich snippets are generated from the markup documents at *indexing* time and are saved into the index. At searching time, rich snippets are simply retrieved and returned to the front page. This implementation makes sure there is no searching time performance penalties incurred by rich snippets.

The code that actually handles the rich snippets is in getDocument() method, as shown in List 17.9 (again, it can be found from the indexer component from the downloaded source code package).

List 17.9 getDocument() method defined in Indexer.java

```
1:     private Document getDocument(File file) throws
1a:                         IOException {
2:
3:         Document doc = new Document();
4:
5:         // get the content from the file
6:         Properties props = new Properties();
7:         props.load(new FileInputStream(file));
8:
9:         // build fields
10:        String title = props.getProperty("title");
11:        String url = props.getProperty("url");
12:        String author = props.getProperty("author");
13:        String content = props.getProperty("content");
```

```
14:
15:     // specify some field type: no indexing, but storing
16:     FieldType fieldType = new FieldType();
17:     fieldType.setIndexed(false);
18:     fieldType.setStored(true);
19:
20:     // add to document
21:     doc.add(new TextField("title", title, Field.Store.YES));
22:     doc.add(new TextField("content", content,
22a:                          Field.Store.YES));
23:     doc.add(new TextField("everything", title+content,
23a:                          Field.Store.NO));
24:     doc.add(new Field("url", url, fieldType));
25:     doc.add(new Field("author", author, fieldType));
26:
27:     // generate the rich snippets
28:     String mfile = file.getAbsolutePath().replaceAll("txt",
28a:                                                       "ttl");
29:     doc.add(new Field("rs", getRichSnippets(mfile),
29a:                       fieldType));
30:
31:     return doc;
32:
33: }
```

As List 17.9 shows, the original document is handled by creating the related fields, with specific indexing and storing options for each field (lines 20–25). With the explanation of List 17.2 in place, understanding these lines should be easy. Note a new everything field is added—this is the *catchAll* field discussed in Sect. 17.2.2.3.

Lines 28 and 29 handle the generation of rich snippets. Line 28 locates the markup file first. Again, the deployment rule is that the original document and its corresponding markup file have exactly the same path, except that the markup file uses ttl as the file extension, indicating that the markup is expressed in Turtle format (more details in Sect. 17.3.2).

Once the markup has been located, rich snippets are generated by using getRichSnippets() method (line 29). Note the generated rich snippets are stored into the index file, but are not indexed (see the settings on FieldType class, lines 16–18). In other words, one cannot search against the rich snippets; they will only be returned together with the search result as a preview of the page content. This is simply a design decision that has been made for this project, and can certainly be made otherwise for different purposes.

17.4.1.2 Converting Semantic Markup to Rich Snippets

Method `getRichSnippets()` converts the semantic markup to rich snippets. List 17.10 shows the details of this method.

List 17.10 `getRichSnippets()` method defined in `Indexer.java`

```
1:   private String getRichSnippets(String fPath) {
2:
3:      String richSnippets = "";
4:      updateModel(fPath);
5:
6:      // find the root element of the markup
7:      RDFNode rootSubject = null;
8:      Property pAbout =
8a:              ResourceFactory.createProperty(schemaAbout);
9:      StmtIterator st = model.listStatements(null, pAbout,
9a:                        (RDFNode)null);
10:     while ( st.hasNext() ) {
11:        Statement statement = st.nextStatement();
12:        rootSubject = statement.getSubject();
13:        break;
14:     }
15:     if ( rootSubject == null ) {
16:        return richSnippets;
17:     }
18:
19:     // find the root type
20:     Resource rootType = null;
21:     st = model.listStatements((Resource)rootSubject, RDF.type,
21a:                        (RDFNode)null);
22:     while ( st.hasNext() ) {
23:        Statement statement = st.nextStatement();
24:        rootType = (Resource)(statement.getObject());
25:        break;
26:     }
27:     richSnippets += rootType.getLocalName() + ": ";
28:
29:     // find the description of root type
30:     Property pDescription =
30a:              ResourceFactory.createProperty(schemaDescription);
31:     st = model.listStatements((Resource)rootSubject,
31a:         pDescription, (RDFNode)null);
```

```
32:    while ( st.hasNext() ) {
33:       Statement statement = st.nextStatement();
34:       if ( statement.getObject().isLiteral() ) {
35:          richSnippets +=
35a:           statement.getObject().asLiteral().getString() + "\n";
36:       }
37:       break;
38:    }
39:
40:    // get into the markup details
41:    String description = "";
42:    NodeIterator nodes = model.listObjectsOfProperty(pAbout);
43:    while ( nodes.hasNext() ) {
44:       description += "About: " +
44a:                      getDescription(nodes.next(),true) + "\n";
45:    }
46:    richSnippets += description;
47:
48:    return richSnippets;
49:
50: }
```

fPath is the path of the markup file, and line 4 uses updateModel() method to read the Turtle statements contained by the markup file and create an RDF model stored in variable model. updateModel() is a utility method that can be found in the downloaded source code, and the same is true of the other utility methods.

Recall all the markup must follow the pattern of "*this page is a* class/type *about a* class/type," and the content page itself (often represented by a blank node) is the root subject. Lines 7–14 try to find this root subject by listing the statements that use schema:about as the predicate. Once such a statement is found, the subject of the statement is considered as the root subject (lines 10–12). What if there is more than one such statement? Their subjects should all be the same, as will be discussed in a later section.

Once the root subject is found, its type is retrieved and used as the start of the rich snippets (lines 20–27). Using the markup shown in List 17.5 as an example, at this point, the rich snippets can tell us, "this page is an schema:Article about ...."

Lines 30–38 find the description of the root subject, and the description is attached to the rich snippets as well. The rich snippet generated so far reads as follows:

```
Article: an article about Roger Federer, the greatest of all time.
```

Starting from line 41, the method tries to find everything about the objects of schema:about. Line 42 retrieves all these objects, and for each one of them, getDescription() method is used to retrieve the details (line 44). The detailed markup is then added to the rich snippets (line 46).

List 17.11 shows the details of getDescription() method.

List 17.11 `getDescription()` method defined in `Indexer.java`

```
1:   private String getDescription(RDFNode node, boolean showType)
1a:                   {
2:
3:     String description = "";
4:
5:     // find its type first
6:     StmtIterator st = model.listStatements((Resource)node,
RDF.type, (RDFNode)null);
7:     while ( st.hasNext() ) {
8:       Statement statement = st.nextStatement();
9:       if ( showType ) {
10:          description += "[" +
10a:   ((Resource)(statement.getObject())).getLocalName() + "] ";
11:      }
12:      break;
13:    }
14:
15:     // find other properties
16:     st = model.listStatements((Resource)node, null,
16a:                               (RDFNode)null);
17:     while ( st.hasNext() ) {
18:       Statement statement = st.nextStatement();
19:       if ( statement.getPredicate().getURI().
19a:           equalsIgnoreCase((RDF.type.getURI())) ){
20:          continue;
21:      }
22:       if ( statement.getPredicate().getURI().
22a:           equalsIgnoreCase((schemaURL)) ) {
23:          continue;
24:      }
25:       RDFNode objectNode = statement.getObject();
26:       if ( objectNode.isLiteral() ) {
27:         description += objectNode.asLiteral().getString()+";";
28:       } else {
29:          description += getDescription(objectNode, false);
30:      }
31:    }
32:
33:   return description.substring(0,description.length()-2);
34:
35: }
```

Method of `getDescription()` is a standard method. It takes a `RDFNode` instance (representing one of the objects of `schema:about` property), and collects everything that has been said about it. More specifically, it first finds the class type of this object (lines 6–13), and then collects all the statements that use this object as the subject (line 16). These statements represent the detailed markup information contained by the markup file. Using list 17.5 as an example, these statements map to lines 7–11 in List 17.5.

For each one of these statements, the object is retrieved. If it has a simple literal value (line 27), the value is retrieved and added to the rich snippets. If it uses another resource as its value, `getDescription()` is called recursively to find all the details about this new resource, as shown by line 29.

Following this pattern, the markup statements are processed one by one. When finished, a rich snippet for this document has been generated. Again, using List 17.5 as the markup example, the generated rich snippet reads as follows:

```
Article: an article about Roger Federer, the greatest of all time.
About: [Person] a record of 17 majors; swiss professional tennis
player; the Greatest of All Time; Federer; Roger
```

Again, the above rich snippet is generated at indexing time, and will be stored into the index, as shown in List 17.9, line 24. Once all the original documents and their markup files are processed, the indexing process stops, and an index file has been created on your local drive, at the location that you have specified.

17.4.1.3   Examining the Generated Index

There are tools one can use to actually examine the generated index file to see if it looks like what we have in mind. One such tool is called Luke—Lucene Index Toolbox.[11] It provides a download page[12] to find different versions one can download. Since Lucene 4.3.1 is the version used for this project, lukeall-4.3.1.jar should be downloaded.

Once download, you can easily use Luke to examine the generated index file. You need to provide the path to Luke for it to know where to find your index. After that, using Luke is quite self-explanatory. Figure 17.2 shows one example of examining the index file we have created for this project.

---

[11] http://code.google.com/p/luke/

[12] https://java.net/projects/opengrok/downloads

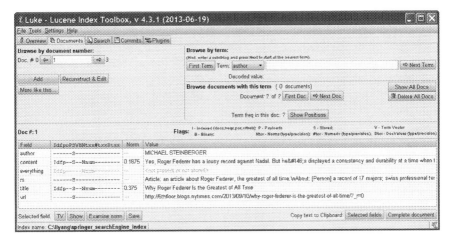

Fig. 17.2 Use Luke to check the index file created by List 17.9

17.4.2 Creating the Searcher

17.4.2.1 The Updated Flow of the Searching Process

The searcher component of this search engine is implemented by `Searcher.java`, which can be found in `Chap17SearchEngineSearcher` package. `Searcher` class has two constructors. The default constructor does not accept any parameter; it uses a hard-coded path as the location of the index file. If this is the constructor to be used, the path to the index file has to be the same as the path used by the indexer. The second constructor takes the path as an input parameter, and therefore offers more flexibility to its users.

For example, the following code can be used to start the searcher:

```
Searcher searcher = new Searcher();
searcher.queryParserSearch("content", searchString);
```

`queryParserSearch()` method actually looks a lot like List 17.4 and will not be discussed here in details Understand that `searchString` is the query string the user enters, and `content` is the name of the field that the searcher will search against. Recall we have actually created a catchAll field called `everything` at indexing time (line 23 in List 17.9), it is therefore a good idea to use this field if it is not possible to tell on-the-fly against which field the search should be conducted.

Finally, note that inside `queryParserSearch()`, `StandardAnalyzer` is used to parse the user query string. The same analyzer is also used by the indexer, as seen in lines 9 and 9a of List 17.1. Although not necessary, it is often the case that both the indexer and the searcher use the same analyzer so that the original document

content and the search sting will be similarly tokenized, therefore maximizing the
chancing of find the right hit.

Compared to List 17.4, our searcher also uses a highlighter.[13] A highlighter can
highlight matching terms in text and further extract the most relevant section from
the text. This is obviously a very useful feature since it directly tells the users why
the underlying document is relevant to the search. Note there are different versions
of highlighters; since we are using Lucene 4.3.1, we therefore should use Lucene
highlighter 4.3.1, which can be downloaded online.[14] List 17.12 shows how the
highlighter is used.

List 17.12 getHighlightText() method defined in Searcher.java

```
1:    private String getHighlightText(Query query, Analyzer
1a:              analyzer, String fieldName, String text)
2:    throws IOException, InvalidTokenOffsetsException {
3:
4:       SimpleHTMLFormatter formatter = new
4a:         SimpleHTMLFormatter("<span
4b:                            class=\"highlight\">","</span>");
5:       TokenStream tokenStream = analyzer.tokenStream(fieldName,
5a:                              new StringReader(text));
6:       QueryScorer scorer = new QueryScorer(query, fieldName);
7:       Fragmenter fragmenter = new SimpleSpanFragmenter(scorer);
8:       Highlighter highlighter = new
8a:              Highlighter(formatter,scorer);
9:       highlighter.setTextFragmenter(fragmenter);
10:
11:      String tmpS = highlighter.getBestFragment(tokenStream,
11a:                 text);
12:
13:      String result = "<style>" + "\n" + ".highlight {" + "\n"
13a:               + " background: yellow; " + "\n" + "}"
13b:               + "\n" + "</style>" + tmpS;
14:      return result;
15:
16:  }
```

---

[13] http://lucene.apache.org/core/4_3_1/highlighter/org/apache/lucene/search/highlight/High
lighter.html

[14] http://grepcode.com/snapshot/repo1.maven.org/maven2/org.apache.lucene/lucene-highlighter/
4.3.1/

As shown in List 17.12, `SimpleHTMLFormatter`, `Fragmenter`, `QueryScorer` and `Highlighter` are all classes defined in the highlighter package, and their usage is quite straightforward. `getBestFragment()` is the key method (line 11); it extracts the most relevant section from the text, and also highlights the matching terms. Note that background yellow is hard-coded as the highlight color (line 13a), but one can easily make it a parameter so the background highlight color can be controlled more dynamically.

Finally, List 17.13 shows how the searcher collects the matching results. With the above discussion in place, it is quite easy to follow.

List 17.13 `showQueryResultWithHighlight()` method defined in Searcher.java

```
1:   private void showQueryResultWithHighlight(IndexSearcher is,
1a:            TopDocs hits, Query query, String fieldName)
1b:            throws IOException, InvalidTokenOffsetsException {
3:
4:      Analyzer analyzer = new
4a:                          StandardAnalyzer(Version.LUCENE_43);
5:      for(ScoreDoc scoreDoc : hits.scoreDocs) {
6:         Document doc = is.doc(scoreDoc.doc);
7:         String url = "<br>" + "<a href=\""+ doc.get("url")
7a:                     + "\">" + doc.get("url") + "</a> </br>";
8:         String tmpResult = url + getHighlightText(query,
8a:               analyzer, fieldName, doc.get(fieldName));
9:         results.add(tmpResult + getRichSnippets(doc,
9a:                             RICH_SNIPPETS));
10:     }
11: }
```

Once the searcher finishes the search, it calls `showQueryResultWith-Highlight()` shown in List 17.13 to collect the matching results. This method loops over all the matching documents (lines 5–10), and for each document, it retrieves the URL of the document (line 7) and the highlighted matching content (line 8a), and stores this information in the `results` array. Note it also makes a call to `getRichSnippets()`, where the rich snippet for each matching document is retrieved and then stored in the result set. Let us take a look at this method in the next section in more detail.

17.4.2.2   Retrieving the Rich Snippets

Method `getRichSnippets()` converts the semantic markup to rich snippets. List 17.14 shows the details of this method.

List 17.14 `getRichSnippets()` method defined in `Searcher.java`

```
1:   private String getRichSnippets(Document doc,
1a:                                  String fieldName) {
2:
3:      String richSnippets = doc.get(fieldName);
4:      if ( richSnippets == null || richSnippets.length() == 0 )
4a:     {
5:         return "";
6:      }
7:
8:      String styleString = "<style>" + "\n" + ".richsnippets {"
8a:                           + "\n" + " color:gray;" + "\n"
8b:                           + "}" + "\n" + "</style>";
9:
10:     if ( richSnippets.contains("\n") == false ) {
11:        return styleString +
11a:           "<br><span class=\"richsnippets\">" +
11b:           richSnippets + "</span></br>";
12:     }
13:
14:     String result = "";
15:     StringTokenizer rs = new StringTokenizer(richSnippets,
15a:                          "\n");
16:     while (rs.hasMoreElements()) {
17:        result += (String)(rs.nextElement()) + "</br>";
18:     }
19:     return styleString + "<br><span class=\"richsnippets\">" +
19a:        result + "</span></br>";
20:
21: }
```

This method first retrieves the rich snippets from the document (line 3). If there is no rich snippet attached to the current document, an empty string is returned (lines 4–6). If there are indeed some rich snippets associated with this document, they are retrieved line by line, with some specific HTML style code embedded for showing them on the front page (line 8–19).

Again, note how rich snippets are processed at searching time: only a simple retrieval is executed, and the rich snippets themselves are prepared and stored at indexing time. This is why supporting rich snippets does not hurt the search performance, as we claimed earlier.

17.4.2.3 Passing the Rich Snippets to the Front

Passing the rich snippets back to the front is very easy. As shown on line 9 of List 17.13, rich snippets is part of the string stored in the `results` array list. Searcher class provides two accessor calls to retrieve the `results` array, as shown in List 17.15.

List 17.15 Accessor methods defined in `Searcher.java` to retrieve results array, which contains rich snippets

```
1:      public String getBestResult() {
2:          if (results.size() > 0 ) {
3:              return results.get(0);
4:          } else {
5:              return "nothing found";
6:          }
7:      }
8:
9:      public List<String> getAllResults() {
10:         return results;
11:     }
```

method `getBestResult()` returns only the best match and its associated rich snippet, and `getAllResults()` returns the top ten matching documents, together with their rich snippets. We will see how these accessor calls can be used when the search engine interface is built in next section.

17.4.3 Using Web Container to Start the Search

17.4.3.1 Using Apache Web Server for the Search Interface

For a Web-based search engine to work, we will need to build an indexer, a searcher and a search interface together with search result rendering. Now that we have developed our indexer and searcher, it is time to create the search interface itself.

The search interface represents the overall look-and-feel of the search engine. It accepts a search string from the user, invokes the searcher, and then renders the search results back to the user. This basic flow can become much more complex in real production. For example, a production-level search engine can handle automatic spelling check, autocomplete (or word completion), or even specific searches such as weather forecasts, home listing, stock quotes, etc.

The search interface itself is often a well-defined Web application, and it therefore requires a Web server as its container. For our purpose, Apache Tomcat is an excellent choice.[15] The code in this chapter has been tested on Apache Tomcat 7.0 server, although other versions should work fine as well.

In general, to make this work, you will have to first download the server from Apache's download page,[16] install the server on your local machine, configure it based on your needs and then test it to make sure it works well. This chapter does not cover these steps in detail, but Apache's documentation site[17] provides plenty of information in this regard.

Once you have Apache Tomcat server ready, we can move on to the development of the search interface (see the next section). The search interface can be implemented by using simple Java Servlets, or some more advanced MVC framework, such as Struts,[18] can be adopted.

The code in this chapter uses the Strut2 framework. You can find all the Java classes and key configuration files in the downloaded code. It requires some knowledge and experience in order to use these configuration files for the Struts2 framework. In addition, you need to understand how to deploy the application to the server. If you decide to use frameworks other than Struts, the Java classes can certainly be reused, but you will need to configure the server yourself.

17.4.3.2 Rendering the Rich Snippets in Search Result

The search interface itself is quite straightforward. List 17.16 shows the start page of the search engine, which accepts a search string from the user.

---

[15] http://tomcat.apache.org/

[16] http://tomcat.apache.org/download-70.cgi

[17] http://tomcat.apache.org/tomcat-7.0-doc/index.html

[18] http://struts.apache.org/

List 17.16 Start page that accepts the search string from the user

```
1: <%@ page language="java" contentType="text/html;
1a:    charset=UTF-8" pageEncoding="UTF-8"%>
2: <%@ taglib prefix="s" uri="/struts-tags"%>
3: <!DOCTYPE html PUBLIC "-//W3C//DTD HTML 4.01 Transitional//EN"
3a:                      "http://www.w3.org/TR/html4/loose.dtd">
4:
5: <html>
6: <head>
7: <title>my search engine</title>
8: <meta http-equiv='Content-Type' content='text/html;
8a:       charset=UTF-8' />
9: </head>
10: <body>
11:
12: <div id="container">
13:
14:    <div id="header" style="background-color:#C8C8C8;
14a:       text-align:center;">
15:      <h3 style="color:#FFFFFF;">  search engine that
15a:          supports rich snippets </h3>
16:    </div>
17:
18:    <div id="content" style="background-color:#F8F8F8;
18a:       text-align:center;">
19:      <form action="search" method="POST">
20:         <input type="text" name="searchString"/>
21:         <input type="submit" value="find"/>
22:      </form>
23:    </div>
24:
25: </div>
26:
27: </body>
28: </html>
```

This does not require much of an explanation. Once the user enters a search string, action search maps to the Java class shown in List 17.17.

List 17.17 `SearchAction` class implements searching against the indexer

```
1: public class SearchAction   {
2:
3:    private String  searchString;
4:    private List<String> searchResults;
5:
6:    public String execute() throws Exception {
7:
8:        Searcher searcher = new Searcher();
9:        try {
10:           searcher.queryParserSearch("content",
10a:                                      searchString);
11:        } catch (Exception e) {
12:            e.printStackTrace();
13:        }
14:        setSearchResults(searcher.getAllResults());
15:        searcher.closeSearcher();
16:        return "success";
17:    }
18:
19:    public List<String> getSearchResults() {
20:        return searchResults;
21:    }
22:
23:    public void setSearchResults(List<String> searchResults) {
24:        this.searchResults = searchResults;
25:    }
26:
27:    public String getSearchString() {
28:        return searchString;
29:    }
30:
31:    public void setSearchString(String searchString) {
32:        this.searchString = searchString;
33:    }
34:
35: }
```

Class `SearchAction` is a typical Struts2 action class. After the search string is submitted by the user, method `execute()` is invoked (lines 6–17). Once the search is finished, success is passed back to the Struts configuration file, and another JSP page is then used to render the result. List 17.18 shows this JSP page.

List 17.18 `SearchResults.jsp` page that renders the search results

```
1: <%@ page contentType="text/html; charset=UTF-8" %>
2: <%@ taglib prefix="s" uri="/struts-tags" %>
3: <%@ taglib prefix="c"
3a:    uri="http://java.sun.com/jsp/jstl/core"%>
4:
5: <html>
6: <head>
7: <title>search results</title>
8: <meta http-equiv='Content-Type' content='text/html;
8a:       charset=UTF-8' />
9: </head>
10:
11: <body>
12:
13: <div id="container">
14:
15:    <div id="header" style="background-color:#C8C8C8;
15a:        text-align:center;">
16:       <h3 style="color:#FFFFFF;">search result</h3>
17:    </div>
18:
19:    <div id="content" style="background-color:#F8F8F8;">
20:       <p> you are searching for: <s:property
20a:          value="searchString" escape="false" /> </p>
21:       <table>
22:          <s:iterator value="searchResults"
22a:                       status="searchResultsStatus">
23:          <tr>
24:            <td><s:property escape="false" /></td>
25:          </tr>
26:          </s:iterator>
27:       </table>
28:       <p></p>
29:       <form action="search" method="POST">
30:          <input type="hidden" name="originalSearch"
30a:               value="true" />
31:          <input type="text" name="searchString"/>
32:          <input type="submit" value="search"/>
33:       </form>
34:    </div>
35:
36: </div>
37:
38: </body>
39: </html>
```

This again is quite straightforward. In addition to Lists 17.16–17.18 as the core components of the search interface, List 17.19 shows the Struts2 configuration file that glues these components together:

List 17.19 `struts.xml` used in our search engine

```
 1: <?xml version="1.0" encoding="UTF-8"?>
 2: <!DOCTYPE struts PUBLIC
 3:  "-//Apache Software Foundation//DTD Struts
3a: Configuration 2.0//EN"
 4:  "http://struts.apache.org/dtds/struts-2.0.dtd">
 5: <struts>
 6:    <constant name="struts.devMode" value="true" />
 7:    <package name="searchWorld" extends="struts-default">
 8:       <action name="search"
 9:         class="springer.book.search.action.SearchAction"
10:         method="execute">
11:         <result name="success">/SearchResults.jsp</result>
12:      </action>
13:    </package>
14: </struts>
```

17.5   Test It Out and Possible Expansions

17.5.1   Test Runs of the Search Engine

Now that we have the search engine ready, we can try it out. Figure 17.3 shows the initial screen of the search engine, where a user can enter a search string to start the search.

Figure 17.4 shows the search result for the search string "roger federer".

As shown in Fig. 17.4, each resulting page is represented by three pieces of information. The first piece is the URL that one can click to go to the original document; the second piece is a summary of the content, with the key matching terms highlighted. The last piece is the rich snippets, which show the *meaning* of each document.

It is obvious how rich snippets can help a user to determine the relevance of a search result page. For example, the last link shows up in the result set only because Roger Federer's name appears in the article; however, the article itself is a news article about a sports event in Shanghai. It has nothing much about Federer as a tennis player. As a comparison, the second result link is an article about Federer as a person, a tennis player who has won 17 major titles. So if a user is looking for some reading about Federer's achievement, the second article is a much better choice.

Fig. 17.3 Initial search engine search screen

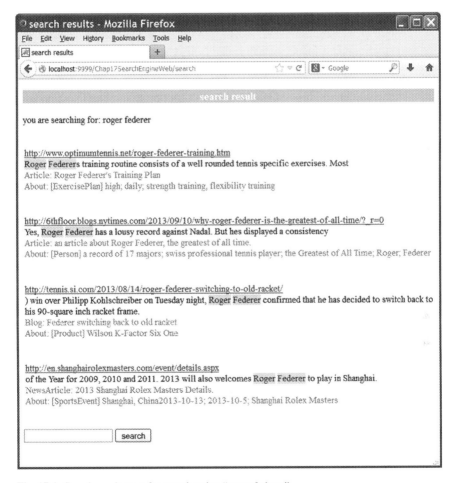

Fig. 17.4 Search result page for search string "roger federer"

17.5.2 Possible Expansions

There are two different types of possible improvements for this search engine. The
first type is about the search engine itself; the second is about the rich snippets—the
semantic part of the search engine.

We are not going to spend too much time on the first type of improvements,
although there is actually a lot of room for this type. For example, one can add
paging control to the search engine. For now, we only search for the top ten results
and we don't offer any paging mechanism at all. What if there are more than ten hits
and we actually have to present the results in multiple pages? Another possible
improvement is about the searching field. In its current version, searching is
implemented against the content field. It could be a better idea to implement the
search against the catchAll field, as we discussed early in this chapter.

The improvements along the rich snippets side will be limited only by our imagination. Let us use two examples to show some possible ones. One possible improvement is to link the markup to the open data cloud, therefore the search engine can use
the markup to create even richer snippets. List 17.20 shows one such example.

List 17.20 Add link to the open data cloud in the markup

```
@prefix schema: <http://schema.org/>.

[] a schema:Article;
   schema:description "an article about Roger Federer, the
greatest of all time.";
   schema:about [
     a schema:Person;
     schema:familyName "Federer";
     schema:givenName "Roger";
     schema:alternateName "the Greatest of All Time";
     schema:jobTitle "swiss professional tennis player";
     schema:sameAs <http://dbpedia.org/resource/Roger_Federer>;
     schema:award "a record of 17 majors"
   ].
```

At indexing time, a search engine can actually use schema:sameAs to
dereference the URL, and therefore to get more structured information about
Federer. The extra information obtained from the open data cloud can then be
added into the generated rich snippets; therefore even richer information can be
presented on the final search result page.

Understand that we have been using anonymous nodes to represent the instance
on page. It is certainly fine to use a specific URI if needed. List 17.21 shows a
markup that uses URI explicitly.

List 17.21 Use URI to explicitly name the instance

```
@prefix schema: <http://schema.org/>.


[] a schema:Article;
   schema:description "an article about Roger Federer, the
greatest of all time.";
   schema:about <http://dbpedia.org/resource/Roger_Federer> .
   <http://dbpedia.org/resource/Roger_Federer> a schema:Person;
      schema:familyName "Federer";
      schema:givenName "Roger";
      schema:award "a record of 17 majors" .
```

Another extension example is to include *multiple* instances in a single markup document. Up to this point, all the markup examples we have been using are about one single instance. What if we wanted to express the fact that one article is about a tennis event, and also about a tennis player named Federer? List 17.22 shows how this can be accomplished.

List 17.22 Describe two instances in a single markup document

```
@prefix schema: <http://schema.org/>.

[] a schema:NewsArticle;
   schema:description "2013 Shanghai Rolex Masters Details.";
   schema:about [
     a schema:SportsEvent;
     schema:url "http://en.shanghairolexmasters.com/index.aspx";
     schema:description "Shanghai Rolex Masters";
     schema:location [
       a schema:Place;
       schema:description: "Shanghai, China"
     ]
   ];
   schema:about [
     a schema:Person;
     schema:familyName "Federer";
     schema:givenName "Roger";
     schema:alternateName "the Greatest of All Time";
     schema:jobTitle "swiss professional tennis player";
     schema:sameAs <http://dbpedia.org/resource/Roger_Federer>;
     schema:award "a record of 17 majors"
   ].
```

There are certainly other extensions one can think of and propose. Again, the goal is to make the final search results as clear as possible to the users, so they understand why a page is important without even clicking though it.

We encourage more extensions, and finally for us, the best extension is to know that you have developed a search engine that supports rich snippets for your own domain, and that search engine is enjoyed and used by many happy customers within your organization.

17.6   Summary

This chapter shows how the Semantic Web idea can be used to enhance the performance of a search engine. In particular, we discuss the details of building a search engine that supports Google-style rich snippets. Its design and implementation are discussed carefully and can be directly used in other projects.

This chapter is closely related to Chap. 10. After reading this chapter, you should be able to understand the implementation presented here in this chapter and you should be able to develop customized search engines that support rich snippets for different organizations.

Chapter 18
More Application Examples
on the Semantic Web

The goal of this chapter is to continue showing you the *How-To* part of the Semantic Web. We will build two application examples, which are more complex than the ones we have created in the last two chapters. To some extent, none of these two applications here is final yet; it is up to you to make them more intelligent and powerful.

By this final chapter of this book, we hope you are convinced that in the Semantic Web, the possibility of developing different applications is only limited by our imaginations. The two application examples presented here should serve as hints, so you can discover and plan your own applications, which I hope, will show more of the value of the Semantic Web.

18.1 Building Your Circle of Trust: A FOAF Agent You Can Use

In the first part of this chapter we build a FOAF agent so you can receive only secured incoming e-mails. The rest of this section presents the details of this agent.

18.1.1 Who Is on Your E-Mail List?

It is safe to say that most of us use at least one e-mail system of some kind. As much as we love e-mail as a communication tool, we also know that there are several things that can threaten the usefulness of a given e-mail system. For example, e-mail bombardment, spamming, phishing (to acquire sensitive information

© Springer-Verlag Berlin Heidelberg 2014   773
L. Yu, *A Developer's Guide to the Semantic Web*,
DOI 10.1007/978-3-662-43796-4_18

fraudulently, such as your user name, password, credit card number, etc.) and certainly, e-mail worms, just to name a few.

To reduce these threats, different e-mail systems have implemented different security measures. One solution is to simply block any e-mail address that has never been used in the system before. For example, if a given incoming e-mail is sent from an e-mail address with whom you have never exchanged e-mail, the system directly routes this e-mail into the spam box.

Obviously, this strategy can result in the loss of some e-mail messages that are actually important. On the other hand, if a given e-mail address is stored in the address book beforehand, the system assumes this e-mail address is trustworthy and does not trash any e-mail message from this address, even if there has never yet been any communication with this address.

Therefore, to take advantage of this security measure and to also make sure that you are getting all your e-mails, a good solution is to add all the trustworthy e-mail addresses into your contact book ahead of time, a process we call "building your circle of trust".

The difficult part of this solution is that you cannot foresee who would send you e-mail, especially those people whom you don't know yet. In addition, manually editing this circle of trust is quite tedious. An automatic way of building the e-mail address directory and also dynamically updating it would be a much better approach.

With help from Semantic Web technology, it is possible to create an automatic tool like this. One solution is based on the linked FOAF documents on the Web, which we discuss in this section. The reason for using linked FOAF data is obvious: it is linked data which machines can process, and it is about human networking with e-mail addresses as one of its common data elements.

18.1.2   The Basic Idea

Let us think about a given FOAF document. Obviously, if its author has indicated that she/he has a friend by using `foaf:knows` property, it is then safe to collect that person's e-mail address into the author's circle of trust.

Based on this approach, when we scan the author's FOAF file, we should at least collect all the e-mail addresses of the friends that have been mentioned in this document. This step can be easily done by following the `foaf:knows` property.

To extend the author's e-mail list, the next step is to explore his/her social network. To do so, the following assumption is made: if any of the author's friends is trustable, this friend's friend should also be trustable, and this friend's friend's friend is also trustable, and so forth, and all their e-mail addresses can be included in the circle of trust. This is a reasonable and plausible assumption—after all, the FOAF project itself is about "Friend of a Friend"!

Therefore, to extend the e-mail list for the author, we take one of the author's friends, and check her/his FOAF document to collect the e-mail addresses of all her/his friends. We then repeat this collection process until all the documents from all the friends of friends have been explored.

To put this idea into action, let us start with Dan Brickley, the creator of the FOAF project. We will use his FOAF file as the starting point and build a trusted e-mail list for him. To see how we are going to proceed, take a look at List 18.1, which is taken from his current FOAF document:

List 18.1 Part of the statements from Dan Brickley's FOAF document

```
1:   <knows>
2:     <Person>
3:       <mbox rdf:resource="mailto:libby.miller@bristol.ac.uk"/>
4:       <mbox rdf:resource="mailto:libby@asemantics.com"/>
5:     </Person>
6:   </knows>
7:
8:   <knows>
9:     <Person
9a:       rdf:about="http://www.w3.org/People/Berners-Lee/card#i">
10:       <name>Tim Berners-Lee</name>
11:       <isPrimaryTopicOf rdf:resource=
11a:             "http://en.wikipedia.org/wiki/Tim_Berners-Lee"/>
12:       <homepage rdf:resource=
12a:             "http://www.w3.org/People/Berners-Lee/"/>
13:       <mbox rdf:resource="mailto:timbl@w3.org"/>
14:       <rdfs:seeAlso rdf:resource=
14a:             "http://www.w3.org/People/Berners-Lee/card"/>
15:     </Person>
16:   </knows>
17:
18:   <knows>
19:     <Person>
20:       <name>Dean Jackson</name>
21:       <rdfs:seeAlso rdf:resource=
21a:             "http://www.grorg.org/dean/foaf.rdf"/>
22:       <mbox rdf:resource="mailto:dean@w3.org"/>
23:       <mbox rdf:resource="mailto:dino@grorg.org"/>
24:       <mbox_sha1sum>
24a:         6de4ff27ef927b9ba21ccc88257e41a2d7e7d293</mbox_sha1sum>
25:       <homepage rdf:resource="http://www.grorg.org/dean/"/>
26:     </Person>
27:   </knows>
```

Notice List 18.1 shows three different ways of adding a friend into a FOAF document:

- Lines 1–6 are the simplest way to add one friend: only the e-mail address is given, no URI is included and no `rdfs:seeAlso` is used when describing the friend.
- Lines 18–27 show the second way of describing a friend: the e-mail address is provided, `rdfs:seeAlso` is used to provide more information about the friend (line 21), however, no URI of the friend is given.
- Lines 8–16 give the third way of adding a friend: the URI of the friend is provided (line 9), the e-mail address is given and `rdfs:seeAlso` is also used (line 14).

These three different ways of describing a friend in a FOAF document have no effect on how we collect the e-mail addresses from these friends, but they do mean different methods of exploring the social network. More specifically, the third method gives us the most information we can use when it come to exploring the network:

- We can dereference the given URI of the friend to get more email addresses.

On the Web of Linked Data, we can assume data publishers follow the principles of Linked Data. As a result, if we deference the URI of a friend, we should get an RDF document that describe this friend, and we can expect to find the e-mail addresses of her/his friends.

For example, in List 18.1, one URI is given by the following (line 9):

```
http://www.w3.org/People/Berners-Lee/card#i
```

and we can get e-mail addresses of Tim Berners-Lee's friends when we dereference this URI.

- We can follow the `rdfs:seeAlso` link to extend the network even more.

`rdfs:seeAlso` does not have formal semantics defined, i.e., its `rdfs:domain` property and `rdfs:range` property are all general `rdfs:Resource` class. However, it does specify another resource that might provide additional information about the subject resource. As a result, we can follow this link, i.e., dereference the object resource, which should provide information about this friend, and it is also possible to locate some more e-mail addresses of this friend's friends. For example, in List 18.1, line 14 provides a URI that can be dereferenced as discussed above.

With this understanding of the third method, the second method (lines 18–27 in List 18.1) is simpler: all we can do is to follow the `rdfs:seeAlso` link since there is no friend's URI we can dereference. Therefore, the second way of adding friends gives us less chance of expanding the e-mail list.

By the same token, the first method (lines 1–6, List 18.1) does not allow us to do any further exploring directly; all we can do is collect the e-mail address there and stop. Notice that theoretically we can still find the FOAF file of this friend (Libby Miller), however, we are not going to do that in this example. Instead, we simply stop exploring the subnetwork headed by this particular friend.

As a side note, how do we find a person's FOAF file if we only have his e-mail address from the `foaf:mbox` property? Since `foaf:mbox` is an inverse functional property, the simplest solution is to visit the Web, and check each and every single FOAF document you can encounter, until you have located one document whose main subject also assumes the same value on `foaf:mbox` property. That main subject, a `foaf:Person` instance, should be the resource you are looking for. As you can tell, the reason why we are not implementing this solution is mainly due to the consideration of the efficiency of our agent. If you ever want to change this example into a real-world application, you might consider implementing this part.

18.1.3 Building the `EmailAddressCollector` Agent

18.1.3.1 `EmailAddressCollector`

Based on our previous discussion, the algorithm of the e-mail list builder agent is fairly straightforward:

0. Make Dan Brickley's URI our `currentURI`
1. Dereference `currentURI`, which gives us an RDF document back that we call `currentRDFDocument`.
2. From `currentRDFDocument`, collect all the e-mail addresses of Dan's friends.
3. For each friend, if she/he has a representing URI, add this URI into `friendsToVisit` (an `URICollection` instance); if she/he also has an `rdfs:seeAlso` property defined, collect the object URI of this property into `friendsToVisit` as well.
4. Repeat step 3 until all friends are covered.
5. Retrieve a new URI from `friendsToVisit` collection, make it `currentURI`, and go back to step 1. If no URI is left in `friendsToVisit` collection, stop.

The code is given in List 18.2.

List 18.2 `EmailAddressCollector.java` definition

```
1: package test;
2:
3: import java.util.HashSet;
4: import java.util.Iterator;
5:
6: import com.hp.hpl.jena.query.Query;
7: import com.hp.hpl.jena.query.QueryExecution;
8: import com.hp.hpl.jena.query.QueryExecutionFactory;
9: import com.hp.hpl.jena.query.QueryFactory;
10: import com.hp.hpl.jena.query.QuerySolution;
11: import com.hp.hpl.jena.query.ResultSet;
12: import com.hp.hpl.jena.rdf.model.Literal;
13: import com.hp.hpl.jena.rdf.model.Model;
14: import com.hp.hpl.jena.rdf.model.ModelFactory;
15: import com.hp.hpl.jena.rdf.model.RDFNode;
16: import com.hp.hpl.jena.rdf.model.Resource;
17: import com.hp.hpl.jena.sparql.vocabulary.FOAF;
18: import com.hp.hpl.jena.vocabulary.RDFS;
19:
20: public class EmailAddressCollector {
21:
22:    private URICollection friendsToVisit = null;
23:    private HashSet emailAddresses = null;
24:
25:    public EmailAddressCollector(String uri) {
26:       emailAddresses = new HashSet();
27:       friendsToVisit = new URICollection();
28:       friendsToVisit.addNewURI(uri);
29:    }
30:
31:    public void work() {
32:
33:      // get the next URI to work on (step 1 in algorithm)
34:      String currentURI = friendsToVisit.getNextURI();
35:      if ( currentURI == null ) {
36:         return;
37:      }
38:
39:      try {
40:         System.out.println("\n...visiting <" +
40a:                              currentURI + ">");
41:
42:         // dereference currentURI (step 1 in algorithm)
43:         Model currentRDFDocument =
43a:                       ModelFactory.createDefaultModel();
```

```
44:          currentRDFDocument.read(currentURI);
45:
46:          // collect everything about currentURI
46a:         // (step 2-4 in algorithm)
47:          int currentSize = friendsToVisit.getSize();
48:          collectData(currentRDFDocument,currentURI);
49:          System.out.println("..." + emailAddresses.size() +
49a:                             " email addresses collected.");
50:          System.out.println("..." + (friendsToVisit.getSize() -
50a:                      currentSize) + " new friends URI added.");
51:          System.out.println("...all together " +
51a:               friendsToVisit.getSize() + " more to visit.");
52:
53:       } catch (Exception e) {
54:          System.out.println("*** errors when handling (" +
54a:                             currentURI + ") ***");
55:       }
56:
57:       // extend the social network by following
57a:       //  friends of friends' (step 5 in algorithm)
58:       work();
59:
60:    }
61:
62:    private void collectData(Model model, String uri) {
63:
64:       if ( uri == null ) {
65:          return;
66:       }
67:
68:       String queryString =
69:        "SELECT ?myself ?who ?email ?seeAlso " +
70:        "WHERE {" +
71:        "  ?myself <" + FOAF.knows + "> ?who. " +
72:        "  optional { ?who <" + FOAF.mbox + "> ?email. }" +
73:        "  optional { ?who <" + RDFS.seeAlso + "> ?seeAlso. }" +
74:        "   }";
75:
76:
77:       Query query = QueryFactory.create(queryString);
78:       QueryExecution qe =
78a:                   QueryExecutionFactory.create(query,model);
79:
80:       try {
```

```
81:         ResultSet results = qe.execSelect();
82:         while ( results.hasNext() ) {
83:
84:           QuerySolution soln = results.nextSolution() ;
85:           Resource who = (Resource)(soln.get("who"));
86:
87:           // step 2 in algorithm
88:           Resource email = (Resource)soln.get("email");
89:           if ( email != null ) {
90:             if ( email.isLiteral() ) {
91:               emailAddresses.add(((Literal)email).
91a:                                  getLexicalForm());
92:             } else if ( email.isResource() ) {
93:               emailAddresses.add(email.getURI());
94:             }
95:           } else {
96:               // there is no foaf:mbox property value
96a:              // for this friend
97:           }
98:
99:           // step 3 in algorithm
100:          if ( who.isAnon() == false ) {
101:             friendsToVisit.addNewURI(who.getURI());
102:          } else {
103:             // there is no URI specified for this friend
104:          }
105:
106:          // step 3 in algorithm
107:          Resource seeAlso = (Resource)soln.get("seeAlso");
108:          if ( seeAlso != null ) {
109:            if ( seeAlso.isLiteral() ) {
110:              friendsToVisit.addNewURI(((Literal)seeAlso).
110a:                                 getLexicalForm());
111:            } else if ( seeAlso.isResource() ) {
112:              friendsToVisit.addNewURI(seeAlso.getURI());
113:            }
114:          } else {
115:             // there is no rdfs:seeAlso property specified
115a:            // for this friend
116:          }
117:
118:        }
119:    }
```

```
120:      catch(Exception e) {
121:         // doing nothing for now
122:      }
123:      finally {
124:         qe.close();
125:      }
126:
127:   }
128:
129:  public void showemailAddresses() {
130:     if ( emailAddresses != null ) {
131:       Iterator it = emailAddresses.iterator();
132:       int counter = 1;
133:       while ( it.hasNext() ) {
134:          System.out.println(counter + ": " +
134a:                             it.next().toString());
135:          counter ++;
136:       }
137:     }
138:   }
139:
140: }
```

Lines 25–29 are the constructor of the EmailAddressCollector agent. The URI that is passed in to this constructor represents the person for whom we would like to create an e-mail list. In our example, this is Dan Brickley's URI given by the following:

http://danbri.org/foaf.rdf#danbri

Line 26 creates a HashSet object, emailAddresses, which holds all the collected e-mail addresses. We use a HashSet to make sure there are no repeated e-mail addresses in this collection.

Line 27 creates another important collection, friendsToVisit, which is an instance of class URICollection. As we discussed earlier, this class uses a stack as its underlying data structure to implement depth-first search. In addition, the implementation of this class makes sure no URI is repeatedly visited. For our application, friendsToVisit holds the URIs that need to be dereferenced next. A given URI in this collection either represents a friend, or an object value of rdfs: seeAlso property. Also notice that at the time the agent gets started, Dan Brickley's URI is the only URI stored in friendsToVisit; it is used as the seed URI (line 28) for the whole collecting process.

Lines 31–60 are the key method, work(), which implements the algorithm presented at the beginning of this section. Line 34 gets the next URI that needs to be dereferenced from the friendsToVisit collection; lines 43–44 dereference this URI and creates a default RDF model in memory. These steps map to step 1 as described in the algorithm.

Line 48 collects the necessary information from the created model, and the details are implemented in `collectData()` method. Once `collectData()` is executed, steps 2–4 as described in our algorithm are complete, and we are ready to move on to the next URI contained in the `friendsToVisit` collection.

Obviously, the handling of the next URI is an exact repeat of the above steps. As a result, we process the next friend's document by recursively calling the `work()` method (line 58). This recursive calling step maps to step 5, as described in our algorithm.

`collectData()` (lines 62–127) is where the data collection work is done. Let us understand it by starting with the SPARQL query string (lines 68–74). List 18.3 shows this query in a more readable format:

List 18.3 SPARQL query used on line 68 of List 18.2

```
1: SELECT ?myself ?who ?email ?seeAlso
2: WHERE {
3:     ?myself <http://xmlns.com/foaf/0.1/knows> ?who.
4:     optional {
5:         ?who <http://xmlns.com/foaf/0.1/mbox> ?email.
6:     }
7:     optional {
8:         ?who <http://www.w3.org/2000/01/rdf-schema#seeAlso>
8a:         ?seeAlso.
9:     }
10: }
```

This query finds all the friends (identified by the `foaf:knows` property) from the current RDF model and also gets their `foaf:mbox` values and `rdfs:seeAlso` values, if available.

To help you understand it better, Table 18.1 shows part of the result if we had written a small separate Java class just to execute the query. Notice that in order to fit into the page, the `?myself` field is not included in Table 18.1.

As shown in Table 18.1, some friends have both `foaf:mbox` and `rdfs:seeAlso` defined (b0, b2 and ***), some only have `foaf:mbox` or `rdfs:seeAlso` defined (b4, b5), and some have no `foaf:mbox` nor `rdfs:seeAlso` defined (b10). In addition, for all the friends he knows, Dan Brickley has not used any URI to represent them, except for Tim Berners-Lee (see the *** line; we put *** there in order to fit onto the page). Therefore, from Dan's FOAF file, that is the only URI that identifies a person; all the other collected URIs come from values of the `rdfs:seeAlso` property.

With an understanding of the query string, the rest of the code is easy to understand. The above query is created and executed (lines 77–78), and the result set is examined line-by-line to get the required information (lines 82–118). More specifically, lines 88–97 implement step 2 as described in our algorithm, where the e-mail addresses are collected. Notice although most FOAF files use a resource as the value of `foaf:mbox` property (lines 92–94), some FOAF files use value string as

Table 18.1 Part of the result when running the query shown in List 18.3

who	email	seeAlso
_: b0	`<mailto:em@w3.org>`	`<http://purl.org/net/eric/` `webwho.xrdf>`
_: b2	`<mailto:barstow@w3.org>`	`<http://www.w3.org/People/` `Barstow/webwho.rdf>`
...		
_: b4	`<mailto:libby.` `miller@bristol.ac.uk>`	
_: b5		`<http://people.w3.org/amy/foaf.` `rdf>`
...		
_: b10		
***	`<mailto:timbl@w3.org>`	`<http://www.w3.org/People/` `Berners-Lee/card>`

***: `http://www.w3.org/People/Berners-Lee/card#i`

its value (lines 90–92). Therefore we need to collect them by using different methods. Either way, the collected e-mail addresses are stored in the `emailAddresses` collection (lines 91, 93).

Lines 100–116 implements step 3 of our algorithm. Since it is perfectly fine not to use any URI to represent a given person, we first have to check whether a friend is identified by a URI or a blank node (line 100). If a friend is identified by a URI, this URI will be visited later to expand the e-mail network, and for now, we simply save it in our `friendsToVisit` collection (line 101). If a friend is represented by a blank node, there is not much we can do (line 103) except to continue checking whether there is an `rdfs:seeAlso` property value we can use to explore the subnetwork that is headed by this friend.

Lines 107–116 are used to check `rdfs:seeAlso` property. Similarly, since the `rdfs:seeAlso` property can use either data type or object type as its value, we need to check both (lines 108–114). Either way, if a value of this property is found, we save it into `friendsToVisit` collection so we can visit it later (lines 110, 112).

The above examination is repeated for all the records in the result set. Once this process is done, we may have gathered a number of e-mail addresses and identified quite a few new URIs yet to visit. This is precisely where the circle of trust is being built and expanded.

At this point, we have discussed the details of our implementation. It is obvious that this way of expanding the e-mail network could result in a fairly deep and wide search tree that needs to be covered. For example, when I ran this collector on my own computer, after an hour or so it ran out of memory, with about 150 e-mail addresses collected, and 1,000 more friends of friends yet to explore.

Unless you have access to large machine which provides much stronger computing power than a home computer, you will want to change the code a little bit, in order to make a complete run. List 18.4 shows the modified definition of `URICollection` class. Since we have seen this class already, only the method with the change is included here.

List 18.4 `URICollection.java` definition

```
1: package test;
2:
3: import java.net.URI;
4: import java.net.URISyntaxException;
5: import java.util.HashSet;
6: import java.util.Iterator;
7: import java.util.Stack;
8:
9: public class URICollection {
10:
11:   private Stack URIs = null;
12:   private HashSet visitedURIs = null;
13:
14:   public URICollection() {
15:     URIs = new Stack();
16:     visitedURIs = new HashSet();
17:   }
18:
19:   public void addNewURI(String uri) {
20:     if ( uri == null ) {
21:       return;
22:     }
23:     // testing purpose: we don't want to go into
23a:    // these social sites
24:     URI myURI = null;
25:     try {
26:       myURI = new URI(uri);
27:       if ( myURI.getHost().contains("my.opera.com") ) {
28:         return;
29:       }
30:       if ( myURI.getHost().contains("identi.ca") ) {
31:         return;
32:       }
33:       if ( myURI.getHost().contains("advogato.org") ) {
34:         return;
35:       }
36:       if ( myURI.getHost().contains("foaf.qdos.com") ) {
37:         return;
38:       }
39:       if ( myURI.getHost().contains("livejournal.com") ) {
40:         return;
41:       }
42:       if ( myURI.getHost().contains("openlinksw.com")) {
43:         return;
44:       }
```

```
45:        if ( myURI.getHost().contains("rdf.opiumfield.com") ) {
46:          return;
47:        }
48:        if ( myURI.getHost().contains("ecademy.com") ) {
49:          return;
50:        }
51:        if ( myURI.getHost().contains("revyu.com") ) {
52:          return;
53:        }
54:        if ( myURI.getHost().contains("xircles.codehaus.org")) {
55:          return;
56:        }
57:      } catch (URISyntaxException e1) {
58:        // e1.printStackTrace();
59:      }
60:      // end of testing purpose: you can clean this part out to
60a:     // do more crawling
61:
62:      try {
63:        if ( visitedURIs.contains(uri) == false ) {
64:          visitedURIs.add(uri);
65:          URIs.push(uri);
66:        }
67:      } catch(Exception e) {};
68:    }
69:
70:   public String getNextURI() {
...
75:    }
76:
...   // other methods you have seen already
103:  }
104:
105:  }
```

As you can tell, lines 23–60 are added to make the crawling process more focused. More specifically, we take a look at the URI that is passed in for collection, and if it is from a social Web site, we simply reject it and move on. In general, these social sites can link quite a large number of people into their networks, and we would not want them to be included in our e-mail list.

With the above change in place, I could finish the run in a little over an hour, with 216 e-mail addresses collected for Dan Brickley.

Finally, List 18.5 is the driver I use to run the collector, and not much explanation is needed here.

List 18.5 Test driver for our email collector

```
1: package test;
2:
3: public class EmailListBuilderTester {
4:
5:     // http://www.w3.org/People/Berners-Lee/card#i
6:     public static final String startURI =
6a:                     "http://danbri.org/foaf.rdf#danbri";
7:
8:     public static void main(String[] args) {
9:
10:         EmailAddressCollector eac =
10a:                             new EmailAddressCollector(startURI);
11:         eac.work();
12:
13:         // here are all the collected email addresses
14:         eac.showemailAddresses();
15:
16:     }
17:
18: }
```

18.1.3.2   Running the `EmailAddressCollector` Agent

Now, find these class definitions from the package you have downloaded:

```
EmailAddressCollector.java
URICollection.java
EmailAddressCollectorTester.java
```

Build the application and fire it up, and you can see the search in action. For example, the following is part of the output when I ran the agent using Dan's FOAF file as the starting point:

```
...visiting <http://danbri.org/foaf.rdf#danbri>
...21 email addresses collected.
...17 new friends URI added.
...all together 17 more to visit.

...visiting <http://heddley.com/edd/foaf.rdf>
...43 email addresses collected.
...10 new friends URI added.
...all together 26 more to visit.

...visiting <http://clark.dallas.tx.us/kendall/foaf.rdf>
```

And you can add more output lines into the source code so you can see more clearly what is happening during the search. The following is part of the collected e-mail addresses:

```
1: mailto:nova@radarnetworks.com
2: mailto:aditkal@yahoo.com
3: mailto:lac@ecs.soton.ac.uk
4: mailto:rafa@sidar.org
5: mailto:et@progos.hu
6: mailto:alerer@mit.edu
7: mailto:kidehen@openlinksw.com
8: mailto:nmg@ecs.soton.ac.uk
9: mailto:mauro.buratti@nontorno.com
10: mailto:stefan.decker@deri.org
11: mailto:wvasconc@csd.abdn.ac.uk
12: mailto:joe.brickley@btopenworld.com
13: mailto:simonstl@simonstl.com
14: mailto:em@zepheira.com
15: mailto:simon.price@bristol.ac.uk
16: mailto:hendler@cs.umd.edu
17: mailto:giles@gilest.org
18: mailto:ian.sealy@bristol.ac.uk
19: mailto:b.j.norton@open.ac.uk
20: mailto:danny666@virgilio.it
21: mailto:ben@benhammersley.com
22: mailto:swh@ecs.soton.ac.uk
23: mailto:elias@torrez.us
24: mailto:dino@w3.org
25: mailto:phil@chimpen.com
...
```

To add these e-mail addresses into your e-mail system's address book, all you need to do is cut-and-paste. And now, you have created your circle of trust based on your FOAF network, and this is made possible by the open Linked Data principles and Semantic Web technologies.

It is also important to realize the dynamic nature of the Web: your friend's circle is growing and so is yours: you will get to know new friends, and your friends' friends will expand their circles, and so on. As a result, it is important to run this agent from time to time, and you will see quick growth of the harvested e-mail addresses.

18.1.4   Can You Do the Same for the Traditional Web?

As usual, try to figure out a plan that helps you implement exactly the same agent on the traditional Web. The truth is, it will be quite difficult, if not completely impossible. And even if you can do it now, wait until you run it again a while later: you will need to make significant changes to make it work again. I will leave this to you to consider, which will for sure make you appreciate the value of the Semantic Web more.

18.2   A ShopBot on the Semantic Web

So far in this chapter, we have built a simple FOAF agent, which works in the environment of the Semantic Web, and exhibits the traits that we have always been looking for from Web agents: a much smarter way of accomplishing the given task, with the required scalability and maintainability. In the second half of this chapter, we are going to create another interesting Web application: a smart ShopBot. We first discuss ShopBots in general, and we will then build a ShopBot step by step in a simulated Semantic Web world. This will not only show you some necessary techniques when it comes to development on the Semantic Web, but will also give you some hints for other possible applications.

18.2.1   A ShopBot We Can Have

A ShopBot is a software agent that works on the Web. For a particular product specified by the consumer, it searches different online stores and retailers, so as to provide the consumer with the prices offered by these stores and retailers.

There are quite a few Web sites powered by ShopBots. For example,

```
www.pricescan.com
www.pricewatch.com
www.dealtime.com
```

You can visit these sites to get a sense of ShopBots.

It is important to realize that ShopBots normally operate by a form of screen-scraping (there have been some changes in recent years, as discussed below), meaning that they download the pages and get the necessary information by parsing the content. In general, screen-scraping is a method used to extract data from a set of Web pages with the goal of consolidating the data in a single Web page, which can then be conveniently viewed by a user.

The fact that ShopBots operate by screen-scraping also dictates their basic assumption during the course of their work. Once a page is downloaded, a ShopBot has to search for the name of the specified product. If it can locate the item successfully, it then searches for the nearest set of characters that has a dollar sign, assuming this set of characters is the price of the item.

Obviously, this solution may not be as robust as we would expect. For instance, imagine on a given Web page, after the name of the product, the first set of characters that has a dollar sign is actually the suggested retail price, and somewhere down the page, another set of characters that also has a dollar sign is the current sale price. A ShopBot may completely miss the target in this case.

To handle the situations like above, a ShopBot just has to be "smarter", either by applying some heuristics that work most of the time, or by processing the pages on a case-by-case basis. In fact, some Web sites powered by ShopBots have established agreements with big retailers to make sure the price information can be correctly obtained.

Recently, some ShopBots have been created based on the Mashup concept we introduced in Chap. 11. Instead of screen-scraping, this new breed of ShopBots obtain the price and related information of a product by consuming the Web services provided by a given retailer. This is certainly a much better solution compared to screen-scraping, since the results from the Web service calls are structured data where no assumption is needed. However, two issues still exist. First, not all the retailers offer Web services. Second, Web services offered by different retailers have to be consumed by using different APIs, therefore the ShopBot development team has to learn a new set of APIs every time a new retailer is considered. As a result, this solution is still not a scalable one.

In fact, even with better Mashup support and smarter heuristics, the ShopBots we can build today can only offer limited usage to us. More specifically, we have to tell the ShopBot exactly what product we are looking for; we cannot simply *describe* what we want to buy.

For example, we cannot tell the ShopBot to search for a camera that is manufactured by Nikon and has at least 6-megapixel picture quality, and can support a lens that has an 18–200 mm zoom. Instead, we have to specifically tell it to find a product that has a model number given by Nikon D200.

This clearly presents some difficulty for probably most of us: quite often, we can only describe what we want and we do not have a particular product in mind. Ideally, a particular product that satisfies our needs should be part of the information we get by using a ShopBot.

To solve this issue, some Web sites powered by ShopBots allow you to search for a product first by using a search-engine-like interface on their sites. For example, you can type in the word camera to start your search. However, it is then up to you to read all the returned items to figure out exactly which product you would like to have. Again, this is a tedious manual process that can take up lots of time before you settle down with one specific product.

The Semantic Web seems to be the right solution for all these issues. By adding semantics to a retailer's Web pages, the content of the Web site becomes understandable to a ShopBot. For example, an added RDF file describing the products is for the ShopBot to read, while the traditional HTML content is still there for human eyes.

In the next few sections, we construct the ShopBot we really want: a ShopBot that can accept our description of a product instead of a specific model number, and a ShopBot that is easy to maintain and that also has excellent scalability.

18.2.2   A ShopBot We Really Want

18.2.2.1   How Does It Understand Our Needs?

To make sure a ShopBot can understand our description about what we want, using an RDF model to express the description is a good choice. Casual users can be presented with an HTML form so he/she can express his/her needs by filling out the form, which is then mapped to an RDF model. In other words, there is no need for a user to learn RDF beforehand.

Now, let us assume we would like to buy a camera, and the following RDF document shown in List 18.6 describes what exactly we want for our ideal camera:

List 18.6 An RDF document describing what camera we are looking for

```
1: <?xml version="1.0" encoding="UTF-8"?>
2: <rdf:RDF
2a:     xmlns:rdf="http://www.w3.org/1999/02/22-rdf-syntax-ns#"
3:      xml:base="http://www.liyangyu.com/shopbot/request">
4:
5:    <!-- here is what I am looking for -->
6:
7:    <Digital rdf:ID="myDigitalCamera"
7a:           xmlns="http://www.liyangyu.com/camera#">
8:
9:      <effectivePixel rdf:datatype=
9a:                 "http://www.liyangyu.com/camera#MegaPixel">
9b:        6.0</effectivePixel>
10:
```

```
11:        <body>
12:          <Body>
13:            <shutterSpeed>
14:              <ValueRange>
15:                <minValue rdf:datatype=
15a:                    "http://www.w3.org/2001/XMLSchema#float">
15b:                  0.0005</minValue>
16:              </ValueRange>
17:            </shutterSpeed>
18:          </Body>
19:        </body>
20:
21:        <lens>
22:          <Lens>
23:            <focalLength rdf:datatype=
23a:                    "http://www.w3.org/2001/XMLSchema#string">
                      18-200mm</focalLength>
24:            <aperture>
25:              <ValueRange>
26:                <minValue rdf:datatype=
26a:                    "http://www.w3.org/2001/XMLSchema#float">
26b:                  1.8</minValue>
27:                <maxValue rdf:datatype=
27a:                    "http://www.w3.org/2001/XMLSchema#float">
27b:                  22</maxValue>
28:              </ValueRange>
29:            </aperture>
30:          </Lens>
31:        </lens>
32:
33:      </Digital>
34:
35: </rdf:RDF>
```

Figure 18.1 represents List 18.6 in an RDF graph format:

Notice that in Fig. 18.1, an oval represents a class and a box represents an instance or resource, and the URI of the resource is included inside the box. If the box represents a blank node, there is no URI given inside the box. Also, if a property value takes a simple string or a float number, the number or string is simply used without having a box.

Since the only purpose of List 18.6 is to describe our target camera, the URI we use to identify this camera will not be reused by anyone, and the properties we have given about this ideal camera are not important to the outside world either. Therefore, we have used an rdf:ID (line 7) together with an xml:base attribute (line 3) to identify the camera, which has the following URI,

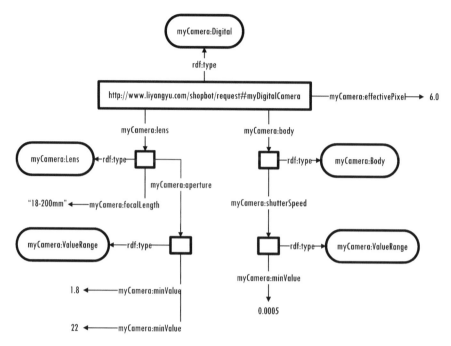

Fig. 18.1 List 18.6 in RDF graph format

```
http://www.liyangyu.com/shopbot/request#myDigitalCamera
```

and all the property values, such as `myCamera:Lens`, `myCamera:Body` and `myCamera:ValueRange`, are represented by blank nodes. Notice that we do use our camera ontology in List 18.6 (the default namespace on line 7), and we will come back to this point later.

Now, based on List 18.6, here is what we are looking for:

- We want a digital camera (line 7).
- The camera should have at least 6.0 megapixel resolution (line 9).
- The shutter speed of the camera should be able to reach as fast as 1/2,000 s (lines 11–19).
- The camera should have a lens that has a zoom range of 18–200 mm, and minimum aperture of 1.8, with a maximum aperture of 22 (lines 21–30).

As you can see, to be able to describe our needs like the above is a great enhancement to the user experience when using the ShopBot. All we have described is a camera that satisfies our needs, and we don't have to specify a product model at all.

Notice that our camera ontology is specified on line 7 by using the following statement,

```
xmlns="http://www.liyangyu.com/camera#"
```

and List 18.6 is equivalent to List 18.7, which probably looks more familiar to you.

List 18.7   An equivalent form of List 18.6

```
 1: <?xml version="1.0" encoding="UTF-8"?>
 2: <rdf:RDF
2a:     xmlns:rdf="http://www.w3.org/1999/02/22-rdf-syntax-ns#"
 3:     xmlns:myCamera="http://www.liyangyu.com/camera#"
 4:     xml:base="http://www.liyangyu.com/shopbot/request">
 5:
 6:   <!-- here is what I am looking for -->
 7:
 8:   <myCamera:Digital rdf:ID="myDigitalCamera">
 9:
10:     <myCamera:effectivePixel rdf:datatype=
10a:                 "http://www.liyangyu.com/camera#MegaPixel">
10b:      6.0</myCamera:effectivePixel>
11:
12:     <myCamera:body>
13:       <myCamera:Body>
14:         <myCamera:shutterSpeed>
15:           <myCamera:ValueRange>
16:             <myCamera:minValue rdf:datatype=
16a:                   "http://www.w3.org/2001/XMLSchema#float">
16b:             0.0005</myCamera:minValue>
17:           </myCamera:ValueRange>
18:         </myCamera:shutterSpeed>
19:       </myCamera:Body>
20:     </myCamera:body>
21:
22:     <myCamera:lens>
23:       <myCamera:Lens>
24:         <myCamera:focalLength rdf:datatype=
24a:                   "http://www.w3.org/2001/XMLSchema#string">
24b:           18-200mm</myCamera:focalLength>
25:         <myCamera:aperture>
26:           <myCamera:ValueRange>
27:             <myCamera:minValue rdf:datatype=
27a:                   "http://www.w3.org/2001/XMLSchema#float">
27b:             1.8</myCamera:minValue>
28:             <myCamera:maxValue rdf:datatype=
28a:                   "http://www.w3.org/2001/XMLSchema#float">
28b:             22</myCamera:maxValue>
29:           </myCamera:ValueRange>
30:         </myCamera:aperture>
31:       </myCamera:Lens>
32:     </myCamera:lens>
33:
34:   </myCamera:Digital>
35:
36: </rdf:RDF>
```

18.2.2.2   How Does It Find the Next Candidate?

Making the ShopBot understand our need is only the first step, the next step is to make it work as we expected. Before we dive into the details, let us summarize our assumptions for our ShopBot:

1. There is a list of retailers that the ShopBot will visit.
2. Each of these retailers publishes its own product catalog documents on the Web by using an RDF model.
3. When it comes to describing cameras in their RDF catalog documents, all of these retailers have agreed to use our camera ontology.

First, the ShopBot in its most general form, to make sure it does not miss any potential retailer and product, must visit the Web just as a crawler does. In this example, we will not ask it to crawl every Web site it has randomly encountered; rather, it will crawl some Web sites from a predefined list that was given to it as part of the input. For instance, this list might include retailers such as BestBuy, RitzCamera or Sam's Club, just to name a few. Obviously, doing so can greatly improve the performance of the ShopBot, and also ensures that our ShopBot only visits the sites that we trust, which is another important issue on the Web.

The second assumption is vital for an agent that works on the Semantic Web. For instance, BestBuy could have one catalog file for all the PCs it sells, another catalog for all the TVs, and another catalog for all the cameras, and so on and so forth. Furthermore, these catalog files are created by using terms defined in some ontologies, and they have to be published by the retailer on its Web site so our ShopBot can access these catalog files. Clearly, this is one big extra step that has to be taken by the retailers.

Once our ShopBot reaches a retailer's Web site, it only inspects the published catalog files and skips all the traditional Web documents that are constructed using HTML on the same Web site. Obviously, this is one important difference between this new ShopBot and the one we currently have on our traditional Web.

The third assumption is to make sure all the retailers share a common vocabulary so it is easier for the ShopBot to work. This is also why ontology reuse is vital in the world of the Semantic Web. However, in reality, it may well be true that some retailer who sells cameras has instead used some other camera ontology to describe his items. We will come back to this point in a later section.

With the above assumptions in place, our ShopBot can continue to locate the next retailer and further decide whether any camera products are offered by this retailer.

In general, a given retailer could have a large number of RDF documents published on its Web site, and only a few of these RDF files are real product catalogs. Therefore, when visiting a retailer's Web site, the first step is to decide, for a given RDF file, whether it contains some description of camera products. If the conclusion is yes, it will then be considered as a candidate that can be potentially collected by our ShopBot.

To make this decision, the following observation is the key: if a given catalog RDF file has made use of our camera ontology, this catalog file is considered as one candidate for further verification. If not, our ShopBot skips this file.

For example, List 18.6 specifies our request, and the terms used in List 18.6 were taken from the following ontology namespaces:

```
http://www.w3.org/1999/02/22-rdf-syntax-ns#
http://www.liyangyu.com/camera#
```

Now, our ShopBot encounters an RDF document as shown in List 18.8 from a retailer's Web site:

List 18.8 An example catalog document in RDF format

```
1: <?xml version="1.0" encoding="UTF-8"?>
2: <rdf:RDF
2a:     xmlns:rdf="http://www.w3.org/1999/02/22-rdf-syntax-ns#"
3:      xml:base="http://www.retailerExample1.com/onlineCatalog">
4:
5:   <Retailer rdf:ID="Retailer-1"
5a:            xmlns="http://www.eBusiness.org/retailer#">
6:
7:     <location>Norcross, GA</location>
8:     <address>6066 Cameron Pointe</address>
9:     <webSite>www.bestStuff.com</webSite>
10:
11:    <catalog rdf:parseType="Collection">
12:
13:      <Notebook rdf:ID="PC_TOP_08"
13a:     xmlns="http://www.ontologyExample.org/ontology/pcspec#">
14:
15:        <memory>
16:          <Memory>
17:            <mem_capacity>1.0GB</mem_capacity>
18:          </Memory>
19:        </memory>
20:
21:        <processor>
22:          <Processor>
23:            <cpu_name>Intel Pentium M processor</cpu_name>
24:            <cpu_speed>2.0GHz</cpu_speed>
```

```
25:            </Processor>
26:          </processor>
27:
28:        <harddisk>
29:          <HardDrive>
30:            <hd_capacity>120GB</hd_capacity>
31:          </HardDrive>
32:        </harddisk>
33:
34:      </Notebook>
35:
36:      <Processor rdf:ID="intel_m"
36a:     xmlns="http://www.ontologyExample.org/ontology/pcspec#">
37:        <cpu_name>Intel Pentium M processor</cpu_name>
38:        <cpu_speed>2.0GHz</cpu_speed>
39:        <cost>
40:          <Money>
41:            <price>$199.99</price>
42:          </Money>
43:        </cost>
44:      </Processor>
45:
46:      <Mointor rdf:ID="Monitor-Hanns-G" xmlns=
46a:      "http://www.ontologyExample.org/ontology/monitorspec#">
47:        <dimension>
48:          <Dimension>
49:            <size>17</size>
50:            <resolution>1440x900</resolution>
51:          </Dimension>
52:        </dimension>
53:      </Mointor>
54:
55:      <DSLR rdf:ID="Nikon_D70"
55a:          xmlns="http://www.liyangyu.com/camera#">
56:        <body>
57:          <Body>
58:            <shutter>
59:              <ValueRange>
60:                <minValue rdf:datatype=
60a:                  "http://www.w3.org/2001/XMLSchema#float">
60b:                  0.00002</minValue>
61:              </ValueRange>
62:            </shutter>
```

```
63:            </Body>
64:          </body>
65:          <lens>
66:            <Lens>
67:              <zoomRange rdf:datatype=
67a:                     "http://www.w3.org/2001/XMLSchema#string">
67b:                18-200mm</zoomRange>
68:            </Lens>
69:          </lens>
70:        </DSLR>
71:
72:      </catalog>
73:
74: </Retailer>
75:
76: </rdf:RDF>
```

Obviously, this retailer is selling more than just cameras; it is also selling computers, processors and monitors. Our ShopBot is able to discover that terms used in this catalog are from the following ontology namespaces:

```
http://www.w3.org/1999/02/22-rdf-syntax-ns#
```
http://www.liyangyu.com/camera#
```
http://www.eBusiness.org/retailer#
http://www.ontologyExample.org/ontology/monitorspec#
http://www.ontologyExample.org/ontology/pcspec#
```

Clearly, our camera ontology namespace,

```
http://www.liyangyu.com/camera#
```

has been used by both the request file (List 18.6) and the catalog file (List 18.8). The ShopBot then treats this catalog file as one candidate and further investigates whether there is a matched camera contained in this catalog file. We discuss the matching process in the next section.

18.2.2.3 How Does It Decide Whether There Is a Match or Not?

First, you might have noticed that in List 18.8, the following property is used (line 67) to describe the Nikon D70 camera:

```
http://www.liyangyu.com/camera#zoomRange
```

and it is not a term from our camera ontology. In fact, in this chapter, in order to make our ShopBot more interesting, we will change our camera ontology a little bit. More specifically, our camera ontology is given in List 5.30, and we will make some changes to several property definitions, as shown in List 18.9:

List 18.9 Property definition changes in our camera ontology (see List 5.30)

```
1:  <owl:ObjectProperty
1a:     rdf:about="http://www.liyangyu.com/camera#effectivePixel">
2:    <owl:equivalentProperty rdf:resource="#resolution"/>
3:    <rdfs:domain rdf:resource="#Digital"/>
4:    <rdfs:range
4a:      rdf:resource="http://www.liyangyu.com/camera#MegaPixel"/>
5:  </owl:ObjectProperty>
6:  <rdfs:Datatype
6a:       rdf:about="http://www.liyangyu.com/camera#MegaPixel">
7:    <rdfs:subClassOf
7a:      rdf:resource="http://www.w3.org/2001/XMLSchema#decimal"/>
8:  </rdfs:Datatype>
9:
10: <owl:ObjectProperty
10a:      rdf:about="http://www.liyangyu.com/camera#shutterSpeed">
11:   <owl:equivalentProperty rdf:resource="#shutter"/>
12:   <rdfs:domain rdf:resource="#Body"/>
13:   <rdfs:range rdf:resource="#ValueRange"/>
14: </owl:ObjectProperty>
15:
16: <owl:DatatypeProperty
16a:      rdf:about="http://www.liyangyu.com/camera#focalLength">
17:   <owl:equivalentProperty rdf:resource="#zoomRange"/>
18:   <rdfs:domain rdf:resource="#Lens"/>
19:   <rdfs:range
19a:      rdf:resource="http://www.w3.org/2001/XMLSchema#string"/>
20: </owl:DatatypeProperty>
21: <rdfs:Datatype
21a:        rdf:about="http://www.w3.org/2001/XMLSchema#string"/>
```

As shown in List 18.9, the only change we have made to the current camera ontology (List 5.30) is on lines 2, 11 and 17. And now, myCamera:effectivePixel is equivalent to myCamera:resolution, myCamera:shutterSpeed is equivalent to myCamera:shutter, and finally, myCamera:focalLength is equivalent to `myCamera:zoomRange`. With these changes, line 67 in List 18.8 simply uses a different term which has the same meaning as `myCamera:focalLength` does.

Now, to further decide whether there is a real match or not, our ShopBot first has to decide which item described in this given catalog could potentially satisfy our needs. In our example, the ShopBot figures out that the Nikon D70 described in the catalog has a type of `DSLR`, which is a subclass of `Digital`. As a result, it can be considered as a candidate product. Also notice that this item is the only product from List 18.8 that is considered further by the ShopBot.

With this potential candidate, the ShopBot has to dive into more details:

- We are looking for a digital camera whose lens has a specific value for its `focalLength` property. In the catalog, Nikon D70's lens has a property called `zoomRange`. With the inferencing power provided by the camera ontology, our ShopBot understands that `focalLength` and `zoomRange` are equivalent properties; therefore, the description of what we are looking for matches the description of the item on sale.
- The same process has to be repeated for other terms. For example, our ShopBot also understands that `shutter` and `shutterSpeed` are also equivalent, and so on. If all the terms match, the given product can be considered as a match to our need.

With all this said, let us move on to the construction of our ShopBot, and you will have another chance to see the inferencing power at work.

18.2.3 Building Our ShopBot

Given the previous discussions, building our ShopBot becomes fairly easy. Let us start with some basic utilities first.

18.2.3.1 Utility Methods and Class

The first utility method we would like to mention is the method shown in List 18.10, which is used to understand our search request.

List 18.10 Method to understand our search need

```
1:   private boolean getItemToSearch(Model m) {
2:
3:      String queryString =
4:              "SELECT ?subject ?predicate ?object " +
5:              "WHERE {" +
6:              "   ?subject <" + RDF.type + "> ?object. " +
7:              "   }";
8:
9:      Query q = QueryFactory.create(queryString);
10:     QueryExecution qe = QueryExecutionFactory.create(q,m);
11:     ResultSet rs = qe.execSelect();
12:
13:     // collect the data type property names
14:     while ( rs.hasNext() ) {
15:       ResultBinding binding = (ResultBinding)rs.next();
16:       RDFNode rn = (RDFNode)binding.get("subject");
17:       if ( rn != null ) {
18:          targetItem = rn.toString();
19:       }
20:       rn = (RDFNode)binding.get("object");
21:       if ( rn != null ) {
22:          targetType = rn.toString();
23:       }
24:     }
25:     qe.close();
26:
27:     if ( targetItem == null || targetItem.length() == 0 ) {
28:       return false;
29:     }
30:     if ( targetType == null || targetType.length() == 0 ) {
31:       return false;
32:     }
33:     return true;
34: }
```

More specifically, we express our need in an RDF document (as shown in Lists 18.6 and 18.7), and we create an RDF model based on this document. This model is then passed to this method so we can have the following two pieces of information:

- The URI that represents the product we are looking for, and
- The type information of the product.

To accomplish this, we run the following SPARQL query against the model that represents our need:

```
SELECT ?subject ?predicate ?object
WHERE {
    ?subject <http://www.w3.org/1999/02/22-rdf-syntax-ns#type>
    ?object.
}
```

and this query is coded on lines 3–7. Once the query is run against the model, we can scan the result for the URI and type information as shown on lines 14–24. Notice it is important to understand the following two assumptions here:

- One request document only describes one item.
- We always give a URI to represent this item; in other words, it is not represented by a blank node.

With these assumptions, the query on lines 3–7 and the scan on lines 14–24 can be find the item and its type. Notice that the URI that represents the item is stored in the variable called `targetItem`, and its type is stored in variable `targetType`.

Once the above is done, both `targetItem` and `targetType` should have their values. If either of them is not populated, a `false` value is returned (lines 27–32), indicating the RDF document that represents the request is not properly created.

If you run the method against the request document shown in List 18.6, these two variables hold the following values when this method finishes:

```
targetItem:
      http://www.liyangyu.com/shopbot/request#myDigitalCamera
targetType:
      http://www.liyangyu.com/camera#Digital
```

The second utility method is used to solve the problem discussed in Sect. 18.2.2.2. This method itself uses another method to accomplish the goal, and these two methods are shown in List 18.11.

List 18.11 Methods used to decide whether a given catalog document should be
further investigated

```
1:   private boolean isCandidate(Model m) {
2:
3:      if ( m == null  ) {
4:         return false;
5:      }
6:
7:      HashSet ns = new HashSet();
8:      this.collectNamespaces(m,ns);
9:      return ns.contains(ontologyNS);
10:
11: }
12:
13: private void collectNamespaces(Model m,HashSet hs) {
14:    if ( hs == null || m == null ) {
15:       return;
16:    }
17:    NsIterator nsi = m.listNameSpaces();
18:    while ( nsi.hasNext() ) {
19:       hs.add(nsi.next().toString());
20:    }
21: }
```

These two methods should be fairly straightforward to follow. Method
collectionNamespaces() uses Jena API listNameSpaces() method to collect
all the namespaces used on a given RDF model (line 17), and these namespaces are
saved in a Hash set as shown on lines 18–20.

Method isCandidate() is called when our ShopBot encounters a new RDF
document. Based on this RDF document, a model is created and passed on to
method isCandidate(). Inside the method, a collection of namespaces used by the
given model is created by calling collectNamespaces() method (line 8). If the
namespace of our camera ontology is one of the namespaces used (line 9), method
isCandidate()returns true, indicating the given RDF document should be further investigated. Notice variable ontologyNS holds the namespace of our camera
ontology.

Another important utility is findCandidateItem() method. Once the ShopBot
has decided that a given RDF document possibly contains products in which we are
interested, it then needs to decide exactly what these products are. This is done by
the findCandidateItem() method. List 18.12 shows the definition of the method.

List 18.12 Method used to find all the candidate products in a given RDF catalog

```
1:   private Vector findCandidateItem(Model m) {
2:
3:     Vector candidates = new Vector();
4:     String queryString =
5:     "SELECT ?candidate " +
6:     "WHERE {" +
7:     "  ?candidate <" + RDF.type + "> <" + targetType + ">. " +
8:     "  }";
9:
10:    Query q = QueryFactory.create(queryString);
11:    QueryExecution qe = QueryExecutionFactory.create(q,m);
12:    ResultSet rs = qe.execSelect();
13:
14:    while ( rs.hasNext() ) {
15:      ResultBinding binding = (ResultBinding)rs.next();
16:      RDFNode rn = (RDFNode)binding.get("candidate");
17:      if ( rn != null && rn.isAnon() == false ) {
18:        candidates.add(rn.toString());
19:      }
20:    }
21:    qe.close();
22:    return candidates;
23: }
```

As you can tell, the idea is very simple: since we know we are looking for something that has http://www.liyangyu.com/camera#Digital as it type, all we need to do is to run the following query against the RDF model that represents the given catalog document:

```
SELECT ?candidate
WHERE {
    ?candidate <http://www.w3.org/1999/02/22-rdf-syntax-ns#type>
    <http://www.liyangyu.com/camera#Digital>.
}
```

Notice this query is implemented by lines 4–8, and variable targetType has http://www.liyangyu.com/camera#Digital as its value.

The rest of the method is quite straightforward: a SPARQL query is created and submitted to run against the catalog (lines 10–11), and the results are analyzed on line 14–20, where the URIs of the candidate products are collected.

Now, the interesting part comes from the fact that if you simply take the RDF catalog shown in List 18.8 and create a simple RDF model from it, and then use method findCandidateItem() on this model, you will not find any candidate product at all. This is not surprising. After all, the Nikon D70 camera described in the catalog has a type of DSLR, and it is not the exact type that we specified in the query. However, as we discussed earlier, DSLR is a subclass of Digital; therefore, Nikon D70 is also an instance of Digital camera, and it should be returned in the query result.

Now, in order for our ShopBot to see this, we cannot use a simple RDF model to represent the catalog file. Instead, we need to create an ontology model that has the inferencing power. More specifically, List 18.13 shows the steps needed:

List 18.13 To find the candidate products from a given catalog document, we need to create a inferencing model

```
1:   Model catalogModel = getModel(catalog);
2:
3:   // create ontology model for inferencing
4:   OntModel ontModel = ModelFactory.createOntologyModel
4a:                    (OntModelSpec.OWL_MEM_RULE_INF,catalogModel);
5:   FileManager.get().readModel(ontModel,ontologyURL);
6:
7:   candidateItems = findCandidateItem(ontModel);
```

First, catalog represents the path of the given RDF catalog file as shown in List 18.8, and ontologyURL is the path of our camera ontology. Line 1 calls another utility method, getModel(), to create a simple RDF model based on the catalog document, and this model is stored in variable catalogModel. Lines 4 and 5 use catalogModel and ontologyURL to create an ontology model, which has the derived statements added by the OWL inferencing engine provided by Jena.

One way to make this more understandable is to print out all the statements about the type of Nikon D70 camera contained in the two models at both line 2 and line 6 in List 18.13. More specifically, line 1 calls getModel() to create a simple RDF model based on the catalog document. If we were to collect all the type statements about Nikon D70 at line 2, we would collect only one such statement:

```
<http://www.retailerExample1.com/onlineCatalog#Nikon_D70>
<http://www.w3.org/1999/02/22-rdf-syntax-ns#type>
<http://www.liyangyu.com/camera#DSLR> .
```

And this is exactly the reason why the query (lines 4–8 in List 18.12) fails to identify Nikon D70 as a potential product for us. Now, if we were to collect the same type statements on line 6 against the ontology model, we would see the following statements:

```
<http://www.retailerExample1.com/onlineCatalog#Nikon_D70>
<http://www.w3.org/1999/02/22-rdf-syntax-ns#type>
<http://www.liyangyu.com/camera#DSLR> .
```

```
<http://www.retailerExample1.com/onlineCatalog#Nikon_D70>
<http://www.w3.org/1999/02/22-rdf-syntax-ns#type>
<http://www.w3.org/2002/07/owl#Thing> .


<http://www.retailerExample1.com/onlineCatalog#Nikon_D70>
<http://www.w3.org/1999/02/22-rdf-syntax-ns#type>
<http://www.liyangyu.com/camera#Camera> .


<http://www.retailerExample1.com/onlineCatalog#Nikon_D70>
<http://www.w3.org/1999/02/22-rdf-syntax-ns#type>
<http://www.liyangyu.com/camera#Digital> .


<http://www.retailerExample1.com/onlineCatalog#Nikon_D70>
<http://www.w3.org/1999/02/22-rdf-syntax-ns#type>
<http://www.w3.org/2000/01/rdf-schema#Resource> .
```

As you can tell, all these statements except the first one are added by Jena's inferencing engine, and they are all contained in the ontology model. Clearly, this is why the query on lines 4–8 (List 18.12) can now successfully identify all the potential products from the given catalog file.

We will see more reasoning power along the same line in the next section. Before we move on, we need to discuss a utility class named `CameraDescription`, and you will see more about its usage in the later sections.

This class has the following private variables for describing a camera:

```
private float pixel;
private float minFocalLength;
private float maxFocalLength;
private float minAperture;
private float maxAperture;
private float minShutterSpeed;
private float maxShutterSpeed;
```

And obviously, each one of these variables represents a property that is defined in our camera ontology. In fact, this class is quite easy to understand once you see its connection to the camera ontology.

A key method we would like to briefly mention is the `sameAs()` method, which tries to decide whether a given camera can satisfy our needs or not. This method takes an instance of `CameraDescription` class and returns `true` if the calling instance is the same as the parameter instance, and returns `false` otherwise. You can check out the method to see how "same as" is defined in the method, but here is one example. The following camera,

```
pixel value is: 6.0^^http://www.liyangyu.com/camera#MegaPixel
focalLength value is:
```

```
    18-200mm^^http://www.w3.org/2001/XMLSchema#string
min aperture value is:
    1.8^^http://www.w3.org/2001/XMLSchema#float
max aperture value is: 22^^http://www.w3.org/2001/XMLSchema#float
min shutterSpeed value is:
    0.0005^^http://www.w3.org/2001/XMLSchema#float
max shutterSpeed value is not specified.
```

and this one,

```
focalLength value is:
    18-200mm^^http://www.w3.org/2001/XMLSchema#string
min aperture value is not specified.
max aperture value is not specified.
min shutterSpeed value is:
    0.00002^^http://www.w3.org/2001/XMLSchema#float
max shutterSpeed value is not specified.
```

are considered to be the same. Notice that only those available properties are taken into account. In other words, if one camera has a pixel value defined and the other one does not, then at least these two cameras are not different on this aspect. In addition, for those available properties, such as shutter speed as an example, if the parameter camera instance is not worse then the calling instance, the method will return a `true` value. Therefore, a `true` value indicates the camera instance passed to the method can be selected as a candidate, since it satisfies our requirements as far as all the explicitly defined properties are concerned.

18.2.3.2   Processing the Catalog Document

Once our ShopBot has decided that the given RDF catalog document contains some products that may potentially be what we are looking for, it starts the process of handling the catalog document. In this section, we discuss the main idea of processing the catalog document and we also see the key method to implement the idea.

The main idea is again closely related to the camera ontology we are using. For a given candidate camera contained in the catalog document, since there is only a fixed number of properties defined in the ontology that can be used to describe a camera, we can query the value of each one of these properties for this candidate camera and store the value of that particular property in a `CameraDescription` instance. Once we are done with all the properties, this `CameraDescription` instance can be used in a comparison to decide whether the given camera is a match or not.

At this point, based on our camera ontology, the following methods defined by `CameraDescription` class can be used to query the property value of a candidate camera:

```
private String getPixel(Model m, String itemURI)
private String getFocalLength(Model m, String itemURI)
private String getAperture(Model m, String itemURI,
                           int minMaxFlag)
private String getShutterSpeed(Model m, String itemURI,
                               int minMaxFlag)
```

Let us take a look at one example. List 18.14 shows the definition of `getPixel`
() method.

List 18.14 Definition of `getPixel()` method

```
1:   private String getPixel(Model m, String itemURI) {
2:
3:     String queryString =
4:         "SELECT ?value " +
5:         "WHERE {" +
6:         "   <" + itemURI +
6a:        "> <http://www.liyangyu.com/camera#effectivePixel>
6b:        ?value. " +
7:         "   }";
8:
9:     Query q = QueryFactory.create(queryString);
10:    QueryExecution qe = QueryExecutionFactory.create(q,m);
11:    ResultSet rs = qe.execSelect();
12:
13:    while ( rs.hasNext() ) {
14:      ResultBinding binding = (ResultBinding)rs.next();
15:      RDFNode rn = (RDFNode)binding.get("value");
16:      if ( rn != null && rn.isAnon() == false ) {
17:        return rn.toString();
18:      }
19:    }
20:    qe.close();
21:    return null;
22:
23: }
```

First, notice that at this point, our ShopBot has decided that the catalog file
(List 18.8) contains a camera that could potentially satisfy our need, and this
camera has the following URI,

```
http://www.retailerExample1.com/onlineCatalog#Nikon_D70
```

which is passed in as the `itemURI` parameter to the method (line 1).

Now, the following SPARQL query is used to get the pixel value of the given
camera:

```
SELECT ?value
WHERE {

   <http://www.retailerExample1.com/onlineCatalog#Nikon_D70>
   <http://www.liyangyu.com/camera#effectivePixel> ?value.
}
```

and this query is coded on lines 3–7 and is submitted to the model on
lines 9–11.

As you can tell, in the query, myCamera:effectivePixel is specified as the
property name. What if some retailer has used other name for the same query?
myCamera:resolution, for example, can be used (see List
18.9).

Again, to handle this issue, we need the inferencing power from the ontology
model. More specifically, the catalog document is represented as a ontology
model (see List 18.13), and it is passed in as the Model m parameter to the
method (line 1). The query shown on lines 3–7 is run against this ontology
model that has all the inferred statements. The final result is our ShopBot
seems to be smart enough to realize myCamera:effectivePixel and
myCamera:resolution are equivalent properties, and the correct property
value is retrieved successfully.

Therefore, using an ontology model that has all the derived statements is the key
to make sure a given query can return all the facts. This is also true for all the other
methods when it comes to handling the catalog document. To see one more
example, List 18.15 shows the method that queries the shutter speed of a given
camera.

List 18.15 Definition of getShutterSpeed() method

```
1:    private String getShutterSpeed(Model m, String itemURI,
1a:                                     int minMaxFlag) {
2:
3:       String queryString = null;
4:       if ( minMaxFlag == MyShopBot.MIN) {
5:         queryString =
6:          "SELECT ?value " +
7:          "WHERE {" +
8:          "   <" + itemURI +
8a:         "> <http://www.liyangyu.com/camera#body> ?tmpValue0. " +
9:          "   ?tmpValue0
9a:         <http://www.liyangyu.com/camera#shutterSpeed>
9b:         ?tmpValue1." +
10:        "   ?tmpValue1 <http://www.liyangyu.com/camera#minValue>
10a:       ?value . " +
11:        "   }";
12:      } else {
```

```
13:      queryString =
14:       "SELECT ?value " +
15:       "WHERE {" +
16:       "   <" + itemURI +
16a:      "> <http://www.liyangyu.com/camera#body> ?tmpValue0. " +
17:       "   ?tmpValue0
17a:      <http://www.liyangyu.com/camera#shutterSpeed>
17b:      ?tmpValue1." +
18:       "   ?tmpValue1
18a:      <http://www.liyangyu.com/camera#maxValue> ?value . " +
19:       "   }";
20:   }
21:
22:   Query q = QueryFactory.create(queryString);
23:   QueryExecution qe = QueryExecutionFactory.create(q,m);
24:   ResultSet rs = qe.execSelect();
25:
26:   String resultStr = "";
27:   while ( rs.hasNext() ) {
28:     ResultBinding binding = (ResultBinding)rs.next();
29:     RDFNode rn = (RDFNode)binding.get("value");
30:     if ( rn != null && rn.isAnon() == false ) {
31:       return rn.toString();
32:     }
33:   }
34:   qe.close();
35:   return null;
36:
37: }
```

Obviously, querying the value of `myCamera:shutterSpeed` property is more complex than querying the value of `myCamera:effectivePixel` property. More specifically, we need the following SPARQL query to accomplish this:

```
SELECT ?value
WHERE {
    <http://www.retailerExample1.com/onlineCatalog#Nikon_D70>
    <http://www.liyangyu.com/camera#body> ?tmpValue0.
    ?tmpValue0
      <http://www.liyangyu.com/camera#shutterSpeed> ?tmpValue1 .
    ?tmpValue1 <http://www.liyangyu.com/camera#minValue> ?value .
}
```

which, in fact, needs a reference chain to reach the required shutter speed value. This chain starts from `myCamera:body` property, which uses a resource as its value. This resource has a `myCamera:Body` type, and bonded to `tmpValue0` variable. Next, this `myCamera:Body` resource has a `myCamera:shutterSpeed` property, which uses another resource as its value, and this new resource is of type `myCamera:ValueRange`, and is bonded to another variable called `tmpValue1`. Finally, resource `tmpValue1` has two properties, and for this query, we use `myCamera:minValue` property, which tells us the minimum shutter speed this camera can offer. Notice this query is coded from lines 5–11 in List 18.15.

Now, what about the maximum shutter speed this camera body can offer? A similar query is used (lines 13–19), with the only difference being that `myCamera:maxValue` property has replaced `myCamera:maxValue` property. To let the method understand which value we need, we have to pass in a third parameter, `minMaxFlag`, as shown on line 1 of this method.

Similar to the query about `myCamera:effectivePixel` property, `myCamera:shutterSpeed` property also has an equivalent property. In order to recognize all the possible terms, we again need to represent our catalog document as an ontology model which has all the inferred statements, and pass it to the method using the `Model m` parameter as shown on line 1.

For our catalog RDF document (List 18.8), `myCamera:shutter` property is used instead of `myCamera:shutterSpeed` (lines 58–62). Since we have passed in the ontology model that represents this catalog, the above query is able to find the shutter speed value. This is another example that shows the reasoning power you gain from an ontology model.

This also shows how much dependency we have on a specific ontology, since the above query is constructed based on the ontology structure. This gives a key reason why ontology reuse is important: applications are often developed to understand some specific ontology; by reusing this ontology, we can quickly develop a new application since a large portion of the existing application can also be reused.

The other methods, namely, `getFocalLength()` and `getAperture()`, are quite similar to List 18.15, and I leave them for you to understand. At this point, we are ready to discuss the overall workflow of our ShopBot, which we cover in next section.

18.2.3.3   The Main Work Flow

With the above discussion, the overall workflow of our ShopBot is quite easy to understand. This workflow is defined in the following `work()` method, as shown in List 18.16.

List 18.16 Main workflow of our ShopBot agent

```
1:    private void work() {
2:
3:      // for the product we are looking for,
3a:     //get its URI and type info
4:      Model requestModel = getModel(requestRdf);
5:      if ( getItemToSearch(requestModel) == false ) {
6:        System.out.println("your request description
6a:                           is not complete!");
7:      }
8:      System.out.println("this URI describes the resource
8a:                         you are looking for:");
9:      System.out.println("<" + targetItem + ">");
10:     System.out.println("its type is given by
10a:                        the following class:");
11:     System.out.println("<" + targetType + ">");
12:
13:     // find all the requested parameters
14:
15:     CameraDescription myCamera = new CameraDescription();
16:
17:     String targetPixel = getPixel(requestModel,targetItem);
18:     myCamera.setPixel(targetPixel);
19:     show("pixel(target)",targetPixel);
20:
21:     String targetFocalLength =
21a:            getFocalLength(requestModel,targetItem);
22:     myCamera.setFocalLength(targetFocalLength);
23:     show("focalLength(target)",targetFocalLength);
24:
25:     String targetAperture =
25a:            getAperture(requestModel,targetItem,MyShopBot.MIN);
26:     myCamera.setMinAperture(targetAperture);
27:     show("min aperture(target)",targetAperture);
28:
29:     targetAperture =
29a:            getAperture(requestModel,targetItem,MyShopBot.MAX);
30:     myCamera.setMaxAperture(targetAperture);
31:     show("max aperture(target)",targetAperture);
32:
33:     String targetShutterSpeed =
33a:          getShutterSpeed(requestModel,targetItem,MyShopBot.MIN);
34:     myCamera.setMinShutterSpeed(targetShutterSpeed);
35:     show("min shutterSpeed(target)",targetShutterSpeed);
36:
```

```
37:     targetShutterSpeed =
37a:       getShutterSpeed(requestModel,targetItem,MyShopBot.MAX);
38:     myCamera.setMaxShutterSpeed(targetShutterSpeed);
39:     show("max shutterSpeed(target)",targetShutterSpeed);
40:
41:     CameraDescription currentCamera = new CameraDescription();
42:     while ( true ) {
43:
44:       Model catalogModel = getModel(catalog);
45:
46:       // see if it has potential candidates
47:       if ( isCandidate(catalogModel) == false ) {
48:         continue;
49:       }
50:
51:       // create ontology model for inferencing
52:       OntModel ontModel = ModelFactory.createOntologyModel
52a:                  (OntModelSpec.OWL_MEM_RULE_INF,catalogModel);
53:       FileManager.get().readModel(ontModel,ontologyURL);
54:
55:       // which item could be it?
56:       candidateItems = findCandidateItem(ontModel);
57:       if ( candidateItems.size() == 0 ) {
58:         continue;
59:       }
60:
61:       for ( int i = 0; i < candidateItems.size(); i ++ ) {
62:
63:         String candidateItem =
63a:                (String)(candidateItems.elementAt(i));
64:         System.out.println("\nFound a candidate: " +
64a:                           candidateItem);
65:         currentCamera.clearAll();
66:
67:         // find the pixel value
68:         String pixel = getPixel(ontModel,candidateItem);
69:         currentCamera.setPixel(pixel);
70:
71:         // find lens:focalLength value
72:         String focalLength =
72a:                getFocalLength(ontModel,candidateItem);
73:         currentCamera.setFocalLength(focalLength);
```

```
74:            show("focalLength",focalLength);
75:
76:            // find lens:aperture value
77:            String aperture =
77a:                getAperture(ontModel,candidateItem,MyShopBot.MIN);
78:            currentCamera.setMinAperture(aperture);
79:            show("min aperture",aperture);
80:            aperture =
80a:                getAperture(ontModel,candidateItem,MyShopBot.MAX);
81:            currentCamera.setMaxAperture(aperture);
82:            show("max aperture",aperture);
83:
84:            // find body:shutterSpeed value
85:            String shutterSpeed =
85a:            getShutterSpeed(ontModel,candidateItem,MyShopBot.MIN);
86:            currentCamera.setMinShutterSpeed(shutterSpeed);
87:            show("min shutterSpeed",shutterSpeed);
88:            shutterSpeed =
88a:            getShutterSpeed(ontModel,candidateItem,MyShopBot.MAX);
89:            currentCamera.setMaxShutterSpeed(shutterSpeed);
90:            show("max shutterSpeed",shutterSpeed);
91:
92:            if ( myCamera.sameAs(currentCamera) == true ) {
93:              System.out.println("found one match!");
93a:             // more interesting action?
94:            }
95:        }
96:
97:      break;  // or next catalog file.
98:    }
99:
100: }
```

The workflow starts from line 4, where an RDF model (requestModel) representing our search request is created. It is then passed into method getItemToSearch() so our ShopBot can understand more about the requirement (line 5).

As we discussed earlier, we describe our need by creating a resource. Method getItemToSearch() looks for the URI that represents this resource (saved in targetItem variable), and it also collects the type information of this resource (saved in targetType variable). If it cannot find these two pieces of information, a false value is returned with an error message shown to the user (lines 5–7). In case of success, targetItem and targetType are echoed back to the user, as shown on lines 8–11.

Once the above is successfully done, our ShopBot creates a new instance of class CameraDescription named myCamera, which represents our detailed requirements about the camera we want to find (line 15). To populate myCamera, the getPixel() method is first called (line 17), with requestModel and targetItem as its parameters. This method returns the value of the myCamera:effectivePixel property, which is then stored in the myCamera instance, as shown on line 18.

Similarly, the ShopBot calls method getFocalLength() and stores the returned value into myCamera (lines 21–23). Then it calls getAperture() method to query both the minimum and maximum aperture values, and these values are again used to populate myCamera instance (lines 25–31). The same is true for shutter speed, as shown from lines 33–39. Once all these are done, our ShopBot has finished the task of understanding our needs, and all our requirements about our camera are now stored in myCamera instance.

At this point, our ShopBot is ready to handle catalog files. To do so, the first thing it does is to create another CameraDescription instance called currentCamera, which is used as a place to hold the descriptions of a potential camera found in a given catalog document (line 41).

Obviously, there are multiple catalog documents our ShopBot needs to visit, and it will visit them one by one, using a loop of some kind. So far, since we have established only one example catalog document (List 18.8), and given the fact that the exact same processing flow will work for any catalog file, I will not create more catalog file examples. Therefore, instead of actually having a list of documents to visit, I will simply use a while() loop (lines 42–98) to represent the idea of having a collection of documents to visit. It is up to you to come up with more example catalog files, and change the while() loop so none of these document are missed.

Now, for a given catalog file on hand, our ShopBot first creates a simple RDF model to represent it (line 44), and then calls isCandidate() method to see whether there is any need to study this catalog more (line 47). If the current catalog file does not have any product that can potentially satisfy our needs, our ShopBot moves on to the next catalog document (line 48).

When the ShopBot decides to investigate more on the current catalog file, it first creates an ontology model based on the catalog document as shown on lines 52–53. As we discussed earlier, this is necessary since the inferencing engine can add derived statements into the model, and it is the reason why all the queries can work correctly.

The ShopBot then tries to find from the catalog document all the products that could be potential matches by calling the findCandidateItem() method (line 56). We discussed this method already, and it returns a collection of URIs (a Vector), with each one of these URIs representing such a potential product. In our example, this collection has only one product, which has the following URI:

http://www.retailerExample1.com/onlineCatalog#Nikon_D70

If the returned collection is empty, meaning the current catalog document does not have any possible matches, our ShopBot skips this catalog and moves on to the next one, as shown in lines 57–59.

It is certainly possible that a given catalog document has more than one cameras that can potentially satisfy our needs. To examine these products one by one, we need to have a loop as shown on lines 61–95.

To start the examination, our ShopBot takes one URI from this collection (line 63). Since we have only one `currrentCamera` instance that holds the description of the current product, it may still contain the description of the previous product. Therefore our ShopBot clears it first, as shown on line 65.

Next, our ShopBot starts to query against the current catalog document to retrieve the values of the applicable properties, namely, pixel value, focal length value, aperture value and shutter speed value. And once a value is retrieved, it is saved into the `currentCamera` instance. This process is shown in lines 67–90, and it is the same process that our ShopBot used to understand the request document (lines 17–39).

Once this process is done, `currentCamera` instance holds the description of the current product. It is then used to compare with `myCamera` instance, which holds our request. If this comparison returns a `true` value, our ShopBot declares that a match has been found (lines 92–94). In our example, to declare a match simply means a system printout is used to alert the user (line 93). You can change this line to whatever you would like to do, for example, collecting the retailer's name and the Web site that describes this product in more detail, including its pricing and shipping information, and so on.

Once all the potential products from the current catalog are examined, our ShopBot should continue on to the next catalog file, which should be done on line 97. Again, for this example, currently only one catalog file is used, so line 97 simply breaks the loop. For you, if you want our ShopBot to visit more catalog documents, this is the line you should change.

At this point, we have finished building our ShopBot. Notice that the classes and methods that we discussed here are the major ones; you can find the complete code from the package you have downloaded. With what we have learned here, you should not have any problem understanding the complete code.

18.2.3.4 Running Our ShopBot

The best way to understand our ShopBot agent is to download the complete code, compile it using your own java project and favorite IDE, and of course, run it.

Also, to make the ShopBot run, I have used the following files:

- Request file: `C:/liyang/myWritings/data/myCameraDescription.rdf`
- Catalog file: `C:/liyang/myWritings/data/catalogExample1.rdf`
- Ontology file: `C:/liyang/myWritings/data/camera.owl`

You should be able to find these files when you download the code for our ShopBot, and you should change the paths of these files so your ShopBot agent can access these files.

List 18.17 shows the driver we use to start the ShopBot.

List 18.17 Test driver for our ShopBot agent

```
1: public static void main(String[] args) {
2:
3:    MyShopBot myShopBot = new MyShopBot();
4:    myShopBot.work();
5:
6: }
```

List 18.18 shows the output you should see when running the ShopBot:

List 18.18 Screen output generated by our ShopBot agent

```
this URI describes the resource you are looking for:
<http://www.liyangyu.com/shopbot/request#myDigitalCamera>
its type is given by the following class:
<http://www.liyangyu.com/camera#Digital>

pixel(target) value is:
6.0^^http://www.liyangyu.com/camera#MegaPixel
focalLength(target) value is:
18-200mm^^http://www.w3.org/2001/XMLSchema#string
min aperture(target) value is:
1.8^^http://www.w3.org/2001/XMLSchema#float
max aperture(target) value is:
22^^http://www.w3.org/2001/XMLSchema#float
min shutterSpeed(target) value is:
0.0005^^http://www.w3.org/2001/XMLSchema#float
max shutterSpeed(target) value is not specified.

Found a candidate:
http://www.retailerExample1.com/onlineCatalog#Nikon_D70
focalLength value is:
18-200mm^^http://www.w3.org/2001/XMLSchema#string
min aperture value is not specified.
max aperture value is not specified.
min shutterSpeed value is:
0.00002^^http://www.w3.org/2001/XMLSchema#float
max shutterSpeed value is not specified.

found one match!
```

After understanding our ShopBot and seeing its example output, you can compile more catalog files for it to understand. Try it out and have fun!

18.2.4   Discussion: From Prototype to Reality

The ShopBot presented in this chapter is a simple prototype, and its goal is to show you another application example on the Semantic Web. You should be able to see the following main points from this example:

- ShopBots created in the Semantic Web environment can do much more than traditional ShopBots. For example, you don't have to only search a specific product; instead, you can describe what you want and let the machine find it for you.
- There is no need to screen-scrape, since the Semantic Web makes it possible to create and run ShopBots in a much more scalable and maintainable way.

There are obviously lots of things you can do to make it better. To name a few:

- A ShopBot should be able to visit the Web to find catalog files from different retailers. In our example, we simply feed it with catalog files.
- For now, the catalog files we are looking for are RDF files. Because of the "scarcity" of these files, what is the best way to find them quickly?
- Instead of editing separate RDF documents, some retailers may decide to use RDFa or microformats to add semantic markup directly into their online HTML documents. How should we change our ShopBot to handle this situation?
- If you run our current ShopBot, you will notice that it runs slower when we have to create ontology models instead of simple RDF models. This might hurt the scalability and efficiency of our ShopBot. How can we make improvements in this direction?

All these questions are important when constructing a real ShopBot. However, from prototype to real application, actually more important issues remain to be solved. For example,

- There has to be a set of ontologies that the whole community accepts.

For a given application domain, a set of ontologies are needed. However, who is responsible for creating these ontologies? How do we reach final agreement on these ontology files? Sometimes, different ontologies might already exist for a given domain. Instead of reinventing the wheel, it might be a good idea to merge these ontologies together to form a standard one. Yet how this merge should be done?

- Each retailer has to semantically mark up his/her catalog, and the markup has to be done based on the standard ontology files.

For the general public on the Web, semantic markup is never an easy process. To mark up a Web document, either a separate RDF document can be created, or RDFa/microformats can be used to embed the markup into the Web document. Whichever method is chosen, there is a learning curve for the users to conquer, and they have to agree to use the terms from the standard ontologies. To overcome the technical challenges and the learning curve, user motivation plays an important role as well.

Besides the above, there are other issues such as security and trust, and whether sharing sensitive data on the public Web is acceptable to each retailer. Also, from a technical perspective, building intelligent agents still has the issues of scalability and efficiency, especially when reasoning on large ontologies is involved.

Clearly, there is still a long way to go before our prototype can finally become a practical application system on a large scale. However, it is our hope that understanding these issues will make our road ahead clear and also give you the motivation to continue the exploration on the Semantic Web, and finally, to turn the idea into a beautiful reality.

18.3   Summary

In this chapter, we created two more applications on the Semantic Web. The first is an agent that works with FOAF documents to create a trustable e-mail list for you, and the second is a ShopBot that understands your needs and tries to find those products that can satisfy your needs. With these examples, you should be able to understand the following:

- The basic steps and patterns when it comes to developing applications on the Semantic Web.
- Soft agents on the Semantic Web can be developed with scalability and efficiency that cannot be matched if the same agents were developed on the traditional document Web.
- In addition, soft agents are extremely suitable for dynamic and distributed data environments, and it is almost effortless to maintain these agents.

Meanwhile, understand that to build production-level soft agents in the real world, quite a few issues have to be addressed first. Noticeably, the development of shared ontologies, the motivation for the general public to mark up their Web documents and the related security/trust issues are the top items on the list.

Finally, congratulations on finishing the whole book. I hope you have learned something from this book, and more importantly, I hope you are now motivated to pursue more of the vision of the Semantic Web, and soon, you will be able to deliver applications on the Web that can make millions of users happy.

Index

© Springer-Verlag Berlin Heidelberg 2014
L. Yu, *A Developer's Guide to the Semantic Web*,
DOI 10.1007/978-3-662-43796-4

Printed in the United States
By Bookmasters